THE CREATION
according to the
Midrash Rabbah

THE CREATION

according to the

Midrash Rabbah

Rendered with Commentary

by

Wilfred Shuchat

P U B L I S H I N G
J E R U S A L E M • N E W   Y O R K

Edited by
Rabbi Dr. Raphael Posner

The Creation According To The Midrash Rabbah
Published by Devora Publishing Company
Text Copyright © 2002 by Wilfred Shuchat

Cover Design: Benjie Herskowitz
Design & Typesetting: Posner & Sons, Jerusalem

Cloth ISBN 1-930143-40-0

For Special Sales contact: Marketing Director
40 East 78th Street, Suite 16D
New York, New York 10021
Tel: (800) 232-2931
Fax: (212) 472-6253
Email: pitspop@netvision.net.il
Web Site: www.pitspopany.com

Printed in Israel

By Way of an Introduction

The publication of a volume does not have to be justified. On the other hand, it does require an explanation.

I became interested in Midrash very early in my rabbinical career. Every rabbi uses Midrash for sermonic purposes. About twenty years ago, however, I began studying Midrash in a serious and systematic way.

It began as a result of an incident. One summer day I walked into the *bet ha-midrash*, the daily chapel of my synagogue and saw a gentleman whom I did not recognize deeply engrossed in study. When he saw me he called me over and introduced himself. He was Rabbi Dr. C. Hillel Kauvar, of Denver, Colorado. I recognized the name because he had been a close friend of my predecessor, Rabbi Dr. Herman Abramowitz. He informed me that he was in Montreal to visit members of his wife's family and then went on to explain what he was studying. He did not follow the schedule of the *Daf Yomi*, the organized method of the daily study of a folio of the Talmud. On the other hand he never allows a day to go by without studying either a side or a folio page of Talmud. He advised me very strongly to do the same, stressing that it would add profundity to everything I did as a rabbi and as a Jew. It didn't have to be Talmud, but he felt that it should be a rabbinic text.

It was then that I began studying the *Midrash Rabbah* on a daily basis. After a while I began realizing that what I was doing was not only helping me, but could help others as well. I then decided to start the *Midrash Rabbah* from the beginning again, but this time to put everything down in writing.

Although I have made some use of the Soncino translation of the *Midrash Rabbah* for this volume and I am grateful to my cousin by marriage, the late Mr Jack Goldman ז״ל of Judaica Press for permission to use it, I realized at the outset that Midrash requires much more than translation; it requires rendering so that the arguments flow gently and meaningfully from one sage to another.

It also requires interpretation. That, however, is many sided which is why I have added *Additional Commentary* which lists interpretations which I have not been able to include, but that I have found useful.

The most important aspect of Midrash, however, is its relevance. The

Rabbis tried to show that Judaism spoke to their generation. That is how I understand Midrash. We should try to do the same thing for ourselves.

I have tried to do this through the *Seed Thoughts* that are to be found after every section of Midrash. Some of them can be used as sermonettes, others can be expanded into essays or full fledged sermons. Others are insights suggested either by the passage in the Midrash itself or by one of its commentators. Those who follow the beautiful custom of delivering words of Torah around the family table or in the community will find a harvest of ideas in these pages.

I have been greatly helped by some of the beautiful Hebrew commentaries that have appeared in our era, such as the work of Aryeh Mirkin and *Ha-Midrash ha-Mevo'ar* edited by Rabbi Avraham Steinberger. I am deeply grateful to Rabbi Steinberger for allowing me to use the diskettes of his vocalized Hebrew text, which saved hours of labour.

The experience with Midrash has been for me the greatest form of spiritual enjoyment. It is my hope to continue this work with *Midrash Rabbah* for as long as the Almighty grants me the years and the energy to do so. I am publishing this work for an audience of one – myself. If others become interested, my spiritual joy will be unbounded.

Midrashic literature generally attempts to explain difficult passages in the Bible and also contains a great deal of aggadic material, much of which also appears in the Talmud. It is believed that the literature was compiled between the sixth and the twelfth centuries in places as far apart as Palestine, Babylonia and Italy. Our text, *Midrash Rabbah* – 'The Great Midrash' – so called because it is the largest of the midrashic collections, contains *midrashim* on the Pentateuch and on each of the five *megillot* – Song of Songs, Ruth, Lamentations, Ecclesiastes and Esther. Scholars believe that *Bereishit Rabbah* was compiled in the sixth century, while other parts of the work were compiled up to the twelfth century.

Before comencing our work, it would be well to say a word about the style of Midrash. In most midrashic passages there is implied a question to which the interpretation is a response. In most instances the question is not expressly posed. In the opening section of our book, the question is the meaning of the word בראשית – *bereishit* – which is the opening word of the Torah. The style of the Midrash is then for a verse to be cited which contains the answer to the question of the *midrash* (in this case, the verse is from the Book of Proverbs). However, it will help us to remember that the Midrash usually does not proceed immediately to the answer which is implied in the verse. Having brought forward the verse, it will then, *en passant,* draw certain conclusions from it, or certain teaching values, that may or may not be related to the immediate question. Only after this is done, does the *midrash* then conclude with the answer to its question.

In order to facilitate easy reading we have given the text of the Midrash in vocalized Hebrew and the translation in bold letters; the rest, in normal characters, is my contribution. The text given is that of *Ha-Midrash ha-Mevo'ar* and I have pointed out where that text differs from other editions. The translation of the Midrash itself tries to follow the Hebrew syntax and style and in many instances elegance has been sacrificed to that purpose. In translating biblical verses I have generally followed the Jewish Publication Society of America's translation (Philadelphia 1962), except when that translation does not agree with the midrashic context. The transliteration used is that of the *Encyclopaedia Judaica,* except for the letter צ which is transliterated at *tz.*

Contents

Some Thoughts on Midrash

In our age the word 'relevance' has taken on an urgent meaning. Human beings are concerned that their lives have meaning, that their behaviour be related to goals which they can accept rationally, and that their education be related to purposes and experiences with which they can identify both emotionally and intellectually.

This is not a new phenomenon. The same urge has existed in most creative generations. In Judaism, the rise of the Oral Law and its traditions is eloquent testimony to the desire of the Talmudic Sages to make the law and its values significant and therefore acceptable as the context of a life-style and the catalyst for sacrifice and dedication.

Probably in no aspect of the tradition was this theme of relevance so obvious and noticeable as in the Midrash. There are many who claim that the Midrash is not really an original branch of Talmudic literature, that many of its greatest insights are either parallel to or an actual duplication of the aggadic or folkloric content of the Talmud. That may be of concern to textual scholars, but not to those who seek a significant way of life and want to know whether Judaism has anything to offer that is relevant to that kind of significance. For if what I am about to describe can be shown to have importance for the vast aggadic element of the Talmud as well, and possibly even to certain aspects of its halakhic development, who would quarrel with such a development?

That which I describe for want of a better term as the Midrashic method was a revolutionary development in Jewish thought. If a way could be found to relate that method to our present-day concerns, we would advance much further in our search for meaning.

What prompts me to write this way now is a most intriguing discussion that I have come across in my reading of *Bereishit Rabbah*. The scene is a dialogue between God and Abraham (Genesis 15) in which Abraham receives a revelation of the role which is reserved for him in the biblical scheme of things. He is informed of a male heir that will carry on his heritage, of a people great in number and significance that will ultimately emerge from his seed. But Abraham wants guarantees, or at least some assurance that the revelation has a basis in reality. According to the text, Abraham asks, במה אדע כי אירשנה, 'How shall I know that I am to possess it' (Genesis 15:8) and there follows, as an answer, the scene of the ברית בין הבתרים, 'the covenant of the parts' – the special offering of Abraham and the prophecy of Jewish suffering in a strange land to be followed by a cosmic deliverance.

Let us now turn our attention to what the Midrash does with certain aspects of this text and scene.

> R. Ḥiyya b. R. Ḥanina said: [When Abraham asked, 'How shall I know that I am to possess it'] he was not being sceptical, but was simply saying, 'What do I have to do to merit such a privilege?'

In other words, Abraham was not asking for a special sign or omen that would in some miraculous way elicit his complete trust and eliminate all his doubts. He trusted God. What he did not trust was himself, that he could transmit such a mission to his children, or that they in turn would have the capacity to carry out the mission in the face of changing circumstances and changing challenges.

Now what prompted R. Ḥiyya to depart from what seems to be the obvious intention of Abraham to seek a sign from God for reassurance, to the newer interpretation that Abraham was seeking an assurance for himself and for his doubts about himself? It can only be that R. Ḥiyya was less interested in solving the problem of the text and more interested in solving the problem of life. He was less interested in what the text said about Abraham and more interested in what he could see in Abraham that would help him, R. Ḥiyya, and everyone like him find help and encouragement for his self-doubts, his spiritual weariness, and the stale arguments that were making his own educational efforts rusty.

This, then, is the first principle that I want to establish in what I regard as the Midrashic method: To be less interested in solving the problem of the biblical text and more interested in solving the problem of life; to see in the biblical text a valuable springboard for the text of life and to regard even such fanciful flights of interpretation as legitimate areas of biblical study and valid approaches in the search for meaning in life and human salvation.

If Abraham's question, according to R. Ḥiyya, related to his own self-doubts and a method whereby the heritage would have a chance for survival in the future, what are we to say about the answer that the text gives?

The Almighty's answer begins, קחה לי עגלה משלשת, 'Bring Me a three-year-old heifer...' and there follow the details of the setting for the great vision.

Now what does R. Ḥiyya do with this text and how does he understand the answer to Abraham's question?

Question: במה אדע כי אירשנה – How will I be able to transmit the heritage? With what merit will I possess the land?

Answer: בזכות הקרבנות – By virtue of the system of sacrifices that I will place before you. He then goes on to examine the text.

Scripture: 'And He said to him, 'Bring Me a three-year-old heifer...''

Midrash: 'He demonstrated to him the three types of offerings in which heifers are used, the three types of offerings in which rams are used and the three types of offerings in which goats are used.'

The first reaction to this interpretation is to raise the question of biblical exegesis. By what right does R. Ḥiyya translate משלש or משלשת as 'three heifers' rather than 'one a three-year-old heifer'?

The Midrashic method is not concerned with a literal interpretation of a text; nor is it correct to say that R. Ḥiyya had something important to say about life and was looking for a textual pretext to which he might attach it. What happened was that the use of the text משלש gave R. Ḥiyya an insight into a larger framework than the text revealed. It became for him a symbol not of one calf, but of the system of offerings of which the present text is only a harbinger.

This insight, which R. Ḥiyya grasped intuitively, suggested a flow of development which fell in line with many of the problems that were of great concern to him as a human being and as a Jew.

Did he first have this insight and then look for a text to buttress it or did the text itself suggest the intuition? This would be a good problem for psychological investigation. At any rate it brings us to the second principle or purpose of the Midrashic method which is to re-open insights on life which were acquired in the Talmudic period and use them to cast new light upon our own experiences and very possibly bring into being new intuitions of our own.

Let us explore this possibility and see where it leads in reflecting upon the Midrash text that has been the subject matter of these remarks. Abraham is asking the question, what assurance do I have that my descendants will carry on my trust? And we are told that he was shown three types of oxen, three types of sheep, and three types of goats.

This allusion to the variegated system of sacrifices – nowadays replaced by the system of prayers – can be understood to refer to that aspect of Jewish worship that makes of it a daily regimen, with a specific form and a way of life.

The Hebrew word for this aspect of worship is קבע, *keva‘*, a word which we might translate as 'an established routine.' There is an aspect of prayer that has to be routine as breathing is routine and eating is routine and brushing one's teeth is routine. Of course there is more to eating than routine and there is more to prayer then routine. There is also, for the sake of the record, spontaneity and meaning and song and ecstasy and protest. But there is *also* routine and that routine nourishes the soul as bread in its routine way nourishes the body, the appetite and the instinct to survive.

Prayer needs routine to sustain it for the very reason that its needs are not only daily, but permanent. Is there a moment in life when it can be argued that one need not think of God or have one's life related to His Essence? On the other hand, it is not to be expected that a human being can maintain peak experiences of sensitivity amid the daily challenges of work, play, suffering and concern. That is why the routine is necessary. Not only does it support that aspect of worship which refines the human soul, it makes it possible for peak experiences to multiply in a fashion that would not happen without the routine, the daily regimen. The spiritual appetite grows with the spiritual eating.

The routine we are talking about must also be understood as being a specifically Jewish routine. That is to say, the routine of prayer three times a day – and more often on festivals – and the system of benedictions and the various table ceremonies make of the routine of prayer a specifically Jewish form and thereby a Jewish way of life to the degree that such worship occupies an important segment of a person's time and therefore his concern. Since the context of Jewish prayer is no longer the bringing of animals as offerings to the Temple, but rather an experience with a text whose contents proclaim the covenant between God and Israel, reiterate the commandments and state the main needs and hopes of the Jewish people as the initiators of prayer, the very routine becomes, in fact, a form of Jewish identification, involvement and renewal of major proportions.

We have now traced two principles in the Midrashic method. The first sees the scriptural text as a commentary on life. The second uses the interpretation as a spring board for a new insight in human problems and we have used the example of prayer in the particular *midrash* that we have chosen as an illustration. The third development of the Midrashic method is the effort and ability to reinterpret. Reinterpretation means taking a concept and transposing it into the octave of our contemporary lives and our own situation.

Not all Midrashic comment is capable of reinterpretation nor are all reinterpretations of equal value. What is so fascinating about Midrashic literature, however, is the degree and extent to which it is open to reinterpretation.

Let us refer again to the text that has been the subject matter of this essay. When Abraham asked the question, 'How do I know that I or my descendants will be able to transmit the heritage?' he was given the answer, בזכות הקרבנות – You can be sure of it 'by reason of the atonement sacrifices.'

What are the atonement sacrifices? They are the guilt offerings, the sin offerings, the doubt offerings, and so forth. In Temple times these dramatized the individual's inadequacies or failures and also his desire for correction and improvement. What Abraham was being told was that his descendants would cling to Judaism if they discovered in it an outlet for their emotional life, a framework within which to work and a community of love and compassion that would forgive their failures and inspire them to reach higher and achieve more.

This emotional therapy so essential to human life was provided by the atonement sacrifices which do not exist today. Is there a way in which we can compensate for their absence?

Can we not reinterpret and say in a general way, that this ought to be the function of religion in our time? Would it not be in order to suggest that the agencies and institutions of Jewish religion, such as the synagogues, the seminaries, the *yeshivot* and the Rabbinate itself ought to be directed not only to the promotion of *mitzvot*, but also to the cultivation of emotional welfare – to the building up of family relationships and the sense of community between individuals, ideologies and groups?

We have ample precedent for this. The prophet Ezekiel chastises the shepherds of Israel, 'The weak you have not strengthened, the sick you have not healed, the wounded you did not bandage, the banished you have not returned and the lost you have not sought' (Ezekiel 34:4). God speaks to the prophet about what spiritual leadership implies.

'As a shepherd leads his flock so will I tend them... the lost will I seek, the driven out I will bring back, the wounded will I bandage, the sick will I strengthen, the bullies will I bring down. I will tend them all with justice' (Ezekiel 34:15).

This re-interpretation in no way alters or perverts the meaning of the text. On the contrary, it gives it a force it did not have before, by making it speak to us, to our personal concerns and to our very existence. In this way, Midrash can speak to us as can no other document – ancient or modern.

We have this vast Midrashic treasure house at our disposal and it is not being used. Midrashic scholars are more concerned with establishing which Midrash manuscript is textually correct and which is corrupt, rather than with interpreting it as a commentary to life..When the *derashah*, formal Jewish preaching, was fashionable some aspects of Midrash insight reached the public. Today synagogue preaching is in great decline, Midrash teaching is rare and, in Israel, the most pulsating Jewish community, the sermon has been virtually eliminated.

We must find a way to reopen the Midrash and meaningfully display its wares.

Midrash as Rabbinic Thought

Bernard Raphael Shuchat

When one approaches the study of Midrash, the basic question is its place in the tradition of Jewish thought. Midrash comes under the larger category of Classical Rabbinic Thought, which includes the Rabbinic works from what can be called the classical period of Judaism, that is, the period of the Mishnah and the Talmud, roughly from 100 B.C.E. until 600 C.E. (Tanna'im, Amora'im, and Savora'im). This is the classic period for the germination and formation of halakhic thinking, as well as for fruitful developments in Aggadah and Midrash. The world of Halakhah is well organized. The process of redaction, turning the theoretical discussions of the Talmud into the categories of the *Rishonim* (the medieval commentators and authorities), the codices of the *Rishonim* in the twelfth to fifteenth centuries, and finally evolving into the *Shulkhan Arukh* in the sixteenth century, is well documented. Despite the effort put into organizing Halakhah, the relation to the Rabbinic thought that is articulated throughout the aggadic literature and *midrashim* was different. Was this due to the Rabbinic edict "לאו שאין בו מעשה אין לוקין עליו," which put the question of personal faith outside the jurisdiction of the courts, or just the difficulty of determining the basis of Rabbinic thinking due to a lack of orderliness of the material? The halakhic process in the Talmud is quite tangential, skipping from topic to topic. The talmudic sages took on a mammoth task when organizing the legal material in the light of the Mishnah, the *beraitot,* and the *Tosefta.* Why was not the same done with Midrash and Aggadah?

The answer to this question cannot be that non-legal Rabbinic thought was taken lightly. Even though Naḥmanides in his famous debate with Pablo Christiani refers to the *midrashim* as "sermons," it is evident from all who study medieval Jewish philosophy that despite the many disputes among the Rabbis of the Middle Ages in the area of Jewish thought, no thinker openly takes issue with the aggadic material of the Talmud or of well-documented, authoritative *midrashim.* The closest to taking issue with Rabbinic thought is Maimonides who, however, only permits himself to reinterpret Midrash or, in extreme cases, to question the authenticity of a

specific *midrash*. We will discuss this opinion in greater length. If this is
the case, obviously, the midrashic literature was considered to be the basis
of the tradition of Jewish thought. Therefore, the obvious question is
whether there existed a consistent train of thought that stood behind the
various collections of Midrash by which all aggadic material could be
understood. The first to make such a claim was the Maharal of Prague,
followed by the Kabbalists, among them R. Moses Ḥayyim Luzzatto
(Ramḥal). Therefore, in order to understand the role of Midrash in Jewish
thought and in order to establish whether it contains a coherent Rabbinic
system of thought, it is important to briefly review the standpoints of both
Maimonides and Ramḥal. These two thinkers – the rationalist and the
mystic – will help us understand the place of Midrash in Jewish thinking.

Maimonides

There are at least three important sources in Rambam's writings concerning Midrash. The first is in his introduction to Perek Ḥelek. There he talks
of three categories of people in relation to Midrash: a) the religious literalists, "who destroy the beauty of Torah and darken its shine"[1] by thinking
that all *midrashim* are to be taken literally; b) the secular literalists, who
use a simplistic understanding of far-fetched *midrashim* to mock the sages;
and c) the true scholars who understand that the Rabbis of the Midrash
"spoke in parables and riddles, for this is the way of great scholars,"[2] as it
is written in the Book of Proverbs, "To understand a parable or clever
remark, the words of sages and their riddles."[3] Rambam claims that most
of the Rabbis of his generation erroneously held the first position[4] and
only a handful held the true position, namely, that the Sages spoke in
parables and that not always are the *midrashim* to be taken literally.[5] What
is the rule? When is a *midrash* speaking literally and when is it a parable?
This we can deduce from what Rambam says about the first group. They
think that the Sages did not understand that certain events are impossible
and stated that "impossible events are [to the sages] all possible. This [mis-
take] is due to the fact that [this group] has no knowledge of wisdom."[6]

---

1   Introduction to Helek, *Hakdamot le-Perush ha-Mishnah*, ed. M. Rabinovitch, Jeru-
    salem 1961, p. 118.
2   Ibid., p. 121.
3   Proverbs 1:7.
4   Introduction to Helek, p. 117.
5   Ibid., p. 121.
6   Ibid., p. 118.

The third group, the true one, knows that certain things are illogical and therefore the sages never meant them to be take literally in the first place.[7] In the end Rambam spells it out. "If you are from the third group [those of the true knowledge] and you see something in their [the sages] words that contradicts reason[8] – dwell on it and know that it is a riddle and a parable."[9] In short, the guiding principle seems to be that a *midrash* is to be taken literally unless it is obviously a parable (e.g., when it says "to what can this be compared") or when it contradicts human reason. When do the Sages talk in riddles and parables? When they speak of the topics of "the Tractate Berakhot, Perek Ḥelek, etc.,"[10] which talk of indescribable metaphysical matters, which are "not comprehensible at first glance"[11] without the proper understanding. Rambam gives examples of this from Scripture where the prophet talks in parables in order to describe metaphysical events (e.g. Ezekial chaps. 1 and 37).[12] Occassionally Rambam attacks a *midrash,* calling it contrary to reason, and reinterprets it according to a scriptural source. Therefore, not only is reason a guideline, but also Scripture. This brings us to our second source. In a letter to Obadiah the proselyte, Rambam discusses the intricate relationship between Midrash, Scripture, and human reason. The background to Obadiah's question is Rambam's statement in *Mishneh Torah* that the concept of free will is "the pillar of Torah and its commandments,"[13] and that in no case does God limit free will.[14] Concerning this issue, Obadiah asks how Rambam's standpoint holds in view of the Rabbinic statement "All is in the hands of heaven except for the fear of heaven,"[15] which seems to imply that human free will is limited to ethical issues. Rambam replies in a twofold fashion. First he gives his interpretation of that *aggadah* in line with his opinion on free will and then he states, based on the assumption that it is illogical that God commands us to do the *mitzvot* without free will to choose: "Anyone who leaves these concepts [of total free will] which are built on eternal foundations, and goes after aggadic or midrashic material or writings of the Ge'onim, that in their literal sense goes against our ideas [on free will]

---

7 Ibid., p. 121.
8 "She-ha-da'at marḥiko."
9 Introduction to Helek, p. 123.
10 Ibid., p. 119.
11 Ibid., p. 123.
12 Ibid., p. 122.
13 Hilkhot Teshuvah, chap. 5:3.
14 Ibid., 5:1–2.
15 Berakhot 33b.

which are words of reason and understanding – is committing [spiritual] suicide."[16] Here there is a definite value to human reason in deciding whether the *midrash* in Tractate Berakhot is to be understood literally. After discussing a second seeming contradiction from Aggadah concerning his ideas on free will, Rambam formulates a general rule: "Something which is explicit in the Torah takes precedence... and if one finds a verse in the prophets or the words of the sages contradicting this dictum, one should meditate and explain [the issue] to understand what the prophet or sage meant. If it harmonizes with the Torah dictum – good, if not, one should say: 'I do not understand its meaning and it is not meant literally'."[17] The principle that seems to come out of this last source is that two things can decide if a *midrash* is not literal: a) if it contradicts Scripture (i.e., the Pentateuch); and b) if it contradicts human reason.[18] At times Rambam finds no way to explain a *midrash* that contradicts reason, but still sees it as a metaphor.[19] In short, for Rambam, the way of Midrash is at times metaphoric and this can be discerned through contradictions with Scripture or human reason. Whether Midrash has an underlying coherent way of thinking is not discussed by Rambam, and sometimes he see a *midrash* as the private view of the sage being quoted.[20] Although, being part of the classical writings of the Sages, all authentic *midrashim* are given full appreciation and cannot be contradicted without valid reason.

Ramḥal

In his *Treatise on the Aggadah*,[21] Ramḥal divides *Aggadah* into two categories: educational *Aggadah* (*Limudiyim*) and exegetical *Aggadah* (*Be'uriyim*). He subdivides the second category into three parts: 1) explanations of scriptural text; 2) traditions concerning the meaning of certain verses; and 3) traditions hinted at in the text. The educational *aggadot* are also subdivided: 1) educational *aggadot* with moral implications and teachings; and 2) educational *aggadot* with metaphysical teachings. It is in this latter sub-category that one finds numerous *aggadot* written in metaphoric lan-

---

16 *Igrot ha-Rambam*, by I. Shilat, Jerusalem 1987, pp. 236–237.
17 Ibid., p. 237.
18 Rambam seems to hold the opinion that even scriptural statements that contradict human reason are not to be understood literally. See *Guide to the Perplexed*, II:25.
19 *Guide*, II:26.
20 Ibid.
21 Ma'amar al ha-Haggadot, *Yalkut Yedi'ot ha-Emet*, vol. 1, pp. 241–249. Also found in the introduction to *Midrash Rabbah*, Vilna Edition, Jerusalem 1975, vol. 1, pp. xiv–xv.

guage with hints and parables. Ramḥal explains this as a necessary method. Even though Rabbi Judah the Prince taught that one might write down the oral traditions of Halakhah in order to teach later generations, explains Ramḥal, with regards to the mysteries of Torah and the metaphysical understandings of text, there was a desire to keep this knowledge limited to select scholars, and therefore it was written in a concealed way.

This explanation, though slightly different than Rambam's, agrees that there are certain *aggadot* – and this would include *midrashim*[22] – that were purposely concealed in metaphors and parables. Ramḥal tells us to use metaphoric exegesis only concerning the midrashic category of metaphysical teachings. The difference between Ramḥal and Rambam's position is that Ramḥal sees Aggadah as a coherent body of knowledge with a complete *weltaunchaung* concealed within.[23] This means that not only does halakhic material contain traditions passed down from generation to generation, but so do the philosophic aspects of Torah. These world views are found in Aggadah and Midrash. It is the task of the interpreter to discover this subterranean level of meaning.[24] The Maharal develops his own numerological system to interpret Midrash, Ramḥal uses the wealth of Kabbalistic literature to understand the metaphysical teachings of Midrash, and Rambam uses reason and Scripture to find new meanings in metaphoric *midrashim.*

The world of Midrash, quite neglected by mainstream Torah scholars, is in need of revival. This work, both translating and offering a selection of some of the more important classical interpretations of Midrash, as well as an attempt to formulate the seeds of new ideas, is a trailblazer in bringing Midrash back to the limelight of Torah scholarship. There can be no better a time than today. As the Midrash itself states: "If you want to discover He who commanded the creation of the world – study Midrash."

---

22 It would seem that the *aggadot* would be the most reliable *midrashim* because they are found in the compilation of the Talmud, edited by the Savoraim. The next best would be the classical *midrashim,* specifically *Midrash Rabbah,* especially the older parts of it quoted by Rashi in the tenth century, like *Bereishit Rabbah* and *Shemot Rabbah,* and *Midrash Tanḥuma* based on the earlier compilation of *Midrash Yelamdenu.*

23 This seems to be the opinion of the Maharal of Prague in his Beure Aggadot.

24 For Ramḥal it is probably important for the interpreter to have knowledge of the mystical traditions handed down for the category of the educational metaphysical *midrashim.* For Rambam, these traditions existed once but were lost in time. See *Guide to the Perplexed* III, introduction.

Acknowledgements

There is no such thing as a solo performance in the area of publishing. Along the way there are friends and helpers who make the work easier for those who are inexperienced.

I am grateful to my friend Ḥaim Tessler of Jerusalem for introducing me to Rabbi Dr. Raphael Posner. Not only is he an outstanding Rabbinical scholar but an editor of great excellence. When he agreed to edit and produce my work on Midrash I knew that I was on the right track.

I am very appreciative of Devora Publishing Company and of its Director, Yaacov Peterseil who sees Jewish books as an opportunity to keep Judaism alive and well.

I want to thank the well-know artist Yehuda Chaki for the use of a section of his tapestry design on the creation that will be found on the cover of this book. The tapestry is on permanent display at the Shaar HaShomayim Synagogue in Montreal.

In the early nineteen fifties I met every Saturday night with a group of college students going over Rabbinic texts. When they graduated in 1953 they presented me with a copy of the Vilna edition of the *Midrash Rabbah.* Little did they or I realize that this gift would ultimately produce this and other works in Midrash. Their names are: Neil Gilman who is today Vice Chancellor of the Jewish Theological Seminary of America and an important name in the world of Jewish philosophy; Nahum Gelber, a lawyer by profession but also an art connoisseur and a philanthropist of world stature; Charles Solomon, an orthodontist by profession who, upon *aliyah* to Israel, became the administrator of the Shalom Hartman Institute; Beruriah Shine Shenton of Washington, D.C.; and Gordon Wasserman, former head of the London Constabulary of London, England.

Three years ago, I suffered a great tragedy in the loss of my precious daughter, Elizabeth. She was not only outstanding in her profession as a social worker where she headed a counselling unit for the Orthodox community of the Five Towns but as a Rebbetzen of the Young Israel of

Oceanside she was a role model for young and old. In dedicating this volume to her life and memory, I pray that her soul will bless all who read this book.

I thank the Holy One, blessed be He, for the privilege of completing this volume and if I am granted more years, I hope to continue my comments to the *Midrash Rabbah* which I consider to be one of the most inspiring documents of Judaism.

Rabbi Wilfred Shuchat

Parashah One, Midrash One

בְּרֵאשִׁית בָּרָא אֱלֹהִים וגו'.... (בראשית א:א)

In the beginning God created... (Genesis 1:1)

רַבִּי הוֹשַׁעְיָה רַבָּה פָּתַח (משלי ח, ל) 'וָאֶהְיֶה אֶצְלוֹ אָמוֹן וָאֶהְיֶה שַׁעֲשׁוּעִים יוֹם יוֹם
וגו''' אָמוֹן פֵּידָגוֹג אָמוֹן מְכֻסֶּה אָמוֹן מְצֻנָּע וְאִית דְּאָמַר אָמוֹן רַבָּתָא

**R. Hoshaya Rabbah commenced [his exposition thus]: 'I was by
Him, as a nursling [*amon*]; and I was daily all delight'** (Proverbs 8:30).
***Amon* means tutor; *amon* means covered; *amon* means hidden; and
some say *amon* means great.**

The formula פָּתַח, *patah*, with which a passage often begins, should be
understood in its technical sense. Coming from the Hebrew root 'to open,'
its implication is the opening of that which otherwise would be closed.
The word thus refers to a solution to a problem. In our passage, R.
Hoshaya comes forward with a solution to the meaning of the word
bereishit ('in the beginning') and he begins by referring to the verse in
Proverbs.

In Proverbs, the general theme is wisdom, which, traditionally means
Torah. How is it that the Torah came to us with the particular kind of
learning and challenge that are associated with it? The answer is found in
the word אמון, *amon*, which is the key word in the verse quoted.

The word *amon* can mean either pedagogy, or covered, or concealed.
The difference between 'covered' and 'concealed' is the difference between an object being before you, but covered with something, and an
object whose whereabouts are completely unknown. The *midrash* goes on
to cite proof-texts for each of these meanings.

אָמוֹן פֵּידָגוֹג הֵיךְ מָה דְּאַתְּ אָמַר (במדבר יא, יב) 'כַּאֲשֶׁר יִשָּׂא הָאֹמֵן אֶת הַיֹּנֵק' אָמוֹן
מְכֻסֶּה הֵיאַךְ מָה דְּאַתְּ אָמַר (איכה ד, ה) 'הָאֱמֻנִים עֲלֵי תוֹלָע וגו''' אָמוֹן מְצֻנָּע הֵיאַךְ
מָה דְּאַתְּ אָמַר (אסתר ב, ז) 'וַיְהִי אֹמֵן אֶת הֲדַסָּה'

***Amon* is a tutor, as in, 'As a nurse [*omen*] carries an infant'** (Numbers
11:12). ***Amon* means covered, as in 'Those who were clad [*ha-emunim*]**

1

in purple' (Lamentations 4:5). *Amon* means hidden, as in, 'And he reared [or concealed, *omen*] Hadassah' (Esther 2:7).

The idea of *amon* meaning 'pedagogical' is from the verse in Numbers where it is used in the sense of bringing up a child. The idea of *amon* as 'covered' is from the verse in Lamentations, which describes those who were clothed in purple (i.e., covered in robes of purple, the attire of the wealthy and illustrious). The idea of *amon* meaning 'concealed' is from the verse in Esther, based on the tradition (Rashi) that when Mordecai heard that Ahasuerus was searching for a queen he hid Esther so that she should not be found, but he did not succeed. In the light of this tradition, *amon* can be translated as 'concealed.'

אָמוֹן רַבְּתָא כְּמָה דְתֵימָא (נחום ג, ח) 'הֲתֵיטְבִי מִנֹּא־אָמוֹן' וּמְתַרְגְּמִינַן הַאַתְּ טָבָא מֵאֲלֶכְּסַנְדְּרִיָּא רַבְּתָא דְּיָתְבָא בֵּין נַהֲרָוָתָא

Amon can also mean great, as in, 'Were you any better than No-Amon' (Nahum 3:8), which is translated into Aramaic as 'Were you any better than the *great* Alexandria that is situated among the rivers?'

The fourth interpretation of *amon* as 'great' refers to the fact that the Torah is greater and deeper than any attempt to reduce it to principles even when lofty ones as we have just mentioned.

What does all this mean?

It is quite obvious that the term 'rearing' cannot apply to the Torah. It can only mean, then, that the Torah prides itself on the fact that it is constantly being renewed and developed by scholars by means of interpretation and insight. The Torah is not an open book — its laws are sometimes completely concealed by the hermeneutic principles according to which it is to be interpreted. Sometimes they can be revealed as mysteries and sometimes revealed through clues, hints, and insights. All this was done in order to create a suitable challenge and a suitable reward for those who study the Torah (*Tiferet Tzion*).

דָּבָר אַחֵר אָמוֹן אֻמָּן הַתּוֹרָה אוֹמֶרֶת אֲנִי הָיִיתִי כְּלִי אֻמָּנוּתוֹ שֶׁל הַקָּדוֹשׁ בָּרוּךְ הוּא בְּנוֹהַג שֶׁבָּעוֹלָם מֶלֶךְ בָּשָׂר וָדָם בּוֹנֶה פָּלְטִין אֵינוֹ בּוֹנֶה אוֹתָהּ מִדַּעַת עַצְמוֹ אֶלָּא מִדַּעַת אֻמָּן וְהָאֻמָּן אֵינוֹ בּוֹנֶה אוֹתָהּ מִדַּעַת עַצְמוֹ אֶלָּא דִּפְתְּרָאוֹת וּפִנְקְסָאוֹת יֶשׁ לוֹ לָדַעַת הֵיאַךְ הוּא עוֹשֶׂה חֲדָרִים הֵיאַךְ הוּא עוֹשֶׂה פִּשְׁפָּשִׁין כָּךְ הָיָה הַקָּדוֹשׁ בָּרוּךְ הוּא מַבִּיט בַּתּוֹרָה וּבוֹרֵא אֶת הָעוֹלָם

Another interpretation: *Amon* is a craftsman [*uman*]. The Torah declares: 'I was the working tool of the Holy One, Blessed be He.' In human practice, when a king builds a palace he builds it not with his own skill, but with the skill of a craftsman, and the craftsman moreover does not design it out of his own head, but employs plans and diagrams to plan the rooms and passageways. Thus God looked into the Torah and created the world.

We now come to the key question that underlies the whole section. Why did the Torah begin with the word *bereishit*? The problem is essentially grammatical. The form of *bereishit* is adjectival and requires the presence of a noun that is not in the verse. For example, the intention might have been, 'In the beginning *of the world*, God created...,' but the phrase 'of the world' is not present. If the intention of *bereishit* is adverbial, as indeed it is usually translated, 'In the beginning,' the Hebrew word chosen should have been *ba-rishonah* or an equivalent whose usage would be more acceptable. Why, then, *bereishit*?

'Well,' says the *midrash*, 'would a person, even a king, in erecting a building, rely completely on his own insights? Would he not, instead, hire an expert, an architect or a craftsman (*amon*) to plan it for him? And the architect, would he not rely on blueprints, which make use of the natural laws of gravity, and of his particular materials?' So too, in creating the world, the Almighty used the Torah as both means and ends. He used it as the means, in the sense that the world is so constituted that the Torah is capable of being observed in it – in fact, it is the world's perfect design; and He used it as the ends, in the sense that the Torah represents the purpose for which the world was created. This is the meaning of the '*amon*' in Proverbs, which should be understood as '*uman*,' a craftsman. God created the world as a craftsman, using materials whose form and content were one, namely, the Torah.

וְהַתּוֹרָה אָמְרָה 'בְּרֵאשִׁית בָּרָא אֱלֹהִים' וְאֵין 'רֵאשִׁית' אֶלָּא תוֹרָה הֵיאַךְ מָה דְּאַתְּ אָמַר (משלי ח, כב) 'ה' קָנָנִי רֵאשִׁית דַּרְכּוֹ'.

And the Torah declares: 'In the beginning God created' (1:1). 'Beginning' refers to the Torah, as in the verse, 'The Lord created me as the beginning [*reishit*] of His course' (Proverbs 8:22).

The word *reishit* can also be an allusion to the Torah, as in the verse in Proverbs, and thus the first verse of Genesis should be translated, 'With the purpose (or by means) of the Torah did God create the heavens and earth.' This is the conclusive answer of this *midrash* to the original question as to why the Torah begins with the word *bereishit*.

* * *

Seed Thoughts

Everything about the natural world is complicated. Its physical location in space is only partly understood. The vast differences in climate and topography and the power of the sun and its satellites are a mystery contained within the miracle of creation. There are also the great natural cataclysms, earthquakes, and storms that seem to be breaking their own natural laws.

Into this most complicated environment of nature, the human being has been catapulted. He is even more complicated than the world. He not only has biological life like the animals; he is also in the divine image, which means that he possesses a mind and has the ability to choose. But he also has an emotional nature, and his emotions are sometimes in conflict with his intellect, and, when not, they are more often than not in conflict with someone else's intellect. Furthermore, if man as an individual is not complicated enough, man in community possesses a group personality of his own. Nationalism can turn him into a tiger; ideals true and false can obsess him. Hatred and anger can transform him into a virtual beast.

How can one manage this complicated world and this complex man? Why should one even try? What possible reason could there be for creating man if this be the nature of his character and environment? The answer is that God created a cure even before the disease was set in motion.

The Torah is as complicated as the world and as inscrutable as man. It possesses great continuity. According to tradition, it was at God's side for 2,000 years before the creation of the world. It has greatness in the sense of tremendous depth. We think we know it, only to discover that our knowledge is only skin deep, and that we have only scratched its surface meaning. The Torah is also mysterious. Its true meaning is hidden but it lends itself to self-revelation by means of study, insight, and scholarship.

Only because of the Torah is the world of man and nature possible. Indeed, God looked into the Torah as an architect looks into his blueprints. It is not merely that the world of nature and man are so constituted as to allow the Torah to function. The Torah is so constituted that by following its direction the world can produce its best and mankind can experience its greatest moments.

'*Be-reishit*'... 'With *reishit*'... or, as one commentator puts it, '*bi-reishit*' – meaning, 'with me' as the beginning – meaning the Torah – and with me as the goal – meaning the Torah – God was able to create the world.

* * *

Additional Commentary

The various meanings of *amon* such as 'pedagogical, 'covered,' and 'concealed' are not separate explanations, but are integrally related. The concept of Torah can be understood as being divided into three categories: judgments, commandments, and statutes. The judgments (*mishpatim*) are civil laws teaching humans how to relate to each other (pedagogical). The commandments (*mitzvot*) are partly revealed because reasons are sometimes given for them, but not always, and therefore it takes investigation to reveal that which is covered (covered, *amunim*). The statutes are completely mysterious in terms of a rationale, they are *omen* – concealed. (*Yefei To'ar*)

*

Amon means great

The new thought here is that in the Torah of the 'upper world' all the laws, *midrashim* and *aggadot* (legends), are included. (See Exodus Rabbah 76:1 as to why they are not included in the written Torah.) It is in this respect that '*amon*' is interpreted as meaning 'great,' referring to that version of the Torah that contains both the hidden and the revealed. This reflects the difference of opinion between R. Eliezer and R. Joshua. The latter says 'it is not in heaven' and the fundamental Torah is that which was given to us on earth. In this view the Torah is described as 'pedagogue,' since it helps man to grow every day. The other opinion follows the view of R. Eliezer that the fundamental Torah is in heaven and therefore, 'let heaven prove who is right.' '*Amon*' interpreted as great means that in heaven it is great and has been from the time of creation. (*Tiferet Tzion*)

*

In human practice

Why does Midrash use parables that relate to 'human practice'? To indicate that God created this world to operate by natural law and everything must be carried on in terms of that principle. The point is that God had to conduct Himself at creation precisely in the way that He had created the world. (*Tiferet Tzion*)

Parashah One, Midrash Two

רַבִּי יְהוֹשֻׁעַ דְּסִכְנִין בְּשֵׁם רַבִּי לֵוִי פָּתַח (תהלים קיא, ו) 'כֹּחַ מַעֲשָׂיו הִגִּיד לְעַמּוֹ לָתֵת לָהֶם נַחֲלַת גּוֹיִם'

R. Joshua of Siknin, quoting R. Levi, commenced his exposition thus: 'He has declared to His people the power of His works in giving them the heritage of the nations' (Psalms 91:6).

R. Joshua exposited on the opening words of the description of the creation by referring to the verse that affirms that God demonstrated His power to the Children of Israel by giving them the Land of Israel, which originally had been occupied by others.

מָה טַעַם גִּלָּה הַקָּדוֹשׁ בָּרוּךְ הוּא לְיִשְׂרָאֵל מַה שֶׁנִּבְרָא בַּיּוֹם הָרִאשׁוֹן וּמָה שֶׁנִּבְרָא בַּיּוֹם הַשֵּׁנִי מִפְּנֵי עוֹבְדֵי כּוֹכָבִים וּמַזָּלוֹת שֶׁלֹּא יִהְיוּ מוֹנִין אֶת יִשְׂרָאֵל וְאוֹמְרִין לָהֶם הֲלוֹא אֻמָּה שֶׁל בָּזוֹזִים אַתֶּם

Why did the Holy One, blessed be He, reveal to Israel what was created on the first day and on the second day? So that the nations of the world would not be able to taunt Israel saying, 'Surely you are a nation of robbers!'

He quoted this verse in response to an unasked question. What need was there for the Torah to describe the creation of the first two days? Since the Torah was meant for the Children of Israel, would it have not been more reasonable for it to begin with the account of the first commandment given to them when they left Egypt? If it is important to establish God as the creator of the universe, is not the statement in the fourth commandment of the Decalogue, '...for in six days the Lord made heaven and earth...,' sufficient? Why all the details of the creation and particularly those of the creation of the physical earth? Basically these are internal questions. The *midrash*, however, focuses on a far more serious point. The verse in Psalms illustrates the need for the description to enable the People of Israel to rebut any claim of the nations of the world to the effect that they stole the Land of Israel from the seven nations who originally occupied it.

6

וְיִשְׂרָאֵל מְשִׁיבִין אוֹתָן וְאוֹמְרִין לָהֶם וְאַתֶּם הֲלוֹא בְזוּזָה הִיא בְּיֶדְכֶם הֲלוֹא (דברים
ב, כג) 'כַּפְתֹּרִים הַיּצְאָים מִכַּפְתֹּר הִשְׁמִידָם וַיֵּשְׁבוּ תַחְתָּם'

But Israel can retort: 'But you hold your countries as spoil, for surely, "…the Caphtorim, who came from Crete, wiped them out and settled in their place"' (Deuteronomy 2:23).

The Bible tells that the inhabitants of neighboring lands originally came from elsewhere and conquered the lands they now live in. For that matter each of the seven nations displaced their predecessors. The verse from Psalms explains why this is possible.

הָעוֹלָם וּמְלוֹאוֹ שֶׁל הַקָּדוֹשׁ בָּרוּךְ הוּא כְּשֶׁרָצָה נְתָנָהּ לָכֶם וּכְשֶׁרָצָה נְטָלָהּ מִכֶּם
וּנְתָנָהּ לָנוּ הֲדָא הוּא דִכְתִיב 'לָתֵת לָהֶם נַחֲלַת גּוֹיִם'

The world and the fullness thereof belong to God. When He wished, He gave it to you: and when He wished, He took it from you and gave it to us. This is what is meant by, 'In giving them the heritage of the nations, He hath declared to His people the power of His works.'

The importance of Genesis goes beyond what happened in the first and other days of creation. The stories of Genesis project not only the creation, but the perfection of the world through the Sabbath, the struggles between good and evil, truth and falsehood, all of which represent the purpose for which God made the world. If that purpose demands that the People of Israel settle and inherit a particular piece of land, we accept that mandate with appreciation and obedience. That is what 'the power of His works' means. We are persuaded that He who has done everything else in the world knows what He is doing in assigning the Jewish people to the Land of Israel.

הִגִּיד לָהֶם אֶת כָּל הַדּוֹרוֹת.

He told them [for] all the generations.

The Ramban (Nahmanides) was one of the first to point out the incorrectness of the Hebrew text in this edition. He claims that it should read הגיד להם הבראשית, 'He therefore told them [Israel] the details of the creation,' as indeed the Soncino translation has it. For, as the Ramban has stated, the power of His works can only refer to creation and not to the generations that are yet to come. However, it is possible to justify our reading: God told them [the details of creation so that it should serve them] in future generations [when the Jewish claim to the Land of Israel would be challenged].

* * *

Seed Thoughts

This *midrash* should be compared with Rashi's comment on the first verse of Genesis, whose source is in *Midrash Tanhuma*. In the *midrash* quoted by Rashi, the question raised is: Why did the Torah not begin with Exodus 12:2, 'This month shall mark for you the beginning of the months,' since that was the first commandment given to the People of Israel?

The question raised by the text before us is why the Torah should have started with the creation story and what importance in general is the whole story of Genesis to the main purpose of the Torah, which is the experience of the People of Israel as God's people.

In actual fact, neither of these questions seems to be fundamental. The claim that the Torah is simply a series of rules and commandments given to Israel is offset by the fact that at least nine commandments are found in the Torah prior to Exodus 12:2 – six commandments to Adam, a seventh to Noah, an eighth to Abraham, and a ninth to Jacob.

The claim that Genesis is unnecessary is surely offset by the overall purpose of the Torah – the proclamation that God is the master of the Universe, creator of humanity. Even though this could have been derived by implication from other areas of the Bible, it is surely important enough to have been 'dealt with' directly – at least with the kind of coverage to be found in Genesis.

This is one of the several occasions in the *midrash* when the answer becomes more important than the question. For, both in *Tanhuma* and in our text, the question is answered by means of the verse in Psalms that says, in essence, that the purpose in the creation story is to lay the foundation for Jewish rights to the Promised Land.

Herein lies one of the great areas of Jewish sensitivity to the claim to Palestine, which dates from the conquest of Joshua. How is that conquest to be justified? Even if the text establishes the Jewish claim to the land, why did it have to be by conquest?

The answer of the *midrash* is that this is part of the divine plan by which the world was created. Just as God had reasons unknown to us why the order of creation had to be what it was, first day, second day, and third day, so too it was part of His design that Israel should become a sacred people, united with this little piece of land so central to the natural geography of the world and to the spiritual topography of humanity. The claim to this land goes beyond history for all to whom the Bible has authority and sanctity.

* * *

Additional Commentary

So that the nations might not taunt Israel
They would continually admonish and chastise Israel, as though they, the nations, were 'holier than thou.' (*Ha-Midrash ha-Mevo'ar*)

*

Because of the nations
There is a difference in conception between Israel and the nations of the world. The heathen nations believe that God did indeed create the world, but that afterwards he handed it over to other powers (*mazalot*) for direction. Every state, therefore, has its own special god or star in accordance with the character of that particular state. The result is that in this connection every nation worships its own god. When Israel took the land belonging to the seven nations, they were accused of taking away lands assigned to those peoples by their gods. We Jews, however, believe that there is only one God and He is the director and manager of the world.

This becomes more obvious when the detail of every day of creation is revealed. Were that not so, He would merely have had to create the original matter that was created in the first day (heaven and earth). After that, the work could have been given over to the constellations (powers) for them to continue the creation from the potential to the actual. From the fact that this was not done, we learn that He was the creator and supervisor of every detail in creation.

The question why this could not have been deduced from the Exodus story and all the other miracles of succeeding generations that the constellations and the other secondary powers could not accomplish, would have to be answered by the argument that God's management is not restricted to Israel, as though the non-Jewish nations are subject to some other power. This is what they claim and therefore maintain that, having placed them under one power who gave them their territory, their rights cannot be changed. We bring testimony from the creation story that He supervises the entire universe and even the subservient cultures of the nations are under His control. That being the case, He can give whatever He wants to whomever He desires. (*Tiferet Tzion*)

Parashah One, Midrash Three

בְּרֵאשִׁית בָּרָא אֱלֹהִים

In the beginning God created

רַבִּי תַּנְחוּמָא פָּתַח (תהלים פו, י) 'כִּי גָדוֹל אַתָּה וְעֹשֵׂה נִפְלָאוֹת [אַתָּה אֱלֹהִים לְבַדֶּךָ']

R. Tanḥuma commenced with the verse: 'For You are great and perform wonders; You alone are God' (Psalms 86:10).

The question treated in this *midrash* is why the name of God, *Elokim*, appears grammatically in the plural form, while the verb, *bara*, created, is in the singular. R. Tanḥuma sees the solution in the wording of the second part of Psalms 86:10 where the same name of God appears in the plural as *Elokim*, but in the first part is addressed as 'You,' *attah*, in the singular. The adverb attached to the name of God, לְבַדֶּךָ, *levadekha*, which means 'alone,' is also in the singular and its very meaning rejects any semblance of divine pluralism. However, the word also has the meaning of uniqueness. In the verse God's uniqueness makes itself manifest in doing wondrous things. A very appropriate example is now brought forward.

אָמַר רַ' תַּנְחוּם הַנּוֹד הַזֶּה אִם יִהְיֶה בּוֹ נֶקֶב כְּחֹד שֶׁל מַחַט כָּל־רוּחוֹ יוֹצֵא מִמֶּנּוּ וְהָאָדָם עָשׂוּי מְחִלִּים מְחִלִּים נְקָבִים נְקָבִים וְאֵין רוּחוֹ יוֹצֵא מִמֶּנּוּ מִי יַעֲשֶׂה כֵן (שם שם, שם) 'אַתָּה אֱלֹהִים לְבַדֶּךָ.'

R. Tanḥum said: If a skin bag has a hole even as small as the eye of a needle, all the air escapes, yet although man is formed with many cavities and orifices [such as the mouth, the nose, and the ears], his breath does not escape through them. Who can do this? 'You God alone' (*ibid.*).

If, indeed, God alone created the universe, the *midrash* now sees another challenge.

אֵימָתַי נִבְרְאוּ הַמַּלְאָכִים

When were the angels created?

After all, Scripture mentions angels many times. Were they in existence

10

before the universe was created? Did they play any part in the act of creation?

ר' יוֹחָנָן אָמַר בְּב' נִבְרְאוּ הַמַּלְאָכִים הֲדָא הוּא דִכְתִיב (שם קד, ג) 'הַמְקָרֶה בַמַּיִם עֲלִיּוֹתָיו וְגוֹ'' וּכְתִיב (שם שם, ד) 'עֹשֶׂה מַלְאָכָיו רוּחוֹת'

R. Joḥanan said: They were created on the second day, as it is written, 'He sets the rafters of His lofts in the waters' (Psalms 104:3) [which continues, 'Who makes the clouds His chariot.' The reference here is to the creation of the firmament, which took place on the second day], which is followed by 'He makes the spirits His angels, [the fiery flames His servants]' (ibid. v. 4).

Thus, the angels were created on the second day.

ר' חֲנִינָא אָמַר בְּה' נִבְרְאוּ מַלְאָכִים הֲדָא הוּא דִכְתִיב (בראשית א, כ) 'וְעוֹף יְעוֹפֵף עַל הָאָרֶץ וְגוֹ'' וּכְתִיב (ישעיה ו, ב) 'וּבִשְׁתַּיִם יְעוֹפֵף'

R. Ḥanina said: They were created on the fifth day, for it is written, 'and birds that fly above the earth' (Genesis. 1:20) and it is written, 'and with two wings would he [the angel] fly' (Isaiah 6:2).

The verse in Genesis describes the fifth day of creation. It uses the word יְעוֹפֵף for 'fly,' which is exactly the word used in the verse from Isaiah in reference to the angels. R. Ḥanina uses this as proof that angels were created on the fifth day.

רַבִּי לוּלְיָנָא בַּר טַבְרִין אָמַר בְּשֵׁם רַבִּי יִצְחָק בֵּין עַל דַּעְתֵּהּ דְּרַבִּי חֲנִינָא בֵּין עַל דַּעְתֵּהּ דְּרַבִּי יוֹחָנָן הַכֹּל מוֹדִים שֶׁלֹּא נִבְרָא בְּיוֹם רִאשׁוֹן כְּלוּם

R. Luliani b. Tabri said in R. Isaac's name: Whether we accept the view of R. Ḥanina or that of R. Joḥanan, all agree that none were created on the first day.

Therefore God could not have had any partners in the act of creation.

שֶׁלֹּא יֹאמְרוּ מִיכָאֵל הָיָה מוֹתֵחַ בִּדְרוֹמוֹ שֶׁל רָקִיעַ וְגַבְרִיאֵל בִּצְפוֹנוֹ וְהַקָּדוֹשׁ בָּרוּךְ הוּא מְמַדֵּד בְּאֶמְצָעוֹ

Thus, people cannot say that Michael pulled at the south end of the firmament and Gabriel at the north while the Holy One, blessed be He, straightened it out in the middle.

There is a *midrash* that says that the angel Michael is on God's right and the angel Gabriel on God's left when they are singing praises to Him, thus one might think that Michael participated in the south, which is the right-hand side, and Gabriel participated in the north.

אֶלָּא (שם מד, כד) 'אָנֹכִי ה' עֹשֶׂה כֹּל נֹטֶה שָׁמַיִם לְבַדִּי וְגו'

Therefore Scripture declares, 'It is I, the Lord, who made every-thing, Who alone stretched out the heavens' (*ibid.* 44:24).

[רֹקַע הָאָרֶץ מֵי אִתִּי] מֵאִתִּי 'מִי אִתִּי' כְּתִיב מִי הָיָה מִי הָיָה עִמִּי שֶׁתָּף עִמִּי בִּבְרִיָּתוֹ שֶׁל עוֹלָם.

[The verse continues, 'and by Myself spread out the earth.'] The word מֵאִתִּי, 'by Myself' is written in the verse as two words which can also be read as מִי אִתִּי, which means 'who was with Me?' – Who was My partner in the creation of the world?!

The *midrash* uses the fairly common phenomenon of *keri* and *ketiv* (words which are written in the Bible in a manner other than that in which they are read) to understand the verse as a proclamation by God Himself that He had no partners in the act of creation, not even the angels.

דָּבָר אַחֵר 'כִּי גָדוֹל אַתָּה וְעֹשֵׂה נִפְלָאוֹת' בְּנֹהֵג שֶׁבָּעוֹלָם מֶלֶךְ בָּשָׂר וָדָם מִתְקַלֵּס בַּמְּדִינָה וּגְדוֹלֵי הַמְּדִינָה מִתְקַלְּסִין עִמּוֹ שֶׁנּוֹשְׂאִין עִמּוֹ בְּמַשָּׂאוֹ אֲבָל הַקָּדוֹשׁ בָּרוּךְ הוּא אֵינוֹ כֵן אֶלָּא הוּא לְבַדּוֹ בָּרָא אֶת הָעוֹלָם הוּא לְבַדּוֹ מִתְקַלֵּס בָּעוֹלָם הוּא לְבַדּוֹ מִתְהַדֵּר בְּעוֹלָמוֹ

Another interpretation: 'For You are great and perform wonders' (Psalms 86:10) – **ordinarily, when a mortal king boasts of his realm, the great men of the realm boast too, because they participated with him in the achievement. But that is not the case with the Holy One, blessed be He. He alone created the world, He alone can boast of it, He alone is glorified by it.**

A mortal ruler operates by delegation, and the assistants bearing a share of the responsibility also deserve some of the praise. Not so God. He created the world unassisted.

אָמַר ר' תַּנְחוּמָא 'כִּי גָדוֹל אַתָּה וְעֹשֵׂה נִפְלָאוֹת' לָמָּה כִּי 'אַתָּה אֱלֹהִים לְבַדֶּךָ' אַתָּה לְבַדְּךָ בָּרָאתָ אֶת הָעוֹלָם.

R. Tanḥuma [concludes this *midrash* with another exposition on the verse with which he began it] and said: 'For You are great and per-

form wonders' (Psalms 86:10). **Why is that so? Because 'You alone are God.' You alone created the world.**

The emphatic conclusion of the *midrash* is better understood as a polemic against dualism or trinitarianism.

* * *

Seed Thoughts

If a skin bottle is perforated, it immediately collapses. The human body is so complex, however, that even though it contains many apertures, openings, and perforations, air or oxygen is still retained within the body to preserve life. But this is only part of the miracle.

The idea of wind, or air, or spirit is a unique phenomenon in life. Can you see air? Can you describe it? Can you grasp it or touch it? Yet this same air has the power to raise a man above the earth and even sustain the power of heaven. The door opens and the wind enters. You can neither see the wind nor describe where it comes from or where it is going. Wind is the symbol of those things in the natural world that are concealed, though their effects are seen and utilized. Similarly, not only the oxygen within the human body, but the very openings and closings in the human body, are concealed from view and yet they are essential for life, and if they do not function properly life is in danger. This is the aspect of creation that is so wonderful, so miraculous, and so inspiring. This is also a symbol of the spiritual life which, though invisible, nonetheless has the power to uplift both body and spirit.

* * *

Additional Commentary

The real problem in this *midrash* is that the word for God, *Elokim*, is in the plural, which might be erroneously understood as meaning that others, i.e., the angels, took part in the act of creation. Indeed this was the view held by many sects. However, the verb 'created' *(bara)* is in the singular. Thus the *midrash* emphasizes that God was alone in the creation.

Another way of understanding the *midrash* is that it was bothered by the fact that *bereishit* is a dependent word (adverb) and therefore the translation should be: '*Before* [anything was formed] God created heaven and earth.' It then became necessary to demonstrate that angels were not yet created and so could not have been involved in creation.

The section about angels is very obscure. Logically, the *midrash* should have begun with a statement to the effect that angels could not have been created on the first day and then gone on to ask when they were created. Our present text, however, might be explained as follows. The *midrash* first brings a proof-verse for God's miraculous powers in the creation of man, which is the beginning of the verse, 'For You are great and perform wonders'; it then proceeds to explain why this is possible, that is, because 'You alone are God.' The final interpretation of the *midrash* deals not with the creation of heaven and earth itself, but with the fact that God sustains and nourishes His works even after they are created. (*Yefei To'ar*)

Parashah One, Midrash Four

בְּרֵאשִׁית בָּרָא אֱלֹהִים

In the beginning God created...

The deeper meaning of this *midrash* is to be found in the fact that some of the basic values of Judaism are not mentioned as part of the creation story. These values are those that come under the general heading of 'spiritual.' In order to confront this question, the *midrash* addresses itself again to the word בְּרֵאשִׁית, *Bereishit*, and reads it as two separate words, בָּרָא, *bara*, and שִׁית, *shit*, meaning, 'created six,' and then lists six values that were created before the material universe.

שִׁשָּׁה דְבָרִים קָדְמוּ לִבְרִיאַת הָעוֹלָם יֵשׁ מֵהֶן שֶׁנִּבְרְאוּ וְיֵשׁ מֵהֶן שֶׁעָלוּ בַּמַּחֲשָׁבָה לְהִבָּרֵאת

Six things preceded the creation of the world; some of them were actually created, while the creation of the others was already contemplated.

The meaning here is that some of these things were created before the world because they were spiritual entities, while others were contemplated but not created because they were actually physical objects.

הַתּוֹרָה וְהַכִּסֵּא הַכָּבוֹד נִבְרָאוּ תּוֹרָה מִנַּיִן שֶׁנֶּאֱמַר (משלי ח, כב) 'ה' קָנָנִי רֵאשִׁית דַּרְכּוֹ [קֶדֶם מִפְעָלָיו מֵאָז]' כִּסֵּא הַכָּבוֹד מִנַּיִן דִּכְתִיב (תהלים צג, ב) 'נָכוֹן כִּסְאֲךָ מֵאָז [מֵעוֹלָם אָתָּה]'

The Torah and the Throne of Glory were created. The Torah, for it is written, 'The Lord created me at the beginning of His course [as the first of His works of old]' (Proverbs 8:22). The Throne of Glory, as it is written, 'Your throne stands firm from of old [from eternity You have existed]' (Psalms 93:2).

The Torah and the Throne of Glory are spiritual values and were therefore created before the world. In the case of Torah, the proof-text from Proverbs contains the word קֶדֶם, *kedem*, which can also mean 'prior to' and

15

the whole context of that section has to do with the priority of the Torah in creation. In the case of the text from Psalms, the word מֵעָז, *mei-oz,* meaning 'from before,' is associated with God's throne in that particular verse and means prior to the creation of the world.

הָאָבוֹת וְיִשְׂרָאֵל וּבֵית הַמִּקְדָּשׁ וּשְׁמוֹ שֶׁל מָשִׁיחַ עָלוּ בַמַּחֲשָׁבָה לְהִבָּרֹאת

The Patriarchs, Israel, the Temple, and the name of Messiah were contemplated.

The Patriarchs, the People of Israel as God's people, the Temple, and the name of Messiah are all tangible concepts and were therefore only contemplated, not actually created, before the world. The 'name' of the Messiah must imply the nature of his mission and the characteristics by which he would be recognized.

הָאָבוֹת מִנַּיִן שֶׁנֶּאֱמַר (הושע ט, י) 'כַּעֲנָבִים בַּמִּדְבָּר וגו''

The creation of the Patriarchs was contemplated as it is written, 'I saw your forefathers as the first ripening of the fig tree in the wilderness at its first season' (Hosea 9:10).

The proof-text for the Patriarchs makes reference to Israel being as precious to God as the first figs to grow on a tree in the aridity of the desert are precious to the farmer. The same text in Hosea includes the word בְּרֵאשִׁיתָהּ, *be-reishitah,* which is interpreted as meaning before everything, that is, the creation of the world.

יִשְׂרָאֵל מִנַּיִן שֶׁנֶּאֱמַר (תהלים עד, ב) 'זְכֹר עֲדָתְךָ קָנִיתָ קֶּדֶם'

The creation of Israel was contemplated as it is written, 'Remember Your community which You made Yours as of old' (Psalms 74:2).

The proof-text for Israel in the verse from Psalms refers to the congregation and also uses the term קֶדֶם, *kedem,* meaning before the creation of the world.

בֵּית הַמִּקְדָּשׁ מִנַּיִן שֶׁנֶּאֱמַר (ירמיה יז, יב) 'כִּסֵּא כָבוֹד מָרוֹם מֵרִאשׁוֹן וגו''

The creation of the Temple was contemplated as it is written, 'Your throne of glory, on high from the beginning, the place of our sanctuary' (Jeremiah 17:12).

The verse from Jeremiah refers to the earthly Temple being prepared by the Temple that already existed in heaven before the world was created.

שְׁמוֹ שֶׁל מָשִׁיחַ מִנַּיִן שֶׁנֶּאֱמַר (תהלים עב, יז) 'יְהִי שְׁמוֹ לְעוֹלָם וְגוֹ''

The name of Messiah was contemplated, as it is written, 'his name existed before the sun' (Psalms 72:17).

In the case of the name of the Messiah, the continuation of the verse mentions the name יִנּוֹן, *yinon*, which is regarded as the name of Messiah. He was created, at least as a concept, before the sun, meaning before the creation of the world.

רַבִּי אַהֲבָה בְּרַבִּי זְעֵירָא אָמַר אַף הַתְּשׁוּבָה שֶׁנֶּאֱמַר (שם צ, ב) 'בְּטֶרֶם הָרִים יֻלָּדוּ'
וְאוֹתָהּ הַשָּׁעָה (שם שם, ג) 'תָּשֵׁב אֱנוֹשׁ עַד דַּכָּא וְגוֹ''

R. Ahava b. R. Ze'ira said: Repentance too, as it is written, 'before the mountains were brought forth etc.' (*ibid.* 90:2) and from that very moment, 'You turn man back to contrition [and say, Repent, you children of men]' (*ibid.* v. 3).

It may seem surprising that R. Ahava adds that repentance was also contemplated before the world, since that, too, is a spiritual value. On the other hand, repentance cannot be separated from man since true repentance can cause anguish and fasting and tribulation. Indeed, the verse quoted from Psalms uses the phrase 'turn back man to contrition,' which indicates how much true repentance can affect a person tangibly.

אֲבָל אֵינִי יוֹדֵעַ אֵיזֶה מֵהֶם קֹדֶם אִם הַתּוֹרָה קָדְמָה לְכִסֵּא הַכָּבוֹד וְאִם כִּסֵּא הַכָּבוֹד
קֹדֶם לַתּוֹרָה אָמַר רַ' אַבָּא בַּר כָּהֲנָא הַתּוֹרָה קָדְמָה לְכִסֵּא הַכָּבוֹד שֶׁנֶּאֱמַר 'ה' קָנָנִי
רֵאשִׁית דַּרְכּוֹ וְגוֹ'' קֹדֶם לְאוֹתוֹ שֶׁכָּתוּב בּוֹ 'נָכוֹן כִּסְאֲךָ מֵאָז'

But I still do not know which was first, whether the Torah preceded the Throne of Glory or the Throne of Glory preceded the Torah. Said R. Abba bar Kahana: The Torah preceded the Throne of Glory, as it is written, 'The Lord created me at the beginning of His course as the first of His works of old' (Proverbs. 8:22), which means, before that of which it is written, 'Your throne stands firm from of old' (Psalms 93:2).

The *midrash* is now trying to establish an order of preference for the six values it has enumerated. It begins with the two spiritual values that were actually created before the world. As between the Throne of God and the Torah, the latter takes precedence. What is the proof? The proof is that in the continuation of the text from Proverbs the word מֵאָז, *mei-oz*, meaning 'of old,' is superfluous because mention is already made in the verse of the beginning of the world. It is put there to inform us that it, the Torah, was created before the other *mei-oz* in Psalms that refers to the Throne of Glory.

רַ' הוּנָא וְרַ' יִרְמְיָה בְּשֵׁם רַבִּי שְׁמוּאֵל בַּר רַ' יִצְחָק אָמְרוּ מַחֲשַׁבְתָּן שֶׁל יִשְׂרָאֵל קָדְמָה לְכָל דָּבָר מָשָׁל לְמֶלֶךְ שֶׁהָיָה נָשׂוּי לְמַטְרוֹנָה אַחַת וְלֹא הָיָה לוֹ מִמֶּנָּה בֵּן פַּעַם אַחַת נִמְצָא הַמֶּלֶךְ עוֹבֵר בַּשּׁוּק אָמַר טְלוּ מֵילָנִין וּקְלָמִין זוֹ לִבְנִי וְהָיוּ הַכֹּל אוֹמְרִין בֵּן אֵין לוֹ וְהוּא אוֹמֵר טְלוּ מֵילָנִין וּקְלָמִין זוֹ לִבְנִי חָזְרוּ וְאָמְרוּ הַמֶּלֶךְ אַסְטְרוֹלוֹגוֹס גָּדוֹל הוּא אִלּוּלֵי שֶׁצָּפָה הַמֶּלֶךְ שֶׁהוּא עָתִיד לְהַעֲמִיד מִמֶּנָּה בֵּן לֹא הָיָה אוֹמֵר טְלוּ מֵילָנִין וּקְלָמִין לִבְנִי כָּךְ אִלּוּלֵי שֶׁצָּפָה הַקָּדוֹשׁ בָּרוּךְ הוּא שֶׁאַחַר כ"ו דוֹרוֹת יִשְׂרָאֵל עֲתִידִין לְקַבֵּל אֶת הַתּוֹרָה לֹא הָיָה כוֹתֵב בַּתּוֹרָה 'צַו אֶת בְּנֵי יִשְׂרָאֵל' 'דַּבֵּר אֶל בְּנֵי יִשְׂרָאֵל'

R. Huna and R. Jeremiah in the name of R. Samuel b. R. Isaac said: The intention to create Israel preceded everything else. This may be illustrated thus: A king was married to a certain lady, but had no son by her. On one occasion the king was in a market and gave orders, 'Take this ink, inkwell, and pen for my son,' at which people remarked, 'He has no son; what does he want with ink and pen?' Subsequently they concluded the king was a great astrologer, and had actually foreseen that he was destined to beget a son! Thus, had the Holy One, blessed be He, not foreseen that after twenty-six generations Israel would receive the Torah, he would not have written therein, 'Command the children of Israel' or 'Speak to children of Israel.'

Is this argument strictly a matter of form? What is its real meaning? Since the Throne of Glory is the source from which justice is meted out, perhaps R. Abba was arguing that Torah is more important than law. It would seem to be so because law is only one facet of Torah. On the other hand, R. Huna and R. Jeremiah maintain that the thought of creating Israel was the most important value because without Israel as a committed people, who would carry out the Torah or carry out the law?

אָמַר רַ' בַּנָּאִי הָעוֹלָם וּמְלוֹאוֹ לֹא נִבְרָא אֶלָּא בִּזְכוּת הַתּוֹרָה שֶׁנֶּאֱמַר (משלי ג, יט) 'ה' בְּחָכְמָה יָסַד אָרֶץ וְגו''

R. Bana'i said: The world and its fullness were created only for the sake of the Torah as it is written, 'The Lord for the sake of wisdom [i.e., the Torah] founded the earth' (Proverbs 3:19).

Some manuscripts (cited by Mirkin) add an interpretation by R. Berekhiah at this point that the world was created for the sake of Israel, based on Jeremiah 2:3 where Israel is described as רֵאשִׁית תְּבוּאָתֹה 'the first of His produce.' But how can you say that Israel is the most important of all created things since it must uphold the Torah? Suppose it does not – which happened often – can the universe have been created for its sake? Israel is important only if it observes the Torah. Therefore, it is the Torah that gives Israel its merit.

רַבִּי בֶּרֶכְיָה אָמַר בִּזְכוּת מֹשֶׁה שֶׁנֶּאֱמַר (דברים לג, כא) 'וַיַּרְא רֵאשִׁית לוֹ'

R. Berekhiah said: For the sake of Moses, as it is written, 'And he saw the beginning [of the creation] for himself, [for there a portion of a lawgiver (Moses) was reserved]' (Deuteronomy 33:21).

How can one explain what R. Berakiah (Some say R. Aḥa – [Mirkin]) means by saying that the world was created for the sake of Moses? It might mean that the goal of creation is to produce the ideal human being. If you can produce a Moses, it makes all of creation worthwhile.

How the *midrash* derives Moses from the verse in Deuteronomy should be spelled out. The verse is part of a section dealing with the portion of the land of Israel assigned to the tribe of Gad. It makes mention of the fact that it contains the hidden burial place of the lawgiver, i.e., Moses. The verse also uses the expression *reishit* – beginning. This provides the fuller development of the idea that the world was created for the sake of Moses.

רַ' הוּנָא בְּשֵׁם רַ' מַתְּנָה אָמַר בִּזְכוּת ג' דְּבָרִים נִבְרָא הָעוֹלָם בִּזְכוּת חַלָּה וּבִזְכוּת מַעֲשְׂרוֹת וּבִזְכוּת בִּכּוּרִים

R. Huna said in R. Mattenah's name: The world was created for the sake of three things: ḥallah, tithes, and first fruits.

In the debate as to which is more important, Israel or Torah, R. Huna introduces a third consideration. The world, he maintains, was created for the purpose of acknowledging God. He makes this statement by referring to the system of tithes: *ḥallah* (a portion of the dough of every baking given to the priests), tithes (includes various portions of the harvest that are given to the priests, the Levites, and the poor) and first fruits (given to the priests in the sanctuary).

וּמַה טַּעַם 'בְּרֵאשִׁית בָּרָא אֱלֹהִים' וְאֵין רֵאשִׁית אֶלָּא חַלָּה שֶׁנֶּאֱמַר (במדבר טו, כ) 'רֵאשִׁית עֲרִסֹתֵיכֶם' וְאֵין רֵאשִׁית אֶלָּא מַעֲשְׂרוֹת הֵיךְ דְּאַתְּ אָמַר (דברים יח, ד)

'רֵאשִׁית דְּגָנְךָ' וְאֵין רֵאשִׁית אֶלָּא בִּכּוּרִים שֶׁנֶּאֱמַר (שמות כג, יט) 'רֵאשִׁית בִּכּוּרֵי אַדְמָתְךָ וְגו'.'

How do we derive this? Because Scripture says, '*With reishit* did God create…' [note how this differs from the accepted translation, 'In the beginning'], and *reishit* alludes to *ḥallah*, as it is written, '…of the first [*reishit*] of your dough' (Numbers 15:20); *reishit* alludes to tithes, as it is written, '…the first fruits (*reishit*) of your corn' (Deuteronomy 18:4) and, finally, *reishit* alludes to first fruits, as it is written, '…the choicest [*reishit*] first fruits of your land' (Exodus 23:19).

All of these special commandments are meant to glorify God and increase His presence in the world. Why are they specified here? Because each proof-text for the various tithes contains the word *reishit*. But the Torah begins with *be-reishit*, the inference being that God created the world for the sake of those gifts that are called *reishit*. The tithes are God's reward, so to speak, for the creation of the world. His reward is to acknowledge and offer our thanksgiving to Him.

* * *

Seed Thoughts

When, in the *Ethics of the Fathers*, Chapter Five, we come upon the passage that describes those biblical events that were created at twilight at the end of the sixth day of creation, the reason is clear. There are a number of stories of miracles in the Bible that clash with natural law. The 'delayed response' of those things created at dusk served to satisfy some of the questioning minds.

What, however, motivated our *midrash* to postulate six concepts as having been created before the world? What problems is the *midrash* trying to solve? We can never know the true answers to these questions but it may be possible, at least, to respond with certain considerations.

For one thing, the moment something is created, it becomes part of the material world and subject to all the natural laws of the world, including gravity, cause and effect, and so forth. It seemed important in the eyes of the Sages that some of the fundamental spiritual concepts should not be included within that framework, but should be free to fulfill their purposes.

Of course, God came before the creation of the world; but God also had to be pictured as the Supreme Being, who is not dependent on the world. We therefore have Him described as the Throne of Glory, representing a seat of judgment, implying that He is constantly occupied, if such a term can be used in association with God.

The concepts of 'Patriarchs' and 'Israel' should also be considered on another level. Even though God foresees everything, freedom of choice is given. 'Patriarchs' and 'Israel' were created as a reserve to be used only if necessary. If, for example, Adam and Eve and their children had succeeded in their mission of world building, the goals of creation could have been achieved without recourse to the Patriarchs or Israel. If Noah had succeeded, a different conclusion would also have been reached in the biblical story. Thus the creation of the Patriarchs and Israel had only to be contemplated before the creation of the world; held, so to speak, in preparation should they be needed. They were.

It is easier to deal with the concept of Torah since *midrash* 1:1 already asserts that the Torah preceded the world. It represents God's divine plan, the architectural blueprint that precedes a building. Granted that the content of the Torah is life centered, it is important that a concept of that magnitude should be given the transcendent position that it deserves.

It would appear that 'Penitence' is a strictly earthly and human phenomenon. But if so, why make the claim that the greatest saint is not worthy to stand in the same place as the repentant sinner? There must be a quality in 'turning' that goes beyond the ability to change, a certain magnetic spark that leads one back to God. *Teshuvah* is a never-ending process. Why should death end what should be transcended? The concept of Messiah is similar to that of *Teshuvah* except that it applies to the world as a whole, society as a whole, or the Jewish people as a whole.

There is a second consideration that has already been referred to in an oblique manner. What happens after a person dies? Believers assert that after the resurrection of the dead, which is a physical resurrection on this earth, there occurs spiritual immortality. The soul lives on. Is it an entity that thinks, speaks, meditates? If not, why yearn for it? If so, what does it do? What is its meaning? Here the six transcendent symbols come to the fore. What does the soul do? It occupies itself with God and the Torah, the Patriarchs and Israel, Penitence and the Messiah. Not a bad way to spend immortality.

* * *

Additional Commentary

Six things
The point here is to explain why the Torah begins with the word *bereishit* and not with *ba-rishonah*, which would be translated 'at first.' The answer

of the *midrash* is that the text wanted to hint at the fact that six concepts were created to operate in a supernatural way. The word *bereishit* achieves this purpose since it consists of two words, *bara shit*, meaning, 'He created six.' Considering that some of them were only creations of the mind and not actually operative, and even those that were created were spiritual and therefore not visible in the world of matter, they were only hinted at by the text. After that, God created the entire universe, which operated in accordance with natural law in relationship to which God is referred to as *Elokim*. (*Tiferet Tzion*)

*

Repentance
God created that power in the world so that by means of repentance men could be rehabilitated as they were before sinning. Otherwise, a person who wanted to repent would not be capable of doing so because of the fact that his sins caused so much turmoil in the upper worlds. If, for example, a man had sexual relations with a woman married to another man who gave birth to an illegitimate child, his repentance would be most difficult since his sin is so visible. Similarly, if the possibility of spiritual rehabilitation by means of repentance did not exist, all sins would remain forever in their inflamed state. (*Tiferet Tzion*)

*

Command the Children of Israel
The problem seems to be that if Israel was created before the world, how then could the Jewish people come to the Torah by choice? If indeed the goal of creation was not the emergence of Israel, why were all the others reduced in importance? As to the tradition that God made the rounds of all the nations and offered them the Torah, it does not mean that He wanted to give them the Torah but only certain particular commandments. (*Tiferet Tzion*)

*

As the first ripening of the fig tree in the wilderness at its first season
It is the nature of a fig tree that its fruits do not ripen at the same time but rather one by one and little by little. In the beginning there are only one, two, or three of them like the Patriarchs. 'At its first season,' *be-reishito*, as in the verse quoted from Psalms, should be seen in association with the phrase '*reishit darko*,' 'the beginning of his course,' in Proverbs as quoted in the text. Just as Torah was conceived before the creation of the world, so was the intention to create the Patriarchs. (RZWE, abridged)

Parashah One, Midrash Five

The question underlying this *midrash* might be formulated in this way: Is it permitted to study the creation story in an intensive, analytical, or philosophical manner?

רַ' הוּנָא בְּשֵׁם בַּר קַפְּרָא פָּתַח (תהלים לא, יט) 'תֵּאָלַמְנָה שִׂפְתֵי שָׁקֶר וְגוֹ'' אִתְפַּרְכָן אִתְחָרְשָׁן אִשְׁתַּתְּקָן

R. Huna commenced (his exposition) in Bar Kappara's name thus: 'Let the lying lips be dumb [*te'alamnah*]' (Psalms 31:19) – this means, Let them be bound, made dumb, and silenced.

In response to the above assumption, R. Huna in the name of Bar Kappara reacts with the verse in Psalms, 'May the lying lips be dumb.' In other words, such study of the creation story should be discouraged. The phrase 'be dumb' used in the verse is given three meanings and all of them apply.

R. Huna then goes on to explain how he derives these three meanings for *te'alamnah*.

אִתְפַּרְכָן אִתְחָרְשָׁן הֵיךְ מָה דְאַתְּ אָמַר (שמות ד, יא) 'אוֹ מִי יָשׂוּם אִלֵּם אוֹ חֵרֵשׁ אוֹ פִקֵּחַ אוֹ עִוֵּר הֲלֹא אָנֹכִי ה'' וְאוֹמֵר (בראשית לז, ז) 'וְהִנֵּה אֲנַחְנוּ מְאַלְּמִים אֲלֻמִּים בְּתוֹךְ הַשָּׂדֶה וְהִנֵּה קָמָה אֲלֻמָּתִי' אִשְׁתַּתְּקָן כְּמַשְׁמָעוֹ

'Let them be bound,' as in the verse, 'Behold, we were binding [*me'allemim*] sheaves' (Genesis 37:7); 'Let them be made dumb' as you read 'Or who made a man dumb [*illem*]' (Exodus 4:11); 'Let them be silenced' is its literal meaning.

Each of these meanings for *te'alamnah* can be inferred from the verses cited. The 'binding' of the verse in Genesis can mean in our context, 'Let their lips be sealed together.' The verse in Exodus gives our term the meaning, 'Let him be struck dumb.' The literal meaning of the term is 'Let him be silenced.'

'הַדִּבְּרוֹת עַל צַדִּיק' חַי הָעוֹלָמִים (תהלים שם, שם) 'עָתָק' שֶׁהֶעְתִּיק בִּבְרִיּוֹתָיו (שם שם, שם) 'בְּגַאֲוָה' אַתְמְהָה בִּשְׁבִיל לְהִתְגָּאוֹת וְלוֹמַר אֲנִי דוֹרֵשׁ בְּמַעֲשֵׂה בְרֵאשִׁית

23

(שם שם, שם) 'וָבוּז' אַתְמָהָה מְבַזֶּה עַל כְּבוֹדִי דַּאֲמַר ר' יוֹסֵי בַּר חֲנִינָא כָּל הַמִּתְכַּבֵּד
בִּקְלוֹן חֲבֵרוֹ אֵין לוֹ חֵלֶק לָעוֹלָם הַבָּא בִּכְבוֹדוֹ שֶׁל מָקוֹם עַל אַחַת כַּמָּה וְכַמָּה
וּמַה כְּתִיב אַחֲרָיו (שם שם, כ) 'מָה רַב טוּבְךָ אֲשֶׁר צָפַנְתָּ לִירֵאֶיךָ' 'לִירֵאֶיךָ' וְלֹא
לְבוֹזִים אֶת מוֹרָאֶךָ [הָרַב] אַל יְהִי בְּ'מָה רַב טוּבְךָ'

'Which speak against the righteous,' i.e., the Eternal One, arrogantly [*atak*], meaning, on matters which He has withheld (*he'etik*) from his creatures. 'With pride,' the verse expresses astonishment! In order to boast and say, 'I discourse on the creation narrative!' 'and with contempt,' the verse expresses astonishment! To think that he contemns My glory! For R. Jose b. R. Hanina said: Whoever elevates himself at the cost of his fellow man's degradation has no share in the world-to-come. How much the more when it is done at the expense of the glory of God! And what is written after it? 'Oh! How abundant is Your goodness, which You have laid up for them that fear You' (*ibid.* v. 20) – for them that fear You, but not for them that contemn the [great] fear of You. Let him have no part of Your abundant goodness!

The *midrash* continues interpreting the verse as referring to persons who insist on analyzing the creation story.

'The righteous' against whom the wicked people speak must be the Eternal One, because it is inconceivable that David, the psalmist, was referring to himself in such terms (RWZE). The word *atak* is interpreted as deriving from a root that means to move something away and is taken to mean the secrets of creation that God has moved away, i.e., hidden from His creatures.

The *midrash* then dwells on the words 'pride' and 'contempt' and explains them in this way. Those who devote their intellectual efforts to investigating the intricate matters of creation do so with pride; they think that they are enhancing their reputation. In actual fact, they are making of themselves objects of derision. After all, if God hid certain things from His creatures it must have been by design and for some important purpose. What right do these people have to research such matters. Do they not realize that they are not God and that they are belittling His design? As R. Jose puts it, personal aggrandizement at the expense of your fellowman is enough to disqualify you from the world-to-come. How much more so, personal aggrandizement at the expense of God.

The verse that follows in Psalms, 'Oh! How abundant is Your goodness, which You have laid up for them that fear You,' implies that those who

do not fear God and insist on investigating the act of creation and, by
doing so, are insulting Him will receive no part of that abundant good.

בְּנוֹהֵג שֶׁבָּעוֹלָם מֶלֶךְ בָּשָׂר וָדָם בּוֹנֶה פָּלָטִין בְּמָקוֹם בְּמָקוֹם הַבִּיבִים וּבִמְקוֹם הָאַשְׁפָּה
וּבִמְקוֹם הַסְּרִיּוֹת כָּל מִי שֶׁהוּא בָּא לוֹמַר פָּלָטִין זוֹ בְּנוּיָה בְּמָקוֹם הַבִּיבִים וּבִמְקוֹם
הָאַשְׁפָּה וּבִמְקוֹם הַסְּרִיּוֹת אֵינוֹ פּוֹגֵם כָּךְ כָּל מִי שֶׁהוּא בָּא לוֹמַר הָעוֹלָם הַזֶּה נִבְרָא
מִתּוֹךְ תֹּהוּ וָבֹהוּ אֵינוֹ פּוֹגֵם אַתְמָהָה

In human practice, if an earthly monarch were to build a palace on
a site of sewers, dunghills, and garbage, and people would come and
say, 'This palace is built on a site of sewers, dunghills, and garbage,'
would they not insult him? So, too, whoever comes to say that this
world was created out of disorder and void, does he not insult
[God]? It is amazing!

Even if the king did build his palace on such an unsavory site, it would
still be insulting to mention it once the palace had been built. How much
more so is it insulting to God to say that the disorder and void existed
before the creation and that God used them as the materials from which
to create the world. Particularly so, since this is not true and before the
creation there was nothing but God.

רַ' הוּנָא בְּשֵׁם בַּר קַפָּרָא אָמַר אִלּוּלֵי שֶׁהַדָּבָר כָּתוּב אִי אֶפְשָׁר לְאָמְרוֹ 'בְּרֵאשִׁית
בָּרָא אֱלֹהִים' מִנַּיִן הֵן 'וְהָאָרֶץ הָיְתָה תֹהוּ וָבֹהוּ.'

R. Huna said in Bar Kappara's name: If it were not written [in the
Torah], it would be impossible [for us] to say – 'In the beginning God
created [heaven and earth].' Out of what? The earth was disorder
[*tohu*] and void [*vohu*].

The last part of this *midrash* is an indirect polemic against the view that
matter existed before the creation of the world, a view which, as we shall
see below, was held by philosophers and various sects. The polemic is
here put rather daringly. The description of the creation begins with 'In
the beginning God created heaven and earth,' and a reader's immediate
reaction would most probably be, 'But from what?' From the continuation, 'and the earth was disordered and void,' one might think that the
disorder and void are material things and God used them as the material
out of which to create the world! However, the truth is that the *tohu* and
vohu were also created, as will be proven in a later *midrash* and that creation was *creatio ex nihilo*, creation out of nothing, and not *creatio ex creatio*,
creation out of something that existed. For the uninitiated the very first

verse of Genesis is dangerous and therefore if it were not written in the Torah, no Jew could dare to say it.

* * *

Seed Thoughts

I have learned as much from the commentators on Midrash as I have from Midrash itself. Good commentators have so absorbed the style and the thought processes of the material they have been studying that they create their own *midrash* without actually knowing it.

This is particularly the case with a metaphor used by the *Tiferet Tzion* (Rabbi Isaac Zvi Yadler, d. 1917). Commenting on the last phrase used in our *midrash* and the question of whether or not *tohu* and *vohu* is or is not a material thing, he writes that it might be compared to the seminal drop (literally, the putrid drop).

What is he trying to say? It would seem that in this respect the commentator follows a middle position. One view affirms that *tohu va-vohu* is a material substance and therefore matter is pre-existent and eternal and God created something out of something. Those who differ maintain that *tohu va-vohu* describes nothing and is indeed the personification of nothing and therefore God created *ex nihilo*. The *Tiferet Tzion* seems to take a middle position.

To describe *tohu va-vohu* as a seminal drop is not to concretize it, but to symbolize its potential. The sperm has miraculous potential, but it must combine with the female egg in order to produce life. Otherwise, it disappears by absorption as billions and billions of sperms have disappeared and always will.

The *tohu va-vohu* had great potential but it was only realized when the spirit of God hovered over it and indeed, it is always realizable when and if the spirit of God activates it. Then it can become a springboard to help create the life of the world. But only then.

Just as God has this power to ignite and make real even the formless and void, so, too, the human being, created in God's image, has been granted something of that power. He can take the formless, the hopeless, the faithless, and the downtrodden and help bring them back to real life. Or, to use the imagery of the commentator, to have them climb the ladder of life that reaches heaven.

* * *

Additional Commentary

May we study the creation story? Now that it is written down, yes! Rav

Huna seems to feel that one should not study the creation story even though it has been written down. (RWZE, abridged)

*

First, one should try to silence such a teacher of the creation story with insult (אתפרכן). If that does not help, then it should be followed by a curse that his power of speech should fail (אתחרשו, meaning literally that his lips should cleave together), and if that does not succeed in deterring him, he should be cursed with paralysis (אשתתקן). (RDL)

*

It should be stated that our *midrash* is dealing with issues that are much more fundamental than meet the eye. The Torah says that the world was created from תהו ובהו, *tohu va-vohu*, roughly translated as chaos. The word תהו, *tohu*, is a derivation of the Hebrew root '*tohe*,' meaning to wonder (at the unknown). That is to say, it describes the unknown – the state of affairs before the creation, which is something completely unknown to humans, and which cannot be described because humans can only describe what they have experienced.

There is a tradition that God created a thin pliant substance that could take any form describable. This was unformed matter, i.e., the *tohu*, and from it He created formed matter such as heaven and earth. The Hebrew word בהו, *vohu*, should be understood as a form of the Hebrew והוא, *ve-hu*, literally, 'and it,' that is, *from it*, the *tohu*, the unformed matter, He created the formed matter. This is stated by Naḥmanides in his commentary to the words *tohu va-vohu*. Nevertheless, all who teach in this manner should understand that they are in some fashion lessening the Creator, and some students might even be tempted to claim that matter existed before creation, which is contrary to Jewish teaching. (*Yefei To'ar*)

*

In human practice
The purpose of this illustration is to explain the prohibition to speculate about those matters of the creation story that He Himself put into writing, namely, what is below and what is above, what is in front (the future) and what is behind (the pre-creation past). The method used is to refer to those aspects of the creation story that we are permitted to interpret, namely, the story in Genesis, and to point out that even there one can find certain nuances that do not contribute to the honor of God. How much more so those aspects of the story that are beyond human intellectual capacity and thus certainly would not honor God. (*Tiferet Tzion*)

Parashah One, Midrash Six

This commentary continues the theme of *Bereishit* and examines what God actually revealed in the creation story.

רַ' יְהוּדָה בַּר סִימוֹן פָּתַח (דניאל ב, כב) 'וְהוּא גָּלֵי עֲמִיקָתָא וּמְסַתְּרָתָא'

R. Judah bar Simon commenced his exposition: 'And He reveals the deep [*amikata*] and hidden [*mesatrata*] things' (Daniel 2:22).

R. Judah bar Simon sees a special significance in the verse from Daniel. It means that the creation story is a vehicle through which some of the most profound theological ideas have reached us. What are some of these ideas?

'הוּא גָּלֵי עֲמִיקָתָא' זוֹ גֵּיהִנָּם שֶׁנֶּאֱמַר (משלי ט, יח) 'וְלֹא יָדַע כִּי רְפָאִים שָׁם' וְאוֹמֵר
(ישעיה ל, לג) 'הֶעֱמִיק הִרְחִב' 'וּמְסַתְּרָתָא' זוֹ גַּן עֵדֶן שֶׁנֶּאֱמַר (שם ד, ו) 'לְמַחְסֶה
וּלְמִסְתּוֹר מִזֶּרֶם וּמִמָּטָר' וְאוֹמֵר (תהלים לא, כא) 'תַּסְתִּירֵם בְּסֵתֶר פָּנֶיךָ'

'The deep things' are Gehenna, as it is written, '...but he does not know that the shades are there; that her guests are in the depth of the nether world [*she'ol*]' (Proverbs 9:18), and it is also written, '[His fire pit] has been made both wide and deep' (Isaiah 30:33). 'Hidden things' refers to the Garden of Eden, as it is written, '...[which shall serve]... and for a refuge and for a covert (*le-mistor*)' (Isaiah 4:6) and it is written 'You grant them the protection of Your presence' (Psalms 31:21).

The first of these great ideas is that of heaven and hell, which are symbols of the doctrine of reward and punishment as motivations for behavior.

The main element of this exegesis is that Daniel used two terms, '*amikata*' and '*mesatrata*.' The interpretation is that Daniel wanted to praise God for having revealed the existence of Gehenna, called '*amikata*,' and Gan Eden, called '*mesatrata*.' These motivate men to become more God fearing either by fear of punishment or a desire for a great reward.

The main question that should be asked is why the *midrash* quotes two verses in connection with hell and then two verses in connection with heaven or Paradise. The *midrash* does not waste words. There has to be a reason.

28

The afflictions of hell apply to people in correspondence with their deeds. They are divided into two categories – those who sin as a result of passion and those who sin as an act of defiance. For this reason R. Judah bar Simon cites two verses. The first (Proverbs 9:18) describes the punishment for sins of passion because the verse deals with a harlot whose motivation is erotic passion and therefore all the verse says is, 'her guests are in the depth of the nether world.' The second verse (Isaiah 30:33) deals with those who sin deliberately and it speaks of Sennacherib who blasphemed and therefore it tells that 'His fire pit has been made both wide and deep, with plenty of fire and firewood, and with the breath of the Lord burning in it like a stream of sulfur.'

Similarly there are two types of Paradise. The first is at the time of Messiah since only then can we be sure that there will be no backsliding. That is why it is called '*mestarta*,' because man is there protected from the onslaughts of time. The second Paradise is the 'upper Gan Eden,' meaning the future world-to-come. That is what is meant by the verse, 'You grant them the protection of Your presence.' (*Tiferet Tzion*)

דָּבָר אַחֵר 'הוּא גָּלֵי עֲמִיקָתָא וּמְסַתְּרָתָא' אֵלּוּ מַעֲשֵׂיהֶם שֶׁל רְשָׁעִים שֶׁנֶּאֱמַר (ישעיה כט, טו) 'הוֹי הַמַּעֲמִיקִים מֵה'' 'וּמְסַתְּרָתָא' אֵלּוּ מַעֲשֵׂיהֶם שֶׁל רְשָׁעִים שֶׁנֶּאֱמַר (שם שם, שם) 'לַסְתִּיר עֵצָה' (דניאל שם, שם) 'יָדַע מָה בַחֲשׁוֹכָא' אֵלּוּ מַעֲשֵׂיהֶם שֶׁל רְשָׁעִים שֶׁנֶּאֱמַר (ישעיה שם, שם) 'וְהָיָה בְמַחְשָׁךְ מַעֲשֵׂיהֶם' (דניאל שם, שם) 'וּנְהוֹרָא עִמֵּהּ שְׁרֵא' אֵלּוּ מַעֲשֵׂיהֶם שֶׁל צַדִּיקִים דִּכְתִיב (משלי ד, יח) 'וְאוֹרַח צַדִּיקִים כְּאוֹר נֹגַהּ' וְאוֹמֵר (תהלים צז, יא) 'אוֹר זָרוּעַ לַצַּדִּיק וְגו''

Another interpretation: 'And He reveals deep things,' refers to the deeds of the wicked, as it is written, 'Woe unto them that hide their plans deep from the Lord' (Isaiah 29:15). 'He knows what is in the darkness' (Daniel 2:22) also refers to the deeds of the wicked, as it is written, 'who do their work in dark places' (Isaiah 29:15). 'And light dwells with him' (Daniel 2:22) refers to the deeds of the righteous as it is written, 'Light is sown for the righteous' (Psalms 97:2).

The second theological idea derived from creation is the question of what is morally good and what is morally evil. Its main thought is that there are many roads that lead to evil, but only one road that leads to good. This is the meaning of the verse in Daniel that has three major expressions for evil, but only one expression was given by Daniel for the good way.

The question can again be raised, why are there three verses for the wicked and only one for the righteous. According to the *Tiferet Tzion* there are three types of wicked. The first says that God does not supervise the world and does not respond to man's behavior. In this connection the Bible says, 'Woe unto them that hide their plans deep from the Lord,' because they believe that their deeds are too deep to be known by God. The second group believes in God's providence over the world, but feels that not every period of time is equal. When God is busy with other things, He has no time to supervise this lowly world. These are the wicked who know how to hide their actions from God and with reference to them it is said 'He knows what is in the darkness.' The third group believes that God does supervise the world at all times, but how can He know what happens in the darkness. The verse therefore says, 'who do their work in dark places.' But God does good to all and wants the wicked to repent, and therefore through His prophets He revealed their wicked ways to the wicked so that they might realize that God does know the deeds and actions of man. (*Tiferet Tzion*)

The second part of this *midrash* was also taught by R. Judah bar Simon, and it deals with the same text in Daniel, but it can be considered a separate teaching.

אָמַר רַ' יְהוּדָה בַּר סִימוֹן מִתְּחִלַּת בְּרִיָּתוֹ שֶׁל עוֹלָם 'הוּא גָּלֵי עֲמִיקָתָא וּמְסַתְּרָתָא'

R. Judah bar Simon said: From the commencement of the world's creation 'He revealed the deep things.'

God created heaven and earth but how and with what ingredients? And furthermore, how can we know about them?

'בְּרֵאשִׁית בָּרָא אֱלֹהִים וְגוֹ'' וְלֹא פֵּירַשׁ וְהֵיכָן פֵּירַשׁ לְהָלָן (שם מ, כב) 'הַנּוֹטֶה כַדֹּק שָׁמַיִם' 'וְאֵת הָאָרֶץ' וְלֹא פֵּירַשׁ וְהֵיכָן פֵּירַשׁ לְהָלָן (איוב לז, ו) 'כִּי לַשֶּׁלֶג יֹאמַר הֱוֵא אָרֶץ' (שם לח, לח) 'בְּצֶקֶת עָפָר לַמּוּצָק וּגְ' וַיֹּאמֶר אֱלֹהִים יְהִי אוֹר' וְלֹא פֵּירַשׁ וְהֵיכָן פֵּירַשׁ (תהלים קד, ב) 'עֹטֶה אוֹר כַּשַּׂלְמָה'.

It is written, 'In the beginning God created the heaven,' but it is not explained how. Where then is it explained? Elsewhere: 'Who spread out the skies like gauze' (Isaiah 40:22); **'and the earth' which is likewise not explained. Where is that explained? Elsewhere: 'He commands the snow, "Fall to the ground!"'** (Job 37:6) **'Whereupon the earth melts into a mass and its clods stick together'** (ibid. 38:38) **'And God said: Let there be light' and the manner of this, too, is not explained. Where is it explained? Elsewhere: '[You are] wrapped in a robe of light'** (Psalms 104:2).

The *midrash* now establishes that although the creation story is told in a general way, its particulars are given elsewhere in the Bible. When it asks the question where is this part of creation specified, it is underlying a very important principle – that everything is explained in Scripture. If it is not explained in the Pentateuch, it is explained in the Prophets or Writings.

That is the meaning of the term *amikata*. God revealed His mysteries somewhere. In the case of heaven, He revealed more in Isaiah; in the case of the creation of earth, He revealed more in the Book of Job; and in the case of the creation of light, he revealed more in Psalms.

In Isaiah, He revealed that, at first, heaven was a very thin substance. Later on, it expanded to encompass the entire earth. By the same token, earth and light were created in stages as the verses reveal.

* * *

Seed Thoughts

One of the key ideas in modern scientific and scholarly thought is the concept of development. Things and beings do not merely grow in size, but in structure and capacity as well. During this process many changes can occur. Is this process something that was there potentially at the beginning, or does it involve something quite new that was added? Did the human being develop from the ape or Neanderthal, man or was he created as a complete human? The debate is perennial.

Coming closer to home, did Jewish law develop over the centuries, or does both the oral and written law come from Sinai? For those who affirm the latter, was the ascription to Sinai potential or actual? Did general principles at Sinai potentially possess all the ingredients of their further development or do we take literally the idea taught in the *Aggada* that Abraham put on *tefilin*, presumably the same kind that we wear today? Here, too, the debate rages on between modernists and fundamentalists.

The *Tiferet Tzion*, in the closing words of his commentary on this particular *midrash*, makes the interesting point that it is not only the earth and material things that experience growth and development. The heavens and the spiritual life also experience development.

What does it mean for spiritual life to develop? Does it mean that new values appear that were not there before? Does it mean that modern technology may have made certain doctrines or practices untenable or requiring new interpretation? Or does it mean that the same great values and ideas encompass more people and that development simply means growth in numbers?

However, a major difference between scientific development and spiritual growth may be defined. In scientific development one generation can learn from the other. Once the cure for polio was found, that knowledge was carried on to the next generation. Once having been discovered, such information is forever part of the daily life experience of all people.

The same cannot be said of the spiritual life. Granted that in the area of religious learning much progress has been made. Rabbinic literature, followed by the philosophical writings and then the codes, were all the works of genius. If this is what is meant by development, then, we can all be in accord. But if spiritual development can only occur with an improvement in the character and personality of man, it is not easy to make a judgment.

Looking at the history of the world, it does not appear as though the generations are improving. On the other hand, every generation has its share of good people, some of them even saintly. The main difference seems to be that, unlike the physical realm, in the realm of the spiritual one generation does not seem capable of learning from the other.

If the goal of history is to be reached, or if the Messiah is to come, based on our efforts, a generation will have to arise that will have such a plethora of good people as never existed before to make it possible. It will have to be one generation because there is no carry-over. Geniuses in learning and ethical achievement have put their thoughts on paper, but it takes a lifetime to read them and then there is hardly time left to put them into action.

Development in terms of spiritual values requires more clarification, not to speak of that strategy that will enable them to be transmitted and lived by the Jewish people and the world.

It is very difficult. Can that be why the Messiah delays his coming?

* * *

Additional Commentary

R. Judah b. R. Simon said

There is a certain methodology to the *midrash* that has to be understood. This *midrash* really is not in place here. However, this is the style when the Midrash wants to bring proof from a particular scriptural text. First it explains the text in many ways that are not relevant to the subject in question, until finally it comes to the point that it needs. (Rashi)

At the beginning of creation the Almighty revealed certain things but did not explain them until later. (Rashi)

*

From the commencement of the world's creation

This teaching is the most important one that belongs here and because of it the rest of the section was brought in by the way. That includes the opening part about revealing deep and hidden things. Note that the language doubles itself. This is meant to indicate that something new has been revealed – the question of how the world was created.

This was revealed in other places in the Torah so that the mystery is only here. (RWZE, abridged)

*

Said R. Abba

The context of the verse from Daniel is the dream of Nebuchadnezer. The preacher now interprets the verse from Daniel as praise to God for having revealed to him the interpretation of the dream. This dream made known the three exiles after that of Babylon and also the coming of Messiah when God's majesty will be revealed. In reference to this he said, 'He reveals deep and hidden things' – the two expressions refer to the exile of the Medes and the Greeks. Their end was also revealed but not that of Rome. Even Daniel did not know that. That is why he said, 'He knows what is in the darkness' – only God knows when the end will come. (*Tiferet Tzion*)

*

From the commencement of the world's creation

'He reveals deep and hidden things.' The interpretation is that even from the beginning of the world when heaven and earth and light were created on the first day as the foundation of all material and spiritual creations, and they were indeed 'deep and hidden things' – hidden from human intelligence – He nevertheless revealed through His prophets the manner of their creation. In this He revealed His love for those who fear Him in the fact that He reveals His secrets. (*Tiferet Tzion*)

*

Where then is it explained?

In connection with the creation of heaven, the question arises how was it actually done? Was it created completely at one time or was it created first partially and later on it was expanded? The Sages explained that heaven and earth continued stretching until God commanded, 'Stop!' This is what the verse quoted in the *midrash* reveals: 'Who spread out the skies like gauze.' In the beginning He stretched it out as a curtain which is very thin and afterwards 'and stretched them out like a tent to dwell in' (which is the continuation of the verse). The heavens increased – i.e., developed – through the power of God's word that was inherent in them from the moment of creation. What is new here is that even in matters affecting the upper worlds – spiritual worlds – even though there is no physical repro- duction (be fruitful and multiply) nevertheless they still have the capacity to grow. Even the special light that is stored up for the righteous has the capacity to grow. This happens through the power that is generated when righteous people perform the commandments. (*Tiferet Tzion*)

Parashah One, Midrash Seven

רַ' יִצְחָק פָּתַח (תהלים קיט, קס) 'רֹאשׁ דְּבָרְךָ אֱמֶת וְגוֹ''

R. Isaac commenced his exposition with the verse 'Truth is the essence of Your word; Your just rules are eternal' (Psalms 119:160).

When R. Isaac interpreted the opening words of Genesis – 'In the beginning God created...' – he referred to this scriptural quotation for two reasons. The first was why the name *Elokim* was used and not *Hashem*, which is the tetragrammaton (i.e., the famous name of four letters). The second reason was the fact that the name of God seems to be written in the plural.

אָמַר רַ' יִצְחָק מִתְּחִלַּת בְּרִיָּתוֹ שֶׁל עוֹלָם 'רֹאשׁ דְּבָרְךָ אֱמֶת' 'בְּרֵאשִׁית בָּרָא אֱלֹהִים'

Said R. Isaac: From the very commencement of the world's creation, 'truth is the essence of Your word,' thus, In the beginning God created.

The last letter of each of the first three words of Genesis makes up the Hebrew word אמת – *emet* – truth. This could only have happened by using the name of God as *Elokim*, otherwise the letter מ would have been lacking. We now have an answer from the style of the text. What about its content?

(ירמיה י, י) 'וַה' אֱלֹהִים אֱמֶת' (תהלים שם, שם) 'וּלְעוֹלָם כָּל מִשְׁפַּט צִדְקֶךָ' שֶׁכָּל גְּזֵרָה וּגְזֵרָה שֶׁאַתָּה גוֹזֵר עַל בְּרִיּוֹתֶיךָ הֵן מַצְדִּיקִין עֲלֵיהֶם אֶת הַדִּין וּמְקַבְּלִין אוֹתוֹ בָּאֱמוּנָה וְאֵין כָּל בְּרִיָּה יְכוֹלָה לוֹמַר שְׁתֵּי רְשֻׁיּוֹת בָּרְאוּ הָעוֹלָם וַיְדַבְּרוּ אֱלֹהִים אֵין כְּתִיב כָּאן אֶלָּא 'וַיְדַבֵּר אֱלֹהִים' וַיֹּאמְרוּ אֱלֹהִים אֵין כְּתִיב כָּאן אֶלָּא 'וַיֹּאמֶר אֱלֹהִים' בְּרֵאשִׁית בָּרְאוּ אֱלֹהִים אֵין כְּתִיב כָּאן אֶלָּא 'בָּרָא אֱלֹהִים.'

'But the Lord God is the true God' (Jeremiah 10:10), and 'Your just rules are eternal' (Psalms 119:160). For with regard to every decree which You promulgate concerning Your creatures, they affirm the righteousness of Your judgment and accept it with faith. And no person can argue that two powers created the world. For [concern-

35

ing the giving of the Torah], 'and the gods spoke' [with the verb
וַיְדַבְּרוּ in the plural] is not written, but 'and God spoke [with the verb
וַיְדַבֵּר' in the singular] all these words' (Exodus 20:1). Similarly, it does
not say 'And *Elokim* said' [וַיֹּאמְרוּ in the plural], but '*Elokim* said' [וַיֹּאמֶר
in the singular]. [And with regard to the creation of the world], 'In
the beginning *Elokim* created' [with the verb בָּרְאוּ in the plural] is not
written here, but 'In the beginning *Elokim* created' [with the verb
בָּרָא in the singular].

In other words if the question is why *Elokim* is used in place of *Hashem*,
the answer is that the name *Elokim* is used elsewhere as a symbol of God's
divine justice – justice based on truth. By understanding that the world is
based on truth, every divine decree, no matter how difficult to understand,
is rationalized and justified by believers in the conviction that truth must
be supported by faith.

We still have not responded to the concern of the name of God being
in the plural. R. Isaac points out that although the name *Elokim* seems to
be in the plural form, because of the יﬦ at the end, the fact that the verbs
used with it are always in the singular, amply demonstrates that in reality
Elokim is one.

* * *

Seed Thoughts

The central idea of this *midrash* is that God's seal is truth. The creation
story begins with truth. God's word is truth.

But what is truth? Is it ever capable of definition? It is probably impossible to get to an ultimate definition, but if we try to respond to this question in several faltering steps, we might acquire a little more illumination
on the subject.

People speak of scientific truth. By that they mean the scientific method
or those things that can be proven by measurement. All scientists will
agree that there is a scientific truth. There is also an aesthetic truth, though
it is less exact, and it represents the criteria by which those who are knowl-
edgeable will identify great art as being truly great. Ethical truth is even
more difficult to define since every society has its own definition, and, as
the *midrash* puts it, justice is the truth of God.

Even though we speak of truth in these limited forms, the problem of
definition is very difficult.

At Expo '67, the Pavilion of Judaism projected a theme which, among
others, included the concepts of truth, justice, and peace. In the case of

truth, the best they could come up with was the choice of twenty-five great Jews and a quotation by each of them under the general rubric of: 'the truths by which we live.'

If truth is an absolute we cannot define it. We can only approach it. That is what we must try to do. The prophet Amos said, 'Seek Me and live.' He did not say, 'Find Me and live.' It is in the seeking that a person finds meaning. We are not called upon to define truth or even to achieve it in its absolute form. But we are called upon to seek it, to approach it with sincerity and devotion, to the best of our ability. According to the present *midrash*, this search is a religious commandment.

* * *

Additional Commentary

From the very commencement

The main point of this *midrash* is directed against the sectarians who believe in many powers. In accordance with that belief there is no true good. The good elements in man come from the 'good creator' and his bad elements comes from 'the creator of evil.' Furthermore, there is no connection between man's behavior and the good or bad that happens to him. Therefore, there is no such thing as true justice. The *midrash* affirms that from the beginning of creation God emphasized that truth must have power in the world. If, indeed, God created, then the rule of the world is truth. This can be proven first from Jeremiah 10:10 where it actually says 'God is truth' and from the fact that the last three letters of *Bereishit Bara Elokim* make up the word *emet*, truth. Based on the verse from Psalms, 'Your just rules are eternal,' it is the duty of man to justify God's truth, which is His justice. So, the first verse quoted, 'truth is the essence of Your word,' means that the fundamental principle is truth. God stands on the principle of truth and his justice endures forever. (Mirkin)

*

Truth is the essence of Your word

The *midrash* is trying to explain why the Torah begins with the name *Elokim* for God, which means justice, and not with the name *Hashem*, which stands for mercy. The question also arises because *Elokim* has a plural form. The answer is that the name *Elokim* is the sign of the world being judged in truth for God (*Elokim*) is truth. The verse is interpreted literally: 'The beginning of Your word is truth and all Your righteous ordinances endure forever.' This means that the Torah, which is God's word, begins with *Elokim* and God is truth. Furthermore, at the giving of the Torah, the text also begins with *Elokim* – 'And *Elokim* spoke all these words' (Exodus 20:1) for the same reason, to indicate that He is a truthful judge even for those who do not observe the Torah, and those who do observe are expected to justify the law even when it applies to them.

There need be no fear of a misunderstanding due to the name *Elokim* appearing at the opening of Scripture and also at the opening of the Ten Commandments seemingly in plural form. No one can claim on the basis of these words that two powers created the world because the verb applying to *Elokim* is always in the singular. (*Tiferet Tzion*)

*

R. Isaac began

The problem is the use of the name *Elokim* in the opening of Genesis since this term is not exclusive to God – judges are so referred to by that appellation. So are the angels, which is why God is referred to as '*Elokei Elokim.*' In response to this problem the verse, 'The beginning of Your word is truth and all Your righteous ordinances endure forever' is to indicate that the special reason for starting the Torah with the name *Elokim* is because this word stands for the quality of truth as explained above. It also implies the quality of justice as also explained above. This cannot be said of the quality of compassion and mercy referred to by God's name, *Hashem* (*Adonai*). This is not the quality of truth (but rather the abrogation of truth in favor of peace).

Since the fundamental reason for the establishment of the world is the quality of truth and the Torah itself is described as truth, and man's behaviour should be based on truth, it is most appropriate that the Torah should begin with this particular name of God, *Elokim*, which stands for truth. (*Tiferet Tzion*)

Parashah One, Midrash Eight

The question again is, why did the Torah begin with the word, *bereishit*, and not, for example, with the word *ba-rishonah*. It implies, as rendered earlier in the *midrash*, that the word, *bereishit*, is a composite of two words, *bara shit* – 'He created six.' From this the *midrash* derives that six items were created before anything else. What were they?

רַבִּי יְהוֹשֻׁעַ בֶּן לֵוִי בְּשֵׁם רַ' לֵוִי אָמַר זֶה שֶׁהוּא בּוֹנֶה צָרִיךְ שִׁשָּׁה דְבָרִים מַיִם וְעָפָר
וְעֵצִים וַאֲבָנִים וְקָנִים וּבַרְזֶל

R. Joshua b. Levi said in the name of R. Levi: A person about to build requires six things: water, earth, timber, stones, canes, and iron.

The poor man requires two types of timber in his house, large logs to hold up the foundations and also soft thatch that can be put in place by plaster or clay. Since a poor man's house is small, he doesn't need a measuring rod.

וְאִם תֹּאמַר עָשִׁיר הוּא וְאֵינוֹ צָרִיךְ לְקָנִים הֲרֵי הוּא צָרִיךְ לִקְנֶה הַמִּדָּה שֶׁנֶּאֱמַר
'וּפְתִיל פִּשְׁתִּים בְּיָדוֹ וּקְנֵה הַמִּדָּה' (יחזקאל מ, ג)

And even if you say he is a wealthy man and does not need canes, yet he surely requires a measuring rod, as it is written, 'and a measuring reed in his hand' (Ezekiel 40:3).

Rich men's houses do not need reeds, but they do need a measuring reed, stones, and earth for the foundation, water to absorb the clay, and iron for strength.

כָּךְ הַתּוֹרָה קָדְמָה אוֹתָן שֵׁשׁ קְדִימוֹת (משלי ח, כא) 'קֶדֶם' וּ'מֵאָז' (שם שם, כב)
וּ'מֵעוֹלָם' וּ'מֵרֹאשׁ' וּ'מִקַּדְמֵי' תְּרֵין בְּפָרְשָׁה (שם שם, כב) 'ה' קָנָנִי.'

Thus the Torah preceded [the creation of the world] by these six things, viz, *kedem* [the first], *me-az* [of old] (Proverbs 8:21), **me-olam [from everlasting]** (*ibid.* v. 22), **me-rosh [from the beginning], and mi-kadmei [from the earliest times], which counts as two.**

Just as a builder needs six things before he can start building, so too the Torah through which the world was created preceded it in six stages, all of which are represented in the book of Proverbs in two verses (8:21-22) up to the word – ארץ – at the end of the sentence. R. Joshua did not list all the words, only those connected with time or with the process of building (RWZE, abridged). The word מקדמי, *mikadmei,* is interpreted as counting for two because it is in the plural.

* * *

Seed Thoughts

Of all the interpretations that try to make sense of this curious *midrash,* the one that appeals to me most is a comment by the *Tiferet Tzion.* He compares the six building materials that preceded the world to the six orders of the Mishnah.

Why the Mishnah? Because the Mishnah is the classic text of the Oral Law and its development poses many unsolved and unresolved questions.

That the Mishnah is a great work is beyond dispute. What is still a puzzle is the development from the Biblical Torah system to the more sophisticated code of the Mishnah. Somehow, the Mishnah appears so advanced that it is hard to find its connection to the scriptural text. I do not use the term advanced in any sense of superiority. I am merely referring to the many laws in the Mishnah that seem to be unrelated to the biblical original. Very often the Sages of the Mishnah could themselves describe the laws as mountains of rulings that depend upon a source as flimsy as a hair.

The Rabbis were sensitive to the problem and to the danger that the Mishnah would be regarded as a later development and not dependent upon its original source. It was very important, therefore, that they seek, find, and postulate a special and legal foundation for the Oral Law. Our *midrash* is one of the ways to achieve this purpose.

The world has to conform to natural law, of course. But spiritual laws are also natural. They are intrinsically a part of the world and were part of the original creation.

The building blocks for the spiritual world of which the Oral Law is the supreme part was already established as of old. God established it as the first and true beginning of the way He wanted for this world.

* * *

Additional Commentary

Needs six things

The interpretation is that when God willed to create the world, He prepared six things, intellectual gifts (acts of grace), the *sefirot* of the building in the words of the Kabbalists. But I am foolish and do not understand these things. However, as we see in human behavior, before a building is begun, six items are prepared and then the building starts. The world of nature resembles the world of the mind as the behavior of an ape resembles the behavior of a human, except that it is done without mind.

Similarly, the behavior of the world of nature resembles the behavior of the upper world. Reflect upon the fact that the human being is called both man and human (*adam*). Similarly the angels are referred to as '*ish*' and '*adam.*' And God Himself, so to speak, is also referred to as '*ish*' and '*adam*,' e.g., 'The Lord is a man of war' and the fact that over the Throne of Glory there was the image of a man. There is an Aramaic saying, 'The lower world resembles the upper world and therefore learn from it' (from the lower world about the upper world). That is why the true Sages of Israel always used parables. From this world we learn about the heavenly world. That is the meaning of the expression so constantly used, בנוהג שבעולם – 'in human practice.' Similarly, in building, the lower world resembles the upper world. However we can only learn in reverse, from the lower to the upper. Whoever knows the science or wisdom of building this world will also know a great deal about building of human relationships as is said in *Exodus Rabbah, parashah* 13, Abba Yosef, the builder knows how the world was built. From these few words you will learn the style in which the Sages used parables to focus on the wisdom of Torah and of God. (RWZE)

*

A builder requires
God created the world for it to operate by natural law. It was therefore necessary that, from the very outset, life should continue as in natural law. (*Tiferet Tzion*)

*

Thus the Torah preceded
The six advanced things correspond to the Oral Torah that is divided into six sections for the main basis of the covenant with God and Israel is through them. Because the Mishnaic orders of *Kedoshim*, holy things, and *Taharot*, laws of ritual purity, are not operative in our day but only while the Temple stands, therefore, Scripture encompassed them in one word, *mi-kadmei.* (*Tiferet Tzion*)

Parashah One, Midrash Nine

How should one interpret the verse, 'And the earth was formless and void,' which implies that it was formless and void before creation? This prompted the question of a philosopher.

פִּילוֹסוֹפִי אֶחָד שָׁאַל אֶת רַבָּן גַּמְלִיאֵל אָמַר לֵהּ צַיָּר גָּדוֹל הוּא אֱלֹהֵיכֶם אֶלָּא שֶׁמָּצָא סַמְמָנִים טוֹבִים שֶׁסִּיְּעוּ אוֹתוֹ תֹּהוּ וָבֹהוּ וְחשֶׁךְ וָרוּחַ וּמַיִם וּתְהוֹמוֹת

A certain philosopher asked Rabban Gamaliel, saying to him: 'Your God is indeed a great artist, but He found good materials which assisted him: *tohu, vohu*, darkness, wind, water, and the deep.'

The philosopher wanted to prove from the verse 'and the earth was formless and void' that the '*tohu* and *vohu*' existed before creation and they, together with the other elements that are listed in the first two verses of Genesis, were the materials out of which God created the world. Rabban Gamaliel proves from Scripture that God created all the items listed in that verse in the same fashion as other creations.

אָמַר לֵהּ תִּפַּח רוּחֵהּ דְּהַהוּא גַּבְרָא כֻּלְּהוֹן כְּתִיב בָּהֶן בְּרִיאָה תֹּהוּ וָבֹהוּ שֶׁנֶּאֱמַר (ישעיה מה, ז) 'עֹשֶׂה שָׁלוֹם וּבוֹרֵא רָע' חֹשֶׁךְ (שם שם, שם) 'יוֹצֵר אוֹר וְגוֹ'' מַיִם (תהלים קמח, ד) 'הַלְלוּהוּ שְׁמֵי הַשָּׁמַיִם וְהַמַּיִם' לָמָּה שֶׁצֻּוָּה וְנִבְרָאוּ' רוּחַ (עמוס ד, יג) 'כִּי הִנֵּה יוֹצֵר הָרִים וּבֹרֵא רוּחַ' תְּהוֹמוֹת (משלי ח, כד) 'בְּאֵין תְּהֹמוֹת חוֹלָלְתִּי.'

He [Rabban Gamaliel] replied: May your spirit blow away! With regards to all of them it is written [in the Bible] that they were created. Emptiness and disorder – 'I make weal and create woe' (Isaiah 45:7); Darkness – 'I form light and create darkness (ibid.); Water – 'Praise Him, highest heavens, and you waters,' Why? 'For it was He who commanded that they be created' (Psalms 145:45); Wind – 'Behold, He who formed the mountains and created the wind' (Amos 4:13); Depths – 'There was still no deep when I [wisdom] was brought forth' (Proverbs 8:24).

This last verse says much more than that the deep was created. It says that the Torah was created before the deep. So all these things were created and we need not worry about the charges of the philosopher. Indeed, as

42

we learned earlier that the word *bereishit* consists of *bara shit* meaning, 'He created six,' in this instance the six elements mentioned in the first two verses, all of which were created.

* * *

Seed Thoughts

This is one of the many places in Midrash and Rabbinic literature in general, where conversations are recorded between a leading non-Jewish scholar usually described as a philosopher, and an outstanding Rabbinic sage. In each case the philosopher poses a challenge to some Jewish doctrine or scriptural text, usually a criticism that is well thought out logically and intellectually. The Rabbi has to use much skill and homiletical ability to counter the arguments and prove again the truth of the Jewish religious position.

The important point to notice is that such contacts existed. The *midrash* could not have happened with the special quality that it possesses in isolation or ghettoization. It required the cross-fertilization of cultures and the challenge and provocation that comes from sincere questioning.

One cannot produce an eschatology or a redeeming document merely by talking to oneself. Contacts are required not only with individuals who differ, but with cultures and traditions of different origins. We need not ever feel that we will suffer by comparison or that we will be theologically demoralized through such interaction. We must have confidence in our beliefs and value system.

The *Ethics of the Fathers* says, 'Know how to answer the heretic.' It might be rendered as meaning: 'Know, learn, and absorb very well whatever are the answers that you use to respond to the heretic.' This will become a most important form of positive reinforcement of the Torah.

* * *

Additional Commentary

The philosopher and Rabban Gamaliel

By *tohu* and *vohu* the philosopher meant primeval matter, without form. Thereupon Rabban Gamaliel quoted: 'I make weal (that which is whole, i.e., what contains both matter and form) and evil, i.e., that which is defective, consisting of matter only without form. Thus, that too was created. (Husik, *A History of Medieval Jewish Philosophy*, p. 29.) Perhaps, too, this is an allusion to the fact that matter is a source of evil.

*

If the world was created from *tohu va-vohu* and we know that they were unformed but real substances, though unknown, does that not mean that something existed before the world was created? This is, basically, the question that the philosopher asked Rabban Gamaliel. Granted that your God is a wonderful artist of creation, but He had good materials existing with which to work. Rabbi Gamaliel's denial takes the form of proving that creation is associated with all the materials listed by the philosopher. (*Ha-Midrash ha-Mevo'ar*)

*

May your spirit blow away!

This kind of language is customary in Midrash when it argues with opponents of Judaism. It would appear that these are not the direct words of Rabban Gamaliel to the philosopher. It is not to be imagined that they would curse such high-ranking people to their faces. These are expressions added by the redactors of Midrash in the spirit of the verse 'the name of evil-doers will rot' and, in this case, because the philosopher denied the creation of the world *ex nihilo*, he was, in fact, denying the newness of the world, '*ḥiddush ha-olam*.' (RWZE)

*

This expression often occurs when a view is expressed that contradicts the faith of Israel. It is not intended to mean that the person should burst and therefore die. It really implies 'May he depart crestfallen, by virtue of having received a decisive and conclusive answer.' (Mirkin, *Peshuto shel Drash*)

*

'I make weal [*shalom*, lit. 'peace'] and create woe [*ra*, lit. 'evil']'

The word *ra* should be understood as meaning not 'evil' as usually understood, but as the opposite of *shalom*, wholeness, meaning complete with form, and is, therefore, incomplete being only in a raw state of matter. (*Yefei To'ar*)

*

The evil is meant as a symbol of *tohu* and *vohu* as in the verse, 'I saw the earth and behold it was *tohu* and *vohu*.' This kind of evil is the way to eternal life as written, 'The way to achieve a good way of life is through constant moral chastisement.' Therefore God created evil so that confronting it would improve us in our latter days. (*Tiferet Tzion*)

*

When there were no depths

The Torah says, 'Before the depths were created.' That means that creation preceded the 'depths.' This is the meaning of *bereishit, bara shit* – God created these six things and someone came along and erroneously claimed that they preceded creation. (*Ha-Midrash ha-Mevo'ar*)

*

A philosopher asked
The philosopher wanted to prove from the verse 'and the earth was formless and void' that the *tohu* and *vohu* were there before God's act of creation. That seems to be the meaning of the verb *hayyeta* – 'was' in the same fashion as other creations. As for the phrase 'and the earth was' it is similar to the expression 'Let there be light and there was light.' Or similar to the expression 'it became melted' meaning that it became something that it was not before. And it means according to the Gaon of Vilna that then, at the moment of that verse, *tohu* and *vohu* and darkness and wind and water all came into being. (*Tiferet Tzion*)

Parashah One, Midrash Ten

The question that this *midrash* addresses is: Why did the Torah start with the letter *bet* and not *aleph*, which is the first letter of the alphabet? Furthermore, what is there so special about the letter *bet* that the Torah begins '*Bereishit bara Elokim*'? Would it not have been more appropriate to begin *Elokim bara bereishit*?

רַבִּי יוֹנָה בְּשֵׁם רַ' לֵוִי אָמַר לָמָה נִבְרָא הָעוֹלָם בְּב' אֶלָּא מַה ב' זֶה סָתוּם מִכָּל צְדָדָיו וּפָתוּחַ מִלְפָנָיו כָּךְ אֵין לְךָ רְשׁוּת לוֹמַר מַה לְמַטָה מַה לְמַעְלָה מַה לְפָנִים מַה לְאָחוֹר אֶלָּא מִיוֹם שֶׁנִבְרָא הָעוֹלָם וּלְהַבָּא

R. Jonah said in R. Levi's name: Why was the world created with a *bet*? Just as the *bet* is closed on all sides and only open in front (at which point the Torah begins), so, too, you are not permitted to speculate on what is above and what is below, what is before and what is behind, but only on the day of creation and onwards.

בַּר קַפָּרָא אָמַר (דברים ד, לב) 'כִּי שְׁאַל נָא לְיָמִים רִאשׁנִים אֲשֶׁר הָיוּ לְפָנֶיךָ' - 'לְמִן הַיּוֹם' שֶׁנִבְרְאוּ אַתָּה דוֹרֵשׁ וְאִי אַתָּה דוֹרֵשׁ לְפָנִים מִכָּאן. (שם שם, שם) 'וּלְמִקְצֵה הַשָּׁמַיִם וְעַד קְצֵה הַשָּׁמָיִם' אַתָּה דוֹרֵשׁ וְחוֹקֵר וְאִי אַתָּה חוֹקֵר לְפָנִים מִכָּאן

Bar Kappara said: 'You have but to inquire about bygone ages that came before you, ever since God created man on earth' (Deuteronomy 4:32) and 'from one end of heaven to the other' (ibid.) – you may inquire regarding that day onwards but you may not speculate about what was before that day.

You might think from this that the permission to speculate is only from the creation of man, which is the sixth day. This explains why Bar Kappara brings the continuation of that verse, meaning: You may speculate from the day that days were created, but you may not speculate on what was before that. You can speculate from day one and do not have to wait until the sixth day (RWZE).

דָּרַשׁ רַבִּי יְהוּדָה בֶּן פָּזִי בְּמַעֲשֵׂה בְרֵאשִׁית בַּהֲדֵיהּ דְּבַר קַפָּרָא

R. Judah b. Pazzi lectured on the creation story, in accordance with this interpretation of Bar Kappara.

46

This report is brought as proof that the interpretation of Bar Kappara was accepted.

The first teaching conveyed by the letter *bet* is the limitation placed upon speculation about creation. Some commentators feel that the names of R. Jonah and Bar Kappara should be interchanged. For our purpose it is enough to know the differences between the two. Both accept the limitation of speculation to the time of the creation of the world and not before it. One view says that even this kind of speculation should be done privately, on an individual basis. The other asserts that it is permitted to teach it publicly. That is what is meant by the phrase דורש וחוקר – 'preach and investigate.' (RWZE, abridged)

לָמָּה נִבְרָא הָעוֹלָם בְּבֵ' לְהוֹדִיעֲךָ שֶׁהֵן שְׁנֵי עוֹלָמִים הָעוֹלָם הַזֶּה וְהָעוֹלָם הַבָּא.

Why was the world created with a *bet*? To teach you that there are two worlds – this world and the world-to-come.

The first interpretation of *bet* had to do with its appearance. The second interpretation has to do with its numerical value of two. There are two worlds, this world and the world-to-come. The world-to-come is mentioned nowhere in Scripture, but this interpretation provides a hint of it. This interpretation was not satisfied with the previous one based on the shape of the letters because we are not certain what the original shape of the letters really was. (*Yefei To'ar*)

דָּבָר אַחֵר וְלָמָּה בְּבֵ' שֶׁהוּא לְשׁוֹן בְּרָכָה וְלָמָּה לֹא בְּאָלֶף שֶׁהוּא לְשׁוֹן אֲרִירָה

Another interpretation: Why with a *bet*? Because *bet* connotes blessing (*berakhah*). And why not with an *aleph*? Because *aleph* connotes cursing (*arirah*).

The third interpretation is that of the *notrikon* method, which means an acrostic. It is a shortened form of writing words by using only the first letter. In English, for example, BBC is an acrostic standing for the British Broadcasting Corporation. A well-known Hebrew acrostic may be found in the Passover Haggadah – ד׳צ׳ך, ע׳ד׳ש וכו' – whose letters stand for the ten plagues of Egypt, but only the initial letters are used. Here, too, the letter *bet* can be used as an acrostic for blessing – *berakhah*. And even though it is possible to find words beginning with *aleph* that are hopeful, and words beginning with *bet* that are pessimistic, the majority are not that way. However, this solution, too, does not seem satisfactory and so a fourth interpretation is offered.

דָּבָר אַחֵר לָמָה לֹא בְּאָל"ף שֶׁלֹּא לִתֵּן פִּתְחוֹן פֶּה לָאֶפִּיקוֹרְסִין לוֹמַר הֵיאַךְ הָעוֹלָם
יָכוֹל לַעֲמֹד שֶׁהוּא נִבְרָא בִּלְשׁוֹן אֲרִירָה אֶלָּא אָמַר הַקָּדוֹשׁ בָּרוּךְ הוּא הֲרֵי אֲנִי
בוֹרֵא אוֹתוֹ בִּלְשׁוֹן בְּרָכָה וְהַלְוַאי יַעֲמֹד.

Another interpretation: Why not with an *aleph*? In order not to provide a justification for heretics to claim: How can the world endure, seeing that it was created with the language of cursing? Hence the Holy One blessed be He, said, 'Lo. I will create it with the language of blessing, and would that it may stand!'

The purpose of the *bet* is to forestall heretical arguments. The meaning here is the view that our fate is predestined for us. If the Torah had started with an *aleph* – the language of curses – it could have been maintained that all the evil of the world was pre-ordained at its creation, and thus man cannot be held responsible for doing evil. Now that the Torah started with *bet* – the language of blessing – evil cannot be ascribed to the world or nature, but only to ourselves and our wicked ways. As for the expression, 'would that it may stand!' that is a challenge to human beings to make this world a blessing.

דָּבָר אַחֵר לָמָה בְּב' אֶלָּא מַה ב' זֶה יֶשׁ לוֹ שְׁנֵי עוֹקְצִין אֶחָד מִלְמַעְלָה וְאֶחָד
מִלְמַטָּה מֵאֲחוֹרָיו אוֹמְרִים לַב' מִי בְרָאֲךָ וְהוּא מַרְאֶה בְּעוֹקְצוֹ מִלְמַעְלָה וְאָמַר זֶה
שֶׁלְמַעְלָה בְּרָאַנִי וּמַה שְּׁמוֹ וְהוּא מַרְאֶה לָהֶן בְּעוֹקְצוֹ שֶׁל אַחֲרָיו וְאוֹמֵר ה' שְׁמוֹ

Another interpretation: Why with a *bet*? Just as the *bet* has two projecting points, one on its top pointing upward and the other, at its bottom, pointing backward, so when it is asked, 'Who created you?' it intimates with its upward point, 'He who is above created me.' And if it is further asked, 'What is His name?' it intimates to us with its back point: 'The Lord is His name.'

A fifth interpretation again makes use of the shape of the letter *bet*, particularly the points jutting upwards, and pointing rearwards. The first points to God; the second points to what is before the *bet*, namely, the *aleph*, and indicates that God is One and His Name One.

אָמַר ר' אֶלְעָזָר בַּר חֲנִינָא בְּשֵׁם ר' אַחָא עֶשְׂרִים וְשִׁשָּׁה דוֹרוֹת הָיְתָה הָאָל"ף קוֹרֵא
תִּגָּר לִפְנֵי כִסְאוֹ שֶׁל הַקָּדוֹשׁ בָּרוּךְ הוּא אָמְרָה לְפָנָיו רִבּוֹנוֹ שֶׁל עוֹלָם אֲנִי רִאשׁוֹן
שֶׁל אוֹתִיּוֹת וְלֹא בָרָאתָ עוֹלָמְךָ בִּי אָמַר לָה הַקָּדוֹשׁ בָּרוּךְ הוּא הָעוֹלָם וּמְלוֹאוֹ לֹא
נִבְרָא אֶלָּא בִזְכוּת הַתּוֹרָה שֶׁנֶּאֱמַר (משלי ג, יט) 'ה' בְּחָכְמָה יָסַד אָרֶץ וְגוֹ'' לְמָחָר
אֲנִי בָא לִתֵּן תּוֹרָה בְּסִינַי וְאֵינִי פּוֹתֵחַ תְּחִלָּה אֶלָּא בָךְ שֶׁנֶּאֱמַר (שמות כ, ב) 'אָנֹכִי
ה' אֱלֹהֶיךָ'

R. Eleazar bar Ḥanina said in R. Aḥa's name: For twenty-six generations the *aleph* complained before the throne of the Holy One, blessed be He, pleading before him: 'Sovereign of the universe! I am the first of the letters, yet You did not create Your world with me! God said to it: 'The world and its fullness were created for the sake of the Torah alone. Tomorrow, when I come to give My Torah at Sinai, I will commence with none but you,' as it is written, 'I [*anokhi*] am the Lord your God.'

The final interpretation, however, completely outshadows all the others, and completes this part of the *midrash.* The Torah begins with *bet* in order to disclose the moral purpose of the creation of the world. That purpose would not fulfill itself in creation but at the time of the giving of the Ten Commandments, which will begin with an *aleph.* Not only is this the purpose of the moral universe; it is also the purpose and goal of the Torah, and the task for Israel to realize and fulfill.

רַבִּי הוֹשַׁעְיָא אוֹמֵר לָמָּה נִקְרָא שְׁמוֹ אָלֶ"ף שֶׁהוּא מַסְכִּים מֵאֶלֶף שֶׁנֶּאֱמַר (תהלים קה, ח) 'דָּבָר צִוָּה לְאֶלֶף דּוֹר.'

R. Hoshaya said: Why is it called *aleph*? Because [God] agreed one thousand generations before Sinai to give the Torah beginning with that letter, as it is written 'the promise He gave for a thousand generations' (Psalms 105:8).

What R. Hoshaya adds is the fact that with the giving of Torah, which began with *aleph,* one thousand (Hebrew *elef*) generations were completed, in fulfillment of the promise that after 1,000 generations the Torah would be revealed. For 974 generations God reflected upon the Torah and intended to reveal it, and 26 generations were completed from Adam to Moses – making 1,000. (*Matnot Kehunah*)

This calculation merely complements the intention of the previous interpretation to make the giving of the moral law the supreme purpose of the world and mankind.

* * *

Seed Thoughts

(1) The *aleph* was weeping for twenty generations because it was upstaged by the letter *bet.* Many people go through life weeping because they too think they have been bypassed.

But the *aleph* had not been bypassed. It was saved for a much greater occasion. Creation was not the goal of the Almighty. Revelation was. And, indeed, there is a goal even beyond revelation, namely redemption and the world-to-come. There are a series of goals in the universe.

But, like so many of us, the *aleph* did not have patience. Very often we do not have faith in a better future for ourselves and therefore we despair. Sometimes we give up hope because mistakenly we think we have missed the boat.

In a parallel *midrash* from another source, the author uses the symbol of the apple tree. It first blossoms and then produces fruit at a later stage. Those not familiar with apple trees will regard the blossom as its purpose. But they are wrong.

So many people misread events because they do not have faith in the future. We need patience, we need steadfastness, we need diligent work, and we need the courage to believe.

*

(2) The Hebrew language is one of Judaism's greatest blessings. It is called the holy tongue and this probably alludes to the fact that the Scriptures were written in the Hebrew language. But if the word 'holy' is used as a metaphor for what is of ultimate importance, one would have to add that Hebrew is holy for a series of reasons.

For one thing, the letters of the Hebrew alphabet have a numerical value. *Aleph* is one; *Bet* is two; and so on. The letters of the Latin alphabet also have a numerical value but they are used only for counting and re-cording dates in the calendar. In Hebrew the numbers are used for pur-poses of meaning. For example: A verse in Isaiah reads, 'I have created this people to tell of My glory.' The word 'this' – זו, *zu* – consists of the letters *zayin* and *vav*, whose numerical values are seven and six, amounting to thirteen. The *midrash* thus renders it, 'I have created this *Bar Mitzvah* people that they should tell of My glory.'

The Hebrew language also uses the device of *notrikon.* That means that acrostics are used to represent other symbols or verses. For example, the verse in Amos reads, 'When the lion roars who will not be afraid?' The Hebrew word for lion is *aryeh,* אריה, which is written *aleph resh yod, heh.* The commentators say *aleph* stands for Elul, אלול (the Hebrew month), *resh* stand for Rosh Hashanah, *yod* stands for Yom Kippur, and *heh* stands for Hoshana Rabba. The meaning is that when this particular time of the year comes around – the period of judgment – who can be so sure of his right-eousness that he is not spiritually afraid?

Another aspect of Hebrew letters made popular by the Kabbalists is *gematria,* which means the study of numbers either in interpreting phrases or adding new layers of meaning. The Ba'al ha-Turim, a commentator on the Pentateuch, specialized in such interpretations. He noticed that when Eve was brought to Adam the word, 'And he brought her' – ויבאה – was written without the second *yod* (after the *bet*). That enabled the letters to add up to 24, which is the number of forms of jewelry and decoration that a bride is supposed to wear when she enters the wedding canopy.

As we have seen, *midrash* seven of *Genesis Rabbah* notes that the letters ending the first three words in Genesis make up the word 'truth' – אמת. Not only is this used to show that truth is the greatest virtue of the Torah, but also that the word *bara*, ברא, 'created,' had to be in the singular and could not possibly be in the plural, and therefore *Elokim* is not a plural form but a singular one.

The Hebrew language is used in so many other ways. Midrash finds a lesson in Hebrew words that seem to be spelled the same even though the literal meaning in the context is quite different. Numerical values are drawn not only from letters but even from the names of letters written out in full such as *bet*, which, written out in full, has the numerical number of 412, not merely 2, and this is used for many homiletical purposes. *Bet* also means a house. So does every other Hebrew letter have a translation and these too are often used homiletically.

The Hebrew language is used to abbreviate words and proper names such as Rashi and Rambam, all of which are acrostics of much lengthier names.

In short, it is possible to learn Judaism in translation. But one who becomes literate in the Hebrew language has acquired a key to in-depth study of the Torah that is indispensable.

* * *

Additional Commentary

Why was the world created with a *bet*

We can derive an answer from the way an infant behaves. Today he is taught that the order is *aleph, bet* and tomorrow, *bet, aleph.* Now the Torah begins with two *bets* and two *alephs* – *bereishit bara Elokim et...* It would seem that the proper way would be the opposite: *Elokim bara*, which is the order of the alphabet and the way a young child is taught. But the main point of the Torah is homiletical interpretation, not a sequential order or simple literalness. That is why even in the beginning it is written *bereishit bara*, in which the *bet* precedes the *aleph* making the point that the fundamental purpose of the Torah is to be interpreted and not to be taken literally or in order. (RWZE)

*

How seriously are we to take the question, Why did the Torah begin with *bet*? Suppose the Torah had begun with an *aleph*, could we not have asked the same question since there is no law that a sacred book must begin with the first letter of the alphabet? Are we to assume that the question was but a pretext for answers that deal with fundamental concerns? Is the *midrash* engaged in play, like the Passover *Haggadah*, to arouse the interests of children?

One must assume that the *midrash* is asking a serious question and investigate the intellectual framework behind it. One source for this way of thinking is the view that the purpose of the Torah is to stimulate inquiry and interpretation far more than literary order. (RWZE, abridged)

*

The particular kind of interpretation that is motivated in this study is that of *gematria* – גימטריא – or the study of numbers. It arises out of the tendency in Scripture for letters to interchange – for rhythmic patterns to appear from time to time in Psalms and elsewhere. Sometimes these appear in alphabetical order, from *aleph* to *tav*, sometimes in reverse, and sometimes in a variation of patterns. This phenomenon has given rise to the belief that letters have hidden meanings, beginnings of sentences have hidden meanings, and certainly the beginning of the Torah text would surely be used to convey such value. This would occur whether or not the Torah began with a *bet*, though the existing situation does lend itself to many interesting possibilities. The world view of those who deal with matters of *gematria* is that letters have a numerical value that gives them meaning, that the order of letters in the alphabet is a source of meaning, and the interchange of letters in different words is a source of meaning. There are many such examples in Hebrew etymology and in the Scriptural text. Furthermore, the view of those who hold such opinions is that these phenomena and their interpretations have authority as though they were transmitted from Sinai.

What meaning does this question have in terms of our knowledge of the history of the Hebrew alphabet? The Talmud itself points to the fact that the Torah was given in one form of Hebrew script, and it was only Ezra who changed the script to what is called the Ashuri type of script. The graphic form of the *bet* in old Hebrew script differs from that of Ashuri script. The difference is only in the fact that in old Hebrew script the *bet* was more circular than square. However, the belief of Ritba (Yom Tov Ishbili, Spanish talmudist, c. 1250–1330) and other authorities is that the discussions in the Talmud refer to Torah scrolls that Jews were writing themselves. Insofar as the original Ten Commandments were concerned, the belief is that they were written in Ashuri script. At any rate, the interpretations given in this *midrash* must be understood in this light. (*Yefei To'ar*)

*

Another interpretation

From the letter *bet* beginning the Torah we learn two fundamental principles of our religion. Not only the Torah and commandments are given by God, but even the form of the Hebrew letters. They were given at Sinai, unlike other languages whose script is based on a social consensus. That is why one can ask of the shape of the letter *bet*, Who created you? Are you the product of a social consensus or are you from Sinai? The *bet* then points to its top upward line to show that He who is above created it. It also affirms that He providentially supervises everything. This is shown by its right rear and lower extension. This demonstrates that God's name begins with an *aleph* – *adnut*– or mastery, which means that God is the master of everything. Since the purpose of creation is for the sake of Torah and faith, the Torah began with *bet* in order to teach us fundamental religious principles. (*Tiferet Tzion*)

Parashah One, Midrash Eleven

This *midrash* continues the discussion of letters of the alphabet begun in the previous one. The question that is now raised is why the Hebrew letters מ, נ, צ, פ, כ each have two graphic forms – one when they occur at the beginning or in the middle of a word, and one when they appear at the end of a word. The first point that is raised is why the letters are expressed in this order and not in alphabetical order.

This knowledge, too, comes to us from Sinai. The order in which the letters are presented alludes to the root of the word, *tzofim* – prophets and seers who transmitted this tradition.

The second point adds the thought that the prophets or teachers re-enacted the alphabetical knowledge after it had been forgotten.

יא. אָמַר רַ' סִימוֹן בְּשֵׁם רַבִּי יְהוֹשֻׁעַ בֶּן לֵוִי מנצפ"ך צוֹפִים אֲמָרוּם הֲלָכָה לְמֹשֶׁה מִסִּינַי רַבִּי יִרְמְיָה בְּשֵׁם רַ' חִיָּא בַּר אַבָּא אָמַר מַה שֶׁהִתְקִינוּ הַצּוֹפִים

R. Simon said in the name of R. Joshua b. Levi: *mnzpkh* was ordained by the *zophim* as a Mosaic enactment from Sinai. R. Jeremiah said in the name of R. Ḥiyya b. Abba: [The order of the letters should be read:] From your *zofim*.

The question is why is this string of letters referred to in the order of מנצפך and not כמנפץ, which is their order in the alphabet? Said R. Simon, it was because the distinction between the two forms of these letters was instituted by prophets as an enactment as given at Sinai. At first it was thought that anyone could decide which of the doubled letters would appear at the middle of a word or which at the end; but the prophets said that it was the law that the open letters would be in the middle and the closed letters at the end. R. Jeremiah adds the thought that this was originally done but then forgotten until the prophets re-instituted the practice, and that the special order of the letters should be understood as making up two words, מן צפך – From your prophets.

מַעֲשֶׂה הָיָה בְּיוֹם סַגְרִיר וְלֹא נִכְנְסוּ חֲכָמִים לְבֵית הַוַּעַד וְהָיוּ שָׁם תִּינוֹקוֹת וְאָמְרוּ בּוֹאוּ וְנַעֲשֶׂה בֵּית הַוַּעַד

It once happened on a stormy day that the Sages did not attend the

house of assembly. Some children were there and they said, 'Come and let us convene an assembly.'

Because of bad weather conditions the Sages were unable to attend the daily assembly in the Bet ha-Midrash at which they discussed Torah matters and decided the law. The children, who did succeed in getting to the Bet ha-Midrash, decided to act as the assembly, because they did not want even a single day to go by without an assembly meeting. The following is the discussion the children, acting as Sages, engaged in.

אָמְרוּ מַה טַעַם כְּתִיב מֵ"ם מֵ"ם מֵ"ם נוּ"ן נוּ"ן צָדֵ"י צָדֵ"י פֵּ"א פֵּ"א כַּ"ף כַּ"ף אֶלָּא
מִמַּאֲמָר לְמַאֲמָר וּמִנֶּאֱמָן לְנֶאֱמָן וּמִצַדִּיק לְצַדִּיק וּמִפֶּה לְפֶה מִכַּף לְכַף

Why are there two forms for *mem, nun, ẓade, peh,* and *kaf*? It teaches [that the Torah was transmitted] from utterance to utterance, from faithful to faithful, from righteous to righteous, from mouth to mouth, and from hand to hand.

The children understood these five letters as being the initial letters of fundamental concepts in the transmission of Torah as is now explained.

מִמַּאֲמָר לְמַאֲמָר מִמַּאֲמָר שֶׁל הַקָּדוֹשׁ בָּרוּךְ הוּא לְמַאֲמָר שֶׁל מֹשֶׁה מִנֶּאֱמָן לְנֶאֱמָן
מֵהַקָּדוֹשׁ בָּרוּךְ הוּא שֶׁנִּקְרָא אֵל מֶלֶךְ נֶאֱמָן לְמֹשֶׁה שֶׁנִּקְרָא נֶאֱמָן דִּכְתִיב (במדבר יב,
ז) 'בְּכָל בֵּיתִי נֶאֱמָן הוּא' מִצַּדִּיק לְצַדִּיק מֵהַקָּדוֹשׁ בָּרוּךְ הוּא שֶׁנִּקְרָא צַדִּיק דִּכְתִיב
(תהלים קמה, יז) 'צַדִּיק ה' בְּכָל דְּרָכָיו' לְמֹשֶׁה שֶׁנִּקְרָא צַדִּיק דִּכְתִיב (דברים לג, כא)
'צִדְקַת ה' עָשָׂה' מִפֶּה לְפֶה מִפִּיו שֶׁל הַקָּדוֹשׁ בָּרוּךְ הוּא לְפִיו שֶׁל מֹשֶׁה מִכַּף לְכַף
מִכַּף יָדוֹ שֶׁל הַקָּדוֹשׁ בָּרוּךְ הוּא לְכַף יָדוֹ שֶׁל מֹשֶׁה שֶׁסִּיְמוּ אוֹתָן וְעָמְדוּ חֲכָמִים
גְּדוֹלִים בְּיִשְׂרָאֵל

From utterance [*Ma'mar*] to utterance – from the utterance of the Holy One, blessed be He, to the utterance of Moses [when he taught the Torah to Israel];
From faithful [*Ne'eman*] to faithful – from the Almighty, who is designated, 'God, faithful king,' to Moses, who is also designated faithful, as it is written, 'he (Moses) is faithful in all my house' (Numbers 12:7);
From righteous [*Tzaddik*] to righteous – from God, who is called righteous, as it is written, 'The Lord is righteous in all His ways' (Psalms 145:17), to Moses who is designated righteous, as it is written 'he executed the righteousness of the Lord' (Deuteronomy 33:21);
From mouth [*Peh*] to mouth – from the mouth of the Holy One, blessed be He, to the mouth of Moses;

From hand [*Kaf*] to hand – from the hand of the Holy One, blessed be He, to the hand of Moses.
[The Sages] took note of the identity of these children and they all grew up to become great Sages.

The story about the children who gave such a beautiful interpretation of the doubled letters is meant as a response to the question why these five letters were chosen to be doubled and not the other letters of the alphabet. The answer is that these letters are a reminder of the special spiritual qualities by which the Torah was transmitted from God to Moses. The interest of this interpretation is to raise the status of Moses above all the other prophets and to emphasize that the Torah that Moses transmitted to the Children of Israel is the authentic Torah given by God Himself to Moses.

וְיֵשׁ אוֹמְרִים רַבִּי אֱלִיעֶזֶר וְרַבִּי יְהוֹשֻׁעַ וְרַ' עֲקִיבָא הָיוּ וְקָרְאוּ עֲלֵיהֶן (משלי כ, יא)
'גַּם בְּמַעֲלָלָיו יִתְנַכֶּר נָעַר וְגוֹ'.'

And some say that the children were R. Eliezer, R. Joshua, and R. Akiva, and [the Sages] applied to them the verse 'Even a child is known by his doings...' (Proverbs 20:11).

This opinion regarding the identity of the children is somewhat problematic. R. Akiva was a disciple of R. Joshua and R. Eliezer. Indeed, in the version of this *midrash* in the Jerusalem Talmud, R. Akiva is not included in this listing. However, our text can be explained in this fashion. As children they had all studied together. R. Joshua had a mother of great foresight who saw to it that he continued to study uninterruptedly. R. Eliezer's father (Hyrkonos) did not want him to continue with higher Jewish studies and was prepared to disinherit him at one stage. So, he abandoned his studies until the age of twenty-eight when he resumed them. R. Akiva also did not begin his studies until the age of forty. At that time he asked his friends to teach him, R. Eliezer (who had been studying for twelve years) and R. Joshua. (RWZE, unabridged)

בְּאָנֹכִי דְּרַבִּי מֵאִיר וְכוּ.'

The *Anokhi* of R. Meir etc.

This phrase is omitted from the Soncino English translation but still appears in all the Hebrew texts. It is omitted by Theodore as a typographical error, whereas others see it as a source reference, i.e., the *midrash* originated in the *midrashim* of R. Meir. RWZE and RDL have interesting explanations but none of them are satisfactory even to their authors.

* * *

Seed Thoughts

The intriguing part of this *midrash* is that its insights and teachings came from the mouths of children. We do not know their ages. They were probably teenagers, maybe younger. It is not only important to note that these interpretations came from children. It should also be noted that these particular children were destined to become great scholars in Israel.

A Jewish child should be exposed to Torah from as young an age as possible. It is quite true that R. Akiva was not motivated to study Torah until the age of forty. He was a great exception. There were and are others like him but they are a minority. The exposure has to begin at an early age.

But what should the child be exposed to? In this respect the modern Jewish day schools have not succeeded nearly as well as the old-fashioned type of *Ḥeder*, or *Talmud Torah*. The modern schools have a tendency to postpone the substantive study of Torah to a later date. There are introductory years of preparation for *ḥumash* as well as for Talmud. Since the average day school goes only to the sixth grade, and there is only one Jewish high school for every five elementary schools, the average child, even of this system, is rarely exposed to Torah in any substantive sense. Only those who stay on through a secondary level have a chance of knowing anything.

There is also the question of what is taught at the high school level and how. Bible is taught, but is it with a methodology that would make it inspirational? Talmud is taught, but does it emerge as an exclusively legal document or is the aggadic material also painstakingly rendered so as to arouse the Jewish soul? I am unaware of any Jewish secondary school that teaches Midrash or even makes an attempt at an exploration of this vast literature.

I recently met a sister and brother who told me that they were the only ones in their respective classes of a well-known Jewish day school who kept kosher. If only the mind is taught and not the soul and not the will, what are we accomplishing?

The *midrash* we studied above helps us move in this positive direction as well. The movement is from '*mem* to *kaf*,' from the intellectual affirmation – the *ma'amar* – to the hand – the *kaf* – that behaves and does.

Parashah One, Midrash Twelve

The question is why the Torah did not begin with the name of God. A secondary aspect of this question, depending upon which interpretation is chosen, would be why the name *Elokim* is chosen and not that of *Adonai* (*Hashem*)

רַבִּי יוּדָן בְּשֵׁם עֲקִילוֹס אָמַר לָזֶה נָאֶה לְקָרְאוֹ אֱלֹהַ בְּנוֹהֵג שֶׁבָּעוֹלָם מֶלֶךְ בָּשָׂר וָדָם מִתְקַלֵּס בַּמְּדִינָה וַעֲדַיִן לֹא בָּנָה לָהּ דִּימוֹסִיּוֹת וַעֲדַיִן לֹא בָּנָה לָהּ פְּרִיבְטָאוֹת בַּתְּחִלָּה מַזְכִּיר שְׁמוֹ וּלְבַסּוֹף קְטִיזְמָא שֶׁלּוֹ בְּרַם יְחִידוֹ שֶׁל עוֹלָם בַּתְּחִלָּה פָּעַל וּלְבַסּוֹף נִתְקַלֵּס

R. Yudan [Judah] said in the name of Akilos: Him it is fitting to designate God. In human practice an earthly king is honoured in his realm even before he has built them public baths or provided them with private baths – first he gives his name and only afterwards does he detail his achievements, but the unique One of the universe [God] first acts and only later is praised.

R. Judah is explaining why the Torah begins *Bereishit bara Elokim* and not *Elokin bara bereishit* considering that it is ordinarily dishonorable to relegate the name of God to the third word in the sentence. He teaches, therefore, that God first wishes to demonstrate His creative powers and only later on allows Himself to be praised, unlike human beings who allow themselves to be praised before they demonstrate their achievements. How much more so should the idolaters feel ashamed whose gods can accomplish nothing. All this is indicated by the order: *Bereishit bara Elokim.* (*Yefei To'ar*)

The sentence, 'first he gives his name and only afterwards does he detail his achievements,' is considered by the commentators to be out of place. They feel it belongs in the next statement by Ben Azzai.

שִׁמְעוֹן בֶּן עַזַּאי אוֹמֵר (שׁ"ב כב, לו) 'וַעֲנֹתְךָ תַּרְבֵּנִי' בָּשָׂר וָדָם מַזְכִּיר שְׁמוֹ וְאַחֲרֵי כֵן שִׁבְחוֹ פְּלָן אֲגוּסְטוֹלִי פְּלָן פְּרָאטָאטָא אֲבָל הַקָּדוֹשׁ בָּרוּךְ הוּא אֵינוֹ כֵן אֶלָּא מִשֶּׁבָּרָא צוֹרְכֵי עוֹלָמוֹ אַחַ"כְ מַזְכִּיר שְׁמוֹ 'בְּרֵאשִׁית בָּרָא' וְאַחַ"כְ 'אֱלֹהִים.'

Simon b. Azzai quoted: 'And Your humility has made me [under-

stand that it is] great' (2 Samuel 22:36) – A human being states his name first and then his title, thus: So-and-so the prince, So-and-so the duke. The Holy One, blessed be He, however, is not so, for He recorded his name only after creating the requirements of His universe: '*Bereishit bara*' and only afterwards '*Elokim*.'

R. Judah's point is that, unlike man, God acts first and only allows Himself to be praised afterwards. But the point remains unclear. In the case of a human being, we can reflect that maybe he will follow up with deeds and maybe therefore he should surely not allow himself to be praised before doing something; but God's word and deed are one. Why, then, should He not allow Himself to be praised? So, R. Simon ben Azzai says that it was only out of humility that God did not mention His name before His praise. It would be an assertion of arrogance to allow the name to come first even though the name is more important than the praise. God does not act that way.

* * *

Seed Thoughts

The tension between pride and humility is one of the interesting syndromes of both the Bible and the Rabbinic writings. Pride, in the sense of arrogance, has always been a target of the prophetic moralizer who sees in it the moving force that leads the individual into so many other forms of temptation. By contrast, humility has always been promoted as the great virtue of human character.

Speaking of humility, it is important not to mistake it for servility. In the Bible, the man who was described as the humblest of all men was Moses. But this same Moses was certainly not servile. In fact, there are moments in which he displayed fierce partisanship, even arrogance, as he fought against his enemies and the enemies of the Children of Israel. How do we reconcile the humble Moses with the not so humble opponent of Korah, of the Amalekites, and the Canaanites? The answer is that humility is not a quality that has to be manifest at all times. It is a quality that should emerge, that must emerge, if it is present at all, at moments of greatness or at moments of crucial importance in the life of an individual or a nation.

It is said of God that wherever you will find His greatness, there you will find His humility. We saw an example of this quality in the *midrash* under discussion – God was content, out of a spirit of humility, to allow His name to appear in Scripture after the words of creation and not before.

It is this principle that we should try to incorporate into human behavior as well. I can think of one splendid illustration that will exemplify this lesson.

David Ben Gurion was the first Prime Minister of Israel and one of its key founders. He was a strong personality. He had many clashes with friend and foe. At times he was arrogant, extremist, and unreasonable. But he did two important things that demonstrated beyond doubt that his greatness was tinged with humility.

Towards the end of his life, he gave up all the symbols of power and moved to the Negev where he lived in the utmost simplicity. He was hoping that others would follow suit and was trying to symbolize his belief that the future of Israel depends upon the settlement of the south.

After his death, the world discovered the following words, which he had ordered to be placed on his tombstone. No panygerics, no encomia, only the following stark lines:

Born 1886

Arrived in Israel 1906

Died 1973

This is the most powerful understatement that I have ever seen a person write about himself. Where greatness abounds, you will find humility.

* * *

Additional Commentary

R. Yudan

At first glance it would appear that there is a contradiction between the views of R. Yudan in the name of Akilos and Ben Azzai. In actual fact, they are asking different questions.

R. Yudan is asking why the name *Elokim* is used for God in the first sentence and not the name *Adonai* and is concerned only secondarily with the order of the words. He seems to be assuming that *Adonai* symbolizes God's essence, while *Elokim* symbolizes God's creative powers. (*Tiferet Tzion*) He thus says, 'To such a one the name *Elokim* properly belongs,' because He wished to be identified by His creative power. That is why His creative powers are mentioned first and only then does the name *Elokim* occur. According to this interpretation מתקלס would not mean to be praised, but to be properly defined.

*

Ben Azzai

Simon b. Azzai feels that the order of the words is most significant. God's name could certainly have appeared as the first word because He, by definition, does not have to prove Himself. Human beings do have to prove themselves first, because one can never be sure that they will achieve what they set out to do.

What God did with the opening words of the Torah, however, says Ben Azzai, is to demonstrate His humility. He deliberately placed His name after the verb and adverb in order to demonstrate that in the very place where His greatness is, so is His humility.

*

Him it is fitting to designate God

The aim of this *midrash* is to explore the reason why the name *Elokim* is used, which is usually an adjectival phrase describing God's acts, and not the name *Adonai (Hashem)*, which is His proper name used by Him exclusively. It was in this connection that he said, 'Him it is fitting to designate *Elokim.*' It is proper to call Him *Elokim*, which describes His works rather than to use the name *Adonai* that refers to His essence. A human king wants only praise and wants it before he has any achievements to his credit. Therefore, he mentions his name first and only afterwards his praise, that is, his title. His main goal is self-aggrandizement. God, however, gives priority to His works to benefit His creatures and therefore His acts precede His name. (*Tiferet Tzion*)

Parashah One, Midrash Thirteen

This *midrash* too relates to the fact that the Torah begins *Bereishit bara Elokim* and not *Elokim bara bereishit*. The name of God is not given first so as to avoid taking the name of God in vain. (*Matnot Kehunah*) This whole issue in now discussed.

תָּנָא רַבִּי שִׁמְעוֹן בֶּן יוֹחַאי מִנַּיִן שֶׁלֹּא יֹאמַר אָדָם לַה' עוֹלָה לַה' מִנְחָה לַה' שְׁלָמִים
אֶלָּא עוֹלָה לַה' מִנְחָה לַה' שְׁלָמִים לַה' תַּלְמוּד לוֹמַר (ויקרא א, ב) 'קָרְבָּן לַה''

R. Simon b. Yoḥai taught: How do we know that one must not declare '[I vow this] to the Lord as a burnt-offering,' or '[I vow this] to the Lord as a meal-offering,' or '[I vow this] to the Lord as a peace-offering'; but must declare: '[This is] a burnt-offering to the Lord,' '[This is] a meal-offering to the Lord,' '[This is] a peace-offering to the Lord'? – Because it is written: 'When any man of you brings an offering unto the Lord' (Leviticus 1:2).

We know that in the case of an offering, one has to begin with the name of the offering and then follow with the phrase 'for the Lord,' and not vice versa. This is done lest otherwise in the interval after having mentioned God's name and before naming the offering he might have a change of heart and would thus have uttered God's name in vain. By the same token, the Torah did not begin with God's name. And whereas, God Himself does not have changes of heart, as does man, it is meant as a warning to all, such as the generation of the Flood and heretics of all ages, not to take the name of the Lord in vain.

וַהֲרֵי דְּבָרִים קַל וָחֹמֶר וּמָה אִם מִי שֶׁהוּא עָתִיד לְהַקְדִּישׁ אָמְרָה תּוֹרָה לֹא יָחוּל
שֵׁם שָׁמַיִם לְהַקְרִיב הַמְחָרְפִים וְהַמְגַדְּפִים וְהָעוֹבְדִים עֲבוֹדַת כּוֹכָבִים עַל אַחַת
כַּמָּה וְכַמָּה שֶׁיִּמָּחוּ מִן הָעוֹלָם.

Now you can surely argue from this: If when one is going to dedicate (a sacrifice) the Torah directs that the divine name should be related to nought but the sacrifice, then how much more so is it true that they who revile, blaspheme, and worship idols will surely be blotted from the world!

This is expressed in the form of *kal ve-ḥomer* קל וחומר, *a fortiori* reasoning. If those whose intention it is to sanctify God are nonetheless warned not to take God's name in vain and will be punished if they do, how much more so will those whose intention it is not to sanctify but to desecrate His name be severely punished.

There is no connection between what follows and what has preceded in this *midrash*. In the manuscript used by the *Tiferet Tzion* the next section is numbered as a separate *midrash*.

רַבָּנָן אָמְרִין בָּשָׂר וָדָם בּוֹנֶה בִּנְיָן בְּשָׁעָה שֶׁהַבִּנְיָן עוֹלֶה בְיָדוֹ הוּא מַרְחִיב וְעוֹלֶה וְאִם לָאו מַרְחִיב מִלְמַטָּה וּמֵצַר מִלְמָעְלָה אֲבָל הַקָּדוֹשׁ בָּרוּךְ הוּא אֵינוֹ כֵן אֶלָּא 'אֶת הַשָּׁמַיִם' שָׁמַיִם שֶׁעָלוּ בַּמַּחֲשָׁבָה 'וְאֵת הָאָרֶץ' אֶרֶץ שֶׁעָלְתָה בַּמַּחֲשָׁבָה

The Rabbis said: When mortal man builds an edifice, during the building process he can decide to widen it as the building rises, or broaden it below and narrow it at the top. The Holy One, blessed be He, is not so, however; He built *the* heaven, that is, the heaven exactly as He had originally contemplated it, and *the* earth, that is, the earth exactly as He had originally contemplated it.

Why does the first verse read 'the heavens and the earth' with the Hebrew style את ה..., *et ha..*, which serves as an emphasized definite article? The answer is that whereas humans introduce modifications in their original plans because those plans were not perfect, God's plans are perfect and the heavens and earth were created exactly as He had planned.

רַב הוּנָא בְּשֵׁם רַבִּי אֱלִיעֶזֶר בְּנוֹ שֶׁל רַ' יוֹסֵי הַגְּלִילִי אָמַר אֲפִלּוּ אוֹתָן שֶׁכָּתוּב בָּהֶן (ישעיה סה, יז) 'כִּי הִנְנִי בוֹרֵא שָׁמַיִם חֲדָשִׁים' כְּבָר הֵן בְּרוּאִין מִשֵּׁשֶׁת יְמֵי בְרֵאשִׁית הֲדָא הוּא דִכְתִיב (שם סו, כו) 'כִּי כַאֲשֶׁר הַשָּׁמַיִם הַחֲדָשִׁים וְהָאָרֶץ הַחֲדָשָׁה' הָאָרֶץ חֲדָשָׁה אֵין כְּתִיב כָּאן אֶלָּא 'הַחֲדָשָׁה.'

R. Huna said in the name of R. Eliezer, the son of R. Jose the Galilean: Even those elements about which it is written, 'For, behold, I am creating a new heaven...' (Isaiah 65:17), were already created in the six days of creation, as it is written, 'For as the new heaven and the new earth [which I will make shall endure by my will]' (*ibid.* 66: 22) – it does not say *a* new earth, but '*the* new earth'

It is not only *et hashomayim* את השמים and *et ha-aretz* את הארץ that should be underlined for its specific meaning, but also the *ha* in *ha*-shomayim and also in connection with *ha*-aretz. The very heavens that were in His mind at creation came into being, and the very new heavens that were also in His mind at creation have not yet come into being but they will come into being in the future. (*Ha-Midrash ha-Mevo'ar*)

* * *

Seed Thoughts

Why is so much concern expressed about the nature of God? Does it really matter to the Almighty if His name is mentioned before or after an offering? And, if it is meant to matter to man, what is its real significance? What does it mean? What is it meant to mean?

The special attitude to the name of God is reflected not only in the *midrash.* It is visible in the laws and folkways of Israel. That we are not permitted to pronounce the Tetragrammaton, the four letter name of God, is well known. But the practice has developed of not pronouncing the substitutes for His name as well. One does not say *Adonai* except in prayer or in quoting from the Bible. Otherwise it is *Hashem* or *Adoshem.* Sometimes even the word God in English is spelled without the middle letter as a sign of reverence.

Let us try to analyze this behavior by referring to the source, which is the third commandment, 'You shall not take the name of the Lord your God in vain for I will not exonerate one who takes My name in vain.'

The first thing to notice is the prohibition to take the name in vain. If the name is not taken in vain, there is no problem. It is important to re-member that. Now let us examine the situations when taking the name in vain might occur.

The use of the name of God is mandatory when it comes to taking an oath. An oath has to be taken by reference to one's highest beliefs. If a person takes such an oath and does not live up to it, he is certainly guilty of taking the name in vain.

A second illustration would be in reference to the concept of *Hillul Hashem,* doing something that would desecrate God's name. Suppose someone had the reputation of being very religious and even wore the outer garb of a very religious person to the point where there can be no mistaken identity, and then it turns out that he is guilty of immoral behav-ior. Such a person makes a mockery of religion and is certainly taking the name of God in vain.

A third area where the name of God is in constant use is that of prayer. If prayer becomes mechanical or merely ritualistic, having no bearing on one's ethical behavior or the performance of other commandments, it would have to be a case of taking the name of God in vain.

There are, of course, other more obvious occurrences when, in personal speech, the name of God is used in swearing and for other pejorative purposes. I leave to those more specialized to explain why it is that the more secular a society the more the name of God seems to be used for imprecations.

All of these are substantive issues where the name of God is associated with some of the delicate and most important aspects of human behavior. The prohibition of taking the name of the Lord in vain is a way of purifying some of these most important human issues, one's word of honor, one's ethical behavior, one's experience of prayer, and the cleanliness of our speech.

Will these be affected whether or not the name of God is used before or after the word *korban* – קרבן – offering? Probably not. However, and this should be emphasized, the power of education reveals itself most when it can be inculcated into human habit. These prohibitions make us conscious of the wider, more substantive issues where God's will should become man's. They make us conscious of ourselves that we are thinking beings not robots and that what we do should reflect our highest purposes.

It may be a far cry from using the name of God before or after the word *korban*, and the great substantive issues of life, but the process invites us to raise the level of our consciousness, which is one of the most vital and most important religious experiences.

* * *

Additional Commentary

Now you can surely argue from this

It would certainly have been clearer for a person to say 'To the Lord as a burnt offering.' For then it would be quite apparent that the offering was to be dedicated to God, whereas in saying 'A burnt offering to the Lord' it is not clear – at least at the beginning of the vow – to whom it is being dedicated. One must say therefore that the reason it was prohibited to say 'To the Lord an offering' was because the Torah suspected that possibly these words were not being said with the proper holiness and that he might be punished that very moment either by death through heavenly decree or a paralysis and it would turn out that he would have pronounced the name of God in vain.

From this we learn how great is the punishment of those who revile and blaspheme. One can argue this way. If in the case of the person who truly wanted to sanctify God's name the Torah hesitated and was concerned lest he may not have mentioned God's name with the proper intention and he might, God forbid, be punished by death, how much more so will be the severity of the punishment meted out to those who revile and blaspheme. And one can say that corresponding to their success in this world so will be their reward (or rather, punishment) in the world-to-come without any hope of amelioration. This explains why the Torah did not begin with the name of *Elokim.* (*Tiferet Tzion*)

*

Builds an edifice

You might think that God had other designs for this world more in keeping with His honor and that these intentions were changed due to the limitations of man, or that He followed the ordinary building procedure of human society that introduces modification while actually building in accordance with new developments that arise. The *midrash* draws our attention to the Torah text that states very clearly that such a change in the divine intention did not occur, but that God created *et* the very heaven and *et* the very earth that had originally been His intention. (*Tiferet Tzion*)

*

A human engineer or architect will adjust his construction to fit the site and the materials. He might widen the foundation and build higher, or modify the foundations and build lower. In no case could he widen the top without adjusting the foundation so that it would maintain the structure. But the miracle of creation is that much greater by virtue of the detail that the heavens were wider than the earth, and yet they could be sustained by the Master Builder. (Mirkin)

*

R. Huna

If the new heaven and earth were already created and simply awaiting their appearance, why does Scripture say, 'Behold I will create a new heaven and a new earth'? What is happening here is that God has prepared an entirely different kind of moral structure for the new heaven and earth. No evil will be found there, nor will there be anything lacking. Only enjoyment will prevail forever. All of this was created long ago at creation. In general, God only influences for good and our Rabbis said that it is incumbent upon a person to recite the blessing 'Blessed be the righteous judge' over sad and even tragic events, as well as the blessing for 'good' (*Hatov ve-Ha-meitiv*). In their origin all things are good. They become evil only in the hands of the recipients. That is because they perceive their good as bad. This may be compared to a king who distributed a present to his children. Those who were in good health used the money for food and drink; those who were ill used it to buy medicines. From the point of view of God, the new heaven and earth with all its glories are already prepared. From our point of view they are not yet available because we still experience evil. In the future, however, there will apply to us the verse 'And I will sprinkle you with pure water and I will give you a new heart.' Then we will experience what for us is a new creation that will include only good and not evil. (*Tifetet Tzion*)

Parashah One, Midrash Fourteen

Why does the preposition indicating a direct object, *et*, appear in the first verse of the Torah '*et* the heavens and *et* the earth.'

רַבִּי יִשְׁמָעֵאל שָׁאַל אֶת רַבִּי עֲקִיבָא אָמַר לוֹ בִּשְׁבִיל שֶׁשִּׁמַּשְׁתָּ אֶת נַחוּם אִישׁ גַּם
זוּ עֶשְׂרִים וּשְׁתַּיִם שָׁנָה 'אַךְ'ין וְ'רַק'ין מְעוּטִין 'אֶת'ין וְ'גַם'ין רִבּוּיִין הָדֵין 'אֶת'
דִּכְתִיב הָכָא מַה הוּא אָמַר לוֹ אִלּוּ נֶאֱמַר בְּרֵאשִׁית בָּרָא אֱלֹהִים שָׁמַיִם וָאָרֶץ הָיִּינוּ
אוֹמְרִים הַשָּׁמַיִם וְהָאָרֶץ אֱלֹהוֹת הֵן

R. Ishmael asked R. Akiva: Since you have studied twenty-two years under Naḥum of Gimzo [who formulated the principle that the prepositions] *akh* (save that) and *rak* (except) are limitations, while *et* and *gam* (also) are extensions, what do the [two] *ets* written here signify? He answered: If it had stated, 'In the beginning created God heaven and earth [without the *ets*],' we might have maintained that heaven and earth too are divine powers.

Naḥum Ish Gimzo specialized in interpreting the prepositions in the Torah as having special and significant meaning. Thus, words like *akh* (nevertheless) or *rak* (only) were meant as restrictive terms limiting the law or the idea to what was listed, while words like *et* (the direct object indicator) and *gam* (also) were meant as expansive or multiplying terms, going beyond what was specifically listed.

Since R. Akiva had been Naḥum's disciple for many years and had, presumably, adopted his technique and theory, he was asked by R. Ishmael for an interpretation of the preposition *et* as it appeared twice in the first verse. His reply was that without *et*, the impression would be created that heaven and earth were also divine powers that took part in the act of creation. This claim is easily understood in the light of the syntactical construction of the first word, which literally reads, 'In the beginning created God heaven and earth,' in that order as though God, heaven, and earth were all equally divine. The insertion of *et* before the words heaven and earth makes such an interpretation impossible.

A misinterpretation of the verse would confirm the heretical view that God handed over the governing of the world to the constellations and that heaven and earth had the ability to bring the world into being after God created the original impulse. This denial is the purpose of the text. (*Tiferet Tzion*)

אָמַר לוֹ (דברים לב, מז) 'כִּי לֹא דָבָר רֵק הוּא מִכֶּם' וְאִם רֵק הוּא מִכֶּם לָמָה שֶׁאֵין
אַתֶּם יוֹדְעִים לִדְרשׁ בְּשָׁעָה שֶׁאִי אַתֶּם יְגֵעִין בּוֹ (שם שם, שם) 'כִּי הוּא חַיֵּיכֶם'
אֵימָתַי הִיא חַיֵּיכֶם בְּשָׁעָה שֶׁאַתֶּם יְגֵעִין בּוֹ אֶלָּא 'אֵת הַשָּׁמַיִם' לְרַבּוֹת חַמָּה
וּלְבָנָה וּמַזָּלוֹת 'וְאֵת הָאָרֶץ' לְרַבּוֹת אִילָנוֹת וּדְשָׁאִין וְגַן עֵדֶן

[R. Ishmael then] said to him [that is the meaning of the verse], 'For this is not a trifling thing for you' (Deuteronomy 32:47), and if it is trifling, it is so on your account, because you do not know how to interpret it because you do not invest sufficient effort; 'It is your very life' (ibid.), when is it your life? When you invest the required effort. [Your explanation is not correct], '*et* the heavens' is to include the sun and moon, the stars and planets; '*ve-et* the earth' is to include trees, herbage, and the Garden of Eden.

R. Ishmael did not accept R. Akiva's explanation and expressed his displeasure, particularly since the latter had been a disciple of Naḥum of Gimzo. Not a single word in the Torah is trifling (literally: empty), that is, without purpose, and you cannot expect to interpret a verse correctly without struggling with it – and R. Akiva's answer did not suggest much effort. That is the meaning of the verse R. Ishmael cited from Deuteronomy. The words 'for you' (*mi-kem*, literally: 'from you') seem to be unnecessary. But the interpretation is that if the Torah or any statement of it appears to be meaningless and empty it is only because of you – because you do not know how to interpret it, which is the result of not investing enough effort.

R. Ishmael, who did not generally subscribe to Naḥum's system of exegesis, went on to suggest an interpretation in Naḥum's spirit: *Et* should be interpreted as having the meaning of 'with' – with the heavens were created everything associated with the heavens, and with the earth were created all those things associated with the earth. These were all created on the first day but emerged in the second or third day, and so forth. (*Matnot Kehunah*)

רַבִּי תַּנְחוּמָא מִשׁוּם רַב הוּנָא אָמַר (שמות לח, כב) וּבְצַלְאֵל בֶּן אוּרִי בֶן חוּר לְמַטֵּה
יְהוּדָה עָשָׂה אֵת אֲשֶׁר צִוָּה אוֹתוֹ מֹשֶׁה לֹא נֶאֱמַר אֶלָּא 'אֵת כָּל אֲשֶׁר צִוָּה ה' אֶת
מֹשֶׁה' אֲפִלּוּ דְּבָרִים שֶׁלֹּא שָׁמַע מִפִּי רַבּוֹ הִסְכִּימָה דַעְתּוֹ לְמַה שֶׁנֶּאֱמַר לְמֹשֶׁה
בְּסִינַי

R. Tanḥuma in the name of Rav Huna said: In Exodus 38:22 it does not say 'And Beẓalel the son of Uri, the son of Hur, of the tribe of Judah, made all that Moses had commanded him' but rather, 'made all that the Lord had commanded Moses' – even those instructions which he had not heard specifically from his teacher [Moses], were views which matched those that were given to Moses at Sinai.

Having mentioned that the Torah can only yield maximum possibilities if great effort is exerted in its study, and then it can become equivalent to life itself, R. Tanḥuma brings an example from Beẓalel, who, as a result of his effort, was able to understand what God wanted without having been instructed by Moses (*Yefei To'ar*). His views matched those of Moses. He made the effort to study the Torah and the divine commands and knew how to draw out homiletical and exegetical possibilities. (RWZE, abridged)

רַבִּי חוּנְיָא בְּשֵׁם רַבִּי אָמַר (מלאכי ב, ו) 'תּוֹרַת אֱמֶת הָיְתָה בְּפִיהוּ' אֵלּוּ דְּבָרִים שֶׁשָּׁמַע מִפִּי רַבּוֹ

R. Ḥunia said in the name of Rabbi [Judah the Patriarch], 'The law of truth was in his mouth' (Malachi 2:6) – refers to the things which he heard from his teacher.

The implication now is that the rest of the verse, 'And falsehood was not found in his lips,' refers to that which he did not learn from his teachers but from his own insight and was not considered a falsehood or misinterpretation. In fact, God helps those who make a maximum effort to achieve results otherwise not thought humanly possible.

In case Beẓalel might not be considered proper evidence for a point of view that one can attain great insights without the instruction or revelation of a teacher, since it was said about Beẓalel that he was filled with the spirit of God, the *midrash* draws upon a text that attributes the same achievement to Aaron. (*Tiferet Tzion*)

וְרַבָּנָן אָמְרִי (משלי ג, כו) 'כִּי ה' יִהְיֶה בְכִסְלֶךָ' אֲפִלּוּ דְּבָרִים שֶׁאַתָּה כְּסִיל בָּהֶן (שם שם, שם) 'וְשָׁמַר רַגְלְךָ מִלָּכֶד' רַבִּי דּוֹסָאי אָמַר מִן הַהוֹרָיָה רַבִּי אַבָּהוּ אָמַר מִן הָעֲבֵרָה ר' לֵוִי אָמַר מִן הַמַּזִּיקִין

And the Rabbis say: 'For the Lord will be your trust' (Proverbs 3:26), even in those areas in which you feel foolish; 'and He will keep your feet from being caught' (ibid.). R. Dosai said: This means He will protect you from the dangers inherent in teaching. R. Abahu said: This

means He will protect you from the dangers of sin. R. Levi said: From the dangers of all external challenges (demons).

This is the interpretation of the verse in Proverbs which can be read as 'The Lord will be with you in your folly.' Even in those areas which are apparently above your intellectual capacity, or where you are not assisted by a tradition from your Rabbis and teachers, God will help you if you make a maximum effort.

Nevertheless there are also risks to too much learning. This is how the *midrash* interprets the second part of the verse from Proverbs, 'He will keep your feet from being caught.' There are three risks in too much effort and success in learning. The first is the rendering of decisions that may be unpopular and sometimes even incorrect. The second is sin; the more ability and knowledge, the more self-confidence and the more arrogance, which is the greatest sin. The third threat is from those who are jealous – *mazikin* – and therefore may try to harm or discredit a man who is more learned than themselves. (*Tiferet Tzion*)

אָמַר רַ' אַבְדִּימוֹס אִם נָתַתָּ מִכִּיסְךָ צְדָקָה הַקָּדוֹשׁ בָּרוּךְ הוּא הוּא מְשַׁמֶּרְךָ מִן הַפִּיסִין וּמִן הַזְּמִיּוֹנוֹת מִן הַגֻּלְגְּלָאוֹת וּמִן הָאַרְנוֹנִית.

Said R. Avidomos: If you have given charity from your pocket, the Holy One, blessed be He, will protect you from security tax, from the sales tax, the head tax, and the property tax.

This is a play on the word בכסלך, *be-kislekha*, which is broken up into two words בכיס שלך, *bekis shelkha*, 'in your pocket.' The correct punctuation would have been *ba-kesilakh*. However, since the text does not use that punctuation but rather *ba-kis-lekha*, it allows for the interpretation of *kis shelkha* – your pocket. The teaching that now comes from it is that giving is a condition and way of behavior. If you give charity from your pocket, that is, from your own funds, then God will protect you from many entrapments. This, by the way, is a typical method of Midrash, to take a letter or word in its sound and punctuation even though it may not fit literally into the context of its original verse, and draw certain lessons from it. (RWZE, abridged)

If God is in your pocket, that is to say, if you give your money to charity, God will protect you from all monetary damage. (*Tiferet Tzion*)

This may be the conclusion of the earlier challenge that the Torah is not an empty thing. On the contrary, it can do all of the above, as a protection to the human being.

* * *

Seed Thoughts

There is an old Yiddish expression that describes a person as 'having God in his pocket.' This refers to a certain type of ultra-religious character who is so arrogant in his piety, so obnoxiously self-confident in his unerring knowledge of the inner mind of God, that he is referred to derisively as acting as though he has God in his pocket.

Ironically we have come to a point in our midrashic studies where it is now possible to have God in our pocket in a most constructive and positive way. If you put your hand in your own pocket and take out your own money and share it with those who are poor and needy and give it with a full heart, you are doing what God wants your pocket to do. In this sense, He gladly allows you to have Him in your pocket.

Giving is living. From time immemorial *tzedakah*, in the sense of sharing, has been a primary religious commandment. To be kind and compassionate was always high on the Jewish religious agenda; but such virtues are best expressed in a tangible sense in the areas of giving by parting with that which seems to matter most to some people.

If anything, charity has become a more important avenue in Judaism today than it ever was in ancient times.

In the past, the various offerings in the Temple were vehicles through which the individual could express his or her joy, thanksgiving, remorse, or even a sense of guilt. Today, the absence of the system of offerings in the Temple makes the resort to any of those procedures impossible. However, charity has come to replace them all. Whether the feelings you wish to convey are joy or sorrow, thanksgiving or remorse, a general state of well-being or its opposite, the best religious advice is to set in motion and experience an act of *tzedakah*.

The maxim that says, 'Charity delivers from death,' is literally accurate when it can be perceived in spiritual terms. I know of at least one case where it delivered a person from physical death. A young man entered the office of a prominent businessman and said, 'I intend to commit suicide, but I have certain instructions which must be carried out for my wife and children. Would you look after them for me?' The friend then said to him, 'I will do whatever you ask, provided you let me have three hours of your time, now, immediately.' That was agreed. The businessman who, as luck would have it, was active in the work of the local School for Crippled Children, immediately took him for a tour of that institution. There he found children of the ages between five and seven having excruciating difficulties with their walking, but trying every exercise, even the most painful, in order to learn how to cope. In another room children who could not speak were opening their mouths and trying to produce sounds. Children without arms or legs would do their best to compensate for their handicap. The would-be suicide watched these efforts with ever greater disbelief. After a while he began to cry. These kids have greater problems than I have. He wanted to know who financed the institution and how he could help. 'You cannot help at all,' said his friend, 'you're about to commit suicide.' 'Oh! No! I'm not,' said the young man. 'You have taught me my greatest lesson. I want to start giving of myself, right now.'

There are eight degrees of charity, said Maimonides, each one greater than the other. The highest form of charity is to help someone be self-sustaining. The second highest is to help a person before he falls and not after. These high forms of charity require more caring, more giving, and ever more time-consuming self-sacrifice.

But, if you want to have God in your pocket, that is the way to go.

* * *

Additional Commentary

For this is not a trifling thing for you
Why did R. Ishmael not explain why he rejected R. Akiva's interpretation?

According to R. Akiva, it would have been sufficient for the first *et* to be written; there was no need for the second and the verse could have read: ...*et ha-shomayim ve-ha-aretz*. One could have said that the style of the text was that because of the first *et*, one might just as well add the second for balance. In response he quoted the verse, 'For this is not a trifling thing...' – the Torah includes nothing that does not have an interpretive purpose and therefore he could not accept the view of R. Akiva. (*Tiferet Tzion*)

*

If it is empty, it is on your account
The word *mi-kem* (it is on your account) is unnecessary. What was the text trying to say that was new in asserting that nothing empty is in the Torah? Did anyone suggest that there was? The answer is that no one should ever say about anything (any text) that it was too difficult to understand. This was not said with reference to those who were great scholars. Therefore the text says, '...it is no empty thing,' meaning that there is nothing in the Torah that anyone in Israel would not be able to understand, since God gave the Torah for all Israel. If it ever seems empty, it is because of you, meaning that if you ever discover something in the Torah that appears to

be superfluous it is because you did not make sufficient effort, for if you had, you would have been able to understand everything in accordance with your own mental capacity.

But how does a person know whether he has made enough of an effort? The verse says 'it is your very life,' meaning it is the way to the fulfillment of your life. That is to say, in the beginning of a study program, Torah exhausts a person; however, after he exhausts himself in this kind of study, the Torah bestows upon him strength and power as it is written, 'for they are life to all that find them and to every flesh healing.' The *midrash* then concludes, 'When is it your life? When you exhaust yourself in its acquisition.' (*Tiferet Tzion*)

Parashah One, Midrash Fifteen

Another question regarding the first verse in Scripture: Was heaven created first or was earth? The problem arises because there are contradictory verses in Scripture, verses where earth precedes heaven, and verses such as the present one where heaven precedes earth.

בֵּית שַׁמַּאי וּבֵית הִלֵּל בֵּית שַׁמַּאי אוֹמְרִים הַשָּׁמַיִם נִבְרְאוּ תְּחִלָּה וְאַחַר כָּךְ נִבְרֵאת הָאָרֶץ וּבֵית הִלֵּל אוֹמְרִים הָאָרֶץ נִבְרֵאת תְּחִלָּה וְאַחַר כָּךְ הַשָּׁמַיִם אֵלּוּ מְבִיאִין טַעַם לְדִבְרֵיהֶם וְאֵלּוּ מְבִיאִין טַעַם לְדִבְרֵיהֶם עַל דַּעְתֵּיהֶן דְּבֵית שַׁמַּאי דְּאִנּוּן אָמְרִין הַשָּׁמַיִם נִבְרְאוּ תְּחִלָּה וְאַחַר כָּךְ הָאָרֶץ מָשָׁל לְמֶלֶךְ שֶׁעָשָׂה לוֹ כִּסֵּא וּמִשֶּׁעֲשָׂאוֹ עָשָׂה אִפִּיפוֹרִין שֶׁלּוֹ כָּךְ אָמַר הַקָּדוֹשׁ בָּרוּךְ הוּא (ישעיה סו, א) 'הַשָּׁמַיִם כִּסְאִי וְהָאָרֶץ הֲדֹם רַגְלָי וְגוֹ'"

[The following was a discussion between] the School of Shammai and the School of Hillel. The School of Shammai maintained that the heavens were created first and afterwards the earth, while the School of Hillel held that the earth was created first and afterwards the heavens. Each gave reasons for its opinion. The School of Shammai supported its view that the heavens were created and afterwards the earth by a parable: A king first builds his throne and only afterwards his footrest. So too the Holy One, blessed be He, who said 'The heaven is my throne, and the earth is My footstool' (Isaiah 66:1).

The view of Beth Shammai is based on the allegory of a throne and its footstool. First you build the throne (heaven) and afterwards you build the footstool (earth).

וְעַל דַּעְתֵּיהֶן דְּבֵית הִלֵּל דְּאִנּוּן אָמְרִין הָאָרֶץ נִבְרֵאת תְּחִלָּה וְאַחַר כָּךְ הַשָּׁמַיִם מָשָׁל לְמֶלֶךְ שֶׁבָּנָה פָּלָטִין מִשֶּׁבָּנָה אֶת הַתַּחְתּוֹנִים אַחַר כָּךְ בָּנָה אֶת הָעֶלְיוֹנִים כָּךְ (בראשית ב, ד) 'בְּיוֹם עֲשׂוֹת ה' אֱלֹהִים אֶרֶץ וְשָׁמָיִם'

And the School of Hillel supported its opinion that first the earth was created and only afterwards the heavens with a parable: A king who builds a palace first build the lower sections and only afterwards the upper parts; thus [it is written], 'On the day that the Lord God made earth and heaven' (Genesis 2:4).

75

The view of Beth Hillel is also based on the allegory. First you build the building, which is earth, and afterwards you build the roof or upper story, which is the heavens.

אָמַר רַבִּי יְהוּדָה בַּר אִלְעַי אַף דֵּין קְרָא מְסַיֵּיעַ לְבֵית הִלֵּל (תהלים קב, כו) 'לְפָנִים הָאָרֶץ יָסַדְתָּ' וְאַחַר כָּךְ (שם שם, שם) 'וּמַעֲשֵׂה יָדֶיךָ שָׁמָיִם' אָמַר ר' חָנִין מִמְּקוֹם שֶׁהַמִּקְרָא מְסַיֵּיעַ לְבֵית שַׁמַּאי מִשָּׁם בֵּית הִלֵּל מְסַלְּקִין אוֹתָן (בראשית א, ב) 'וְהָאָרֶץ הָיְתָה' כְּבָר הָיְתָה

R. Judah bar Ilai said: This verse supports the view of the School of Hillel, 'Of old You established the earth' which is followed by, 'and the heavens are the work of Your hands' (Psalms 102:26). R. Ḥanin said: From the very text that supports the School of Shammai, the School of Hillel refutes them, 'and the earth was' (Genesis 1:2) meaning that it had already existed [before the heavens].

What the latter point means is that Beth Shammai based their entire argument on the opening verse, 'In the beginning God created heaven and earth,' as stated in the opening lines of this *midrash*. But this is immediately refuted by what follows immediately, 'and the earth was formless...' which implies that it already existed.

In truth, these parables – whether of the chair or throne according to the School of Shammai or the palace or building according to the School of Hillel – do not adequately explain why God created the world in this particular way. For, even if the carpenter has to build a throne before he can know the measurements for the footstool that will stand before it and the builder of the palace has to build the lower story before the upper, such consideration cannot apply to God who knows all these things in advance. Both the School of Hillel and the School of Shammai chose their parables from verses already appearing in the Bible. The latter from the verse 'heaven is My throne,' which leads to the parable of the throne and the former from the verse, 'the day on which God made earth and heaven,' which seems to imply building a building. So each interpreter explained the creation in terms of those workmen and that kind of workmanship with which the Torah itself illustrated the creation.

ר' יוֹחָנָן בְּשֵׁם חֲכָמִים אָמַר לַבְּרִיאָה שָׁמַיִם קָדְמוּ וְלַשִׁכְלוּל הָאָרֶץ קָדְמָה אָמַר רַבִּי תַּנְחוּמָא אֲנָא אֲמָרִי טַעְמָא לַבְּרִיאָה הַשָּׁמַיִם קָדְמוּ שֶׁנֶּאֱמַר 'בְּרֵאשִׁית בָּרָא אֱלֹהִים' וְלַשִׁכְלוּל הָאָרֶץ קָדְמָה שֶׁנֶּאֱמַר 'בְּיוֹם עֲשׂוֹת ה' אֱלֹהִים אֶרֶץ וְשָׁמָיִם'

R. Joḥanan in the name of the Sages said: As regards creation, heaven was first; as regards completion, earth was first. R. Tanḥuma: I can give the grounds [of this opinion]: As regards creation heaven was first, as it is written, 'In the beginning God created the heaven'; whereas in respect of completion, earth took precedence, for it is written, 'On the day that the Lord God made earth and heaven.'

R. Joḥanan makes the point that 'heaven' was first in terms of creation but earth was first in terms of being completed, *shikhlul.* In essence, that gives man primacy because only he is capable of improvement, since heaven is already perfect by definition. This is the interpretation that R. Tanḥuma gives to the verse 'On the day that God made earth and heaven' – 'made' here, means *tikkun u-gemar,* that is, improvement and completion. (RDL)

אָמַר רַ' שִׁמְעוֹן בֶּן יוֹחַאי תָּמֵהַּ אֲנִי הֵיאַךְ נֶחְלְקוּ אֲבוֹת הָעוֹלָם בֵּית שַׁמַּאי וּבֵית הִלֵּל עַל בְּרִיַּת שָׁמַיִם וָאָרֶץ אֶלָּא אֲנִי שֶׁאֲנִי אוֹמֵר שְׁנֵיהֶם לֹא נִבְרְאוּ אֶלָּא כְּאִלְפָּס וְכִסּוּיָהּ שֶׁנֶּאֱמַר (ישעיה מח, יג) 'קֹרֵא אֲנִי אֲלֵיהֶם יַעַמְדוּ יַחְדָּו'

R. Simon b. Yoḥai observed: I am amazed that the fathers of the world, the Schools of Shammai and Hillel, should engage in controversy over the creation of heaven and earth. I say that they both of them were created like a pot and its lid [i.e., simultaneously], as it is written, 'I call unto them [i.e., heaven and earth], let them stand up together' (Isaiah 48:13).

When R. Simon bar Yoḥai ponders the difference of opinion between the two schools, his real concern is to find a spiritual role for man. If the primacy of the world is heavenly, what role is there for man? And if the primacy of the world is man, why is he animal and driven? His solution is that heaven and earth were created simultaneously and interdependently, like a pot and its cover. This means in essence that the earth also possesses heavenly characteristics and possibilities. Heaven and earth are like all the other pairs in creation in which each complements and supplements the other, even though their characteristics are different. So man, even though earth born, has the ability and potentiality to purify himself and raise himself to great spiritual heights. (*Tiferet Tzion*)

The use of terms like 'pot and its cover' or 'stand up together,' should not be understood as meaning that they were created instantaneously. Both heaven and earth began their creation process together, but their development unfolded in a process that required time and not the same time for each. (*Yefei To'ar*)

אָמַר רַבִּי אֶלְעָזָר בְּ"ר שִׁמְעוֹן אִם כִּדְעַת אַבָּא לָמָּה פְּעָמִים שֶׁהוּא מַקְדִּים אֶרֶץ
לְשָׁמַיִם וּפְעָמִים שֶׁהוּא מַקְדִּים שָׁמַיִם לָאָרֶץ אֶלָּא מְלַמֵּד שֶׁשְּׁנֵיהֶן שְׁקוּלִין זֶה כָּזֶה

**R. Eleazar b. R. Simon observed: If my father's view is correct, why
is earth sometimes mentioned before heaven, and sometimes
heaven before earth? It teaches that they are equal to each other.**

R. Eleazar, R. Simon b. Yoḥai's son, assumed that no one would try to
question his father's view that both heaven and earth were created and
perfected together, and that makes the question of the *midrash* that much
more focused. The fact, however, that at creation heaven was mentioned
first and in connection with completion earth was mentioned first only
shows that they are equal in status.

He now brings five examples of biblical characters that are equal to
each other even though one contains advantages that the other does not.

בְּכָל מָקוֹם הוּא מַקְדִּים אַבְרָהָם לְיִצְחָק וְיַעֲקֹב וּבְמָקוֹם אֶחָד הוּא אוֹמֵר (ויקרא
כו, מב) 'וְזָכַרְתִּי אֶת בְּרִיתִי יַעֲקוֹב וְגוֹ'' מְלַמֵּד שֶׁשְּׁלָשְׁתָּן שְׁקוּלִין זֶה כָּזֶה

**Everywhere Abraham is mentioned before Isaac and Jacob; yet in
one place it says, 'Then I will remember My covenant with Jacob, [I
will remember also My covenant with Isaac, and also My covenant
with Abraham]** (Leviticus 26:42) – **this teaches that the three are equal
to one another.**

Abraham had to sanctify and purify himself (he was 48 years old when he
first recognized God), but Jacob was holy from birth and indeed had no
defect in him at all as it is said, 'his bed was whole.' Nevertheless they are
equal. Not only that, but Abraham is mentioned first since his status was
higher because he had to sanctify himself.

בְּכָל מָקוֹם הוּא מַקְדִּים מֹשֶׁה לְאַהֲרֹן וּבְמָקוֹם אֶחָד הוּא אוֹמֵר (שמות ו, כו) 'הוּא
אַהֲרֹן וּמֹשֶׁה' מְלַמֵּד שֶׁשְּׁנֵיהֶן שְׁקוּלִין זֶה כָּזֶה

**Everywhere Moses is mentioned before Aaron, yet in one place it
says, 'It is the same Aaron and Moses...'** (Exodus 6:26); **this teaches
that they were equal to one another.**

In connection with point two, reference is made to Aaron, who was considered equal to Moses even though Moses is considered the father of all
the prophets and sages and there was no one else like him. Nevertheless,
they were put on an equal footing since the goal of both of them was to
deliver Israel out of Egypt.

בְּכָל מָקוֹם הוּא מַקְדִּים יְהוֹשֻׁעַ לְכָלֵב וּבְמָקוֹם אֶחָד הוּא אוֹמֵר (במדבר יד, ל) 'כִּי
אִם כָּלֵב בֶּן יְפֻנֶּה הַקְּנִזִּי וִיהוֹשֻׁעַ בִּן נוּן' מַגִּיד שֶׁשְּׁנֵיהֶן שְׁקוּלִין זֶה כָּזֶה

Everywhere Joshua is mentioned before Caleb, yet in one place it
says, 'none except Caleb the son of Jephunneh the Kenizzite and
Joshua the son of Nun' (Numbers 32:12); this teaches that they are on
a par.

In connection with point three evidence is brought from Caleb. Although
Joshua was a prophet and therefore closer to God than Caleb, as an angel
is closer than man (and the prophets were called angels). Nevertheless
they were considered equal since God used them both to bring Israel into
the promised land and they were the elders that remained from the generation of the wilderness. Also through them was implanted in Israel a
great faith in the conquest and acquisition of the land.

בְּכָל מָקוֹם הוּא מַקְדִּים תּוֹרִין לִבְנֵי יוֹנָה וּבְמָקוֹם אֶחָד הוּא אוֹמֵר (ויקרא יב, ו) 'וּבֶן
יוֹנָה אוֹ תֹר לְחַטָּאת' מַגִּיד שֶׁשְּׁנֵיהֶם שְׁקוּלִין זֶה כָּזֶה

Everywhere turtledoves are mentioned before pigeons but in one
place it says, 'and a pigeon or a turtledove for a sin offering' (Leviticus
12:6); this teaches that they are on a par.

As for point four, an example is brought from the pigeons. Even though
they were small they were considered as equal to the turtledoves, which
are bigger because their atonement powers are equal.

בְּכָל מָקוֹם הוּא מַקְדִּים כְּבוּד אָב לָאֵם וּבְמָקוֹם אֶחָד הוּא אוֹמֵר (שם יט, ג) 'אִישׁ
אִמּוֹ וְאָבִיו תִּירָאוּ' מַגִּיד שֶׁשְּׁנֵיהֶן שְׁקוּלִין זֶה כָּזֶה אֲבָל אָמְרוּ חֲכָמִים הָאָב קוֹדֵם
לָאֵם מִפְּנֵי שֶׁהוּא וְאִמּוֹ חַיָּבִין בִּכְבוֹד אָבִיו

Everywhere a father's honor is mentioned before the mother's
honor, but in one place it says, 'You shall each revere his mother
and his father' (Leviticus 19:3); this teaches that they are equal to one
another. However, the Sages say that the father takes precedence
because the child and the mother are obligated to honor him.

The commandment to honor father and mother is brought as a fifth point.
Even though she is the recipient and he is the initiator, nevertheless they
are considered equal because birth is impossible without her. As for the
view of the Sages, this should be understood as applying only to cases in
which there is a conflict between the two, where a child cannot honor both
of them. This was strictly for the purpose of *shalom bayit*, household peace.

In all normal respects, however, father and mother, men and women, are of equal worth.

בְּכָל מָקוֹם הוּא מַקְדִּים בְּרִיאַת שָׁמַיִם לָאָרֶץ וּבְמָקוֹם אֶחָד הוּא אוֹמֵר (בראשית ב, ד) 'בְּיוֹם עֲשׂוֹת ה' אֱלֹהִים אֶרֶץ וְשָׁמַיִם' מַגִּיד שֶׁשְּׁנֵיהֶם שְׁקוּלִין זֶה כָּזֶה.

Everywhere the creation of heaven precedes that of earth, yet in one place it says, 'On the day that the Lord God created earth and heaven' (Genesis 2:4); this teaches that they are equal.

The *midrash* now returns to its point of departure – heaven and earth. Even though heaven possesses the five qualities listed above, nevertheless, God could not fulfill the purpose of the world without the earth and therefore heaven and earth are considered equal. (The running commentary for this *midrash* is from *Tiferet Tzion.*)

* * *

A Homily

The expression 'equally balanced' – שקולים – means that they equal each other in worth irrespective of the number of times each may be mentioned in the Torah and in what order of precedence.

Many commentators regard the fact that five examples were given of other places in the Torah where precedence was interchangeable as being of more than passing significance.

There are five ways in which a person or event can be considered more important than another.

1. Cause and effect. The sun comes before light and therefore can be considered more important. A father precedes a son since he is the cause of the son and not vice versa. Lest you might think that as between heaven and earth there might be a relationship of cause and effect, and one therefore has precedence over the other, therefore the verse in illustration is brought to the effect that Abraham, Isaac, and Jacob are equal in value and purpose even though one was grandfather and father and therefore the cause of the others.

2. Power. If a person represents a strong power, or authority, the authority behind the representative is more highly regarded than the representative. Lest you think that this is the relationship between heaven and earth, the verse in illustration is brought to show that Aaron is equal to Moses even though he is only the latter's mouthpiece or representative.

3. Importance. One who has greater status or dignity is more highly regarded than one of lower class. For example, the wise man is preferred

to the fool. Lest you think that heaven and earth relate to each other with these criteria of importance, the verse in illustration is brought to show that even though Joshua as the successor to Moses had greater status and responsibility, he and Caleb were equal.

4. Time. Time is sometimes an influence in establishing priorities. For example, an elder has chronological priority over a youth. Lest you think that this chronological difference separates heaven and earth, the verse is brought in illustration to show that even though pigeons were older than turtledoves, insofar as the Temple offerings were concerned, they were equal.

5. Place. Position is sometimes a factor in establishing priorities. The next in command comes before the second in command, or third in command, and so on. Lest you think that this is the relationship of heaven and earth, the verse is brought in illustration to show that even though a father is before a mother in position, since his male initiative in providing seed comes before her female function of procreating the seed, nevertheless, in God's eyes they are equal.

In conclusion, in the eyes of God all who do His will are equal, even though some may possess characteristics or qualities that in one way or other give them priority in the eyes of man. However, God looks only to the quality of purpose and the purpose of every living thing is to fulfill the will or the command of the Creator. Whoever fulfills His command is equal in His eyes to one who might seem to be on a higher level and who also fulfills the command of His creator. (*Yefei To'ar*)

* * *

Seed Thoughts

On the scale of worth, heaven is equal to earth but it is not the same as earth. On the scale of values, Abraham, Isaac, and Jacob are of equal worth but they are not identical. They differ in temperament and even in their conception of God. To follow the style of the *midrash*, turtledoves and pigeons are also of equal worth but they, too, have their differences. A father and a mother are equal but their roles are different.

Equality is not sameness and was never meant to be. Equality is not to be confused with egalitarianism, whose purpose seems to be to treat every- one as though they are the same.

The rise of the feminist movement, important as it is, has blurred the concept of equality and has sometimes confused it with sameness. Male and female differ in gender, in biology, in sexual roles, and in some social roles that derive from the former. They do not differ in worth or in equality.

Nevertheless, it seems that the difference between equality and sameness still has to be argued.

As I write these words, a feminist lobby in Canada is petitioning for women to have a combat role in the Canadian Army. Why? Is there a dearth of recruits that makes their inclusion mandatory? Can it be that a combat role will help certain women fulfill themselves? Or is the only principle at stake the fact that men have combat roles and women need them in order to emphasize their equality. But will it be equality that will be achieved or will it be sameness?

What about the arguments that have been used by the same feminist group that women have a greater propensity for peace, for sensitive human relations, and for emphasizing the personal above the collectivity? Is it worthwhile to jeopardize this myth in order to create a new myth of sameness?

It is an aggravating question not yet resolved. Only one point is beyond dispute. Equality is not sameness.

* * *

Additional Commentary

The School of Shammai and the School of Hillel

In order to discover a theoretical justification or analytical purpose to the controversy between the School of Shammai and the School of Hillel, one has to probe much deeper. It could be said that in the view of Bet Shammai, the foundation of creation and its purpose is to be found in the throne of glory of God and His ministering angels in the world above. Therefore, God created heaven first since that was the purpose and the main idea. And from their creation there emerged earth and its creatures, who were secondary to the upper world inhabitants.

The School of Hillel, on the other hand, followed the view that the purpose of creation was man. Therefore God first created earth, which contains man's environment and tools for his needs and, of course, man himself; and only after that did the Almighty create heaven and its satellites that, in any event, were to be considered secondary to man.

Even though both opinions have verses to support them, one cannot look for convincing proof from verses. Verses can be interpreted as opposing the views of one or the other. The real difference of opinion has already been stated and each side will interpret the verses to suit his position. (*Yefei To'ar*)

*

As regards creation, heaven was first

There was a certain advantage to heaven at the beginning of creation because it served God in holiness and purity unlike man, who at his creation was a wild ass wanting only to cater to his instincts. However, when the goal was not creation but perfection, earth had primacy because after man corrects and improves his behavior he is even higher than the angels. An angel is an angel from the very start but man must fight battles against his evil inclination and replace it with the love of God. That makes him higher. (*Tiferet Tzion*)

Parashah Two, Midrash One

What is the meaning of *tohu va-vohu* (Genesis 1:2)? Translated as formlessness and void, is it a situation that existed before the creation of the world or after? If after, why does Scripture not say that *tohu va-vohu* was created? What, in general, was its purpose?

וְהָאָרֶץ הָיְתָה תֹהוּ וָבֹהוּ רַבִּי בֶּרֶכְיָה פָּתַח (משלי כ, יא) 'גַּם בְּמַעֲלָלָיו יִתְנַכֶּר נָעַר'

'Now the earth was unformed and void [and darkness was upon the face of the deep; and the spirit of God hovered over the face of the waters]' (Genesis 1:2). R. Berekhiah began [his exposition]: 'Even a child is known by his doings, whether his work be pure, and whether it be right' (Proverbs 20:11).

From the verse in Proverbs we learn that when a child is small we can already discern the kind of character he will possess as an adult. The same thing can be said about the world. God deliberately made it desolate in its beginning so that man can see the state to which the world can revert if his sins bring about its destruction.

אָמַר רַבִּי בֶּרֶכְיָה עַד דְּהִיא פַּגָּה אַפֵּיקַת כּוּבַיָּא הוּא מַה שֶׁהַנָּבִיא עָתִיד לְהִתְנַבֵּאת עָלֶיהָ בְּסוֹף (ירמיה ד, כג) 'רָאִיתִי אֶת הָאָרֶץ וְהִנֵּה תֹהוּ וָבֹהוּ'

Said R. Berekhiah: While [the earth] was as yet immature, it produced thorns; and so the prophet was one day destined to prophesy of it, 'I look at the earth; it is unformed and void' (Jeremiah 4:23).

R. Berekhiah illustrates this truth from the bramble that reveals its thorns even before it ripens, before its trunk is revealed. Similarly, the moment the world was created, the *tohu va-vohu* revealed itself to indicate what might happen in the future.

The very use of terms like *tohu va-vohu* are a direct reference to the destruction of the Temple as a result of Israel's sins. This is mentioned specifically by the prophet Jeremiah in the verse quoted. In fact, according to the *Malbim*, the prophet was referring to the entire creation in saying that when destruction occurs, either of the Temple or the world, it will revert back to *tohu va-vohu.*

* * *

Seed Thoughts

The chaos that existed before the creation of the world was not a danger to mankind. This is so even if you look upon the unformed matter as being the building materials of the new world.

Not so the chaos that might obtain after the world was created. That would be a mortal danger for that would be due only to man's moral failures or incompetence.

Therefore, look upon the opening verse of Scripture as a warning amidst the excitement of creation. It can fail. Make sure it doesn't.

* * *

Additional Commentary

The term *tohu va-vohu* really stands for unformed material, which was earth in its original state. Creation made of it formed material. (*Yefei To'ar*)

*

It is in the nature of growing things that at the very beginning of their growth they give indication of what they will look like towards the end. Similarly, it is the nature of the earth to return to its unformed state, that is why it was made unformed immediately after its creation. In this manner God was able to indicate to man that he must be very careful in his actions lest he destroy the world, since the earth has the tendency to return to its unformed stage and only by virtue of God's great love does He bestow upon it the abundance of its nourishment to its inhabitants. However, if man perverts his ways, it will then be necessary for God to remove His love from the universe, at which point earth will return to its unformed state in accordance with its nature. It therefore becomes incumbent upon every human being to walk in the way of life, for this was the real purpose of creation. (*Tiferet Tzion*)

*

The Bible used the term 'the earth *was* unformed' and not '*created* unformed' to indicate that some day, if human beings do not live up to the challenge of creation and the form it gave to the material essence, the earth will revert to its original unformed condition. The verse from Proverbs is meant to illustrate that *tohu va-vohu* was the early primitive state of earth, and the verse from Jeremiah indicates that mankind can revert to such a stage. (*Tiferet Tzion*)

Parashah Two, Midrash Two

This *midrash* continues the discussion of the meaning of *tohu va-vohu* and interprets it as meaning 'confusion.' Earth was and is completely confused and desolate at the contrast between its fate and that of heaven. Both were created together, but what a difference there is between them.

רַבִּי אַבָּהוּ וְרַבִּי יְהוּדָה בַּר סִימוֹן רַבִּי אַבָּהוּ אָמַר מָשָׁל לְמֶלֶךְ שֶׁקָּנָה לוֹ שְׁנֵי עֲבָדִים
שְׁנֵיהֶם בְּאוֹנִי אַחַת וּבִטִימִי אַחַת עַל אֶחָד גָּזַר שֶׁיְּהֵא נִזּוֹן מִטַּמְיוֹן וְעַל אֶחָד גָּזַר
שֶׁיְּהֵא יָגֵעַ וְאוֹכֵל יָשַׁב לוֹ אוֹתוֹ תּוֹהֵא וּבוֹהֵא אָמַר שְׁנֵינוּ בְּאוֹנִי אַחַת וּבִטִימִי
אַחַת זֶה נִזּוֹן מִטַּמְיוֹן וַאֲנִי אִם אֵינִי יָגֵעַ אֵינִי אוֹכֵל כָּךְ יָשְׁבָה הָאָרֶץ תּוֹהָא וּבוֹהָא
אָמְרָה הָעֶלְיוֹנִים וְהַתַּחְתּוֹנִים נִבְרְאוּ בְּבַת אַחַת הָעֶלְיוֹנִים נִזּוֹנִין מִזִּיו הַשְּׁכִינָה
הַתַּחְתּוֹנִים אִם אֵינָם יְגֵעִים אֵינָם אוֹכְלִים

R. Abbahu and R. Judah bar Simon [discussed the matter]. R. Abbahu said: It can be compared to a king who acquired two slaves with one bill of sale and one payment. He ordered one to be maintained from the royal treasury [without having to work for a living] and the other to work [if he wanted] to eat. The latter sat desolate and confused and said: Both of us were acquired by the king with one bill of sale and one payment, yet one of us is maintained by the royal treasury [without having to work], while in my case, if I do not work, I will not eat. Similarly, earth sat desolate and confused; it said: The upper creatures and the lower creatures were created at the same time; yet the upper creatures are nourished [directly] from the radiance of the divine Presence, but lower creatures – if they do not work they will not eat.

As described at the end of the first *parashah*, heaven and earth were created at the same time. Yet the celestial creatures, the angels, are sustained by the light of the divine Presence; they have no need to struggle for a livelihood, nor to struggle with the burden of the commandments, nor to control their evil inclination. But the 'lower creatures,' that is, human beings have to earn their bread or they do not eat. This parable is based on a play on words: The Hebrew that we translated as 'desolate and confused' is derived from the same roots as *tohu* and *vohu*. Thus the term *tohu va-vohu* is given an entirely different interpretation.

86

וְר' יְהוּדָה בַּר סִימוֹן אָמַר מָשָׁל לְמֶלֶךְ שֶׁקָּנָה לוֹ שְׁתֵּי שְׁפָחוֹת שְׁתֵּיהֶן בְּאוֹנִי אַחַת
וּבְטִימִי אַחַת עַל אַחַת גָּזַר שֶׁלֹּא תָּזוּז מִפְּלָטִין וְעַל אַחַת גָּזַר טְרוּדִין יָשְׁבָה לָהּ
אוֹתָהּ הַשִּׁפְחָה תּוֹהָא וּבוֹהָא אָמְרָה שְׁנֵינוּ בְּאוֹנִי אַחַת וּבְטִימִי אַחַת זוֹ אֵינָהּ
יוֹצְאָה וְזֶה מִפְּלָטִין וְעָלַי גּוֹזֵר טְרוּדִין כָּךְ יָשְׁבָה לָהּ הָאָרֶץ תּוֹהָא וּבוֹהָא אָמְרָה
הָעֶלְיוֹנִים וְהַתַּחְתּוֹנִים נִבְרְאוּ בְּבַת אַחַת הָעֶלְיוֹנִים חַיִּים וְהַתַּחְתּוֹנִים מֵתִים
לְפִיכָךְ 'וְהָאָרֶץ הָיְתָה תֹהוּ וָבֹהוּ'

But R. Judah bar Simon said: It can be compared to a king who acquired two maidservants with one bill of sale and one payment. He ordered one never to leave the palace whereas the other was commanded to leave the palace. The latter sat desolate and confused and said: Both of us were acquired by the king with one bill of sale and one payment, yet, one of us never leaves the palace, but I was ordered to leave. Similarly, earth sat desolate and confused. It complained: The upper creatures live [forever], but the lower creatures die. Therefore the earth was *tohu va-vohu* – desolate and confused.

R. Judah bases his parable on the same play on words as R. Abbahu, but he does not regard the necessity to work for a living as being something to complain about. On the contrary, to maintain yourself and eat by the work of your hands might be considered a superior achievement (RDL). What bothers R. Judah is the fact that the angels do not know of death, whereas all men must die. This was why the earth was *tohu va-vohu*. As for R. Abbahu, it is his opinion that the disintegration of the body is not something to lament. After all, the soul then returns to its source to receive its reward and radiate in God's presence.

אָמַר רַבִּי תַּנְחוּמָא לְבֶן מֶלֶךְ שֶׁהָיָה יָשֵׁן עַל גַּבֵּי עֲרִיסָה וְהָיְתָה מֵנִיקָתוֹ תּוֹהָא
וּבוֹהָא לָמָּה שֶׁהָיְתָה יוֹדַעַת שֶׁהִיא עֲתִידָה לִטֹּל אֶת שֶׁלָּהּ מִתַּחַת יָדֶיהָ כָּךְ צָפְתָה
הָאָרֶץ שֶׁהִיא עֲתִידָה לִטֹּל אֶת שֶׁלָּהּ מִתַּחַת יָדָיו שֶׁל אָדָם שֶׁנֶּאֱמַר (בראשית ג, יז)
'אֲרוּרָה הָאֲדָמָה בַּעֲבוּרֶךָ' לְפִיכָךְ 'וְהָאָרֶץ הָיְתָה תֹהוּ וָבֹהוּ.'

R. Tanḥuma said: [The matter should be compared] to an infant son of the king sleeping in his cradle. His wet nurse sits desolate and confused [at her lot]. Why? Because she knows that she will be punished for anything wrong the prince does. So, too, the earth realized that it would receive its punishment by the hand of man, as it is written 'Cursed be the ground because of you' (Genesis 3:17). Therefore the earth was desolate and confused.

R. Tanḥuma believes that neither work nor death was what bothered the earth. The earth knew that it was fated to be cursed by God because of Adam and Eve's sin in eating the fruit of the Tree of Knowledge, just as the infant's nurse knows that she will be punished for anything the infant does wrong although she is not directly to blame, because she is responsible for educating the infant and if he behaves badly she will be blamed. The earth was *tohu va-vohu* because it knew it would have to bear the sins of mankind at all times, as indeed it did at the time of the great Deluge, when Sodom was destroyed, when the Ten Plagues were inflicted on Egypt, and when the Temple was destroyed. Scripture is full of such incidents. (*Ha-Midrash ha-Mevo'ar*)

We can now sense the power of R. Tanḥuma's argument. Earth worried about the harm man would do to it through war, pollution, and mismanagement of the environment. This is incorporated in the verse, 'Cursed be the ground because of you.'

* * *

Seed Thoughts

[1] Did the Rabbis really believe that earth was jealous of heaven? Remember, we are speaking of a moment before man was created. The answer is, probably not. But this text gave them an opportunity to say a few things about jealousy and what it can do to human beings, and they would certainly not miss such an opportunity.

There are many people who go through life with feelings of insecurity. They lack confidence in themselves and are uncertain of their place in society and even of what they should be doing. If such people are envious of others, it is at least understandable, though not necessarily justifiable.

However, what are we to say about achievers, whose material success is quite overwhelming, but who grow green with envy because someone they know seems to have done even better and the grass is always greener on the other side of the fence? How do they know that the objects of their jealousy are truly to be envied? Maybe something has happened, or is happening in their lives that belies their outer status. One never knows the degree of someone else's heartbreak.

The best cure for envy is thanksgiving. Visit a school for crippled children. Visit a home for the blind. The more you start appreciating your own blessings, the less you will be disposed to envy.

A folk legend tells about an angel who gathered up everybody's '*tzores*' (that is the Yiddish term for trials and tribulations) and stored them in bundles around a great tree. He then invited the community to come forward and pick whatever '*tzores*' they chose. Every person, upon examination, re-chose his own package of '*tzores*.'

*

[2] It is fascinating to note in this *midrash* the assertion that God created twin worlds at the same time – this world and the world above. The picturesque language of rabbinic thought speaks of the lower world and the upper world.

Why should it matter that twin worlds were created? Because hope matters and the upper world gives us hope. We have been offered a share not only in time but in eternity.

It is standard in scholarly circles that the concept of immortality and the world-to-come was a later development in Judaism. Here we can see the strenuous efforts of the Sages to project the concept all the way back to the creation of the world.

If, as Rabbi Abbahu suggests, work is a form of drudgery, we have another world to look forward to that is free of work and thus far better. Even if work is not looked upon as a form of drudgery, this is a mortal world, finite, while the upper world is enduring, and a fitting reward for our labor here.

It is useless to ask why God needed two worlds. We may well ask why He needed any world at all. The important point is that we need it. Let us accept the 'thought' and be grateful for it.

*

[3] One of the greatest threats of modern times is the damage that is being done to the environment. We have experienced the industrial age, the technological age, and now are in the midst of the electronic age. These developments are so amazing and so overpowering that they have created a euphoria in the human psyche. Not so in the world of nature. Nature has paid a heavy price for this progress. The very physical world that has produced this great bounty has paid the price of human mismanagement of these very resources.

The paper industry has contributed to the deforestation of our woodlands and only now is trying to make amends. The chemical industry has polluted some of the great waterways of the world. The automobile industry has poisoned the atmosphere, and nuclear power is a permanent threat to the stability of the world. Only now is the threat of 'global warming' being appreciated.

The *midrash*, with great foresight, sees this problem not as something new but as one of the original threats to creation. 'Cursed be the ground because of you.' But, if the threat of pollution to the environment, which is what the curse is all about, is because of us, maybe that can also be the source of its blessing. Maybe because of us, we can restore the environment to what it was meant to be – the proper habitat for mankind.

* * *

Additional Commentary

R. Abbahu and R. Berekhiah

The difference between the approach of R. Abbahu in this *midrash* and R. Berekhiah in the previous *midrash* is that the first deals with the theme of earth descriptively and the second, psychologically. The creatures on earth were jealous of those in heaven, who were sustained by a central fund and lived forever, and because they were consumed by jealousy they became desolate, which is what *tohu va-vohu* means. This sometimes happens when a person grieves because of the great elevation of a colleague and becomes dejected, as it is written, 'jealousy makes the bones rot.' Because man has this tendency to jealousy, which can sometimes remove a person from the world, the text wants to tell us how bad it can be – because of jealousy creation became *tohu va-vohu*, dejected and desolate. All this happened before living things emerged, and it was enough to bring darkness over the face of the deep. This is the very opposite of creation and light. The text wants us to know that we can never benefit from jealousy; on the contrary, through it we can lose whatever has already been achieved. This is like the story of the camel who was jealous of the animals with horns. The result is that his ears were also removed from him and, somehow, God in His mercy directs him along the right paths. (*Tiferet Tzion*)

*

R. Abbahu and R. Judah

The difference in the parables used by R. Abbahu and R. Judah can be explained in this way. To R. Abbahu the most important weakness in creation was work and the effort to earn a livelihood. Death in this kind of world is a blessing, since it leads one to an eternal life of peace. To R. Judah, however, the effort or work is a blessing and the only liability in creation was death. (*Yefei To'ar*)

Parashah Two, Midrash Three

The discussion continues on the meaning of the term, *tohu va-vohu*. This time the explanation interprets the words as referring to generational time. The earth was chaotic because the right human beings had not appeared to perfect it. That would only happen with Abraham. It is as though the text were asking the question, why is the earth *tohu va-vohu*?

רַבִּי יְהוּדָה בַּר סִימוֹן פָּתַר קְרָיָא בַּדּוֹרוֹת 'וְהָאָרֶץ הָיְתָה תֹהוּ' זֶה אָדָם הָרִאשׁוֹן שֶׁהָיָה לְלָמָה וְלֹא כְלוּם

R. Judah bar Simon interpreted the text as referring to the generations: 'And the earth was *tohu*' – this refers to Adam who was empty and amounted to nothing.

R. Judah b. Simon interpreted all the terms and phrases in the second verse of Genesis as hints referring to the generations to come. These are now listed. *Tohu* refers to Adam, who was reduced to complete nothingness. The Hebrew term *lamah* is often used by *Targum Yonatan* as in Jeremiah 5:13 to mean nothingness. Adam amounted to nothing because he sinned with the fruit of the Tree of Knowledge on the very day he was created and was punished by having all his special uniqueness and splendor taken away from him.

'וָבֹהוּ' זֶה קַיִן שֶׁבִּקֵּשׁ לְהַחֲזִיר אֶת הָעוֹלָם לְבֹהוּ

'*Va-vohu*' refers to Cain, who wanted to turn the world into *vohu*.

This is a play on words, in which *vohu* is seen as being made up of the words *bo hu*, 'in which only he.' By killing Abel, Cain wanted to make sure that only he would inherit the earth. He brought murder into the world, the most destructive force of all.

'וְחֹשֶׁךְ' זֶה דּוֹרוֹ שֶׁל אֱנוֹשׁ עַל שֵׁם (ישעיה כט, טו) 'וְהָיָה בְמַחְשָׁךְ מַעֲשֵׂיהֶם וַיֹּאמְרוּ מִי וְגוֹ''

'And darkness' refers to the generation of Enosh, as it is written, '[Ha! Those who would hide their plans deep from the Lord!] who do their work in dark places and say, "Who [sees us, who takes note of us?]"' (Isaiah 29:15).

Scripture describes the generation of Enosh as 'It was then that men began to call on the name of the Lord' (Genesis 4:26). According to rabbinic tradition this is interpreted as meaning that in that generation people began worshipping idols; the word 'began' – *huḥal* – is understood as being connected to the word *ḥullin*, meaning secular. The verse would thus be rendered, 'They secularized the name of the Lord' and this would make it correspond with the verse in Isaiah that the works of idolaters are in dark places and with the original scriptural text of 'darkness.' (RWZE)

'עַל פְּנֵי תְהוֹם' זֶה דוֹר הַמַּבּוּל שֶׁנֶּאֱמַר (בראשית ז, יא) 'בַּיוֹם הַזֶּה נִבְקְעוּ כָּל מַעְיְנוֹת תְּהוֹם'

'Upon the face of the deep' refers to the generation of the flood, as it is written 'On that day all the fountains of the great deep burst apart' (Genesis 7:11).

The proof-text for this interpretation, Genesis 7:11 which also employs the word 'deep' – *tehom*, is describing the onset of the great deluge, which was brought about by the sins and corruption of the generation.

'וְרוּחַ אֱלֹהִים מְרַחֶפֶת עַל פְּנֵי הַמָּיִם' עַל שֵׁם (שם ח, א) 'וַיַּעֲבֵר אֱלֹהִים רוּחַ עַל הָאָרֶץ'

'And the spirit of God hovered over the water,' as it is written, 'And God caused a wind to blow across the earth' (Genesis 8:1).

This also refers to the generation of the Flood; the proof-text uses the same word for 'wind' – *ru'aḥ* – as does our verse for 'spirit.' The reference here is to Noah who, by his righteousness, saved the world from destruction. However, Noah's generation was followed by the generation of the Tower of Babel and another ten generations that angered the Lord.

אָמַר הַקָּדוֹשׁ בָּרוּךְ הוּא עַד מָתַי יְהֵא הָעוֹלָם מִתְנַהֵג בַּאֲפֵלָה תָּבוֹא הָאוֹרָה 'וַיֹּאמֶר אֱלֹהִים יְהִי אוֹר' זֶה אַבְרָהָם הֲדָא הוּא דִכְתִיב (ישעיה מא, ב) 'מִי הֵעִיר מִמִּזְרָח צֶדֶק וְגוֹ'' אַל תִּקְרָא 'הֵעִיר' אֶלָּא הֵאִיר

Said the Holy One, blessed be He: How long shall the universe go on in darkness? Let the light come! 'And God said: Let there be light' – [this light] is Abraham as it is written, 'Who has raised [הֵעִיר] one up from the east whom He called in righteousness to His service' (Isaiah 41:2) – **Do not read הֵעִיר [with an *ayin* meaning to 'arouse'], but rather הֵאִיר [with an *alef* meaning to 'illuminate'].**

Abraham came from the east – Ur of the Chaldees to Canaan and stirred up the whole world to the knowledge of God. Who motivated him to do so? None other than God. 'Light' refers to Abraham because he was the first to bring the light of God to the world.

'וַיִּקְרָא אֱלֹהִים לָאוֹר יוֹם' זֶה יַעֲקֹב 'וְלַחשֶׁךְ קָרָא לָיְלָה' זֶה עֵשָׂו 'וַיְהִי עֶרֶב' זֶה עֵשָׂו 'וַיְהִי בֹקֶר' זֶה יַעֲקֹב 'וַיְהִי עֶרֶב' עַרְבּוֹ שֶׁל עֵשָׂו 'וַיְהִי בֹקֶר' בּוֹקְרוֹ שֶׁל יַעֲקֹב 'יוֹם אֶחָד' שֶׁנֶּאֱמַר (זכריה יד, ז) 'וְהָיָה יוֹם אֶחָד הוּא יִוָּדַע לַה' לֹא יוֹם וְלֹא לָיְלָה וְגוֹ'.'

'And God called the light day' – this refers to Jacob, 'and the darkness He called night' – this is Esau; 'and there was evening' refers to Esau, 'and there was morning' refers to Jacob. 'And there was evening' – the evening of Esau; 'and there was morning' – the morning of Jacob. 'One day,' as it is written, 'But it shall be a continuous day – only the Lord knows when – of neither day nor night, [and there shall be light at eventide]' (Zechariah 14:7).

How do we know that day symbolizes Jacob? One interpretation is that in *parashah* eight of *Bereishit Rabbah,* Jacob is referred to as the sun – and sun and day are often used as synonyms. And why is Esau called night? One interpretation is the verse in Isaiah 21:11 where Esau is referred to by the name of his land Seir and with the night, 'He called to me out of Seir, watchman what of the night?' Another interpretation is that the numerical value of the name Esau is 376, which is the same as that for קָרָא לָיְלָה, which means 'he called night.' Evening comes before morning and this indicates that Esau will come to power first, but Jacob will achieve power ultimately. Another interpretation: Esau will achieve power in this world but Jacob will achieve ascendancy in the world-to-come.

The *midrash* continues its imagery: The time will come when the power of Esau will reach its evening and start to diminish and the power of Jacob will reach its morning and start to ascend. When will that time be? The *midrash* gives the verse from Zechariah in answer. There will be 'a continuous day,' without day or night. This means that a time will come, presumably in the world-to-come, when there will no longer be the division of night and day but that it will be all day or all light and that is the meaning of 'a continuous day' – one that shall last forever.

דָּבָר אַחֵר 'יוֹם אֶחָד' שֶׁנָּתַן לוֹ הַקָּדוֹשׁ בָּרוּךְ הוּא וְאֵיזֶה זֶה יוֹם הַכִּפּוּרִים.

Another interpretation: 'One day' – one particular day that God has

**given him [Jacob, i.e., Israel, even during the ascendancy of Esau].
Which day is that? The Day of Atonement.**

We do not have to wait until the end of days in order to experience the great fulfillment of the world-to-come. We can experience it every Yom Kippur, which prepares us and renders us worthy of the great redemption yet to come.

* * *

Seed Thoughts

Yom Kippur has not yet even been mentioned in the text of Scripture and already it has become a central theme in the Torah. Why? Because man requires regeneration. Man is not a static being but a dynamic one. He can go forward or backward, advance along the path of ethical truth or slip backward.

One of the main forms of regeneration is through a great personality, one such as Abraham, who can turn history around. Abraham for his descendants is a memory and a teaching that requires study of which not everyone is capable. It has to be supplemented by an ongoing experience. Yom Kippur provides such an experience. However, special precaution and preparation are required lest even Yom Kippur degenerates into a mechanical or ritual performance. It requires the use of all of Yom Kippur's unique concepts of cleansing, fasting, atonement, purification, confession, and forgiveness. It will then become for us a vehicle for great spiritual regeneration.

* * *

Additional Commentary

Generational time

Whatever the text says about the world at its beginnings is a sign and reflection of what will happen in the generations to come. Just as the confusion of *tohu va-vohu* was clarified by the coming of light, so will the inadequacies of Adam, Enosh, Cain, and others listed, be compensated for by Abraham and, eventually, Yom Kippur will annually give everyone a new start. (*Ha-Midrash ha-Mevo'ar*)

*

And there was evening and there was morning

The problem in this verse is that evening, unlike night, is not close to morning. Evening is the end of the day and the beginning of night. How could the text say 'And there was evening' after having just said 'And the darkness He called night.' Surely, it should first have described evening and then described night.

It is for this reason that the *midrash* must offer a new interpretation for the word *erev*, 'evening.' This is why it says 'the evening of Esau,' and, later, 'the morning of Jacob.' Here, *erev* has the meaning of 'end.' Evening is used as being the end of night in the same way as it is ordinarily used as being the end of day. This is also the interpretation of *erev* in the verse quoted from Zechariah 14:7 – at the end of the night (of Esau in this world) there will be the light (of Jacob in the world-to-come). (RWZE)

Parashah Two, Midrash Four

The following *midrash* offers another interpretation of the phrase *tohu va-vohu*, usually translated as formless and void.

ר' שִׁמְעוֹן בֶּן לָקִישׁ פָּתַר קְרָיָא בַּגָּלֻיּוֹת 'וְהָאָרֶץ הָיְתָה תֹהוּ' זֶה גָּלוּת בָּבֶל שֶׁנֶּאֱמַר
(ירמיה ד, כג) 'רָאִיתִי אֶת הָאָרֶץ וְהִנֵּה תֹהוּ'

R. Simon b. Lakish interpreted the verse 'And the earth was formless and void' as applying to [the various] exiles [experienced by the Jews]. 'And the earth was *tohu*' refers to Babylon, as it is written, 'I look at the earth, it is unformed [*tohu*] and void' (Jeremiah 4:23).

Our verse, as well as subsequent verses, will be searched for hints about the future history of the Jews. Some texts of the *midrash*, like ours, read, *galuyot* – exiles – putting the emphasis on the condition of the Jewish people; others, considered more authentic, read *malkhuyot* – kingships with the emphasis on the foreign power themselves. These foreign powers were destined to rule over Israel and the world. What probably happened was that the original *malkhuyot* was changed to *galuyot* by the censors for public relations reasons.

The Babylon of Nebuchadnezzar destroyed the Temple and the land of Israel and threw the world into chaos – *tohu*. The verse from Jeremiah that speaks of *tohu* as waste was spoken during the destruction of the first Temple and is thus most appropriate.

(אסתר ו, יד) 'וָבֹהוּ' זֶה גָּלוּת מָדַי 'וַיַּבְהִלוּ לְהָבִיא אֶת הָמָן'

'and *vohu*' refers to Media [as it is written], '...and hurriedly [*va-yavhillu*] to brought Haman' (Esther 6:14).

This is the Media of the time of Ahasuerus who reigned over the Jews exiled in Persia after the Babylonian period. Ahasuerus decreed the destruction of Persian Jewry but in the confusion of his rule Queen Esther was able to rescue her people. The word, *va-yavhillu*, in the verse quoted resembles *vohu* in both sound and meaning. From the banquet that Esther prepared for Haman there began that series of events that delivered Israel.

96

'וְחֹשֶׁךְ' זֶה גָּלוּת יָוָן שֶׁהֶחֱשִׁיכָה עֵינֵיהֶם שֶׁל יִשְׂרָאֵל בִּגְזֵרוֹתֵיהֶן שֶׁהָיְתָה אוֹמֶרֶת לָהֶם כִּתְבוּ עַל קֶרֶן הַשּׁוֹר שֶׁאֵין לָכֶם חֵלֶק בֵּאלֹהֵי יִשְׂרָאֵל

'And darkness' refers to Greece, which darkened the eyes of Israel with its decrees, ordering them [the Jews] to write on the horn of an ox that you have no portion in the God of Israel.

The reference here is to the time of Antiochus, in the period after Persia. This kingdom darkened the eyes of the Jews from the light of Torah and faith in God as a result of its evil decrees. The Jews were ordered to write the slogan on the horns of oxen in order to give the widest possible exposure to their humiliation.

'עַל פְּנֵי תְהוֹם' זֶה גָּלוּת מַמְלֶכֶת הָרְשָׁעָה שֶׁאֵין לָהֶם חֵקֶר כְּמוֹ הַתְּהוֹם מָה הַתְּהוֹם הַזֶּה אֵין לוֹ חֵקֶר אַף הָרְשָׁעִים כֵּן

'Upon the face of the deep,' refers to the exile inflicted by the evil empire, which was boundless. Just as there are no limits to the deep, so too those evil people knew no limits.

This refers to Rome, usually referred to as the evil empire. Rome occupied Israel, destroying the Temple, devastating the land, and exiling its population. At the time of R. Simon b. Lakish's exposition, the end of the exile imposed by Rome was not yet in sight. That explains how the text was interpreted to mean that we cannot plumb the depths of this evil empire, meaning that no one knows when its end will come.

We have now named the various exiles. The fact that Rome is not mentioned by name has added significance in that it can stand for all the tyrannies that succeeded it, such as the Spanish Inquisition and in modern times the Holocaust. But what will follow the tyrannies? The Messianic age.

'וְרוּחַ אֱלֹהִים מְרַחֶפֶת' זֶה רוּחוֹ שֶׁל מֶלֶךְ הַמָּשִׁיחַ הֵיאַךְ מַה דְּאַתְּ אָמַר 'וְנָחָה עָלָיו רוּחַ ה'' בְּאֵיזוֹ זְכוּת מְמַשְׁמֶשֶׁת וּבָאָה ה'מְרַחֶפֶת עַל פְּנֵי הַמָּיִם' (ישעיה יא, ב) בִּזְכוּת הַתְּשׁוּבָה שֶׁנִּמְשְׁלָה כְמַיִם כְּמָה שֶׁנֶּאֱמַר 'שִׁפְכִי כַמַּיִם לִבֵּךְ' (איכה ב, יט)

'And the spirit [ru'aḥ] of God hovered...' alludes to the spirit of the King Messiah, as it says, 'And the spirit [ru'aḥ] of the Lord shall rest upon him' (Isaiah 11:2). In the merit of what will this spirit come sooner? [The verse explains: By the merit of that which] 'hovers over the face of the waters,' i.e., by the merit of repentance, which is likened to water, as it is written, 'Pour out your heart like water' (Lamentations 2:19).

The reference to the Messiah is based on the correspondence of the Hebrew word *ru'aḥ* in the Genesis text as well as in the Isaiah text. This means further that the age of Messiah is not a time period, but rather a condition of man. Man will then respond to the spirit of wisdom and understanding, the spirit of counsel and might, the spirit of knowledge and of the fear of the Lord.

What can man do to bring the coming of the Messiah closer? The answer is repentance. Man's condition will change for the better when he learns to repent. Repentance is that beautiful quality that softens the heart of the sinner so that it becomes like water and is flexible and responsive. 'Pour out your heart like water' and repent. Everything depends upon repentance, which is another way of saying, everything depends upon ourselves.

So far we have been given an interpretation of the word *ru'aḥ*, spirit, and the word 'water' from the same text in Genesis. What about the word *meraḥefet* – 'hovered'?

רַבִּי חַגַּי בְּשֵׁם רַבִּי פְּדָת אָמַר בְּרִית כְּרוּתָה לַמַּיִם שֶׁאֲפִלּוּ בִּשְׁעַת שָׁרָב רוּחָה שְׁיָפָה

R. Ḥaggai said in the name of R. Pedat: A covenant was made with water that even in the hot season a breeze stirs over it.

The word *meraḥefet* (hovered) is understood in this exposition to be referring to the present, not the past. It means, says R. Ḥaggai, that the waters will always provide the quality of coolness and freshness. This is especially appreciated during the summer heat and is one of the great gifts of God caused by His wind that hovers over the water and caresses it. From this interpretation we derive that 'hovers' means caressing in the sense of touching. Ben Zoma, however, later gives a different interpretation to the effect that 'hovers' means separation, that is, without touching. But first, we are told an interesting anecdote.

וּכְבָר הָיָה רַ' שִׁמְעוֹן בֶּן זוֹמָא יוֹשֵׁב וְתוֹהֵא וְעָבַר רַבִּי יְהוֹשֻׁעַ וְשָׁאַל בִּשְׁלוֹמוֹ פַּעַם וּשְׁתַּיִם וְלֹא הֱשִׁיבוֹ בַּשְּׁלִישִׁית הֱשִׁיבוֹ בִּבְהִילוּת אָמַר לוֹ בֶּן זוֹמָא מֵאַיִן הָרַגְלַיִם אָמַר לוֹ מְעַיֵּן הָיִיתִי אָמַר לוֹ מֵעִיד אֲנִי עָלַי שָׁמַיִם וָאָרֶץ שֶׁאֵינִי זָז מִכָּאן עַד שֶׁתּוֹדִיעֵנִי מֵאַיִן הָרַגְלַיִם אָמַר לוֹ מִסְתַּכֵּל הָיִיתִי בְּמַעֲשֵׂה בְרֵאשִׁית וְלֹא הָיָה בֵין מַיִם הָעֶלְיוֹנִים לְמַיִם הַתַּחְתּוֹנִים אֶלָּא כִּשְׁתַּיִם וְשָׁלֹשׁ אֶצְבָּעוֹת וְרוּחַ אֱלֹהִים מְנַשֶּׁבֶת אֵין כְּתִיב כָּאן אֶלָּא 'מְרַחֶפֶת' כָּעוֹף הַזֶּה שֶׁהוּא מְרַפְרֵף בִּכְנָפָיו וּכְנָפָיו נוֹגְעוֹת וְאֵינָן נוֹגְעוֹת נֶהְפַּךְ רַבִּי יְהוֹשֻׁעַ וְאָמַר לְתַלְמִידָיו הָלַךְ לוֹ בֶּן זוֹמָא וְלֹא שָׁהוּ יָמִים מוּעָטִים וּבֶן זוֹמָא בָּעוֹלָם.

It happened that R. Simon ben Zoma was sitting and meditating. R. Joshua passed by and greeted him, a first time and then a second time, but he did not reply. After the third greeting he answered brusquely. [R. Joshua] said to him, 'Ben Zoma, from where have your legs brought you?' [What have you been thinking about so deeply?] He answered, 'I was meditating.' Said R. Joshua to him, 'I call heaven and earth to witness that I will not move from this place until you tell me from where your legs have taken you' [i.e., what you were thinking about]. [Ben Zoma] replied, 'I had a vision of the creation and the separation between the upper waters and the lower waters was only two or three finger-breadths wide. Scripture does not say that the spirit of God *blew* over the waters, but *hovered*, like a bird that hovers in flight [over its nest] with its wings fluttering, touching and not touching.' R. Joshua turned away and said to his disciples, 'Ben Zoma has gone away [from the true understanding of the verse].' Not many days passed and Ben Zoma departed this world.

Ben Zoma explains *merahefet* by noticing the similarity used elsewhere in the Pentateuch in connection with the eagle as *merahefet*, meaning that the eagle hovers over its young without touching them. In the same way, there is always a separation between the upper waters and lower waters, meaning the horizon. That the upper and lower waters separated during the second day of creation is a fact of Scripture. What that means in terms of Ben Zoma's vision is hard to understand. It was probably a mystical experience of tremendous power. When Ben Zoma died after giving this explanation, it was said that he had become much too involved in speculation about the creation, far beyond man's capability. R. Joshua realized that something was very wrong with Ben Zoma, since the 'spirit hovered' on the very first day of creation, but the waters – both upper and lower – were only created later.

Having said this, I would like to suggest that what Ben Zoma saw was an insight that the separation of the upper and lower waters had to be permanent because it was indispensable for the world. Without it the world would be constantly flooded. God's 'hovering' over the universe means that He protected the world by keeping the upper waters always at a distance, however slight it be, from the lower waters. This is what the verse means when it says, 'The spirit of God hovered over the waters.'

* * *

Seed Thoughts

What is most impressive in this text is the interpretation that the verb, *hayetah*, '*was* formless and void,' is not an expression referring to the past, but a style that makes it valid in the present. The world was formless and void not merely before, but also during its creation. In fact, the return to chaos is endemic; it is part of the condition of man.

The world has returned to chaos many times, under the Babylonians, the Persians, the Greeks, the Romans, wherever a great power lords it over the world and also oppresses the Jewish people. Will it happen again in the future? Probably.

Will it ever come to a stop? Only with the advent of Messiah. What does that mean in pragmatic terms? It means the coming of righteousness, justice, true wisdom, and the courage to realize these great ideals. It means the replacement of material goals by spiritual ones.

Will that ever happen? The *midrash* is silent on that question. It merely asserts that Messiah will, of course, come if only to stop the world from its perpetual return to chaos.

* * *

Additional Commentary

R. Simon ben Lakish

The interpretation of R. Simon b. Lakish expresses the thought that the purpose of creation is the coming of Messiah. Then the earth will be filled with the knowledge of the Lord. Therefore he did not concern himself with the intervening years so full of oppression and slavery, for a day would come when the light of the Lord would illumine the earth. (*Yefei To'ar*)

*

And the earth was *tohu* – chaos = exile

The earth was forced to be chaos at the beginning because it was destined to be chaos throughout its existence. The reason is that the purpose of the world is the existence of Israel. Thus, when Israel is in exile the earth has to reflect that exile. It is the purpose of the world to prepare Israel, meaning to improve Israel, so that it could reach the level of its great purpose. One of the ways to that improvement is to preserve faith during the time that His face is hidden, namely, during the darkness of exile when it appears that there is no hope for those who uphold the truth of the Torah. Despite this, we give our lives over every day for the uniqueness of His name and Torah and service. In this way the *galut* is hinted at from the early beginnings of creation, for the road to the giving of Torah leads through the slavery of Egypt. (*Tiferet Tzion*)

The horn of an ox
The idea of writing their spiritual surrender on the horn of an ox was a special form of humiliation. It had symbolic overtones of great irony since it was a reminder of the infamous moment when Israel built a golden calf. Even for those who would obey the decree there were considerable physical dangers from the animal itself to anyone who would try to write on the horn of an ox. (*Tiferet Tzion*)

*

By what merit will it come hurriedly?
Redemption will come in one of two ways, either *be'ito* – in God's own good time – or, *yahishenu* – 'He will hurry it.' If it is hurried, it can only happen by means of the repentance of Israel to make themselves worthy. This is what the *midrash* means by relating repentance to the verse, 'and the spirit of God was hovering over the waters.' The spirit of God hovers over the time of redemption, which could become a reality, even now, by our repentance. (*Tiferet Tzion*)

The spirit of God hovers
'The earth was chaos,' is written in the past tense. 'The spirit of God hovers,' is written in the present tense. This means that the spirit of God always hovers over the waters to protect them even in times of drought. (RWZE)

Parashah Two, Midrash Five

Differing views are here recorded between R. Abbahu and R. Ḥiyya Rabbah on the purpose of creation as reflected in the first verses of Genesis. R. Abbahu sees in these verses an indication that the purpose of creation was to make possible a moral way of life. R. Ḥiyya Rabbah sees the purpose of creation as establishing a spiritual life for the world through the people of Israel.

רַבִּי אַבָּהוּ וְרַ' חִיָּא רַבָּה רַבִּי אַבָּהוּ אָמַר מִתְּחִלַּת בְּרִיָּתוּ שֶׁל עוֹלָם צָפָה הַקָּדוֹשׁ בָּרוּךְ הוּא בְּמַעֲשֵׂיהֶן שֶׁל צַדִּיקִים וּמַעֲשֵׂיהֶן שֶׁל רְשָׁעִים הָדָא הוּא דִכְתִיב 'כִּי יוֹדֵעַ ה' דֶּרֶךְ צַדִּיקִים וְגוֹ'' (תהלים א, ו)

R. Abbahu and R. Ḥiyya Rabbah [were engaged in discussion]. R. Abbahu said, from the very beginning of the world's creation the Holy One, blessed be He, foresaw the deeds of the righteous and the deeds of the wicked, as it is written, 'For the Lord cherishes the way of the righteous, [but the way of the wicked is doomed]' (Psalms 1:6).

From the very beginning, free will to choose his way of life was given to man. That is why some are referred to as 'righteous' and some as 'wicked.' God knows in advance that this is going to happen, but that does not affect freedom of choice. As stated in the *Ethics of the Fathers*, 'Everything is foreseen but freedom of choice is given.' (Avot 3:15)

'וְהָאָרֶץ הָיְתָה תֹהוּ וָבֹהוּ' אֵלּוּ מַעֲשֵׂיהֶן שֶׁל רְשָׁעִים 'וַיֹּאמֶר אֱלֹהִים יְהִי אוֹר' אֵלּוּ מַעֲשֵׂיהֶן שֶׁל צַדִּיקִים

[Thus,] 'And now the earth was formless and void' alludes to the deeds of the wicked; 'And God said let there be light' alludes to the actions of the righteous.

The wicked cause chaos in the world, but the righteous bring light into the world. The point to note is that at the very beginning of the creation God foresees both these actions and ways, which raises the question of free will and God's foreknowledge. Therefore, some people might be misled into believing that since God influences all these actions, the question to be asked is: Whose actions does He prefer?

אֲבָל אֵינִי יוֹדֵעַ בְּאֵיזֶה מֵהֶם חָפֵץ אִם בְּמַעֲשֵׂה אֵלּוּ וְאִם בְּמַעֲשֵׂה אֵלּוּ כֵּיוָן דִּכְתִיב
'וַיַּרְא אֱלֹהִים אֶת הָאוֹר כִּי טוֹב' הֱוֵי בְּמַעֲשֵׂיהֶן שֶׁל צַדִּיקִים חָפֵץ וְאֵינוֹ חָפֵץ
בְּמַעֲשֵׂיהֶן שֶׁל רְשָׁעִים

However, I do not know whether God approves the actions of these or these. Since it is written, 'And God saw the light that it was good' (1:4) it follows that He desires the deeds of the righteous, and not the deeds of the wicked.

Could there possibly be a doubt as to whether God prefers the righteous to the wicked? Here are some of the considerations: 1. There are those who believe that God's knowledge of the future prevents free will and the wicked cannot therefore be blamed. This is rejected by the verse, 'but the way of the wicked is doomed.' 2. Does God prefer the righteous who never sin or the wicked who, after sinning, repent and become righteous? The answer is that he prefers those who are righteous always.

Of course, we assume that God prefers the righteous to the wicked. Nevertheless, it is important, for those less informed, to have a verse in support. That verse is, 'And God saw the light that it was good.'

אָמַר רַ' חִיָּא רַבָּה מִתְּחִלַּת בְּרִיָּתוֹ שֶׁל עוֹלָם צָפָה הַקָּדוֹשׁ בָּרוּךְ הוּא בֵּית הַמִּקְדָּשׁ
בָּנוּי וְחָרֵב וּבָנוּי 'בְּרֵאשִׁית בָּרָא אֱלֹהִים' הֲרֵי בָנוּי הֵיאַךְ מָה דְּאַתְּ אָמַר 'לִנְטֹעַ
שָׁמַיִם וְלִיסֹד אָרֶץ וְגוֹ'" (ישעיה נא, טז)

R. Ḥiyya Rabbah said: From the very beginning of the world's creation the Holy One, blessed be He, foresaw that the temple would be built, destroyed, and rebuilt. 'In the beginning God created' symbolizes the temple built, as it is said, 'I, who planted the heavens and made firm the earth and have said to Zion: You are My people' (Isaiah 51:16).

This verse signifies the Temple built because it describes the Lord abiding in Zion, which is the function of the Temple.

The view of R. Ḥiyya Rabbah is based on the style of the early verses in Genesis – the first verse is positive, the second negative, and the third, positive. The first, 'In the beginning God created,' is positive. 'And the earth was unformed and void,' is negative. 'And God said let there be light' is the positive again. These accentuations mean something.

'וְהָאָרֶץ הָיְתָה תֹהוּ וָבֹהוּ' הֲרֵי חָרֵב הֵיאַךְ מָה דְּאַתְּ אָמַר 'רָאִיתִי אֶת הָאָרֶץ וְהִנֵּה
תֹהוּ וָבֹהוּ' (ירמיה ד, כג) 'וַיֹּאמֶר אֱלֹהִים יְהִי אוֹר' הֲרֵי בָנוּי וּמְשֻׁכְלָל לֶעָתִיד לָבוֹא

הֵיךְ מָה דְּאַתְּ אָמַר 'קוּמִי אוֹרִי כִּי בָא אוֹרֵךְ' (ישעיה ס, א) וּכְתִיב 'כִּי הִנֵּה הַחשֶׁךְ
יְכַסֶּה אֶרֶץ וְגוֹ'" (שם שם, ב)

'Now the earth was *tohu va-vohu*' alludes to the temple destroyed as you read, 'I look at the earth, it is unformed and void' (Jeremiah 4:23). 'And God said: Let there be light' alludes to the Temple rebuilt and firmly established in the messianic era as it says, 'Arise, shine, for your light has dawned; the Presence of Lord has shone upon you' (Isaiah 60:1) and it is also written, 'Behold! Darkness shall cover the earth, [and thick clouds the people; but upon you the Lord will shine and His Presence will be seen over you]' (ibid. v. 2).

The verse in Jeremiah was said in the context of the destruction of the Temple and compares that catastrophic even to the destruction of all creation. Just as the Temple was the climax of creation so was its destruction the removal of all light, as the verse continues, '[I look] at the skies, and their light is gone.' 'Let there be light' refers to the third Temple that will appear in full splendor during the messianic age. The goal of history and creation will be fulfilled at this restoration, for this Temple will possess all the ingredients that the second Temple lacked. The added verse, which does not appear in some editions, indicates that Israel will be redeemed even when 'Darkness shall cover the earth, and thick clouds the people,' that is, the other nations. It symbolizes the redemption of the Jewish people as the pilot people who will bring all of mankind with them in the recognition of the one God.

* * *

Seed Thoughts

The *Tiferet Tzion* (see Additional Commentary) offers the astute observation that God also looks for the good being done by the wicked.

This is an important point. Too often in the classic rabbinic literature and in the prophets as well, the moral temperature is described as black or white. Either the people are sinners beyond the capacity of redemption or saints who can do no wrong.

Most of us are neither angels nor demons. We are creatures of flesh and blood. We go forward at times and we go backward many times.

The whole classification of people into the categories of righteous and wicked leaves a lot to be desired. One can understand the *midrash* using such terms because it is a literature that is trying to set standards, but we who are its readers and students have to know that human beings are too complex to be fitted into a system of righteous and wicked without any other qualifications.

The Kotzker Rebbe refused to accept the views of his disciples that he was a *tzaddik* – 'a righteous man.' 'I cannot accept it,' he said, 'and I do not believe it. Indeed, even if the Almighty Himself were to appear to me in a dream and say to me, "Reb Mendl you are a *tzaddik!*" I would believe it only for that fleeting moment. For how can I know how I will act in the face of the next challenge?'

One thing is certain. No human being has a right to divide people into the categories of righteous and wicked. That is exclusively God's jurisdiction, His exclusive right. He is the only one who knows the complete story and has the complete picture. All we can see are outward manifestations.

It is our job to do the best we can and to criticize whenever necessary. The only rule to remember is the responsibility to criticize ourselves first before assessing others.

* * *

Additional Commentary

The righteous and the wicked

In order to make sense out of these exchanges between R. Abbahu and R. Ḥiyya Rabbah, we have to enter an area well worked on by many researchers and try to reconcile man's freedom of choice with God's omniscience. For, after all, if God knows in advance man's thoughts and deeds, from first to last, there is simply no way to account for man's freedom of choice to do or not to do. Many fine minds have erroneously concluded that one of these alternatives has to be rejected. Either free choice has to be rejected and we are left with the conclusion that man's actions are determined by God's knowledge of them or we must reject the idea of God's omnipotence and admit that God has removed Himself from the moral universe.

The latter view is supported by two misleading observations. One, the fact that we observe the same fate overtaking both righteous and wicked, and why then did God create the wicked if they were destined to sin. Secondly, it is well known from Scripture that God performed miracles for Israel, for example, taking them out of Egypt, bringing them to the Promised Land, building a Temple on a site of His choice, and so forth. Afterwards, because of Israel's sins, they were exiled from their land and the Sanctuary was destroyed, which means that all of God's doings amounted to no effect.

In truth, this whole problem of choosing between God's omniscience and man's freedom was already solved beautifully by the Rivash (R. Isaac b. Sheshet Perfet; 1326–1408, a Spanish talmudist) who observed that God's omniscience is not the same as His omnipotence. That is, it does not force man to act in one way or the other. It simply means that He knows in advance how men will act and, if man changes his mind and acts differently, God also knows that in advance.

As to the argument about the same fate awaiting the righteous and the wicked, R. Abbahu evokes from the verses of creation that God knows in advance the way of the righteous and also, that the way of the wicked leads to ruination. This knowledge, however, does not determine whether men will do good or do evil. As for the argument about God's miracles being in vain, R. Hiyya Rabbah observes that God certainly knew in advance the various stages the Temple would go through in history, but He also knew that in the end it would be re-established. All of these in-between stages and transformations are necessary for the perfection of the human species or for some other purpose that God is so far keeping from our knowledge. (*Yefei To'ar*)

*

I do not know which way God prefers

It is quite astonishing for the text to pretend that God might prefer the way of the wicked. One must therefore conclude that the question really is: Does God prefer the wicked who repents and thus changes his way for the better or does He prefer the righteous who never sins? One would conclude from the discussion that God prefers the permanently righteous to the repentant sinner. But that does not seem to be the literal interpretation of the text. Literally, the text is asking not whether God prefers the righteous way or the wicked way, but rather: How come the early verses do not say specifically which way He prefers? The answer of the text is to quote the verse, 'And God saw the light that it was good' as a proof-text for this purpose. (*Yefei To'ar*)

*

Righteous and wicked – another interpretation

What does it mean that God evaluated the way of the wicked? It means that He took cognizance of the good that even the wicked sometimes do. Of course, no comparisons between the righteous and the wicked can be drawn. The good of the wicked in comparison to the righteous would be as a candle burning at midday when there is a strong sun. The candle would hardly be noticed, but God notices everything. It is the nature of divine justice that God did not want to leave out of the picture even the small good that the wicked sometimes do. (*Tiferet Tzion*)

Parashah Three, Midrash One

וַיֹּאמֶר אֱלֹהִים יְהִי אוֹר רַבִּי יִצְחָק פָּתַח 'פֵּתַח דְּבָרֶיךָ יָאִיר מֵבִין וְגוֹ'' (תהלים קיט,
קל)

**'And God said: Let there be light.' R. Isaac began [his exposition]:
'The opening of Your word gives light, [and grants understanding
to the simple]' (Psalms 119:130).**

Do we read the first verse of Genesis as it is ordinarily understood and
translated or do we regard the word *Bereishit* as a preposition so that the
verse would be translated as follows: 'In the beginning, before God
created heaven and earth and while the earth was still formless and void,
God said, "Let there be light."'

The question arises because a command in the creation story is usually
followed by the expression *va-yehi ken* – 'and it was so.' In connection
with light, however, it says, 'And there was light.' Also because *va-yomer*
'and He said' is the first imperative to be found in the Torah. In the case
of the creation of heaven and earth, there is no commanding verb.

The verse quoted by R. Isaac both opens and closes this *midrash*. It
means that from the moment God spoke and even before His declaration
was completed, light had entered the world. This seems to back the view
of R. Judah, which the next *midrash* brings.

רַ' יְהוּדָה וְרַ' נְחֶמְיָה רַ' יְהוּדָה אוֹמֵר הָאוֹרָה נִבְרֵאת תְּחִלָּה מָשָׁל לְמֶלֶךְ שֶׁבִּקֵּשׁ
לִבְנוֹת פָּלָטִין וְהָיָה אוֹתוֹ מָקוֹם אָפֵל מֶה עָשָׂה הִדְלִיק נֵרוֹת וּפָנָסִין לֵידַע הֵיאַךְ
הוּא קוֹבֵעַ תֵּימְלְיוֹסִים כָּךְ הָאוֹרָה נִבְרֵאת תְּחִלָּה

**R. Judah and R. Neḥemiah [disagree]. R. Judah maintains light was
created first [before heaven and earth]. The question may be
compared to a king who wished to build a palace, but the site was a
dark one. What did he do? He lit lamps and lanterns to know where
to lay the foundations. In like manner was the light created first.**

Though it might seem obvious from the text in Genesis that heaven and
earth were created before light, R. Judah bases his opinion on Psalms
104:2 where light is mentioned first and only afterwards heaven:

'Wrapped in a robe of light, You spread the heavens like a tent cloth.' This conception leads R. Judah to interpret the first verse of Genesis in the manner suggested above.

וְרַ' נְחֶמְיָה אָמַר הָעוֹלָם נִבְרָא תְּחִלָּה מָשָׁל לְמֶלֶךְ שֶׁבָּנָה פָּלָטִין וְעִטְּרָהּ בְּנֵרוֹת וּפָנָסִין

R. Neḥemiah said: The world was created first. The matter can be compared to a king who [first] builds a palace and then decorates it with candles and lanterns.

Both parables are very effective. How, then, does one conclude?

עַד כָּאן דָּרַשׁ רַבִּי יוּדָן

Thus far did R. Judan exposit.

R. Judan's exposition was that the verse from Psalms cited at the beginning of the *midrash* by R. Isaac, 'The opening of Your word gives light, [and grants understanding to the simple],' conforms to R. Judah's understanding of the first verse of Genesis. But what does R. Neḥemiah do with the verse from Psalms?

אֲתָא רַ' פִּינְחָס וְרַ' יְהוּדָה בַּר רַבִּי סִימוֹן וְרַבִּי חָנוּן בְּשֵׁם רַ' שְׁמוּאֵל בַּר רַב יִצְחָק פָּתַח 'פֵּתַח דְּבָרֶיךָ יָאִיר מֵבִין פְּתָיִים' מִפְתַּח פִּמָּךְ לָן הֲוָה נְהוֹרָא 'וַיֹּמֶר אֱלֹהִים יְהִי אוֹר וְגוֹ'.'.

R. Pinḥas and R. Judah b. R. Simon came, and R. Ḥanin in the name of R. Samuel b. R. Isaac and began [his exposition with the same verse as R. Isaac, but interpreted it differently]; 'The opening of Your word gives light, and grants understanding to the simple': the opening of Your mouth was light to us – 'And God said: 'Let there be light.'

This interpretation of the verse from Psalms completely bypasses the question of the priorities in the creation of the world. It understands the verse to be saying that the first *statement* by God was to give light to the world, since there is no mention of God having *said* anything when He created the heavens and the earth. That is to say, light was created by a special pronouncement, the first such declaratory statement from God in Scripture, although the heavens and the earth were created earlier. We now see that the same verse originally interpreted to strengthen the view of R. Judah can also be used in support of R. Neḥemiah.

* * *

Seed Thoughts

The observation of the *Yefei To'ar*, that light in our *midrash* cannot possibly be the light with which we are familiar, is a very astute one. After all, the luminaries, which give the light we are accustomed to, were only created on the fourth day. The light we are talking about has to be a symbol of something. In his view it symbolizes the world-to-come.

The controversy in our *midrash* then takes on a completely different form. R. Judah would maintain that the world-to-come was created first because it represents purpose. R. Neḥemiah asserts that this world was created first because one has to earn in this world that merit that leads to the world-to-come.

This interpretation changes the character of our *midrash* dramatically; but that is what makes the study of this material so exciting and unexpected.

From the point of view of the kabbalists, the controversy as now stated is not a controversy at all. One view simply supplements the other.

The kabbalists would ask: Which world-to-come are you talking about? They speak of many worlds-to-come, all of which are manifestations or qualities of the human soul. Indeed, the very worlds themselves are worlds of the soul, *nefesh, neshamah, ḥaya, yeḥidah.* According to this doctrine, the soul begins its journey in this world but has to go through the other worlds on its journey through eternity.

There is a line in the memorial prayer that reads, 'May the soul (of so-and-so) be bound up in the bond of eternal life.' This is a kabbalistic doctrine and what it expresses is the hope that the soul may ascend from the world of *neshamah*, which is this world, to the world of *ḥayyim*, before it goes even further. This comes about not only through one's own merit, but also when those close to the deceased perform acts of merit in his or her honor, such as reciting *kaddish*, giving charity, or carrying out any of the commandments. This is known as the doctrine of the 'ascent of soul.'

The world to come may have been created first, but it is also last in terms of purpose. This world may have been created last, but it is always first in that it is the setting, the spiritual battleground in which the ascent of soul can be pursued.

* * *

Additional Commentary

Before God created heaven and earth.

R. Judah's view demands a new translation of the first verse of Genesis. It would imply that before the creation of heaven and earth and before the earth was unformed and void that God said, in advance, 'Let there be light,' and there was light. According to this interpretation light preceded not only heaven and earth but also *tohu va-vohu* and darkness. It should also be pointed out that the light referred to has nothing to do with the lights of sun and moon and stars that were created on the fourth day. (*Yefei To'ar*)

*

What is the light?

Light represents 'form' and the world represents 'matter.' The dispute between R. Judah and R. Nehemiah centers around the question whether form precedes matter in priority or whether matter preceded form because it is permanent and can assume many forms. So writes the author of *Goleh Amukim.* But it seems easier for me to explain that light represents the world-to-come and matter – this world. R. Judah feels that the world-to-come is the goal of creation and therefore was created first. That explains the parable of the palace built in a place of darkness whose goal is the light of the world-to-come. So, light was created first.

R. Nehemiah feels that since man has to earn his right to the world-to-come by good deeds in this world, the cause has to come before the effect, just as the palace comes before the lights that are to decorate it. (*Yefei To'ar*)

Parashah Three, Midrash Two

The motivation behind this *midrash* is the fact that the text reads: 'And there was light' and, not as is usually the case, 'and it was so.' In order to explain this variant a verse from Psalms is brought.

רַבִּי בֶּרֶכְיָה בְּשֵׁם רַבִּי יְהוּדָה בַּר סִימוֹן פָּתַח 'בִּדְבַר ה' שָׁמַיִם נַעֲשׂוּ וְגוֹ'' (תהלים לג, ו)

R. Berakhiah commenced in the name of R. Judah bar Simon: 'By the word of the Lord the heavens were made, [and by the breath of His mouth all their host]' (Psalms 33:6).

Notice that it does not say, 'He made the heavens by His word,' but that they were automatically made the moment His word was uttered.

רַבִּי יְהוּדָה בַּר סִימוֹן אָמַר לֹא בְעָמָל וְלֹא בִיגִיעָה בָּרָא הַקָּדוֹשׁ בָּרוּךְ הוּא אֶת עוֹלָמוֹ אֶלָּא 'בִּדְבַר ה'' וּכְבָר 'שָׁמַיִם נַעֲשׂוּ' אַף הָכָא וְהָיָה אוֹר אֵין כְּתִיב כָּאן אֶלָּא 'וַיְהִי אוֹר' כְּבָר הָיָה.

R. Judah b. R. Simon said: Not by labor or toil did the Holy One, blessed be He, create His world, but only by 'the word of the Lord.' So here, too, it is not written *ve-hayah or*, but *va-yehi or* – there already was [light].

The word והיה implies a process of development and emerging; ויהי means that the act was instantaneous. The lesson here is the same, but the emphasis is on the difference between man and God. Anything man does requires an expenditure of energy, even that which we describe as being effortless. But in the case of God the concept of work does not exist. He creates by divine fiat.

* * *

Seed Thoughts

The contrast between God and man is here expressed in a new dimension. God creates by divine fiat; neither labor nor toil is required. But man must labor and toil.

In the beginning this was looked upon as a curse, the punishment of

111

Adam. But the Psalmist already perceived that it could be a source of blessing. 'You shall enjoy the fruit of your labors; you shall be happy and you shall prosper' (Psalms 128:2). Work and effort and toil are the condition of man. But they can become a blessing. It all depends upon why you toil and for whom.

The story is told of three workmen engaged in a construction project. A newspaper reporter watched them and noticed a disparity of mood. The first one seemed to be quite discontented. The second worked with great determination. The third person sang and whistled as he worked. Intrigued by what he sensed could be a good story, the reporter struck up a conversation with them.

'What are you building?' he asked the first one. 'A job is a job,' he replied, 'We're putting up a building. Who cares what kind?'

He then approached the second workman. 'What are you building?' he asked. 'I'm building a future for my wife and children,' he replied.

'What about you?' he asked the third one. 'I'm building a Sanctuary,' he replied. No wonder he was able to sing and whistle. He not only had long-term goals, he had an immediate vision of what he was doing so that every move he made was part of an overall significance.

Work is man's role on earth. It may have started out as a curse, but it can be transformed into a blessing.

* * *

Additional Commentary

And there was light

This *midrash* might relate to the previous discussion as to which came first, the light or the world. The answer here would be that both were created with the same divine fiat and created instantaneously without need of any further physical development.

*

Usually the term *ve-haya,* והיה, is explained as the language of joy and *va-yehi,* ויהי (both mean 'and there was') as the language of sorrow. Joy would certainly be more appropriate for the creation of the world than sorrow. This is what prompts the *midrash* to make its comments.

*

Although previous comments of the *midrash* used parallels of creation that related to human life, this comment wishes to underscore that God's creation and man's creation are not to be compared. God created this world by divine fiat, which required no physical effort, unlike the creativity of man, which is all effort.

*

Va-yehi is usually used to indicate sadness and the creation of light was certainly an occasion for joy. But sadness reigned because the light was to be hidden from the world until the appropriate time. (*Yefei To'ar*)

Parashah Three, Midrash Three

This *midrash* is based on the text, 'And God said: Let there be light.' Why was God's first word uttered with regard to light? Why not with regard to the creation of heaven and earth?

רַ' שִׁמְעוֹן בֶּן יוֹחַאי פָּתַח 'שִׂמְחָה לָאִישׁ בְּמַעֲנֵה פִיו וְדָבָר בְּעִתּוֹ מַה טּוֹב' (משלי
טו, כג) 'שִׂמְחָה לָאִישׁ' זֶה הַקָּדוֹשׁ בָּרוּךְ הוּא שֶׁנֶּאֱמַר 'ה' אִישׁ מִלְחָמָה ה' שְׁמוֹ'
(שמות טו, ג) 'בְּמַעֲנֵה פִיו' 'וַיֹּאמֶר אֱלֹהִים יְהִי אוֹר' 'וְדָבָר בְּעִתּוֹ מַה טּוֹב' 'וַיַּרְא
אֱלֹהִים אֶת הָאוֹר כִּי טוֹב'

R. Simon b. Yoḥai commenced: 'A man has joy in the answer of his mouth and a word in season, how good it is' (Proverbs 15: 23). 'A man has joy' alludes to the Holy One, blessed be He, as it is written, 'The Lord is a *man* of war' (Exodus 15:3); 'in the answer of his mouth' – 'and God said: Let there be light'; 'and a word in season how good it is' – 'and God saw the light that it was good.'

R. Simon b. Yoḥai used this verse to help explain our text. We all know how much joy a person has when he has the right answer to a question. This joy is even greater when the answer comes at the right time because timing is everything in life. Let us now see how this insight helps explain our text.

The correspondence between these two verses is the word אִישׁ, *ish* – 'man.' Furthermore, in the phrase 'A man has joy' the Hebrew is לָאִישׁ, *la-ish* (literally: 'to the man'), implying that a particular man is intended. The *midrash* implies that the man intended is no other than God, and applies the verse to the words with which God began the creation of the world, namely, 'Let there be light.'

Now light is often connected with joy as in Proverbs 13:9, 'The light of the righteous will rejoice.' God's greatest joy was the experience of uttering the commandment of light. God realized that He had created the light at the right time and that the light would endure.

Another interpretation: Having created many worlds and destroyed them, God was satisfied that this world would endure. That is what is meant by 'And God saw the light and it was good.'

* * *

Seed Thoughts

God was delighted with the world that He had created. He was so proud of His achievement that He showed it off to others, presumably the angelic beings. That is the meaning of the phrase, 'And behold! It was good.' It was good in every way.

Never mind that the joy was short-lived. Never mind that the behavior of Adam and of mankind that followed him was enough to drive the world to destruction. The original assessment that this world is good and timely and proper and truly the best is a motivation that we could dearly use.

It would make us more sensitive to our blessings and more thankful for them. It would even make us feel sorry for those fools who don't appreciate the blessings of life and the world.

God was happy with His world when He created it. Maybe we can still do something with it that will make Him happy again.

* * *

Additional Commentary

And God saw that it was good

The impression from this verse is that God saw something new that He had not seen before, but how can that be? This would apply to the style of the other six days as well. The answer is that the expression 'And the Lord *saw* the light' should be interpreted that God *showed* (which comes from the same Hebrew root as 'saw') the light to the whole world. The verb *va-yar* is transitive and takes an object; it is also directed to someone and the reason He showed the light to the whole world is because it was good. That it was good also means that it was timely and that was the most propitious time to reveal this wonderful thing. This is the meaning of the proof-text from Proverbs. (*Tiferet Tzion*)

Parashah Three, Midrash Four

Since the light that is described in the third verse of Genesis is not the same light given by the great luminaries, the sun and the moon to be described later, and was not attached to any material thing, the question arises as to its source.

ר׳ שִׁמְעוֹן בֶּן יְהוֹצָדָק שָׁאַל לְרַבִּי שְׁמוּאֵל בַּר נַחְמָן אָמַר לוֹ מִפְּנֵי שֶׁשָּׁמַעְתִּי עָלֶיךָ שֶׁאַתָּה בַּעַל אַגָּדָה מֵהֵיכָן נִבְרֵאת הָאוֹרָה

R. Simon b. Jehozadak asked R. Samuel b. Naḥman [a question]. He said to him: Since I have heard that you are a master of *aggadah*, whence was the light created?

R. Samuel b. Naḥman is referred to as a master of *aggadah*, which means folklore and wisdom of the oral law. He would then be familiar with sources that go beyond the written biblical text, which is why the question was posed to him.

אָמַר לֵהּ מְלַמֵּד שֶׁנִּתְעַטֵּף בָּהּ הַקָּדוֹשׁ בָּרוּךְ הוּא כַּשַּׂלְמָה וְהִבְהִיק זִיו הֲדָרוֹ מִסּוֹף הָעוֹלָם וְעַד סוֹפוֹ

He replied: [The verse] teaches us that the Holy One, blessed be He, wrapped himself in it as in a robe and irradiated with the luster of his majesty the whole world from one end to the other.

R. Samuel b. Naḥman did not quote a source for this teaching, but merely repeated it as he had heard it.

אָמְרָהּ לֵהּ בִּלְחִישָׁה אָמַר לֵהּ מִקְרָא מָלֵא הוּא (תהלים קד, ב) 'עֹטֶה אוֹר כַּשַּׂלְמָה' וְאַתְּ אֲמַרְתְּ לִי בִּלְחִישָׁה אַתְמְהָא אָמַר לֵהּ כְּשֵׁם שֶׁשְּׁמַעְתִּיהָ בִּלְחִישָׁה כָּךְ אֲמַרְתִּיהָ לָךְ בִּלְחִישָׁה אָמַר רַבִּי בֶּרֶכְיָה אִלּוּלֵי שֶׁדְּרָשָׁהּ רַבִּי יִצְחָק בָּרַבִּים לֹא הָיָה אֶפְשָׁר לְאוֹמְרָהּ

Now he had answered him in a whisper, [whereupon] [R. Simon] said to him: There is an explicit verse [to that effect], 'Who is wrapped in a robe of light' (Psalms 104:2), yet you say it in a whisper! He [R. Samuel] answered him: Just as I heard it in a whisper, so I

116

told it to you in a whisper. R. Berakhiah said: If R. Isaac had not expounded [this doctrine] in public, it would be impossible to say it.

The word לחישה, 'whisper,' indicates that R. Samuel believed that he was transmitting an esoteric speculation regarding the creation, which type of activity was frowned upon. R. Simon responded that this teaching was not an esoteric speculation, but an explicit verse in the Bible and that there was no need to transmit it in a whisper. R. Samuel b. Naḥman responded that it had been told to him in a whisper, which seems to imply that the verse in Psalms is not explicit. How do we know that it is dealing with the light of the first day? Maybe something else is implied. Furthermore, the verse itself is anthropomorphic and should be treated as though it were speculative. R. Berekhiah's remark seems to confirm this. Since R. Isaac's name has not yet appeared in this *midrash*, it is logical to assume that what R. Berekhiah said applied to the interpretation that follows. However, Rashi and others refer it to the interpretation above. (*Ha-Midrash ha-Mevo'ar*)

מִקַּמֵּי כֵן מָה הָיוּ אָמְרִין רַבִּי בֶּרֶכְיָה בְּשֵׁם רַ' יִצְחָק אָמַר מִמְּקוֹם בֵּית הַמִּקְדָּשׁ נִבְרֵאת הָאוֹרָה הֲדָא הוּא דִכְתִיב (יחזקאל מג, ב) 'וְהִנֵּה כְבוֹד אֱלֹהֵי יִשְׂרָאֵל בָּא מִדֶּרֶךְ הַקָּדִים' וְאֵין כְּבוֹדוֹ אֶלָּא בֵּית הַמִּקְדָּשׁ כְּמָה דְאַתְּ אָמַר (ירמיה יז, יב) 'כִּסֵּא כָבוֹד מָרוֹם מֵרִאשׁוֹן מְקוֹם מִקְדָּשֵׁנוּ וְגוֹ''

Before this [above exposition] what did [the Sages] say [on the matter]? R. Berekhiah said in the name of R. Isaac: The light was created from the place of the Temple, as it is written, 'And behold, the glory of the God of Israel came from the east, [with roar like the roar of mighty waters, and the earth was lit up by His glory]' (Ezekiel 43:2) and 'His glory' always refers to the Temple, as it is said, 'O Throne of Glory exalted from of old, our Sacred Shrine' (Jeremiah 17:12).

The phrase in the proof-text from Ezekiel, 'from the east,' is a translation of the Hebrew מקדם, *mi-kedem*, which can also mean 'of old.' Thus the verse is to be understood that the world was lit up of old, that is, at the time of the creation, by God's glory which, as the proof-text from Jeremiah shows, means that it came from the site of the Temple. The Temple is the place where God's glory is to be found and from it was light created. This is based on the view of R. Neḥemiah cited above, that the world was created first and only then was light created. (*Ha-Midrash ha-Mevo'ar*)

* * *

Seed Thoughts

The light that was created before the world or before the luminaries were created is something not physical but spiritual. In using the expression that God clothed Himself with light as with a garment or even the interpretation that light emerged from the site of the Temple, we see attempts to interpret the world as a spiritual universe. More than the laws of physics make this world run. There is another world of spirit that also has its rules and to which we have to accommodate our talents and our intentions.

Parashah Three, Midrash Five

In the scriptural text the word 'light,' אור – *or*, appears five times and apparently unnecessarily. The style could easily have been shortened after the original sentence, 'Let there be light,' such as 'and it was so,' or 'and God saw that it was good.' Why, then, is the word repeated five times? The answer of the *midrash* is that Scripture is here hinting at lights and revelations yet to come (*Tiferet Tzion*). These revelations yet to come emerge in the five books of Moses; through them God's great light will be revealed to the whole world, which is the purpose of creation.

אָמַר רַ' סִימוֹן ה' פְּעָמִים כְּתִיב כָּאן אוֹרָה כְּנֶגֶד חֲמִשָּׁה חֻמְשֵׁי תוֹרָה 'וַיֹּאמֶר אֱלֹהִים יְהִי אוֹר' כְּנֶגֶד סֵפֶר בְּרֵאשִׁית שֶׁבּוֹ נִתְעַסֵּק הַקָּדוֹשׁ בָּרוּךְ הוּא וּבָרָא אֶת עוֹלָמוֹ

R. Simon said: [The word] 'light' is here written five times corresponding to the five books of the Torah. 'And God said: Let there be light' corresponds to Genesis, with which the Holy One, blessed be He, was engaged and created His world.

It must be remembered that it was for the sake of Torah and by means of the Torah that the world was created. The imagery here is that God was engaged in the study of Genesis when He created the world.

'וַיְהִי אוֹר' כְּנֶגֶד סֵפֶר וְאֵלֶּה שְׁמוֹת שֶׁבּוֹ יָצְאוּ יִשְׂרָאֵל מֵאֲפֵלָה לְאוֹרָה

'And there was light' corresponds to the Book of Exodus in which Israelites went forth [from Egypt], out of darkness into light.

The second mention of the word light corresponds to the Book of Exodus, which describes the exodus of the Children of Israel from Egypt as being from darkness to light.

'וַיַּרְא אֱלֹהִים אֶת הָאוֹר כִּי טוֹב' כְּנֶגֶד סֵפֶר וַיִּקְרָא שֶׁהוּא מָלֵא הֲלָכוֹת רַבּוֹת

'And God saw the light that it was good' corresponds to the Book of Leviticus, which is replete with numerous laws.

The third mention of light corresponds to Leviticus, with its wide variety of laws. The Jew is required to walk the path of life by the light of those

119

laws and therefore the description 'that it was good' can certainly be associated with Leviticus.

'וַיַּבְדֵּל אֱלֹהִים בֵּין הָאוֹר וּבֵין הַחֹשֶׁךְ' כְּנֶגֶד סֵפֶר בְּמִדְבַּר שֶׁהוּא מַבְדִּיל בֵּין יוֹצְאֵי מִצְרַיִם לְבָאֵי הָאָרֶץ

'And God separated the light from the darkness' corresponds to the Book of Numbers, which separates those who left Egypt from those who entered the [promised] land.

The fourth reference is to Numbers, which also contains the element of separation – between the generation that was condemned to die in the wilderness and that which actually entered the promised land.

'וַיִּקְרָא אֱלֹהִים לָאוֹר יוֹם' כְּנֶגֶד סֵפֶר מִשְׁנֵה תוֹרָה שֶׁהוּא מָלֵא הֲלָכוֹת רַבּוֹת

'And God called the light day' corresponds to the Book of Deuteronomy, which is replete with numerous laws.

The fifth reference is to Deuteronomy, which not only has new laws but also repeats many laws from the earlier books. That is why the expression associated with it includes both words – 'light' and 'day.'

מְתִיבִין חַבְרַיָּא לְרַבִּי סִימוֹן וַהֲלֹוא סֵפֶר וַיִּקְרָא מָלֵא הֲלָכוֹת רַבּוֹת אָמַר לָהֶן אַף הוּא שָׁנָה בּוֹ דָבָר

However, [his colleagues] objected [to the last identification]: 'Is it not Leviticus that is filled with numerous laws?' He said to them: '[Deuteronomy] also contains repetitions.'

There are many ways of interpreting this passage. One possibility is that the objection was that Leviticus contains more laws than Deuteronomy and that therefore the sentence that contains 'light' and 'day,' that is, a double portion of light, should be associated with the Book that contains more laws. His answer was that the superiority of Deuteronomy resides in the fact that in addition to containing many new laws it also repeats many others. (RDL)

Another possible interpretation: R. Simon said that in connection with Deuteronomy you will notice a change because it says 'And God called the light day' and while it may appear that 'light' and 'day' are one and the same, when it is repeated twice as it is here, it indicates that Deuteronomy also has many laws. In this interpretation, the word *shanah* שנה, which is normally understood to mean 'repeat,' is rendered as *shinah*, meaning 'to make a change.' (Mirkin)

Yet another possible interpretation. Since every one of the Books of the Pentateuch is given an appropriate description by means of the verse chosen for it, Leviticus should have been given some special consideration that would reflect the fact that it possesses many laws. The terms 'light' and 'good' do not reflect this. The answer seems to be that 'light' and 'day' that are assigned to Deuteronomy are in actuality the same thing and so merely a repetition. On the other hand, 'light' and 'good' are distinct and unique and give Leviticus all the distinction it needs. (*Tiferet Tzion*)

* * *

Seed Thoughts

Two ideas emerge as central in this *midrash*. The first is the idea of progressive revelation. True, the earlier verses hint at what is to come, but the important point to consider is the view here being expressed that the fullness of the teaching of the purpose of creation is yet to come. The second aspect of this attitude is the view that the five Books of the Pentateuch are the repository of this greater revelation. This is in line with the rabbinic view that the *Humash*, or Pentateuch, stands way above the rest of the Books of the *Tanakh* (an acronym for Torah, *Nevi'im, Ketuvim*, Torah, Prophets, and Writings) not only in terms of *halakhah*, which is the category of Jewish law and legislation, but also in terms of *aggada*, which is the category of Jewish thought, theology, and imagination.

The *midrash* is not merely interested in showing that the various nuances of the phrases that contain the word *or* can be related rationally to the four Books (the fifth is a recapitulation); it wants us to continue to study the *Humash* with the same thoughts in mind. It will then have an existential relationship to us and we will surely discover again and again echoes of that greater light, which gives the world meaning and substance.

* * *

Additional Commentary

There are four different meanings associated with the word 'light.' Firstly, there is the difference between the potential and the actual. In this sense 'darkness' represents the potential that is hidden and mysterious while 'light' represents the actual, which is revealed. This is represented in the Book of Genesis, which is the story of creation, of the generations and tribes, the building of the world, and the building of Israel.

The second meaning is that of salvation. Trouble or crisis is 'darkness' while deliverance or salvation is 'light.' 'Light' as deliverance is the symbol of the Book of Exodus.

The third meaning of 'light' is that of intelligence while 'darkness' symbolizes folly or stupidity This kind of 'light' is represented in Leviticus because the laws are evidence of wisdom and intelligence.

The fourth meaning of 'light' is as symbol of life while 'darkness' is symbolic of death. This is the Book of Numbers because it records the death of the generation that left Egypt. (*Tiferet Tzion*)

Parashah Three, Midrash Six

The basic problem that motivates this *midrash* is the fact that the light was called 'day.' In the case of dry land, *yabashah*, being given the name *eretz*, there is some significance since the name *eretz* derives from the root *ratzah*, which means to want or desire – the dry land *wanted* to do God's will. In the case of the firmament, *raki'a*, being called *shomayim*, the significance is even more obvious, since the word *shomayim* can be understood to be two words, *sham mayim* – water is there. But the word 'day' seems to be synonymous with 'light' and has no special significance.

וַיִּקְרָא אֱלֹהִים לָאוֹר יוֹם לֹא הוּא אוֹר וְלֹא הוּא יוֹם אֶתָּמְהָא

'And God called the light day,' but are not light and day the same thing? I am amazed.

The word *yom*, day, is not to be understood here as being a name for day. If that had been the intention, the text would have read 'And God called *ha-or*...' and not *la-or*. The use of the letter *lamed* – *la* – seems to indicate that God called out to the light and said, 'I want you to shine during the day.'

(Some manuscripts only begin the *midrash* here.)

תְּנֵי אוֹרָה שֶׁנִּבְרֵאת בְּשֵׁשֶׁת יְמֵי בְרֵאשִׁית לְהָאִיר בַּיּוֹם אֵינָהּ יְכוֹלָה שֶׁהִיא מַכְהָה גַּלְגַּל הַחַמָּה וּבַלַּיְלָה אֵינָהּ יְכוֹלָה שֶׁלֹּא נִבְרֵאת לְהָאִיר אֶלָּא בַּיּוֹם

It was taught: The light that was created in the six days of creation cannot illumine by day, because it would darken the light of the sun, nor by night because it was created only to illumine by day.

The light that was created on the first day is not the light from the luminaries that were created on the fourth day. That light could not function on the fourth day when the luminaries were in existence because in the daytime it would have completely overshadowed the sun. Nor could it function at night since it was created expressly for the day.

וְהֵיכָן הִיא נִגְנְזָה וְהִיא מְתֻקֶּנֶת לַצַּדִּיקִים לֶעָתִיד לָבוֹא שֶׁנֶּאֱמַר 'וְהָיָה אוֹר הַלְּבָנָה כְּאוֹר הַחַמָּה וְאוֹר הַחַמָּה יִהְיֶה שִׁבְעָתַיִם כְּאוֹר שִׁבְעַת הַיָּמִים' (ישעיה ל, כו)

Then where is it stored? It is ready for the righteous in the messianic future, as it is written, 'And the light of the moon shall become like the light of the sun, and the light of the sun shall become sevenfold, like the light of the seven days' (Isaiah 30:26).

What happened to this light after the creation of the sun? It was hidden in Paradise waiting for the redemption of Israel when it will function again. In that day the light of the moon will be equal to the light of the sun today and the light of the sun will be seven times as strong as it is today. Both lights will then function in unison and that is what is meant in saying that God called this particular light 'day'. (*Ha-Midrash ha-Mevo'ar*)

אַתְמָהָא 'שִׁבְעַת' וְלֹא שְׁלֹשָׁה הֵן וַהֲלוֹא בָּרְבִיעִי נִבְרְאוּ הַמְּאוֹרוֹת אֶלָּא כְּאִינָשׁ דְּאָמַר כֵּן וְכֵן אֲנָא מְפַקֵּד לְשִׁבְעַת יוֹמַיָא דְמִשְׁתּוֹתִי

I am amazed! Seven! Surely there were but three, seeing that the luminaries were created on the fourth day! It is like a man who says, 'I am providing so much for the seven days of my wedding feast.'

Why did the verse in Isaiah use the number seven when the original light only lasted three days? It was merely an idiomatic expression, as when a person sets aside provisions for one of the seven days of festivity, but says, 'I am setting this aside for the seven days,' although he means only one of the days. Another example of such usage is that a person is said to be sitting *shiva* (literally: seven) in mourning even though it is interrupted by a festival so that he only sits four days. Nevertheless, he would use the term *shiva* or seven to describe the wedding days of feasting even though only three such days were observed. In the same way, Scripture used the term 'seven' when actually it means 'three.'

רַבִּי נְחֶמְיָה אָמַר אֵלּוּ שִׁבְעַת יְמֵי אֲבֵלוּת שֶׁל מְתוּשֶׁלַח הַצַּדִּיק שֶׁהִשְׁפִּיעַ לָהֶן הַקָּדוֹשׁ בָּרוּךְ הוּא אוֹרָה.

R. Neḥemiah said: It refers to the seven days of mourning for righteous Methuselaḥ, when the Holy One, blessed be He, lavished light upon them.

The Flood was delayed seven days because of the death of Methuselaḥ and as a reward to that generation for mourning him with great respect. In other words, 'And God saw the light that it was good,' refers to the good man Methuselaḥ.

וַיַּרְא אֱלֹהִים אֶת הָאוֹר כִּי טוֹב

And God saw the light that it was good.

This verse is followed by 'And God separated the light from the darkness.' In the other stages of creation the action usually comes first and then the expression, 'and God saw that it was good.' Why was there a change here? This prompts an interpretation.

רַבִּי זְעֵירָא בְּרֵהּ דְּרַבִּי אַבָּהוּ דָּרַשׁ בְּקֵיסָרִין מְנַיִן שֶׁאֵין מְבָרְכִין עַל הַנֵּר עַד שֶׁיֵּאוֹתוּ לְאוֹרוֹ מִן הָכָא 'וַיַּרְא' 'וַיַּבְדֵּל'

R. Ze'ira the son of R. Abbahu preached in Caesarea: Whence do we know that you should not recite a blessing over a candle until you enjoy its light? From here – [first] 'and He saw' and [only afterwards] 'He separated.'

We know from the Talmud that you do not recite a blessing over the *havdalah* candle until you benefit from its light, but what is its scriptural source? It is the order of the verses in Genesis where it first says 'He saw' and only afterwards 'and He separated.'

רַבִּי יְהוּדָה בַּר סִימוֹן אָמַר הִבְדִּילוֹ לוֹ

R. Judah b. R. Simon said: He [God] set it apart for Himself.

God separated the light for Himself so that only He might use it and not anyone else.

רַבָּנָן אָמְרִי הִבְדִּילוֹ לַצַּדִּיקִים לֶעָתִיד לָבוֹא מָשָׁל לְמֶלֶךְ שֶׁהָיָה לוֹ מָנָה יָפָה וְהִפְרִישָׁהּ לִבְנוֹ

The Rabbis said: He set it apart for the righteous in the future, just like a king who had a goodly portion and sets it aside for his son.

The Rabbis add the thought that God did not set aside the light for Himself, but for the righteous in the future. As the Psalmist says, 'Light is sown for the righteous' (Psalms 97:11) and even in the verse, 'and God saw the light that it was good' the word 'good' is taken as referring to the righteous (*Exodus Rabbah* 35:1).

אָמַר רַבִּי בֶּרֶכְיָה כָּךְ דָּרְשׁוּ שְׁנֵי גְּדוֹלֵי עוֹלָם רַבִּי יוֹחָנָן וְר' שִׁמְעוֹן בֶּן לָקִישׁ 'וַיַּבְדֵּל' הַבְדָּלָה מַמָּשׁ

R. Berekhiah said: Thus did two men of world renown, R. Johanan

and R. Simon b. Lakish, expound it: 'and He divided' connotes a physical separation.

This is unlike the interpretation given above that the verse means a separation for a higher purpose. It means, say these two great men, a literal separation between night and day.

מָשָׁל לְמֶלֶךְ שֶׁהָיָה לוֹ שְׁנֵי אִיסְטְרַטֵיגִין אֶחָד שַׁלִּיט בַּיּוֹם וְאֶחָד שַׁלִּיט בַּלַּיְלָה וְהָיוּ
שְׁנֵיהֶם מִדַּיְּנִין זֶה עִם זֶה זֶה אוֹמֵר בַּיּוֹם אֲנִי שׁוֹלֵט וְזֶה אוֹמֵר בַּיּוֹם אֲנִי שׁוֹלֵט
קָרָא הַמֶּלֶךְ לָרִאשׁוֹן אָמַר לוֹ פְּלוֹנִי יוֹם יְהֵא תְחוּמֶךָ וְכֵן לַשֵּׁנִי אָמַר לוֹ פְּלוֹנִי לַיְלָה
יְהֵא תְחוּמֶךָ כָּךְ 'וַיִּקְרָא אֱלֹהִים לָאוֹר יוֹם' אָמַר לוֹ יוֹם יְהֵא תְחוּמֶךָ 'וְלַחֹשֶׁךְ קָרָא
לַיְלָה' אָמַר לֵהּ לַיְלָה יְהֵא תְחוּמֶךָ

Imagine a king who had two commanders [in charge of the country], one in command by day and the other in command at night, who used to quarrel with one another, each claiming, 'I must have command by day.' Thereupon the king summoned the first and said to him, 'So and so, the day shall be your province'; summoning the second he addressed him, 'So and so, night shall be your province.' Similarly, 'God called the light day,' saying to it, 'The day shall be your province'; 'and the darkness He called night,' saying to it, 'Night shall be your province.'

Apparently they felt that the day was most important and that night had an inferior status. In other words we are not dealing with areas of time but areas of jurisdiction. According to this interpretation, calling the light day was not giving a name to a period of time but merely a command to this creation called light to serve God in this manner and at this particular time and the same for night.

אָמַר רַבִּי יוֹחָנָן הוּא שֶׁהַקָּדוֹשׁ בָּרוּךְ הוּא אוֹמֵר לְאִיּוֹב 'הַמִיָּמֶיךָ צִוִּיתָ בֹּקֶר יִדַּעְתָּ
הַשַּׁחַר מְקֹמוֹ' (איוב לח, יב) הֲיִדַעְתָּ מְקוֹמוֹ אֵי זֶה הוּא אַתְמָהָא

R. Johanan observed: That is what the Holy One, blessed be He, said to Job: 'Have you ever commanded the morning, assigned the dawn its place?' (Job 33:12) It would be amazing if you were capable of letting it know its place!

R. Johanan was pointing out that God Himself had challenged Job with exactly the point our *midrash* is making. Notice should be taken of the rare grammatical form, *yidata*, meaning 'Did you inform day of its place the way I did.'

אָמַר רַבִּי תַּנְחוּמָא אֲנָא אמָרִי טַעְמָא 'יוֹצֵר אוֹר וּבוֹרֵא חֹשֶׁךְ עֹשֶׂה שָׁלוֹם' (ישעיה
מה, ז) מִשֶּׁנִּבְרְאוּ 'עֹשֶׂה שָׁלוֹם.'

**R. Tanḥuma said: I can give the grounds [for this statement]: 'I form
the light, and create darkness, I make peace'** (Isaiah 45:7) – **having
created them, I made peace between them.**

In connection with the reference above to the fact that day and night were
quarreling with each other until God separated them, R. Tanḥuma
interprets the verse from Isaiah to explain the idea beautifully. The verse
says that God creates light and darkness and peace. What is the
connection between light and darkness on the one hand and peace? Only
that when light and darkness were created, God made peace between
them.

וַיִּקְרָא אֱלֹהִים לָאוֹר יוֹם אָמַר רַ' אֶלְעָזָר לְעוֹלָם אֵין הַקָּדוֹשׁ בָּרוּךְ הוּא מְיַחֵד שְׁמוֹ
עַל הָרָעָה אֶלָּא עַל הַטּוֹבָה וַיִּקְרָא אֱלֹהִים לָאוֹר יוֹם וְלַחֹשֶׁךְ קָרָא אֱלֹהִים לַיְלָה
אֵין כְּתִיב כָּאן אֶלָּא 'וְלַחֹשֶׁךְ קָרָא לַיְלָה'

**'And God called the light day.' R. Eleazar said: The Holy One,
blessed be He, does not allow His name to be connected with evil,
but only with good. Thus it is not written here, 'And God called the
light day and God called darkness night,' but 'And the darkness *He*
called night.'**

The point to be noted here is that in the verse quoted, the name of God
is associated with 'light,' but not with 'darkness.'

* * *

Seed Thoughts

The *midrash* asserts that God's name is not associated with darkness, but
with light. The *Tiferet Tzion* (see Additional Commentary) interprets this
as meaning that only good emanates from God.

That being the case, what about evil? How do we explain it? Evil is
something that is allowed by God in order that the good should become
manifest and known. According to the kabbalists, God appointed a special angel, Satan, to perform a terrible function. It is the function of Satan
to challenge that good, even as Job was challenged in his classic encounter.

Just as light is only appreciated by contact with darkness, so, too, good
is only appreciated by contrast with evil. Is that contest between good and
evil unequal? Not necessarily. Man is created in the image of God and
therefore good emanates from him as it does from His Maker.

Some years ago Ashley Montague, the well-known psychologist, performed a number of experiments that proved that cooperation is more natural to the human species than competition. The human being responds well to the challenge of good. It is the only way to confront evil.

Nor is this a mere individual challenge. The human being is a political and social animal. He has the brains and the technology to organize a social system that will eliminate poverty and advance social justice.

That is our never-ending task. And, concludes the *Tiferet Tzion*, the time will come when God will be one and His name one. Then, as he so beautifully interprets it, God's quality of mercy will be manifest and everyone in the world will know that only good comes from Him.

* * *

Additional Commentary

Methuselah

The attribution of Methuselah to the age of the Flood is based on the following calculation. Methuselah lived 969 years and fathered Lemekh when he was 187 years old. Lemekh then fathered Noah at the age of 182 years. Together this adds up to 369. This means that Methuselah lived 600 years during the lifetime of Noah which brings him up to the time of the Flood – 'Noah was 600 years old when the Flood came' (Genesis 7:6). Apparently Methuselah was judged a *tzaddik* because he died before the Flood. The Flood was delayed for seven days because of him and also as a reward to that generation for mourning him with great respect. (RWZE)

*

The Flood and the light

In the case of light (Isaiah 10:26) there is the expression *Shivat ha-yamim* – '*the* seven days' with the definite article implying some specific event. In the story of the Flood there is also the expression *le-shivat ha-yamim*. By the exegetical principle of *gezeirah shavah* – similar linguistic expressions – the flood is thus connected with the creation of light. (*Tiferet Tzion*)

*

The good light

A further concern of this *midrash* is the use of the phrase, '...that it was good,' in connection with the light. Why should the element of light be good in a way that darkness is not? In general, how can the term 'good' be applied to anything that is strictly physical? It is this consideration that prompted the *midrash* to a conception of light that is spiritual – that light which is destined for the righteous in the world to come. Of such a light it can be said that it is good. This also motivated the comment that the

Flood was delayed a week so that Methuselah, the good man, would receive the kind of mourning that befitted his dignity. If light could be used for such a purpose it could be described as 'good.' (*Tiferet Tzion*)

*

The name of God and the night
The abundance that is received from God is only good. It is the recipient who transforms the good into bad. A parent sets aside an equal sum of money for each of his children. The healthy ones use the money for food and drink and pleasures. The sick ones are forced to use the money for medicines that will restore their health. Similarly, God bestows upon everyone an abundance of good and only he who is sick physically and spiritually forces this abundance to be transformed into suffering and affliction that have healing purposes.

When the verse says 'On that day shall the Lord be One and His Name One,' it means that the day will come when true knowledge will be abundant and that all will understand that God bestows only good upon the world. This is indicated by the verse's use of the four-letter name for God (what is known as the Tetragrammaton י־ה־ו־ה, derived from the root meaning 'to be' and, except in prayer, usually articulated as *ha-shem*, meaning *the* name), which stands for the quality of mercy. Only we, by virtue of our affliction, transform the abundance into bitterness. For this reason, God does not allow His name to be connected with evil because evil does not issue from Him. (*Tiferet Tzion*)

Parashah Three, Midrash Seven

אָמַר רַבִּי יְהוּדָה בַּר סִימוֹן יְהִי עֶרֶב אֵין כְּתִיב כָּאן אֶלָּא 'וַיְהִי עֶרֶב' מִכָּאן שֶׁהָיָה
סֵדֶר זְמַנִּים קֹדֶם לָכֵן

R. Judah b. Simon said: 'Let there be evening' is not written here, but 'and there was evening' – from this [you can infer] that a time-order existed before this.

The time structure that may have existed earlier is hinted at in various parts of the tradition. One is the idea that there were two thousand years of Torah before the creation of the world. Another is the statement that one thousand years in God's eyes are as one day.

אָמַר רַבִּי אַבָּהוּ מְלַמֵּד שֶׁהָיָה בּוֹרֵא עוֹלָמוֹת וּמַחֲרִיבָן עַד שֶׁבָּרָא אֶת אֵלּוּ אָמַר
דֵּין הֲנָיָן לִי יָתְהוֹן לָא הֲנָיָן לִי

R. Abbahu said: This teaches that the Holy One, blessed be He, went on creating worlds and destroying them until He created this one when He declared, 'This one pleases me; those did not please me.'

God destroyed the previous worlds that He had made because their inhabitants acted perversely. According to the *Anaf Yosef*, these worlds were not actually created but were simply in God's mind, part of His program that was not carried out.

אָמַר רַ' פִּינְחָס טַעְמֵהּ דְּרַ' אַבָּהוּ (בראשית א, לא) 'וַיַּרְא אֱלֹהִים אֵת כָּל אֲשֶׁר עָשָׂה
וְהִנֵּה טוֹב מְאֹד' דֵּין הֲנָיָן לִי יָתְהוֹן לָא הֲנָיָן לִי.

R. Phinḥas said: R. Abbahu's reason [for his teaching in the previous *midrash*] is: 'And God saw everything that he had made and behold it was very good' (Genesis 1:31), which he took to mean 'This pleases me, but those did not please me.'

The fact that the verse says that God saw *everything* that He had made seems to imply that He included everything – even what predated the world. The word *ve-hinei*, והנה, refers to the present and implies that it is much better than what went before it, the latest creation, was very good.

* * *

Seed Thoughts

Are the remains of dinosaurs discovered by scientists in conflict with the creation story? What about the Bronze Age Man and other such relics of ancient times, how are they to be explained by Bible advocates?

It should always be stated when such questions are posed that the Bible is not a scientific manual. Its purpose is not to explain the 'how' of the world, but the 'why'! Only statements about the physical universe that can set the stage of the moral universe are made.

Having said this, the questioning intellectual mind of man must see and understand whatever information comes to light about the human condition past and present. Those who take the Bible literally need such a perspective the most. But even those who see the Bible as metaphor and symbol need a framework not only for their thoughts but for the whole biblical system as well.

That is why a *midrash* such as this one has so much to tell us. This world was not the first in the divine agenda. There were many before it, seven in all, according to one interpretation.

Could not the dinosaurs have been part of these worlds? And is it not possible to incorporate the basic principles of Darwinism into those worlds, that were created and destroyed in order to perfect the human being and create a more favorable environment for man?

This *midrash* should be treasured. It offers a key that can unlock many mysteries.

* * *

Additional Commentary

Creating and destroying worlds

It should not be thought that in the process of creating and destroying worlds God was changing His mind and regretting His former decisions. This should be looked upon as a process of refinement until there emerged a world that had a chance of permanence. (RWZE)

*

Rabbenu Baḥya revealed a great secret in the name of the kabbalists. Based on the verse, 'and the earth shall observe a Sabbath to the Lord,' he taught that the world will be rebuilt and destroyed seven times corresponding to the seven Sabbatical cycles within the Jubilee cycle – together making up forty-nine thousand years. At every Sabbatical (seven thousand years), the world is destroyed and rebuilt. Each rebuilding is an improvement and a completion of the original intent, until finally the perfected world will return to its Creator ready to be settled by man. This is what the *midrash* is saying: Worlds were built and destroyed in order to improve them. Consider it this way. In the beginning God created heaven and earth. Then the earth was empty and void because it was destroyed. After that God said, 'Let there be light,' and this was the first creation of this world. And God accepted this world as being what He desired. (*Tiferet Tzion*)

*

When the verse says '*Va-yehi erev*,' 'and it was evening,' it should be understood as meaning '*va-yehi **od** erev*' – and it was evening again, meaning that there were former worlds that preceded this one. (Mirkin)

Parashah Three, Midrash Eight

This text is similar to the material that has already been studied in *Parashah 2 Midrash 5*. See the notes and comments on that material.

אָמַר רַ' יַנַּאי מִתְּחִלַּת בְּרִיָּתוֹ שֶׁל עוֹלָם צָפָה הַקָּדוֹשׁ בָּרוּךְ הוּא מַעֲשֵׂיהֶן שֶׁל צַדִּיקִים וּמַעֲשֵׂיהֶם שֶׁל רְשָׁעִים

R. Jannai said: From the very beginning of the world's creation the Holy One, blessed be He, foresaw the deeds of the righteous and the deeds of the wicked.

God knows in advance the behavior of all His creatures. He even knows the free choices they will make (but this knowledge in no way affects their freedom of choice). All this is reflected in the opening verses of Genesis.

'וְהָאָרֶץ הָיְתָה תֹהוּ' אֵלּוּ מַעֲשֵׂיהֶם שֶׁל רְשָׁעִים 'וַיֹּאמֶר אֱלֹהִים יְהִי אוֹר' אֵלּוּ מַעֲשֵׂיהֶן שֶׁל צַדִּיקִים

'And the earth was desolate' alludes to the deeds of the wicked; 'And God said: Let there be light,' alludes to those of the righteous.

The behavior of the wicked is like the darkness because they live without regard for purpose. The righteous are compared to light because they try to conform to what God wants.

The distinction between the righteous and the wicked has to be seen as interpreted in *Parashah 2 Midrash 5* – the good done by the wicked cannot compare to the good done by the righteous. That is the meaning of the verse, 'And God saw the light, that it was good' alludes to the deeds of the righteous.

'וַיַּבְדֵּל אֱלֹהִים בֵּין הָאוֹר וּבֵין הַחשֶׁךְ' בֵּין מַעֲשֵׂיהֶן שֶׁל צַדִּיקִים לְמַעֲשֵׂיהֶן שֶׁל רְשָׁעִים

'And God made a division between the light and the darkness': between the deeds of the righteous and those of the wicked.

Obviously the division was made to show God's preference for the righteous over the wicked.

133

'וַיִּקְרָא אֱלֹהִים לָאוֹר יוֹם' אֵלּוּ מַעֲשֵׂיהֶן שֶׁל צַדִּיקִים 'וְלַחֹשֶׁךְ קָרָא לָיְלָה' אֵלּוּ מַעֲשֵׂיהֶן שֶׁל רְשָׁעִים

'And God called the light "day"' alludes to the deeds of the righteous, 'and the darkness He called "night"' to those of the wicked.

God desired the way of the righteous, which is why He referred to them as day, the time frame of doing and action, whereas He designated the wicked as the night signifying desolation.

'וַיְהִי עֶרֶב' אֵלּוּ מַעֲשֵׂיהֶן שֶׁל רְשָׁעִים 'וַיְהִי בֹקֶר' אֵלּוּ מַעֲשֵׂיהֶן שֶׁל צַדִּיקִים

'And it was evening,' refers to the deeds of the wicked, 'and it was morning,' to those of the righteous.

What this means is that the behavior of the wicked will have a bearing on their future that will ultimately decline as will the behavior of the righteous, who will ultimately be vindicated.

'יוֹם אֶחָד' שֶׁנָּתַן לָהֶם הַקָּדוֹשׁ בָּרוּךְ הוּא יוֹם אֶחָד וְאֵיזֶה זֶה יוֹם הַכִּפּוּרִים

'One day' – the Holy One, blessed be He, gave them one day, and which is that? It is the Day of Atonement.

The question preoccupying this section is why the text reads יום אחד, 'one day' and not, יום הראשון, 'the first day.'

The first interpretation is that, *eḥad*, means 'unique.' There is one day in the Jewish calendar that is truly unique in that it unites the wicked and the righteous. On that day the wicked become righteous through penitence. On that day Satan has no power over them. The numerical value of the word Satan is 364, meaning that he has mastery over all the days of the year except one, Yom Kippur, the Day of Atonement.

אָמַר ר' תַּנְחוּם בַּר יִרְמִיָה שֶׁבּוֹ נִבְרְאוּ אַרְבָּעָה דְבָרִים הָרִים שָׁמַיִם וְאֶרֶץ וְאוֹרָה

R. Tanḥum bar Jeremiah said: It was the day on which four things were created, that is, mountains, heaven, earth, and light.

R. Tanḥum offers another interpretation of *eḥad* – on that first day four of the most important creations took place. The mountains are the deep that is under the waters. All the other three are specifically mentioned. These four represent the very basis of the world and life. That is why the first day is called *eḥad* – it was unique because of what was created on it.

אָמַר רַ' יוּדָן שֶׁבּוֹ הָיָה הַקָּדוֹשׁ בָּרוּךְ הוּא יְחִידִי בְּעוֹלָמוֹ שֶׁלֹּא הָיָה בְּעוֹלָמוֹ אֶלָּא
הוּא

R. Judan said: [It was the day] in which the Holy One, blessed be He, was alone in His universe, there was nothing in His world but Him.

R. Judan interprets *yom eḥad* as meaning 'the day of the One,' because on the first day of creation God was still alone in the universe. Not even the angels were created. The Midrash will discuss whether the angels were created on the second or the fifth day. On the first day, however, according to all opinions, God was alone – He was *eḥad* in the universe.

אָתְיָא כְּרַ' יוֹחָנָן וְלֹא אָתְיָא כְּרַבִּי חֲנִינָא רַ' יוֹחָנָן אָמַר בַּשֵּׁנִי נִבְרְאוּ הַמַּלְאָכִים
הֲדָא הוּא דִכְתִיב (תהלים קד, ג) 'הַמְקָרֶה בַמַּיִם עֲלִיּוֹתָיו הַשָּׂם עָבִים רְכוּבוֹ הַמְהַלֵּךְ
עַל כַּנְפֵי רוּחַ' וּכְתִיב (שם שם, ד) 'עֹשֶׂה מַלְאָכָיו רוּחוֹת'

This agrees with R. Joḥanan but not with R. Ḥanina, for R. Joḥanan said [above in *midrash* 1:3] that the angels were created on the second day, as it is written, 'He sets the rafters of His lofts in the waters, Who makes the clouds His chariot' (Psalms 104:3), which is followed by 'He makes the spirits His angels' (ibid. v. 4).

The verse in Psalms refers to the creation of the firmament that separated the upper and lower waters and that took place on the second day. The following verse describes the creation of the angels, which indicates that the angels were created on the same day.

רַבִּי חֲנִינָא אָמַר בַּחֲמִישִׁי נִבְרְאוּ מַלְאָכִים שֶׁנֶּאֱמַר (בראשית א, כ) 'וְעוֹף יְעוֹפֵף עַל
הָאָרֶץ' וּכְתִיב (ישעיה ו, ב) 'וּבִשְׁתַּיִם יְעוֹפֵף'

[But] R. Ḥanina said: The angels were created on the fifth day as it is written, '[Let the waters bring forth swarms of living creatures...] and birds that fly above the earth' (Genesis 1:20) and it is also written, '... and with two he would fly' (Isaiah 6:2).

R. Ḥanina, however, taught that the angels were created on the fifth day by an analogy based on the word יעופף, 'fly,' in the description of the creation of the birds and the same word used in Isaiah's description of the angels he saw in his vision. If the angels were only created on the fifth day, then God was alone for more than one day and thus R. Judan's interpretation of יום אחד can only be valid according to R. Joḥanan's opinion.

רַ' לוּלְיָנִי בַּר טַבְרָאי בְּשֵׁם רַבִּי יִצְחָק אָמַר בֵּין עַל דַּעְתֵּהּ דְּרַבִּי חֲנִינָא בֵּין עַל
דַּעְתֵּהּ דְּרַ' יוֹחָנָן הַכֹּל מוֹדִים שֶׁלֹּא נִבְרָא בַּיּוֹם הָרִאשׁוֹן כְּלוּם שֶׁלֹּא תֹאמַר מִיכָאֵל
הָיָה מוֹתֵחַ בִּדְרוֹמוֹ שֶׁל רָקִיעַ וְגַבְרִיאֵל בִּצְפוֹנוֹ וְהַקָּדוֹשׁ בָּרוּךְ הוּא מְמַדֵּד
בָּאֶמְצָעִיתוֹ אֶלָּא (ישעיה מד, כד) 'אָנֹכִי ה' עֹשֶׂה כֹּל נֹטֶה שָׁמַיִם לְבַדִּי רֹקַע הָאָרֶץ
מֵאִתִּי' 'מִי אִתִּי' כְּתִיב מִי הָיָה שֻׁתָּף עִמִּי בִּבְרִיָּתוֹ שֶׁל עוֹלָם.

R. Luliani b. Tabri said in the name of R. Isaac: Whether we accept
the view of R. Ḥanina or that of R. Joḥanan, all agree that none were
created on the first day, so that you should not be able to say, 'The
angel Michael pulled at the south end of the firmament and Gabriel
at the north while the Holy One, blessed be He, straightened it out
in the middle.' Rather, 'It is I, the Lord, who made everything, Who
alone stretched out the heavens and by Myself spread out the earth'
(Isaiah 44:24). The word מֵאִתִּי, 'by Myself' is written in the verse as two
words, which can also be read as מִי אִתִּי, which means 'who was with
Me?' – Who was My partner in the creation of the world?!

R. Luliani does not address the question of why the term יום אחד is used
rather than יום הראשון. He is more concerned about the substance of the
first day and goes to great lengths to reiterate that it was God and God
alone who created the world. This is specifically aimed at the heretical
view (held by the Gnostics) that the angels played a role in the creation.

* * *

Seed Thoughts

This *midrash* should be compared with similar material that we examined
in *Parashah* One *Midrash* Three and *Parashah* Two *Midrash* Five. There the
midrashim try to examine the difficult problem of judging between good
people who also sin because they are human and evil people who also,
though infrequently, perform good deeds. There are many legends in
aggadic folklore that suggest that God favors an evil-doer who repents or
does good things. In the earlier *midrash* an assertion is made that good
people, even with their faults, are on a higher level than wicked people
even with their good points. The assertion is merely stated without proof.
The present *midrash* is a little more troubled by this dilemma. It proposes
that the term 'one day' (instead of the 'first day,' which would be
grammatically more correct) refers to Yom Kippur. That day should be
used by the *tzaddikim* (good people) and the *resha'im* (wicked) to reflect
upon the fact that in the eyes of God the differences between them are not
so significant. Yom Kippur should be looked upon as an occasion to break

through their labels and former lifestyle and start afresh in recreating that good light, which is the purpose for which life is formed.

* * *

Additional Commentary

The actions of the righteous and the wicked

Right from the start, the Holy One, blessed be He, recognized the difference between the good done by the righteous and the good done by the wicked. The righteous do good for its own sake; the wicked, for their own personal advantage in material terms. God, therefore, made a distinction in their rewards. The righteous were given the world-to-come, symbolized by the term 'day.' The wicked will ultimately use up whatever advantage they get from doing good for selfish purposes and will then have nothing. This is symbolized by the term 'night.' The symbolism of the first verses continues in this sense. When will the true reward of the righteous begin? Just at the moment when the wicked use up all of their spiritual capital from their good deeds. The symbol for that is '*boker*' – 'morning' – for the righteous. For the wicked the symbol is evening – the end – the beginning of their decline. Since even the righteous have their faults and sins, we were all provided with one day to make up our deficiencies – the Day of Atonement. (*Tiferet Tzion*)

Parashah Three, Midrash Nine

This *midrash* proposes another explanation for the use of יוֹם אֶחָד instead of the expected יוֹם רִאשׁוֹן.

אָמַר ר' שְׁמוּאֵל בַּר אַמִּי מִתְּחִלַּת בְּרִיָּתוֹ שֶׁל עוֹלָם נִתְאַוָּה הַקָּדוֹשׁ בָּרוּךְ הוּא
לַעֲשׂוֹת שֻׁתָּפוּת בַּתַּחְתּוֹנִים

R. Samuel b. Ammi said: From the beginning of the world's creation the Holy One, blessed be He, longed to enter into partnership with the mortals.

From the very beginning of creation God wanted His Heavenly Presence to be on earth. Therefore the world was never regarded as complete until the Sanctuary – the Tabernacle in the wilderness – was completed and God's Presence resided in it. On the basis of this idea R. Samuel will interpret the extraordinary use of the word אֶחָד regarding the first day of creation.

מַה נַּפְשָׁךְ אִם לְעִנְיַן הַחֶשְׁבּוֹן לֹא הָיָה צָרִיךְ לְמֵימַר אֶלָּא אֶחָד אֶחָד שְׁנַיִם שְׁלֹשָׁה אוֹ
רִאשׁוֹן שֵׁנִי וּשְׁלִישִׁי שֶׁמָּא אֶחָד שֵׁנִי שְׁלִישִׁי אַתְמָהָא

For what will you; if it was a matter of time reckoning, it should have said either one, two, three or first, second, third, but surely not, one, second, third. It is amazing!

If the purpose of the early verses was merely to indicate the passage of the days, all the numbers should have been cardinal numbers, and if the purpose of the text were to indicate the relationship between the days, ordinal numbers – first, second, and third – should have been used. But who ever heard of such a series – one, second, third?

אֵימָתַי פָּרַע לָהֶם הַקָּדוֹשׁ בָּרוּךְ הוּא לְהַלָּן בַּהֲקָמַת הַמִּשְׁכָּן שֶׁנֶּאֱמַר (במדבר ז, יב)
'וַיְהִי הַמַּקְרִיב בַּיּוֹם הָרִאשׁוֹן אֶת קָרְבָּנוֹ' רִאשׁוֹן לִבְרִיָּתוֹ שֶׁל עוֹלָם אָמַר הַקָּדוֹשׁ
בָּרוּךְ הוּא כְּאִלּוּ בְּאוֹתוֹ יוֹם בָּרָאתִי אֶת עוֹלָמִי

When did the Holy One, blessed be He, repay them? Later, at the erection of the Tabernacle as it is said, 'The one who presented his

offering on the first day...' (Numbers 8:12), meaning, the first of the
world's creation. For God said, 'It is as though on that day I created
my world.'

This beautiful exposition is based on the use of the term 'first day' in the
verse in Numbers describing the offerings brought by the leaders of the
tribes of Israel upon the completion of the Tabernacle in the wilderness
and the inauguration of the *kohanim*, the priests. Actually, the first offering
was presented on the eighth day of the inauguration, which itself took
seven days. Why then does the verse say 'on the first day'? So long as God
was alone in the world, the first day was noted as *eḥad* – 'one,' alone with
God. It was only when the Tabernacle – God's residence, so to speak, on
earth – was completed that the purpose of day one of the creation was
realized, for that was the day when God achieved His desire to be united
with His earthly creatures. At that time God repaid the creation days for
having robbed them of a 'first' relationship. So that when '*rishon*' is used
in connection with the Tabernacle, the meaning is the first day of the
creation of the world, which was only truly completed when the first
Sanctuary was complete. The *midrash* continues to extoll that special day:

תְּנֵי עֶשֶׂר עֲטָרוֹת נָטַל אוֹתוֹ הַיּוֹם רִאשׁוֹן לְמַעֲשֵׂה בְרֵאשִׁית רִאשׁוֹן לַמְּלָכִים
רִאשׁוֹן לַנְּשִׂיאִים רִאשׁוֹן לַכְּהֻנָּה רִאשׁוֹן לַשְּׁכִינָה שֶׁנֶּאֱמַר (שמות כה, ח) 'וְעָשׂוּ לִי
מִקְדָּשׁ' רִאשׁוֹן לַבְּרָכָה רִאשׁוֹן לָעֲבוֹדָה רִאשׁוֹן לְאִסּוּר הַבָּמָה רִאשׁוֹן לַשְּׁחִיטָה
בַּצָּפוֹן רִאשׁוֹן לִירִידַת הָאֵשׁ שֶׁנֶּאֱמַר (ויקרא ט, כד) 'וַתֵּצֵא אֵשׁ מִלִּפְנֵי ה' וְגוֹ'.'

That day took ten crowns: it was the first of the creation; first in
respect of kings; first in respect of the princes; first in respect of the
priesthood; first in respect of the *shekhinah*, as it says, 'They shall
make me a sanctuary' (Exodus 25:8); first in respect of blessing; first in
respect of sacrificial service; first with respect to the prohibition of
high places; first with respect to slaughtering at the north side of the
altar; first with respect to the descending of fire, as it is written, 'And
there came forth fire from before the Lord' (Leviticus 9:24).

The term 'crown' denotes something of prime importance, a 'first.'

The day that is described as the first in the presentation of the tribal
princes' offerings was a 'first' for ten things in all. It was the first of the
creation, because it was a Sunday, the first day of the week; it was first in
respect of kings, because it was also the first of Nisan, the day from which
the reign of a monarch is counted, even though he may have begun to
reign prior to that date; it was first in respect of the twelve days of the

offerings of the princes; it was first in respect of the priesthood, because from this day on the *kohanim* replaced the first-born sons at the altar; it was first in respect of the *shekhinah*, because from this day God's Presence remained in the Tabernacle; it was first in respect of blessing, since from this day the priests began to bless the people; it was first in respect of sacrificial service, because the communal offerings began on this day; it was first with respect to the prohibition of high places – from then on offerings were no longer permitted outside the Sanctuary; it was first with respect to slaughtering sacrifices at the north side of the altar, which new restriction began on this day; and it was first with respect to the descent of fire upon the altar, a miracle that continued in the future.

There are thus ten crowns, but first among them all is the 'first' of the creation story, which was fulfilled only when the Children of Israel completed the erection of the Tabernacle and the dedication of the priests.

* * *

Seed Thoughts

Much has been made in the material here presented as to when the actual act of creation was completed. It would appear from the discussion that the main lesson to be learned is something quite unexpected. Creation was not completed at all. It is an ongoing process.

Surely that is what is behind the *midrash* – that true creation was completed when the *Mishkan*, the Tabernacle, was erected and then filled with the Divine Presence. But what was the function of the *Mishkan*? How did it operate? What did it do?

It was a vehicle through which to foster inspiration. The ritual, the sacrifices, the Levitical choristers, even if we were to leave out the miracle of the descending fire, were meant to give the individual a sense of depth and a conception of destiny in which he could fit.

Not creation is the name of this process but re-creation! That was the function of the Sanctuary (Tabernacle and, later, the Temple) in ancient times. It is the function of the Jewish calendar, the festivals, and the commandments today. It is the true function of the synagogue today and at all times.

* * *

Additional Commentary

When Israel occupies itself with Torah and *Avodah* (worship) it sustains the world and is entitled to be described as God's partner. This was not fulfilled until Israel received the Torah and erected the *Mishkan*, at which time they began Torah and *Avodah* together – then they became true partners with God. (*Tiferet Tzion*)

*

The whole purpose of the creation of the world was for the *tahtonim* (those who occupy the lower sphere – earth) to sustain the world by their good deeds. Since that did not happen on the first day, it could not really be said that the world was created on that first day, but only on the day on which the *Mishkan* was dedicated. That was the first day of the true creation and fulfilment of the world. (*Tiferet Tzion*)

Parashah Four, Midrash One

It is one of the principles of Midrash that what is unexplained in the first five Books of the Torah can be understood from later Books of the Bible. This *midrash* is an example.

(תהלים קד, ג) וַיֹּאמֶר אֱלֹהִים יְהִי רָקִיעַ (בראשית א, ו) כְּתִיב 'הַמְקָרֶה בַמַּיִם עֲלִיּוֹתָיו'

'And God said: Let there be a firmament in the midst of the waters'
(Genesis 1:6). It is written, 'He sets the rafters of His lofts in the waters'
(Psalms 104:3).

The text in Genesis does not explain what a firmament is nor what it is made of; but the Psalmist does have an explanation. The firmament is a ceiling for the world and it is made of water. Why water?

בְּנוֹהֵג שֶׁבָּעוֹלָם מֶלֶךְ בָּשָׂר וָדָם בּוֹנֶה פָּלָטִין וּמְקָרֶה בָּאֲבָנִים וּבְעֵצִים וּבְעָפָר אֲבָל הַקָּדוֹשׁ בָּרוּךְ הוּא לֹא קֵרָה אֶת עוֹלָמוֹ אֶלָּא בַּמַּיִם שֶׁנֶּאֱמַר 'הַמְקָרֶה בַמַּיִם עֲלִיּוֹתָיו.'

In human practice, a mortal king builds a palace and roofs it over with stones, timber, and earth. But the Holy One, blessed be He, roofed over His world with nothing but water, as it is said, 'He sets the rafters of His lofts in the waters.'

The purpose of a roof is to protect the building and its inhabitants from damage caused by rains, winds, and excessive water from whatever source. However, in God's building – the world – the roof is made of water, for this is what the entire firmament was made of. In human terms, water would clearly be the last material to use for a roof. How would it remain there? But God is not limited by the physical laws of the planet. All of this was to declare His glory.

*

Seed Thoughts

I am frightened of miracles. I know they exist. I know they have to exist. But I am frightened of them because man has no way to relate to a miracle. There is no response to it.

The *Tiferet Tzion* (see Additional Commentary) makes the point that God has no need of the world but that the world has need of God. Why is that such a great teaching? If God had no need of man, why then did He create him?

In his introduction to the wisdom of the Kabbalah, Rabbi Ashlag makes a somewhat different observation. Although we can never know the essence of God, there is a generalization that we are entitled to make. It is the nature of God always to want to bestow. By the same token it is the nature of man to have the need to receive. According to this teaching God created man because He had a divine need to bestow and man needed God because of his innate need to receive.

The connecting link between God and man is here not the miraculous, although everything about it is miracle. The real quality that emerges is thanksgiving. This is the bedrock upon which can be built a real relationship between man and God.

* * *

Additional Commentary

He sets the rafters of His lofts in the waters

It is the intention of this *midrash* to explain why God commanded that the firmament be placed *within* the waters and did not create it above the waters. To this end the verse, 'Who sets the rafters...,' is brought. It was His desire that the roof of the world be made of water and therefore the rafters were created within the waters. In this fashion the upper waters became the ceiling for the heavens. But why did God do this? Does He need ceilings? It is in this connection that the *midrash* answers, 'In human practice, a mortal king...,' which means that the Holy One, blessed be He, is teaching man a fundamental principle of faith. He, the Almighty, has no need for this world but this world has a great need of Him. A king of flesh and blood has to be protected from flooding and rain and from any and all mishaps. Therefore, he covers his home with a cupola of stones and his summer palace with wood and earth to offer protection against tempests and winds. But God does not need His world for protection; on the contrary, His world needs His protection. If, heaven forfend, God were to remove His concern from the world for even one second the whole world would become a non-entity, as we know from the philosophers who seek the truth. It is for this reason that He made the ceiling of the world out of water. It is the nature of water to flow downwards; but the waters stand suspended because of His word, blessed be He. On realizing this, man should reflect that all of God's commands and deeds are solely for man's benefit – to improve him for his destiny, which is the fundamental principle of religion. (*Tiferet Tzion*)

Parashah Four, Midrash Two

וַיֹּאמֶר אֱלֹהִים יְהִי רָקִיעַ בְּתוֹךְ הַמָּיִם

And God said: 'Let there be a firmament in the midst of the waters.'

The question raised by this text is: What is the meaning of the phrase 'in the midst of the waters'?

רַבָּנָן אָמְרִין לַהּ בְּשֵׁם רַבִּי חֲנִינָא וְרַ' פִּינְחָס וְרַבִּי יַעֲקֹב בְּרַ' אָבִין בְּשֵׁם רַבִּי שְׁמוּאֵל בַּר נַחְמָן בְּשָׁעָה שֶׁאָמַר הַקָּדוֹשׁ בָּרוּךְ הוּא 'יְהִי רָקִיעַ בְּתוֹךְ הַמָּיִם' גָּלְדָה טִפָּה הָאֶמְצָעִית וְנַעֲשׂוּ הַשָּׁמַיִם הַתַּחְתּוֹנִים וּשְׁמֵי שָׁמַיִם הָעֶלְיוֹנִים

Our Rabbis said the following in the name of R. Ḥanina, while R. Pinḥas and R. Jacob b. R. Avin said it in the name of R. Samuel b. Naḥman: When the Holy One, blessed be He, ordered, 'Let there be a firmament in the midst of the waters,' the middle layer of water solidified, and the nether heavens and the uppermost heavens were formed.

According to the ancients the heavens that we are able to see are the lower heavens. Above them and beyond our view are the upper heavens often referred to as the heaven of heavens. Our *midrash* is now explaining that a line was drawn between the upper and lower heavens. This is one interpretation of 'in the midst of the waters.'

רַב אָמַר לַחִים הָיוּ מַעֲשֵׂיהֶם בַּיּוֹם הָרִאשׁוֹן וּבַשֵּׁנִי קָרְשׁוּ 'יְהִי רָקִיעַ' יֶחֱזַק הָרָקִיעַ

Rav said: [God's] handiwork [the heavens] was in fluid form and on the second day it congealed. Thus, 'Let there be a firmament...' [means], 'Let the firmament become strong.'

Rav's opinion follows the view of Shammai that the heavens were created on the first day in opposition to the view of Hillel reflected in the interpretation offered by the Rabbis quoted above. The heavens congealed on the second day of creation, but they were actually created on the first day.

רַ' יְהוּדָה בְּרַ' סִימוֹן אָמַר יֵעָשֶׂה מַטְלִית לָרָקִיעַ הֵיךְ מַה דְּאַתְּ אָמַר 'וַיְרַקְּעוּ אֶת פַּחֵי הַזָּהָב' (שמות לט, ג)

145

Rabbi Judah b. R. Simon said: [The verse means], 'Let a lining be made for the firmament,' as it says, 'They hammered out sheets of gold [into thin plates]' (Exodus 39:3).

Rabbi Judah is suggesting a different interpretation of the command, 'Let there be a firmament…' The Hebrew for firmament is רקיע, *raki'a*, which is from the same root as וירקעו, *va-yerak'u*, which in the verse in Exodus means 'They hammered out the gold into thin plates.' Based upon this, R. Judah proposes that the command on the second day was for a thin lining to be created and placed in the sky. When we look up, it is that lining that we see.

אָמַר רַבִּי חֲנִינָא יָצְאָה הָאֵשׁ מִלְמַעְלָה וְלִחֲכָה אֶת פְּנֵי הָרָקִיעַ רַבִּי יוֹחָנָן כְּשֶׁהָיָה מַגִּיעַ לְפָסוּק זֶה 'בְּרוּחוֹ שָׁמַיִם שִׁפְרָה' (איוב כו, יג) הָיָה אוֹמֵר יָפֶה לִמְּדַנִי רַבִּי חֲנִינָא.

R. Ḥanina said: Fire came forth from above and dried up the face of the firmament. When R. Joḥanan came to the verse, 'By his breath the heavens were calmed' (Job 26:13), he would say: R. Ḥanina taught me well.

R. Ḥanina's view regarding the way in which the firmament was created concurs with the opinion that the heavens were created on the first day. R. Joḥanan found support for R. Ḥanina's interpretation in the verse cited from the Book of Job, which seems to be a perfect proof-text for it, and pithily remarked, 'R. Ḥanina taught me well.'

אָמַר רַ' יוּדָן בְּרַבִּי שִׁמְעוֹן יָצְאַת הָאֵשׁ מִלְמַעְלָה וְלִהֲטָה פְּנֵי רָקִיעַ

R. Judan b. R. Simon said: Fire came forth from above and burnished the face of the firmament.

The difference between R. Ḥanina and R. Judan is that the former uses the word לחכה, *liḥakah* – the fire licked the heavens making it hard and strong, and R. Judan uses the word להטה, *lihatah* – meaning that the fire made the heavens sparkle and glisten.

We have now seen several explanations of the phrase 'in the midst of the waters,' but only now does the *midrash* come to the main point of its teaching.

ר' בֶּרֶכְיָה בְּשֵׁם רַבִּי אַבָּא בַּר כָּהֲנָא אָמַר בָּא מַעֲשֶׂה בְּרֵאשִׁית לְלַמֵּד עַל מַתַּן תּוֹרָה וְנִמְצָא לָמֵד מִמֶּנָּה 'כְּקִדֹחַ אֵשׁ הֲמָסִים' (ישעיה סד, א)

R. Berakhiah, in the name of R. Abba b. R. Kahana, said: The

creation story was used [by the prophet] to throw light on revelation, but was itself explained thereby: 'As when the blazing fire melted [and divided the waters into two]' (Isaiah 64:1).

The creation story was meant to teach us about the eventual giving of the Torah, and it turns out that we can learn about the creation story from the story of the revelation at Sinai. The prophet Isaiah described the revelation scene, 'As when the blazing fire melted and divided the waters into two,' that is, the fire divided between the upper and the nether waters. Notice that the prophet uses the expression 'as when,' comparing the occasion to something else. But to what? This becomes understandable when we refer to the verse in Isaiah [63:19] that immediately precedes the one quoted by our *midrash*, 'If You would but tear open the heavens and come down, so that mountains would flow down before You.' The Hebrew expression הרים נזולו, 'so that mountains would flow down,' has a parallel in Judges [5:5] .... זה סיני ה' מפני נזולו הרים 'The mountains melted before the Lord, even thou, Sinai.' It now becomes clear that the verse in Isaiah is referring to Sinai. Furthermore, at Sinai there was חמסים אש – a fire that divided the upper and the lower heavens, as it is written, 'And the mountains burned with fire unto the midst of the heavens' (Deuteronomy 4:11). We can now make the appropriate comparison. Fire divided the upper and lower heavens at Sinai 'As when the blazing fire melted and divided the waters into two,' i.e., at the time of creation. (Mirkin)

אֵימָתַי חָצָה הָאֵשׁ בֵּין הָעֶלְיוֹנִים לַתַּחְתּוֹנִים לֹא בְמַתַּן תּוֹרָה אַתְמָהָא כָּךְ הָיְתָה בִּבְרִיָּתוֹ שֶׁל עוֹלָם.

When did the fire divide between the upper and the nether [waters]? Surely not at the revelation! It was at the creation of the world.

We were supposed to learn the conditions present at the giving of the Torah from the description of the creation of the world – after all, the creation came first. But it has turned out that we have learned from the giving of the Torah about creation.

* * *

Seed Thoughts

Is cosmogony a factor in evaluating what a *midrash* has to say? The text speaks of the upper waters and the lower waters. What would such a text state if it were written in modern times? Would it not speak of an outer stratosphere that we call outer space and an inner stratosphere, namely, earth space, which is governed by the laws of gravity?

The cosmogony is different. But does it really matter? Are the Rabbis in our *midrash* trying to teach us cosmogony? Would you not say that they are trying to teach us that there is a connection between creation and the giving of Torah, between the spiritual and the physical world? Let us grant that not all the elements here described may be needed for the physical world. But for the spiritual world! For that world we will always need those very same qualities of conviction, belief, enthusiasm, and dedication.

* * *

Additional Commentary

Creation and the giving of the Torah

The revelation on Mt. Sinai resembled the creation of the world since at that time the world was strengthened. As the Rabbis say on the verse 'I created pillars...,' by means of receiving the Torah the pillars of the world were strengthened for without it the world would be destroyed.

We are therefore to conclude that when Scripture compares this fire [Sinai] with the fire that was before, the reference is to the fire that was needed to perfect the world. In the creation story itself the only place where fire is indicated as having a role in forming the material world is in connection with שמים, *sha-mayim*, which is interpreted as being made up of אש, *esh*, and מים, *mayim*. Thus, the Hebrew word for heaven is a combination of fire and water. (*Tiferet Tzion*)

*

Let there be a firmament

Before this divine command there was no heaven at all, but the waters of the entire universe were one mass. When God said, 'Let there be a firmament' the middle layer of water congealed and the firmament of heaven came into being. Therefore the material from which the earth was created and the material from which heaven was created are one and the same, since both originate in the same waters that were in the universe. This disagrees with the view of scientists who claim that the materials of the heavens and outer space are completely new and different. Later on in the Midrash (*Parashah* 12), R. Eliezer will state that whatever is in the heavens in terms of substance has its origin in the heavens. [*Yefei To'ar*]

*

Special note

Whatever is spoken about in the biblical verses or subject to exegesis in the Rabbinic writings on subjects such as the upper waters and the heavens being made up of water and fire and about rains that come from the upper waters are all meant to be perceived as spiritual matters and are spoken of in this fashion simply as a way of speaking. In actual fact there are no material substances at all in what we call today outer space. All this is emphasized in the sacred books and should be an important principle when approaching these matters. See *A Guide to the Perplexed,* II, 30. (*Ha-Midrash ha-Mevo'ar*)

Parashah Four, Midrash Three

What is the meaning of the phrase, 'in the midst of the waters'?

רַבִּי פִּינְחָס בְּשֵׁם רַבִּי הוֹשַׁעְיָא אָמַר כְּחָלָל שֶׁבֵּין הָאָרֶץ לָרָקִיעַ כָּךְ יֵשׁ בֵּין הָרָקִיעַ
לַמַּיִם הָעֶלְיוֹנִים 'יְהִי רָקִיעַ בְּתוֹךְ הַמַּיִם' בֵּינַיִם וּבֵינְתַיִם

R. Pinhas said in the name of R. Hoshaya: Just as there is a void
between the earth and the firmament, so too there is a void between
the firmament and the upper waters, as it is written, 'Let there be a
firmament in the midst of the waters,' meaning, midway between
them.

R. Hoshaya was interpreting the word בתוך, 'in the midst of,' which is
where, according to the verse, the firmament was to be placed. One must
try to envisage the state of affairs before this happened – a huge mass of
water that the firmament divided into two. According to R. Hoshaya, the
division was equal. Indeed, the Jerusalem Talmud (Berakhot 1:1) has it
that the two spaces – above and below the firmament – are of equal size,
which is five hundred light years. The word בתוך thus means exactly in
the middle of the upper and lower waters.

אָמַר רַבִּי תַּנְחוּמָא אֲנָא אֲמַרִי טַעְמָא אֵלּוּ נֶאֱמַר וַיַּעַשׂ אֱלֹהִים אֶת הָרָקִיעַ וַיַּבְדֵּל
בֵּין הַמַּיִם אֲשֶׁר עַל הָרָקִיעַ הָיִיתִי אוֹמֵר עַל גּוּפוֹ שֶׁל רָקִיעַ הַמַּיִם נְתוּנִים וּכְשֶׁהוּא
אוֹמֵר 'וּבֵין הַמַּיִם אֲשֶׁר מֵעַל לָרָקִיעַ' הֲרֵי הַמַּיִם הָעֶלְיוֹנִים תְּלוּיִים בְּמַאֲמָר

R. Tanhuma said: I will state the proof [for R. Hoshaya's
interpretation]. If the verse had said, 'and God made the firmament,
and He divided between the waters which are upon [על] the
firmament,' I would have said that the waters lay directly *upon* the
body of the firmament itself. Since, however, it is stated, 'and
between the waters which are above [מעל] the firmament,' it follows
that the upper waters are suspended by the word [of God].

The proof is based on the difference between *al*, which means 'upon,' and
me'al, which means 'above.' The upper waters are suspended above the
firmament in some miraculous fashion. It would then mean 'in between'
but not necessarily in the middle.

אָמַר רַבִּי אֲחָא כְּהָדֵין קַנְדִּילָא וּפֵרוֹתֵיהֶם אֵלוּ מֵי גְשָׁמִים.

R. Aḥa said: [The firmament suspended between the upper and lower waters] can be compared to [the flame of] a candle, and their fruits [i.e., of the upper waters] are the water [which comes down as] the rain.

The flame of a candle seems to be suspended in mid-air. The upper waters are seen as the repository from which God sends the rain.

* * *

Seed Thoughts

The idea of a candle in the distant stratosphere separating the upper and the lower waters is only an analogy. It is used by this *midrash* to help us understand its conception of how the two worlds are separated and intertwined at one point.

But the human imagination cannot be stifled. The candle is an analogy. It therefore exists only in our minds. But our minds can just as easily project the symbol of God's light shining as a beacon in outer space, not only separating the upper and lower worlds but reminding them that they were created and that their Creator is ever-present.

When the first Russian astronaut returned from outer space in the Sputnik, he reported that God did not exist. He looked for Him and could not find Him. What was he looking for? No one seems to know. Too bad he was not told of the candle that separates the worlds. Too bad he was not told that this exists in the mind's eye, that God's existence goes beyond the visual to those deep penetrations of the human soul where believing is seeing.

* * *

Additional Commentary

In the midst of the waters
The interpretations we have just read are meant to cope with difficulties in the scriptural text. *Betokh ha-mayim* could be translated as meaning 'in the midst of the waters,' which could refer to any place within the waters. However, R. Hoshaya specifies that it does not mean that, but that the firmament was located exactly between the lower waters and the upper waters. scriptural support for this view is not very strong if based only on the word *betokh*, since the upper waters might easily have rested on the firmament as they did at creation. This is the reason for R. Tanḥuma's

additional comment, which adds scriptural confirmation to R. Hoshaya's view.

*

The candle and its fruits

There are several possibilities to explain this imagery. It could be that of an ordinary candle, which gives the impression from a distance that the flame is burning in mid-air [Rashi]. It could also refer to the wickless oil lamp where water is first placed on the container as a foundation upon which oil is then poured and the oil then kindled. The impression is as though the flame were flickering in mid-air [RWZE]. The more probable explanation is that of an oil lamp with a wick within a container. From a distance it looks as though the flame were hovering in mid-air (just as the upper waters hover over the heavens) and, more important, considering part two of the imagery, the smoke gathers along the walls of the glass lamp; at one time they used to use the layer of soot created to manufacture ink. The soot is thus the fruit of the flame and in the same way the separation of the upper waters by space is the procedure through some form of condensation whereby rain is produced for the earth. (*Tiferet Tzion*)

*

The universe

We are given an interesting conception here of how the Talmudic sages viewed the universe, astronomically speaking. There are those who calculate that the distance between earth and heaven is five hundred light years and that, similarly, this is the difference between heaven and the edge of the upper waters. Above these waters are a series of upper galaxies (*galgalim*), and the difference between each one of them and the other is also that of five hundred light years. Furthermore, the earth is a thick sort of matter while above is a thin or fragile type of matter. Heaven is also a thick form of matter, which is why the heavens had to be separated from the earth. But the thick matter of the heavens (which became thick when it congealed; see *Midrash* 2 of this chapter) has above it a very thin ethereal type of matter. When they describe the *hallal*, the void or space, between earth and heaven as being similar to the *hallal* between heaven and the upper heavens, they are also describing their space content as being identical. [*Yefei To'ar*]

Parashah Four, Midrash Four

This *midrash* continues with a discussion of 'in the midst of the waters.'

כּוּתִי אֶחָד שָׁאַל אֶת ר' מֵאִיר אָמַר לוֹ אֶפְשָׁר הַמַּיִם הָעֶלְיוֹנִים תְּלוּיִים בְּמַאֲמָר
אָמַר לוֹ הֵן אָמַר לוֹ הָבֵא לִי אֲפַרְכָּס הֵבִיא לוֹ אֲפַרְכָּס נָתַן עָלֶיהָ טַס שֶׁל זָהָב וְלֹא
עָמְדוּ מַיִם טַס שֶׁל כֶּסֶף וְלֹא עָמְדוּ מַיִם כֵּיוָן שֶׁנָּתַן אֶצְבָּעוֹ עָמְדוּ מַיִם אָמַר לוֹ
אֶצְבָּעֲךָ אַתְּ נוֹתֵן אָמַר לוֹ מָה אֲנִי שֶׁאֲנִי בָּשָׂר וָדָם אֶצְבָּעִי מַעֲמֶדֶת מַיִם אֶצְבָּעוֹ
שֶׁל הַקָּדוֹשׁ בָּרוּךְ הוּא עַל אַחַת כַּמָּה וְכַמָּה הֱוֵי מַיִם הָעֶלְיוֹנִים תְּלוּיִים בְּמַאֲמָר

A Samaritan asked R. Meir: 'Is it possible that the upper water is suspended by God's word?' 'Yes,' he answered. [Then R. Meir] said, 'Bring me a funnel.' When he brought it, he placed a gold plate upon it, but the water did not stop [flowing downwards]; then a silver plate, but the water did not stop [flowing downwards]. But when he placed his finger [upon the upper] aperture, the water stopped [flowing downwards]. 'But you have put your finger there,' [the Samaritan] objected. [R. Meir] answered: 'If my finger stays the water, though I am but flesh and blood, how much more so the finger of the Holy One, blessed be He!' Hence the upper waters are suspended by [God's] word.

Neither the gold plate nor the silver plate could close the upper aperture hermetically, but the soft flesh of the finger could, and so the water ceased to flow. The question of the Samaritan [Cuthite] can be stated in this fashion. We accept that God created the world *ex nihilo* in miraculous fashion. However, we were told that henceforth creation would follow natural law. But if God sustains the upper worlds by divine fiat, He is interfering in the course of natural law. R. Meir's answer was that natural law is not being interrupted but followed – in the principle of the vacuum. [*Yefei To'ar*]

אָמַר לוֹ אֶפְשָׁר אוֹתוֹ שֶׁכָּתוּב בּוֹ (ירמיה כג, כד) 'הֲלוֹא אֶת הַשָּׁמַיִם וְאֶת הָאָרֶץ אֲנִי
מָלֵא' הָיָה מְדַבֵּר עִם מֹשֶׁה מִבֵּין שְׁנֵי בַּדֵּי הָאָרוֹן אָמַר לוֹ הָבֵא לִי מַרְאוֹת גְּדוֹלוֹת
אָמַר לוֹ רְאֵה בָּבוּאָה שֶׁלְּךָ בָּהֶן רָאָה אוֹתָהּ גְּדוֹלָה אָמַר לוֹ הָבֵא לִי מַרְאוֹת קְטַנּוֹת
הֵבִיא לוֹ מַרְאוֹת קְטַנּוֹת אָמַר לוֹ רְאֵה בָּבוּאָה שֶׁלְּךָ בָּהֶן רָאָה אוֹתָהּ קְטַנָּה אָמַר

153

לוֹ מָה אִם אַתָּה שֶׁאַתָּה בָּשָׂר וָדָם אַתָּה מְשַׁנֶּה עַצְמְךָ בְּכָל מַה שֶׁתִּרְצֶה מִי שֶׁאָמַר
וְהָיָה הָעוֹלָם בָּרוּךְ הוּא עַל אַחַת כַּמָּה וְכַמָּה הֲוֵי כְּשֶׁהוּא רוֹצֶה 'הֲלוֹא אֶת הַשָּׁמַיִם
וְאֶת הָאָרֶץ אֲנִי מָלֵא' וּכְשֶׁהוּא רוֹצֶה הָיָה מְדַבֵּר עִם מֹשֶׁה מִבֵּין שְׁנֵי בַּדֵּי הָאָרוֹן

[The Samaritan then] said to him: 'Is it possible that He of whom it
is written, "For I fill both heaven and earth" (Jeremiah 23:24) spoke to
Moses from between the two staves of the ark [which was a very
small area]?' 'Bring me large mirrors,' said [R. Meir]. [When he
brought them, R. Meir] said to him, 'Look at your reflection,' and
[the Samaritan] saw that it was large. [Then R. Meir] said 'Bring me
small mirrors.' [When he brought them, R. Meir] said to him, 'Look
at your reflection,' and [the Samaritan] saw that it was small. [R.
Meir then] said, 'If you, who are but flesh and blood, can change
yourself at will, how much more so can He at whose word the world
came into existence, blessed be He, expand his presence when He
so desires or contract it! When He wishes – "For I fill both heaven
and earth"; and when He so wishes He speaks to Moses from
between the staves of the ark.'

Here again, what appears to be a supernatural phenomenon turns out to
have its counterpart in the natural world by means of mirrors. The
principle is thus maintained that God used supernatural means only in the
original act of creation, not in the events that followed.

אָמַר רַ' חֲנִינָא בַּר אִיסֵי פְּעָמִים שֶׁאֵין הָעוֹלָם וּמְלוֹאוֹ מַחֲזִיקִים כְּבוֹד אֱלֹהוּתוֹ
פְּעָמִים שֶׁהוּא מְדַבֵּר עִם הָאָדָם מִבֵּין שַׂעֲרוֹת רֹאשׁוֹ הָדָא הוּא דִכְתִיב 'וַיַּעַן ה'
אֶת אִיּוֹב מִן הַסְּעָרָה וְגוֹ'' (איוב לח, א) מִבֵּין שַׂעֲרוֹת רֹאשׁוֹ

R. Ḥanina b. Issi said: At times the world and its fullness cannot
contain His divine glory, yet at times He speaks to man from
between the hairs of his head, as it is written, 'Then the Lord
answered Job out of the whirlwind [*sa'arah*]' (Job 38;1), [which can be
read *sa'arot*] meaning from between the hairs of his head.

This remark interrupts the series of questions the Samaritan asked R. Meir
and posits a new principle – that of *tzimtzum*, God's ability to expand or
contract Himself at will. A mirror is limited to the physical laws of
refraction, but God can extend Himself or contract Himself at will. It is
this additional nuance that differentiates this additional point to what was
said immediately above. The proof-text is actually a play on words:
sa'arah, which means 'storm' or 'whirlwind,' is written with ס (*samekh*) and

if the *samekh* is changed to שׁ (*sin*) the pronunciation remains the same but then the word means 'hair.' The passage in Job might also reflect the story in 1 Kings 19:11 where God did not appear in the whirlwind, but in the still small voice (Mirkin). The Samaritan continues his questioning:

וְעוֹד שְׁאֵלוֹ אָמַר לוֹ אֶפְשָׁר 'פֶּלֶג אֱלֹהִים מָלֵא מָיִם' (תהלים סה, י) מִשֵּׁשֶׁת יְמֵי
בְרֵאשִׁית וְלֹא חָסֵר כְּלוּם אַתְמָהָא אָמַר לוֹ הִכָּנֵס וּרְחוֹץ וּשְׁקוֹל עַצְמְךָ עַד שֶׁלֹא
תִכָּנֵס וּמֵאַחַר שֶׁתִּכָּנֵס הָלַךְ כֵּיוָן שֶׁיָּצָא וְשָׁקַל עַצְמוֹ לֹא חָסֵר כְּלוּם אָמַר לוֹ כָּל
אוֹתָהּ הַזֵּעָה שֶׁיָּצֵאת לֹא מִמְּךָ יָצֵאת אָמַר לוֹ הֵן אָמַר לוֹ וּמָה אַתָּה שֶׁאַתָּה בָּשָׂר
וָדָם לֹא חָסֵר מַעְיָנְךָ כְּלוּם מַעְיָינוֹ שֶׁל הַקָּדוֹשׁ בָּרוּךְ הוּא עַל אַחַת כַּמָּה וְכַמָּה הֱוֵי
'פֶּלֶג אֱלֹהִים מָלֵא מָיִם' מִשֵּׁשֶׁת יְמֵי בְרֵאשִׁית וְלֹא חָסֵר כְּלוּם

[The Samaritan] said to him: 'Is it possible that "the channel of God is full of water" (Psalms 65:10) since the six days of creation and has not been diminished at all? It is incredible!' [R. Meir] said to him: 'Go into [the bathhouse] and bathe. Weigh yourself before you enter and after you have gone in.' [The Samaritan] went and weighed himself and his weight had not diminished at all. [R. Meir then] said to him: 'Did not all that perspiration come from you?' 'Yes,' he answered. 'Then if your fountain [of perspiration] did not in any way diminish, though you are but a mere mortal, how much the more is this true of the fountain of the Holy One, blessed be He! That is why "the channel of God has been full of water" since the six days of creation and has not been diminished at all.'

Anyone who is familiar with a steambath knows that there is a difference in the weight of a person before and after, precisely for the reason described – the loss of perspiration. One can only assume, therefore, that in that region of the world the heat was so intense that whether the bath were indoors or in the open air the drinking of water was a must and this explains why there was no loss of weight. Hence, 'the channel of God' is as full today as it was at creation despite the rain that God has taken from it to make the earth fruitful.

אָמַר רַבִּי יוֹחָנָן נָטַל הַקָּדוֹשׁ בָּרוּךְ הוּא כָּל מֵימֵי בְרֵאשִׁית וּנְתָנָם חֲצִים בָּרָקִיעַ
וְחֲצִים בָּאוֹקְיָנוֹס הֲדָא הוּא דִכְתִיב 'פֶּלֶג אֱלֹהִים מָלֵא מָיִם' פַּלְגָּא

R. Joḥanan said: The Holy One, blessed be He, took all the primeval water and put half in the firmament and half into the ocean. This is what is written, 'The channel [פלג, *peleg*] is full of water,' *peleg* means *palga* [half].

R. Joḥanan uses a different translation of the word *peleg* – not 'channel' or 'river,' but 'half.' This is done to make the point that the original waters were divided into two. One half was poured into the upper waters and the other half into the oceans. Thus we have a new interpretation of the text: 'a firmament in the midst of the waters.'

* * *

Seed Thoughts

For the first time in my experience I have found an error of fact in the Midrash. I am not referring to different ways of viewing the universe. The fact that midrashic cosmogony is pre-modern astronomy is not a criticism. I am referring to something quite pragmatic – the claim of this *midrash* that if you weigh yourself before and after a steambath there is no loss of weight. This is not a mere statement. It is used by R. Meir to prove a serious theological point. But his illustration is incorrect. A lifetime of experience with steambaths proves him to be wrong.

What am I now supposed to do with this information? Am I to surmise that the Rabbis had little experience with steambaths, or that their scales for measuring weights were not precise, or that the *midrash* is not to be relied upon?

My reaction has not been critical at all. In fact, I experienced a great sense of relief. Here I was in such overwhelming awe of R. Meir who produced an entire Mishnah and seemed to be worlds apart from the ordinary scholar. But at last I discover that even R. Meir can make a mistake. He is human. Maybe some of his other more controversial opinions might also be tinged with human frailty.

Does this lessen the importance of Midrash? On the contrary! It is a repository of great human beings who tried to reach the highest possibilities of which they were capable in understanding God and His demands upon man. They were willing to risk all, including mistakes that might jeopardize their reputation, to achieve this goal.

In this respect, I think I now have a higher appreciation of R. Meir's mistakes and all.

* * *

Additional Commentary

אֲפַרְכָּס —funnel or water-clock

Jastrow translates אֲפַרְכָּס as water-clock; Mirkin translates it as funnel with an opening at the top larger than the opening at the bottom.

A water-clock is a vessel with several holes in it and an opening at the top the size of a finger. It can then be filled with water. If, however, the opening above is blocked by a finger, then water will not exit through the lower openings. The moment the finger is removed, however, the water pours out from all the lower openings. (*Matnot Kehunah*)

Parashah Four, Midrash Five

The text of 'a firmament in the midst of the waters' is now used to explain the phenomenon of rain.

הָרָקִיעַ דּוֹמֶה לִבְרֵכָה וּלְמַעְלָה מִן הַבְּרֵכָה כִּפָּה וּמֵחֲמַת שֶׁהַבְּרֵכָה מַזַּעַת טִפִּים
עָבוֹת וְהֵן יוֹרְדִין לְתוֹךְ מַיִם הַמְּלוּחִים וְאֵינָן מִתְעָרְבִין

The firmament is like a pool and above the pool is a vault; because of the heat of the pool [the vault] perspires [and exudes] heavy drops of water, which descend into the salt water yet do not combine with it.

The firmament is not actually a pool, but it encompasses a pool as though the waters were held aloft by pillars. The vault above it also contains water, but it is enclosed in a tent-like apparatus and because of the heat of the pool the vault exudes moisture. We learned earlier that the heavens are made up of fire and water. Thus the fire of the firmament–pool heats up the water contained in the vault, which creates a condensation on the outside of the vault and drops of water begin oozing out and fall into the salt water of the oceans, but do not combine with it. Presumably, the clouds then absorb this sweet water, which then becomes rain.

The explanation here is that the heat that causes moisture to exude also sweetens that water. What happens is that the water in the upper vault is sweet while the water in the lake-firmament is salty. The sweet waters have to pass through the salt waters, which are also the source for the ocean waters [*RaSHaL*]. The question that follows is: How do the drops of fresh water retain their sweetness?

אָמַר רַ' יוֹנָה אַל תִּתְמַהּ הָדֵין יַרְדְּנָא עָבַר בְּיַמָּא דִטְבֶרְיָא וְלָא מִתְעָרֵב בֵּהּ מַעֲשֵׂה
נִסִּים יֵשׁ בַּדָּבָר אָדָם כּוֹבֵר חִטִּים אוֹ תֶבֶן בִּכְבָרָה עַד שֶׁלֹּא יָרְדוּ שְׁתַּיִם וְשָׁלֹש
אֶצְבָּעוֹת הֵן מִתְעָרְבִין וְאֵלּוּ מְהַלְּכִין מַהֲלַךְ כַּמָּה שָׁנִים וְאֵין מִתְעָרְבִין

R. Jonah observed: Do not be amazed [at this phenomenon]. The River Jordan passes through the Sea of Tiberias yet does not mingle with it. The thing is indeed miraculous! When a man is sifting wheat or stubble in a sieve, before they have dropped a distance of two or

three fingerbreadths they intermingle, yet [these raindrops] have been travelling many years without intermingling.

This illustration is problematic. Was R. Jonah unaware that the Sea of Tiberias – what is known today as the Kinneret – is a freshwater lake? Perhaps the reference is to the hot springs of Tiberias, which contain many chemicals. Another possible explanation is that R. Jonah was not referring to the question of sweet water mingling with salt water, but was pointing out that the course of the Jordan can be clearly observed as it passes through the Kinneret. According to one midrashic source the rain drops travel for five hundred light years before they reach the earth.

רַבִּי יוּדָן בַּר' שִׁמְעוֹן אוֹמֵר שֶׁהוּא מוֹרִידָן בְּמִדָּה שֶׁנֶּאֱמַר 'כִּי יְגָרַע נִטְפֵי מָיִם' (איוב לו, כז) הֵיךְ מַה דְּאַתְּ אָמַר 'וְנִגְרַע מֵעֶרְכֶּךָ' (ויקרא כז, יח)

R. Judan b. R. Simon said: [The reason] is that He brings [the rain] down in measure, as it is written, 'For He draws away [*yegora*] the drops of water' (Job 36:27), where the verb is used in the sense of 'and its assessment shall be reduced [*ve-nigra*]' (Leviticus 27:18).

This is another miracle that is associated with rain – only enough rain falls as is required. The water is drawn or reduced from the upper lake. The use of the term 'reduce' also implies a specific measure – in the case of rain, whatever earth requires. Some commentators cite an explanation from the Jerusalem Talmud and other *midrashim*: The allusion to the term in Leviticus also indicates that God *gore'a* – prevents the raindrops from touching each other.

כְּעוֹבְיָהּ שֶׁל אֶרֶץ כָּךְ עוֹבְיָהּ שֶׁל רָקִיעַ שֶׁנֶּאֱמַר 'הַשֵּׁב עַל חוּג הָאָרֶץ וְגוֹ'' (ישעיה מ, כב) 'וְחוּג שָׁמַיִם יִתְהַלָּךְ' (איוב כב, יד) 'וְחוּג' 'חוּג' לִגְזֵרָה שָׁוָה אָמַר רַ' אֲחָא בְּשֵׁם רַבִּי חֲנִינָא כַּטַּס הַזֶּה רַבִּי יְהוֹשֻׁעַ בַּר' ר' נְחֶמְיָה אָמַר כִּשְׁתַּיִם וְשָׁלֹשׁ אֶצְבָּעוֹת

The thickness of the firmament equals that of the earth, as it is written, 'It is He who sits above the circle [*ḥug*] of the earth' (Isaiah 40:22) and it is also written, 'And He walks in the circuit [*ḥug*] of the heaven' (Job 22:14). The appearance of *ḥug* in both verses is for the purpose of making an analogy [i.e., that the firmament and the earth are alike in their thickness]. R. Aḥa said in R. Ḥanina's name: It is but as thick as this [metal] plate. R. Joshua b. R. Neḥemiah said: It is about two or three fingers in thickness.

The first opinion in the *midrash* sees the firmament as it is today. The view of R. Aḥa represents how the firmament was at creation. The word *raki'a* meaning firmament, when used as a verb means 'to beat out' as with a metal plate. It was quite thin at creation, but later on was made thicker as befitting the divine intention. [*Tiferet Tzion*] The third view proposed by R. Joshua probably represents the differing opinion of Ben Zoma in an earlier *midrash* that there was a separation between the upper and lower heavens that the firmament filled. It is described as two fingers in width. [*Tiferet Tzion*]

רַבִּי שִׁמְעוֹן בֶּן פָּזִי אָמַר הַמַּיִם הָעֶלְיוֹנִים יְתֵרִין עַל הַתַּחְתּוֹנִים כִּשְׁלֹשִׁים כְּסוּסְטָאוֹת 'בֵּין מַיִם לָמָיִם' לְמַד תִּלְתִין רַבָּנָן אָמְרִין מֶחֱצָה עַל מֶחֱצָה

R. Simon b. Pazi said: The upper waters exceed the lower ones by about thirty *xestes* [Hebrew: כסוסטא, approximately equivalent to a pint], for it is written 'Let it [the firmament] divide the waters from the waters [*la-mayim*]'; *lamed* [of *la-mayim*] is thirty. The Rabbis said: They [the upper and lower waters] are half and half.

Note that the Hebrew is not בין מים ומים meaning between 'water and water,' but בין מים למים; the use of the unnecessary *lamed*, the numerical value of which is 30, is the motivation for this derivation. The Rabbis disagree, as they disagreed in an earlier *midrash* with the view of R. Joḥanan and the school of Shammai, who maintained that the upper waters were superior and required the extra amount to prove that point. That extra amount does not exist, the Rabbis say.

* * *

Seed Thoughts

The *Tiferet Tzion* [see Additional Commentary] reflects a view that is found in both Bible and Rabbinic writings. Rain is not looked upon as merely a natural phenomenon. It is perceived as a resource that God uses for His purposes. If man acts properly, rainfall will be plentiful; if not, it will be sparse. It is not appropriate or helpful to investigate whether or not historical evidence bears out this claim. Let us say that in our tradition rainfall has been seen as a reward for moral behavior.

Having said this, it is important to add that this teaching is much more complicated than it appears on the surface. Rain is much more than a reward. It is also a motivation for moral behavior. On the day of Shemini Atzeret the liturgy calls for a Prayer for Rain. But is it only rain for which we beseech God? A close examination of the prayer materials reveal that we pray also for the blessings of Torah, for which water is symbolic.

Consider, furthermore, how the prophet Isaiah (44:3) projects a view of the Messianic age: 'Even as I pour water on thirsty soil, and rain upon dry ground, so I will pour My spirit on your offspring, My blessings upon your posterity.' Malbim, the great Bible commentator, interprets these verses as follows: God's abundance does not rest only on those who are invited or in need of it, in the same way that rain does not fall only because of the crops that need it. When the rain falls, it benefits not only those who need it, but also those not yet ready for it such as the streets of the cities, the wide places, and so forth. In the same manner God's blessing falls not only upon those who are spiritually prepared for it, but also on those who are associated with them. In other words, if Jews prepared well to receive the Torah, the whole world would benefit with them, as in the case of rain. So, the symbol of rain now becomes a clarion call for the salvation of the world.

One further development, again from Isaiah (45:8): 'Pour down, O skies, from above! Let the heavens rain down victory! Let the earth open up and triumph sprout. Yes, let vindication spring up.' Malbim has something to say about this verse too: When rain falls, the earth has to be prepared to receive it. If the fields are not ploughed and sown, of what benefit is the rain? Indeed, it is the earth alone that can be blamed if it is not ready and prepared to receive the good. So, if righteousness and spiritual opportunity pour down from above, it can only be a blessing if man is prepared with wholesome relationships between man and God and between man and man.

In the light of this teaching, rain also becomes a symbol and challenge to prepare for the moral and ethical life.

* * *

Additional Commentary

Like a pool

There should be a different reading. It should really read, 'The firmament might be compared to a cupola above which is a lake. The heat of the lake (its condensation) produces drops of rain.' The early scholars in *Baraita de-Shmuel* add that the lake is the lake of the upper waters and from its condensation rainfall occurs. (RDL)

*

This would also explain the reference to the time the rainfall takes to complete its descent. The firmament holds the lake in its grasp and since the firmament consists of the element of fire, this explains how the lake of the upper waters heats up and its condensation produces rainfall. (*Yefei To'ar*)

*

The firmament with the lower waters resembles a lake with a covering or cupola. The lower waters are the oceans, which look like a lake. The firmament is rounded and looks like a vault. The clouds and dampness (moisture) from the lake to the vault condense and then return as water to the lake or ocean. The clouds attract water from the ocean that is salty but the rain water returns sweet. The sweetness comes from their being in the firmament. Now when the salt drops and the raindrops return to the ocean, they remain separate. The clouds now only absorb the fresh water and return it as rain. (RWZE)

*

Yet they do not mingle
On the question as to how the upper waters that are sweet are able to pass through the lower waters that are salty, two answers are given. The first is the example of the Jordan river that passes through Lake Tiberias and still emerges as the Jordan river. The second answer assumes that there is no intrinsic difference between the rain waters in the upper spheres and the rain water when it descends from the clouds. The whole question of rain water from the point of view of the *midrash* is not part of the natural order of things. Rainfall is in the moral decision-making powers of man. When men walk in God's ways rain falls in its appointed time. When men corrupt their ways, the heavens block themselves off, as the Torah maintains in many places. Therefore, all rainfall is by definition miraculous, not merely the process of salt and sweet water described in this *midrash.* (*Tiferet Tzion*)

Parashah Four, Midrash Six

וַיַּעַשׂ אֱלֹהִים אֶת הָרָקִיעַ זֶה אֶחָד מִן הַמִּקְרָאוֹת שֶׁהִרְעִישׁ בֶּן זוֹמָא אֶת הָעוֹלָם 'וַיַּעַשׂ' אִתְמָהָא וַהֲלוֹא בְּמַאֲמָר הֵן הֱוֵי 'בִּדְבַר ה' שָׁמַיִם נַעֲשׂוּ וּבְרוּחַ פִּיו כָּל צְבָאָם' (תהלים לג, ו)

'And God made the firmament' (1:7) – this is one of the verses over which Ben Zoma raised a commotion: He made?! How remarkable! Surely it came into existence at God's word! As in the verse, 'By the *word* of the Lord were heavens *made*, and all their host by the breath of His mouth' (Psalms 33:6).

How could the Torah have said ויעש, *va-ya'as*, 'He made,' when everything was created by God's word? The answer is found in the verse quoted in Psalms. Yes, the world was created by God's word, but this was regarded by the Psalmist as equal to being made.

לָמָּה אֵין כָּתִיב בַּשֵּׁנִי 'כִּי טוֹב' רַבִּי יוֹחָנָן תָּנֵי לַהּ בְּשֵׁם רַבִּי יוֹסֵי בַּר חֲלַפְתָּא שֶׁבּוֹ נִבְרֵאת גֵּיהִנָּם שֶׁנֶּאֱמַר 'כִּי עָרוּךְ מֵאֶתְמוּל תָּפְתֶּה' (ישעיה ל, לג) יוֹם שֶׁיֵּשׁ בּוֹ אֶתְמוֹל וְאֵין בּוֹ שִׁלְשׁם

Why is '[And God saw} that it was good' not written in connection with the second day [of creation]? R. Joḥanan taught in the name of R. Jose b. R. Ḥalafta: Because on it Gehenna was created, as it is written [regarding hell], 'For the *Tofet* has been ready since yesterday' (Isaiah 30:33), which signifies a day to which there was a yesterday but not a day before yesterday.

The phrase, 'and God saw that it was good,' appears with every day of the creation except the second. Rabbi Joḥanan explains the exception by saying that hell was created on the second day and that, therefore, the phrase 'and it was good' is not fitting. The proof-text is that the *Tofet*, which is another name for hell, is described by Isaiah as being long ready – since yesterday. Only the second day of creation had a yesterday, but not a day-before-yesterday.

רַבִּי חֲנִינָא אוֹמֵר שֶׁבּוֹ נִבְרֵאת מַחֲלֹקֶת שֶׁנֶּאֱמַר 'וִיהִי מַבְדִּיל בֵּין מַיִם לָמָיִם' אָמַר

ר' טַבְיוֹמֵי אִם מַחֲלֹקֶת שֶׁהִיא לְתִקּוּנוֹ שֶׁל עוֹלָם וּלְיִשּׁוּבוֹ אֵין בָּהּ 'כִּי טוֹב'
מַחֲלֹקֶת שֶׁהִיא לְעִרוּבּוּבוֹ עַל אַחַת כַּמָּה וְכַמָּה

R. Ḥanina said: Because on it schism was created, as it is written, 'and let it [the firmament] *divide* the waters.' R. Tavyomei remarked: If, because of a division made for the good of the world and its ability to be populated, 'for it was good' is not [written in connection with that day], then how much the more should this apply to a schism which leads to the confusion [of the world].

One of the important rules that can help interpret this *midrash* is to understand that a second interpretation of a verse or maxim is offered only if the first is found to be either unsatisfactory or inadequate. For example, in our *midrash* R. Ḥanina did not accept the view of R. Joḥanan that hell was created on the second day because there is a section in the Babylonian Talmud (Tractate Pesaḥim) that uses the very same verse of our *midrash* to prove that Gehenna was created before the world. (*Tiferet Tzion*) Therefore R. Ḥanina proposed a different explanation. R. Tavyomei adds that if 'it was good' is not fitting for the day on which the waters were separated, an act that was essential for the good of the world, how much more would 'it was good' not apply to human controversies that can produce so much bitterness.

אָמַר ר' שְׁמוּאֵל בַּר נַחְמָן לְפִי שֶׁלֹּא נִגְמְרָה מְלֶאכֶת הַמַּיִם לְפִיכָךְ כָּתוּב בַּשְּׁלִישִׁי
'כִּי טוֹב' שְׁנֵי פְעָמִים אֶחָד לִמְלֶאכֶת הַמַּיִם וְאֶחָד לִמְלַאכְתּוֹ שֶׁל יוֹם

R. Samuel b. Naḥman said: Because the making of the waters was not finished; consequently 'for it was good' is written twice in connection with the third day, once in respect of the making of the waters and a second time on account of the work done on that day.

R. Samuel could not accept that it was because of the schism or division that the phrase was not mentioned regarding the second day, because even on the first day of creation there was division. He is quoting the view of Ben Zoma mentioned in *midrash* 2:6. (*Tiferet Tzion*) He therefore offered his own explanation: The division of the waters was not completed on the second day, but only on the third, where it is written, 'Let the water below the sky be gathered into one area, that the dry land may appear.' It was not appropriate to say 'it was good' on something which was incomplete, therefore on the third day it says it twice – once for the second day and once for the third.

שָׁאֲלָה מַטְרוֹנָה אַחַת אֶת רַבִּי יוֹסֵי אָמְרָה לוֹ לָמָה אֵין כְּתִיב בַּשֵּׁנִי 'כִּי טוֹב' אָמַר
לָהּ אַף עַל פִּי כֵן חָזַר וּכְלָלוֹ כֻּלוֹ בַּסּוֹף שֶׁנֶּאֱמַר 'וַיַּרְא אֱלֹהִים אֶת כָּל אֲשֶׁר עָשָׂה
וְהִנֵּה טוֹב מְאֹד' (בראשית א, לא) אָמְרָה לֵהּ מָשָׁל שִׁשָּׁה בְנֵי אָדָם בָּאִין אֶצְלְךָ וְאַתְּ
נוֹתֵן לְכָל אֶחָד וְאֶחָד מָנֶה וּלְאֶחָד אֵין אַתְּ נוֹתֵן מָנֶה וְאַתְּ חוֹזֵר וְנוֹתֵן לְכֻלָּם מָנֶה
אֶחָד לֹא נִמְצָא בְּיַד כָּל אֶחָד מָנֶה וּשְׁתוּת וּבְיַד אֶחָד אֶחָד שְׁתוּת אַתְמָהָא

A Roman matron asked R. Jose a question. She said: 'Why is "it was
good" not written in connection with the second day?' 'Even so,'
replied he, '[the text] subsequently included them all in this
description, for it is said, "and God saw everything that He had
made, and, behold, it was very good"' (Genesis 1:31). Said she to him:
'Supposing six men came to you and you gave a *maneh* [a large sum
of money] to each of them except one, and then you gave a second
maneh to all of them jointly. Would not each now have one and a
sixth *manehs*, while the one would only have one sixth of a *maneh*?!
[Your answer] is amazing.'

The distinguished Roman lady is not satisfied because both hell and
division have good aspects to them and have as their goals moral and
ethical motivations. One can discern from her analogy of the workmen
that she considers the second day of equal importance to any of the other
days.

While R. Jose tries to argue with the wise Roman lady that there is a
difference between something that is good in itself and something that is
only contributory to the good (hell and division), he nonetheless accepts
the merits of her arguments and therefore has recourse to the view of R.
Samuel. (*Tiferet Tzion*)

חָזַר וְאָמַר לָהּ כְּהַהוּא דְּאָמַר ר' שְׁמוּאֵל בַּר נַחְמָן לְפִי שֶׁלֹּא נִגְמְרָה מְלֶאכֶת הַמַּיִם
לְפִיכָךְ כְּתִיב בַּשְּׁלִישִׁי ב' פְּעָמִים 'כִּי טוֹב' אַחַת לִמְלֶאכֶת הַמַּיִם וְאַחַת לִמְלֶאכֶת
הַיּוֹם

Then he explained it a second time in the same way as R. Samuel b.
Naḥman, viz. because the making of the water was not completed
on the second day, and therefore 'for it was good' is written twice in
connection with the third day, once on account of the making of the
waters and a second time on account of the work done on that day.

The implication of R. Jose's repetition of R. Samuel's argument is to
establish the new thought that both hell and division were good for the
world and therefore their creation on the second day does not constitute

an adequate explanation for the absence of 'it was good' from the account
of that day. This answer apparently satisfied the Roman matron.

רַבִּי לֵוִי בְּשֵׁם רַבִּי תַּנְחוּם בַּר חֲנִילָאִי אָמַר כְּתִיב 'מַגִּיד מֵרֵאשִׁית אַחֲרִית' (ישעיה
מו, י) מִתְחִלַּת בְּרִיתוֹ שֶׁל עוֹלָם צָפָה הַקָּדוֹשׁ בָּרוּךְ הוּא מֹשֶׁה קָרוּי 'טוֹב' (שמות ב,
ב) וְעָתִיד לִטֹּל אֶת שֶׁלּוֹ מִתַּחַת יְדֵיהֶם לְפִיכָךְ לֹא כָתִיב בָּהֶם 'כִּי טוֹב'

**R. Levi said in the name of R. Tanḥum b. Ḥanilai: It is written, 'I
foretell the end from the beginning' (Isaiah 46:10). From the very
beginning of the world's creation God foresaw the existence of
Moses who was called 'good' (Exodus 2:2) and that he was destined to
be punished through them [i.e., water]; therefore, 'for it was good'
is not written in connection therewith.**

R. Jose, above, seems to indicate from his response that something that
merely contributes to the good is of the same merit as that which is good
in itself. R. Levi is dissatisfied with that interpretation. The purpose of the
world is Torah. Moses, who symbolized Torah, was referred to as *tov*,
'good' in the story of his birth. But he was punished by not being allowed
the enter the Promised Land when he struck the rock to bring forth water
instead of talking to it. It is not appropriate, therefore, that 'it was good'
should be mentioned with regards to the division of the waters on the
second day. Division is sometimes good, but it was not in the case of
Moses. So, that which contributes to the good is not always on the same
level as that which is good intrinsically.

But the water itself is not intrinsically bad. Another interpretation is
needed to underscore this fact. This is brought out by R. Simon.

רַבִּי סִימוֹן בְּשֵׁם רַ' יְהוֹשֻׁעַ בֶּן לֵוִי אָמַר מָשָׁל לְמֶלֶךְ שֶׁהָיָה לוֹ לִגְיוֹן קָשֶׁה אָמַר
הַמֶּלֶךְ הוֹאִיל וְלִגְיוֹן זֶה קָשֶׁה אַל יִכָּתֵב שְׁמִי עָלָיו כָּךְ אָמַר הַקָּדוֹשׁ בָּרוּךְ הוּא
הוֹאִיל וְהַמַּיִם הַלָּלוּ לָקוּ בָהֶם דּוֹר הַמַּבּוּל וְדוֹר אֱנוֹשׁ וְדוֹר הַפְּלָגָה לְפִיכָךְ אַל
יִכָּתֵב בָּהֶן 'כִּי טוֹב'

**R. Simon said in the name of R. Joshua b. Levi: This is similar to an
emperor who had a very cruel legion, and said, 'Since this legion is
so cruel, let my name not be written on [its banner].' Thus the Holy
One, blessed be He, said, 'Since the generation of Enosh, the
generation of the Deluge, and the generation of the separation of
races were punished through them [the waters], let "it was good"
not be written in connection therewith.'**

The source for the Deluge is the Bible; the source for Enosh and the

Tower of Babel being associated with water is later on in *Midrash Rabbah.* What is the lesson? The evil that comes to man is not brought about by God's desire, but by man's wrongdoing. That is why His name, *ki tov* – 'it was good' – had to be removed from water on the second day, which so often is the symbol of man's self-destruction. (*Tiferet Tzion*)

* * *

Seed Thoughts

Rashi notes that Ben Zoma died shortly after the episode in which his world was 'shaken up' by some of the biblical interpretations of which he disapproved. This is said many times of Ben Zoma (see *Parashah* Two, *Midrash* Four).

We all know why these statements were made. They were due to a tendency on the part of the Rabbis to set boundaries to mystical study, especially on subjects such as the creation of the world. The more one sees of the effort, the more one is convinced of its very opposite. Indeed, one of the most impressive aspects of Midrash is that it is brimful not only of speculation, but of a drive to learn more and more about more and more.

Of the four who entered *Pardes,* a term used for the study of mystical literature, and Ben Zoma was one of them, only R. Akiva, we are told, emerged whole and fulfilled. Does that mean that R. Akiva speculated less? He was responsible for the ingenious process of interpreting every *akh* and *rak* conjunction in the Torah.

Suppose Ben Zoma had ceased his speculation. Would he have lived longer? The connection between intellectuality and personal physical survival has not yet been proven.

A life of study has its frustrations, even its crises. But then again, so has every other form of endeavor. There is even a view that Ben Zoma died young because he was unmarried. People use even sacred texts to prove their prejudices.

Ben Zoma's premature death was a great loss. But it should discourage no one from the study of Torah, even the speculative study of Torah.

* * *

Additional Commentary

And God made
Ben Zoma's question is not only on this particular use of the term, 'and God made,' but is directed to every time that verb is used in the creation story. That is why it says specifically that this is but one of the verses about which Ben Zoma made such a commotion. (*Yefei To'ar*)

*

According to Rashi, Ben Zoma's question is never answered. RWZE points out that the answer is to be found at the end of Chapter Ten in *Bereishit Rabbah* where the term 'work' is defined as being quite different when applied to God than when applied to man.

*

Essentially God's work is by means of His word. (Mirkin)

*

Most commentators view Ben Zoma's question as extending up to the phrase 'the breath of his mouth' but not including it and the commotion he raised had to do with the use of the term *va-ya'as*. But it appears to me that his question ends with the phrase 'he made... how remarkable!' The commotion he caused should be interpreted as explained by Rashi that he was trying too hard to understand everything about the creation story. We had some intimation of this tendency in an earlier *midrash* in which he was trying to ascertain the space between the upper and lower waters. The expression 'he made a commotion' really means that he departed from this world. What then follows 'And He made... how remarkable!' is a teaching by itself and not an answer to his question. We find this formulation many times. (*Yedei Moshe*)

*

What we have translated as 'he made a commotion' is literally 'he shook up the world' and the reference is to 'this' world that was upset. He shook up his world, his life, and his days by these questionings and died. (Rashi and others)

*

In the case of human beings, the king first issues his commands, after which his subjects carry them out. In the case of the Holy One, blessed be He, the work of creation was not done by His subjects, but by Himself. The very words He utters are also the work and the doing of the work. When the word has been spoken it also means that the work has been accomplished. Thus *va-ya'as* means that the work was accomplished by God by means of His word. That is why it says 'And it was so.' No real work was done in the sense that we understand the concept. But it was done by means of His word. This is the meaning of the verse 'By God's word heaven was created' – the word was the act and the act was completed when the word was uttered. (*Tiferet Tzion*)

Parashah Four, Midrash Seven

וַיִּקְרָא אֱלֹהִים לָרָקִיעַ שָׁמָיִם:

And God called the firmament heaven.

Names that are given in Scripture usually tell us something about the content and make-up of that which bears the name. What was the name given to the firmament meant to teach?

רַב אָמַר אֵשׁ וָמָיִם

Rav said: [The word *shamayim* is a composite of] *esh* [fire] and *mayim* [water].

But these have opposite characteristics. What is the explanation?

רַבִּי אַבָּא בַּר כָּהֲנָא אָמַר מִשׁוּם רַב נָטַל הַקָּדוֹשׁ בָּרוּךְ הוּא אֵשׁ וּמַיִם וּפְתָכָן זֶה בְּזֶה וּמֵהֶן נַעֲשׂוּ שָׁמָיִם

R. Abba b. Kahana said in the name of Rav: The Holy One, blessed be He, took fire and water and mixed them up together and from them the heaven was made.

God showed that it was even possible to mix opposites together and that is what the name *sha-mayim* is meant to teach.

דָּבָר אַחֵר 'שָׁמַיִם' כְּתִיב שֶׁהֵן שָׁמִים מַעֲשֵׂיהֶן שֶׁל בְּרִיּוֹת אִם זָכוּ 'וְהִגִּידוּ שָׁמַיִם צִדְקוֹ' (תהלים צז, ו) וְאִם לָאו 'יְגַלּוּ שָׁמַיִם עֲוֹנוֹ' (איוב כ, כז)

Another interpretation: [The word] is written as *shamim*, meaning that they evaluate the deeds of human beings. If they have merit, 'The heavens declare their righteousness' (Psalms 97:6); and if not, 'The heavens shall reveal his iniquity' (Job 20:27).

This interpretation is based on an alternative reading of שמים, ignoring the existing vowel signs. In fact, in modern Hebrew, in which words are printed without vowel signs as opposed to the Hebrew of the Bible, the word would be read as *shamim*, which means 'they assess' or 'they evaluate.' This together with the two verses cited makes up the interpretation.

דָּבָר אַחֵר 'שָׁמַיִם' שֶׁהַבְּרִיּוֹת מִשְׁתּוֹמְמִים עֲלֵיהֶן לֵאמֹר שֶׁל מָה הֵן שֶׁל אֵשׁ הֵן שֶׁל מַיִם הֵן אַתְמָהָא!

Another interpretation: [The heavens were called] *shamayim* because people wonder [*mishtomemim*] at them, saying, 'Of what are they composed? Of fire? Of water? 'Tis a mystery!'

All Hebrew words have a grammatical root form from which they are derived. This interpretation takes the root שמ"ם as being that of *shamayim*; it is also the root of *mishtomemim*, which means 'they are amazed.'

ר' פִּינְחָס בְּשֵׁם רַבִּי לֵוִי אָמַר הוּא אָתָא וְקָם עָלָיו 'הַמְקָרֶה בַמַּיִם עֲלִיּוֹתָיו' (תהלים קד, ג) הֲוֵי שֶׁל מַיִם הֵן

R. Pinḥas in the name of R. Levi said: [Scripture] comes and explains it: 'He sets the rafters of His lofts in water' (Psalms 104:3), which shows that [the heavens are made of] water.

R. Pinḥas apparently agrees with the previous interpretation of the name *shamayim* and adds that in the verse cited the Psalmist is answering the wonderment of people.

'סַמִּים' מַה סַּמִּים הַלָּלוּ מֵהֶן יְרָקִין וּמֵהֶם אֲדָמִים מֵהֶם שְׁחוֹרִים וּמֵהֶם לְבָנִים כָּךְ שָׁמַיִם פְּעָמִים יְרָקִין וְכוּ'

[The word *shamayim* can be read as] *samim* [chemicals or pigments]. Just as some pigments are blue, others red, some black, and others white, so are the heavens – parts are blue, [parts are red, parts are black, and parts are white].

In midrashic interpretation the letters שׁ (*shin*), שׂ (*sin*), and ס (*samekh*) are frequently seen as interchangeable because of the similar pronunciation. If we replace the *shin* of *shamayim* with a *samekh* we get the word סמים, which means 'chemicals' or, in talmudic usage, 'pigments.' Thus, the changing colors of the sky are explained. Not only do these colors bespeak the artistic majesty of God's wonders, they also convey a remarkably pluralistic message that all individuals and people have their own unique individuality to which the heavens attest. (*Tiferet Tzion*)

רַבִּי יִצְחָק אָמַר 'שָׁמַיִם' שָׂא מַיִם טְעוֹן מָיִם

R. Isaac said: [The word] *shamayim* means *sa mayim*, carrying water, laden with water.

This interpretation is another play on words and involves replacing the *shin* with *sin*. R. Isaac was apparently addressing himself to the *function* of the heavens – providing the rain that makes the earth fruitful. It is as though God commanded the second day and said, 'I order you to carry water' or 'I assure you that you will be able to carry water.' The *midrash* now goes on to describe the solidification process of the 'liquid' heavens.

מָשָׁל לְחָלָב שֶׁהָיָה נָתוּן בִּקְעָרָה עַד שֶׁלֹּא תֵרֵד לְתוֹכוֹ טִפָּה אַחַת שֶׁל מָסוֹ הוּא מְרַפֵּף כֵּיוָן שֶׁיָּרֵד לְתוֹכוֹ טִפָּה אַחַת שֶׁל מָסוֹ מִיָּד הוּא קוֹפֵא וְעוֹמֵד כָּךְ 'עַמּוּדֵי שָׁמַיִם יְרוֹפָפוּ' (איוב כו, יא) עָמְדוּ שָׁמַיִם נִתַּן בָּהֶם אֶת הַמָּסוֹ

The matter can be compared to milk in a bowl. Before a drop of rennet falls into it, it quivers, but as soon as a drop of rennet falls into it, it immediately curdles and stands still. Similarly, 'The pillars of heaven quiver' (Job 26:13) until the solidifying substance was infused into them.

In other words, until a drop of the coagulant is dropped into it , the milk is fluid. The moment a congealing fluid is dropped into it, it congeals. The *midrash* completely changes the literal meaning of the verse brought as the proof-text. The word *amudei* is not translated as 'pillars,' but as the verb 'to stand,' and the verse is then understood as saying 'the quivering heavens stood firm.' This reading is substantiated by the second half of the verse, 'and are astonished at His reproof.' In a similar manner, the heavens quivered on the first day, but on the second day they congealed. The *parashah* ends with the concluding verse of the second day of creation.

'וַיְהִי עֶרֶב וַיְהִי בֹקֶר יוֹם שֵׁנִי' אָתְיָא כְּדַאֲמַר רַב לַחִים הָיוּ בָרִאשׁוֹן וּבַשֵּׁנִי קָרְשׁוּ

'And there was evening and there was morning, a second day' (Genesis 1:8). This agrees with Rav's dictum: The heavens were liquid on the first day and on the second day they congealed.

RDL comments that the verse quoted should have been, 'And God said, Let there be a firmament...'

* * *

Seed Thoughts

Nature as a spiritual symbol

Why were the heavens given a special name in the creation story? What was wrong with the name *raki‘a* that it had to be changed to *shamayim*? The answer is that the new name was intended to convey a spiritual message about the meaning of nature, at least as expressed by the heavens.

The first idea that *shamayim* brings to the sensitive mind is that it is made up of the words *esh* and *mayim*. Fire and water in many respects possess opposite characteristics, but they share in common the fact that they are the sources of the greatest physical power in the universe. The main sources of energy in the physical world are from fire and water. At the same time, both of these terms have been used in the Rabbinic writings to symbolize moral and ethical values – water as the symbol of Torah and fire as the symbol of moral passion, or, sometimes, fire as the symbol of the quality of justice and water as the symbol of the quality of mercy. These ideas have great implications for the human race.

For one thing, it evokes a great sense of wonder. This is the interpretation that sees in the name *shamayim* the same root as *hishtomemut* meaning amazement or what the philosopher Abraham Joshua Heschel has called 'radical amazement.' How great is God to have created a universe with such power and how great is man to have been entrusted with this almost divine power. We look at the heavens and are constantly bewildered at whom to marvel about first, God in His infinite majesty or man in his extraordinary potentiality. The sense of wonder always leads – or certainly should always lead – to thanksgiving and then to humility. These are the first spiritual benefits that nature can confer upon us.

But these tremendous physical and moral powers clearly spell out another claim – the call to responsibility. This is the interpretation that reads the word *shamayim* as *shamim*, meaning to evaluate or to assess. We should feel as though the heavens are constantly sitting in judgment upon us. How are we using the great trust of our spiritual powers? Are we developing them? Are we using the resources of energy for private gain or for public service? Are we respecting the physical environment, which is also part of our responsibility, or wasting it to the point where it will be unavailable for future generations?

Even more pointed than our responsibilities to the great physical powers in our possession is the challenge to our fellow human beings – our human relationships. We possess great moral powers. Are we aware of them? Are we using them? Do we understand them? This is the interpretation of those who read the word *shamayim* as *sammim*, meaning drugs or medicaments, possibly a shortened form of the word *besomim* often used for spices. The heavens represent a flowering of colors and hues. These are a reflection of the multicultural and ethnic variation that defines human civilization. It is also a symbol of the uniqueness and infinite variety of the individual human being. God is aware of this variation and does not always apply absolute standards in relationship to different groups and peoples. Just as a physician knows that a cure that will work for one will not always work for another and therefore has to vary his prescriptions of *samim*, his medicine or herbs, so too should human beings learn to respect the individuality of groups – ethnic, religious, or cultural – and the uniqueness of the individual.

More, however, than tolerance is called for. Morality means to accept heavy burdens. Certainly that is the role and burden of Israel as interpreted in the Torah and prophets. This thought is alluded to on the part of those who read the word *shamayim* as *sa mayim*, which literally means, 'carry water.' It is as though God ordered the heavens to carry water as He orders us to carry the life-giving waters of Torah. The Torah offers us a framework, a life system, and a series of goals through which to fulfill our obligations to both the physical and moral universe.

* * *

Additional Commentary

Fire and water

The intention here is to indicate that *shamayim* was not *creatio ex nihilo*, but *creatio ex creatio*, that is, from the elements, fire and water, that had already been created. (*Yefei To'ar*)

*

What special meaning did Rav have in mind in specifying that *shamayim* consisted of *esh* and *mayim*? He had in mind the interpretation given by MaHarSha in Tractate Ḥagigah (12) of the Babylonian Talmud: Fire symbolizes Divine judgment (*din*) and water symbolizes Divine mercy (*raḥamim*). Since God rules His world with both these qualities, they had to be reflected in the creation of *shamayim*. (*Tiferet Tzion*)

*

Mishtomemim – amazement

This interpretation was offered in opposition to the view of Rav that *shamayim* consisted of *esh* and *mayim*. People know that fire travels upward and water tends to flow downward, so that *shamayim* could not contain both. (RWZE)

*

The rules for operating the ethical universe are way beyond man's capacity. Are they motivated by strict justice or by quality of mercy? The point of the *midrash* is that by far the dominant element is the quality of compassion. This is the meaning of the conclusion that heaven is from water. *Shamayim* – שם מים – *shom mayim*, meaning, over there is water. (*Yefei To'ar*)

*

Shomim – evaluation

The interpretation of *shamayim* as evaluation is meant to emphasize that the concept of fate does not apply in Judaism. Everything depends upon what a human being does with his ethical choices. (*Tiferet Tzion*)

*

Samim – medicaments

The fact that we seem to discern different standards in God's judgment might be explained by the fact that a good physician adapts his cures to suit the individual patient and does not have a cure-all that applies to everyone. (*Tiferet Tzion*)

Parashah Five, Midrash One

וַיֹּאמֶר אֱלֹהִים יִקָּווּ הַמַּיִם (א, ט) כְּתִיב 'מִן גַּעֲרָתְךָ יְנוּסוּן מִקּוֹל וְגוֹ'' (תהלים קד, ז)

And God said: 'Let the waters under the heaven be gathered together [unto one place and let the dry land appear]' (Genesis 1:9). It is written, 'At Your rebuke they [the waters] fled' (Psalms 104:7).

The text, however, does not explain just how the waters were gathered together. In the style of Midrash, however, what is not found in the Torah text is sought elsewhere in Scripture and a proof-text is found in Psalms. The text explains that at God's word the waters were dispersed over the mountains to end up in the valleys and in one special place that became the ocean.

רַבִּי בֶּרֶכְיָה בְּשֵׁם רַבִּי אַבָּא בַּר אַמִּי אָמַר יֵעָשֶׂה מִדָּה לַמַּיִם וְהֵיךְ מַה דְּאַתְּ אָמַר 'וְקָו יִנָּטֶה עַל יְרוּשָׁלָם' (זכריה א, טז)

R. Berekhiah in the name of R. Abba b. Ammi said: [The verse means] let there be a measure set for the water, as you read, 'The measuring line [kav] is being applied to Jerusalem' (Zechariah 1:16).

The next question being asked is, what is the meaning of the word yikkavu? If it merely meant 'let them be gathered,' there are simpler Hebrew words, such as yikonsu and yei'osfu, both of which mean to be gathered. R. Berekhiah proposes that the significance of the choice of the word yikkavu is that it is derived from the same root as the word kav, which means 'a line' or 'a boundary.' Thus the divine command to the water was that a boundary – the oceans and rivers – had been set for it and that it was not to venture outside that boundary.

רַבִּי אַבָּא בַּר כָּהֲנָא בְּשֵׁם רַבִּי לֵוִי אָמַר אָמַר הַקָּדוֹשׁ בָּרוּךְ הוּא יְקַווּ לִי הַמַּיִם מַה שֶׁאֲנִי עָתִיד לַעֲשׂוֹת בָּהֶם

R. Abba b. Kahana in the name of R. Levi said: The Holy One, blessed be He, said, 'Let the waters expect what I am to use them for in the future.'

A second explanation is now offered for the word yikkavu as being from

175

the same root as *tikvah*, which means 'hope' or 'expectation.' Even though I created a boundary (*kav*) for the waters beyond which they cannot go, they should nevertheless realize that I will some day use them as a warning and even as a vehicle for dire punishment, which will mean moving them outside their boundaries (*Ha-midrash ha-Mevo'an*). This, of course, is referring to the great Deluge, a parable for which is given in the next passage.

מָשָׁל לְמֶלֶךְ שֶׁבָּנָה פַּלְטְרִין וְהוֹשִׁיב בְּתוֹכָהּ אִלְמִים וְהָיוּ מַשְׁכִּימִין וְשׁוֹאֲלִים בִּשְׁלוֹמוֹ שֶׁל מֶלֶךְ בִּרְמִיזָה וּבְאֶצְבַּע וּבְמַנְוָולִין אָמַר הַמֶּלֶךְ אִלּוּ הָיוּ פִּקְחִין עַל אַחַת כַּמָּה וְכַמָּה אַתְמָהָא

Compare this to a king who built a palace and tenanted it with dumb people. They used to rise early and greet the king with gestures, with their fingers and [by waving] handkerchiefs. The king said, '[If these creatures rise early to pay their respects, notwithstanding their limitations], if they were in possession of faculties, how much more would they [respect me]! Is it not amazing [that I have not done so]?!'

The first part of this parable refers to the world at creation before man was created. The waters acknowledged God's ownership of the world.

הוֹשִׁיב בָּהּ הַמֶּלֶךְ דִּיוֹרִין פִּקְחִין עָמְדוּ וְהֶחֱזִיקוּ בַּפַּלְטִין אָמְרוּ אֵין פַּלְטִין זוֹ שֶׁל מֶלֶךְ שֶׁלָּנוּ הִיא אָמַר הַמֶּלֶךְ תַּחֲזֹר פַּלְטִין לִכְמוֹ שֶׁהָיְתָה

Thereupon the king tenanted [the palace] with persons capable of speech, but they arose and seized the palace asserting, 'This is not the king's palace: it belongs to us!' The king [therefore] decreed, 'Let the palace return to its original state!'

The gifted people were then ordered out and the original dumb people placed back within the palace.

כָּךְ מִתְּחִלַּת בְּרִיָּתוֹ שֶׁל עוֹלָם לֹא הָיָה קִלּוּסוֹ שֶׁל הַקָּדוֹשׁ בָּרוּךְ הוּא עוֹלֶה אֶלָּא מִן הַמַּיִם הֲדָא הוּא דִכְתִיב 'מִקֹּלוֹת מַיִם רַבִּים אַדִּירִים מִשְׁבְּרֵי יָם' (תהלים צג, ד) וּמֶה הָיוּ אוֹמְרִים 'אַדִּיר בַּמָּרוֹם ה'' (שם שם, שם)

Similarly, at the very beginning of the world's creation the praise of the Almighty ascended only from the waters, as it is written, 'From the voices of many waters' (Psalms 93:4). What did they proclaim? 'The Lord on high is mighty' (ibid.).

The verse preceding the one quoted reads, 'Your throne stands firm from of old,' which teaches that from the very beginning of the world God was praised, and since man had not yet been created the praise must have come from the waters.

אָמַר הַקָּדוֹשׁ בָּרוּךְ הוּא מָה אִם אֵלּוּ שֶׁאֵין לָהֶן לֹא פֶה וְלֹא אֲמִירָה וְלֹא דִבּוּר וַהֲרֵי הֵן מְקַלְּסִין אוֹתִי כְּשֶׁאֶבְרָא אָדָם עַל אַחַת כַּמָּה וְכַמָּה

Said the Holy One, blessed be He, 'If these, which have neither mouth nor discourse nor speech, praise me, how much more [will I be praised] when I create man!'

It was indeed for precisely this purpose that man was created. Imagine the divine disappointment with what later happened.

עָמַד דוֹר הַמַּבּוּל וּמָרַד בּוֹ עָמַד דוֹר אֱנוֹשׁ וּמָרַד בּוֹ דוֹר הַפְּלָגָה וּמָרַד בּוֹ

The generation of the Flood arose and rebelled against Him; the generation of Enosh arose and rebelled against Him; the generation of the Tower of Babel arose and rebelled against him.

With regards to the great Deluge, Scripture records, 'The earth became corrupt before God; the earth was filled with lawlessness' (Genesis 6:11). Until the generation of Enosh, all humans had worshipped the one God. The Torah says of Enosh, 'It was then that men began to invoke God by name' (ibid. 4:26), which the Rabbis interpreted as meaning that they began to worship many gods. The Tower of Babel was built as an act of open defiance against God. Mankind wanted to make a 'tower with its top in the sky, to make a name for ourselves' (ibid. 11:4), that is, to challenge the Almighty in heaven.

אָמַר הַקָּדוֹשׁ בָּרוּךְ הוּא יְפַנּוּ אֵלּוּ וְיַעַמְדוּ וְיָבוֹאוּ אוֹתָן שֶׁיָּשְׁבוּ בָהֶן מִקֹּדֶם הָדָא הוּא דִכְתִיב 'וַיְהִי הַגֶּשֶׁם עַל הָאָרֶץ אַרְבָּעִים יוֹם וְאַרְבָּעִים לַיְלָה' (בראשית ז, יב)

Thereupon the Holy One, blessed be He, said: Let these be removed and the former ones who lived there earlier come in their place. Hence it is written, 'And the rain fell upon the earth forty days and forty nights' (Genesis 7:12).

All of the above human rebellions were punished by water that dispossessed them. There is a tradition that part of the earth was flooded after the rebellion of Enosh and it became the locale for the Mediterranean Sea.

It seems that the *midrash* is following an important exegetical principle here: There is no chronological order in the Torah, since the Tower of Babel appears after the great Flood and there is no indication in the text of the Torah that it too was punished by a flood.

The Hebrew says הגשם, *the* rain, with the definite article, signifying that well-known rain, that had existed before man, returned to its original place. It was not merely any waters that flooded the earth at the time of the Flood. It was the very waters set aside for this very purpose at the beginning, which God had told those waters to expect.

* * *

Seed Thoughts

In the parable of this *midrash*, the first thing man does when he is given the authority of decision-making is to take control of the palace and claim that it is his. Visions of modern times immediately flash into one's mind – strikers occupying the plants that they are picketing; employers locking out striking employees; students occupying campus buildings; hijackers taking over an aircraft; prisoners taking guards as hostages. All of these represent the breakdown of authority. But authority is a major necessity if there is not to be anarchy and lawlessness. But how can one ever come to such an authority by agreement?

The Rabbis used the story of Noah to formulate the seven Noachide laws, which were intended to formulate the minimum basis of values that all mankind would have to accept in order to maintain a civilized society. This is still a most desirable goal and all educational efforts should be directed to its achievement. Until that goal is reached, however, and possibly in order to reach it, the world has discovered one other precious formula. It is called democracy, and it gives every person the right to choose the authority to whom he will gladly submit.

Democracy may not necessarily produce the highest form of government but it is the best we have, so far. It also gives those who know and love Torah the opportunity to spread its message to the world.

* * *

Additional Commentary

Yikkavu – hope or expect
The word *yikkavu* – let them be gathered together – is interpreted by R. Abba b. Kahana as deriving from the same root as *tikvah*, meaning hope or expectation. God had high hopes for man as indicated in the midrashic parable of the palace occupied by the dumb.

God set the waters aside in one place hopefully, while waiting to see how the world would respond to the challenge of creation. When, however, He saw the behavior of the generation of the Deluge and of the tower of Babel, He removed His restrictions from the waters and allowed them to flood the universe as before creation. (*Yedei Moshe*)

Parashah Five, Midrash Two

אֶל מָקוֹם אֶחָד רַבִּי יוּדָן בְּשֵׁם רַבִּי לֵוִי וְרַבִּי בֶּרֶכְיָה בְּשֵׁם רַבִּי יוּדָן בַּר' שִׁמְעוֹן
אוֹמֵר כָּל הָעוֹלָם כֻּלּוֹ מַיִם בְּמַיִם וְאַתָּה אוֹמֵר 'אֶל מָקוֹם אֶחָד' אַתְמָהָא

'Unto one place' (Genesis 1:9) – R. Judan in the name of R. Levi and
R. Berekhiah in the name of R. Judan b. R. Simon said: The whole
world was one mass of water yet you actually say 'in one place'?
Amazing!

Where were they to go? And what about the waters that already occupied
the space of what we today call the ocean?

Two questions are here being asked. The first has to do with the meaning of water. What is it? Of what does it consist? Secondly, if the whole
world was filled with water, how could it be gathered into one place?
These questions are now answered by means of a parable.

מָשָׁל לְעֶשֶׂר נוֹדוֹת נְפוּחוֹת מְנָחוֹת בְּטְרַקְלִין נִצְרַךְ הַמֶּלֶךְ לִמְקוֹמָן מַה הוּא עוֹשֶׂה
לָהֶן מַתִּירָן וּמוֹצִיא אֶת רוּחָן וּמְסַלְּקָן בְּזָוִית אֶחָד

This may be compared to ten inflated wine-skins lying in a chamber.
When the king needs their place, what does he do to them? He
unties them, permits their air to escape, and removes them [all] into
a corner.

We now have the answer to the first question above. The water spoken of
before creation was not the water that we recognize, but a misty or foggy
substance intermixed with air. When the air was removed from it, the
volume of water was considerably reduced as was the space that it
occupied.

כָּךְ דָּרַךְ הַקָּדוֹשׁ בָּרוּךְ הוּא עַל מֵי בְרֵאשִׁית וְסִלְּקָן בְּיָם אוֹקְיָנוֹס הֲדָא הוּא דִּכְתִיב
'הֵן יַעֲצֹר בַּמַּיִם וְיִבָשׁוּ וְגוֹ' (איוב יב, טו) 'וְדוֹרֵךְ עַל בָּמֳתֵי יָם' (שם ט, ח)

Even so did the Holy One, blessed be He, tread down all the
primeval waters and remove them into the ocean, as it is written,
'When He holds back the waters, they dry up, [when He lets them
loose, they tear up the land]' (Job. 12:15), and [it also says], 'And He
trod upon the waves of the sea' (ibid. 9:8).

This becomes the answer to the second question. By removing the air from the water, it was possible to move it to one place, namely, that now occupied by the ocean. The Hebrew word יעצור, *ya'atzor*, translated here as 'He holds back,' is translated by the Targum as meaning, 'He squeezes,' which is an excellent parallel to 'removing the air' from the water.

God removes the air from the waters as a treader removes the juice from the grapes or the air from a water flask whose opening has been released. The use of the verb 'tread' in Job makes this an appropriate proof-text. There is also an additional verse not here quoted – כונס כנד מי הים – 'He gathers the waters as though they were a water flask' (Psalms 33:7), that is, He deflated the water.

* * *

Seed Thoughts

By definition, God, being all-powerful, can do anything. He could certainly create an ocean when and if He so desired. Nor would it be difficult for the believing reader to accept that kind of act of creation in the same spirit as the other miracles.

Somehow or the other, however, the midrashic sages for all their faith, were not prepared to accept God as some kind of divine magician. It was not enough to accept God as Creator. They had to know exactly how He performed these acts; not because they ever hoped to emulate them, which was clearly impossible, but in order to understand what happened and impart this understanding to others.

They also assumed, and this is very important in understanding the *midrash* we have just studied, that every act of creation had to be done in accordance with those very laws that God Himself had established for the natural world. They assumed that God would not contravene these laws for anything less than an emergency of a salvational nature. Such emergencies did not pertain at the beginning of things.

Parashah Five, Midrash Three

The text is the same as the previous *midrash* – 'gathered unto one place.' Which place? And how did the waters know which place?

אָמַר רַבִּי לֵוִי הַמַּיִם הָיוּ אוֹמְרִים אֵלּוּ לְאֵלּוּ נֵלֵךְ וְנַעֲשֶׂה קִילֶוֹסִין לְהַקָּדוֹשׁ בָּרוּךְ הוּא הֲדָא הוּא דִכְתִיב 'נָשְׂאוּ נְהָרוֹת ה' נָשְׂאוּ נְהָרוֹת קוֹלָם וְגוֹ'' (תהלים צג, ג)

R. Levi said: The waters said to each other, 'Let us go and offer praise to the Holy One, blessed be He,' as it is written, 'The floods lifted their voice...' (Psalms 93:3).

Some commentators connect this *midrash* with the preceding one where the verse from Job is quoted, 'When He holds back the waters, they dry up...' The waters were being gathered into the oceans, which were becoming very high and in danger of flooding the world, so God held them back. 'And He trod upon the waves of the sea' so that this would be prevented. At first, the waters did not wish to be gathered into one place, but when they realized that this would add honor to God, who would demonstrate His restraining powers, they agreed to go to the oceans in obedience to God. (*Tiferet Tzion*) The phrase 'lifted their voice' refers to the sounds of the waves as the waters wended their way to the ocean at creation.

The verse cited from Psalms continues יִשְׂאוּ נְהָרוֹת דָּכְיָם, the translation of which is 'the floods lifted their waves,' and the following section of the *midrash* interprets the word דכים, *dokhyam*, in various ways to answer a question that is not asked explicitly – How did the waters know where to go? – to which God replied, 'Let the floods lift דכים!'

ר' לֵוִי אָמַר דֶּרֶךְ הַיָּם דֶּרֶךְ הַיָּם ר' אַבָּא בַּר כַּהֲנָא אָמַר לְדוּכְתָּא פְּלוֹנִית וּלְזָוִית פְּלוֹנִיתָא גַּלְגְּלָא פְּלָנִיתָא

R. Levi said: [*Dokhyam*] means '*derekh yam*' [to the way of the sea]. R. Abba b. Kahana said: To such and such a *dukhta* (place), to such and such a corner should each specific wave go.

The waters were whispering to each other and saying let us go towards the sea. R. Levi interprets *dokhyam* not with its literal meaning, but as

182

though it were a shortened form of דרך ים, *derekh yam*, meaning 'towards the sea.'

R. Abba sees the word as being derived from the Aramaic word דוכתא, *dukhta*, which means 'place.' He adds the thought that each stream in the floods had a specific location to go to. Thus, the waters testify to God's prowess not only by going to the oceans, but also because water is found in every crevice hidden or revealed on earth. Water has been directed to each region to conform to its peculiar character. Even the taste and color of the water is variegated in accordance with God's plan.

רַב הוּנָא אָמַר לְהָדֵךְ יַמָּא לְהָדֵךְ יַמָּא

R. Huna said: [*Dokhyam*] means 'to *hadakh yama*' (this sea).

He explains *dokhyam* as coming from the Aramaic words הדך ימא, *hadakh yama*, meaning 'this sea,' as though the waters were telling each other where to go. It could mean that the waters knew the specific area to which they were heading (*Ha-Midrash ha-Mevo'ar*) or it could imply their confidence that even though all the waters were running into the sea, the sea would never become full. Somehow God had given the sea power to absorb them. (*Tiferet Tzion*)

רַ' יְהוֹשֻׁעַ בַּר' חֲנִינָא אָמַר לְדְכְסָאִים לְדְכְסָאִים

R. Joshua b. Hananiah said: [*Dokhyam*] means 'to *duksa'im duksa'im*' (receptacles).

R. Joshua understands *dokhyam* as being derived from the Greek *duksamon*, which means 'a place where waters gather.' He is adding the thought that although the waters travel long distances, those that are of a different character do not intermingle. *Duksa'im* is here to be understood as 'lane' or 'track.' (*Tiferet Tzion*)

רַ' אֱלִיעֶזֶר אָמַר קְלָטָן הַיָּם הֵיךְ מַה דְּאַתְּ אָמַר 'הֲבָאתָ עַד נִבְכֵי יָם' (איוב לח, טז) עַד קְלוֹטִין דְּיַמָּא

R. Eliezer said: The sea absorbed them, as it is said, 'Have you penetrated to the sources of the sea' (Job 38:16), [which the Targum translates as meaning] 'to the waters absorbed by the sea.'

R. Eliezer adds that the waters did not just head towards the sea, somehow the sea attracted them almost as though it had a magnetic power. He relates the term נבכי ים, *nivkhei yam*, in the verse from Job to *dokhyam*, which now becomes the area of the sea that attracts.

רַבָּנָן אָמְרִי דּוֹכִים קַבְּלוּנוּ מְדֻכָּנִים אָנוּ קַבְּלוּנוּ

The Rabbis say: [*Dokhyam*] means 'We are crushed (*dokhim*), receive us; We are beaten (*medukanim*), receive us!'

Dokhyam is now translated as deriving from the root הכה, 'to hit' or 'to press out.' The Rabbis say, not only was the air squeezed out of the waters of the world, but also from the waters of the oceans. That is why they had room to accept more. One set of waters said to the other, we are pressed out, so you can accept us.

אָמַר ר' יְהוֹשֻׁעַ בַּר' נְחֶמְיָה הַמַּיִם הָיוּ עוֹלִים הָרִים וְיוֹרְדִים תְּהוֹמוֹת עַד שֶׁהִגִּיעוּ
לְאוֹקְיָנוֹס הָדָא הוּא דִכְתִיב "יַעֲלוּ הָרִים יֵרְדוּ וְגוֹ'" (תהלים קד, ח) אֵיזֶה מָקוֹם יָסַדְתָּ
לָהֶם זֶה אוֹקְיָנוֹס

R. Joshua b. R. Neḥemiah said: The waters ascended mountains and descended into the depths, until they came to the ocean, as it is written, 'They ascended the mountains, they descended into valleys into the place which You founded for them' (Psalms 104:8). Which place did You found for them? The ocean.

R. Joshua ben Neḥemiah says that God's handiwork was reflected in the waters by virtue of the fact that the waters climbed mountains, which is against the laws of nature since water does not, of itself, flow upwards. All this because they hurried to do God's work and chose the shortest route. (*Tiferet Tzion*)

דָּרַשׁ רַבִּי אַבָּהוּ אוֹקְיָנוֹס גָּבוֹהַּ מִכָּל הָעוֹלָם כֻּלּוֹ וְכָל הָעוֹלָם כֻּלּוֹ מֵימָיו הֵם
שׁוֹתִים

R. Abahu exposited: The ocean is higher than the entire world and still the whole world drinks its waters.

R. Abahu's point is that God's might is shown in the waters by virtue of the fact that the oceans are higher than the earth and yet do not flood it. On the contrary, the world uses its waters. This is only possible because the water ascends into clouds that both protect the earth and sustain it with rain. (*Ha-Midrash ha-Mevo'ar*)

* * *

Seed Thoughts

One of the great miracles of creation is the fact that the oceans do not flood the earth. The rivers that pour into the oceans have reason to declare the glory of God for they have been used as His instruments.

I was listening to a symposium on the dangers now occurring to man because the ozone layer has been pierced. No one is, as yet, sure of the consequences. One participant, speaking about Africa, was concerned that one of the effects of the damage to the ozone layer would be that the sea might rise one or two meters. If that were to happen the continent of Africa might be flooded and even eventually disappear.

What about God's covenant with creation? His promises not to flood the earth? His restraining of the oceans? All of these covenants are in place. Unfortunately, it is man who has changed everything. Man's creative genius, coupled with his greed and/or his ignorance of the consequences of his behavior, threaten the balancing factors of the universe.

These can still be corrected if only we will work together with nature, and not in opposition to it.

Parashah Five, Midrash Four

This *midrash* is a continuation of the previous one. It relates to the same text – 'Let the waters be gathered.'

אָמַר ר' לֵוִי יֵשׁ מִן הַדַּרְשָׁנִים שֶׁהֵם דּוֹרְשִׁים כְּגוֹן בֶּן עַזַּאי וּבֶן זוֹמָא נַעֲשָׂה קוֹלוֹ
שֶׁל הַקָּדוֹשׁ בָּרוּךְ הוּא מֶטַטְרוֹן לְמֹשֶׁה בְּשָׁעָה שֶׁאָמַר לוֹ 'עֲלֵה אֶל הַר הָעֲבָרִים'
(דברים לב, מט) נַעֲשָׂה קוֹלוֹ שֶׁל הַקָּדוֹשׁ בָּרוּךְ הוּא מֶטַטְרוֹן עַל הַמַּיִם הָדָא הוּא
דִכְתִיב 'קוֹל ה' עַל הַמָּיִם' (תהלים כט, ג)

R. Levi said: Some of the interpreters, such as Ben Azzai and Ben Zoma interpret: The voice of the Lord became a guide to Moses when He said to him, 'Ascend these heights of Avarim to Mount Nevo' (Deuteronomy 32:49); the voice of the Lord became a guide to the waters, as it is written, 'The voice of the Lord is over the waters' (Psalms 29:3).

Mount Nevo was to be the burial place of Moses, but the verse does not specify an exact location. However, the voice of God guided Moses, who followed its sound wherever it led. Similarly, when the command came for the waters to gather, no specific place was mentioned, and the voice of God became a guide that the waters followed. Note that it does not say אל המים, *el ha-mayim*, 'to the waters,' which would mean that God spoke to the waters, but על המים, *al ha-mayim*, 'on the waters,' as though the voice of God was above them guiding them to their destination.

אָמַר רַבִּי בֶּרֶכְיָה לֹא פֵּירְשׁוּ הַמַּיִם הַתַּחְתּוֹנִים מִן הָעֶלְיוֹנִים אֶלָּא בִּבְכִיָּה הָדָא
הוּא דִכְתִיב (איוב כח, יא) 'מִבְּכִי נְהָרוֹת חִבֵּשׁ'

R. Berekhiah said: The nether waters only parted from the upper waters with weeping, as it is written, 'He binds the streams from weeping' (Job 28:11).

The point that is being made here is that the waters did not separate cheerfully. The waters are here personified as having a will of their own. Just as earlier it was indicated that the separation of the waters brought division and controversy into the world, so it is maintained that the lower waters separated from the upper waters resentfully. (Mirkin)

רַ' תַּנְחוּם מַיְתֵי לַהּ מִן הָכָא 'עשֶׁה אֶרֶץ בְּכחוֹ וְגוֹ' לְקוֹל תִּתּוֹ הֲמוֹן מַיִם וְגוֹ'' (ירמיה
י, יב־יג) וְאֵין לְקוֹל אֶלָּא בְּכִי הֵיךְ מַה דְּאַתְּ אָמַר 'קוֹל בְּרָמָה נִשְׁמָע' (שם לא, יד)

R. Tanḥum adduced this [idea] from the following: 'He made the
earth by his might... when He gives [His command] there is the
voice of a multitude of waters in the heavens' (Jeremiah 10:12) – now
'voice' only refers to weeping, as it says, 'A voice is heard in Ramah,
wailing, bitter weeping' (ibid. 31:15).

R. Tanḥum's additional proof seems to consist of the fact that the word
קול, 'a voice,' is often used in the Bible in the context of weeping.
According to the plain meaning of the first verse cited, the word קול refers
to God's voice.

* * *

Seed Thoughts

'Now "voice" only refers to weeping...'

Perhaps a better translation of this phrase would be that the only attribute possessed by a human being in relationship to God is its voice when,
as a cry, it indicates penitence or a desire for forgiveness. (*Tiferet Tzion*)

We are told in the text that the use of voice in Scripture implies a 'cry.'
But when we reflect upon how 'cry' is interpreted in the quotation above,
we realize that what is being referred to is actually prayer. God hearkens
to the cry of man because that cry is the cry of prayer.

Prayer is the pouring out of the human heart before God. It involves
complete exposure not only of our weaknesses, but also of our strengths.
It is not done in order to change the will of God, but to change our will
so that we may be brought into closer conformity with God's desires.

It can be taken for granted that the person who prays looks upon himself as a penitent. It can be taken for granted that the person who prays
has a desire for forgiveness.

These are the traits that God seeks most from man.

That is why the voice of prayer must be cultivated and cherished by
man. It is to be found not only in words, but also in deeds and in the
reflections of a contrite heart.

* * *

Additional Commentary

Darshanim – homiletists

Both Ben Azzai and Ben Zoma are consistent in their opposition to an-
thropomorphisms and any material way of expressing the Godhead. The

quotation from Deuteronomy is a vision whereby Moses is shown the entire land of Israel before he dies. The vision presumably implies an index finger pointing out the various sights to Moses. Ben Azzai and Ben Zoma insist that this was done not by a finger but by a voice. (Mirkin)

*

He binds the streams from weeping

מבכי נהרות חבש, *mi-bekhi naharot ḥibeish*, should most probably be emended to מנבכי נהרות חבש, *mi-**nivkhei** naharot ḥibeish*, as in Job 38:16 – *nivkhei yam* meaning springs of water and referring to the creation. That is why the homiletists tried to render it as 'cry' since the letters of *bekhi* are found in each of the words. (RWZE)

*

Our *midrash* urges man to cry and protest at anything that draws him away from God. Take a lesson from the inanimate waters, which were only created to serve man. The moment they were separated from the upper waters and were no longer immediate servants of heaven, they burst into tears. How much more so should man, whose sole purpose it is to serve God, protest when the times in which he lives interfere with his religious obligations. (*Tiferet Tzion*)

Parashah Five, Midrash Five

אָמַר רַ' יוֹחָנָן תְּנָאִין הִתְנָה הַקָּדוֹשׁ בָּרוּךְ הוּא עִם הַיָּם שֶׁיְּהֵא נִקְרָע לִפְנֵי יִשְׂרָאֵל
הָדָא הוּא דִכְתִיב 'וַיָּשָׁב הַיָּם לְאֵיתָנוֹ' (שמות יד, כז) לִתְנָאוֹ שֶׁהִתְנָה עִמּוֹ

R. Joḥanan said: The Holy One, blessed be He, made a stipulation with the sea that it should divide before Israel, as it is written, 'And the sea returned to its normal state (*le-eitano*)' (Exodus 14:27) — in accordance with its agreement (*li-tena'o*).

In the first *midrash* of this *Parashah*, R. Abba b. Kahana interpreted the phrase *yikkavu ha-mayim*, 'Let the waters be gathered,' not according to the plain meaning, but as 'Let the waters expect what I am to use them for in the future.' R. Joḥanan now comes to show how that 'expectation' was fulfilled. The waters became God's instrument at the Red Sea when they parted in order to allow the Children of Israel to pass through and joined together again to drown the Egyptian hosts.

The verse says that the sea returned to its natural state. With a change in the order of the letters, the word איתנו can be read תנאיו, meaning, 'its condition.'

אָמַר רַבִּי יִרְמְיָה בֶּן אֶלְעָזָר לֹא עִם הַיָּם בִּלְבַד הִתְנָה הַקָּדוֹשׁ בָּרוּךְ הוּא אֶלָּא עִם
כָּל מַה שֶּׁנִּבְרָא בְּשֵׁשֶׁת יְמֵי בְרֵאשִׁית הָדָא הוּא דִכְתִיב 'אֲנִי יָדַי נָטוּ שָׁמַיִם וְכָל
צְבָאָם צִוֵּיתִי' (ישעיה מה, יב)

R. Jeremiah b. Eleazar said: Not with the sea alone did the Holy One, blessed be He, make a stipulation, but with everything which was created in the six days of creation, as it is written, 'My own hands stretched out the heavens and I commanded all their host' (Isaiah 45:12).

The apparent interferences with nature that took place in the Bible are not interventions at all, but rather conditions built in at the moment of their creation. The first part of the verse quoted, 'It was I who made the earth and created man upon it,' is to be understood as meaning 'at that time I commanded them all even to go against natural law if I so desire.'

מִידֵי נָטוּ שָׁמַיִם וְכָל צְבָאָם צִוִּיתִי צִוִּיתִי אֶת הַיָּם שֶׁיִּהְיֶה נִקְרָע לִפְנֵי יִשְׂרָאֵל
צִוִּיתִי אֶת הַשָּׁמַיִם וְאֶת הָאָרֶץ שֶׁיִּשְׁתְּקוּ לִפְנֵי מֹשֶׁה שֶׁנֶּאֱמַר 'הַאֲזִינוּ הַשָּׁמַיִם וְגוֹ''

(דברים לב, א)

**When My hands stretched out the heavens and I commanded all
their host: I commanded the sea to divide before Israel; I
commanded the heavens and the earth to be silent before Moses as
it says, 'Give ear, O heavens, let me speak' (Deuteronomy 32:1).**

These are the first two of the eight illustrations brought in this *midrash* to
show how God's stipulation at the time of creation was for the purpose of
miracles that happened much later. They are meant to demonstrate the
great spiritual purposes that motivated this delayed power to be revealed
at that particular time. The first was the miracle needed to strengthen
belief in the prophet Moses. This took place at the Red Sea, regarding
which it is written, 'And they [the Children of Israel] believed in God and
in His servant Moses.' The purpose of the second quotation is to teach
respect for the prophet and regard his word as having eternal value. This
occurred when God silenced heaven and earth so that the song of Moses,
Ha'azinu, could be heard.

צִוִּיתִי אֶת הַשֶּׁמֶשׁ וְאֶת הַיָּרֵחַ שֶׁיַּעַמְדוּ לִפְנֵי יְהוֹשֻׁעַ שֶׁנֶּאֱמַר 'שֶׁמֶשׁ בְּגִבְעוֹן דּוֹם'

(יהושע י, יב)

**I commanded the sun and the moon to stand before Joshua, as it is
written, 'Stand still, O sun, at Giveon, [O moon, in the Valley of
Ayalon]' (Joshua 10:12).**

This event was to wreak vengeance on the enemies of Israel during the
time of Joshua.

צִוִּיתִי אֶת הָעוֹרְבִים שֶׁיְּכַלְכְּלוּ אֶת אֵלִיָּהוּ שֶׁנֶּאֱמַר (מ"א יז, ו) 'וְהָעֹרְבִים מְבִיאִים
לוֹ וְגוֹ''

**I commanded the ravens to feed Elijah, as it is written, 'And the
ravens brought him...' (1 Kings 14:6).**

When God told Elijah to hide in the cave, He said, 'You will drink from
the wadi, and I have commanded the ravens to feed you there' (1 Kings
14:4). The verse cited in the *midrash* records that the ravens did indeed do
God's will. Ravens have the reputation of being cruel and merciless
animals, so that accomplishing their mission involved a complete change
in their nature.

צִוִּיתִי אֶת הָאוּר שֶׁלֹּא תַזִּיק לַחֲנַנְיָה מִישָׁאֵל וַעֲזַרְיָה

I commanded the fire to do no harm to Ḥananiah, Mishael, and Azariah.

No proof-text is brought for this and the next incidents. The story is in Daniel Chapter 3. The purpose of the miracle was to proclaim God's providential care and power in the world.

צִוִּיתִי אֶת הָאֲרָיוֹת שֶׁלֹּא יַזִּיקוּ אֶת דָּנִיֵּאל

I commanded the lions not to harm Daniel.

This miracle is recorded in Daniel Chapter 6. God designed creation so that a righteous man could be delivered from persecution, as in the case of Daniel.

צִוִּיתִי אֶת הַשָּׁמַיִם שֶׁיִּפָּתְחוּ לְקוֹל יְחֶזְקֵאל שֶׁנֶּאֱמַר 'נִפְתְּחוּ הַשָּׁמַיִם וְגוֹ'' (יחזקאל א, א)

I commanded the heavens to open before Ezekiel, as it is written, 'The heavens were opened [and I saw visions of God]' (Ezekiel 1:1).

Another purpose was to teach the saintly some of God's mysteries, as in the vision of Ezekiel.

צִוִּיתִי אֶת הַדָּג שֶׁיָּקִיא אֶת יוֹנָה שֶׁנֶּאֱמַר 'וַיֹּאמֶר ה' לַדָּג וַיָּקֵא אֶת יוֹנָה' (יונה ב, יא)

I commanded the fish to vomit forth Jonah as it is written, 'The Lord commanded the fish and it spewed Jonah out upon the dry land' (Jonah 2:11).

The final miracle was wrought to motivate an entire people to repent, which was accomplished through the miracle of Jonah's survival in the body of the fish. (The above running commentary is from *Yefei To'ar*.)

* * *

Alternative Commentary

Tiferet Tzion approaches the theme and the text of our *midrash* with a very different analysis.

The problem is not to preserve the integrity of God's will and demonstrate that His will is not a whim that changes. On the contrary, the changeability of God's will is precisely the condition established at creation. God will, indeed, change His will if there are overriding spiritual implications motivating Him to do so.

The *midrash* lists seven situations where natural law cannot be allowed to be dominant. At such times God will indeed intervene, and this intervention is the very condition and warning established at creation. What are these situations?

A time will come when God will want to reveal His glory in the world and this will not be possible without suspending or changing a natural law. This will prove conclusively that His hand rules. This was already indicated at the dividing of the sea: 'And the Children of Israel saw the mighty hand... and they believed in God and in Moses His servant.' This one act really encompassed or summarized all the miracles of Egypt, whose purpose it was to implant in the hearts of Israel the belief that God is the ruler of the universe, as it is written, 'That you might narrate in the ears of your son and son's son that which I performed in Egypt... that you should know that I am the Lord.' Always remember, as indicated above, that the miracles are repeatable in time.

A second situation can occur where nature should not be allowed to dominate, and this concerns those who study the Torah in order to ascertain its truth. It is impossible for anyone to study the Torah or to merit its crown other than by extraordinary effort and utter exhaustion. Commenting on the verse, 'This is the Torah: if a man dies in a tent...,' the Rabbis say that one cannot achieve the crown of Torah without figuratively killing oneself in the process, for this is surely above the ordinary capacity of a human being, way beyond any natural effort. It may even be termed superhuman or supernatural in the sense that its great profundity can only be acquired by the gift of prophecy. Even though we are told that prophecy was removed from the prophets, it was not removed from the Sages, for it is simply not possible to acquire Torah without this gift. God even assists the true believer in worldly matters: 'Whosoever occupies himself with Torah will become prosperous in ways beyond human achievement' (Babylonian Talmud, Tractate Avodah Zarah 19b). And so, at the close of the Torah, which is the song of *Ha'azinu* and testifies how Israel will blossom when it fulfills the Torah and vice versa, God made heaven and earth become silent before Moses to show Israel that nature has no authority over the one who exhausts himself in the study of Torah.

The state of the Land of Israel is another situation that has to be approached from the supernatural point of view as it is written, 'The eyes of the Lord your God are upon it from the beginning of the year to the end of the year.' Therefore, when Joshua conquered the land of Israel, the sun and the moon were made to stand still in order to demonstrate that the guiding principles for the land of Israel transcend the laws of nature.

Human livelihood is also governed by considerations beyond nature. This was demonstrated by the ravens who fed Elijah. We know that by nature the ravens are very cruel even towards their own young, nevertheless Elijah was sustained by them to prove that there can be no obstacle to God's will when He wants to sustain His creatures, except man's sins. So the Rabbis say, three keys cannot be delivered by a messenger or representative and one of them is earning a livelihood.

Nature also does not triumph over those righteous men who are able to discipline their passions. Since, basically, they are disciplining their passions in order to serve their Father in heaven, nature has no power over them. Proof is brought from the stories of Ḥananya, Mishael, and Azariah, who were delivered from the fiery furnace and Daniel from the lions' den. (*Tiferet Tzion* sees Ḥananiah and Daniel as one illustration.)

Furthermore, whenever a person is in trouble and cries out to God, nature cannot conquer him. Even if he does not succeed entirely by means of natural causes to deliver himself, the doors are not closed for him to benefit from powers that are beyond nature. This was demonstrated in the life of Ezekiel, who was exiled to Babylon and cried out to God to have mercy on Israel in time of trouble, and God opened the heavens to prove that nature is not all-determinant.

The concept of nature also cannot exert its power over one who wants to return in penitence. From the point of view of natural law, it is impossible for a person to repent. After all, what is done is done. However, from the very beginning of creation nature was not allowed to impose its will upon man who might want to repent. That is why, as was said earlier in *Bereishit Rabbah*, repentance was created before the creation of the world so that nature when created would not have power over it. This was illustrated by Jonah, who was sent to Nineveh to persuade an entire people to repent. God helped him in many ways to convince the people of Nineveh that their situation was not inevitable and could be changed by their transformation.

* * *

Seed Thoughts

A human being is made up of nature and of what is more than nature. Our natural endowments and our natural environment are indispensable to our comfort and well-being. But they can also be very limiting.

That is why the human aspect of our condition is so important. There are times and occasions when we have to go beyond nature and even oppose it. In fact, God Himself has set such a precedent in the biblical miracles. That does not mean that we can be so egocentric as to expect God to intervene on our behalf.

On the other hand, we can make a major effort in those areas of life that are threatened by dehumanization. The exhaustive study of Torah is one of those areas that can truly make us sensitive humans; the urge to repent and change for the better is another; the heroism that is required to withstand tyranny is another. Sometimes we despair that we can ever overcome the natural limitations that seem to restrain us. But often, though not always, the universe responds and we discover sources of power we had not anticipated before.

Rabbi Yitzḥak Ze'ev Yadler, author of the remarkable commentary on the *Midrash Rabbah* known as *Tiferet Tzion*, describes how this phenomenon affected him. He struggled for fourteen years on the commentary. Often he would spend hours trying to figure out a difficult passage and, then, he writes, 'Suddenly, the Holy One, blessed be He, revealed His light to me to understand that which heretofore I was not able to understand by my own intellectual powers. The Rabbis say, "If you find an answer after much intellectual struggle, believe that it is possible." But I say that first you must struggle intellectually and then God rewards that struggle with the light of His holiness that no man is able to achieve on his own.'

* * *

Additional Commentary

God imposed conditions

The Sages intended by means of this interpretation of the 'conditions' to remove and eliminate from the concept of God any semblance of the changing of God's will. If we take the position that at the time of a miracle something new has entered experience that had not been willed before, that would imply a change of God's will from what He had previously intended. They therefore expounded that at the creation of the world this power or will was concealed to be revealed or put into effect at a later date. For example, we know that iron is heavy and will fall to the ground by the propulsion of gravity unless it is tightly fastened. But if a person were to place a powerful magnet in the vicinity of the iron it would be drawn to it, and the iron would not fall. This would not mean that the iron had changed its nature, because this quality of being attracted to a magnetic force was concealed within it from the beginning and only revealed at the appropriate time. Similarly, God implanted certain powers in every created thing that righteous people can influence and motivate to operate.

This does not indicate a new form of creation or intervention in the world, but rather the unfolding of a quality hidden there from the outset. The eight illustrations in the *midrash* show how this delayed creation operated in biblical times. (*Yefei To'ar*)

*

In accordance with its agreement (condition)
The idea here is that even after the sea fulfilled its promise by dividing before the Children of Israel, it did not return to its former state but remained in readiness with the understanding that it would still have to live up to a condition in the future. This is because all the miracles that were performed for our ancestors in Egypt will be repeated by the Holy One, blessed be He, speedily and in our day at the time of the final redemption. It has thus been written, 'As the days of your exodus from Egypt, so will I perform wondrous things,' which means that although the condition was fulfilled at the Red Sea, it will have to be repeated at the time of the final redemption. (*Tiferet Tzion*)

Parashah Five, Midrash Six

אָמַר רַ' אֶלְעָזָר מִתְּחִלַּת בְּרִיָּתוֹ שֶׁל עוֹלָם גָּזַר הַקָּדוֹשׁ בָּרוּךְ הוּא וְאָמַר 'יִקָּווּ
הַמַּיִם' לָמָּה 'הַקּוֹרֵא לְמֵי הַיָּם' (עמוס ה, ח) 'הַקּוֹרֵא לְמֵי הַיָּם' (שם ט, ו) ב' פְּעָמִים
אַחַת בְּדוֹר הַמַּבּוּל וְאַחַת בְּדוֹר אֱנוֹשׁ בִּשְׁבִיל 'וְהָאֱלֹהִים עָשָׂה שֶׁיִּרְאוּ מִלְּפָנָיו'
(קהלת ג, יד)

R. Eleazar said: From the very beginning of the world's creation the Holy One, blessed be He, issued a decree saying, 'Let the waters be gathered together.' Why, then, is it twice written, 'Who summons the waters of the sea [and pours them out upon the earth]' (Amos 5:8; 9:6)? Once in the generation of the Flood and a second time in the generation of Enosh, because 'God has done it so that men should fear Him' (Ecclesiastes 3:14).

The point of R. Eleazar's question is that God arranged for the waters to be collected once and for all time and we know that God, by definition, does not change His mind. How then can the references in Amos 8:5 and 9:6 that God flooded the earth twice be explained? Furthermore, it should be noted that the verses in Amos are in the present tense as though to indicate that God is poised with these interventions at any time. The answer seems to be that one cannot compare a threat or punishment that is visible to one that is invisible. When it is not always visible the heart of the sinner is not that fearful. For this reason God arranged for the waters to be higher than the earth so that its natural tendency would be to overflow the earth at least potentially so that this threat would always be visible (see *Tiferet Tzion* in Additional Commentary).

The verse from Ecclesiastes is quoted to say even though, ordinarily, God would not change His intention, this had to be done so that mankind would have the proper respect and fear.

מָשָׁל לִמְדִינָה שֶׁמָּרְדָה בַּמֶּלֶךְ שָׁלַח הַמֶּלֶךְ לִגְיוֹן קָשֶׁה וְהִקִּיפָהּ כְּדֵי שֶׁיִּרְאוּ אוֹתוֹ
בְּנֵי הַמְּדִינָה וְיִתְיָרְאוּ מִלְּפָנָיו כָּךְ לָמָּה 'כֹּנֵס כַּנֵּד מֵי הַיָּם' (תהלים לג, ז) בִּשְׁבִיל
'וְיִירְאוּ מֵ' כָּל הָאָרֶץ וְגוֹ'' (שם שם, ח)

This can be compared to a country that rebelled against its king. The king sent a cruel legion and surrounded it, so that the

196

inhabitants might see it and fear him. So, too, why does 'He heap up the ocean like a mound' (Psalms. 33:7)? In order that 'all the inhabitants should dread Him' (ibid. v. 8).

God surrounded the earth with water so that the inhabitants would fear Him. Furthermore, He would not have to flood the world again as in the previous generations, the potential fear alone would create respect. This is now the answer to the original question. Why does the verse say, 'that the dry land should appear.' Is that not obvious? Not necessarily. The word ותראה (*ve-teira'eh*), 'appear,' is of the same root as ייראו (*yir'u*), meaning 'to fear.' The inhabitants would see the land as it was surrounded by the tremendous power of the oceans and be very fearful.

* * *

Seed Thoughts

The story is told of parents who were having great difficulty in disciplining their ten-year-old child. After much soul searching, they sought the aid of a famous child psychologist. The child was brought for an interview that lasted a relatively short time. Just before they parted, the psychologist bent over and whispered something into the boy's ear. Whatever it was worked like magic. The child was obedient, dutiful, and most considerate. A friend of the family could not restrain himself. He called up the psychologist and asked what were the magic words he used that made such an impression. The psychologist replied, 'I said to him, if you don't follow my instructions, I will break every bone in your body.'

Fear is not a noble motivation. We do not like to use it. We know it is not progressive. But we also know that it works. Maybe not all the time, but often enough to make a difference.

The Almighty also seems to have acknowledged the reality of fear. He created the world in such a way that the oceans would surround the earth, thus putting the fear of God in man.

* * *

Additional Commentary

Rabbi Eleazar said

The fundamental thrust of R. Eleazar's question has to be properly understood. At the creation of the world, it was established as a natural law that the waters were to be gathered into one place. It also seems to have been established as a natural law that the waters would overwhelm the earth at God's command. This appears to be the meaning of the verses in

Amos that are in the present tense. Why was such divine intervention necessary? Why could not God have arranged the punishment of evil-doers in purely natural ways? The answer seems to be that you cannot compare a threat or punishment that is visible to that which is not always visible. When it is not always visible, the heart of the sinner is not that fearful. For this reason God arranged for the waters to be higher than the earth so that its natural tendency would be to overflow the earth, so that this threat would always be visible. This is the appropriateness of the parable of the king and the rebellious province. Sending the legion was in order to instill fear. The continuous presence of the army would make the fear last longer. It was thus God's intention that the world should fear His potential punishment and merit the ultimate good that was His main purpose in creating the world. That purpose was to bestow good upon His creatures in this world and in the world-to-come. (*Tiferet Tzion*)

*

Explaining Amos

A fuller explanation of our *midrash* is found in *Deuteronomy Rabbah* 10:2. There the *midrash* interprets Ecclesiastes 3:14: 'I realized, too, that whatever God has brought to pass will recur evermore: Nothing can be added to it and nothing taken from it – and God has brought to pass that men revere Him.' On the face of it, the first part of the verse contradicts the second part. However, the letter *vav* in *ve-ha'elohim asa* 'and what God has brought to pass' is to be seen as a *vav ha-mehapekh* – the conversive *vav*, which inverts the meaning of what follows to 'and God will bring it to pass...' Thus, God sometimes intervenes in nature so that men should fear His punishment. A sample of God's intervention are the verses in Amos quoted above. (RZWE)

Parashah Five, Midrash Seven

בְּנוֹהֵג שֶׁבָּעוֹלָם אָדָם מְפַנֶּה כְּלִי מָלֵא בְּתוֹךְ כְּלִי רֵיקָן שֶׁמָּא כְּלִי מָלֵא בְּתוֹךְ כְּלִי
מָלֵא כָּל הָעוֹלָם כֻּלּוֹ מַיִם בְּמַיִם וְאַתְּ אוֹמֵר 'אֶל מָקוֹם אֶחָד' אֶלָּא מִכָּאן שֶׁהֶחֱזִיק
מוּעָט אֶת הַמְּרֻבֶּה

**In human practice, a man empties a full vessel into an empty one;
does he ever empty a full vessel into a full vessel? The world was
water in water and yet you say '[Let the waters be gathered] unto
one place!' From this [we learn] that the little held the much.**

The text being discussed here is 'Let the waters be gathered unto one
place.' But how can that be possible if the whole world consisted of water.
From this, however, a new principle emerges: A small area was able to
encompass a very large amount. That is to say, the area we now call the
ocean was able to encompass all the waters that were in the world in some
miraculous way.

There now follow a series of biblical illustrations that show that this
phenomenon repeats itself many times.

וְדִכְוָתַהּ 'וַיַּקְהִלוּ מֹשֶׁה וְאַהֲרֹן' (במדבר כ, י) אָמַר רַבִּי חֲנִינָא כִּמְלוֹא פִּי כְּבָרָה קְטַנָּה
הָיְתָה בָּהּ וְכָל יִשְׂרָאֵל עוֹמְדִין בָּהּ אֶלָּא מִכָּאן שֶׁהֶחֱזִיק מוּעָט אֶת הַמְּרֻבֶּה

**Similarly, 'Moses and Aaron assembled the congregation in front of
the rock' (Numbers 20:10). R. Ḥanina said: It was only the size of a
small sieve, yet all Israel stood there?! From this [we learn] that the
little held the much.**

R. Ḥanina had a tradition that the area in front of Miriam's Well was the
size of the mouth of a small sieve. But how could all of Israel, 600,000 of
them, stand in such a small space! Tradition even has it that a person
regarded himself as though he were standing on the rock. The explanation
is that a miracle happened – a small area was able to encompass a greater
amount.

וְדִכְוָתַהּ 'וַיֹּאמֶר ה' אֶל מֹשֶׁה וְאֶל אַהֲרֹן קְחוּ לָכֶם' (שמות ט, ח) אָמַר רַ' הוּנָא וְכִי
חָפְנוֹ שֶׁל מֹשֶׁה הָיְתָה מַחֲזֶקֶת שְׁמוֹנָה קְמָצִים אַתְמְהָא לָא דָּמֵי הַהוּא דְּחָפַן

לְהַהוּא דְּקָמֵץ הַהוּא דְּחָפַן תְּרֵי מֵהַהוּא דְּקָמֵץ וּכְתִיב 'וּזְרָקוֹ מֹשֶׁה' נִמְצֵאת חָפְנוֹ
שֶׁל מֹשֶׁה הָיְתָה מַחֲזֶקֶת שְׁמוֹנָה קְמָצִים אֶלָּא מִכָּאן שֶׁהֶחֱזִיק מוּעָט אֶת הַמְרֻבֶּה

**Similarly, 'Then the Lord said to Moses and Aaron, "Each of you
take [handfuls of soot from the kiln, and let Moses throw it towards
the sky in the sight of Pharaoh...]"' (Exodus 9:8). R. Huna said:
Could one fistful of Moses contain eight handfuls! I am amazed! For
a fistful is not the same as a handful, one fistful equalling two
handfuls, yet it is written, 'and let Moses throw *it*' – thus one fistful
of Moses actually contained eight handfuls! From this [we learn] that
the little held the much.**

There is a difference between חופן (*hofen*), a handful, and קומץ (*kometz*), a
fistful. A handful contains twice as much as a fistful. Since Moses and
Aaron each took two handfuls of the soot, as they were ordered to do by
God, together they held four handfuls = eight fistfuls. We are then told
that Moses threw all the soot (referred to by the singular, *it*) into the air
and throwing is usually done with one hand, clenched as a fist. The only
possible explanation can be that the fist of Moses was able to hold four
handfuls – an instance of a small area encompassing much more.

וְדִכְוָתָהּ אָמַר רַ' יוֹסֵי בַּר' חֲלַפְתָּא 'אֹרֶךְ הֶחָצֵר מֵאָה בָאַמָּה וְרֹחַב חֲמִשִּׁים
בַּחֲמִשִּׁים' (שם כז, יח) וְכָל יִשְׂרָאֵל עוֹמְדִים שָׁם אִתְמָהָא אֶלָּא מִכָּאן שֶׁהֶחֱזִיק
מוּעָט אֶת הַמְרֻבֶּה

**Similarly R. Jose b. R. Halafta observed: 'The length of the court
shall be a hundred cubits' (Exodus 27:18), yet all Israel stood there!
From this [we learn] that the little held the much.**

The length of the court was one hundred cubits; it included the tabernacle
which itself was fifty cubits in length. The width of the court was fifty
cubits, which meant that the tabernacle was fifty by fifty. Yet, at the time
of the dedication of the Tabernacle (Lev. 8:3-4), it could accommodate all
Israel! This illustration is similar to the ones above. How was it possible
for all of Israel to gather in the Tabernacle court? Because, miraculously,
a small area encompassed a greater amount.

וְדִכְוָתָהּ 'וַיֹּאמֶר יְהוֹשֻׁעַ אֶל בְּנֵי יִשְׂרָאֵל גֹּשׁוּ הֵנָּה וְגוֹ'' (יהושע ג, ט) רַ' הוּנָא אָמַר
זָקְפָן בֵּין שְׁנֵי בַּדֵּי הָאָרוֹן אָמַר רַבִּי אַחָא בְּרַבִּי חֲנִינָא סָמְכָן בֵּין שְׁנֵי בַּדֵּי הָאָרוֹן
רַבָּנָן אָמְרִין צִמְצְמָן בֵּין שְׁנֵי בַּדֵּי הָאָרוֹן

Similarly, 'And Joshua said unto the Children of Israel: Come

hither...' (Joshua 3:9). R. Huna said: He made them stand between the staves of the ark. R. Aḥa b. R. Ḥanina said: He crowded them between the staves of the ark. The Rabbis said: He squeezed them between the two staves of the ark.

How did Joshua arrange for the Children of Israel to cross the Jordan and at the same time pass through the staves of the ark? R. Huna says that they walked through erect and not crowded. R. Aḥa said that the miracle was even greater. As they approached the staves they were able to be seated in a comfortable position, each in accordance with his rank. The Rabbis said they were crowded together without space between them. That is why it says in the Joshua text גשו, *goshu*, meaning, 'come close together.'

אָמַר לָהֶן יְהוֹשֻׁעַ מִמַּה שֶּׁהֶחֱזִיקוּ שְׁנֵי בַדֵּי הָאָרוֹן אֶתְכֶם אַתֶּם יוֹדְעִים שֶׁשְּׁכִינָתוֹ שֶׁל הַקָּדוֹשׁ בָּרוּךְ הוּא בֵּינֵיכֶם הָדָא הוּא דִכְתִיב 'וַיֹּאמֶר יְהוֹשֻׁעַ בְּזֹאת תֵּדְעוּן כִּי אֵל חַי בְּקִרְבְּכֶם' (שם שם, י) וְאַף בִּירוּשָׁלַיִם דִּתְנַן עוֹמְדִים צְפוּפִים וּמִשְׁתַּחֲוִים רְוָחִים

Joshua said to them, 'From the fact that the two staves of the ark were able to encompass you, you should know that the Presence of the Holy One, blessed be He, is among you,' as it is written, 'And Joshua said to them: "By this you shall know that the living God is among you' (Joshua 3:10). [Such a miracle occurred] also in Jerusalem, as it was taught in a *mishnah*, 'They stood pressed together, yet, when they prostrated themselves each had ample space.'

By virtue of the fact that all of you have been accommodated in this small space, you should realize that a miracle has been wrought by the Divine Presence. This is another example of 'the little encompassing the much.'

The source referred to for the miracle in the Temple in Jerusalem is Tractate Avot 5:5. Since the Temple was the permanent home of the Ark, it is entirely appropriate that mention should be made of it here.

רַבִּי שְׁמוּאֵל בְּרַבִּי חָנָא בְּשֵׁם רַבִּי אַחָא אָמַר אַרְבַּע אַמּוֹת לְכָל אֶחָד וְאַמָּה מִכָּל צַד כְּדֵי שֶׁלֹּא יְהֵא אָדָם שׁוֹמֵעַ תְּפִלָּתוֹ שֶׁל חֲבֵרוֹ וְאַף לֶעָתִיד לָבוֹא כֵּן שֶׁנֶּאֱמַר 'בָּעֵת הַהִיא יִקְרְאוּ לִירוּשָׁלַיִם כִּסֵּא ה' וְגוֹ'' (ירמיה ג, יז)

R. Samuel b. R. Jonah said: [In the Temple] each had four cubits, and a cubit space on each side, so that none should hear his neighbor's prayer. And in the future, too, it shall be thus, as it is said, 'At that time they shall call Jerusalem "Throne of the Lord" [and all nations shall assemble there]' (Jeremiah 3:17).

Four cubits, approximately six feet, is considered the measure of 'personal
space,' since when a person prostrates himself on the ground he takes up
that much space. R. Samuel is, in fact, extending the scope of the miracle
in the Temple; not only could each worshipper prostrate himself in comfort, there was even space on each side to ensure his privacy.

The same will happen in the future when all the nations will come to
Jerusalem; the Temple courtyard will be able to contain the whole of mankind! Note that in the verse cited from Jeremiah, 'At that time they shall
call Jerusalem "Throne of the Lord" and all nations shall assemble there,'
the Hebrew for 'assemble' is וְנִקְווּ, *ve-nikvu*, from the same root as *yikkovu*,
in our text in Genesis. Then, too, the principle will apply – the small area
will encompass the greater number.

רַבִּי יוֹחָנָן סָלִיק לְמִשְׁאַל לְמִשְׁאָל שְׁלָמֵהּ דְּר' חֲנִינָא אַשְׁכְּחֵהּ דְּיָתֵב וְדָרֵשׁ בְּהָדֵין פְּסוּק
'בָּעֵת הַהִיא יִקְרְאוּ לִירוּשָׁלַיִם כִּסֵּא ה'' אָמַר לוֹ רַבִּי וְכִי מַחֲזֶקֶת הִיא יְרוּשָׁלַיִם
כִּסֵּא ה' אֲמַר לֵהּ הַקָּדוֹשׁ בָּרוּךְ הוּא אֲמַר לַהּ הַאֲרִיכִי הַרְחִיבִי קַבְּלִי אוּכְלוּסַיִךְ הֲדָא
הוּא דִכְתִיב 'הַרְחִיבִי מְקוֹם אָהֳלֵךְ' (ישעיה נד, ב) לָמָה 'כִּי יָמִין וּשְׂמֹאול תִּפְרֹצִי וְגוֹ'''
(שם שם, ג)

**R. Joḥanan went to inquire after the well-being of R. Ḥanina, and
he found him sitting and lecturing on this verse: 'At that time they
shall call Jerusalem "Throne of the Lord" [and all nations shall
assemble there]' (Jeremiah 3:17). Said he to him: 'Rabbi, can it
[Jerusalem] then hold "Throne of the Lord" [i.e., all the nations]?!'
[R. Ḥanina] answered him: 'The Holy One, blessed be He, will say
to it [Jerusalem], "Become longer! Become wider! And receive your
populations!" as it is said, "Enlarge the site of your tent" (Isaiah 54:2).
Why? "For you shall spread out to the right and the left"' (ibid. v. 3).**

The difference between this section and the former is the teaching that in
the future Jerusalem will not have to expand miraculously on the principle
of the 'small encompassing the much,' but rather Jerusalem will expand
its borders physically. 'Enlarge the site of your tent' means 'enlarge your
borders.' (Malbim)

* * *

Seed Thoughts

That which has been described as a miracle of 'the little sustaining the
much' may, indeed, be regarded as a miracle from the material point of
view, but, in terms of the spiritual life and even in terms of human nature,

it is not really a miracle at all. It is a principle of human behavior and human potentiality. In this respect we ought to change the translation and render it as the principle of the 'minority sustaining the majority.' Looked upon in this light, we recognize this phenomenon as having occurred time and again in human history.

Who was responsible for Greek civilization other than a handful of Athenians, great personalities in philosophy, science, and art, who lifted up the masses of unlearned Greeks and their barbarian slaves to a status that they themselves had never earned.

The first chapter of Tractate Avot in the Mishnah lists the handful of great men, from Moses to the Men of the Great Assembly, who were responsible for the transmission of the Torah tradition that literally created the Jewish people anew. Again, it was a minority that sustained the majority.

No revolution ever really starts with the masses. It is sparked by a dedicated few, selflessly devoted to an ideal or purpose for the achievement of which they are ready to give their lives. Their energy is so overwhelming and so contagious that it is enough to inspire a mass following that will last so long as the leadership is capable of maintaining its inspiration. This was the story behind the Maccabean revolution, the French, the American, the Marxist – indeed of all sorts of national and religious re-awakenings. It is always the minority that sustains the majority.

This ought to be a source of hope to all who struggle for human freedom and dignity. There is no reason to despair because the whole world has not been won over to the cause of truth. The whole world is not necessary. Only a dedicated few prepared to make the necessary sacrifices are an indispensable ingredient. There will always be the many ready to follow the dedicated few.

This ought also to come as a welcome teaching to the Jewish people. The Jewish people has always been a minority in the world, with a covenant and a mission to mankind that have always appeared to be too overwhelming for such a small entity. But a Jewish people committed to the ideals of the prophets and the obligation to become a kingdom of priests and a holy nation could indeed change the world if they were truly dedicated. It is always 'the minority that sustains the majority,' the 'little that encompasses the much.'

This should also bring a message to the lone individual fighting a seemingly hopeless battle for the moral life against an indifferent society. Even a minority of one can be a powerful influence in motivating and sustaining the many.

This principle of the 'little' or the 'minority' sustaining 'the much' or 'the majority' was deeply imbedded into the very nature of the world, when the universe of water within water was gathered into one place.

It was restated again and again in the experience of Moses and Joshua. It is the vital experience of human faith.

* * *

Additional Commentary

Zekafan, and so forth

The expressions *zekafan*, *semakhan*, and *tzimtzeman*, used in this *midrash* in connection with the text from Joshua, should be taken metaphorically. It is the purpose of Torah to eliminate jealousy, lust, and false pursuit of honor that destroy human beings. In opposition to honor, *kavod*, the *midrash* says *zekafan*, that the Torah will lift up those who learn it and give them all the honor they will ever need. In opposition to jealousy, *kinah*, the *midrash* says *tzemadan* (an alternative reading for *semakhan*). The Torah teaches everyone to know and value his place and not to desire that which belongs to his neighbor. In opposition to lust, *ta'avah*, the Torah teaches everyone to discipline himself, *tzimtzeman*, to practice austerity and make do with what he has. (*Yefei To'ar*)

*

So that none should hear his neighbor's prayer

From this we can derive that a public form of liturgy took place even during the days of the Second Temple. (*Yefei To'ar*)

Parashah Five, Midrash Eight

וַיִּקְרָא אֱלֹהִים לַיַּבָּשָׁה אֶרֶץ לָמָּה נִקְרָא שְׁמָהּ אֶרֶץ שֶׁרָצְתָה לַעֲשׂוֹת רְצוֹן קוֹנָהּ

'And God called the dry land *eretz* – Earth' (Genesis 1:10). **Why was it called *eretz*? Because it desired [*ratzetah*] to do the will [*ratzon*] of its owner.**

Eretz can be understood as deriving from the root רוץ, *rutz,* as which it will mean 'I will run,' or from the root רצה, *ratzah,* when it will mean 'I will want' or 'desire.' Both indicate a preparedness to do God's will.

רַבִּי נָתָן בְּשֵׁם רַ' אַחָא וְר' בֶּרֶכְיָה בְּשֵׁם רַבִּי יִצְחָק אָמַר 'אֲנִי אֵל שַׁדַּי' (בראשית יז,
א) אֲנִי שֶׁאָמַרְתִּי לַשָּׁמַיִם וָאָרֶץ דַּי שֶׁאִלְמָלֵא כֵן הָיוּ מוֹתְחִים וְהוֹלְכִין עַד עַכְשָׁו

R. Natan said in the name of R. Aḥa, and R. Berekhiah said in the name of R. Isaac: 'I am El Shaddai' (Genesis 17:1) – It was I who said to heaven and earth 'Dai!' [Enough!], because otherwise they would have continued to expand even until now.

The name 'El Shaddai,' which is translated in non-Jewish English translations of the Bible as 'Almighty God,' is understood here as meaning 'I am God, who said "Dai!"' An indication of heaven and earth's love of God was their desire to continue the process of creation and would have continued it indefinitely had not God intervened and put a stop to it.

וּלְמִקְוֵה הַמַּיִם קָרָא יַמִּים אָמַר ר' יוֹסֵי בַּר' חֲלַפְתָּא וַהֲלוֹא יָם אֶחָד הוּא וּמַה
תַּלְמוּד לוֹמַר 'יַמִּים' אֶלָּא אֵינוֹ דוֹמֶה טַעַם דָּג הָעוֹלֶה מֵעַכּוֹ לָעוֹלֶה מִצִּידוֹן
וְלָעוֹלֶה מֵאַסְפַּמְיָא

'And the gathering waters He called *yamim* – Seas' (Genesis 1:10). **R. Jose b. R. Ḥalafta said: But surely there is only one sea? Why then does it say 'Seas'? [The reason is] because the taste of a fish caught at Acre is not the same as that of one caught at Sidon or Aspamia.**

The question arises because the word for the gathering of waters, *mikveh,* is written in the singular, while the word *yamim,* seas, is in plural. The answer that fish from different places have a different taste even though they are the very same breed of fish implies that although there

205

is only one body of water in the world, that is, the sea, various localities have unique characteristics.

* * *

Seed Thoughts

It is a beautiful thought to realize that the root of the Hebrew word for earth, *Eretz*, has the meaning of loving God and running to do His will. But, if the earth, by its very definition, wants and loves God, man's mandate should be to love the earth and then, by implication, to love God as well.

This business of loving the earth is no longer a matter of rhetoric. Concern for the environment has now become a priority in all civilized nations. The earth was meant to be exploited for man's use, but not for his destruction. What sense does it make to use the blessings of the earth to develop a paper mill, for example, and allow its waste to pollute the rivers. In the long run we are destroying ourselves, because the earth is man's habitat.

It should be possible for public and private jurisdictions to develop a policy that will *use* the earth and not *abuse* it, cultivate it, but also respect it.

This is what it means to love the earth in our day. We will thus be helping the earth love God as well.

* * *

Additional Commentary

Shaddai
If both heaven and earth responded to God's word, heaven should also have been given a name like *Eretz*, meaning favorable to God. However, heaven is by definition closer to spiritual things and earth is closer to material things. It is as though earth has to make a special effort that merits recognition. (*Tiferet Tzion*)

*

Aspamia
Some say that Aspamia refers to that body of land that we today call Spain. It would thus refer to the Atlantic ocean in addition to the Mediterranean. Others render Aspamia as referring to Pamias, a town north of Israel. (Theodore, quoted by Mirkin)

Parashah Five, Midrash Nine

וַיֹּאמֶר אֱלֹהִים תַּדְשֵׁא הָאָרֶץ תְּנֵי בְּשֵׁם רַ' נָתָן שְׁלֹשָׁה נִכְנְסוּ לַדִּין וְאַרְבָּעָה יָצְאוּ
מְחֻיָּבִין וְאֵלּוּ הֵן אָדָם וְחַוָּה וְנָחָשׁ נִכְנְסוּ לַדִּין וְנִתְקַלְלָה הָאָרֶץ עִמָּהֶן שֶׁנֶּאֱמַר
'אֲרוּרָה הָאֲדָמָה בַּעֲבוּרֶךְ' (בראשית ג, יז) שֶׁתְּהֵא מַעֲלָה לְךָ דְּבָרִים אֲרוּרִים כְּגוֹן
יִתוּשִׁים וּזְבוּבִין פַּרְעוֹשִׁין אָמַר רַ' יִצְחָק מִגְדַלָאָה אַף הֵן יֶשׁ בָּהֶן הֲנָאָה

'And God said: Let the earth sprout vegetation...' (Genesis 1:11). It was taught in the name of R. Natan: Three entered for judgment yet four came out guilty and these are they: Adam and Eve and the serpent entered for judgment, whereas the earth was ruined [punished] with them, as it is written, 'Cursed be the ground because of you' (Genesis 3:17), which means that it would produce accursed things for him [Adam] such as gnats, insects, and fleas. R. Isaac of Magdala said: In them, too, there is benefit.

R. Natan seems to feel that the earth was punished because of Adam and Eve's sin in eating from the Tree of Knowledge at the instigation of the serpent. The earth was thus cursed in so far as man is concerned, in that it produces insects that disturb his comfort. The Theodore-Albeck edition of *Bereishit Rabbah* has the reading ותעלה לו גמל, 'and it will produce a camel,' presumably meaning that the earth would produce pests as big as a camel, thus making the punishment be even more striking.

R. Isaac comments that everything created has a purpose, as indeed the Talmud assures us (Tractate Shabbat 47b), and that the production of the gnats and insects cannot be seen as a punishment.

However, according to R. Natan, why was the earth punished?

וְלָמָּה נִתְקַלְלָה רַ' יְהוּדָה בַּר' (שמעון) [שָׁלוֹם] וְרַ' פִּינְחָס בַּר' יְהוּדָה בַּר' (שמעון)
[שָׁלוֹם] אָמַר שֶׁעָבְרָה עַל הַצִּוּוּי שֶׁכַּךְ אָמַר לָהּ הַקָּדוֹשׁ בָּרוּךְ הוּא 'תַּדְשֵׁא הָאָרֶץ
דֶּשֶׁא וְגו'' מַה הַפְּרִי נֶאֱכָל אַף הָעֵץ נֶאֱכָל וְהִיא לֹא עָשְׂתָה כֵּן אֶלָּא 'וַתּוֹצֵא הָאָרֶץ
דֶּשֶׁא וְגו'' הַפְּרִי נֶאֱכָל וְהָעֵץ אֵינוֹ נֶאֱכָל רַ' פִּינְחָס אָמַר אַף הוֹסִיפָה עַל הַצִּוּוּי
סָמְכָה לַעֲשׂוֹת רְצוֹן בּוֹרְאָהּ 'עֵץ עֹשֶׂה פְּרִי' אֲפִלּוּ אִילָנֵי סְרָק עָשׂוּ פֵּרוֹת

Now why was the earth punished? R. Judah b. R. (Simon) [Shalom] and R. Pinḥas [disagreed on this matter]. R. Judah b. R. (Simon) [Shalom] said: Because it disobeyed God's command. The Holy

One, blessed be He said thus: 'Let the earth sprout vegetation...' – Just as the fruit can be eaten, so too should the tree be edible. It [the earth] did not do so, but 'The earth brought forth...' (Genesis 1:12): the fruit could be eaten but not the tree. R. Pinḥas said: It [the earth] exceeded His command, thinking to do the will of its Creator: [It brought forth] 'trees making fruit' – even fruitless trees yielded fruit.

R. Judah and R. Pinḥas disagree on the reason for the earth's punishment. R. Judah said the earth was cursed because it transgressed the specific commandment directed to it. Genesis 1:11 reads in full 'And God said: Let the earth sprout vegetation: seed-bearing plants, fruit trees of every kind on earth that bear fruit with the seed in it.' R. Judah points out that the order to produce fruit trees meant that the tree should have the same taste as its fruit and the earth disobeyed the order, for the text continues, 'The earth brought forth... trees of every kind bearing fruit,' i.e., the taste was only in the fruit. Therefore, the earth deserved punishment.

R. Pinḥas, however, believes that some trees do have the same taste as their fruit (such as, according to the Talmud in Tractate Sukkah 35a, the etrog tree) and that that was not the earth's sin. He said that the problem was that the earth added to the commandment much more than it had been commanded. It so delighted to fulfill the will of its Creator of a tree yielding fruit, that even the barren trees that had not been commanded to produce fruit (1:11) did indeed produce fruit in those days.

עַל דַּעְתֵּהּ דְּרַ' יְהוּדָה בֵּר שִׁמְעוֹן נִיחָא אֶלָּא עַל דַּעְתֵּהּ דְּרַ' פִּינְחָס לָמָּה נִתְקַלְלָה אֶלָּא כְּאִינָשׁ דְּאָמַר יְהוֹן לִיטִין בִּזַּיָּא דְּהָדֵין מְנִיק

According to R. Judah's view [the punishment] is understandable, but according to R. Pinḥas' view, why was it cursed? It is as one might say: 'Cursed be the breasts that suckled such a one as this.'

From the point of view of R. Judah we can understand why the earth was cursed. It transgressed a commandment. But from the point of view of R. Pinḥas, that it did even more than commanded, why was it cursed? This can be answered in terms of the folk-saying: 'May the breasts be cursed that nursed this one.' The mother is cursed even though she may have been an outstanding person, because she had an indirect share of responsibility for her child, having brought him to life. Similarly, the earth is the nourisher of man and has to bear a share of the responsibility for man's evil doing even though she was only minimally contributory to it.

* * *

Seed Thoughts

Concern for the environment is not a twentieth-century phenomenon. As we can see from the *midrash*, man's need for the environment and his responsibility for it date from his very creation.

Is the earth cursed or is man cursed? The use of the term 'cursed' is meant to indicate the difficulties and challenges that face man's existence, particularly in his confrontation with nature.

When the world was created, it was intended that the earth yield of its abundance easily and swiftly. As a result of Adam's sin, the timing of this abundance was changed and it required struggle and toil on the part of man. This is what Scripture means by the term 'curse.'

The amazing story of man's development is the history of how the curse was overcome. Commenting on the verse about Noah, 'This one shall comfort us in our work and in the toil of our hands which comes from the ground which the Lord has cursed' (Genesis 5:29), Rashi makes the point that Noah invented the first plough. If, indeed, the technological revolution begins with Noah, it is certainly man's greatest accomplishment to date. In effect, it has removed the curse from the earth and transformed it into a blessing.

In this connection, notice should be taken of a new environmental revolution in our day that seems to have as its goal the belittling of technology and the return to some kind of more primitive lifestyle. This is a major error of judgment. What has actually happened is that the technological revolution has been too successful.

The great corporations of midwest America did not have as their goal the production of acid rain. Their goal was to produce a product that would meet the needs of the masses of people and make a profit within the structure of a capitalist economy. The fact that a consequence of this productivity is the creation of acid rain is a very serious matter. The solution is not to stop technology, which would be a disservice to the world, but to work out ways and means of protecting the environment. It should be possible for man's unique technology to save the environment as well.

Is the world cursed or is man cursed? The answer here is the same as in most things. It depends on what we do.

* * *

Additional Commentary

This is the explanation. There are three types of people in the world – the completely righteous, the completely wicked, and the in-betweeners.

Nothing will ever change or divert the completely righteous. Nothing will ever change or divert the completely wicked. The in-betweeners, however, may start in a very corrupt way, but they have the possibility of redemption and rehabilitation. Since the Bible often compares man to a tree, the present discussion is symbolized by three trees. The etrog is a tree that not only produces a fruit that is edible, but the tree itself is edible. The etrog, therefore, symbolizes the completely righteous, body and spirit completely holy to God. The pepper tree is one that produces a fruit, but the tree itself is not edible. The taste of the pepper tree is completely bitter. This tree therefore symbolizes the completely wicked, rebellious in body and spirit. The in-betweeners are the great majority and for that reason in the case of most trees the taste of the fruit and the tree are not alike. (*Tiferet Tzion*)

Parashah Five, Midrash Ten

וַיְהִי עֶרֶב וַיְהִי בֹקֶר יוֹם שְׁלִישִׁי יוֹם שֶׁנִּבְרְאוּ בּוֹ גִּבּוֹרִים הֵיךְ מַה דְּאַתְּ אָמַר
'שָׁלִשִׁים וּקְרוּאִים רֹכְבֵי סוּסִים כֻּלָּם' (יחזקאל כג, כג)

'And there was evening and there was morning, a third day [*shelishi*]' (Genesis 1:13) – the day in which strong ones were created, as it says, 'Captains (*shalishim*) and councillors, all of them riding upon horses' (Ezekiel 23:23).

The question motivating this *midrash* appears to be: Why is the third day described as *shelishi*, meaning 'third,' and not *sheloshah*, meaning day three. This is similar to *ehad* being used for day one, rather than *rishon*, which would mean the first day. In the case of *sheni*, the second day is a continuation of the first and therefore second might be appropriate. But the third day is not a continuity for it describes the earth in general.

The word *shalishim* bears a close resemblance to the word *shelishi*, which is why the verse is so appropriate. The question of *shelishi* had to be answered in terms of something created that was specifically new and therefore was interpreted as referring to iron, which was created on the third day together with the mountains where it is deposited. Iron was among the 'strong ones' created on the third day.

כֵּיוָן שֶׁנִּבְרָא הַבַּרְזֶל הִתְחִילוּ הָאִילָנוֹת מְרַתְּתִים אָמַר לָהֶן מַה לָכֶם מְרַתְּתִים עֵץ
מִכֶּם אַל יִכָּנֵס בִּי וְאֵין אֶחָד מִכֶּם נִזּוֹק

When iron was created, the trees began to tremble. [The iron] said to them, 'Why do you tremble? Let none of you[r wood] enter me, and not one of you shall be harmed.'

The trees realized that the iron would be used to make the axes that would cut them down. Therefore they trembled in fear. The iron, however, pointed out to them that axes need hafts to be used and if the trees refused to be used as hafts they would have nothing to fear. In modern terminology we would say that destructive strength of the iron depends upon its being manipulated by man.

* * *

211

Seed Thoughts

Interpreting the parable of the wood and the iron takes many forms. The more prevalent view seems to be that it resembles the verse, 'Your destroyers shall come from within you.' If the wood hadn't joined with the iron the trees would have had nothing to fear. The Jewish people have to fear most when their own people join their enemies, whether these are to be found in the new religious cults or the anti-Jewish New Left or the anti-Israel bandwagon. Jewish alienation that reaches its ultimate in joining the forces of anti-Jewish political or religious action or even the alienation that leads to indifference, assimilation, or intermarriage, or the other forms of Jewish erosion, is the greatest danger to the Jewish body politic.

Another interpretation renders this parable within the framework of sin and repentance. The tree represents man and the iron represents the evil inclination. The human being always fears that the evil inclination will destroy him. This teaching offers man the hope that he can overcome it. The evil inclination depends upon man's cooperation. First it appears as a passerby, than it is accepted as a guest in the household, and then it takes over as proprietor of the house. But even in the latter case the Almighty has created an antidote in the form of repentance, which was created before the world and is therefore beyond nature and capable of confronting and surmounting the evil inclination. Even when man is already in the grasp of the *yetzer ha-ra*, he still has the power through repentance to overcome the evil inclination and to climb the ladder that leads to heaven – May our Father and King so privilege us. (*Tiferet Tzion*)

It seems to me, however, that this parable has to be seen within a much larger context. Man is a tool-making animal, a manipulator whose mind is capable of creative invention, but who is also capable of making moral decisions. We make the mistake of identifying the bomb with the destruction that it produces, or the printed word with its sometimes pornographic product, or television with the violence it often shows. But in all these cases it is man who makes the crucial decisions. The only thing we have to fear is fear itself; that is to say, sinful man is our only threat or enemy. It is in our hands to use properly not only the iron of the world or the wood, but all of the energy resources. Righteousness is the only true goal and when justice obtains neither the iron, or the wood, or the human being nor the Jewish people will ever have any reason to fear.

* * *

Additional Commentary

Gibborim

What can it possibly mean that on the third day, the 'strong,' *gibborim*, were created. After all, we know for a fact that on the third day trees, grasses, and vegetation were created. But I remember a passage in *Midrash Konnen* that I studied in my youth, and there it stated that on the third day trees and vegetation were created, at which point the cedars of Lebanon noticed that they were taller than all other creatures. The trees immediately became arrogant. When the Holy One, blessed be He, noticed their arrogance, He created iron in opposition to them. This made the trees tremble, at which point He said, 'Let not your wood enter the iron and you have nothing to fear.' (RZWE)

*

Perhaps the reading should be not *gibborim*, but *gevohim*, meaning high or tall, and referring to the trees. (RDL)

*

In what respect does *gibborim* refer to *barzel*, iron. For one thing the strong men of war use iron either as sword or spear. However, it could be added that the creation of iron fits properly into the third day. For when the waters were gathered to one place and earth appeared, a natural process appeared whereby earth and air combined to (oxidize) produce metal and especially iron. Since the charioteers, known as *shalishim*, were taller or higher than anyone else, the text from Ezekiel was brought as proof-text. (RDL)

Parashah Six, Midrash One

וַיֹּאמֶר אֱלֹהִים יְהִי מְאֹרֹת (א, יד)

And God said: Let there be lights (1:14).

The verse then goes on to explain that the purpose of the lights was firstly to provide illumination and then to be a reminder of the festivals. R. Joḥanan now poses an interesting question. He is motivated by the fact that *me'orot* is written minus the *vav*, thereby giving the impression of being singular, and thus referring to one light or, by the verb *yehi*, which is also in the singular.

ר' יוֹחָנָן פָּתַח 'עָשָׂה יָרֵחַ לְמוֹעֲדִים' (תהלים קד, יט) אָמַר רַבִּי יוֹחָנָן לֹא נִבְרָא לְהָאִיר אֶלָּא גַּלְגַּל חַמָּה בִּלְבָד אִם כֵּן לָמָּה נִבְרֵאת לְבָנָה 'לְמוֹעֲדִים' כְּדֵי לְחַדֵּשׁ בְּחֶשְׁבּוֹנָהּ רָאשֵׁי חֳדָשִׁים וְשָׁנִים

R. Joḥanan began [his exposition] thus: 'He made the moon to mark the seasons' (Psalms 104:19). R. Joḥanan commented: The orb of the sun alone was created to give light. If so why was the moon created? 'For seasons' – in order to calculate thereby the sanctification of new months and years.

It is a well-known axiom of *midrash* that problems in understanding verses in the Torah can often be explained in the other Books of the Bible. Thus R. Joḥanan resorts to the verse in Psalms to help solve the problem. There was only one light created to provide illumination – the sun, which explains the use of the singular. As for the moon, says the Psalmist, its purpose was to establish the dates of the festivals, which are all fixed according to the lunar calendar.

רַבִּי שִׁילָה דִכְפַר תְּמַרְתָּא בְּשֵׁם רַ' יוֹחָנָן אָמַר אַף עַל פִּי שֶׁ'עָשָׂה יָרֵחַ לְמוֹעֲדִים' 'שֶׁמֶשׁ יָדַע מְבוֹאוֹ' (שם שם, שם) מִשֶּׁמֶשׁ יָדַע מְבוֹאוֹ אֵין מוֹנִין לַלְּבָנָה אֶלָּא מִשֶּׁתִּשְׁקַע הַחַמָּה

R. Shila of Kefar Temarta said in R. Joḥanan's name: Although 'He made the moon to mark the seasons,' even so, 'the sun knows

its coming' (ibid.); from the sun one knows [the month's] coming, for we count the beginning of the month only from sunset.

The entire verse reads, 'He made the moon to mark the seasons; the sun knows when to set.' The Hebrew for 'when to set' is *mevo'o*, which can also mean 'its coming,' that is, the coming of each festival, since the sun also plays a role in the calculation of the month. If the new moon is sighted at midday, the month does not begin until nightfall, that is, when the sun goes down. Days are counted by the moon but not hours, so that both the sun and the moon are required 'for seasons, for days, and for years.'

יוֹסְטִי חַבְרָא בְּשֵׁם רַבִּי בֶּרֶכְיָה אָמַר הֲרֵי הוּא אוֹמֵר 'וַיִּסְעוּ מֵרַעְמְסֵס בַּחֹדֶשׁ הָרִאשׁוֹן בַּחֲמִשָּׁה עָשָׂר לַחֹדֶשׁ' (במדבר לג, ג) וְאִם לַלְּבָנָה אַתָּה מוֹנֶה עַד כַּדּוּן לֵית לֵהּ אֶלָּא אַרְבַּע עֶשְׂרֵה מַטְמוֹעִין הֲוֵי אֵין מוֹנִין לַלְּבָנָה אֶלָּא מִשֶּׁתִּשְׁקַע הַחַמָּה

Justi Ḥavra said in R. Berekhiah's name: It is written, 'And they journeyed from Rameses in the first month, on the fifteenth day of the month' (Numbers 33:3). However, if you count by the moon, then so far there were only fourteen sunsets? Hence it follows that we only count according to the moon after sunset.

The question of exactly how the months and festivals are fixed according to the moon is clearly of great importance and Justi Ḥavra – he was called Ḥavra, the Aramaic of *Haver*, because of his great piety – brings the following proof that although the rising of the new moon fixes the first day of the month, that day starts only after sunset. The proof is from the account of the Exodus in the Book of Numbers. We know from tradition that in the month of Nisan before the first Passover the moon rose – known by the term *molad* – on a Wednesday at noon. The Jews left Egypt the day after the Paschal Lamb was slaughtered on the fourteenth of Nisan, thus the Torah describes the day of the Exodus as the fifteenth of Nisan, which was a Thursday. It follows that although the moon was sighted on Wednesday at noon, it was not Wednesday that was declared Rosh Ḥodesh, but Thursday. This proves that the first day of the lunar month is only calculated after nightfall.

רַבִּי עֲזַרְיָה בְּשֵׁם רַבִּי חֲנִינָא אָמַר לֹא נִבְרָא לְהָאִיר אֶלָּא גַּלְגַּל חַמָּה בִּלְבָד אִם כֵּן לָמָּה נִבְרֵאת לְבָנָה אֶלָּא מְלַמֵּד שֶׁצָּפָה הַקָּדוֹשׁ בָּרוּךְ הוּא שֶׁעֲתִידִין עוֹבְדֵי כּוֹכָבִים לַעֲשׂוֹתָן אֱלֹהוֹת אָמַר הַקָּדוֹשׁ בָּרוּךְ הוּא מָה אִם מִשֶּׁהֵן שְׁנַיִם מַכְחִישִׁין זֶה אֶת זֶה עוֹבְדֵי כּוֹכָבִים עוֹשִׂין אוֹתָן אֱלֹהוֹת אִלּוּ הָיוּ אֶחָד עַל אַחַת כַּמָּה וְכַמָּה

R. Azariah said in R. Ḥanina's name: The orb of the sun alone was

created to give light; yet if so, why was the moon created? Because the Holy One, blessed be He, foresaw that the peoples of the world would treat them as deities. Said the Holy One, blessed be He: 'If the two luminaries, which are opposed to each other, are worshipped as gods by the idolaters, how much more would they do so if there was only one!'

The first reason given for the creation of the moon is inadequate since the sun is also required to establish the festivals. Therefore a unique role still has to be found for the moon. R. Azariah provides an explanation. He argues that the moon's role is to try to prevent idolatry. Those who believe the sun is a god will change their mind when the sun goes down and the moon appears and vice versa. Some commentators interpret the contradiction between the sun and the moon as referring to eclipses – when the sun covers the moon and when the moon covers the sun. God foresaw that even though they were two they would still be worshipped, but at least their joint and contradictory existence would give true believers the argument against idolatry.

רַבִּי בֶּרֶכְיָה בְּשֵׁם רַ' סִימוֹן אָמַר שְׁנֵיהֶם נִבְרְאוּ לְהָאִיר שֶׁנֶּאֱמַר 'וְהָיוּ לִמְאֹרֹת' (בראשית א, טו) 'וַיִּתֵּן אֹתָם אֱלֹהִים בִּרְקִיעַ הַשָּׁמַיִם' (שם שם, יז). 'וְהָיוּ לְאֹתֹת' אֵלּוּ שַׁבָּתוֹת 'וּלְמוֹעֲדִים' אֵלּוּ שָׁלֹשׁ רְגָלִים 'וּלְיָמִים' אֵלּוּ רָאשֵׁי חֳדָשִׁים 'וְלְשָׁנִים' זֶה קִדּוּשׁ שָׁנִים

R. Berekhiah said in R. Simon's name: Both were created in order to give light, as it says, 'And they shall serve as lights' (Genesis 1:15); 'And God set them in the expanse of the sky' (ibid., verse 17); 'They shall serve as signs' (ibid., verse 14) refers to the sabbaths; 'and for seasons' (ibid.) refers to the three pilgrimage festivals; 'and for the days' (ibid.) refers to the New Moons; 'and years' (ibid.) refers to the sanctification of the years.

Neither the view of R. Joḥanan that the moon is for festivals or the view of R. Azariah that it is a factor in preventing idolatry are acceptable to R. Berekhiah. Rather both were meant to give light. We see this from the next verse where the words are in the plural: *ve-hayu* and *me'orot*. Furthermore, the continuation is explicit: 'And God set *them* in the expanse of the sky *to shine* upon the earth.' R. Berekhiah therefore interprets the verses differently. 'They shall serve as signs (*otot*)' means that they will serve to show us which day is the Sabbath, since Shabbat is also called an *ot*; 'seasons' (*mo'adim*) refers to the three pilgrim festivals,

Passover, Shavuot, and Sukkot, which are also called *mo'adim*; 'days' (*yamim*) is New Moons, since a month is called *ḥodesh yamim*; and 'years' refers to the New Year and the announcement of leap years. All these elements of the Jewish calendar are fixed in accordance with the cycles of the moon or the sun or both.

* * *

Seed Thoughts

The moon was not needed for light. The moon was only needed for festivals as the Psalmist puts it, 'He created the moon for festivals.' The text in Genesis says it even more forcefully, though it applies it also to the sun, 'They shall serve as signs for the seasons, for days, and for years.'

There probably are other people in the world who take these verses seriously, but none as seriously as the Sages of Israel. They looked upon these verses not as proclamations of fact, but as an order and so, based on it they created that most remarkable institution, the Jewish calendar.

The Jewish calendar is lunar, that is, based on the cycles of the moon. Sabbaths and festivals begin in the evening. That is already stated in the creation story: 'and there was evening and there was morning, a first day.'

What has made the design of the calendar so challenging and difficult is the fact that Judaism also requires a certain measure of conformity to the solar cycle. Passover must occur in the spring and Sukkot must occur in the fall. The calendar must therefore be intercalated with this in mind. This does not happen with the Moslems, who also use a lunar calendar only. Sometimes Ramadan can occur in the springtime and sometimes in the winter. It depends on the lunar calendar.

Another problem that the Jewish calendar had to resolve was the fact that Hoshanah Rabbah must never occur on Shabbat and Yom Kippur can never fall on a Friday or a Sunday.

These difficult problems were resolved by a process of intercalation when six times in every cycle of nineteen years a leap year is established in which one extra month is added. This brings the lunar year into conformity with the solar year.

The second resolution of the problem was to add an extra day to certain months in the form of a second-day Rosh Ḥodesh. This is not the place to elaborate on these calculations except to say that in the opinion of the writer in the *Jewish Encyclopedia*, the Jewish calendar is the most accurate of all the calendars that are known.

Our *midrash* claims that the moon is not needed for light but rather to serve as a sign of the seasons. In fact, although the light we see from the moon is a reflection of the sun's light, the moon provides a tremendous light, the light of renewal – חדש, *ḥadash* – at every month and at every reappearance.

Parashah Six, Midrash Two

לְךָ יוֹם אַף לְךָ לָיְלָה (תהלים עד, טז) לְךָ הַיּוֹם מְקַלֵּס וּלְךָ הַלַּיְלָה מְקַלֵּס מָה הַיּוֹם
בִּרְשׁוּתֶךָ אַף הַלַּיְלָה בִּרְשׁוּתֶךָ

'The day is Yours, the night also' (Psalms. 74:16) – the day gives praise to You and the night gives praise to You. Just as the day is under Your control, so too is the night under Your control.

This *midrash* continues the discussion that started in the previous one and indirectly provides another answer to the question why the two great lights were necessary since we know that it is only the sun that is the source of light and that the moon is merely a reflector.

In true midrashic style, a solution is sought from another scriptural source, in this case, Psalm 74. That psalm lists many acts of creation in the form of active verbs: 'It was you who drove back the sea... who smashed the heads of the monsters' (verse 13), 'It was You who crushed...' (verse 14), 'It was You who released...' (verse 15). The sequence is then interrupted by the verse that begins this *midrash*, 'The day is Yours, the night also,' after which the Psalm returns to it original style, 'It was you who set in place the orb of the sun.'

Why the interruption? The change in style seems to imply that the psalm is not just listing God's creation when it comes to night and day. Our *midrash* now proceeds to offer an interpretation. The first is praise. Night and day are personified as praising God. This follows the idea expressed in Psalm 19, 'Day to day makes utterance, night to night speaks out.' (*Ha-Midrash ha-Mevo'ar*)

Another interpretation of the *midrash* focuses on the word אף – *af*, 'also' or 'even.' That day is in God's jurisdiction is understandable because day is usually associated with things that are good, but night is associated with darkness and terror. That, too, however, is in God's domain and merits our praise.

However, this interpretation seems inadequate since praise is not an act of creation and does not fit in with the general context of the psalm. (*Yefei To'ar*) It is humans who give praise, and so the *midrash* continues along that line.

בְּשָׁעָה שֶׁאַתָּה עוֹשֶׂה לָנוּ נִסִּים בַּיּוֹם 'לְךָ יוֹם' וּבְשָׁעָה שֶׁאַתָּה עוֹשֶׂה לָנוּ נִסִּים בַּלַּיְלָה 'אַף לְךָ לָיְלָה' בְּשָׁעָה שֶׁאַתָּה עוֹשֶׂה לָנוּ נִסִּים בַּיּוֹם אָנוּ אוֹמְרִים לְפָנֶיךָ שִׁירָה בַיּוֹם וּבְשָׁעָה שֶׁאַתָּה עוֹשֶׂה לָנוּ נִסִּים בַּלַּיְלָה אָנוּ אוֹמְרִים לְפָנֶיךָ שִׁירָה בַלַּיְלָה

When You perform miracles for us by day, 'The day is Yours' and when You perform miracles for us by night, 'the night also.' When You perform miracles for us by day we utter song before You in daytime, and when You perform miracles for us by night, we utter song to You at night.

The *midrash* now continues to supply examples of this notion.

עָשִׂיתָ לָנוּ נִסִּים בַּיּוֹם וְאָמַרְנוּ לְפָנֶיךָ שִׁירָה בַיּוֹם 'וַתָּשַׁר דְּבוֹרָה וּבָרָק בֶּן אֲבִינֹעַם בַּיּוֹם וְגוֹ'' (שופטים ה, א) עָשִׂיתָ לָנוּ נִסִּים בַּלַּיְלָה וְאָמַרְנוּ לְפָנֶיךָ שִׁירָה בַלַּיְלָה 'הַשִּׁיר יִהְיֶה לָכֶם כְּלֵיל הִתְקַדֶּשׁ חָג' (ישעיה ל, כט)

You performed miracles for us by day, and we uttered song to You by day, thus, 'On that *day* Deborah and Barak the son of Avinoam sang' (Judges 5:1). You performed miracles for us by night and we uttered song to You by night: 'For you, there shall be singing as on a *night* when a festival is hallowed' (Isaiah 30:29).

The meaning of the verse from Isaiah is that a celebration would be held upon the defeat of Sennacherib, which would be as festive as the eve of the departure from Egypt. When Sennacherib besieged Jerusalem in the days of King Hezekiah, God performed a miracle for the Jews and 'that night an angel of the Lord went out and struck down one hundred and eighty-five thousand in the Assyrian camp, and the following morning they were all dead corpses' (II Kings 19:35). Since the miracle took place at night, the celebration of it and the song of praise to Him who wrought it would also be at night.

לְךָ נָאֶה לוֹמַר שִׁירָה בַיּוֹם לְךָ נָאֶה לוֹמַר שִׁירָה בַּלַּיְלָה לָמָּה שֶׁ'אַתָּה הֲכִינוֹתָ מָאוֹר וָשָׁמֶשׁ' (תהלים שם, שם) וְאַתָּה עָשִׂיתָ אֶת שְׁנֵי הַמְּאוֹרוֹת שֶׁנֶּאֱמַר 'וַיַּעַשׂ אֱלֹהִים אֶת שְׁנֵי הַמְּאֹרֹת הַגְּדֹלִים וְגוֹ'' (בראשית א, טז)

To You it is becoming to utter song by day and by night. Why is this so? Because 'It was You who set in place the orb of the sun' (Psalms 74:16) and You made the two luminaries, as it is written 'God made the two great lights' (Genesis 1:16).

Thus the lights have not only a physical purpose but a spiritual one as well and that is why both of them are needed. The spiritual purpose is that of constantly renewing the universe.

* * *

Seed Thoughts

The Rabbis would not have devoted so much time and energy to the phenomena of day and night unless to them these had symbolic meaning. Day represented that which was good and beautiful; night, that which was dark and evil.

We, who live in the age of electricity, find it much harder to relate to the night as an environment of terror. When sporting events are held at night and the miracle of electricity literally transforms night into day, it is not easy to imagine a time when night meant only darkness.

Mind you, this can happen even in the age of the electric light as well. I remember landing at Lod airport in Israel on the third night of the Yom Kippur war during a blackout when even the headlights of automobiles had to be shaded and all one could see was utter and total blackness.

The Rabbis, however, associated night with more than physical terror. They associated it with evil.

In questioning the jurisdiction of God over day and night they were wrestling with the problem of evil. Of course God is associated with the good; but how can He be divested of a relationship with evil. Did He not create man with all the limitations of mortality and an animal nature? Even if the ills of mankind are due to man's wrong choices, how can God be exonerated from a relationship to evil as Creator of the world?

He cannot be. Therefore, the *midrash* is forced to admit without too much comprehension that we have to thank God even for evil and its challenges as much as we have to thank Him for the good.

Let us go further and acknowledge that night also stands as a symbol for dimensions more complicated than raw evil. It also stands for ageing, sickness, and death. The Book of Ecclesiastes refers to these matters with the symbols of darkness and black clouds that gather over human life.

At such moments we need God and we seek Him, and we place our lives in His trust for He who created the light also created the darkness. He even created evil, or, as the verse in Isaiah (45:7) is emended by the Rabbis in the prayer book, He is the creator of everything.

As the last verse of *Adon Olam* reads: 'Into His hand I will commit my spirit when I arise and when I awake and with my spirit my body also. The Lord is with me, I shall not fear.'

* * *

Additional Commentary

The aim of this *midrash* is to explain the statement in the Pentateuch that the Almighty made two great lights, when we know that only the sun can provide light while the moon receives its light from the sun. Nevertheless, all of this is divinely motivated. God gave the power of light to the sun and it was He who arranged for the sun to give light to the moon. In that sense, both the day and the night are indebted to God and are under His authority. (*Tiferet Tzion*)

*

Night is also in Your power

This statement is meant to contradict those who maintain that night is simply the absence of light and not something that was created as a separate entity. (RDL)

*

The day is Yours, and the night also

The name of God was not associated with the creation of night but only with the creation of day or light (Genesis 1:3). The reason the name of God is not specified with night is because night is often the symbol of evil and God is not to be associated with evil. But it should never be imagined that night has any special powers. On the contrary, God uses time, which includes night and day, for His purposes. That is what the verse of our *midrash* now specifies, 'And God made two great lights' and that is why the verses in Psalm 74 are interrupted in their style by 'the day is Yours, and the night also.' (*Yedei Moshe*)

Parashah Six, Midrash Three

רַבִּי יוּדָן בְּשֵׁם רַבִּי תַּנְחוּם בְּ"רַ' חִיָּא וְרַבִּי פִּינְחָס בְּשֵׁם רַ' סִימוֹן אָמַר מֵאַחַר
שֶׁהוּא קוֹרֵא אוֹתָן גְּדוֹלִים הוּא חוֹזֵר וּפוֹגֵם אוֹתָם 'אֶת הַמָּאוֹר הַגָּדֹל לְמֶמְשֶׁלֶת
הַיּוֹם וְאֶת הַמָּאוֹר הַקָּטֹן לְמֶמְשֶׁלֶת הַלַּיְלָה' אַתְמָהָא אֶלָּא עַל יְדֵי שֶׁנִּכְנַס בִּתְחוּמוֹ
שֶׁל חֲבֵרוֹ

R. Yudan in the name of R. Tanḥum and R. Pinḥas in R. Simon's
name said: After calling them great, He diminished [one of] them
[by writing], 'The greater light to dominate the day and the lesser
light to dominate the night' (1:16). This is strange! [The reason is]
because it [the moon] trespassed on its neighbor's territory.

This *midrash* is addressing what seems to be a contradiction in the account
of the creation of sun and moon. The verse first states that on the fourth
day 'God made the two great lights,' which seems to suggest that they were
equally great. But the verse then goes on to describe the sun as 'the greater
light' and the moon as 'the lesser light.' The explanation is that when they
were created they were indeed equal, but the moon was later diminished
as a punishment for trespassing on the territory of the sun, by being visible
also during the day.

אָמַר רַבִּי פִּינְחָס בְּכָל הַקָּרְבָּנוֹת כְּתִיב 'שְׂעִיר עִזִּים אֶחָד חַטָּאת' וּבְרֹאשׁ חֹדֶשׁ
כְּתִיב 'שְׂעִיר עִזִּים אֶחָד חַטָּאת לַה'' (במדבר כח, טו) אָמַר הַקָּדוֹשׁ בָּרוּךְ הוּא הָבִיאוּ
כַּפָּרָה עָלַי שֶׁמִּעַטְתִּי אֶת הַיָּרֵחַ שֶׁאֲנִי הוּא שֶׁגָּרַמְתִּי לוֹ לְהִכָּנֵס בִּתְחוּמוֹ שֶׁל חֲבֵרוֹ
וּמָה אִם זֶה שֶׁנִּכְנַס בִּרְשׁוּת כָּךְ פְּגָמוֹ הַכָּתוּב הַנִּכְנָס שֶׁלֹּא בִּרְשׁוּת עַל אַחַת כַּמָּה
וְכַמָּה

R. Pinḥas said: In respect of all other sacrifices it is written, 'There
shall be one goat for a sin offering' (Numbers 28:22, 29:5, *et al*),
whereas in respect of the New Moon it is written, 'And here shall be
one goat as a sin offering *for the Lord*' (Numbers 28:15). [It is as
though] the Holy One, blessed be He, said: 'Bring [a sacrifice as] an
atonement for Me for having diminished the moon. Because it was
I who caused it to enter its colleague's domain.' If [the moon] which
entered [the sun's domain] with permission was thus disparaged by

holy writ, think how much more so is one who enters without permission deserving [of disparagement].

The plain meaning of 'for the Lord' is that the sin offering is brought to the Lord to atone for the sins of Israel. However it is strange that the phrase appears only with regard to the additional offering of the New Moon. The *midrash*, therefore, offers a novel and extremely daring interpretation: On the one hand, the moon had to be punished for its transgression, but God, as it were, also felt a measure of responsibility for the transgression because He permitted it and therefore He needed a sacrifice to atone for His part in the transgression. The lesson for humans to learn from this is that encroaching upon another's domain is a very serious sin.

רַבִּי לֵוִי בְּשֵׁם רַבִּי יוֹסֵי בַּר אִלְעַאי אָמַר דֶּרֶךְ אֶרֶץ הוּא שֶׁיְּהֵא הַגָּדוֹל מוֹנֶה לַגָּדוֹל וְהַקָּטָן מוֹנֶה לַקָּטָן עֵשָׂו מוֹנֶה לַחַמָּה שֶׁהִיא גְדוֹלָה וְיַעֲקֹב מוֹנֶה לַלְּבָנָה שֶׁהִיא קְטַנָּה

R. Levi said in the name of R. Jose b. Ila'i: It is only proper that the great should count by the great and the small by the small. Esau counts [time] by the sun, which is large, and Jacob by the moon, which is small

This *midrash* makes an interesting comment on the fact that the sun is larger than the moon. Esau was the older son of Isaac and Rebecca and Jacob was the younger. The Roman calendar – the Romans and other Western nations are considered by Jewish tradition to be descendants of Esau – is a solar calendar, whereas the Jews – the descendants of Jacob – have a lunar calendar.

אָמַר רַב נַחְמָן וְהוּא סִמָּן טָב עֵשָׂו מוֹנֶה לַחַמָּה שֶׁהִיא גְדוֹלָה מָה חַמָּה הַזֹּאת שׁוֹלֶטֶת בַּיּוֹם וְאֵינָה שׁוֹלֶטֶת בַּלַּיְלָה כָּךְ עֵשָׂו יֵשׁ לוֹ חֵלֶק בָּעוֹלָם הַזֶּה וְאֵין לוֹ חֵלֶק לָעוֹלָם הַבָּא יַעֲקֹב מוֹנֶה לַלְּבָנָה שֶׁהִיא קְטַנָּה מָה הַלְּבָנָה הַזוֹ שׁוֹלֶטֶת בַּלַּיְלָה וּבַיּוֹם כָּךְ יַעֲקֹב יֵשׁ לוֹ חֵלֶק בָּעוֹלָם הַזֶּה וְלָעוֹלָם הַבָּא

Said R. Naḥman: This is a good augury [for Israel]. Esau counts [time] by the sun, which is large; just as the sun dominates the day but does not rule the night, so too Esau has a share in this world, but has no share in the world-to-come. Jacob counts [time] by the moon, which is small; just as the moon rules by night and by day, so too Jacob has a portion in this world and in the world-to-come.

Although the moon was punished for encroaching on the domain of the sun in that it also appears during the day, R. Naḥman finds a good omen in its smallness. He sees day and the solar calendar as the symbol of this world and night and the lunar calendar as the symbol of this world and the world-to-come.

רַב נַחְמָן אָמַר כָּל זְמַן שֶׁאוֹרוֹ שֶׁל גָּדוֹל קַיָּם אֵין אוֹרוֹ שֶׁל קָטָן מִתְפַּרְסֵם שָׁקַע אוֹרוֹ שֶׁל גָּדוֹל מִתְפַּרְסֵם אוֹרוֹ שֶׁל קָטָן כָּךְ כָּל זְמַן שֶׁאוֹרוֹ שֶׁל עֵשָׂו קַיָּם אֵין אוֹרוֹ שֶׁל יַעֲקֹב מִתְפַּרְסֵם שָׁקַע אוֹרוֹ שֶׁל עֵשָׂו מִתְפַּרְסֵם אוֹרוֹ שֶׁל יַעֲקֹב הָדָא הוּא דִכְתִיב 'קוּמִי אוֹרִי כִּי בָא אוֹרֵךְ כִּי הִנֵּה הַחֹשֶׁךְ יְכַסֶּה אֶרֶץ וְגוֹ'' (ישעיה ס, א-ב)

R. Naḥman [further] said: As long as the light of the greater [i.e., the sun] functions, the light of the smaller [i.e., the moon] is not noticeable, but when the light of the greater sets [at night], the light of the smaller becomes noticeable. So too, as long as the light of Esau prevails, the light of Jacob cannot be noticed, but when the light of Esau sets [in messianic times] that of Jacob shall be noticed. This is the meaning of that which is written, 'Arise, shine, for your light has dawned... Behold, darkness shall cover the earth, [and thick clouds the peoples, but upon you the Lord will shine, and His Presence will be seen over you]' (Isaiah 60:1).

The struggle between Jacob and Esau is a very widespread theme in rabbinic literature, and our *midrash* sees it as a confrontation between two worlds – this world and the world-to-come. The verse in Isaiah is clearly referring to the days of the Messiah when the moon – and the Jewish people – will come into their own.

* *

Seed Thoughts

The idea of God making a mistake or being guilty of a sin is, by definition, impossible and therefore, preposterous. The *midrash*, however, makes God go through the pretense of pleading guilty to a decision that seems to appear wrong even though it was not wrong in fact. This attribution of human inadequacies to God even though by pretense is done in order to provide a lesson for man. Things must not only be right and just; they also have to appear to be right and just. Even God commanded that a sin offering be brought for Him when it appeared as though the moon had been treated unfairly. How much more so must sinful man be sensitive to the feelings of his fellow man.

* * *

Additional Commentary

Bring an atonement for Me

The idea of the moon entering the area of the sun by appearing in the daytime should be understood as a symbol of Israel living in the midst of the nations of the world. The idea of *galut*, exile, began with the sin of the Golden Calf. In this connection certain rules have to be understood. Israel receives its salvation and abundance directly from God but only if it remains within the Land of Israel. Outside its land Israel is like one without God. The nations of the world receive their abundance from nature. Now God knew that Israel was going to deserve the punishment of exile and therefore had to create a structure in which Israel would be able to survive even in exile. It was therefore necessary for the Holy One to create the moon (symbol of Israel) in such a way as to have it enter the domain of its colleague so that in this way Israel would develop the capacity to gather influence from the natural powers for as long as they were away from the Land of Israel.

Not only was the sin of the Golden Calf the main cause of Exile, it was also responsible for depriving Israel of the New Moons that were originally intended to be the major festivals, and instead these were reduced to the three pilgrimage festivals. For this reason the Holy One commanded that on Rosh Ḥodesh a sin offering should be offered up to atone for the fact that we made it necessary for God to diminish the moon, and with it the great festivals of Rosh Ḥodesh, in order for Israel to be sustained in exile.

It was Israel that forced God into diminishing the moon, but God ascribes it to himself as would a parent for a child. We have to understand, however, that it is our doing. Israel and only Israel must bring this sin offering on Rosh Ḥodesh. (*Tiferet Tzion*)

*

Derekh eretz – The way of the world

This teaching is meant as a form of appeasement of the sun as to why it was diminished. After all, as a result of that diminution, Israel counted its way of life by means of the moon. It is also a form of consolation to Israel for having to follow the lesser of the two luminaries. The consolation derives from the fact that Israel will rule in both this world and the world-to-come, just as the moon is visible in both day and night. This world is compared to the day, because it is visible to all. The world-to-come is compared to night, because it is hidden and mysterious, as is the night. There is a lesson in all this because if a person experiences suffering and depression in this world he should not complain against God. It is no different or better in the heavens. The sun and the moon are unequal and one enters the space of the other. At least, man is mortal and suffers only temporarily. For the sun and the moon the arrangement is forever. (*Yefei To'ar*)

Parashah Six, Midrash Four

'וְאֵת הַכּוֹכָבִים' (בראשית א, טז) אָמַר רַ' אֲחָא מָשָׁל לְמֶלֶךְ שֶׁהָיוּ לוֹ שְׁנֵי אֶפּוֹטְרוֹפִין אֶחָד שׁוֹלֵט בָּעִיר וְאֶחָד שׁוֹלֵט בַּמְּדִינָה אָמַר הַמֶּלֶךְ הוֹאִיל וּמִעֵט עַצְמוֹ זֶה לִהְיוֹת שׁוֹלֵט בָּעִיר גּוֹזֵר אֲנִי עָלָיו בְּשָׁעָה שֶׁהוּא יוֹצֵא תְּהֵא כָּל אוּכְלוּסָא יוֹצְאָה עִמּוֹ וּבְשָׁעָה שֶׁיְּהֵא נִכְנָס תְּהֵא בּוֹלִי וְדִימוֹס נִכְנָסָה עִמּוֹ כָּךְ אָמַר הַקָּדוֹשׁ בָּרוּךְ הוּא הוֹאִיל וְהַלְּבָנָה הַזּוֹ מִעֲטָה עַצְמָהּ לִהְיוֹת שׁוֹלֶטֶת בַּלַּיְלָה גּוֹזֵר אֲנִי עָלֶיהָ בְּשָׁעָה שֶׁהִיא יוֹצֵאת שֶׁיְּהוּ הַכּוֹכָבִים יוֹצְאִין עִמָּהּ בְּשָׁעָה שֶׁהִיא נִכְנֶסֶת יְהוּ הַכּוֹכָבִים נִכְנָסִים עִמָּהּ

'And the stars' (1:16). R. Aḥa said: This can be compared to a king who had two governors, one ruling a city and the other a province. The king said, 'Since the former has humbled himself [and is prepared] to rule a city only, I decree that whenever he goes out [of his residence] the whole population [of the city] go out [of their houses] with him. And whenever he enters [his residence], the city council and a guard of honor shall enter with him.' Thus did the Holy One, blessed be He, say: 'Since the moon humbled itself willingly to rule only by night, I decree that when it comes out [i.e., rises], the stars shall come out with it, and when it goes in [i.e., sets] the stars shall go in with it.

Why is the phrase 'and the stars' added to the description of the lesser light, the moon? The parable compares the sun and the moon to two governors appointed by a king. The fact that one of them was prepared to diminish his own stature and accept the governorship of a city, which is a far less important post than the governorship of a province, led the king to grant him very special marks of honor. The answer to our question is now clear. The stars constitute a guard of honor for the moon in tribute to its humility. The importance of humility is reiterated in the continuation.

וְדִכְוָתָהּ 'וְשֵׁם אָחִיו יָקְטָן' (בראשית י, כה) אָמַר רַבִּי אֲחָא לָמָּה נִקְרָא שְׁמוֹ יָקְטָן שֶׁהָיָה מַקְטִין אֶת עֲסָקָיו מַה זָכָה זָכָה לְהַעֲמִיד שְׁלֹשׁ עֶשְׂרֵה מִשְׁפָּחוֹת גְּדוֹלוֹת וּמָה אִם יָקְטָן עַל יְדֵי שֶׁהָיָה מַקְטִין אֶת עֲסָקָיו כָּךְ גָּדוֹל שֶׁהוּא מַקְטִין אֶת עֲסָקָיו עַל אַחַת כַּמָּה וְכַמָּה

Similarly we read, 'And the name of his brother was Joktan' (Genesis
10:25). R. Aḥa commented: Why was he called Joktan? Because he
diminished his behavior. What did he merit thereby? He was privileged to establish thirteen great clans. Now, if this is so with regard
to the smaller, who diminished himself, how much more so will it
be true of a great man who diminishes himself.

The full verse quoted reads as follows: 'Two sons were born to Ever: the
name of the first was Peleg, for in his days the earth was divided; and the
name of his brother was Joktan.' This is part of the great genealogical list
in the Book of Genesis and R. Aḥa was commenting on the fact that
whereas a reason is given for the older brother's name – the Hebrew root
PLG means to divide or split – no reason is given for the name of the
younger brother, Joktan, which derives from the root *KTN*. R. Aḥa also
noticed that no descendants are listed for Peleg, whereas the following
verse lists no less than thirteen sons of Joktan, all of whom became major
clans. It was this juxtapositioning and the root from which Joktan's name
is derived that led to this homily and the moral to be learned from it.

וְדִכְוָתַהּ 'וַיִּשְׁלַח יִשְׂרָאֵל אֶת יְמִינוֹ וַיָּשֶׁת עַל רֹאשׁ אֶפְרַיִם וְהוּא הַצָּעִיר' (שם מח,
יד) אָמַר רַבִּי חוּנְיָא וְכִי מִן הַתּוֹלָדוֹת אֵין אָנוּ יוֹדְעִים שֶׁהוּא הַצָּעִיר אֶלָּא מַה 'הוּא
הַצָּעִיר' שֶׁהָיָה מַצְעִיר אֶת עֲסָקָיו מַה זָּכָה זָכָה לַבְּכוֹרָה וּמָה אִם הַצָּעִיר עַל יְדֵי
שֶׁהָיָה מַצְעִיר אֶת עֲסָקָיו זָכָה לַבְּכוֹרָה הַגָּדוֹל שֶׁהוּא מַצְעִיר אֶת עֲסָקָיו עַל אַחַת
כַּמָּה וְכַמָּה אַתְמְהָא

Similarly, 'But Israel stretched out his right hand, and laid it upon
Ephraim's head, though he was the younger' (Genesis 48:14). Said R.
Ḥunia: Do we not know from the birth records that he was the
younger? What does 'he was the younger *(tzaʿir)*' mean? He
diminished *(matzʿir)* his behavior. What did he merit thereby? He
merited the birthright. Now, if this is so with regard to the younger,
who diminished himself, how much more so will it be true of the
older brother who diminishes himself. This is wondrous.

Jacob, when blessing Joseph's two sons, placed his right hand on the head
of Ephraim, who, we are told in the verse, was the younger. R. Ḥunia
remarked that there was no need to inform us of this fact since we already
know it from the account given of their birth. His answer is similar to that
in the previous passage. The Hebrew for younger is *tzaʿir*, the root of
which can also mean to make small or diminish. Ephraim's reward for
humbling himself was that he is considered Joseph's firstborn – in all

places where the two sons are mentioned Ephraim takes precedence over his older brother, Manasseh.

* * *

Seed Thoughts

The human quality most admired by the Bible is humility. This seems to be the main lesson of our *midrash*. What makes humility so important?

If one takes the position that that which is spiritual is separate and apart from that which is natural in the sense of one's animal nature, then humility is probably the most spiritual of all the virtues.

To be humble is not natural. Nature wants us to be self-centered, assertive, egotistical and, if you like, egomaniacs. Survival of the fittest is the most famous of the Darwinian slogans.

Along comes the Torah and warns us that the goal of life is not to survive but to serve; not self-fulfillment but altruism. Pride, particularly self-pride, interferes with our ability to serve. It has to be replaced by altruism.

How interesting that the *midrash* was not satisfied with the illustration of Joktan. Joktan, as his name implies, was meant to be the number two personality in his circle. The fact that he accepted this role with humility and understanding is most commendable. But Ephraim was of a different calibre. Already in his early youth he was informed by his grandfather, Jacob, that he and not his elder brother would be the leader of the Joseph tribes. Nevertheless, despite this advance knowledge, he understood that it was his role to serve. He became a leader who exemplified humility, altruism, and empathy, not because he had to, but out of noblesse oblige.

This, then, became the cardinal virtue. Most exemplary in this regard was Moses, of whom it was said that he was the humblest man on earth. However, the *midrash* is proud to find others and pass this knowledge over to us for our edification and imitation.

Parashah Six, Midrash Five

'וַיִּתֵּן אֹתָם אֱלֹהִים בִּרְקִיעַ הַשָּׁמָיִם' (בראשית א, יז) אָמַר רַבִּי יוֹחָנָן שְׁלֹשָׁה דְבָרִים נִתְּנוּ מַתָּנָה לָעוֹלָם וְאֵלּוּ הֵן הַתּוֹרָה וְהַמְּאוֹרוֹת וְהַגְּשָׁמִים

'And God set them in the expanse of the sky' (Genesis 1:17). R. Joḥanan said: Three things were given as a gift to the world and these are they: the Torah, the luminaries, and rain.

The problem that R. Joḥanan is addressing in this *midrash* is the fact that the sun and the moon were created in the heavens, as is clearly stated at the beginning of the fourth day of the creation: 'God said, 'Let there be lights in the expanse of the sky' (verse 14). What, then, should be understood by 'And God set them in the expanse of the sky' (verse 17)? Furthermore, the use of the term *va-yiten* implies that they had been elsewhere and God moved them to the sky. Note that the word *va-yiten* is derived from the same root as *matanah*, meaning a gift. Note also that the term gift in this instance refers to something most precious, not replaceable, and not attainable by man through his own efforts. Objects like the Torah, the luminaries, and the rains fit into these categories and all of them have the root *NTN* in their scriptural sources.

הַתּוֹרָה מִנַּיִן שֶׁנֶּאֱמַר 'וַיִּתֵּן אֶל מֹשֶׁה וְגוֹ'' (שמות לא, יח) הַמְּאוֹרוֹת מִנַּיִן שֶׁנֶּאֱמַר 'וַיִּתֵּן אֹתָם אֱלֹהִים בִּרְקִיעַ הַשָּׁמָיִם' גְּשָׁמִים מִנַּיִן שֶׁנֶּאֱמַר 'וְנָתַתִּי גִשְׁמֵיכֶם בְּעִתָּם' (ויקרא כו, ד)

Whence do we know this of the Torah? 'And He gave (*va-yiten*) Moses the two tablets of the covenant...' (Exodus 31:18). The luminaries – 'And God set (*va-yiten*) them in the expanse of the sky.' Rain – 'I will grant (*ve-natati*) your rains in their season' (Leviticus 26:4).

Regarding the Torah, the full verse reads (in its Hebrew order): 'And He gave Moses, when He finished speaking with him, the two tablets of the covenant, stone tablets inscribed with the finger of God.' The expected order should have been: 'He gave Moses the two tablets of the covenant when He finished speaking with him...' The change leads the *midrash* to

231

the interpretation that 'He gave' does not mean 'He handed over' but rather 'He granted as a gift.' (*Ha-Midrash ha-Mevo'ar*) The luminaries came into existence in the sky, therefore 'And God set them' can only mean 'He gave them as a gift.' In the matter of rain, the verbal form used, *ve-natati*, is in the past tense, 'I have already given,' implying as a gift.

רַבִּי עֲזַרְיָה בְּשֵׁם רַבִּי יְהוּדָה בְּ"ר סִימוֹן אוֹמֵר אַף הַשָּׁלוֹם שֶׁנֶּאֱמַר 'וְנָתַתִּי שָׁלוֹם בָּאָרֶץ' (שם שם, ו) רַבִּי יְהוֹשֻׁעַ בְּרַבִּי נְחֶמְיָה אָמַר אַף הַיְשׁוּעָה שֶׁנֶּאֱמַר 'וַתִּתֶּן לִי מָגֵן יִשְׁעֶךָ' (ש"ב כב, לו; תהלים יח, לו) רַבִּי תַּנְחוּמָא אָמַר אַף אֶרֶץ יִשְׂרָאֵל שֶׁנֶּאֱמַר 'וַיִּתֶּן לָהֶם אַרְצוֹת גּוֹיִם וְגוֹ'' (תהלים קה, מד) וְיֵשׁ אוֹמְרִים אַף הַנְּקָמָה בֶּאֱדוֹם שֶׁנֶּאֱמַר 'וְנָתַתִּי נִקְמָתִי בֶּאֱדוֹם וְגוֹ'' (יחזקל כה, יד) רַבָּנָן אָמְרֵי אַף הָרַחֲמִים שֶׁנֶּאֱמַר 'וַיִּתֵּן אוֹתָם לְרַחֲמִים לִפְנֵי כָּל שׁוֹבֵיהֶם' (תהלים קו, מו) רַבִּי יִצְחָק בַּר מַרְיוֹן אוֹמֵר אַף הַפְרָשַׁת הַיָּם הַגָּדוֹל שֶׁנֶּאֱמַר 'כֹּה אָמַר ה' הַנּוֹתֵן בַּיָּם דָּרֶךְ וְגוֹ'' (ישעיה מג, טז) רַבָּנָן אָמְרֵי 'הַנּוֹתֵן בַּיָּם דָּרֶךְ' מֵעֲצֶרֶת וְעַד הֶחָג 'וּבְמַיִם עַזִּים נְתִיבָה' מִן הֶחָג וְעַד הַחֲנֻכָּה

R. Azariah said in the name of R. Judah b. R. Simon: Peace, too [was given as a gift] as it says, 'And I will give (*ve-natati*) you peace' (Leviticus 26:6). R. Joshua b. R. Neḥemiah said: Salvation too [was given as a gift] as it says, 'You have given (*va-titen*) the shield of your protection' (II Samuel 22:36, Psalms 18:36). R. Tanḥuma said: The Land of Israel too [was given as a gift] as it says, 'He gave (*va-yiten*) them the lands of the nations' (Psalms 110:44). Some say, vengeance on Edom, too, [was given as a gift] as it says, 'I will wreak (*ve-natati*) My vengeance on Edom' (Ezekiel 25:14). Our Rabbis say: Compassion, too, [was given as a gift] as it says, 'He made (*va-yiten*) all their captors kindly disposed toward them' (Psalms 106:46). R. Isaac b. Marion said: Even travel by sea [was given as a gift] as it says, 'Thus said the Lord, who made (*ha-noten*) a road through the sea…' (Isaiah 43:16). Our rabbis say: [The first part of that verse], 'who made a road through the sea' [refers to the calm period of time] from Shavuot to Sukkot; [the second part], 'And path through mighty waters' [refers to the stormy period] from Sukkot to Ḥanukkah.

This *midrash* continues with the idea that when a derivative of the Hebrew verb *natan* appears where the subject is God and the object is something that humans are unable to attain by their own efforts, the intention is that that object was given to humanity as a gift. Humans are by nature quarrelsome, competitive, and egoistic and would be unable to make peace between themselves, if God had not given peace to mankind as a gift. Salvation, too, is a gift from God because human salvation is false and meaningless. The Land of Israel was conquered miraculously. Vengeance, too, particularly against Edom, that is, Rome, which destroyed the Temple, is also something which cannot be achieved by human efforts and some day that will be avenged as God's gift to the Jewish people. The fact that Israel's enemies sometimes showed compassion to them when they had Israel in captivity was also a gift from God. Safe travel by ship is also a gift of God. On this last item the Rabbis commented that even when the sea is calm (from April/May until September), the fact that a ship can navigate its way over vast, unmarked stretches of ocean is a gift from God and that is certainly so in the stormy season (September until December). Thus they interpret the parallelism of the verse in Isaiah. There is, however, a period in the year when it is not safe to travel by sea at all – from Ḥanukkah (December) until Shavuot (April\May). (*Yefei To'ar*)

R. Joḥanan who began our *midrash* listing the three great gifts, does not consider the qualities listed by the others above, such as peace, salvation, the Land of Israel, vengeance, compassion and sea travel, to be gifts from God, because all of them can sometimes be achieved by human beings as a result of their own efforts and planning. The other Sages who do list these qualities do so because they do not believe that humans can achieve them on their own (*Yefei To'ar*).

רַבִּי נָתָן כֹּהֵן אֲחוּהָ דְּרַבִּי חִיָּא בַּר אַבָּא הֲוֵי מְפָרֵשׁ בְּיַמָּא אֲמַר לֵהּ לַאֲחוּי צַלִּי עֲלַי אֲמַר לֵהּ מַה נְּצַלֵּי עֲלָךְ מִן דְּאַתְּ קָטַר לוּלָבָךְ קְטוֹר רַגְלָיךְ אִין עֲיַלְתְּ לִכְנִשְׁתָּא וּשְׁמַעְתּוּן מְצַלְּיִן עַל מִטְרָא לָא תִסְמוֹךְ עַל צְלוֹתִי

R. Nathan Kohen, the brother of R. Ḥiyya b. R. Abba, was setting out on a sea voyage. 'Pray for me,' he asked his brother. 'How can I pray for you?' replied he, 'When you bind up your palm branch, bind your feet! [Furthermore], if you enter the synagogue and hear the congregation praying for rain, do not rely upon my prayers.'

This anecdote is an example of the principle laid down in the previous *midrash*. Sea travel between Sukkot and Ḥanukkah is dangerous, and it was in that period that R. Nathan was planning his trip. He realized that he was putting himself in a dangerous position and so he requested his brother to pray for his safety. The brother replied that he could not do so because the principle was that when you bind up the *lulav*, used in the ceremonies of the Sukkot festival, you should bind your feet, that is, you should not undertake any sea journeys. He also pointed out that it is during the Sukkot festival (on Hoshanah Rabbah or Shemini Atzeret) that the congregation prays for rain and stormy weather, and therefore his prayers for R. Nathan's welfare would be unavailing, since the prayers of the congregation always take precedence over the prayers of an individual.

רַ' יְהוֹשֻׁעַ בְּרֵהּ דְּרַבִּי תַּנְחוּמָא בַּר חִיָּא דִּכְפַר חָנוּן הֲוָה בְּאַסְיָא בְּעָא דִּיפְרוֹשׁ אָמְרָה לֵהּ מַטְרוֹנָה בְּאִלֵּין יוֹמַיָּא פָּרְשֵׁי אַתְמְהָא אִתְחֲזֵי לֵהּ אֲבוּי בְּחֶלְמָא אָמַר לֵהּ בְּרִי בְּלָא קְבוּרָה שֶׁנֶּאֱמַר 'גַּם קְבוּרָה לֹא הָיְתָה לוֹ' (קהלת ו, ג) וְלָא שְׁמַע לְמִלֵּי דְּדֵין וְלָא לְמִלֵּי דְּדֵין וְכֵן הֲוַת לֵהּ

R. Joshua b. Tanḥum b. R. Ḥiyya of Kefar Ḥanun was in Asia Minor and wished to embark on a sea journey. A [Roman] matron said to him, 'I am astonished that one should set out at this time of the year.' His father appeared to him in a dream and said to him, 'My son, [would you die] without burial, as it is written "I was not even accorded a burial" (Ecclesiastes 6:3)!' But he paid no heed to the words either of the matron or his father and that fate did befall him.

R. Joshua was also contemplating a sea journey from Asia Minor (present-day Turkey) in the dangerous period of the year, between Sukkot and Ḥanukkah, apparently in pursuit of his business interests. The Roman matron is brought into the anecdote to illustrate that you do not have to be a sage to know that you should not undertake sea travel at this time of the year. The first part of the verses quoted by R. Joshua's father in the dream reads, 'Even if a man should beget a hundred children and live many years… if his gullet is not sated through his wealth, I say: The stillbirth, though it was not even accorded a burial, is more fortunate than he.' The moral being that the temptation to make more money will lead a man into disaster.

* * *

Seed Thoughts

It is of interest to note that of all the qualities listed as gifts to mankind, freedom is conspicuously absent. Freedom is not a gift. It has to be earned and continually earned, time and time again. Independence can be granted to people, but unless these concepts are internalized and become part of a way of life and incorporated into a system of law and order, they will not yield positive human results.

* * *

Additional Commentary

Three things as gifts

R. Joḥanan lists three things that are of benefit to the entire world and that cannot be acquired even with the greatest amount of money, but which God has freely given to us and without any intercession. The Torah was given freely in accordance with the maxim, considering that I, God, come to you freely, how much more so My Torah. And so were the luminaries and the rains. Qualities such as wisdom, riches, and strength were not listed because they are gifts to individuals and not the world. He also did not list basic essentials like fire, water, and earth because they are in never-ending supply. (*Yefei To'ar*)

*

The limitations of prayer

The main reason for telling the story about R. Nathan Kohen is to indicate the parameters of prayer and the limitations of its power. There are two reasons why R. Ḥiyya refused to pray for his brother. The first is that prayer can only help in situations that come upon a person inadvertently and not where a person endangers his life by his own choice. The second is that prayer cannot help where the general public is praying for the very opposite to happen.

There is a third area where prayer is ineffective and that is in a situation that can be described as *shekhiḥah hezekah*, where the whole atmosphere is potentially hazardous. It has to be assumed that R. Joshua must have had very important business to transact for him to have risked travel by sea at an inappropriate season. He was relying on the principle that those engaged in a *mitzvah* mission are never harmed. However, he failed to realize that in a situation that is potentially hazardous, not even a *mitzvah* mission is able to be protective.

The fact that prayer has mystical elements about it does not mean that the individual has the right to introduce irrational behavior into its orbit. Prayer was never intended to fly in the face of a reality, but to help the individual face the real world with courage but not with recklessness. (Partially from *Tiferet Tzion*)

Parashah Six, Midrash Six

הֵיכָן גַּלְגַּל הַחַמָּה וּלְבָנָה נְתוּנִים בָּרָקִיעַ הַשֵּׁנִי שֶׁנֶּאֱמַר 'וַיִּתֵּן אֹתָם אֱלֹהִים בִּרְקִיעַ הַשָּׁמָיִם' (בראשית א, יז)

Where are the spheres of the sun and the moon set? In the second firmament (*raki'a*), as it says, 'And God set them in the firmament of the heaven' (Genesis 1:17).

The question is, where, exactly, were the luminaries placed within the firmament. Rashi notes that the verse could have read firmament / heaven or heaven / firmament, but it reads instead 'the firmament of the heaven (*ha-shomayim*).' Firmament of the heaven means firmament above the heaven and therefore, the second heaven. It should also be noticed that the word *shomayim* is a plural form, indicating, in rabbinic cosmogony, that there is more than one.

רַבִּי פִּינְחָס בְּשֵׁם רַבִּי אַבָּהוּ אָמַר מִקְרָא מָלֵא הוּא וְאַנְשֵׁי כְּנֶסֶת הַגְּדוֹלָה פֵּירְשׁוּ אוֹתוֹ 'אַתָּה הוּא ה' לְבַדֶּךָ אַתָּה עָשִׂיתָ אֶת הַשָּׁמַיִם שְׁמֵי הַשָּׁמַיִם וְכָל צְבָאָם וְגו'' (נחמיה ט, ו) הֵיכָן הוּא 'כָּל צְבָאָם' נְתוּנִים בָּרָקִיעַ שֶׁהוּא לְמַעְלָה מִן הַשָּׁמָיִם

R. Pinḥas said in R. Abbahu's name: There is an explicit verse [on the subject] and the Men of the Great Assembly interpreted it: 'You alone are the Lord, You made the heavens, the heaven of heavens, and all their host' (Nehemiah 9:6). Where are 'all their host' set? In the firmament which is above the heaven.

The verse cited is from the Book of Nehemiah and the interpretation is ascribed to the Men of the Great Assembly, of which group Nehemiah was a member. If, as has now been established, there are at least two firmaments, one on top of the other, it would be most helpful to know how far one was from the other. We would then be able to establish exactly where the firmament is.

וּמִן הָאָרֶץ וְעַד הָרָקִיעַ מַהֲלַךְ חֲמֵשׁ מֵאוֹת שָׁנָה וְעוֹבְיוֹ שֶׁל רָקִיעַ מַהֲלַךְ חֲמֵשׁ מֵאוֹת שָׁנָה וּמֵרְקִיעַ עַד הָרָקִיעַ מַהֲלַךְ חֲמֵשׁ מֵאוֹת שָׁנָה רְאֵה כַּמָּה הוּא גָבוֹהַּ וּתְנַן בְּאֶחָד בִּתְקוּפַת תַּמּוּז אֵין צֵל לְכָל בְּרִיָּה דִּכְתִיב 'וְאֵין נִסְתָּר מֵחַמָּתוֹ' (תהלים יט, ז)

236

From the earth to the firmament is a five hundred years' journey (by foot), and the thickness of the firmament is a five hundred years' journey, and from the first firmament to the next firmament is a five hundred years' journey. See then how high [the sun] is! Yet it was taught: On the first day of the cycle of Tammuz [i.e., summer] no creature has a shadow for it is written, 'Nothing escapes its heat' (Psalms 19:7).

The calculation of a five hundred years' journey by foot is based on the formula that one day equals ten parasangs and each parasang is approximately four kilometers. According to this the sun is at least 21,900,000 kilometers distant from the earth. Despite this enormous distance the sun is still powerful. On the first day of the summer solstice, there is no shade for any creature. The meaning seems to be that despite the distance, when the sun is directly at the center, the high point of its position over the earth, there is no shadow or hardly any shade for protection and even the shade itself is extremely hot. This is the reason why the luminaries were placed in the second heaven, as a protection for man and all other creatures. Of course, with regard to astronomical distances, the Rabbis did not have the benefit of modern methods of calculation, but had to rely on the scientific data available in their day.

גַּלְגַּל חַמָּה יֵשׁ לוֹ נַרְתִּיק שֶׁנֶּאֱמַר 'לַשֶּׁמֶשׁ שָׂם אֹהֶל בָּהֶם' (שם שם, ה) וּבְרֵכָה שֶׁל מַיִם לְפָנָיו בְּשָׁעָה שֶׁהוּא יוֹצֵא הַקָּדוֹשׁ בָּרוּךְ הוּא מַתִּישׁ כֹּחוֹ בַּמַּיִם שֶׁלֹּא יֵצֵא וְיִשְׂרֹף אֶת הָעוֹלָם אֲבָל לֶעָתִיד לָבוֹא הַקָּדוֹשׁ בָּרוּךְ הוּא מְעַרְטְלוֹ מִנַּרְתִּיקוֹ וּמְלַהֵט בּוֹ אֶת הָרְשָׁעִים שֶׁנֶּאֱמַר 'וְלִהַט אוֹתָם הַיּוֹם הַבָּא' (מלאכי ג, יט)

The globe of the sun has a sheath, as it is written, 'He placed in them [the heavens] a tent for the sun' (Psalms 19:5). And there is a lake of water before it [the tent]. And when [the sun] goes forth, the Holy One, blessed be He, weakens its strength in the water, lest it go forth and burn up the world. But in the future, the Holy One, blessed be He, will take it from its sheath and burn up the wicked with it, as it is written, 'And the day that is coming, said the Lord of Hosts, shall burn them into ashes' (Malachi 3:19).

The Creator went even further to protect man than establishing a vast distance between man and the sun. The constellation of the sun has a special enclosure around the sun as a sort of covering. There is even a lake between the first and second heavens for this same purpose, namely to prevent the sun from burning man. But at the Day of Judgment, when

God renders judgment over all mankind, He will use the sun in its undiluted strength to punish the wicked.

רַבִּי יַנַּאי וְרַ' שִׁמְעוֹן תַּרְוַיְיהוֹן אָמְרִין אֵין גֵּיהִנָּם אֶלָּא יוֹם שֶׁהוּא מְלַהֵט אֶת הָרְשָׁעִים מַה טַּעַם 'הִנֵּה יוֹם בָּא בֹּעֵר כַּתַּנּוּר וְגוֹ'' (שם שם, שם) רַבָּנָן אָמְרִי יֵשׁ גֵּיהִנָּם שֶׁנֶּאֱמַר 'נְאֻם ה' אֲשֶׁר אוּר לוֹ בְּצִיּוֹן וְגוֹ'' (ישעיה לא, ט)

R. Jannai and R. Simon b. Lakish said: There is no other Gehenna (in the future) save a day which will burn up the wicked. What is the proof? 'And the day that is coming, said the Lord of Hosts, shall burn them into ashes' (Malachi 3:19). Our Rabbis maintain: There will be a Gehenna, for it is said, 'Declares the Lord who has a fire in Zion, who has an oven in Jerusalem' (Isaiah 31:9).

When R. Jannai and R. Simon b. Lakish say there is no Gehenna, they are referring to what will come after the resurrection of the dead. Up to the time of the resurrection, Gehenna will function as a holding place for the wicked, but afterwards the sun will come in its full force and judgment will be rendered to the wicked immediately and therefore Gehenna will no longer be required. The Rabbis taught that there was no difference between our world and that of the world-to-come except for the cessation of Jewish persecution. Therefore everything will remain in place as before, including Gehenna, and the righteous will only get their final judgment at the end of days. The oven in Jerusalem is a permanent fixture.

רַ' יְהוּדָה בַּר אִלְעָאי אוֹמֵר לֹא יוֹם וְלֹא גֵּיהִנָּם אֶלָּא אֵשׁ שֶׁהִיא יוֹצֵאת מִגּוּפָן שֶׁל רְשָׁעִים וּמְלַהֶטֶת אוֹתָם מַה טַּעַם דִּכְתִיב 'תַּהֲרוּ חֲשַׁשׁ תֵּלְדוּ קַשׁ רוּחֲכֶם אֵשׁ תֹּאכַלְכֶם' (שם לג, יא)

R. Judah b. R. Ila'i said: There will be neither such a day nor a Gehenna, but a fire shall come forth from the bodies of the wicked themselves and burn them up. What is the proof? 'You shall conceive hay, give birth to straw; your breath will devour you like fire' (Isaiah 33:11).

According to R. Judah b. R. Ila'i, there is no such judgment day on which God will use the sun to destroy the wicked; neither is there Gehenna. He believes that the wicked will self-destruct. Perhaps he means that since the wicked have conceived a way of life as insignificant as chaff, like chaff eventually becomes stubble easily burned, so too will their lives just simply disappear, which will be their true punishment.

רַבִּי יְהוֹשֻׁעַ בַּר אָבִין אָמַר 'וַיַּגִּידוּ שָׁמַיִם צִדְקוֹ' (תהלים נ, ו) לֶעָתִיד לָבוֹא שָׁמַיִם
מְתַנִּים צְדָקָה שֶׁעָשָׂה הַקָּדוֹשׁ בָּרוּךְ הוּא עִם עוֹלָמוֹ שֶׁלֹּא נְתָנָם בָּרָקִיעַ הָרִאשׁוֹן
שֶׁאִלּוּ נְתָנָם בָּרָקִיעַ הָרִאשׁוֹן לֹא הָיְתָה בְּרִיָּה יְכוֹלָה לַעֲמֹד מֵאִשּׁוֹ שֶׁל יוֹם

**R. Joshua b. R. Avin quoted: 'Then the heavens proclaim His
righteousness' (Psalms 50:6). In the future the heavens will declare the
righteousness [charity] which the Lord did for His world in not
setting them [the luminaries] in the first firmament, for had He set
them in the first firmament, no creature could have endured, on
account of the burning heat of the day.**

This *midrash* now returns to the first point and emphasizes God's kindness
to humanity. The word 'Then' in the verse quoted refers to the end of days
when the sun will be released from its second heaven so that its rays will
shine with tremendous burning power that will wreak punishment on the
wicked. At that time even the heavens will realize God's kindness in not
setting the luminaries in the first firmament.

* * *

Seed Thoughts

How are we to understand the concept of the second firmament and its
use by the Sages? Is it simply their inferior knowledge of cosmogony?
Were they forced to this conclusion because of their interpretation of the
biblical verses? It seems to me that the Sages were far too sophisticated
to be evaluated in such restrictive terms. They were trying to reach out
into higher realms of the human personality.

In a later generation, Freud and Jung would speak of the unconscious
and teach that there is a realm of experience and power that goes beyond
our conscious awareness and collects memories from every aspect of our
lifetime (Freud), or that it includes influences that reach back to primor-
dial sources (Jung).

The Rabbis were projecting to the outer world the same kind of depth
and extra energy that the analysts of the twentieth century detected in our
psychic experience. They felt the same calls to infinity, but projected them
outward to the world. The second heaven is not a cosmological fact, but
rather a psychic experience. It is part of the human imagination, a way of
reaching out to the infinite in a manner that Jung would describe as myth-
ological. The whole Midrash commentary to Genesis can be understood
with great new freshness in this light.

* * *

Additional Commentary

Five hundred years

The Jerusalem Talmud comments on the verse, 'In order that you and your children may endure, as long as the heavens are over the earth' (Deuteronomy 11:21) and calculates that the life span of the patriarchs taken together was five hundred years: Abraham 175, Isaac 180, and Jacob 117. All together 502, which is pretty close to 500. This is probably why the tradition arose that 'as the days (i.e., distance) of heavens over the earth' is 500 years. (Mirkin)

*

Heavens will declare (the condition of) the righteous

The word מתנין, *matnin* – from the same root as תנאי, condition – should actually be the word מחכים, *maḥkim*, which in Arabic means to recognize or acknowledge. In the future, heaven will acknowledge God's goodness in placing the luminaries in the second firmament. This reading was later found in *Midrash Shoḥer Tov*. (*Yedei Moshe*)

*

Gehenna

The use of the term גהינם, Gehenna (hell or purgatory), and the arguments surrounding its existence have to be understood in relation to God's judgment. In our day, human nature is in the grip of inclinations and passions that are stronger than our intellect and wisdom, which are weak. By right, God should punish every sin immediately, but the world could not survive under such a system. So God gives us until the day of our death to repent. Even after death it would not be right to punish us immediately because we have been in the grip of this passion, this *yetzer*. Therefore, God has created a situation called Gehenna – not necessarily a place as much as a time slot to purify the individual soul. In the future yet to come, however, there will be no *yetzer*, and therefore, man will receive his reward or punishment immediately. That is why R. Jannai and R. Simon both state that there will be no Gehenna in the world-to-come. The Rabbis feel that the only difference between our time and the Messianic age will be the absence of Jewish persecution, but that the *yetzer* will still exist and therefore Gehenna will be needed until the end of that period. R. Judah b. Ila'i not only affirms that there will be no need for Gehenna in the world-to-come because there will be no *yetzer*, there will also not be any external punishment. Rather, from the bodies of the wicked will emerge a fire that will consume them. This fire will not purify them; it will destroy them. (*Tiferet Tzion*)

Parashah Six, Midrash Seven

אָמַר רַבִּי לֵוִי שְׁלֹשָׁה דְבָרִים קוֹלָן הוֹלֵךְ מִסּוֹף הָעוֹלָם וְעַד סוֹפוֹ וְהַבְּרִיּוֹת בֵּינְתַיִם וְאֵינָם מַרְגִּישִׁים וְאֵלּוּ הֵן הַיּוֹם וְהַגְּשָׁמִים וְהַנֶּפֶשׁ בְּשָׁעָה שֶׁהִיא יוֹצֵאת מִן הַגּוּף

R. Levi said: The sound of three things travels from one end of the world to the other, between which there are creatures but none of them are aware of it, and these are they: the day, the rain, and the soul as it leaves the body.

This *midrash* should be understood as a further commentary to the verse 'And God set them in the firmament of the heavens' (Genesis 1:17). The previous *midrashin* have interpreted the term *raki'a* as meaning a firmament, and state that there are more than one above the earth. The depths of the firmaments are, as we have seen, each five hundred years journey by foot and a similar distance separates between them. God put the luminaries inside the second firmament, for our protection, so to speak. The result is that human beings cannot hear sounds being made there. If humans were able to hear the sounds made in the second firmament they would not be able to concentrate on anything else and would not be able to continue their normal activities (*Tiferet Tzion*). The 'day' referred to by R. Levi means the sun, that is, the sound of the sun in its orbit, and 'rain' means the sound of cosmic rain as it falls through space.

הַיּוֹם מִנַּיִן אָמַר רַ' יְהוּדָה אַתְּ סָבוּר שֶׁהוּא שָׁף בָּרָקִיעַ וְאֵינוֹ אֶלָּא כַּמַּסָּר הַזֶּה שֶׁהוּא נוֹסֵר בָּעֵץ הַגְּשָׁמִים מִנַּיִן אָמַר רַבִּי לֵוִי 'תְּהוֹם אֶל תְּהוֹם קוֹרֵא לְקוֹל וְגו'"
(תהלים מב, ח)

Whence do we know this of the day? R. Judah said: You may think that [the sun] floats through the heavens, but that is not so; it is rather like a saw sawing through wood. Whence do we know it of the rain? R. Levi said: [It is written], 'Where deep calls to deep in the roar of Your cataracts' (Psalms 42:8).

According to R. Judah, the passage of the sun through space is not silent but is as noisy as a saw going through wood. We know that from

241

the fact that the sun is in the center of the second firmament and the firmament has a kind of solidity to it, and as it goes through the sun makes a noise, but we do not hear it. As for rain, the meaning of the verse quoted is that the upper waters are calling to the lower waters, that is, the oceans, 'Send us your waters to irrigate the earth,' to which the lower waters reply, 'Send water down and we will come up to meet it.' This communication between them is like a roar but we do not hear it.

וְהַנֶּפֶשׁ בְּשָׁעָה שֶׁהִיא יוֹצֵאת מִן הַגּוּף מִנַּיִן דְּרַבִּי שְׁמוּאֵל אֲחוּי דְּרַבִּי פִּינְחָס בְּ"ר'
חָמָא הֲוֵי דָמִיךְ בְּצִפּוֹרִי וְהַוְיָן חַבְרַיָּה יְתִיבִין גַּבֵּהּ אַתַת מִלְּתָא וְשָׁרְיָן גָּחֲכִין אֲמַר
לְהוֹן כַּמָּה נַפְשֵׁהּ דַּאֲחוּהּ דְּהַהוּא גַּבְרָא מְקַצְצָה אַרְזִין וּמְקַצְצָה אִילָנוֹת וְאַתּוּן
יָתְבִין גָּחֲכוּן וְלָא יָדְעִין

And whence do we know it of the soul as it leaves the body? From [the story of] R. Samuel, the brother of R. Pinḥas b. R. Ḥama. He was dying in Sepphoris and a group of Sages were sitting with [R. Pinḥas]. Something happened to make them laugh and [R. Pinḥas] said to them, 'How the soul of that man's brother [i.e., his own brother] is breaking down cedars and breaking down [other] trees and you are sitting and laughing and are unaware of it.

Although he was in a different place, R. Pinḥas suddenly felt that his brother, R. Samuel, had died in Sepphoris, but the other Sages with him were unaware of it. For R. Pinḥas, the soul of his brother made a tremendous noise, comparable to the breaking of cedars and other trees, when it left his body, but only he heard it. The other Sages who were laughing at something comical they had heard were totally unaware. All these metaphors are intended to convey the thought that the Almighty, in His great kindness, spares us the terrible sounds of death. It also points to the fact that special and sensitive individuals can hear the actual sounds to which others are deaf.

There are several different versions of this story in various manuscripts and printed editions. In some R. Pinḥas and his colleagues were together with R. Samuel when he died.

* * *

Seed Thoughts

The most important events in our universe are not accompanied by sound, but rather by silence. Nowadays, I suppose, you could call this phenomenon 'the sound of silence.' Those events do not require public relations or advance publicity. All they require is reflection and understanding.

The most obvious of these great events is the journeyings of the sun through space. The sun is the central factor in the system that bears its name – the solar system. It is responsible for all those enabling influences such as heat, light, and power, which allow the physical universe to function together with its human and animal kingdom.

The second most important phenomenon is rain. Water is, by far, the preponderant material in the universe and, together with the sun, is responsible for sustaining life.

But the most sensational event of all is the separation of the soul from the human body at death. This goes beyond the sun and the rain, for they are natural phenomena, but this one is supernatural. The former relate to the natural world, but the latter releases the spiritual into eternity.

This remarkable event occurs whenever someone dies. It becomes even more meaningful when the one who leaves the earth is like the brother of R. Pinḥas, who has earned his way into the world-to-come by virtue of his good deeds.

This phenomenon is silent to our ears; to God, however, it is as though the whole world is shaken, as it was at Mt. Sinai at the giving of the Torah. Indeed, the return of the soul to God is equivalent to the return of the Torah to its Giver. Such is its transcendental significance.

What can we learn from this remarkable wonder? To try to see the world from God's perspective and change our scale of values; to try to cultivate a sensitive ear and listen to the 'sounds of silence' that can so deeply stir the human soul.

When a human being dies, a part of the Torah is returned with him. But when a great Torah scholar dies, more of the Torah is left behind than he takes with him. This is because he has fulfilled the greatest of all roles and has transmitted the Torah's message to other souls whom he has taught.

* * *

Additional Commentary

Sounds
Our unawareness of these sounds is not meant as a criticism of mankind. To the contrary, it emphasizes the grace of the Almighty who realized that human beings could not withstand the power of such sounds. (*Yefei To'ar*)

*

The first two sounds are natural sounds and therefore human beings take them for granted and they are not perceived. The sound of the soul departing the human body, however, is a supernatural sound and only true servants of the Lord, such as R. Pinḥas, are privileged to discern them. (RZWE)

*

The sound of the soul

The explanation of the sound of the soul leaving the body is based on the talmudic saying (Tractate Ketubot 17a) that by right 600,000 people should be present at the departure of the soul to correspond to the 600,000 that were present at the giving of the soul. The point is that when the soul leaves the body so does the Torah, since the dead are not obliged to study Torah, only the living. Furthermore, in the account of the giving of the Torah we read, 'The blare of the horn grew louder and louder' (Exodus 19:19) and another verse, which is interpreted as referring to the giving of the Torah, reads, 'The voice of the Lord shatters the cedars of Lebanon' (Psalms 29:5). Thus, when the soul leaves the body it makes a sound like the shattering of the cedars of Lebanon, because with it the Torah returns to God, and regarding Torah the same circumstance should surround its departure as surrounded its arrival.

It should also be added that as long as the soul is in the body it cannot use its great powers except in conformity with the weak powers of the body that encloses it, since all its activities must be through the body. After it leaves the body, however, its strength is as unlimited as the source from which it was drawn. It therefore has the power to shatter the cedars of Lebanon, renowned for their beauty and strength, by the mere sound of its voice. (*Tiferet Tzion*)

Parashah Six, Midrash Eight

According to the cosmogony of the Rabbis, the world is flat and surrounded on all sides by the oceans. The heavens are spread over it like a
canopy. The ends of the earth will thus touch the circular covering of the
heavens. The shape of the heavens was one half of a ball or sphere, like a
spherical vault (*kippah*) suspended above the earth. Thus the oceans find
themselves between the ends of the earth and the ends of the heavens.
This helps us understand what is now being asked. (RZWE)

'וַיִּתֵּן אֹתָם אֱלֹהִים בִּרְקִיעַ הַשָּׁמָיִם' (בראשית א, יז) כֵּיצַד גַּלְגַּל חַמָּה וּלְבָנָה שׁוֹקְעִים
בָּרָקִיעַ ר' יְהוּדָה בַּר אִלְעַאי וְרַבָּנָן רַבָּנָן אָמְרִין מֵאֲחוֹרֵי הַכִּפָּה וּלְמָטָה וְר' יְהוּדָה
בַּר אִלְעַאי אָמַר מֵאֲחוֹרֵי הַכִּפָּה וּלְמָעְלָה

**'And God set them in the firmament of the heavens' (Genesis 1:17).
How do the orbs of the sun and the moon set? R. Judah b. R. Ila'i and
the Rabbis disagree. The Rabbis maintained: Behind the vault and
below it. R. Judah said: Behind the vault and above it.**

This *midrash* returns to the text treated at the beginning of *Midrash Five*,
above, but discusses what happens to the sun and the moon when they
set, that is, when they are no longer visible. Rabbi Judah b. Ila'i holds that
the luminaries, after disappearing from view, then rise above the vault of
the heavens and head towards the east where they begin their orbit again.
The Rabbis, like most of the non-Jewish astronomers of their time, held
the view that at night the sun sinks below the horizon, travels under the
earth towards the east where it rises again the following day.

אָמַר ר' יוֹחָנָן נְרָאִין דִּבְרֵי ר' יְהוּדָה בַּר אִלְעַאי דְּהוּא אָמַר מֵאֲחוֹרֵי הַכִּפָּה וּלְמָעְלָה
בִּימוֹת הַחַמָּה שֶׁכָּל הָעוֹלָם כֻּלּוֹ רוֹתֵחַ וּמַעְיָנוֹת צוֹנְנִין וּמִלְּהוֹן דְּרַבָּנָן דְּאָמְרִין
מֵאֲחוֹרֵי הַכִּפָּה וּלְמָטָה בִּימוֹת הַגְּשָׁמִים שֶׁכָּל הָעוֹלָם כֻּלּוֹ צוֹנֵן וּמַעְיָנוֹת פּוֹשְׁרִין

**R. Joḥanan said: The view of R. Judah b. R. Ila'i that it is behind the
vault and above it is preferable in summertime, when the whole
world is hot while the wells are cold; and the opinion of the Rabbis
that it is behind the vault and below appears correct in respect of
winter, when the whole world is cold and the wells are tepid.**

245

The assumption here is that the sun remains hot even during the night, except that its heat does not reach the surface of the earth. Thus R. Joḥanan, observing the change in the natural phenomena in summer and winter, came to the following conclusions. In summer the wells are cold, which means that the sun cannot be under the earth, since then it would heat up the wells. Thus, it must be above the vault of the sky where its heat cannot affect the wells. In winter however, the temperature of the water in the wells is higher than that on the surface of the earth, therefore it must have been warmed by the sun, which is under the earth.

אָמַר רַבִּי שִׁמְעוֹן בֶּן יוֹחַאי אֵין אָנוּ יוֹדְעִין אִם פּוֹרְחִין הֵן בָּאֲוִיר וְאִם שָׁפִין בָּרָקִיעַ וְאִם מְהַלְּכִין הֵן כְּדַרְכָּן הַדָּבָר קָשֶׁה מְאֹד וְאִי אֶפְשָׁר לַבְּרִיּוֹת לַעֲמֹד עָלָיו

R. Simon b. Yoḥai said: We do not know whether [the sun and the moon] fly through the air, glide in the heavens, or travel in their usual manner. This is an exceedingly difficult matter; and no person can fathom it.

R. Simon b. Yoḥai makes the point that even when they are visible to the eye, we do not understand the mechanics of the movements of the sun or the moon, and we certainly cannot understand how they move when they are invisible. He therefore adopts a more realistic view.

* * *

Seed Thoughts

Said R. Simon b. Yoḥai: The whole question of the constellations is a very difficult matter and no person can fathom it.

Does that mean that we are not supposed to try? The saying of R. Simon b. Yoḥai comes after a number of Sages have already given their opinions. They tried but their answers were not universally accepted.

In many places it is suggested to us that speculation on metaphysical things is unproductive and will never create significant results. On the other hand there is something about the restlessness and curiosity of the human being that they themselves experienced. From time to time the Rabbis discouraged it, knowing full well that once the faucet of intellectual thinking is turned on it can never be turned off.

* * *

Additional Commentary

Summer and winter
The differentiation made by R. Joḥanan about the rainy season and the

summer season is above my comprehension; may God illumine our eyes. (RZWE)

*

A difficult problem
You will discover that the Holy Zohar clarifies this problem in a way that is acceptable to our generation. It has thus been revealed to us. (*Ha-Midrash ha-Mevo'ar*)

*

Additional thought
The disagreement between R. Judah bar Ila'i and the Sages reflects a difference of opinion on how God conducts the world. The Sages feel that the world is conducted as set up at creation, namely, by means of the operation of natural laws. This is the interpretation of 'behind the *kippah* and below it.' R. Judah bar Ila'i affirms that God's ways are determined by man's behavior and these are not fixed by any constellation. Thus, 'behind the *kippah* and above it' is where natural laws do not apply.

As to the distinctions made by R. Johanan about summer and winter, these should be understood as affirming that God responds to man's behavior even in times of difficulties. Thus, according to R. Johanan, the place of the constellations may be both above and below the horizon, but Israel is not affected by it. The laws of providence will operate.

R. Simon bar Yohai's observation should also be perceived in the same light. The three possible methods of movement in space that he describes reflect the various conditions of man. Those who seem to float in space are the most successful in life. There are those who seem to have only bad luck and suffering, as though their fortune is constantly being depressed. Finally, there are the average persons who sometimes do better and sometimes do worse. Unfortunately, we can never know which of these conditions will apply to whom. (*Tiferet Tzion*)

Parashah Six, Midrash Nine

וְלִמְשֹׁל בַּיּוֹם וּבַלַּיְלָה וְגוֹ' אָמַר רַ' אִילְפָא אִם לְעָנְיַן הַמְּאוֹרוֹת הֲלוֹא כְבָר נֶאֱמַר
'אֶת הַמָּאוֹר הַגָּדוֹל לְמֶמְשֶׁלֶת הַיּוֹם' וּמַה תַּלְמוּד לוֹמַר 'וְלִמְשֹׁל בַּיּוֹם וּבַלַּיְלָה'
אֶלָּא אֵלּוּ הַצַּדִּיקִים שֶׁהֵן שׁוֹלְטִין בַּמֶּה שֶׁנִּבְרָא לְהָאִיר בַּיּוֹם וּבַמֶּה שֶׁנִּבְרָא לְהָאִיר
בַּלַּיְלָה הָדָא הוּא דִּכְתִיב 'וַיִּדֹּם הַשֶּׁמֶשׁ וְיָרֵחַ עָמָד עַד יִקֹּם גּוֹי אֹיְבָיו הֲלֹא הִיא
כְתוּבָה עַל סֵפֶר הַיָּשָׁר' (יהושע י, יג) מַאי 'סֵפֶר הַיָּשָׁר' סֵפֶר אַבְרָהָם יִצְחָק וְיַעֲקֹב
וְאַמַּאי קָרֵי לֵהּ 'סֵפֶר הַיָּשָׁר' דִּכְתִיב 'תָּמֹת נַפְשִׁי מוֹת יְשָׁרִים' (במדבר כג, י)

'And to dominate the day and the night' (Genesis 1:18). R. Ilfa said: If
this refers to the luminaries, surely it has already been stated, 'The
greater light to dominate the day...' (verse 16). What then is taught by
'And to dominate the day and the night'? It refers to the righteous,
who have power over what was created to give light by day and
what was created to give light by night, as it is written, 'And the sun
stood still and the moon halted... is it not so written in the Book of
Yashar' (Joshua 10:13). What is 'the Book of Yashar'? It is the book of
Abraham, Isaac, and Jacob (i.e., Genesis). And why is it called 'the
Book of Yashar'? Because it is written [in Balaam's prophecy], 'May
I die the death of the righteous [yesharim]' (Numbers 23:10).

The proof-verse from Joshua not only shows that Joshua could control the
sun and the moon, it also gives as the source for such authority the Book
of Yashar. R. Ilfa identifies that book with Genesis because the context of
Balaam's wish to die the death of the righteous (yesharim, the plural form
of yashar) is a reference to the Patriarchs. In the previous verse Balaam
says, 'From the top of the rocks [צוּרִים, tzurim] I see [the Children of Israel]'
and צוּר is a reference to the Patriarchs and Matriarch as in Isaiah 51:1-2,
'Look to the rock (tzur) you were hewn from... look back to Abraham
your father....' The conclusion to be drawn is that the verse with which
this midrash began is the source of Joshua's authority.

רַ' חֲלַפְתָּא מַיְתֵי לֵהּ מִן הָכָא 'וְלִמְשֹׁל בַּיּוֹם וּבַלַּיְלָה' רַבִּי חָנִין בְּשֵׁם רַבִּי שְׁמוּאֵל
מַיְתֵי לַהּ מִסֵּיפָא דִּסְפָרָא 'וְאוּלָם אָחִיו הַקָּטֹן יִגְדַּל מִמֶּנּוּ' (בראשית מח, יט) וְאֶפְשָׁר
כֵּן אֶלָּא זֶה יְהוֹשֻׁעַ שֶׁהוּא עוֹמֵד מִמֶּנּוּ שֶׁהוּא מַעֲמִיד גַּלְגַּל חַמָּה וּלְבָנָה שֶׁהֵן
שׁוֹלְטִין מִסּוֹף הָעוֹלָם וְעַד סוֹפוֹ

R. Ḥalafta [also sees the source of Joshua's ability to control the sun and the moon as being] from 'And to dominate the day and the night.' R. Ḥanin in the name of R. Samuel finds the source [in a verse] at the end of the Book [of Genesis]: 'Yet his younger brother [Ephraim] shall be greater than he [Manasseh] and his offspring shall become a multitude of nations' (Genesis 48:19). Now, is it possible [that the offspring of one son can fill up the entire world]? Hence this must refer to Joshua, who was a descendant [of Ephraim] who would stay the sun and the moon, which rule from one end of the world to the other.

The miracle of the sun and moon stopping in their tracks, which was brought about by Joshua, affected the whole world and thus Jacob's blessing for Ephraim was fulfilled, since Joshua was of the tribe of Ephraim. R. Ḥanin agrees that the Book of Yashar, mentioned in Joshua, is Genesis, but claims that the reference is not to Genesis 1:18 at the beginning of the Book, but rather to 48:19, near the end.

רַבִּי חָנָן בְּשֵׁם ר' שְׁמוּאֵל בַּר רַב יִצְחָק מַיְתֵי לַהּ מִסּוֹפָא דְאוֹרְיְתָא 'בְּכוֹר שׁוֹרוֹ הָדָר לוֹ' (דברים לג, יז) אֶפְשָׁר כֵּן אֶלָּא זֶה יְהוֹשֻׁעַ שֶׁהוּא עוֹמֵד מִמֶּנּוּ שֶׁהוּא מַעֲמִיד גַּלְגַּל חַמָּה וּלְבָנָה שֶׁהֵן שׁוֹלְטִין מִסּוֹף הָעוֹלָם וְעַד סוֹפוֹ

R. Ḥanan in the name of R. Samuel b. R. Isaac identified [the source in a verse] from the end of the Torah: 'Like a firstling bull in his majesty, he has horns like the horns of the wild ox; with them he gores the peoples, the ends of the earth one and all. These are the myriads of Ephraim' (Deuteronomy 33:17). Is that possible? Hence it refers to Joshua who would spring from [Joseph] and stay the sun and the moon, which rule from one end of the world to the other.

R. Ḥanan claims that the Book of Yashar is Deuteronomy and not Genesis. He reaches this conclusion because Deuteronomy contains the word ישר, *Yashar*, no less than five times in commandments such as 'Do what is right [*ha-yashar*] and good in the sight of the Lord' (Deuteronomy 6:18; also 12:8, 12:25, 13:19, 21:9). Therefore, if any Book deserves to be called Yashar it must be Deuteronomy. The proof-text is from Moses' blessing for the tribes of Joseph, to one of which, Ephraim, Joshua belonged.

  In addition to this indication that the Book of Yashar refers to Deuteronomy, the next *midrash* brings further evidence of Joshua's connection with that Book.

דְּאָמַר רַבִּי שִׁמְעוֹן בֶּן יוֹחַאי סֵפֶר מִשְׁנֵה תוֹרָה הָיָה סִגְנוֹן לִיהוֹשֻׁעַ בְּשָׁעָה שֶׁנִּגְלָה
עָלָיו הַקָּדוֹשׁ בָּרוּךְ הוּא מְצָאוֹ יוֹשֵׁב וְסֵפֶר מִשְׁנֵה תוֹרָה בְּיָדוֹ אָמַר לוֹ חֲזַק יְהוֹשֻׁעַ
אֱמַץ יְהוֹשֻׁעַ 'לֹא יָמוּשׁ סֵפֶר הַתּוֹרָה הַזֶּה וְגוֹ'' (יהושע א, ח) נְטָלוֹ וְהֶרְאָהוּ אוֹתוֹ
לְגַלְגַּל חַמָּה אָמַר לוֹ כְּשֵׁם שֶׁלֹּא דוֹמַמְתִּי מִזֶּה אַף אַתָּה דֹּם מִלְּפָנַי מִיָּד 'וַיִּדֹּם
הַשֶּׁמֶשׁ וְיָרֵחַ עָמָד' (שם י, יג)

R. Simon b. Yoḥai said: 'The Book of Deuteronomy was Joshua's style. When the Holy One, blessed be He, revealed Himself to [Joshua], He found him sitting with the Book of Deuteronomy in his hand. [God] said to him, 'Be strong, Joshua! Be of good courage, Joshua!' (Joshua 1:6). And it is also written, 'This Book of the Torah shall not cease from your lips' (ibid., verse 8). Thereupon, [Joshua] took it and showed it to the orb of the sun and said: 'Just as I have not stood still from studying this, so you, too, stand still before me!' Straightway, 'And the sun stood still' (ibid. 10:13).

According to R. Simon b. Yoḥai, Joshua had a special connection to Deuteronomy. It was like a flag and on that flag there was written the entire Book of Deuteronomy (Mirkin), so that when it says as quoted above, 'with them he shall gore peoples,' the meaning is with the Book of Deuteronomy that was inscribed on his flag. Joshua had the status of a king according to RDL and a king is required by Torah law to keep a copy of Deuteronomy with him at all times. Since there is no evidence of a scroll in his possession, this must refer to the flag on which was written the Book of Deuteronomy. Joshua's argument to the sun was: I have never ceased to study the Torah and that gives me the right to command you to desist. (*Yefei To'ar*)

However, the sun did not take kindly to this order and had to be spoken to very sharply. (RZWE)

אָמַר ר' יִצְחָק אֲמַר לֵהּ עַבְדָּא בִישָׁא לָא זְבִינָא דְּאַבָּא אַתְּ לֹא כָּךְ רָאָה אוֹתְךָ אַבָּא
בַּחֲלוֹם 'וְהִנֵּה הַשֶּׁמֶשׁ וְהַיָּרֵחַ וְגוֹ'' (בראשית לז, ט) מִיָּד 'וַיִּדֹּם הַשֶּׁמֶשׁ וְיָרֵחַ וְגוֹמֵר'

R. Isaac said: [Joshua] said to [the sun], 'You are a bad servant; were you not the chattel of my ancestor [Joseph]; did not my ancestor see you thus in a dream, "The sun and the moon and eleven stars bowed down to me" (Genesis 37:9).' Immediately, 'And the sun stood still' (Joshua 10:13).

Joshua reminded the sun and the moon that they had already been under the control of his ancestor, Joseph, in homage to whom they bowed down.

Therefore they were obliged to obey the order given to them by Joseph's descendant, Joshua. The luminaries found this argument irrefutable and immediately did Joshua's will.

* * *

Seed Thoughts (1)

In connection with the creation of light, the verb *va-yiten* is used. It means to set or to place, but it is also the verb from which *matanah*, gift, is derived. The teaching here is that light is God's great gift to the world but is the kind of gift that has special meaning for the righteous. The gifts of light and darkness are tremendous blessings but they can be abused. Therefore, power was given to the righteous to dominate them.

The *Tiferet Tzion* commentary explains it this way: God has given to the righteous the gift of light including all of the physical enjoyments that light brings with it, because a righteous person will use even physical enjoyment for the purpose of serving God.

From the homiletical point of view, this should be seen as a lesson of what ought to happen and might be compared with the *Ethics of the Fathers* (5:8): 'Beauty, vigour, affluence, honor, wisdom, old age, and children are an adornment for the righteous and an adornment for the world.' The meaning is that these qualities or achievements are only good for the world when they are in the possession of the righteous.

Most of the problems of society would be manageable if good people were willing to come forward, take leadership, and assume power when necessary with all its challenges, including the risks of corruption. Light was given as a challenge to the righteous to come forward and do their share for the community. As the *Ethics of the Fathers* also says (2:6): 'In a place where there are no right people, you try to be the right one.'

* * *

Seed Thoughts (2)

These words are written at a time when concern for the environment is sweeping the world. The pollution of the atmosphere and the alleged damage to the ozone layer have made sensitive people alert to the dangers now facing the world as man's natural habitat.

That man is more important than nature is granted. But does that give man the right to pollute natural resources that ultimately lead to sickness and the destruction of the very human beings who are supposed to be superior to nature?

Environmentalism has also given rise to the animal rights movement.

This movement has already wrought havoc with the fur industry, has interfered with trapping, and has thus tampered with the way of life of the aboriginal peoples. In short, it has tried to raise animals to the status of human beings.

Granted that animals should not be made to suffer or be confined to one spot all their lives as is alleged in the production of veal, for example, and other forms of modern farming technology. On the other hand, is it not a fact that animals were meant to serve man and not the other way around?

The question can, however, be seriously asked whether man can be relied upon to know the difference between the use of animals and their abuse. That is why the *midrash* makes the important point that it is not ordinary man who is meant to dominate nature but the *tzaddik*, the righteous person. The good human being would have the sensitivity and the moral dimension to do with nature, with animal nature and with human nature, that which is right and good.

* * *

Additional Commentary

The righteous
The fundamental teaching of this *midrash* is the fact that the righteous person is meant to dominate the sun and the moon and not the other way around. This has already been stated. The reference to Abraham is most significant. Attention should be called to the vision of Abraham, who was called outside and asked to look heavenwards. A *midrash* says that God placed Abraham somewhere in outer space at a vantage point from which he could see the earth below him. This is the dramatic demonstration that the good man is meant to dominate the natural world and he is called upon to do so. (RZWE)

Parashah Seven, Midrash One

'וַיֹּאמֶר אֱלֹהִים יִשְׁרְצוּ הַמַּיִם' (א, כ) כְּתִיב 'אֵין כָּמוֹךָ בָאֱלֹהִים וְגוֹ'' (תהלים פו, ח)
בְּנוֹהֵג שֶׁבָּעוֹלָם בָּשָׂר וָדָם צָר צוּרָה בַּיַּבָּשָׁה אֲבָל הַקָּדוֹשׁ בָּרוּךְ הוּא צָר צוּרָה
בַּמַּיִם שֶׁנֶּאֱמַר 'וַיֹּאמֶר אֱלֹהִים יִשְׁרְצוּ הַמַּיִם שֶׁרֶץ נֶפֶשׁ חַיָּה'

'And God said: "Let the waters swarm with swarms of living
creatures" (1:20).' It is written, 'There is none like You among the
gods, O Lord, and there are no deeds like Yours' (Psalms 86:8). In
human practice a mortal king draws a figure on dry land, but the
Holy One, blessed be He, created figures in water as it is said, 'And
God said: "Let the waters swarm…"'

The point to note from this text is that the fish were created from the water
and not from the land at the sea bottom. The emphasis of the verse from
Psalms is not merely that there is none like God, but that there are no
works that can compare with His. The key words are 'There are no deeds
like Yours.' A human being can only create a form from a solid, not from
water, which is a liquid, because the water will dissipate whatever the
person makes in it. But God can do that as well. So, when the text says,
'Let the waters produce fish,' it means that the act of creation was in the
water itself. From then on the fish would reproduce on their own.

* * *

Seed Thoughts

That man is not God is incontrovertible. That there is no one like God is
beyond dispute. That God's works are beyond man's possibilities is also
a contention that is beyond argument.

On the other hand, the greatest of God's works is man. Man, through
his unique endowments, has been able to do many more things than the
writers of the *midrash* thought possible. One of these might even be described as creating form in water.

I am thinking, at the moment, of *in vitro* fertilization, where it is possible
to produce life outside the womb. This is not to be compared with what
God can do, but it is nonetheless, an impressive display of how close man
can come in imitating his Maker.

Maybe that is one of the reasons why the verse from Psalms that begins 'There is none like You among the gods' is used as an introduction to the Torah service in the synagogue. God has given man tremendous power, but He has also given him a Torah so that his power may be used above all other things to spiritualize man.

* * *

Additional Commentary

Draws a figure

Human beings can only create something from something. They can only do so in a place where there is visibility such as land, and where there is air and not water. The Holy One, blessed be He, however, can create *ex nihilo* (something from nothing) and does so unconditionally whether in darkness or water, and so forth. (RZWE)

*

An additional miracle is hinted at here. God's logic does not follow that of man. You would have imagined that first, fish would have been created and only then would the fish have been commanded to multiply. But God skipped over the intermediary step so that not only 'There is none like You among the gods,' but also 'And there are no deeds like Yours.' (*Tiferet Tzion*)

Parashah Seven, Midrash Two

יַעֲקֹב אִישׁ כְּפַר נְבוֹרָאִי הוֹרָה בְּצוֹר דָּגִים טְעוּנִין שְׁחִיטָה שָׁמַע ר' חַגַּי שָׁלַח לֵהּ
תָּא לְקֵי אֲמַר לֵהּ בַּר אֵינָשׁ דְּאָמַר מִלְתָּא מִן אוֹרְיְתָא לְקֵי אֲמַר לֵהּ מְנַיִן הִיא
דְאוֹרְיְתָא אֲמַר לֵהּ מִן הָדָא דִכְתִיב 'וַיֹּאמֶר אֱלֹהִים יִשְׁרְצוּ הַמַּיִם שֶׁרֶץ נֶפֶשׁ חַיָּה
וְעוֹף יְעוֹפֵף עַל הָאָרֶץ' וּמָה עוֹף טָעוּן שְׁחִיטָה אַף דָּגִים טְעוּנִין שְׁחִיטָה אֲמַר לֵהּ
לָא הוֹרֵית טָב אֲמַר לֵהּ מְנַיִן אַתְּ מוֹדַע לִי אֲמַר לֵהּ רְבַע וַאֲנָא מוֹדַע לָךְ דִּכְתִיב
'הֲצֹאן וּבָקָר יִשָּׁחֵט לָהֶם וּמָצָא לָהֶם וְאִם אֶת כָּל דְּגֵי הַיָּם יֵאָסֵף לָהֶם וּמָצָא לָהֶם'
(במדבר יא, כב) יִשָּׁחֵט אֵין כְּתִיב כָּאן אֶלָּא 'יֵאָסֵף' אָמַר חֲבוֹט חֲבָטָךְ רְצוֹף רְצָפֵּךְ
דְּהִיא טָבָא לְאוּלְפָנָא

Jacob of Kefar Nevora'i gave a ruling in Tyre that fish must be ritually slaughtered. R. Ḥaggai heard [of this ruling] and sent him a message: 'Come and be flagellated.' [Jacob] said to him, 'When a man gives a ruling from the Torah is he to be flagellated?!' [R. Ḥaggai] asked him, 'What is the Scriptural source?' He answered 'Because it is written, "Let the waters swarm with swarms of living creatures, and birds that fly above the earth" – just as birds must be ritually slaughtered, so too must fish be ritually slaughtered.' 'You have not ruled correctly,' said [R. Ḥaggai] to him. [Jacob then] said 'What is the source of what you tell me?' [R. Ḥaggai] answered, 'Crouch down [to be lashed] and I will tell you. It is written, "Could enough flocks and herds be slaughtered to suffice them? Or could all the fish of the sea be gathered for them to suffice them?" (Numbers 11:22) – "slaughter" is not written here [regarding fish], but "gathered"!' [Jacob] said, 'Strike me with your blows, force me to lie down; it is good [for me] to learn!'

R. Jacob was guilty of giving an halakhic decision not in accordance with the law, for which the punishment is flagellation. He had based his ruling on his own interpretation of the verse and asked, 'Can I be punished for interpreting the Torah?' The answer is, 'Yes,' for one is not permitted to interpret the Scriptures in opposition to the tradition. From our text R. Jacob tried to make a comparison between fowl and fish. R. Ḥaggai, however, offered much better scriptural proof for the law that fish do not require *sheḥita*, a proof that is also given in the Talmud: In the case of fish, 'gathering them' is all that is required for fish to be kosher for eating. This was not the only instance in which Jacob handed down incorrect halakhic decisions, as we shall now see.

יַעֲקֹב אִישׁ כְּפַר נְבוֹרָאִי הוֹרָה בְּצוֹר מֻתָּר לָמוּל בְּנָהּ שֶׁל נָכְרִית בְּשַׁבָּת שָׁמַע רַבִּי חַגַּי שָׁלַח לֵהּ תָּא לְקִי אֲמַר לֵהּ בַּר נָשׁ דְּאָמַר מִלְתָּא דְאוֹרָיְתָא לָקֵי אֲמַר לֵהּ וּמַן הִיא דְאוֹרָיְתָא אֲמַר לֵהּ 'וַיִּתְיַלְדוּ עַל מִשְׁפְּחֹתָם לְבֵית אֲבֹתָם' (שם א, יח) מִשְׁפַּחַת אָב קְרוּיָה מִשְׁפָּחָה מִשְׁפַּחַת אֵם אֵינָהּ קְרוּיָה מִשְׁפָּחָה אֲמַר לֵהּ לָא הוֹרֵית טָב אֲמַר לֵהּ וּמִנַּיִן אַתְּ מוֹדַע לִי אֲמַר לֵהּ רְבִיע וַאֲנָא מוֹדַע לָךְ אֲמַר אִם אֲתֵי בַּר עֲבוֹדַת כּוֹכָבִים לְגַבָּךְ וְיֹאמַר לָךְ אֲנָא בָּעֵי מִתְעַבְּדָא יְהוּדִי עַל מְנָת לְמִגְזְרָה בְּיוֹמָא דְשַׁבְּתָא אוֹ בְּיוֹמָא דְכִפּוּרַיָּא מְחַלְּלִין אוֹתוֹ עָלָיו וַהֲלוֹא אֵין מְחַלְּלִין שַׁבָּת וְיוֹם הַכִּפּוּרִים אֶלָּא עַל בְּנָהּ שֶׁל בַּת יִשְׂרְאֵלִית בִּלְבָד אֲמַר לֵהּ וּמִנַּיִן לָךְ מִן הָדָא דִכְתִיב 'וְעַתָּה נִכְרָת בְּרִית לֵאלֹהֵינוּ לְהוֹצִיא כָל נָשִׁים וְהַנּוֹלָד מֵהֶם בַּעֲצַת ה' וְגוֹ'' (עזרא י, ג) אֲמַר לֵהּ רַבִּי וּמִן הַקַּבָּלָה אַתָּה מַלְקֵנִי

Jacob of Kefar Nevora'i gave a ruling in Tyre that it is permitted to circumcise the infant son of a gentile woman [and a Jewish father] on the Sabbath. When R. Ḥaggai heard [of this ruling] and sent him a message: 'Come and be flagellated.' [Jacob] said to him, 'When a man gives a ruling from the Torah is he to be flagellated?!' [R. Ḥaggai] asked him, 'What is the scriptural source?' He answered 'Because it is written, "[They convoked the whole community] who were registered according to their fathers' clans" (Numbers 1:18) – the family [or clan] of the father is called family; the family of the mother is not called family.' 'You have not ruled correctly,' said [R. Ḥaggai] to him. [Jacob then] said 'What is the source of what you tell me?' [R. Ḥaggai] answered, 'Crouch down [to be lashed] and I will tell you. If a non-Jew approached you and said, "I wish to become a Jew on condition that I be circumcised on the Sabbath or on the Day of Atonement," would you desecrate that holy day for him? Surely the Sabbath and the Day of Atonement can only be violated for circumcision in the case of the son of a Jewish woman alone!' [Jacob then] asked, 'What is your source [for that]?' [To which R. Ḥaggai replied], 'It is written, "Now then, let us make a covenant with our God to expel all these [non-Jewish] women, and those who have been born to them" (Ezra 10:3).' [Jacob] protested, 'Rabbi, will you actually punish me on the strength of tradition?!'

Jacob had interpreted the verse from Numbers to mean that the religion

of a child is fixed according to his father. This means that a child born of
a Jewish father and Gentile mother is a Jew and if a male, he should be
circumcised on the eighth day of his birth even if that day is Shabbat or
the Day of Atonement. This is not in accordance with the *halakhah*, which
rules that it is the mother's status that establishes whether the child is a
Jew or not. This was exactly the thrust of R. Ḥaggai's question, 'If a
non-Jew approached you and said, "I wish to become a Jew...."' Since the
would-be convert is not Jewish, obviously it is not permitted to desecrate
Shabbat in order to circumcise him. Jacob challenged this comparison of
the child of a Gentile woman to a non-Jew and asked for the source for
that ruling. Jacob agreed that a Gentile who comes for conversion cannot
be circumcised on Shabbat; however, he argued that the child of a Jewish
father and Gentile mother is Jewish. Rabbi Ḥaggai then brought the verse
from Ezra in which a covenant was made between the people and God
according to which the non-Jewish wives *and their children* were expelled
from the community. This proves that the children of a Gentile wife are
not considered Jews. R. Jacob objected that he could not be condemned
on the basis of a verse from the Book of Ezra, which does not have the
authority of the Torah.

אָמַר לֵהּ וְהָכְתִיב תַּמָּן 'וְכַתּוֹרָה יֵעָשֶׂה' (שם שם, שם) אָמַר לֵהּ מֵאֵיזוֹ תּוֹרָה אָמַר
לֵהּ מִן הַהוּא דַּאֲמַר רַבִּי יוֹחָנָן בְּשֵׁם רַבִּי שִׁמְעוֹן בֶּן יוֹחַאי 'וְלֹא תִתְחַתֵּן וְגוֹ'' (דברים
ז, ג) מִפְּנֵי מָה 'כִּי יָסִיר אֶת בִּנְךָ מֵאַחֲרַי' (שם שם, ד) בִּנְךָ הַבָּא מִיִּשְׂרְאֵלִית קָרוּי בִּנְךָ
וְאֵין בִּנְךָ הַבָּא מִן עוֹבֶדֶת כּוֹכָבִים קָרוּי בִּנְךָ אָמַר לֵהּ חֲבוֹט חֲבָטָךְ דְּהִיא טָבָא
בְּקוּלְטָא וּרְצוֹף רְצָפָּךְ דְּהִיא טָבָא בְּאוּלְפָנָא

**R. Ḥaggai retorted, 'In [that very verse in Ezra] it is written "Let it
be done according to the Torah" (ibid.).' [Jacob, however,] insisted,
'From which [verse in] the Torah?' [R. Ḥaggai] answered, 'From that
which R. Joḥanan said in the name of R. Simon bar Yoḥai: "You
shall not intermarry with them [i.e., the Canaanite peoples]"
(Deuteronomy 7:3). And why is that? "For he [the Gentile] will turn
your son away from Me" (ibid. 7:4). The son that issues from a Jewish
mother is considered "your" son, but the son issuing from a
non-Jewish mother is not considered "your" son.' [Jacob then]
conceded, 'Strike me with your blows, which is good to make me
absorb [what you have just said], force me to lie down; it is good [for
me] to learn!'**

R. Ḥaggai pointed out that the very verse from Ezra that ordered the
expulsion of the Gentile wives and their children stated that it was accord-

ing to Torah law, and when Jacob insisted and asked where is such a thing stated in the Torah, R. Ḥaggai apprised him of R. Simon bar Yoḥai's exposition on the verse from Deuteronomy. That verse states that the Gentile father will turn your son away from God, but it does not say that the Gentile mother will do so, for the simple reason that the son of a Gentile mother is not Jewish and cannot therefore be turned away from God. This source for the law that the status of a child follows it mother's status is also given in the Talmud.

* * *

Seed Thoughts

Two different issues are raised here. Why should not fish require slaughter since this could be derived by implication from a biblical verse? Secondly, why not accept the child of a Jewish father and a non-Jewish mother as Jewish since there seems to be a biblical source for ruling that a child's religious status follows that of his father.

Notice that in each case the representative of the tradition not only gives an appropriate answer, but becomes very emphatic and asserts that the question alone merits punishment. R. Ḥaggai was not only annoyed that Jacob of Kfar Nevora'i had misinterpreted a biblical verse, but more so because he was unaware that there was a tradition, meaning the Oral Law, that he should have known about.

This *midrash* offers us a rare look at the meaning of the oral tradition. For the Sages of the Talmud, the oral tradition was first and foremost a tradition handed down as the legitimate interpretation of Scripture.

The attempt to argue tradition from Scripture was a secondary step. R. Ḥaggai is emphasizing this source as well as trying to trace this specific tradition even to biblical verses as demonstrated in the Book of Ezra. The proofs from Scripture or from reason are used to strengthen the tradition.

Once again the tradition is being challenged by the Reform movement that has affirmed patrilineal descent as an acceptable form of Jewish status.

Whenever a doctrine becomes polemical, it is not enough to assert the law. Arguments are required. The arguments are not the reason for the law, but if they are cogent, they can help defend it.

My own view is that the Jewish people are fortunate to have a doctrine like matrilineal descent as the criterion for Jewish status for the following reasons: One always knows who the mother of a child is but not always who the father is. Furthermore, generally speaking, a mother spends more time with her child and is therefore usually the most influential in determining his or her development, including the religious upbringing. It is also a tremendous form of recognition of Jewish womanhood to acknowledge that Jewish status depends entirely upon her.

The bottom line is that the future of the Jewish people depends upon Jewish marriage and that means the marriage of a Jewish man to a Jewish woman. Every effort should be made to make such marriages as numerous and as successful as possible.

A Jewish child requires a father and a mother who share the same ideals and the Jewish way of life.

* * *

Additional Commentary

Living creatures and fowl
The main motivation for this *midrash* is the verse in Genesis that mentions living creatures in one part of the verse and fowl in the other. The point is that the *gezeirah shavah*, the hermeneutic principle of analogy, is not to be used. (*Tiferet Tzion*)

*

Kabbalah... tradition
The Books of the Prophets and the Books of the Writings are referred to as *divrei kabbalah*, 'teachings of tradition,' which have received their guidance from previous generations. Even though, in Jewish law, the Oral Law is given the same authority as the Written Law, it may be different in this case because of the verse in Numbers with patrilineal emphasis that seems to contradict the accepted tradition. It is now necessary to accommodate the rendition to the biblical source, possibly indicating that one was meant only for its own time and the other for all the generations. (Mirkin)

Parashah Seven, Midrash Three

'וְעוֹף יְעוֹפֵף' (א, כ) בְּנוֹהַג שֶׁבָּעוֹלָם מֶלֶךְ בָּשָׂר וָדָם בּוֹנֶה פְּלָטִין וּמַשְׂרֶה דִיוֹרִין
בָּעֶלְיוֹנִים וּבַתַּחְתּוֹנִים שֶׁמָּא בֶּחָלָל אֲבָל הַקָּדוֹשׁ בָּרוּךְ הוּא מַשְׂרֶה דִיוֹרִין בֶּחָלָל
כִּדְכְתִיב 'וְעוֹף יְעוֹפֵף עַל הָאָרֶץ וְגוֹ''

'And let birds fly above the earth' (Genesis 1:20). In human practice a
mortal king builds a palace and tenants the upper and the lower
stories, but can he tenant the space between? [Surely not!] But the
Holy One, blessed be He, placed denizens in the space between, as
it is said, 'And let birds fly above the earth.'

This *midrash* relates to the continuation of the verse discussed in the first
midrash of this *Parashah*. Space is not only the place where birds fly, it is
their natural habitat, where they live. Even a king can do no more than
build additional stories for his family and guests; he cannot place anyone
in space. Only God can place occupants in space as demonstrated by the
birds who fly above the earth.

* * *

Seed Thoughts

This is another of those *midrashim* that make us realize what enormous
strides man has made. We were not created with wings and we cannot fly
individually, as do the birds. But collectively we have been able to master
technology that enables us to fly in airplanes and helicopters and even in
satellites circling the earth in space. And we can make others fly. As these
words are being written, Voyageur 2, in its twelfth year of research flight,
is passing the planet Neptune and taking photographs of it for the first
time ever.

Is this a tribute to the greatness of man? Is it not rather a tribute to the
greatness of God? We are not birds, but we have special talents because
we are made in the image of God. These enable us not only to fly, but to
do many other things as well. What is called for on our part is an appreciation of the Divine source from which our intellectual abilities and our
special talents come.

* * *

Additional Commentary

The verse should have read, 'And let fowl fly in the air.' Why does it say 'above the earth'? Because birds are able to walk on the earth and also fly in the air. This is something that man cannot do and is another tribute to the supernatural capacities of God as written, 'There is none like You among the gods, O Lord, and there are no deeds like Yours.' (*Tiferet Tzion*)

Parashah Seven, Midrash Four

'וַיִּבְרָא אֱלֹהִים אֶת הַתַּנִּינִם' (א, כא) רַבִּי פִּינְחָס בְּשֵׁם רַבִּי אַחָא אָמַר 'תַּנִּינִם' כְּתִיב
זֶה בְּהֵמוֹת וְלִוְיָתָן שֶׁאֵין לָהֶם בֶּן זוּגוֹת אָמַר רַבִּי שִׁמְעוֹן בֶּן לָקִישׁ בְּהֵמוֹת יֵשׁ לוֹ
בֶּן זוּג וְאֵין לוֹ תַּאֲוָה שֶׁנֶּאֱמַר 'גִּידֵי פַחֲדָו יְשֹׂרָגוּ' (איוב מ, יז)

'And God created the great sea monsters [*taninim*]' (1:21). R. Pinḥas
said in R. Idi's name: *Taninm* is written [without the last *yod*,
indicating the plural form]; it refers to behemoth and leviathan,
which have no mates. R. Simon b. Lakish said: Behemoth has a
mate, but it has no desire, as it is said, 'The sinews of his thighs are
knit together' (Job 40:17).

The fact that *taninim* is written without the second *yod* might indicate that
it is singular and refers to one particular type of animal. R. Pinḥas argued
that it refers to a particular animal as in Psalms (50:10) where the phrase
בהמות בהררי יער should not be read as 'cattle upon a thousand hills' but
rather, בהמה אחת היא, one particular animal whose name is Behemoth.
This animal as well as the Leviathan, mentioned in Isaiah 27:1, has no
female counterpart. Like all the other animals, they were created male and
female, but God realized that if they were to have offspring, these
enormous animals would put the rest of the world in jeopardy, so the
female was killed and the male castrated and set aside for the great festive
meal of the righteous in the world-to-come. And, because it was the only
one left of its kind, it was referred to as *Taninm* without the last *yod*.
(*Ha-Midrash ha-Mevo'ar*) R. Simon b. Lakish holds that this animal does
have a female counterpart; however, for the same reason as mentioned
above, God castrated the male and made the female frigid. In short, the
female counterpart is there, but there is no sexual desire. (*Ha-Midrash
ha-Mevo'ar*) The verse from Job, which specifically relates to the
behemoth, means that the tubes into the testicles are knit together and the
sexual drive cannot be aroused. These mammals also demonstrate the
wonders of the Almighty.

רַב הוּנָא בְּשֵׁם רַב מַתְנָא אָמַר הַצָּבוּעַ הַזֶּה מִטִּפָּה שֶׁל לָבָן הוּא וְיֵשׁ לוֹ שְׁלֹשׁ מֵאוֹת
וְשִׁשִּׁים וַחֲמִשָּׁה מִינֵי צִבְעוֹנִים כְּמִנְיַן יְמוֹת הַשָּׁנָה שֶׁל חַמָּה

R. Huna said in the name of R. Matna: The peacock is formed from a white drop [of semen], but it contains three hundred and sixty-five different colors, as many as the days of the solar year.

This exposition is based on the fact that in the verse, 'And let birds fly above the earth,' the Hebrew for 'birds' is in the singular, *of*, used, according to the plain meaning, in the collective sense. Our *midrash* understands it to refer to one specific bird, the *tzavu'a*, which we, following *Ha-Midrash ha-Mevo'ar*, have translated as peacock (a note in the Soncino translation suggests it is either the leopard or the striped hyena; but clearly the reference is to a bird). This animal, like all others, is created from a single white drop but possesses three hundred and sixty-five colors corresponding to the days of the year.

רַבִּי יִרְמְיָה [אָמַר] כָּהֲנָא שָׁאַל לְר' שִׁמְעוֹן בֶּן לָקִישׁ הַמַּרְבִּיעַ מֵחַיַּת הַיָּם מַהוּ אָמַר לֵהּ אַף הֵן כְּתִיב בָּהֶן 'לְמִינֵהֶם' בְּהָדָא פְּרַס בֶּן לָקִישׁ מְצוּדָתֵהּ לְכָהֲנָא אוֹתִיב כָּהֲנָא וַהֲלוֹא אַף הַדָּגִים כְּתִיב בָּהֶן לְמִינֵהֶן בְּהָא פְּרַס כָּהֲנָא מְצוּדְתֵהּ עַל רַ' שִׁמְעוֹן בֶּן לָקִישׁ

R. Jeremiah said: R. Kahana asked R. Simon b. Lakish: 'What [is the law] regarding the crossbreeding of different sea species?' He answered him: 'Regarding them, too, it is written, "after their kind".' With this the son of Lakish spread his net over Kahana [i.e., caught him out]. R. Kahana, however, refuted him: 'But is not "after their kind" also written with regards to fish?!' With this, Kahana spread his net over the son of Lakish.

This *midrash* is relating to the continuation of the verse (1:21) discussed in the previous *midrash*. On the text, 'which the waters brought forth after their own kind,' the question arises: Is it permitted to crossbreed sea animals? Crossbreeding land animals is expressly forbidden and constitutes what is called *kila'im*, mixing. Does this rule apply to marine animals as well? R. Simon b. Lakish held that it does, since the same term is stated with regards to them as is stated with regards to land animals, 'after their own kind.' From the statement about casting his net, it seems that R. Kahana had been arguing that the rule did not apply and that R. Simon b. Lakish 'caught him out.' R. Kahana, however, responded by observing that the phrase is written regarding fish, too, and it is ludicrous to imagine that the prohibition of crossbreeding should apply to them since they reproduce in an entirely different fashion. This riposte 'caught out' R. Simon b. Lakish.

וְהֵיךְ עֲבִידָא אָמַר ר' יוֹנָה יָכוֹל אֲנִי מְקַיֵּם לָהּ מִשׁוּם מַנְהִיג מֵבִיא שְׁנֵי דָגִים חַד
מַיִּירֹן וְחַד אַסְפְּרוֹן וְקַשְׁרָן בִּגְמִי וּמַמְשִׁיכוֹ בַּנָּהָר אוֹ בַיָּם וְאָסוּר כֵּן מִשׁוּם
כִּלְאַיִם דְּתְנַן כִּלְאַיִם שֶׁאָמְרוּ הַנּוֹהֵג בָּהֶן אֲסוּרִין לַחֲרֹשׁ וְלִמְשֹׁךְ וְלִנְהֹג יַחְדָּו
שֶׁנֶּאֱמַר 'וְאֵת כָּל נֶפֶשׁ הַחַיָּה הָרֹמֶשֶׂת אֲשֶׁר שָׁרְצוּ הַמַּיִם לְמִינֵהֶן'

**Now how can the matter be resolved? R. Jonah said: I can apply [the
law of *kila'im* to fish] with regard to the prohibition of driving: a
person takes two separate kinds of fish, one white and the other
black, ties them together with a reed and pulls them through a river
or a sea. It is forbidden to do so because of the law of *kila'im*, for we
learned: The law of *kila'im* which [the Sages] enacted applies to
leading them, which is forbidden, ploughing with them, pulling
them or driving them, as it is written, 'and all the living creatures
that creep, which the waters brought forth, *according to their kind.'***

R. Jonah's solution is that the law of *kila'im* applies not only to crossbreeding, which is impossible with regards to fish, but also to having two
animals from different species yoked together. The prohibition applies to
all activities, ploughing together, pulling together, driving, steering, or
binding together. The two different species of fish named in the *midrash*
are not identified; our translation follows the Dictionary of Midrashic
Literature by Marcus Jastrow.

וְאֵת כָּל עוֹף כָּנָף זֶה הַטַּוָס

**'And all the living creatures that creep and every winged fowl': this
is the peacock.**

The same interpretation of the many-colored bird described above is now
applied to a different text. It is maintained that the peacock contains the
color of every winged fowl that exists. The proper place for R. Huna's
statement (above) is at the end of this paragraph and not in the middle,
where it is presently placed. (*Tiferet Tzion*)

* * *

Seed Thoughts

'And every winged fowl after its kind.' The word 'winged' is superfluous
since every bird has wings. That is why the *midrash* suggests that what is
meant here is the peacock. The reason being that this bird has exceptional
wings. To strengthen the intention of Scripture and the Almighty's
purpose in creating such a beautiful bird is the statement of R. Huna that

this bird has three hundred and sixty-five colors, corresponding to the days of the year.

There is a lesson to man in this teaching. Don't let the evil inclination seduce you into believing that we cannot aspire to a life of Torah that requires such great sophistication, seeing that we are produced by one seminal drop, and that we should not, therefore, attempt such an undertaking. For this reason God created the peacock, with all of its many colors, which is also produced from one seminal drop. The small beginning does not prevent nature from unfolding in all its fullness. How much more so we, the children of Israel, who contain the soul of the Divine within us. The number 365 should also be a reminder to adorn ourselves each day with those good deeds that befit the day as it is written, 'Bless the Lord every day.' (*Tiferet Tzion*)

* * *

Additional Commentary

Have no female counterpart
These two animals, Behemoth and the Leviathan, are therefore lacking, as the Hebrew word תנינם, *taninm*, is lacking the *yod*. The reason why the Behemoth and the Leviathan were so created is the fear that if, indeed, they could procreate in normal fashion, they would destroy the world because of their vast size. (*Tiferet Tzion*)

*

R. Jonah said
R. Simon ben Lakish had a tradition from his teacher, to apply the hermeneutical rule of the *gezeirah shavah*, the analogy, to the word *leminah*, 'to its kind,' with the result that the prohibition of *kila'im* applies to animals of the sea. (*Tiferet Tzion*)

Parashah Seven, Midrash Five

וַיֹּאמֶר אֱלֹהִים תּוֹצֵא הָאָרֶץ וְגוֹ' (את כד) אָמַר ר' אֶלְעָזָר 'נֶפֶשׁ חַיָּה' זֶה רוּחוֹ שֶׁל
אָדָם הָרִאשׁוֹן

**'And God said: Let the earth bring forth the living creature… (1:24).'
R. Eleazar said: 'Living creature' means the soul of Adam.**

Genesis 1:24 reads, in full, 'And God said, let the earth bring forth the
living creature after his kind, cattle, and creeping things, and beasts of the
earth after its kind.' There are four items listed here. Some commentators,
among them Rashi, feel that the first item, 'the living creature after its
kind,' is an all-inclusive generalization that includes the three items that
follow. Others believe that 'the living creature after its kind' is a separate
item. But, if that is the case, the verse that follows (Genesis 1:25), 'God
made the beast of the earth after its kind, and cattle after their kind and
everything that creeps on the earth after its kind,' only lists three items.
What happened to 'the living creature'? To answer this question R.
Eleazar says that 'the living creature' refers to man, whose creation follows
immediately in verse 26. In fact, Genesis 2:7 describes man specifically as
'a living soul.'

וַיַּעַשׂ אֱלֹהִים אֶת חַיַּת הָאָרֶץ לְמִינָהּ (א, כה) ר' הוֹשַׁעְיָא רַבָּה אָמַר זֶה הַנָּחָשׁ

**'And God made wild beasts of every kind' (1:25). R. Hoshaya Rabbah
said: This is the serpent.**

Another question arises from the fact that in verse 24 the last item listed
is 'wild beasts,' whereas in verse 25 'wild beasts' is given as the first item.
To this question R. Hoshaya Rabbah (literally: 'the great,' perhaps
meaning 'the elder') responds that the reference is to the serpent. The
serpent was originally the most important of all the animals, but after the
incident with Eve and the Tree of Knowledge it was discredited. Verse 25
describes the serpent at its creation when its status was high, whereas verse
24 describes the serpent in God's thought, as it were, where the serpent is
listed in the position it would ultimately occupy in the animal hierarchy.
(*Ha-Midrash ha-Mevo'ar*)

266

אָמַר רַבִּי חָמָא בַּר הוֹשַׁעְיָא בַּנְּפָשׁוֹת אוֹמֵר אַרְבַּע כְּשֶׁנִּבְרְאוּ הוּא אוֹמֵר 'חַיַּת
הָאָרֶץ לְמִינָהּ וְאֶת הַבְּהֵמָה וְאֶת כָּל רֶמֶשׂ הָאֲדָמָה' אַתְמְהָא

R. Ḥama b. R. Hoshaya said: In speaking of souls it enumerates four, but in speaking of their actual creation only three! It is strange.

R. Ḥama is reiterating the question raised at the beginning of this *midrash*. Verse 24, describing God's statement, 'Let the earth bring forth...,' lists four kinds of creatures, but verse 25, which describes the implementation of that statement, lists only three items. The first section of this *midrash* solved the problem by stating that the fourth item is the soul of Adam. In this section of the *midrash* a different solution is proposed.

ר' אוֹמֵר אֵלּוּ הַשֵּׁדִים שֶׁבָּרָא הַקָּדוֹשׁ בָּרוּךְ הוּא אֶת נִשְׁמָתָן וּבָא לִבְרֹאת אֶת גּוּפָן
וְקָדַשׁ הַשַּׁבָּת וְלֹא בְרָאָן לְלַמֶּדְךָ דֶּרֶךְ אֶרֶץ מִן הַשֵּׁדִים שֶׁאִם יִהְיֶה בְּיַד אָדָם חֵפֶץ
טוֹב אוֹ מַרְגָּלִית עֶרֶב שַׁבָּת עִם חֲשֵׁכָה אוֹמְרִים לוֹ הַשְׁלֵךְ מִמְּךָ שֶׁמִּי שֶׁאָמַר וְהָיָה
הָעוֹלָם הָיָה עָסוּק בִּבְרִיָּתוֹ שֶׁל עוֹלָם וּבָרָא אֶת נִשְׁמָתָן בָּא לִבְרֹאת אֶת גּוּפָן
וְקָדַשׁ שַׁבָּת וְלֹא בְרָאָן

Rabbi said: This [extra soul is that of] the demons which the Holy One, blessed be He, created. But when He came to create their bodies, the Sabbath commenced and he could not create them. [God did] this in order to teach you proper behavior from the case of the demons. If a person is holding in his hand a costly article or a precious stone on the eve of the Sabbath at twilight, we say to him, 'Throw it away, for He at whose behest the world came into existence was engaged in the creation of the world and had already created their souls [i.e., of the demons], but when He came to create their bodies the Sabbath commenced and he did not create them.'

Rabbi Judah the Prince maintains that the item of which God said, 'Let the earth bring forth...' but which was not actually created is the 'demons' or spirits. God did not complete the creation of the demons and they were left as ghosts in an incomplete state. This is hinted at in the word *la-asot* (Genesis 2:3), which can be translated as 'intended to make,' which implies that the intention was never implemented because of the Sabbath (RZWE). Any act of creation on the Sabbath is forbidden and the reference to the costly article or precious stone should be understood as referring to a case in which the person is unable to get the article to his home without transgressing the laws of Shabbat.

* * *

Seed Thoughts

The humanization of God is a phenomenon that is often discerned in rabbinic writings. By that I mean the effort to endow the Divine with human attributes to make it easier for mortal man to imitate Him.

Consider what has happened in this *midrash*. We know that the Sabbath emerged because God had finished His work of creation. But if God had not finished His work, the Sabbath would have been delayed. It might have occurred on the eighth or ninth day.

If God had truly wanted to create demons, He would certainly have delayed the Sabbath. But note what the Rabbis have projected. Once the Sabbath was decided upon, God Himself was subject to its authority. It is not the Sabbath that has to be flexible before man, but man, and even God, must adapt themselves to the requirements of the Sabbath.

The Sabbath, therefore, emerges not merely as a day of rest, but as a day of spiritual power. Temporal and physical power must give way before it. Only in that way can the Sabbath be a form of rejuvenation that will enable the individual and the Jewish people to make a more enthusiastic effort in the week ahead.

God Himself has set the example for man to follow.

* * *

Additional Commentary

The serpent
The reason why חית הארץ, the beasts of the earth, is interpreted as serpent is because in Arabic the word *ḥavaya* means serpent. (Mirkin)

*

The demons and spirits
In connection with the whole subject of spirits, Rabbis have differed throughout the ages. Some believe in their existence and claim that they consist of two of the four elementary substances of creation, earth, fire, water, and air. There are others who say that they are merely symbols of spiritual powers. Still others deny their existence completely. Each side argues strenuously to prove its point and to explain away the views of the Talmudic Sages that disagree with their point of view. Nevertheless, if we examine the statement before us literally, and similar statements scattered in different parts of the Talmud, one would have to conclude that at least some of the Talmudic Sages did believe in spirits and looked upon them as ethereal creatures without bodies, as is explained in this *midrash*. (*Yefei To'ar*)

Parashah Eight, Midrash One

וַיֹּאמֶר אֱלֹהִים נַעֲשֶׂה אָדָם בְּצַלְמֵנוּ כִּדְמוּתֵנוּ רַבִּי יוֹחָנָן פָּתַח 'אָחוֹר וָקֶדֶם צַרְתָּנִי
וְגוֹ'' (תהלים קלט, ה) אָמַר רַ' יוֹחָנָן אִם זָכָה אָדָם אוֹכֵל שְׁנֵי עוֹלָמוֹת שֶׁנֶּאֱמַר 'אָחוֹר
וָקֶדֶם צַרְתָּנִי' וְאִם לָאו הוּא בָא לִתֵּן דִּין וְחֶשְׁבּוֹן שֶׁנֶּאֱמַר 'וַתָּשֶׁת עָלַי כַּפֶּכָה'

'And God said: "Let us make man in Our image, after Our likeness"'
(1:26). R. Joḥanan commenced [his discourse on this verse]: 'You
form me [*tzartani*] behind and before' (Psalms 139:5). Said R. Joḥanan:
If a man is worthy enough, he enjoys two worlds, for it says, 'You
hedge me behind [the world-to-come] and before [this world]'; but,
if not he will have to render an account [of his misdeeds], as [the
verse] continues, 'You lay Your hand upon me.'

According to *Yefei To'ar*, the main question motivating this *midrash* is why
man was created last. According to RZWE and others, the main point is
to fathom the meaning of the term 'after Our likeness.' Which likeness?
Actually, both themes will be addressed.

In the verse from Psalms, R. Joḥanan interprets the verb *tzartani* as
meaning 'You have formed me' (although its accepted meaning is 'You
have hedged me' or 'You have beset me') and as such the verse is contradictory. On the one hand it affirms that man will rule over what is before
him and what is behind him, but on the other hand, God's hand will
always be there to call him to an accounting. Surely, if man rules over all,
he is not accountable for his actions! R. Joḥanan solves this contradiction
by interpreting 'before' and 'behind' as referring to this world and the
next, respectively, and by understanding the whole verse as a moralistic
warning to man given at his very creation.

אָמַר רַבִּי יִרְמְיָה בֶּן אֶלְעָזָר בְּשָׁעָה שֶׁבָּרָא הַקָּדוֹשׁ בָּרוּךְ הוּא אֶת אָדָם הָרִאשׁוֹן
אַנְדְּרוֹגִינוֹס בְּרָאוֹ הֲדָא הוּא דִכְתִיב 'זָכָר וּנְקֵבָה בְּרָאָם' (בראשית ה, ב)

**R. Jeremiah b. Eleazar said: When the Holy One, blessed be He,
created Adam, He created him an hermaphrodite, as it is said, 'Male
and female He created them...' (Genesis 5:2).**

R. Jeremiah is suggesting another interpretation of the verse used by R.

269

Joḥanan to open his exposition. He interprets 'behind' and 'before' as
indicating that when man was first created he possessed both male and
female reproductive organs. According to R. Jeremiah, this is the meaning
of the verse (5:2), 'Male and female He created them and called their [in
the plural] name Adam,' that is, one human being. So we see that the first
human was of both sexes. Thus *aḥor*, behind, and *kedem*, before, in the
verse from Psalms are referring to the front and back of the first human,
an oblique reference to 'its' double sexuality.

אָמַר ר' שְׁמוּאֵל בַּר נַחְמָן בְּשָׁעָה שֶׁבָּרָא הַקָּדוֹשׁ בָּרוּךְ הוּא אֶת אָדָם הָרִאשׁוֹן דְּיוֹ
פַּרְצוּפִים בְּרָאוֹ וְנִסְּרוֹ וַעֲשָׂאוֹ גַּבַּיִם גַּב לְכָאן וְגַב לְכָאן אֵיתִיבוּן לֵהּ וְהָא כְתִיב
'וַיִּקַּח אַחַת מִצַּלְעֹתָיו' (שם ב, כא) אֲמַר לְהוֹן מִתְּרֵין סִטְרוֹהִי הֵיךְ מַה דְּאַתְּ אָמַר
'וּלְצֶלַע הַמִּשְׁכָּן' (שמות כו, כ) דְּמִתַרְגְּמִינַן 'וְלִסְטַר מַשְׁכְּנָא וְגוֹ''

**R. Samuel b. Naḥman said: When the Holy One, blessed be He,
created Adam he created him double-faced, then he split him and
made him of two backs, one back on this side and one back on the
other side. [His colleagues] objected: But it is written, 'He took one
of his ribs [*mi-tzal'otav*]...' (Genesis. 2:21)?! He replied [*mi-tzal'otav*
means] one of his two sides, as you read, 'And for the other side
[*tzel'a*] of the tabernacle...' (Exodus 26:20).**

R. Samuel maintains that the first human was a sort of Siamese twin,
composed of a male and a female connected at their backs. This, of
course, is a perfect interpretation of the verse cited above, 'Male and
female He created them and called their [in the plural] name Adam.' The
objection to this is that in the account of the creation of Eve it says
explicitly that God took one of Adam's ribs and created Eve out of it,
whereas according to R. Samuel's interpretation what God did was to
execute a surgical operation and cut them apart. R. Samuel answered this
objection by pointing out that the Hebrew for 'rib,' צלע, can also mean
'side,' as he demonstrates from the verse in Exodus concerning the
Tabernacle in the wilderness, and that, therefore, his interpretation can
stand.

רַבִּי תַּנְחוּמָא בְּשֵׁם רַבִּי בִּנְיָה וְרַבִּי בֶּרֶכְיָה בְּשֵׁם ר' אֶלְעָזָר אָמַר בְּשָׁעָה שֶׁבָּרָא
הַקָּדוֹשׁ בָּרוּךְ הוּא אֶת אָדָם הָרִאשׁוֹן גֹּלֶם בְּרָאוֹ וְהָיָה מוּטָל מִסּוֹף הָעוֹלָם וְעַד
סוֹפוֹ הֲדָא הוּא דִכְתִיב 'גָּלְמִי רָאוּ עֵינֶיךָ וְגוֹ'' (תהלים קלט, טז)

**R. Tanḥuma in the name of R. Benayah and R. Berekhiah in the
name of R. Eleazar said: When the Holy One, blessed be He,**

created Adam, He created him as a lifeless mass [*golem*] and he was laid out from one end of the world to the other, as it is written, 'Your eyes saw my unformed substance' (Psalms 139:16).

Golem means an unfinished product. 'Before' and 'behind,' according to this interpretation, refer to the two ends of the earth from which he was suspended. The form of both was completed when woman was created. (*Ha-Midrash ha-Mevo'ar*)

רַבִּי יְהוֹשֻׁעַ בַּר נְחֶמְיָה וְרַבִּי יְהוּדָה בַּר סִימוֹן בְּשֵׁם רַבִּי אֶלְעָזָר אָמַר מְלֹא כָל הָעוֹלָם בְּרָאוֹ מִן הַמִּזְרָח לַמַּעֲרָב מִנַּיִן שֶׁנֶּאֱמַר 'אָחוֹר וָקֶדֶם צַרְתָּנִי וְגוֹ'' מִצָּפוֹן לַדָּרוֹם מִנַּיִן שֶׁנֶּאֱמַר 'וּלְמִקְצֵה הַשָּׁמַיִם וְעַד קְצֵה הַשָּׁמָיִם' (דברים ד, לב) וּמִנַּיִן אַף בַּחֲלָלוֹ שֶׁל עוֹלָם שֶׁנֶּאֱמַר 'וַתָּשֶׁת עָלַי כַּפֶּכָה' כְּמָה דְאַתְּ אָמַר 'כַּפְּךָ מֵעָלַי הַרְחַק' (איוב יג, כא)

R. Joshua b. R. Nehemiah and R. Judah b. R. Simon in R. Eleazar's name said: He created him filling the whole world. What is the source [that he stretched] from east to west? As it is said, 'You have formed me behind (*ahor*) and before (*kedem*).' From north to south? Because it says, 'Ever since God created man on earth, from one end of the heaven to the other' (Deuteronomy 4:32). And how do we know that he filled the empty spaces of the world? From the verse, 'And You laid Your hand upon me' as you read, 'Your hand is far from me' (Job 13:21).

The terms 'behind' and 'before' in our original verse from Psalms are here interpreted as meaning that the body of the first man stretched across the whole world from east to west, since *kedem* can also mean 'east.' What about north and south? The proof-verse from Deuteronomy states that when Adam was created he stretched from one end of the heaven to the other, and since we already know that he stretched from east to west it must mean that he also stretched from north to south.

And what about space? The Hebrew for 'You laid' ותשת, *va-tashet*, indicates close proximity. This is verified by the verse from Job, where Job complains that God's hand is far away from him, an ordinary human being, implying that for Adam the hand was close. This shows that Adam reached up through space to God's hand. A further interpretation is that the Hebrew for 'hand' in the original proof-verse is *kapekha*, which is taken to be derived from the Hebrew *kippah*, which, as we have seen previously, means the vault of the heavens.

אָמַר רַ' אֶלְעָזָר 'אָחוֹר' לְמַעֲשֵׂה יוֹם הָרִאשׁוֹן 'וָקֶדֶם' לְמַעֲשֵׂה יוֹם הָאַחֲרוֹן הוּא
דַעְתֵּהּ דְּרַבִּי אֶלְעָזָר דַּאֲמַר רַבִּי אֶלְעָזָר (בראשית א, כד) 'תּוֹצֵא הָאָרֶץ נֶפֶשׁ חַיָּה
לְמִינָהּ' זֶה רוּחוֹ שֶׁל אָדָם הָרִאשׁוֹן

R. Eleazar said: [Adam] was the last (*aḥor*) in the creation of the first day and the first (*kedem*) in the creation of the last day. This is R. Eleazar's view, for he said: 'Let the earth bring forth the living creature…' (Genesis 1:24) refers to the soul of Adam.

The Hebrew phrase, *ma'aseh yom rishon*, 'the creation of the first day,' should be understood as referring to the entire creation story. There is an opinion that everything created in the six days was already created on the first day and merely refined on the rest of the days (*Ha-Midrash ha-Mevo'ar*). The thought of man was in the mind of the Creator from the very outset as the goal of creation, even though in actual fact he was the last to be created. By the same token he was the first to be created on the last day, the sixth day, before the other animal creations. This is yet another interpretation of *aḥor* and *kedem*, based on R. Eleazar's view, which was discussed in *Parashah Seven, Midrash Five*. It is possible that R. Eleazar is indicating a separation of the concepts of body and soul – the body of man was created last but the spirit of man first.

אָמַר רַ' שִׁמְעוֹן בֶּן לָקִישׁ 'אָחוֹר' לְמַעֲשֵׂה יוֹם הָאַחֲרוֹן 'וָקֶדֶם' לְמַעֲשֵׂה יוֹם
הָרִאשׁוֹן הוּא דַעְתֵּהּ דְּרֵ"שׁ בֶּן לָקִישׁ דַּאֲמַר רֵישׁ לָקִישׁ 'וְרוּחַ אֱלֹהִים מְרַחֶפֶת עַל
פְּנֵי הַמַּיִם' (שם א, ב) זוֹ רוּחוֹ שֶׁל מֶלֶךְ הַמָּשִׁיחַ הֵיךְ מַה דְּאַתְּ אָמַר 'וְנָחָה עָלָיו רוּחַ
ה'' (ישעיה יא, ב) אִם זָכָה אָדָם אוֹמְרִים לוֹ אַתָּה קָדַמְתָּ לְמַלְאֲכֵי הַשָּׁרֵת וְאִם לָאו
אוֹמְרִים לוֹ זְבוּב קְדָמְךָ יְתוּשׁ קְדָמְךָ שִׁלְשׁוּל זֶה קְדָמֶךָ

R. Simon b. Lakish said: [Man] was the last [*aḥor*] in the creation of the last day and the first [*kedem*] in the creation of the first day. This is consistent with [another] view of R. Simon b. Lakish, for he said: 'And the spirit of God hovered over the waters' (Genesis 1:2) refers to the King-Messiah as you read, 'And the spirit of the Lord shall rest upon him' (Isaiah 11:2). If man has merit, they will say to him, 'You preceded in creation even the ministering angels'; but, if not, they will tell him, 'A fly preceded you, an insect preceded you, a worm preceded you.'

Resh Lakish applies the terms in reverse: last on the last day and first on the first day. 'The spirit of God hovering' is an allusion to the spirit of God mentioned in Isaiah as resting on the Messiah, who, in Jewish theology,

will be a man of flesh and blood. In R. Simon b. Lakish's opinion this
comes to teach us a sublime doctrine. Man has the capacity to be greater
than the ministering angels, but he can also be lower than the lowest
insect. It all depends on him.

אָמַר רַב נַחְמָן 'אָחוֹר' לְכָל הַמַּעֲשִׂים 'וָקֶדֶם' לְכָל עוֹנָשִׁין אָמַר רַבִּי שְׁמוּאֵל אַף
בְּקִלּוּס אֵינוֹ בָא אֶלָא בָּאַחֲרוֹנָה הֲדָא הוּא דִכְתִיב 'הַלְלוּ אֶת ה' מִן הַשָּׁמַיִם וְגוֹ''
(תהלים קמח) וְאוֹמֵר כָּל הַפָּרָשָׁה וְאַחַר כָּךְ 'הַלְלוּ אֶת ה' מִן הָאָרֶץ וְגוֹ'' וְאוֹמֵר כָּל
הַפָּרָשָׁה וְאַחַר כָּךְ אוֹמֵר 'מַלְכֵי אֶרֶץ וְכָל לְאָמִּים בַּחוּרִים וְגַם בְּתוּלוֹת' (שם שם)

R. Naḥman said: [Man is] last (*aḥor*) in creation but first (*kedem*) for
all punishment. R. Samuel b. R. Tanḥum said: Even in his praise [of
God, man] comes only at the last, as it is written, 'Hallelujah, Praise
the Lord from the heavens...' (Psalms 148:1-6); the passage continues
until 'Praise the Lord, O you who are on earth...' (ibid. verse 7) and
only after that, 'All kings of the earth and all peoples, youths and
maidens alike' (ibid. verses 11-12).

The final interpretation of the significance of *aḥor* and *kedem* is that man
was last in creation, but is first in line for punishment. Man is, on the one
hand, commanded and, on the other hand, possesses free will. Therefore,
his chief quality is responsibility. He is also last in praising God because
the other creatures do that instinctively, but man can only do it out of
conviction. This last idea is derived from Psalm 148, which calls upon all
to praise God. It begins with the angels and, verse by verse, works its way
down to man.

אָמַר ר' שַׂמְלַאי כְּשֵׁם שֶׁקִּלּוּסוֹ אֵינה אֶלָא אַחַר בְּהֵמָה חַיָּה וָעוֹף כָּךְ בְּרִיָּתוֹ אֵינָה
אֶלָא אַחַר בְּהֵמָה חַיָּה וָעוֹף מַה טַעְמָה שֶׁנֶּאֱמַר 'וַיֹּאמֶר אֱלֹהִים יִשְׁרְצוּ הַמַּיִם'
(בראשית א, כ) וְאַחַר כָּךְ 'וַיֹּאמֶר אֱלֹהִים תּוֹצֵא הָאָרֶץ וְגוֹ'' (שם שם, כד) וְאַחַר כָּךְ
'וַיֹּאמֶר אֱלֹהִים נַעֲשֶׂה אָדָם וְגוֹ'' (שם שם, כו)

R. Simlai said: Just as the praise [man offers to God] comes after that
of cattle, beasts, and fowls, so does his creation come after that of
cattle, beasts, and fowl, as it says, 'And God said, "Let the waters
bring forth swarms of living creatures"' (Genesis 1:20), and after that
'And God said, "Let the earth bring forth..."' (ibid 1:24), and only
after that, 'And God said, "Let us make man..."' (ibid. 1:26).

R. Simlai disagrees with the previous opinions that man's spirit or soul
was created on the first day. He claims that man – body and soul – was

created on the last day, and his proof is from the continuation, 'The Lord God formed man from the dust of the earth. He blew into his nostrils the living soul' (Genesis 2:7-8), which clearly means that man received his soul after his body had been created. (*Ha-Midrash ha-Mevo'ar*)

* * *

Seed Thoughts

The biblical story of the creation of woman is not well received in modern times. Feminists, even those who are far from being radical, see it as a playing down of woman's role in society. If woman is only a rib out of Adam's totality, is not that a patronizing way of identifying her as a human being?

In this respect the *midrash* offers an interpretation that can only be described as sensational. R. Jeremiah asserts that the first human being was created an *adroginos*, meaning hermaphrodite, having both male and female reproductive organs. This is quite an improvement over the original text in the sense that woman's stature is no less than that of the males, in that God's creation of the first human being was a mixture of male and female.

R. Samuel b. Naḥman goes even further and says that the first human being had two bodies joined together. The story of the rib was not that at all, but their separation into two distinct entities.

This view is not the individual aberration of one sage. It became the normative view and the only way to explain the remarkable verse, 'Male and female He created them (plural) and He called their (also plural) name Adam,' meaning, one human being.

First and foremost, this passage establishes forever the equal worth of man and woman in Judaism. This should not be misunderstood. Talmudic legislation abounds in commandments that are the exclusive responsibility of women and other more numerous commandments that are the exclusive domain of men. This has to do with the differentiation of roles, a phenomenon that has taken place in every society in one form or another, including modern times. You may agree or disagree with the concept of role differentiation, but none of this has anything to do with the essential value and equal worth of men and women as created in the image of God. Men and women from the early pages of Genesis are equal to each other and so are equal in the eyes of God.

There is another implication of this teaching that offers a particular view of the institution of marriage. 'Male and female He created them and He called their name *one human being*.' Let me put it this way. The goal of life is not celibacy, though many are forced into it through a lack of opportunity or other circumstances. The goal of life is man and woman related to each other sexually and in every other dimension of life. Marriage has been created as the structure to make this goal feasible and acceptable.

The Kabbalists, elaborating upon this text, say that God did not create human souls as individuals but as couples. The goal of life is for each soul, each human being, to seek their *tikkun* – their completion or perfection with their counterparts of the opposite sex. Hopefully, they will succeed and, if they have merit, they will create that Adam, that one complete human, which represents man at his highest.

* * *

Additional Commentary

Golem
The term *golem* is used to describe any creation that is not finished. It is a *golem* when it is in an unfinished state. (*Yefei To'ar*)

*

Androginus
When R. Samuel b. Naḥman and some say R. Simon b. Gamaliel added the remark that Adam was created *du-partzufin,* Siamese twins, he was merely trying to interpret what R. Jeremiah meant in saying that man was created hermaphrodite. R. Jeremiah really meant to say that he was created with two bodies (or, two faces), which seems to be the meaning of the verse, 'Male and female He created them,' apparently with two bodies. This may seem to contradict the verse later on 'And the Lord created a deep sleep to fall upon the man and took one of his ribs…' However, this would have to be interpreted that he separated the two bodies and created two backs and thus, two separate people. How then do you explain the verse, 'For Adam there was not found a helpmate'? That means that she was not *ke-negdo,* 'facing him,' since the faces of the two bodies projected outward, and that was not satisfactory. Why then did God create them that way in the first place? Because it was His desire that man would also cleave in loyalty and faithfulness to his partner and not like the other members of the animal kingdom who were not so restricted. He created them with two bodies attached to teach the lesson that all creatures were intended to function as they were originally created and monogamous faithfulness was how man and woman were created. There is now a special meaning attached to the key verse in our *midrash,* 'You form me behind and before,' with the two bodies, one facing behind and one facing in front. Therefore, 'You placed Your hand upon me,' meaning that from

the very beginning of creation each of us was admonished to cleave to his own wife and not to someone else's, the penalty for which transgression is death. But then, by natural instinct implanted in Adam, God made it easy for man to observe this restriction and the main point of Scripture is to convey to us God's loving mercy in that we were created in such a way that it is possible to observe and fulfill this commandment. (*Tiferet Tzion*)

*

Why was man first created as a *golem*?

If man were to be created in only one country or one place in the world, his nature might only have allowed him to live there, but not, for example, in cold climates if he were accustomed to hot. There are certain animals, for example, which can only live in cold climates and others that can only live in hot. Since it was God's desire that the entire earth be populated by humans, He created the *golem*, which consisted of the basic body of man and hurled or suspended it in such a way as to reach all parts of the earth in its orbit. Thus the particular needs and immunization required by various climates could be incorporated into his system. Thus, his descendants could settle everywhere.

It was for this reason that R. Joshua b. Neḥemia added the thought that Adam was created to fill the whole world, meaning that the human body was designed to adapt to any part of the world, even to space. (*Tiferet Tzion*)

*

Behind the first day of creation

It is nature's way to produce first the blossom that protects the fruit and, at a later stage, the fruit itself. When the fruit is ripe, the owner of the land first gathers the fruit and later, if he so desires, the leaves that protect the fruit. In a similar manner, when God created the earth on the first day and imbued it with the power of growth for all life, he did not give it the power to produce man, the main fruit of creation, until the very end. On the sixth day of the week when the process of creation was nearing completion, God then went about harvesting the main fruit, which was the life and soul of man. Therefore R. Eleazar was able to say, 'behind the last act of the first day and before the first act of the last day.' All of this was to indicate the greatness of man, even his animal side. (*Tiferet Tzion*)

*

Behind the events of the last day

What R. Simon b. Lakish said should not be seen as in disagreement with R. Eleazar. He reaffirms that spiritual man was created on the first day before everything else, but he held that bodily man was created on the last day after everything else.

Insofar as the verse is concerned, 'the spirit of God hovered over the waters,' one might ask why this detail was specified over all others. One has to deduce that what is being spoken of is the spirit of holiness, as written, 'And the spirit of the Lord rested upon him.' Apparently, the verse is telling us that the spirit of holiness will not reveal itself in the world except by a spiritual regeneration, or, in Hebrew, *teshuvah*. R. Simon sees this concept of regeneration in the very opening words of Genesis. The concept and verse of 'spirit hovering' can imply either the first man or Messiah, because only the human being can be the instrument of this kind of true spiritual transformation. (*Tiferet Tzion*)

*

A fly, an insect, a worm

Human arrogance can be traced to three important influences: man's knowledge, his power, and his wealth. In this respect Scripture says, 'Let not the wise man glory in his wisdom nor the man of strength in his power or the man of wealth in his riches.' In this connection, the *midrash* speaks of three things: a fly, an insect, and a worm.

If a person is too proud of his wisdom he is chided, even a fly was created before you. As the wisest of all men wrote in Ecclesiastes, 'Dead flies turn the perfumer's ointment fetid and putrid; so a little folly outweighs massive wisdom' (10:1). Just as a fly can destroy the best efforts of a wise artisan who makes the beautiful perfume, so a little folly can destroy good deeds that are done with great wisdom. So, from a fly you learn not to be arrogant about your knowledge.

From an insect we can learn not to be arrogant about our power. The Roman, Titus, was very arrogant about his power. The Holy One fought with him by means of an insect, the weakest of all the animals, to show that if God wills it the weakest can be more powerful than the strongest. In the case of Titus the insect entered through his ear to the brain, ultimately causing his death.

Worms remind us not to be too impressed with our wealth. The immediate desire of wealth displays itself in much eating and drinking, which makes one fatter and ultimately produces more worms in the grave. The more flesh, the more worms. (*Tiferet Tzion*)

*

Praise and creation

R. Samuel made the point that man's being created last indicated his great importance. By the same token, his praise of God coming after others was also a tribute to his great importance. The chain of praise must have an order of importance so that that which comes later must be more important, otherwise why would it be needed? So, if the earth is engaged in praise the order would be first vegetation, then animals or creatures who praise in terms of their capacity, and finally, man created in God's image so that his ability to praise God is that much greater. Therefore, he comes last because of his importance.

But the *midrash* now asks: Why? Of what importance is it for man to be mentioned last? The answer is derived from the very order of creation. The verses read in the following order: first, 'Let the waters swarm with swarms of living creatures'; then, 'Let the earth bring forth living creatures; and, finally, 'And God said, "Let us make man in Our image".' It then continues 'They shall rule the fish of the sea, the birds of the sky, the cattle, the whole earth...' So, man's importance derives from his being created at the end, after all the rest had been created, otherwise they would not have been in existence for man to have dominion over. In the case of the arrival of a king, first comes his entourage and only at the end, the king. Just as there is no king without subjects, so, after the creation of all living things, there should come the being who will rule over them. (*Tiferet Tzion*)

Parashah Eight, Midrash Two

רַבִּי חָמָא בַּר חֲנִינָא פָּתַח 'הֲזֹאת יָדַעְתָּ מִנִּי וְגוֹ'' (איוב כ, ד)

R. Ḥama b. R. Ḥanina began [his exposition with the verse], 'Do you not know this, that from time immemorial, since man was set on earth' (Job 20:4).

The basic text is, 'Let us make man in Our image' (Genesis 1:26). The verse, however, suggests that God consulted with others as to whether man should be created. This presents a very serious theological problem since it means that God was not alone in the act of creation and, furthermore, there is no such implication in the accounts of any of the other things created. In response to this question, R. Ḥama quotes a verse from Job that also appears to be contradictory. On the one hand man is described as being the oldest in creation – *mini 'ad*, from the very earliest time – and on the other hand, the last in creation, which is the meaning of 'since man was set on earth.' He then goes on to present his solution.

אָמַר רַבִּי חָמָא בַּר חֲנִינָא מָשָׁל לִמְדִינָה שֶׁהָיְתָה מִסְתַּפֶּקֶת מִן הַחַמָּרִין וְהָיוּ שׁוֹאֲלִין אֵלוּ לָאֵלוּ מַה שְּׁבְרוֹן נַעֲשָׂה בַּמְּדִינָה הַיּוֹם שֶׁל שִׁשִּׁי הָיוּ שׁוֹאֲלִין שֶׁל חֲמִישִׁי וְשֶׁל חֲמִישִׁי שֶׁל רְבִיעִי וְשֶׁל רְבִיעִי שֶׁל שְׁלִישִׁי וְשֶׁל שְׁלִישִׁי שֶׁל שֵׁנִי וְשֶׁל שֵׁנִי שֶׁל רִאשׁוֹן וְשֶׁל רִאשׁוֹן לְמִי הָיָה לוֹ לִשְׁאֹל וְלֹא לִבְנֵי הַמְּדִינָה שֶׁהָיוּ עֲסוּקִין בְּדִימוֹסָה שֶׁל מְדִינָה

R. Ḥama b. R. Ḥanina said: The matter may be compared to a city which received its supplies from donkey drivers [who brought in produce from the surrounding villages]. They used to ask each other [i.e., the incoming and outgoing suppliers], 'What market price [have the authorities fixed]?' [Thus those who supplied on] Friday would ask of those [who supplied] on Thursday; Thursday's [suppliers] would ask of those of Wednesday; Wednesday's would ask Tuesday's; Tuesday's would ask Monday's; Monday's would ask Sunday's. But who could Sunday's [suppliers] ask? Surely [they had to ask] the citizens who were engaged in the public affairs of the city.

Similarly in the creation story.

אַף כָּאן כָּל מַעֲשֶׂה שֶׁל כָּל יוֹם וָיוֹם הָיוּ שׁוֹאֲלִין אֵלּוּ לָאֵלּוּ מַה בְּרִיּוֹת בָּרָא הַקָּדוֹשׁ
בָּרוּךְ הוּא בָּכֶם הַיּוֹם שֶׁל שִׁשִּׁי שׁוֹאֵל שֶׁל חֲמִישִׁי וְכוּ' עַד לָרִאשׁוֹן לְמִי הָיוּ שׁוֹאֲלִין
לֹא לַתּוֹרָה שֶׁקָּדְמָה לִבְרִיָּתוֹ שֶׁל עוֹלָם

**Here, too, the works of each day asked one another, 'Which
creatures did the Holy One, blessed be He, create among you?' The
[works of] the sixth day asked those of the fifth, and so on. But who
could the first day ask? Surely the Torah, which preceded the
creation of the world by two thousand years.**

The Talmud rules that it is permitted to speculate about the creation from
the first day on, but it is forbidden to speculate as to what happened before
the first day. Thus, the creatures and the various phenomena created on
each of the days could ask regarding the creations of the previous days.
However, those created on the first day had none to ask since nothing was
created before them. Just as the donkey drivers of Sunday had to ask the
authorities in the city who fixed the market prices, so too the creations of
the first day had to ask the Torah, the creation of which preceded that of
the world. The *midrash* goes on to explain the source for this.

דַּאֲמַר ר' שִׁמְעוֹן בֶּן לָקִישׁ שְׁנֵי אֲלָפִים שָׁנָה קָדְמָה הַתּוֹרָה לִבְרִיָּתוֹ שֶׁל עוֹלָם הֲדָא
הוּא דִּכְתִיב 'וָאֶהְיֶה אֶצְלוֹ אָמוֹן וְגוֹ'' (משלי ח, לב) וְיוֹמוֹ שֶׁל הַקָּדוֹשׁ בָּרוּךְ הוּא אֶלֶף
שָׁנִים דִּכְתִיב 'כִּי אֶלֶף שָׁנִים בְּעֵינֶיךָ כְּיוֹם אֶתְמוֹל' (תהלים צ, ד) הֲוֵי 'הֲזֹאת יָדַעְתָּ
מִנִּי עַד וְגוֹ'' (איוב כ, ד) הַתּוֹרָה יוֹדַעַת מַה קֹדֶם בְּרִיָּתוֹ שֶׁל עוֹלָם אֲבָל אַתָּה אֵין
לְךָ עֵסֶק לִדְרֹשׁ אֶלָּא 'מִנִּי שִׂים אָדָם עֲלֵי אָרֶץ'

**As R. Simon b. Lakish said: The Torah preceded the creation of the
world by two thousand years, as it is written, 'I [the Torah] was by
Him, as a nursling [*amon*]; and I was all delight day after day'
(Proverbs 8:30). ['Day after day' means at least two days] and the day
of the Holy One, blessed be He, is a thousand years, as it is written,
'For in Your sight a thousand years are like yesterday that has past'
(Psalms 90:4). That is the meaning of 'Do you not know this, that from
time immemorial' (Job 20:4). The Torah knows what was before the
creation of the world, but you can speculate about what happened
only 'since man was set upon the earth' (ibid.).**

R. Simon b. Lakish's source verse is the verse with which *Bereishit Rabbah*
begins. See *Parashah One, Midrash One* for a full discussion. The Hebrew
for 'this' in the verse from Job is *zot* and refers, by association to the Torah,
as is learned from the phrase *ve-zot ha-torah*, 'and *this* is the Torah,' in

Deuteronomy 4:44. This exposition also answers the question: With whom did God consult when He said, 'Let us make man…' – He consulted with the Torah. Having reached the above conclusion, the *midrash* now continues that the Torah knows what happened before the creation of the world and that humans must not speculate about it. We have the right to study what happened since the moment man was created.

ר' אֶלְעָזָר בְּשֵׁם בֶּן סִירָא אָמַר בְּגָדוֹל מִמְּךָ אַל תִּדְרֹשׁ בְּחָזָק מִמְּךָ בַּל תַּחְקֹר בְּמֻפְלָא מִמְּךָ בַּל תֵּדַע בִּמְכֻסֶּה מִמְּךָ אַל תִּשְׁאַל בַּמֶּה שֶׁהֻרְשֵׁיתָ הִתְבּוֹנֵן וְאֵין לְךָ עֵסֶק בַּנִּסְתָּרוֹת

R. Eleazar said in Ben Sira's name: About that which is greater than you do not inquire; that which is stronger than you do not investigate; about that which is separate from you do not try to know; of that which is hidden from you do not ask. Contemplate on that which is permitted to you; you have no business with hidden things.

The Book of Ben Sira is an apocryphal work and not included in the canon of the Bible. It is therefore not quoted as a source text, but rather as the opinion of Ben Sira. What he says constitutes a summation of what we have just learned. Man should study what is permitted, namely, from the creation story and onwards. 'Hidden things' refers to the details of creation and to the descriptions of the divine chariot as seen in Ezekiel's visions.

* * *

Seed Thoughts

What is meant by the assertion that the Torah existed before the creation of the world, that God consulted with it in the act of creation, particularly that of man? Does it mean that the document in our possession existed then, that the words were written on parchment and the whole history of what was to be was already known?

While all kinds of miracles are possible and God can do anything, it seems hardly likely that this is what is meant. After all, the Midrash states in many places that other things were created before the creation of the world such as the throne of God, Israel, and the concept of Messiah (see *Parashah One, Midrash Four*). What our *midrash* seems to be saying is that when the world was created, God had the purpose of Torah in mind. Not only was the Torah the purpose that existed before creation, the world was so constituted that the Torah could be observed in it. Nay, more so.

The world was so constituted that it would yield its highest spiritual dividends if the ideals of the Torah became its ideals, that is to say, the ideals of individuals and societies. Furthermore, the claim would be that the human being is himself so constituted that he will realize his potential if he adopts the ideals of the Torah. As for the Jewish people as a whole, that is unquestionably so.

It is not to be understood, therefore, that Torah as a document existed before creation. What is being told to us is that the purpose of Torah became the purpose of creation. Now that we know the destiny and character of the world, we should steer the ship of our lives in its direction.

* * *

Additional Commentary

R. Ḥama commenced

From the verse 'Let us make man in our image,' it would appear that God consulted with someone on the question of man's creation. This idea presents an enormous theological difficulty. How and why would God consult with anyone on the creation of man? If man were not to be created, what would be the point of the creation of the universe? It was this latter kind of question that prompted R. Ḥama to start with this particular verse, 'Do you not know...,' from which we deduced that the Torah knew what happened before creation, but we are not entitled to enquire except from, 'Since the time man was set on the earth.' Therefore we are not allowed to speculate even about questions, such as what meaning would creation have without the creation of man, because that is beyond human understanding. (*Tiferet Tzion*)

*

The Torah knows

Zophar the Naamathite responds to Job with the words quoted above, 'Do you not know this, that from time immemorial...' when Job questioned the ways of God. His point was that when you see someone doing something that appears improper, you cannot begin to question his behavior unless you know the purpose behind the actions and what his intentions are. Similarly, one cannot question God's ways since we do not know His purpose in creating the world and man. We have no choice but to act as the Torah instructs us, because the Torah does know the purpose of creation and can thus bring us to a point where our actions will also conform to this purpose. If, however, the human being acts only in accord with his own reason, he is certain to err and find himself in darkness and on a slippery path.

So the *midrash* now comes to its conclusion. No one has the right to speculate, for your reason will surely mislead you. True, you can learn something from those who came earlier in the process of creation as you can learn from those who preceded you in life; but from this knowledge you will learn only physical things. The real purpose of the world in so far as spiritual matters are concerned we can only discern from the Torah, which is the supreme wisdom upon which the world was founded. (*Tiferet Tzion*)

*

Ben Sira – why the four?

Even in matters that are in the purview of human reason, there are different gradations and different levels of human comprehension. Some people are able to comprehend matters that are completely hidden from others, indeed, from any other living persons, as, for example, the great discoverers. There are others whose mental capacity cannot grasp even obvious things. The *midrash* lists these categories. Some areas of thought may not appear to be too complicated, but because the subject matter is so important such as, for example, the life force, we cannot comprehend it. In such matters as are greater than you, be very careful. Sometimes the subject matter is very minor, but can become complicated and abstruse. In this respect, the *midrash* warns you to stay away from what is stronger than you, that is, too hard for you, do not investigate. However, when it comes to those miraculous areas where only God can function – what is separate from you – you should not even try to know. A special category, all on its own, is those things that are hidden from us such as the story of Ezekiel's chariot, the story of creation, and other themes that God has kept hidden from man. Do not even ask about these things except in a general way. And do not worry that if you miss out on these things you will be deprived of a sufficient intellectual challenge. You have enough to exhaust yourself through your lifetime in what you have culturally inherited. Study what has been revealed. Do not pursue that which is hidden. (*Tiferet Tzion*)

Parashah Eight, Midrash Three

'וַיֹּאמֶר אֱלֹהִים נַעֲשֶׂה אָדָם' (בראשית א, כו) בְּמִי נִמְלַךְ רַבִּי יְהוֹשֻׁעַ בְּשֵׁם רַ' לֵוִי אָמַר
בִּמְלֶאכֶת הַשָּׁמַיִם וְהָאָרֶץ נִמְלַךְ מָשָׁל לְמֶלֶךְ שֶׁהָיוּ לוֹ שְׁנֵי סַנְקְלִיטִים וְלֹא הָיָה
עוֹשֶׂה דָּבָר חוּץ מִדַּעְתָּן

'And God said: "Let us make man"' (Genesis 1:26). **With whom did he take counsel? R. Joshua b. Levi said: He took counsel with the work of heaven and earth, like a king who had two ministers in council and never did anything without their consent.**

The question that was posed obliquely in the first two *midrashim* of this *parashah* is now asked explicitly. The question is of extreme importance theologically and indeed has bothered theologians throughout the ages. R. Joshua, giving a parable in true midrashic fashion, claims that He consulted with the works of heaven and earth. He gives a parable because the matter is beyond human comprehension and, indeed, in the previous *midrash* we were told that we must not even think of the question. R. Joshua obviously disagrees. In the light of the next passage, *Ha-Midrash ha-Mevo'ar* comments that God consulted with heaven and earth together, not separately. As we shall see below, other Sages proposed different explanations.

רַבִּי שְׁמוּאֵל בַּר נַחְמָן אָמַר בְּמַעֲשֶׂה כָּל יוֹם וָיוֹם נִמְלַךְ מָשָׁל לְמֶלֶךְ שֶׁהָיָה לוֹ
סַנְקְתֶּדְרוֹן וְלֹא הָיָה עוֹשֶׂה דָּבָר חוּץ מִדַּעְתּוֹ

R. Samuel b. Naḥman said: He took counsel with the works of each day, like a king who had an associate without whose agreement he did nothing.

A second view was that God consulted with the works of each day of creation individually and privately. They were therefore not a council and their views were consultative, not binding.

רַ' אַמִּי אָמַר בְּלִבּוֹ נִמְלַךְ מָשָׁל לְמֶלֶךְ שֶׁבָּנָה פָּלְטִין עַל יְדֵי אַרְדִיכָל רָאָה אוֹתָהּ וְלֹא
עָרְבָה לוֹ עַל מִי יֵשׁ לוֹ לְהִתְרָעֵם לֹא עַל אַרְדִיכָל אַתְמָהָא הֱוֵי 'וַיִּתְעַצֵּב אֶל לִבּוֹ'
(בראשית ו, ו)

R. Ammi said: He took counsel with his own heart. The matter can be compared to a king who had a palace built by an architect, but when he saw it, it did not please him. With whom is he to be indignant? Surely with the architect! Thus, 'And it grieved Him in His heart' (Genesis 6:6).

R. Ammi's exposition is more orthodox than the previous two. God's heart is an integral part of Him and not something separate like heaven and earth or the works of all the days. Thus R. Ammi removes any hint that might lessen the Almighty's uniqueness. When God saw that human beings were degrading their possibilities, He realized that the responsibility lay with the 'architect' who planned the creation of man – His own heart.

אָמַר רַ' אַסֵי מָשָׁל לְמֶלֶךְ שֶׁעָשָׂה לוֹ סְחוֹרָה עַל יְדֵי סַרְסוּר וְהִפְסִיד עַל מִי יֵשׁ לוֹ
לְהִתְרָעֵם לֹא עַל הַסַּרְסוּר אַתְמָהָא הֲוֵי 'וַיִּתְעַצֵּב אֶל לִבּוֹ'

R. Assi said: It may be compared to a king who conducted business through an agent and suffered loss. With whom is he to be indignant? Surely with the agent! Thus, 'And it grieved Him in His heart' (Genesis 6:6).

R. Assi is unhappy with his colleague's metaphor of an architect. When one consults a professional expert, one is surely bound to accept his advice or decisions. It is inconceivable that the Almighty is bound to do anything. Therefore R. Assi considers God's heart to be an agent, that is, someone who is entirely dependent on his principal. God's consultation should be regarded not as consultation but as reflection. RZWE understands the heart to mean the Torah, since, in traditional rabbinic thought, the heart is the seat of wisdom. When, therefore, it turned out that God regretted man's evil behavior, His anger was directed against His advisors, His heart or His Torah depending upon how the phrase is interpreted.

* * *

Seed Thoughts

'Let us make man in our image.' From this verse the *midrash* deduces that God consulted before He went about creating man. With whom did He consult? There are three views and, according to the *Yefei To'ar* in a brilliant insight, the consultations were a way of revealing the nature and purpose of man.

The first view that is presented to us is that God consulted with heaven and earth. That is to say, there is something about man that is connected with heaven. Man connects the upper spiritual world with the lower material world. Man cannot be judged merely in terms of his animal nature. More has been put into him and more is expected of him.

I find that the best way to illustrate the difference is to compare views on sexuality. Those who view man in purely secular terms will see sexuality as a function not too different from eating, and in that light human sexual attitudes would differ only in degree from those of animals. Those who see man as a cosmic phenomenon will view sexuality as a holy experience since it deals with those aspects of experience that are ultimate in terms of importance, reproducing new generations and educating them to ideals. The 1987 controversy about AIDS illustrates this point very well. Those who want a media barrage advocating the use of a particular male contraceptive as a way of preventing AIDS have no qualms about the fact that they will be condoning sexual promiscuity as being perfectly natural and in order. Those who look upon this development in horror and advocate sexual abstinence outside of marriage – at least as an option that can be talked about – fear that the social and ethical problems produced by promiscuity are as bad as AIDS. In fact, it was permissiveness that produced AIDS in the first place. Man is more than animal. He is a spiritual being.

The second opinion in the *midrash* brings to our attention that God consulted with all creation because man was to be its crowning achievement, the world in miniature. Who can contemplate this universe without a sense of wonder? But our real sense of wonder should be not the beauties of nature, but rather the wonder and mystery of human nature. When Abraham was asked to go outside and try to count the stars, we might imagine that the lesson being taught to him was the glory of the universe. But the word that came to him was: Look at the stars and remember that your descendants will be as many. Your descendants will be the real stars far greater than the natural ones.

Much effort has gone into teaching us about the glory of man. Unfortunately, our very glory contains the seeds of our own destruction because we possess not only spirit but also animal nature. The animal in us wants to fight. It wants power, sovereignty, territory, resources. We have experienced a First World War, a second, and a Holocaust of unbelievable proportions. Have we learned from these experiences? There has hardly been a moment in the twentieth century when wars of one kind or another were not being waged in some corner of the world. Just look at the history of modern Israel and what it has been forced to undergo in order to survive. Why is there so much hatred, so much anger, and so much bloodthirstiness? Because too many people are too convinced of the rightness of their cause, and whenever people are too convinced of their rightness, beware! It always spells danger.

In contrast to these terrible manifestations of human madness, I was filled with admiration when I read a little essay on Zamenhoff, the creator of Esperanto. Zamenhoff was looking for a way to bring brotherhood to the world. He thought that a universal language would do it. Would you believe that his first thought was that Yiddish was simple enough to become that language? He only changed his strategy when it was pointed out to him that he might be accused of ethnic arrogance. He chose the name Esperanto because it means hope. At first the movement spread like wildfire and a considerable literature developed. All of this was stopped and ruined by the outbreak of World War I. I saw a letter that Zamenhoff published, an open letter, crying at the impending destruction and warning the world that nothing that they might achieve would be worth the destruction and the loss of life. It is the Zamenhoff type that is truly the hope of the world.

The third view brought to our attention is that God consulted with Himself. The moral here is that man has the power to make decisions with his own conscience despite what may happen elsewhere. This is truly a message of hope because the individual is the source of hope. When Hillel Zeitlin, the great Yiddish writer and scholar who perished in the Holocaust, realized that the world would not change no matter what, he never lost faith that he might change. That might be what we are called upon to do when all else fails – to change ourselves and improve ourselves.

A youngster was annoying his father, who was anxious to read the evening newspaper. He gave the boy a complicated puzzle of the map of the world, hoping that that would divert his attention for a considerable time. Imagine his surprise when his son finished the puzzle in a few minutes. 'How did you do it so quickly?' asked the father. And the boy replied, 'I noticed that there was a picture of a man on the other side. All I did was put the man together and I was able to put the world together.' Maybe that is what we ought to be doing.

* * *

Additional Commentary

With whom did God consult?

Maybe consult is not the right word. God had to make certain arrangements so that His plan for man as a moral being would materialize. On the one hand, He had to establish conditions for man's material abundance. He wanted that to depend on man's moral behavior. That is why God consulted heaven and earth, to make sure that rain would fall when morally earned and not fall when undeserved. On the other hand, He had to make sure that man understood the possibilities of his own nature and that other creations that preceded man also understood this. It is man's uniqueness that he is able to change himself, to transform his character from anger to pity. The same applies to every attribute. This is man's uniqueness. It was necessary to get the consent of the works of everyday not to stand in the way of man's self-transforming power.

God didn't have to consult in order to bring about this state of affairs, but because consultation is the best way for political states to follow, He established the precedent to enable and encourage human political leaders to act in the same way. (*Tiferet Tzion*)

*

Sankilitim and sankatadron

The term *sankelitim*, used as a metaphor for heaven and earth, refers to a court. A court must rule in accordance with law without any discretionary ability. So heaven and earth obey God's rules and conditions without any discretionary powers.

Sankatadron, the metaphor for the works of each day, are advisors with discretionary powers. The nature and role of the human being is to change and improve the world so that it transcends the original nature of each set day of creation. (*Tiferet Tzion*)

*

R. Ammi said

How can it be said that God speaks to His heart? The heart is the dwelling place for wisdom, as the verse says, 'In the heart of every wise man I have placed wisdom.' Therefore, the highest form of wisdom, which is Torah, is sometimes called 'heart.' In this connection the *midrash* uses the parable of the architect. A king uses an architect to build. The Torah was God's architect as in *Parashah One, Midrash One*. God looked into the blueprints of Torah and built the world. The consultation was not necessarily to create man or not, as the biblical verse seems to suggest, but what particular character should man be endowed with. After all, an architect is used both for the design of a building as well as the decision whether it should be built at all.

The issue here is one that God wanted decided by someone else (although of course He knew the right decision). Would it be better for man to be free from material concerns in order to study Torah? God therefore consulted with Torah since the world was created for the sake of Torah. The Torah advised to create man with as few material problems as possible. God listened and created a situation where man sowed seed only once in forty years and, even then, for less than one hour, and produced the cedars of Lebanon, and the wild beasts were not a threat at all. They had a beautiful climate from Passover to Shemini Atzeret, and all this so that man should study Torah without interruption. During the time of the Flood, however, it was obvious that the system was not working. God showed the Torah that its advice was not good and the Torah was forced to admit this and acknowledge that man needs the persuasion of austerity and challenge to function well. When the verse says, 'He was saddened in His heart' it means that the Torah was sad in that it had to change life in this world so that man could be motivated for Torah study. Many of the forty-eight ways of acquiring the Torah, listed in the last chapter of the *Ethics of the Fathers*, have to do with suffering. Bread and water shall you drink and the life of austerity shall you live. It is sad to realize that suffering is needed in order to raise the level of Torah. (*Tiferet Tzion*)

*

R. Assi and the metaphor of the agent

'And he was sad in his heart' refers to man. The comparison is that of an agent. Man is God's agent, who was given control over all the world's creatures and, based on his good deeds, this world can rise higher and higher. Man became sad because he did not succeed and the world's destruction was decreed through the Flood.

R. Assi does not disagree with R. Ammi, who says that the Torah was sad. God often says one thing from which we learn two.

*

With whom did He consult?

Rashi, in his commentary to the Pentateuch, interpreted our *midrash* as a controversy on the question: For what purpose was man created?

R. Joshua in the name of R. Levi said: He consulted heaven and earth. This teaches that the purpose of man is to show that the higher world is connected with the lower world. They are indeed connected, as we can see from man. There is within him a part that is earthy, namely his body, together with a part of his soul, which represents heaven. In man heaven and earth are connected.

R. Samuel b. Naḥman, who said that God consulted with the works of every day, implies that within man all of creation and all of the world may be found. That includes the heritage of the plant world and all the rest of creation, for man is 'the world in miniature.' In man we can see that all that has been created is interconnected and indissoluble.

R. Ammi, who says that God consulted with Himself, is asserting that the greatness of man is his ability to choose and exercise free will. That is what is meant by 'He consulted with His heart.' He did all things by the free will of His own decision-making. This decision comes from the heart and depends upon one's heart. Man should not have to make decisions based on the rules of nature as do other creatures who cannot change. That is his greatness. (*Yefei To'ar*)

*

This consultation took place on the sixth day when all else had been created. God wanted to counsel with all of them about man because he wanted man to rule over them all. As each creature came into being, God explained its purpose and added that man would be ruler over them all and asked for their consent. (RZWE)

Parashah Eight, Midrash Four

אָמַר רַבִּי בֶּרֶכְיָה בְּשָׁעָה שֶׁבָּא הַקָּדוֹשׁ בָּרוּךְ הוּא לִבְרֹאת אֶת אָדָם הָרִאשׁוֹן רָאָה
צַדִּיקִים וּרְשָׁעִים יוֹצְאִים מִמֶּנּוּ אָמַר אִם אֲנִי בוֹרֵא אוֹתוֹ רְשָׁעִים יוֹצְאִים מִמֶּנּוּ
וְאִם לֹא אֶבְרָא אוֹתוֹ הֵיאַךְ צַדִּיקִים יוֹצְאִים מִמֶּנּוּ מֶה עָשָׂה הַקָּדוֹשׁ בָּרוּךְ הוּא
הִפְלִיג דַּרְכָּן שֶׁל רְשָׁעִים מִכְּנֶגֶד פָּנָיו וְשִׁתֵּף בּוֹ מִדַּת רַחֲמִים וּבְרָאוֹ הֲדָא הוּא
דִּכְתִיב 'כִּי יוֹדֵעַ ה' דֶּרֶךְ צַדִּיקִים וְדֶרֶךְ רְשָׁעִים תֹּאבֵד' (תהלים א, ו) אִבְּדָהּ מִכְּנֶגֶד
פָּנָיו וְשִׁתֵּף בּוֹ מִדַּת רַחֲמִים וּבְרָאוֹ

R. Berekhiah said: When the Holy One, blessed be He, came to create Adam, he saw the righteous and the wicked issuing from him.
He said: 'If I create him, wicked men will issue from him, but if I do
not create him, how are the righteous to issue from him?' What then
did the Holy One, blessed be He, do? He removed the way of the
wicked out of his sight and associated the quality of mercy with
Himself and created him. This is what is meant by the verse 'For the
Lord cherishes the way of the righteous, but the way of the wicked
shall perish (to'veid)' (Psalms 1:6). [What does to'veid mean?] He
destroyed (ibbedah) [the way of the wicked] from his sight and
associated the quality of mercy with Himself and created him.

The text for this *midrash* is the verse, 'Let us make man...' and R.
Berekhiah seems to agree with R. Ammi in the previous *midrash* that God
took counsel with Himself. What was the nature of His reflections? God
ignored the fact that there would be wicked people among the progeny
of Adam. How could He do that? By allowing the attribute of mercy to
be involved in the creation of man. That is the meaning of the verse from
Psalms quoted, 'the way of the wicked shall perish,' in which 'the way of
the wicked' as the subject of the verb, is now re-interpreted to mean that
God removed the way of the wicked from His sight when He decided to
create man. In general, the acts of creation were done with the attribute
of justice, which explains the use of the term *Elokim* everywhere in the
creation story. In the case of man's creation, however, the attribute of
mercy was introduced, which explains the use of *Hashem* and *Elokim* in
the verse, 'Then the *Lord God* formed man' (Genesis 2:7). That now
becomes the meaning of, 'Let us make man.' The use of the plural form

refers to the decision of God to allow the attribute of mercy to be involved in the creation of man.

רַ' חֲנִינָא לֹא אָמַר כֵּן אֶלָּא בְּשָׁעָה שֶׁבָּא לִבְרֹאת אֶת אָדָם הָרִאשׁוֹן נִמְלַךְ בְּמַלְאֲכֵי הַשָּׁרֵת וְאָמַר לָהֶן 'נַעֲשֶׂה אָדָם בְּצַלְמֵנוּ כִדְמוּתֵנוּ' אָמְרוּ לוֹ אָדָם זֶה מַה טִיבוֹ אָמַר לָהֶן צַדִּיקִים עוֹמְדִים מִמֶּנּוּ הָדָא הוּא דִכְתִיב 'כִּי יוֹדֵעַ ה' דֶּרֶךְ צַדִּיקִים' כִּי הוֹדִיעַ ה' דֶּרֶךְ הַצַּדִּיקִים לְמַלְאֲכֵי הַשָּׁרֵת 'וְדֶרֶךְ רְשָׁעִים תֹּאבֵד' אִבְּדָהּ מֵהֶם גִּלָּה לָהֶם שֶׁהַצַּדִּיקִים עוֹמְדִים מִמֶּנּוּ וְלֹא גִלָּה לָהֶם שֶׁהָרְשָׁעִים עוֹמְדִים הֵימֶנּוּ שֶׁאִלּוּ גִלָּה לָהֶם שֶׁהָרְשָׁעִים עוֹמְדִים הֵימֶנּוּ לֹא הָיְתָה מִדַּת הַדִּין נוֹתֶנֶת שֶׁיִּבָּרֵא

R. Ḥanina did not say this, rather [he said that] when He came to create Adam, He consulted the ministering angels, saying to them, 'Let us make man.' They asked, 'What shall his character be?' and [God] replied, 'Righteous men shall spring from him.' [This is as it is written, 'For the Lord knows (*yode'a*) the way of the righteous,' which means that the Lord made known (*hodi'a*) the way of the righteous to the ministering angels; 'but the way of the wicked shall perish' – He destroyed [i.e., concealed] it from them. He revealed to them that righteous men would arise from [Adam], but He did not reveal to them that wicked men would [also] spring from him; for if he had revealed to them that the wicked would spring from him, the quality of justice would not have permitted him to be created.

R. Ḥanina did not accept the view that God consulted with Himself, that is, engaged in reflection. It was his view that God took counsel with the angels. Apparently, He had already decided to create man and the question under discussion in the consultation was what should the qualities of the man to be created be. Should man have only spiritual qualities like the angels, or should he be a blend of the spiritual and the material, as indeed, he was ultimately created? The angels, who saw themselves as the ideal creatures, then inquired about man's behavior. God revealed that righteous people would spring from him, but He did not mention that evil-doers would also arise. According to R. Ḥanina, this is the correct interpretation of the verse in Psalms; 'the way of the wicked shall perish' is now interpreted as 'He concealed the way of wicked.' R. Ḥanina then continued that only thus could man have been created, because had the angels known that there would be wicked among Adam's progeny, they would not have agreed to his creation and God, in His attribute of justice, would have had to conform.

* * *

Seed Thoughts

We can detect in this *midrash* not only the sadness of the Sages in acknowledging the evil of man and the world. We perceive in their interpretation that God Himself was saddened by this development.

The idea that evil-doers will be punished by letting them have no portion in the world-to-come and will be thus cut off from eternity is theoretically very appropriate, but offers no comfort to those who suffer from the evil in this world.

Can it be changed? Not if you value freedom. For that is the bottom line of this discussion. Without evil there can be no good – not merely by contrast, but by virtue of the very nature of man as a being who has choice.

Can evil be overcome within the context of freedom? Only by doing good, by the example of good people, by the cooperative efforts of good individuals and mature societies.

When all is said and done, the attribute of mercy has to work hand in hand with the attribute of justice.

* * *

Additional Commentary

Said R. Berakhiah

The implication of the verse 'Let us make man' can now be explained as follows: All creatures were created with only one attribute. That includes the angels, who possessed either the quality of justice or mercy but not both. That is why an angel cannot be entrusted with more than one mission, since for an additional mission the angel would require more than one attribute. The same holds true of the animal world. But the human being was born with the potential of all the attributes. He can choose to be whatever he wants to be. He can also possess and behave in terms of more than one attribute at any one time, whether to be merciful or just. In this respect man truly resembles God, who uses all the attributes. Because God communicated with His attributes the verse reads, 'Let us make man' and also why He said, 'in Our image after Our likeness.' (*Tiferet Tzion*)

*

The Lord knows (cherishes)

The question arises, what new angle is brought to our attention by quoting the verse that the Lord knows the way of the righteous? The implication seems to be that He does not know the way of the wicked (heaven forfend). Therefore the word *yode'a*, 'know,' is translated in a transitive sense.

The intent of the verse would then be that God 'made known' to the angels the way of the righteous but not of the way of the wicked. The reason for this was that the consultations with the angels was to indicate that man's actions would determine the behavior of all the world including the angels. He wanted their consent to have man rule over them, just as in the building of the Tabernacle God consulted with Moses about Bezalel and with Israel. One does not appoint a leader over a community without the consent of that community. Furthermore, He only had to inform the angels about those people who would have a share in building the world, but the wicked are considered dead in their lifetime since their actions have no effect beyond this world and, therefore, their existence was not brought to the attention of the angels. (*Tiferet Tzion*)

Parashah Eight, Midrash Five

אָמַר רַבִּי סִימוֹן בְּשָׁעָה שֶׁבָּא הַקָּדוֹשׁ בָּרוּךְ הוּא לִבְרֹאת אֶת אָדָם הָרִאשׁוֹן נַעֲשׂוּ מַלְאֲכֵי הַשָּׁרֵת כִּתִּים כִּתִּים וַחֲבוּרוֹת חֲבוּרוֹת מֵהֶם אוֹמְרִים אַל יִבָּרֵא וּמֵהֶם אוֹמְרִים יִבָּרֵא הֲדָא הוּא דִכְתִיב 'חֶסֶד וֶאֱמֶת נִפְגָּשׁוּ צֶדֶק וְשָׁלוֹם נָשָׁקוּ' (תהלים פה, יא)

R. Simon said: When the Holy One, blessed be He, came to create Adam, the ministering angels formed themselves into groups and parties, some of them saying, 'Let him be not created,' whilst others urged, 'Let him be created.' Thus it is written, 'Loving-kindness and truth fought together, justice and peace combatted each other' (Psalms 85:11).

The text for this *midrash* is, 'Let us make man...' and R. Simon follows the view that God consulted with the angels. The disagreement among the angels as to whether or not man should be created is based on a new interpretation of Psalm 85. This is not how the verse is usually translated. The word נשקו, *nashaku*, is here translated not as 'kissed,' but as deriving from the word נשק, *neshek*, meaning weapons. The word נפגשו, *nifgashu*, meaning 'meet,' is here rendered as meeting in combat. This new interpretation gives the arguments very great force. What were the arguments?

'חֶסֶד' אוֹמֵר יִבָּרֵא שֶׁהוּא גּוֹמֵל חֲסָדִים 'וֶאֱמֶת' אוֹמֵר אַל יִבָּרֵא שֶׁכֻּלּוֹ שְׁקָרִים 'צֶדֶק' אוֹמֵר יִבָּרֵא שֶׁהוּא עוֹשֶׂה צְדָקוֹת 'שָׁלוֹם' אוֹמֵר אַל יִבָּרֵא דְּכֻלֵּהּ קְטָטָה מֶה עָשָׂה הַקָּדוֹשׁ בָּרוּךְ הוּא נָטַל 'אֱמֶת' וְהִשְׁלִיכוֹ לָאָרֶץ הֲדָא הוּא דִכְתִיב 'וְתַשְׁלֵךְ אֱמֶת אַרְצָה' (דניאל ח, יב)

Loving-kindness (*ḥesed*) said, 'Let him be created, because he will dispense acts of kindness'; truth (*emet*) said, 'Let him not be created, because he is compounded of falsehood'; justice (*tzedek*) said, 'Let him be created, because he will perform righteous deeds (*tzedakot*)'; peace (*shalom*) said, 'Let him not be created, because he is full of strife.' What did the Holy One, blessed be He do? He took truth and cast it to the ground as it is written, 'He hurled truth down to the earth' (Daniel 8:12).

295

Ḥesed – 'loving-kindness' or 'mercy' – emphasized man's good qualities, such as lending money to the needy, giving food, and various forms of personal service to others. *Emet* thought in absolute terms and saw no value in good deeds if they were accompanied by lies. *Tzedek* – 'justice' or 'righteousness' – said, 'Create him, for he will be a force for good,' whereas peace could only see man as a quarreller. God solved the argument by sending 'truth' down to earth and thus not having to be concerned with its opinion. The same was not done with peace because it was not as forceful. After the expulsion of 'truth' from the consultation, there was a majority decision in favor of the creation of man, but the angels protested.

אָמְרוּ מַלְאֲכֵי הַשָּׁרֵת לִפְנֵי הַקָּדוֹשׁ בָּרוּךְ הוּא רִבּוֹן הָעוֹלָמִים מָה אַתָּה מְבַזֶּה תַּכְסִיס אַלְטִיכְסִיָּה שֶׁלָּךְ תַּעֲלֶה אֱמֶת מִן הָאָרֶץ הֲדָא הוּא דִכְתִיב 'אֱמֶת מֵאֶרֶץ תִּצְמָח' (תהלים פה, יב)

Said the ministering angels before the Holy One, blessed be He, 'Sovereign of the universe! How can You despise Your seal?' [God said to them], 'Let truth rise from the earth!' hence it is written, 'Truth springs up from the earth' (Psalms 85:12).

The angels protested that by demeaning truth, God was demeaning a major part of Himself, since 'truth' is his seal. The Hebrew, תַּכְסִיס אַלְטִיכְסִיָּה, is difficult since both words are variations of the same word. The Theodor-Albeck edition of *Bereishit Rabbah* has only the second word, which is translated by Jastrow as 'the chief of the court ceremonies.' It is possible that our reading is the result of a copyist's error. The angels therefore requested the return of truth, to which God acquiesced, based on the second part of the verse from Psalms that was interpreted as the source of the consultation above.

רַבָּנָן אָמְרֵי לַהּ בְּשֵׁם רַ' חֲנִינָא בַּר אִידִי וְרַבִּי פִּינְחָס וְרַבִּי חִלְקִיָּה בְּשֵׁם רַבִּי סִימוֹן אָמַר 'מְאֹד' הוּא 'אָדָם' הֲדָא הוּא דִכְתִיב 'וַיַּרְא אֱלֹהִים אֶת כָּל אֲשֶׁר עָשָׂה וְהִנֵּה טוֹב מְאֹד' (בראשית א, לא) וְהִנֵּה טוֹב אָדָם

The Rabbis said the following in the name of R. Ḥanina, and R. Pinḥas and R. Ḥilkiah said it in the name of R. Simon: The word *me'od*, meaning 'very,' is identical with *Adam*, which is the meaning of that which is written, 'And God saw everything that He had made, and, behold, it was very (*me'od*) good' (Genesis 1:31) – and, behold, Adam was good.

The letters of מאד, meaning 'very,' are the same the letters as Adam, אדם,

meaning man, except in a different order. The point of this lovely interpretation is to indicate that while God consulted the angels, He didn't need their advice at all. He knew in advance that the creation of man was a good thing and had not intended to accept their advice.

ר' הוּנָא רַבָּה שֶׁל צִפּוֹרִין אָמַר עַד שֶׁמַּלְאֲכֵי הַשָּׁרֵת מִדַּיְּנִין אֵלּוּ עִם אֵלּוּ וּמִתְעַסְּקִין אֵלּוּ עִם אֵלּוּ בְּרָאוֹ הַקָּדוֹשׁ בָּרוּךְ הוּא אָמַר לָהֶן מָה אַתֶּם מִדַּיְּנִין כְּבָר נַעֲשָׂה אָדָם

R. Ḥuna, the Rabbi of Sepphoris, said: While the ministering angels were arguing with each other and disputing with each other, the Holy One, blessed be He, created him [Adam]. Said He to them, 'What are you discussing? Man has already been created!'

God's intention to create man despite the opinion of the angels is here demonstrated conclusively. While they were arguing, He created man. Thus we have a new interpretation of the word נעשה, *na'aseh*; it is not to be understood as being future ('Let us make man'), but as a passive verb in the past tense – 'He is already made.' This is not an emendation of the biblical text since exactly the same spelling with the same vocalization can have both meanings.

* * *

Seed Thoughts

Psalm 85:11 reads, 'Loving-kindness and truth meet; justice and peace kiss.' Our *midrash* had rendered the verb, *nashaku*, not as meaning 'kiss,' but as deriving from the word *neshek*, which means weapons or armaments. This changes the whole meaning of the verse, which is now rendered, 'Loving-kindness and truth have fought each other, justice and peace are in combat.' The new interpretation is fantastic! It gives tremendous power to the biblical verse and fills it with a great sense of realism.

An employer was seized with a perplexing dilemma. The young man he had recently hired was not proving to be satisfactory. He tried hard but did not seem to have the knack of working with people. On the other hand, he needed the job and the employer happened to know that due to certain events he was now his mother's sole means of support. He probably could straighten him out but it would take weeks, possibly months of personal guidance and time he could ill afford. Should he decide on the basis of truth and give him notice or on the basis of mercy and struggle with him?

A teenager was caught shoplifting. The routine procedure is for the store detective to call the police and level a charge. It so happened that the manager of the store heard of the incident. He discovered that the boy's family was well known to him. What should he do: judge by virtue of truth and let whatever happens happen, or, in terms of mercy, if not for the sake of the boy then at least for his parents?

These dilemmas face us at every turn and in every relationship. There are no rules to aid us in particular situations because every case is so different and we usually have to do our best with our own resources. The dilemma between justice and peace is of the same order, except that it usually takes place on a wider canvas.

Every conflict that leads to war can be described as a confrontation between justice and peace.

As I write these words the U.N. just completed a cease-fire between Iran and Iraq. At first Iran did not accept. Did that mean it did not want peace? What about justice? After all, Iraq started the war and if those who start wars are not punished in some fashion, where is justice?

Those who try to move in the direction of peace in the Near East are aware of this dilemma. Most Arabs declare that they want peace, but they also want justice. In their eyes justice would be some kind of Palestinian entity with compensation for refugees, restitution of certain lands, and so forth. On the Israeli side the claim is also for justice. For Israel justice will include security, and no return to the *status quo antebellum*. The conceptions of justice differ and seem to be incompatible.

Is there any way out of these dilemmas? Maybe it would help if we established some ground rules. First, both sides of a major argument cannot be right. Secondly, one side of a major confrontation also cannnot be entirely right. Once people can agree to these propositions, they are well on their way to the resolution of even the greatest dilemmas. Unfortunately, in this age of religious fundamentalism and political extremism, one would be hard put to find an acceptance of even these so harmless and so seemingly logical propositions, and so the confrontations continue.

Notice how the *midrash* tries to approach these problems. It is truth that gives way; it is cast down to the earth. If one were to try to re-interpret this concept, it would be as though every protagonist would say, 'Let's forget about our ideological commitments and see if we can come to an agreement on bordering issues.' That was the unique achievement of the Camp David Accords. There was a clause that said, despite the competing claims to the territory of the West Bank, they would try first to solve all tangential problems. Hopefully, they would develop a working relationship that would eventually help them confront the larger, thornier issues.

In the beautiful insight of the *Yefei To'ar*, when truth is sent to the earth, it is not truth in its universal expression, but Truth as Torah. How can Torah help in resolving the great dilemmas of human experience? By creating a new order of priorities, a new sense of what is and what is not important. In this new order, power and territory and dominance would take a back seat.

Not to have but to be, that is what Torah would try to achieve. Possibly we might be restored to a spiritual condition where the old translation of the Psalmist might suit a new generation: 'Loving-kindness and truth meet; justice and peace kiss.'

* * *

Additional Commentary

He took truth and cast it to the earth

The angels are spiritual entities with no conception of material things. They do not have the sophistication to comprehend that sometimes righteous people can perfect themselves even through (what we sometimes refer to as 'white') lies. As the Sages put it, it is permitted to change the truth for the sake of peace. The proof of this is that God Himself altered the truth slightly when He told Abraham that Sarah had said that she (not Abraham, which she had in fact said) was too old to have children.

'He threw the truth down to the earth' means that He clothed truth with material form (i.e., brought it down to earth, made it flexible) so that it should reflect on the fact that sometimes falsehood (up to a point, i.e., not revealing everything) can become more important than truth and eventually, having been 'educated,' truth would agree with the creation of man. When truth did consent, the angels then requested that he be raised again heavenwards and spiritualized as before. That is the meaning of, 'Let truth spring up from the earth.' (*Tiferet Tzion*)

*

Let truth spring up

The fact that truth was thrown to the earth and then ascended to the high heavens contains a lesson for human beings. Always remember that when you think you have reached rock bottom, the very lowest you think you can descend, that is precisely the moment when you can start rising again. That is why the verse says that truth springs up from the earth. That is always the way from generation to generation.

*

The Rabbis said

R. Simon brings as proof of his views that God wanted the angels to agree to the creation of man, the fact that He threw truth to the ground. This is based on the verse, 'And God saw everything that He had made, and behold, it was very good.' It may be questioned why the verse made reference to all of creation seeing that after every day God said, 'and the Lord saw that it was good.' Furthermore, why did it say at this point, '*very* good'? The answer is that the verb וירא, *va-ya'ar*, is here used in the transitive sense as though it meant, 'He showed (*her'ah*) the angels and all the other creatures what He had made, and, behold, man was very good' and they all agreed. (*Tiferet Tzion*)

*

Arguing about man

Truth argued on the basis of law. The law says not to lie and when one lies there is a transgression against the commandment, 'You must not utter falsehood.' Since man would lie, he should not be created.

Peace, however, could not argue on the basis of law. The fact that it argued as though the law were on its side did not mean that its position was based on law, only that the very fact of quarrel or argument interferes with the attribute of peace.

It thus turns out that *hesed* and truth were arguing with each other on the basis of Torah Law, but that justice and peace were merely engaged in discussion. That is why God created man in the interim, and it was not an insult to them. (*Tiferet Tzion*)

*

The ministering angels formed themselves into groups

The point is that when God was about to create man He placed before Himself all the elements required for the building and, if necessary, the destruction of the world. All of these elements of His thought He referred to and described as angels – ministering angels whom He actually called by the names of these abstract concepts (Mercy, Truth, etc.). Since truth was the main obstacle from the outset to man's creation on the ground that all men are liars and full of falsehood, he threw it to the ground and there remained only mercy, justice, and peace before Him. Therefore, God followed the majority and created man. There was no reason to send peace away since its views were cancelled out by the majority.

We should add that this *midrash* is also commenting on the descent of the soul from the holy place of heaven in order to join the body, at which point the soul is close to being a liability. In this connection mercy said, 'Let man be created,' because he will do acts of loving-kindness and will thus acquire much merit through good deeds that will then bring the soul back to its original spiritual position. By contrast, now, only mercy gives man any acknowledgment. Truth, however, said, 'Let man not be created,' and let not the soul descend because the earth is full of lies and falsehoods, and, as a result, the soul may be destroyed by the environment in the material world. Righteousness said, 'Let man be created,' for in the world of action he will perfect and fulfill himself through deeds, and, by reason of doing righteous acts since righteousness is the greatest of all human attributes. Peace then said, 'Let man not be created,' for he is full of quarrels, strife, and disagreements, and the body will be forever in confrontation with the soul and will persuade it to sin.

Let us try to understand this a little better.

What, actually, did God do? He took truth, which is the Torah, and threw it down to earth so that it could act as a guardian or protector to destroy the evil inclination. The Torah is the complete healing and the elixir for the passions of the body. When the ministering angels said to God, 'What a shame that the most precious Torah should have to dwell among material beings prone to sin,' the Almighty answered, 'Indeed! That is its greatest glory. Truth will spring forth from the earth and therefore the true place of Torah is among human beings who dwell on earth.' It was in this spirit that Moses answered the angels when he ascended to heaven to receive the Torah. (*Yefei To'ar*)

Parashah Eight, Midrash Six

ר' הוּנָא בְּשֵׁם רַבִּי אַיְבוּ אָמַר בְּדַעַת בְּרָאוֹ שֶׁבָּרָא צָרְכֵי מְזוֹנוֹתָיו וְאַחַר כָּךְ בְּרָאוֹ
אָמְרוּ מַלְאֲכֵי הַשָּׁרֵת לִפְנֵי הַקָּדוֹשׁ בָּרוּךְ הוּא רִבּוֹן הָעוֹלָם 'מָה אֱנוֹשׁ כִּי תִזְכְּרֶנּוּ
וּבֶן אָדָם כִּי תִפְקְדֶנּוּ' (תהלים ח, ה) הָדָא עָקְתָא לְהָן מִבַּרְיָא אֲמַר לְהוֹן אִם כֵּן 'צֹנֶה
וַאֲלָפִים כֻּלָם וְגוֹ'' (שם שם, ח) לָמָה נִבְרָא 'צִפֹּר שָׁמַיִם וּדְגֵי הַיָּם' (שם שם, ט) לָמָה
נִבְרָאוּ

R. Huna said in R. Aibu's name: He created him with due
deliberation: He [first] created his food requirements and only then
did He create him. The ministering angels said to the Holy One,
blessed be He, 'Sovereign of the universe! "What is man, that You
have been mindful of him, and the son of man that You have taken
note of him?" (Psalms. 8:5). This trouble, for what has it been created?'
He said to them, 'If so, why were "Sheep and oxen, all of them" (ibid.
verse 8) created? Why were "The birds of the heaven and the fish of
the sea" (ibid. verse 9) created?'

This *midrash* seems to be a continuation of God's discussion with the
ministering angels and, indeed, some editions have it as part of *Midrash
Five*. The point here is that the Almighty did not enter into discussion with
the angels in order to reach a decision. He had already decided to create
man as the goal of His enterprise from the very beginning. That is, He
had prepared man's food first, in the early days of creation, long before
man arrived. The angels noticed this and protested. 'Why waste your time
on man,' they said in Psalm 8, 'Concentrate your handiwork on the
heavens and its glories. Man is only a trouble maker.' God's reply to this
argument was, 'I have created sheep in their thousands. Why? Only
because of man. What other purpose would there be for them?'

מָשָׁל לְמֶלֶךְ שֶׁהָיָה לוֹ מִגְדָל מָלֵא כָל טוּב וְאֵין לוֹ אוֹרְחִים מַה הֲנָאָה יֵשׁ לַמֶּלֶךְ
שֶׁמְּלָאוֹ אָמְרוּ לְפָנָיו רִבּוֹנוֹ שֶׁל עוֹלָם 'ה' אֲדֹנֵינוּ מָה אַדִּיר שִׁמְךָ בְּכָל הָאָרֶץ' (שם
שם, י) עֲבַד מַה דַּהֲנֵי לָךְ

This can be compared to a king who builds a tower full of good
things, but has no guests. What pleasure can the king have in having

302

filled it? The angels said to him, 'O Lord, our Lord, how majestic is Your name throughout the earth' (ibid. verse 10); **do what is pleasing in Your eyes!**

The parable is meant to establish that the world was created for man. It doesn't mean that man is interested only in food and good things, but that he would use all these good things as a way of honoring God. Finally, the angels understood and acknowledged the majesty of God, but also the supremacy over them of man. A side product of this *midrash* – if not its motivation – is that it presents a logical sequence for the verses in Psalm 8. According to this *midrash*, the psalm presents a coherent account of God's discussion with the angels regarding the creation of man.

* * *

Seed Thoughts

This *midrash* is a beautiful interpretation of Psalm 8 as a hymn to human potentiality.

From the physical point of view, why would God bother to create man? Human infancy is the weakest and the longest of the animal kingdom. But, in man's development as a spiritual being, he is only a little lower than the angels.

Even though man is worthless when compared to God, man's existence is a great tribute to his Creator. As the Psalmist puts it, 'How majestic is Your name throughout the earth!' (8:2)

Imagine if man were to live up to this potentiality in word and deed! It would be the ultimate tribute of all.

* * *

Additional Commentary

The parable of the king

The text of the *midrash* up to this point creates a problem. Just because food for man was now available, must he be created? Is it being suggested that the whole purpose of man is to eat? After all, this was the argument by which the angels were convinced. Not so. The parable of the king sets the argument straight. Visitors who are invited to the king are not there simply to eat and drink. The palace is not a hotel. It is a place to which not the general public is invited, but rather the princes and officers of the realm, who come not only to honor the king, but also to seek his counsel in running the affairs of state. It is for this purpose that the king prepares food and lavish hospitality. If the preparations had been made and no one showed up, all would have been wasted. God acts in the same way. The purpose of man's creation was to honor God, to study His Torah, to serve Him, and to influence others in the way of eternal life. For this purpose He created the entire universe. If man were not now to be created, all the creations of the first six days would have been in vain. (*Tiferet Tzion*)

*

With deliberation

The mood in the previous *midrash* is that God created man in a hurry. He didn't wait for the angels to conclude their discussions. Instead He confronted them with a *fait accompli* and said, 'Man is already created.' Our *midrash* provides us with a different view. God created man not in a hurry but with great deliberation. *Da'at*, דעת, should be seen as meaning not 'knowledge,' which is the usual translation, but rather, *yishuv ha-da'at*, which means, great care and deliberation. (Rashi)

*

What is man, that You have been mindful of him

What prompted the *midrash* to have the angels quote Psalm 8, 'What is man...'? If the psalm had been personalized by David, as the Psalmist, it should have read, 'What am I that you have been mindful of me' or 'What are we that you have been mindful of us?' Since it has not been personalized, but is written in the third person, it must be understood as having been spoken by someone who was not man – the angels. (RZWE)

Parashah Eight, Midrash Seven

רַבִּי יְהוֹשֻׁעַ דְּסִכְנִין בְּשֵׁם רַבִּי לֵוִי אָמַר בְּנַפְשׁוֹתָן שֶׁל צַדִּיקִים נִמְלַךְ הָדָא הוּא
דִכְתִיב 'הֵמָּה הַיּוֹצְרִים וְיֹשְׁבֵי נְטָעִים וּגְדֵרָה עִם הַמֶּלֶךְ בִּמְלַאכְתּוֹ יָשְׁבוּ שָׁמָּה'
(דה"א ד, כג)

R. Joshua of Sikhnin said in R. Levi's name: He took counsel with
the souls of the righteous as it is written, '[And the records are
ancient]. These were the potters and those that dwell at Netaim and
Gederah; they dwelt there in the king's service' (I Chronicles 4:23).

The text is 'Let us make man' and the *midrash* continues the series of
interpretations in response to the question, 'With whom did God consult?'
Here, God is described as having consulted the righteous based on the
idea that the righteous were created before the world (see *Parashah One,
Midrash Four*). When God saw their good works, He created man. They
outweighed the possibilities for evil. According to this, the proof-verse
should be interpreted, as the *midrash* continues.

'הֵמָּה הַיּוֹצְרִים' עַל שֵׁם 'וַיִּיצֶר ה' אֱלֹהִים אֶת הָאָדָם עָפָר מִן הָאֲדָמָה' (בראשית ב, ז)

'These were the potters (Hebrew: *yotzerim*, literally 'makers' or
'formers').' They are so termed on account of the verse, 'The Lord
formed [*va-yitzer*] man from the dust of the earth' (Genesis 2:7).

The Hebrew term יוצרים generally means 'potters,' but it derives from the
same Hebrew root used in the verse quoted. The phrase וְהַדְּבָרִים עַתִּיקִים,
'And the records are ancient,' which appears at the end of I Chronicles
4:22, is interpreted to refer to the creation of the world. Since יוצר, 'to
form,' is applied to God in Genesis and to the righteous היוצרים in
Chronicles, this is seen as proof that God consulted with the righteous in
creating the world.

'יוֹשְׁבֵי נְטָעִים' עַל שֵׁם 'וַיִּטַּע ה' אֱלֹהִים גַּן בְּעֵדֶן מִקֶּדֶם' (שם שם, ח)

'And those that dwell at Netaim' corresponds to 'And the Lord God
planted a garden in Eden, in the East' (ibid. verse 8).

According to the plain meaning of the text, Netaim is a place name, but the *midrash* associates it with the use of the same root in the verse from Genesis, thus 'those that dwell at Netaim' is understood to refer to the Garden of Eden. *Yotzerim* from the verse in I Chronicles and 'God formed (*va-yitzer*) man' in Genesis and the verse, 'Let us make man,' must indicate a partnership between God and the righteous. (RZWE) The Garden of Eden is, of course, meant to be the abode for the righteous.

'וּגְדֵרָה' עַל שֵׁם 'אֲשֶׁר שַׂמְתִּי חוֹל גְּבוּל לַיָּם' (ירמיה ה, כב)

'And Gederah' is an allusion to 'Who set the sand as a boundary to the sea' (Jeremiah 5:22).

Gederah, literally a place name, is also understood as reference to the righteous who, from the verse in Jeremiah, were the reason God set a boundary to the sea so that it could not overflow the world as a result of the sins of the wicked. The word *gederah* derives from the root גדר, which means 'to set a boundary.'

'עִם הַמֶּלֶךְ בִּמְלַאכְתּוֹ יָשְׁבוּ' עִם הַמֶּלֶךְ מֶלֶךְ מַלְכֵי הַמְּלָכִים הַקָּדוֹשׁ בָּרוּךְ הוּא יָשְׁבוּ נְפָשׁוֹת שֶׁל צַדִּיקִים שֶׁבָּהֶן נִמְלַךְ הַקָּדוֹשׁ בָּרוּךְ הוּא וּבָרָא אֶת הָעוֹלָם

'They dwelt there in the king's service' means that the souls of the righteous dwelt there with the supreme King of Kings, the Holy One, blessed be He, with whom He took counsel, and created the world.

The literal translation of the conclusion of the verse in I Chronicles is 'They sat with the king in his work.' The verse does not specify which king and so the *midrash* interprets the king as the Holy One, blessed be He. 'His work' must only mean the act of creation and the place was, as explained in the previous section of the *midrash*, the Garden of Eden, where the souls of the righteous live.

* * *

Seed Thoughts

How are we to understand the statement of the *Tiferet Tzion* that the *tzaddik*, the righteous person, is often made to atone for the sins of his generation? This view is found frequently in Talmudic literature, but its application to this *midrash* is quite original.

There is a modern comparison that comes to mind that may help us make some sense out of a concept that is, otherwise, way beyond our depth.

Those who follow professional sports are familiar with a pattern I will now describe, but are also very often puzzled by it. A baseball team finishes the season in third or fourth place in its division, but has in its ranks a player with the highest batting average and an excellent fielding record. To the astonishment of the general public, this outstanding player will often be traded for three or four players of lesser caliber whom the management feel will help the club grow. Very often they are proven right. How do they explain it? Obviously, the club has gone as far as it can go with the star on its roster. If it had unlimited financial capital it would keep the star and seek additional help. Most businesses – and professional sport is a business – cannot afford this. Their only asset is the star, and, by trading him, they can sometimes strengthen other parts of the team.

Similarly, the Sages seem to be telling us that God sometimes trades humanity's greatest asset, the *tzaddik*, or saintly individual, through the latter's suffering or his removal to a higher world. This is done in order to strengthen the teamwork of a particular generation and allow it a second chance. Nor is this to be looked upon as a punishment for the *tzaddik*, but, rather his premature reward of the world-to-come in the presence of the Eternal. For the generation left behind, it often becomes a tremendous stimulation for repentance and regeneration. This thought can become a source of consolation and gratitude even for the family of the *tzaddik*, who have to suffer the most painful loss of their most important personal guiding light.

* * *

Additional Commentary

He took counsel with the souls of the righteous
It is the role of the righteous to atone for their generation. Sometimes this happens by means of suffering; other times, by means of their death. This thought is found in *Shir Hashirim Rabbah* where it says, 'If God sees that the generation is very liable under the law, He removes one *tzaddik* from their midst who is equal in worth to all of them together.' By doing so, God can say to the attribute of justice, 'You have done enough.' Thus, one righteous person can atone for the entire generation. It was, therefore, necessary for God to consult the souls of the righteous to see whether they would accept the bearing of such a heavy yoke. (*Tiferet Tzion*)

*

They were the makers...
Since the righteous accepted upon themselves to atone for the entire generation, on the basis of which God created man, they are described as the

builders (makers). Through this they earned the merit of two advantages. For one thing, they earned the merit of living in the Garden of Eden, for one cannot earn this status other than through Torah and good deeds in this world. Secondly, through their merit, they protect the world from evil decrees. As for the verse, 'I set the sand as a boundary to the sea,' the implication is just as the sand is like the army of God protecting the land, so are the righteous God's army who ward off all evil decrees by their good deeds. (*Tiferet Tzion*)

*

They sat with the king in his work

As for the expression 'in his work,' this refers to the verse, 'He rested from all His work.' The creation of man is called 'all his work.' Also the verse, 'and everything which He had made' is a reference to man who was the end purpose of His work, all of which was created for man. This is similar to the expression, 'For this is all of man,' namely, that the entire world was created for him. (RZWE)

*

And created the world

Notice that it says, 'And created *the world*,' and not, 'And created *man*,' although the context of the consultation with the souls of the righteous is the creation of man. The solution is that God began with man and ended up by creating the world. That would imply that people (souls) were created before the rest of the world. We learned in *Parashah One, Midrash Four* of our text that the Patriarchs, Israel, and the Messiah were in God's mind to be created even before He created the world, though they had, in fact, not been created. In that same chapter of the Midrash, the verse, 'And the spirit of God hovered over the waters' was interpreted as referring to the spirit of King Messiah and also as being the spirit of man. From this one would discern that the souls were created on the first day and therefore not before the world was created. How then could God consult with them? The answer is that all the souls were incorporated in the creation of the first man on day six. In a parallel passage in *Ruth Rabbah* it does not say, as in our *midrash*, at the very end 'and created the world,' it says rather, 'and He created His world.' This must refer to the special kind of providential relationship God created for man with miraculous intervention and supreme providential and personal care. For the righteous, that is the true world and not the world of nature. (RZWE)

Parashah Eight, Midrash Eight

רַבִּי שְׁמוּאֵל בַּר נַחְמָן בְּשֵׁם רַבִּי יוֹנָתָן אָמַר בְּשָׁעָה שֶׁהָיָה מֹשֶׁה כּוֹתֵב אֶת הַתּוֹרָה
הָיָה כּוֹתֵב מַעֲשֵׂה כָל יוֹם וָיוֹם כֵּיוָן שֶׁהִגִּיעַ לַפָּסוּק הַזֶּה שֶׁנֶּאֱמַר 'וַיֹּאמֶר אֱלֹהִים
נַעֲשֶׂה אָדָם בְּצַלְמֵנוּ כִּדְמוּתֵנוּ' אָמַר לְפָנָיו רִבּוֹן הָעוֹלָם מָה אַתָּה נוֹתֵן פִּתְחוֹן פֶּה
לַמִּינִים אַתְמָהָא אָמַר לוֹ כְּתֹב וְהָרוֹצֶה לִטְעוֹת יִטְעֶה

R. Samuel b. Naḥman said in R. Jonathan's name: When Moses was
engaged in writing the Torah he had to write the work of each day.
When he reached this verse, which says, 'And God said: "Let us
make man in Our image, after Our likeness"' (1:26), he said to Him,
'Sovereign of the universe! Why do You furnish an excuse to
heretics? I am amazed!' [God] replied, 'Write [it]! Whoever wishes
to err may err.'

Moses, it seems, was struck by the fact that only this verse is couched in
the plural. If all the days had been in the plural, there would have been
no question since it would have implied the royal 'we' at all times. But
with only the creation of man associated with a plural verb, there is a wide
opening for heretics to maintain that a dualistic universe exists in
Scripture, that another power exists in addition to God with whom He
consults. The Almighty's answer was that heresy depends on the desires
of the person and implies that He was giving those who have a tendency
to heresy the chance to articulate that heresy and, of course, to be
punished for it.

אָמַר לוֹ הַקָּדוֹשׁ בָּרוּךְ הוּא מֹשֶׁה הָאָדָם הַזֶּה שֶׁבָּרֵאתִי לֹא גְדוֹלִים וּקְטַנִּים אֲנִי
מַעֲמִיד מִמֶּנּוּ שֶׁאִם יָבוֹא הַגָּדוֹל לִטֹּל רְשׁוּת מִן הַקָּטָן מִמֶּנּוּ וְהוּא אוֹמֵר מָה אֲנִי
צָרִיךְ לִטֹּל רְשׁוּת מִן הַקָּטָן מִמֶּנִּי וְהֵן אוֹמְרִים לוֹ לְמוֹד מִבּוֹרַאֲךָ שֶׁהוּא בָרָא אֶת
הָעֶלְיוֹנִים וְאֶת הַתַּחְתּוֹנִים כֵּיוָן שֶׁבָּא לִבְרֹאת אֶת הָאָדָם נִמְלַךְ בְּמַלְאֲכֵי הַשָּׁרֵת

'Moses,' said the Holy One, blessed be He, to him, '[regarding] this
man that I have created, do I not cause both great and small men to
spring from him? Now if a great man has to ask permission [for a
proposed action] from one that is less than he, and he says, "Why
should I ask permission from my inferior!" they can answer him,

"Learn from your Creator, who created all that is above and below, yet when He came to create man He took counsel with the ministering angels."'

The continuation of this *midrash* adds another dimension. The Torah uses the plural form in the creation of man in order to teach man a lesson by example. The great should be willing to learn even from the small, just as God was willing to consult with those whom He Himself had created who were, by definition, inferior to Him. It's not only a question of learning but of receiving permission when necessary.

אָמַר רַ' לֵוִי לֵית הָכָא מַלְכוּ אֶלָּא מָשָׁל לְמֶלֶךְ שֶׁהָיָה מְטַיֵּל בְּפֶתַח פָּלָטִין שֶׁלּוֹ וְרָאָה בָּלוֹרִין אַחַת מֻשְׁלֶכֶת אָמַר מַה נַּעֲשֶׂה בָּהּ מֵהֶן אוֹמְרִים דִּימוֹסִיּוֹת וּמֵהֶן אוֹמְרִים פְּרִיבָטָאוֹת אָמַר הַמֶּלֶךְ אִינְדַרְטִין אֲנִי עוֹשֶׂה אוֹתָהּ מִי מְעַכֵּב

R. Levi said: There was no taking counsel here. The matter may be compared to a king who was strolling at the door of his palace when he saw hewn stone[s] lying about. He said [to his courtiers], 'What shall we do with it?' Some answered, '[Use them to build] a public bath-house'; others answered: 'Private baths.' The king said, 'I will make a monument of it. Who can stop [me]?!'

R. Levi absolutely denies that there was any consultation regarding the creation of man. In the parable, the king was not really interested in the advice of his courtiers. He had already decided what to do. They felt that the stone or stones that they had come across were too trivial and unimportant to make anything of real significance out of them, and so they answered what they answered. The king, however, had decided to make a monument to himself, with his own features inscribed on it – man, who is created in the image of God (*Etz Yosef*). [In his *Dictionary of the Midrash*, Jastrow translates the phrase בלורין אחת משלכת as 'a collapsed bath-house,' which of course fits nicely with the courtiers' suggestions.]

* * *

Seed Thoughts

The expression, 'Man in the image of God,' has been interpreted by the Sages in spiritual terms. 'As He is merciful, be you merciful, as He is gracious, so be you gracious.' This is the supreme principle of the imitation of God – *imitatio dei*.

What is happening in this *midrash* is a movement in the opposite direction. It is not that God is in the image of man, heaven forfend. It is, rather, that God is mediated in the world by man. We are His representatives. People learn about God by the behavior of His creatures.

The text of the Kaddish prayer says, 'Yitgadal… shmeih rabbah,' meaning, 'May God's name be magnified and sanctified in the world.' How can that be done? By acting in a way that is righteous, merciful, and truthful.

In this respect God depends upon man. That is possibly the interpretation of the verse, 'If you will be My people, then I will be your God.'

* * *

Additional Commentary

Great and small

People differ from one another in all ways. Sometimes one who is small in height may be strong in other qualities. Therefore a great man sometimes has to take counsel from one who may be his lesser in some respects. The Psalmist says, 'I have learned from all my teachers.' It was important for God to set this example from creation so that this trait might be engraved in all humans to act in this spirit. It was God's intention to use His behavior at the creation as a model for man to follow, for it to become second nature. The *midrash* says, 'They can answer him…' Who are the 'they'? They are the very natural instincts that we possess who will say to man, 'Do as God does.' (*Tiferet Tzion*)

*

Let us make man

Having made a model of man in bodily form, God was asking the heavenly court what, in their opinion, should be done with this creation – man. He was testing their ability and judgment. By offering as an example that man would be to God what the statue of a king is to a king, man is thus interpreted as God's messenger on earth. The *midrash* is also a reminder not to be concerned about what the heretics or unbelievers may say. (RZWE)

Parashah Eight, Midrash Nine

The problem being discussed in this text is the apparent plural use of the name of God. You have it in two instances. The first is the name *Elohim*, which has a plural ending. The second is the phrase 'Let *us* make,' indicating that God consulted, presumably with an equal partner. Both of these phrases are now discussed.

שָׁאֲלוּ הַמִּינִים אֶת רַבִּי שַׂמְלַאי כַּמָּה אֱלֹהוֹת בָּרְאוּ אֶת הָעוֹלָם אָמַר לָהֶם אֲנִי
וְאַתֶּם נִשְׁאַל לְיָמִים הָרִאשׁוֹנִים הָדָא הוּא דִכְתִיב 'כִּי שְׁאַל נָא לְיָמִים רִאשֹׁנִים
לְמִן הַיּוֹם אֲשֶׁר בָּרָא אֱלֹהִים אָדָם' (דברים ד, לב) אֲשֶׁר בָּרְאוּ אֵין כְּתִיב כָּאן אֶלָּא
'אֲשֶׁר בָּרָא' חָזְרוּ וְשָׁאֲלוּ אוֹתוֹ אָמְרוּ לוֹ מַה הוּא דֵין דִּכְתִיב 'בְּרֵאשִׁית בָּרָא
אֱלֹהִים' אָמַר לָהֶם בָּרְאוּ אֱלֹהִים אֵין כְּתִיב כָּאן אֶלָּא 'בָּרָא אֱלֹהִים'

Sectarians asked R. Simlai: 'How many deities created the world?' He replied, 'I and you must inquire of the bygone ages, as it is written, "You have but to inquire about bygone ages that came before you, ever since God created (*bara*) man [on earth]" (Deuteronomy 4:32). [They] created (*bar'u* – in the plural) is not written here, but [He] created (*bara* – in the singular). They again questioned [R. Simlai] and said, 'Why is it written "In the beginning *elohim* (with the plural suffix) created?"' He replied, '*Bar'u* [plural] *elohim* is not written here, but *bara* [singular] *elohim*.'

In the very first verse of the Torah, 'In the beginning God created the heavens and the earth,' the term for God is *Elohim* with a plural ending. This suggests duality. Of interest is the fact that the sectarians apparently believed in the Bible, otherwise they would not have based their questions on it and would not have accepted R. Simlai's answer, which was also based on a biblical text. It is therefore likely that the sectarians were Jewish sectarians, perhaps Christians. R. Simlai's answer was that although the term for God is in the plural, the verb governing it is in the singular, thus there is no room for error.

אָמַר רַבִּי שַׂמְלַאי בְּכָל מָקוֹם שֶׁאַתָּה מוֹצֵא פִּתְחוֹן פֶּה לַמִּינִין אַתָּה מוֹצֵא תְּשׁוּבָה
בְּצִדָּה חָזְרוּ וְשָׁאֲלוּ אוֹתוֹ אָמְרוּ לוֹ מַה הוּא דֵין דִּכְתִיב 'נַעֲשֶׂה אָדָם בְּצַלְמֵנוּ

312

כִּדְמוּתֵנוּ' אָמַר לְהוֹן קְרָאוּן מַה דְּבַתְרֵהּ וַיִּבְרְאוּ אֱלֹהִים אֶת הָאָדָם בְּצַלְמֵיהֶם לֹא
נֶאֱמַר אֶלָּא (בראשית א, כז) 'וַיִּבְרָא אֱלֹהִים אֶת הָאָדָם בְּצַלְמוֹ'

**R. Simlai commented: Wherever you find an opportunity for the
sectarians [to attack], you find the refutation at its side. The
sectarians again questioned him and said, 'What is meant by "And
God said, 'Let us make man'?"' He replied, 'Read what follows it. It
is not written "And the gods created (*va-yivr'u* – plural) man in their
(plural) image," but "God created (*va-yivra* – singular) in His
(singular) image"' (Genesis 1:27).**

R. Simlai's comment was aimed at the sectarians. He was telling them that
you cannot reach a conclusion based on a single word, but that you must
examine the general context. Their next question was more difficult, since
the verse 'And God said, "Let *us* make man in *our* image according to *our*
likeness"' is completely in the plural. His rebuttal was also based on the
context. The very next verse, which records the actual creation of man, is
entirely in the singular.

וְכֵיוָן שֶׁיָּצְאוּ אָמְרוּ לוֹ תַלְמִידָיו רַבִּי לְאֵלּוּ דָּחִיתָ בְּקָנֶה לָנוּ מָה אַתְּ מֵשִׁיב אָמַר
לָהֶם לְשֶׁעָבַר אָדָם נִבְרָא מִן הָאֲדָמָה חַוָּה נִבְרָאת מִן הָאָדָם מִכָּאן וָאֵילָךְ 'בְּצַלְמֵנוּ
כִּדְמוּתֵנוּ' לֹא אִישׁ בְּלֹא אִשָּׁה וְלֹא אִשָּׁה בְּלֹא אִישׁ וְלֹא שְׁנֵיהֶם בְּלֹא שְׁכִינָה

**When [the sectarians] departed, [R. Simlai's] disciples said to him:
'You dismissed them with a mere reed, but what answer can you
give us?' He said to them: 'In the past [at creation] Adam was created
from the earth and Eve was created from Adam; but henceforth it
shall be "in our image, after our likeness": neither man without
woman nor woman without man, nor both of them without the
Divine Presence.'**

R. Simlai's disciples, who had been witnesses to the confrontation with
the sectarians, were unwilling to accept their master's rebuttal, which was
based on grammatical forms and which they described as a reed, that is,
a makeshift answer. They wanted a 'real' answer to the questions the
sectarians had posed. He replied that the phrase, 'in our image, according
to our likeness' came to teach a fundamental of faith. Adam had been
created by God from the earth; Eve had been created from Adam – but
that was a one-time event that would never be repeated. From creation
onwards man can only be created from a union of male and female with
the blessing of the Divine Presence. Why did R. Simlai not give this

interpretation to the sectarians? It seems that his interpretation was aimed against the Christian doctrine of the virgin birth and that he did not want to attack the sectarians on such a fundamental dogma of their faith, either out of fear of reprisals or out of good manners.

חָזְרוּ וְשָׁאֲלוּ אוֹתוֹ אָמְרוּ לֵהּ מַה דֵין דִּכְתִיב 'אֵל אֱלֹהִים ה' וְגוֹ' (יהושע כב, כב) אָמַר
לָהֶם הֵם יוֹדְעִים אֵין כְּתִיב כָּאן אֶלָּא 'הוּא יָדַע' (שם שם, שם) אָמְרוּ לוֹ תַלְמִידָיו
לְאֵלּוּ דָחִיתָ בְּקָנֶה לָנוּ מָה אַתָּה מֵשִׁיב אָמַר לָהֶם שְׁלָשְׁתָּן שֵׁם אֱלֹהִים הֵן כְּאִינָשׁ
דְּאָמַר בָּסִילוֹגוֹס קֵיסָר אַגוּסְטוֹס קֵיסָר חָזְרוּ וְשָׁאֲלוּ לוֹ אָמְרוּ לוֹ מַה הוּא דֵין
דִּכְתִיב 'כִּי אֱלֹהִים קְדֹשִׁים הוּא' אָמַר לָהֶן קְדוֹשִׁים הֵמָּה אֵין כְּתִיב אֶלָּא 'קְדֹשִׁים
הוּא' (שם כד, יט)

The [sectarians] again questioned him and said to him, 'What is the meaning of "God, the Lord God" (Joshua 22:22)?' He answered, 'It does not continue "they know," but "He knows."' His disciples then said, 'You dismissed them with a mere reed, but what answer can you give us?' He answered, 'All three are the names of God, as people say Basilogus Caesar, Augustus Caesar.' The [sectarians] again questioned him and said to him, 'What is the meaning of, "For He is a holy (*kedoshim* – plural) God" (Joshua 24:19)?' He answered, 'It is not written "For *they are* (*heimah* – plural) holy gods," but rather "For *He is* (*hu* – singular) a holy God."'

The verse cited by the sectarians from the Book of Joshua uses three separate terms for God – *El, Elohim,* and *Hashem.* Thus this verse too seems to imply plurality in God. R. Simlai's answer was once again based on the verb in the verse, which is in the singular. To his disciples he gave a simple rational explanation – all three terms are alternative names of the one God, just as the same Caesar is known by different names. Of interest is the fact that this answer seemed to satisfy his disciple as well.

* * *

Seed Thoughts

That man and woman are needed for procreation is central to the world. Man and woman need each other. Since, in terms of life, birthing and nurturing are indispensable to one another, there must be a partnership of husband and wife.

What is the nature of this partnership? It is governed by the fact that a third partner is present. God is responsible for the creation of the soul of man while man and woman are responsible for the body. This, however, though it is so stated in the words of the *midrash* as interpreted by Rashi, is far from simplistic.

If God functions through man and woman in creating the body, surely God functions through man and woman in creating the soul. The sacred and intimate partnership of man and woman to each other (in marriage) surely goes beyond the body and physical things. They are God's instruments for creating the soul, nurturing it, sustaining it, and honoring it.

Is the soul an entity or is it a process? If it is an entity, it exists even when the human being is comatose. If it is a process, does that mean that it is only a function of the body? These are some of the questions for which there are no ready answers.

It appears from the attribution of soul-creating to God, that the *midrash* sees the soul as an entity. Much more thought is required along these lines lest we enter into areas that encroach upon the scientific and make claims that cannot be substantiated.

There are many questions. If the soul is an entity, does it exist at birth or, as the Code of Jewish Law seems to suggest, only after thirty days? If the soul is an entity, does it exist in the fetus, and is that a factor in rendering a judgment on abortion? When the body dies, what happens to that which we call soul? Does it return immediately to God, and, if not, what are its journeyings and the sources for those journeyings?

The point is that when God is affirmed as a third partner in marriage and in procreation, more is involved than a mere figure of speech or a beautiful turn of phrase. What is being expressed is the fundamental meaning of the phrase that man is created in the image of God.

* * *

Additional Commentary

Let us make man in our image
This is directed to the father and mother, who in the future will create man. (*Matnot Kehunah*; Mirkin)

*

Neither man without woman
Notice the change in the order of the verses. Verse 27 deals with the creation of man and woman. If verse 26 is interpreted as a special command to man and woman entrusting procreation and education to them, it would have had to be placed after verse 27 and not before. There is no explanation other than to note the fact that this is what the *midrash* has done.

*

People say Basilogus Caesar, Augustus Caesar

Basilogus conquered the Romans, who remained under him as a result of his power. Augustus reigned after him and conducted the affairs of state with great wisdom. Thereafter all Roman rulers who showed courage were called Basilogus Caesar and all rulers who showed wisdom were called Augustus Caesar. Similarly, our Father and King is the creator, leader, and ruler of every individual, and His name is called in accordance with how He rules. If He rules with power He is called *Elokim*, if with love and mercy He is called *Hashem*. And all of this is determined by the recipients since we do not know the relationship between justice and mercy. God's name is therefore determined by our own limited perception, and the names are changeable such as *Elokim* and *Hashem*. In the days to come, however, when knowledge increases, all will recognize that whatever God does is love and compassion and therefore He will be one and His name one. (*Tiferet Tzion*)

*

For He is a holy God

This answer is repeated in the Jerusalem Talmud (Berakhot 8:9) that God is holy with all manner of holiness. The meaning is that all who were created have the amount of holiness to which they are entitled, either through their deeds or the intrinsic holiness given to them at birth, and all receive their holiness from God as it is written, 'For I am the God that sanctifies you.' That is why God is described as *kedoshim*, in the plural, to show that He is holy with every manner of sanctification and bestows upon everyone that holiness to which he is entitled. (*Tiferet Tzion*)

Parashah Eight, Midrash Ten

אָמַר רַבִּי הוֹשַׁעְיָא בְּשָׁעָה שֶׁבָּרָא הַקָּדוֹשׁ בָּרוּךְ הוּא אָדָם הָרִאשׁוֹן טָעוּ מַלְאֲכֵי הַשָּׁרֵת וּבִקְשׁוּ לוֹמַר לְפָנָיו קָדוֹשׁ

R. Hoshaya said: When the Holy One, blessed be He, created Adam, the ministering angels mistook him (for a divine being) and wished to exclaim 'Holy!' before him.

This has to be understood in relationship to the text, 'And God created man in His own image, in the image of God He created him' (Genesis 1:27). The picture of man standing on two feet so different from the animals gave an impression to the angels of godliness, and they wanted to adore him as God was adored in the sixth chapter of Isaiah by saying, 'Holy, holy, holy!'

מָשָׁל לְמֶלֶךְ וְאֶפַּרְכוֹס שֶׁהָיוּ בְּקָרוֹכִין וְהָיוּ בְּנֵי הַמְּדִינָה מְבַקְשִׁין לוֹמַר לַמֶּלֶךְ דּוֹמִינוֹ וְלֹא הָיוּ יוֹדְעִין אֵיזֶהוּ מֶה עָשָׂה הַמֶּלֶךְ דְּחָפוֹ וְהוֹצִיאוֹ חוּץ לְקָרוֹכִין וְיָדְעוּ הַכֹּל שֶׁהוּא אִיפַּרְכוֹס

To what can this be compared? To a king and a governor who were in the [royal] carriage and the citizens wished to say to the king, 'Domini! [Hail!],' but they did not know who he was. What did the king do? He pushed the governor out of the chariot, and so they knew who was the king.

The king and his chief officer were riding together in a chariot of honor. The king presumably was not wearing a crown and from a distance the people could not tell the difference. They wanted to hail the king, but they could not identify him. However, when the king pushed his chief officer out of the carriage the people realized that he was the king.

כָּךְ בְּשָׁעָה שֶׁבָּרָא הַקָּדוֹשׁ בָּרוּךְ הוּא אֶת אָדָם הָרִאשׁוֹן טָעוּ בוֹ מַלְאֲכֵי הַשָּׁרֵת וּבִקְשׁוּ לוֹמַר לְפָנָיו קָדוֹשׁ מֶה עָשָׂה הַקָּדוֹשׁ בָּרוּךְ הוּא הִפִּיל עָלָיו תַּרְדֵּמָה וְיָדְעוּ הַכֹּל שֶׁהוּא אָדָם הֲדָא הוּא דִכְתִיב 'חִדְלוּ לָכֶם מִן הָאָדָם אֲשֶׁר נְשָׁמָה בְּאַפּוֹ כִּי בַמֶּה נֶחְשָׁב הוּא' (ישעיה ב, כב)

Similarly, when the Holy One, blessed be He, created Adam, the

317

angels mistook him (for a divine being) and wanted to say 'Holy!' before him. What did the Holy One, blessed be He, do? He caused a deep sleep to fall upon him and then all knew that he was man. Thus it is written, 'Oh, cease to glorify man, who has only a breath in his nostrils! For by what does he merit esteem?' (Isaiah 2:22)

Since the angels had been told that man was to rule over all the worlds including that of the angels, and since they saw that man was so different from all the other created animals, they mistook him for a divine being and wanted to adore him with the same adoration due to God. In order to differentiate between Himself and man, God placed man in a deep sleep (see Genesis 2:21) and thus it became clear to the ministering angels that man was mortal. The use in the *midrash* of the term הפיל, *hipil*, from the root 'to fall,' gives the impression of man being lowered from his illusory status. That is how the verse in Isaiah is interpreted.

* * *

Seed Thoughts

The important warning that emerges from this *midrash* is not the error that the angels made, but rather the mistakes we are likely to make regarding one another. The angels had difficulty in sizing up the human being because they were overwhelmed by his power of free choice, the greatest and most unique feature that makes us human.

The Psalmist said, 'What is man that You take regard of him' and on the other hand, 'You made him a little lower than the angels.' Our danger is that we may fall into the trap of believing that man is God. We fall into this trap in a number of ways. Individuals who acquire great power through wealth or political authority often believe their own rhetoric and act as though ultimate authority is theirs; societies that determine that they set the norms of morality and are not bound by the moral axioms that they assign to a previous age; scientists who dare to go beyond the bounds of the giving and taking of life, where the possibility of manipulating man so that free choice is removed from him becomes a real danger.

One way of protecting ourselves even as we celebrate man's great virtues is to be conscious of his weaknesses as well. 'Sleep' in this *midrash* is a reminder of the sleep of death that is part and parcel of life. We are mortal, and that is our great weakness. What, then, do we want to leave behind, a record of power and dominance or one of service and healing?

A little humility is the greatest protector of our gift of freedom.

* * *

Additional Commentary

Oh, cease to glorify man

This *midrash* brings together a number of difficult and disparate elements and tries to bring some order to them. 'Oh, cease to glorify man' – but is not the soul the fundamental nature of man and the principle source of his importance? Furthermore, to whom was this command directed?

It would not seem to make sense that this command is directed to human beings. Would you say to humans, 'Cease to glorify man,' as though you were dealing with another type of creature whom you are warning to beware of this particular creation? One can only conclude that the angels erred about man. They were ready to adore man with 'Holy, Holy, Holy!' as they adore God. The result was that God caused a deep sleep to fall upon him.

According to this *midrash* there is no connection between this deep sleep and the creation of Eve. They are simply two events covered by the same verse.

The verse in Isaiah is directed to the angels. The meaning is, 'Cease to glorify man who bears no resemblance to the Holy One, blessed be He, because there is breath in his nostrils.' During sleep this becomes obvious. (Mirkin)

*

A king and a governor

It was the way of kings to appoint governors over their realms who would then conduct the government according to the rules laid down by the king. However, when the populace saw that the king and the governor were in one and the same carriage with no distinguishing marks of rank to identify them, there was room for them to err and to conclude that the great king had given authority to the governor to rule the country as he wished. They would thus be required to salute him, the little king, with the greeting 'Hail my lord!' or 'Hail my sovereign!' since they were in his territory and under his jurisdiction. Similarly, the human being is the governor of the King of Kings, the Holy One, blessed be He, who gave him dominance over all living creatures, for example, 'Rule over the fish of the sea,' and so forth. When the angels saw that the 'carriage' of man was the same as the carriage of God, they concluded that just as God operates His great carriage by means of free choice, so is man free in both his actions and behavior. Their mistake was in believing that God had given exclusive power to man to run this world as God runs His worlds. Therefore, they wanted to adore him as 'Holy.' Since from this error they could easily fall into the trap of idolatry, God showed them that man also possessed natural attributes over which he had no control, not even through his powers of free choice. The best proof was sleep, which comes upon man beyond his control. They would then know that man is dependent upon God for his sustenance and his protection like other creatures of flesh and blood. When he is asleep he is like an inert stone with only breath in his nostrils. How then is it within his powers to dominate angels? (*Tiferet Tzion*)

Parashah Eight, Midrash Eleven

זָכָר וּנְקֵבָה בְּרָאָם (בראשית ה, ב) זֶה אֶחָד מִן הַדְּבָרִים שֶׁשִּׁנּוּ לְתַלְמַי הַמֶּלֶךְ זָכָר וּנְקוּבָיו בְּרָאָם

'Male and female (*nekevah*) He created them' (Genesis 5:2). This is one of the things which they altered for King Ptolemy: Male with his apertures (*nekuvav*) He created them.

Although Genesis 1:27 also records the same idea, the exact wording of the quote in this *midrash* is from Genesis 5:2. It could very well be that this is a scribal error, since the Midrash has not yet completed Chapter 1 of Genesis. Indeed, the Soncino edition gives the verse as coming from Genesis 1:2. However, 1:27 reads בְּרָא אֹתָם, where the object of the verb is clearly in the plural, whereas 5:2 reads בְּרָאָם, which, although a plural form, could be understood as meaning that male and female refers to one person. According to rabbinic tradition, the Egyptian king, Ptolemy, invited seventy-two rabbis to translate the Bible for him into Greek. The translators were isolated from each other, but produced identical texts, even of the verses that they deliberately 'mistranslated.' The Greek version of the Bible is known as the *Septuagint*, meaning 'the translation of the seventy.' The account is given in the Babylonian Talmud (Tractate Megillah), where the day the translation was completed is described as 'a very bad day' for Judaism. With regard to our verse, the translators were afraid that Ptolemy might get the impression that God is also male and female or that Scripture is in error when it describes the creation of woman as being a later stage in creation.

רַבִּי יְהוֹשֻׁעַ בַּר נְחֶמְיָה בְּשֵׁם רַבִּי חֲנִינָא בַּר יִצְחָק וְרַבָּנָן בְּשֵׁם ר' אֶלְעָזָר אָמְרִי בְּרָא בוֹ אַרְבַּע בְּרִיּוֹת מִלְמַעְלָה וְאַרְבַּע מִלְמַטָּן אוֹכֵל וְשׁוֹתֶה כַּבְּהֵמָה פָּרֶה וְרָבֶה כַּבְּהֵמָה וּמֵטִיל גְּלָלִים כַּבְּהֵמָה וּמֵת כַּבְּהֵמָה מִלְמַעְלָה עוֹמֵד כְּמַלְאֲכֵי הַשָּׁרֵת מְדַבֵּר כְּמַלְאֲכֵי הַשָּׁרֵת יֵשׁ בּוֹ דַעַת כְּמַלְאֲכֵי הַשָּׁרֵת וְרוֹאֶה כְּמַלְאֲכֵי הַשָּׁרֵת וּבְהֵמָה אֵינוֹ רוֹאֶה אַתְמְהָא אֶלָּא זֶה מִצֵּדַד

R. Joshua b. R. Nehemiah said in the name of R. Ḥanina b. R. Isaac, and some Rabbis in the name of R. Eleazar said: He created him with four attributes of the higher beings [i.e., angels] and four

attributes of the lower beings [i.e., animals]. He eats and drinks like an animal; procreates like an animal; excretes like an animal; and dies like an animal. [The four attributes of] the higher beings are: he stands upright like the ministering angels; he speaks like the ministering angels; he understands like the ministering angels; and he sees like the ministering angels. But do animals not see? I am amazed! [It means] that he has peripheral vision.

When Scripture says, 'In the image of God He created him,' it is referring to man's resemblance to the higher beings. When Scripture says 'Male and female created He them,' it is referring to their resemblance to the lower animal beings. On the question as to whether an animal can see, the thought is that humans can see on their sides (peripheral vision) even while their eyes are focused forward, but animals have to turn their heads in order to see sideways.

רַ' תִּפְדַּאי בְּשֵׁם רַ' אַחָא הָעֶלְיוֹנִים נִבְרְאוּ בְצֶלֶם וּבִדְמוּת וְאֵינָן פָּרִין וְרָבִין וְהַתַּחְתּוֹנִים פָּרִים וְרָבִים וְלֹא נִבְרְאוּ בְצֶלֶם וּבִדְמוּת אָמַר הַקָּדוֹשׁ בָּרוּךְ הוּא הֲרֵינִי בוֹרֵא אוֹתוֹ בְּצֶלֶם וּבִדְמוּת מִן הָעֶלְיוֹנִים פָּרֶה וְרָבֶה מִן הַתַּחְתּוֹנִים

R. Tifdai said in R. Aḥa's name: The celestial beings were created in the image and likeness [of God], but do not procreate, while the terrestrial creatures [dumb animals] procreate, but were not created in [His] image and likeness. The Holy One, blessed be He, declared: 'Behold, I will create him [man] in [My] image and likeness, [so that he will partake] of the [character of the] celestial beings, but he will procreate, [after the nature] of the terrestrial beings.'

The human being thus became a unique creation – a combination of the upper and lower worlds, a person with the attributes of knowledge, speech, upright stature, and vision like the angels, combined with a sexual and, therefore, mortal nature like the animal world.

רַבִּי תִּפְדַּאי בְּשֵׁם רַ' אַחָא אָמַר אָמַר הַקָּדוֹשׁ בָּרוּךְ הוּא אִם בּוֹרֵא אֲנִי אוֹתוֹ מִן הָעֶלְיוֹנִים הוּא חַי וְאֵינוֹ מֵת מִן הַתַּחְתּוֹנִים הוּא מֵת וְאֵינוֹ חַי אֶלָּא הֲרֵי אֲנִי בוֹרֵא אוֹתוֹ מִן הָעֶלְיוֹנִים וּמִן הַתַּחְתּוֹנִים אִם יֶחֱטָא יָמוּת וְאִם לֹא יֶחֱטָא יִחְיֶה

R. Tifdai said in R. Aḥa's name: The Holy One, blessed be He, said, 'If I create him of the celestial elements, he will live and not die, and [if I create him] of the terrestrial elements, he will die and not live [in a future life]. Therefore, I will create him of the upper and the

lower elements; if he sins he will die, while if he does not sin, he will live.'

So man was created both with 'His image and likeness' and also with sexuality. Both 'in the image of God' and also 'male and female.' As a result, man's survival as a species will forever depend upon his moral nature and moral choices. He will be capable of moral choices, but will also have to bear the consequences of his choices in terms of reward and punishment.

* * *

Seed Thoughts

Only with man could the thought have occurred of having a being with higher and lower qualities. The fact that the human being shares some qualities with animals and other qualities unquestionably superior is a favorite theme of the Midrash and of most Rabbinic writings. However, when we examine this particular *midrash* and reflect upon those qualities that are distinctly man's, we are less than impressed. So many others are left out.

To stand upright may be an important quality enabling man to do many things, but some animals stand upright too – the kangaroo, for example. Human speech is a great achievement, but many animals have forms of communication – the whales and dolphins, for example. The *midrash* comments on the question of which qualities animals also have. Understanding is, of course, a quality that sets man apart, even when we do grant that certain animals can be taught many things.

More than understanding is involved in man's uniqueness: It is the understanding that makes us capable of moral choices. Furthermore, the whole area of the soul and of immortality as being part of what is involved in being created in God's image is not listed or even alluded to.

It seems that there is so much that differentiates the human being, that even when expressed modestly in terms of these functions that animals also possess, the differences in degree are as sensational as the differences in kind.

* * *

Additional Commentary

One of the expressions altered for King Ptolemy

When the Torah was translated into Greek at the behest of King Ptolemy, the Rabbis who executed the translation changed the meaning in several places in order for the text to make a good impression on the king. Instead of 'male and female He created them,' they translated 'male and his bodily openings' – a play on a similar sounding Hebrew word, *nekuvov*. The reason for this was to obviate the question that the verse above could provoke, namely that there were two separate creations of man and woman, which would contradict the story that Eve was created from Adam's rib. In the latter case, the creation of woman was not a completely separate act. Without doubt the earlier verse, 'male and female He created them' (Genesis 1:27), with the predicate completely spelled out, was also changed but the *midrash* deals with the later verse (5:2) since it occurs after the creation of Eve. (Mirkin)

*

He created him with four attributes

What is involved here is the pinpointing of several expressions: 'and God created man in His image,' 'in the image of God He created him,' 'male and female He created them.' Why 'him' in one case and 'them' in another? The verse could so easily have been simplified. All of this is to teach that there were many acts of creation: 1. 'in the image of God He created him' refers to the creation of the upper spheres; 2. 'male and female He created them' refers to creation in the lower spheres. (Mirkin)

*

Be fruitful and multiply

Since man was fated to die, God gave him the ability to survive, in some sense, through the species and the commandment to be fruitful and multiply. After the statement that He created them in His image, comes the admonition, 'be fruitful and multiply.' (RZWE)

Parashah Eight, Midrash Twelve

וּרְדוּ בִּדְגַת הַיָּם (בראשית א, כח) אָמַר רַבִּי חֲנִינָא אִם זָכָה 'וּרְדוּ' וְאִם לָאו יֵרְדוּ אָמַר
רַבִּי יַעֲקֹב דְּכְפַר חָנִין אֶת שֶׁהוּא 'בְּצַלְמֵנוּ כִּדְמוּתֵנוּ' 'וּרְדוּ' אֶת שֶׁאֵינוֹ 'בְּצַלְמֵנוּ
כִּדְמוּתֵנוּ' יֵרְדוּ רַבִּי יַעֲקֹב דְּמִן כְּפַר חָנָן אָמַר יָבוֹא צַלְמֵנוּ וּדְמוּתֵנוּ וְיִרְדֶּה לְשֶׁאֵינוֹ
דוֹמֶה לְצַלְמֵנוּ כִּדְמוּתֵנוּ

'And rule (*u-redu*) the fish of the sea' (Genesis 1:28). R. Ḥanina said: If
[man] merits it, [the Almighty says] '*u-redu* – rule!' But if not, [the
Almighty says] '*yeradu* – they shall be ruled!' R. Jacob of Kefar Ḥanin
said: To him who is 'in Our image and likeness' [applies] '*u-redu* –
rule!' but to him who is not 'in Our image and likeness' [applies]
'*yeradu* – they shall be ruled!' R. Jacob of Kefar Ḥanan said: [The
Almighty is saying,] 'Let he who is "in Our image and Our likeness"
come and have dominion over that which is not "in Our image and
Our likeness"!'

Here we have a classic midrashic play on words. The word וּרְדוּ, *u-redu*,
appears in this verse and means 'Rule over' or 'Have dominion over.' The
same idea is expressed in verse 26 of the same chapter, but this time as
וְיִרְדּוּ, *ve-yirdu*, which means 'and they shall have dominion over,' but it
can be vocalized as וְיֵרָדוּ, *ve-yeradu*, which means 'and they will be ruled.'
In verse 26 the word is immediately preceded by 'Let us make man in our
image and our likeness,' which R. Jacob of Kefar Ḥanin saw as a basic
condition for 'and they shall have dominion over the fish.' R. Jacob of
Kefar Ḥanan, however, exposited without the play on word, and relied
solely on the sequence in verse 26.

וַיְבָרֶךְ אֹתָם אֱלֹהִים תַּמָּן תְּנֵינָא בְּתוּלָה נִשֵּׂאת לְיוֹם רְבִיעִי וְאַלְמָנָה לְיוֹם חֲמִישִׁי
לָמָּה שֶׁכָּתוּב בָּהֶן בְּרָכָה וַהֲלֹוא אֵין כְּתִיב בְּרָכָה אֶלָּא בַּחֲמִישִׁי וּבַשִּׁשִּׁי בַּר קַפָּרָא
אָמַר רְבִיעִי אוֹר לַחֲמִישִׁי וַחֲמִישִׁי אוֹר לַשִּׁשִּׁי

'And God blessed them' (Genesis 1:28). It is taught elsewhere: A virgin
should be married on the fourth day of the week (i.e., on a
Wednesday), and a widow on the fifth day (i.e., on a Thursday).
Why? Because a blessing is written in connection with these days.
But surely a blessing is written only in connection with the fifth and

325

the sixth days?! Bar Kappara explained: The fourth day means the eve of the fifth, and the fifth means the eve of the sixth.

A virgin should be married on a Wednesday so that on Wednesday night, which belongs to the fifth day, she will enter her husband's home and begin marital relations on a day that God blessed in the days of the creation. A widow should be married on a Thursday, in order for the marriage to be consumated on that night, which belongs to Friday and is the other day on which there was a blessing. The reverse order was not acceptable. A virgin was not to be married on the sixth say in case her virginity was challenged by the groom and he claimed that he was cheated in that he was assured his wife was a virgin. Such a claim would have to be brought to the Bet Din, which would not have time to meet before the Sabbath. A widow was to be married on the sixth day because the blessing to man is the stronger one and furthermore the couple would have more time for each other and not be tempted to go to work, if it were mid-week.

רַ' אֶלְעָזָר בְּשֵׁם רַבִּי יוֹסֵי בֶּן זִמְרָה 'וְכִבְשָׁהָ' 'וְכִבְשָׁהּ' כְּתִיב הָאִישׁ מְצֻוֶּה עַל פְּרִיָה
וּרְבִיָה אֲבָל לֹא הָאִשָּׁה רַ' יוֹחָנָן בֶּן בְּרוֹקָה אוֹמֵר אֶחָד הָאִישׁ וְאֶחָד הָאִשָּׁה עַל
שְׁנֵיהֶם הוּא אוֹמֵר 'וַיְבָרֶךְ אֹתָם אֱלֹהִים וְגוֹ''

R. Eleazar said in the name of R. Jose b. Zimra: 'And master it (in the plural: *ve-khivshuhah*)' (Genesis 1:28); the actual spelling is *ve-khivshah* (in the singular). [From this we can learn that] man is commanded regarding procreation but not woman. R. Johanan b. Berokah said: Both man and woman [are commanded to procreate] because regarding both it is written 'and God blessed them.'

The plain translation of verse 28 is: 'God blessed them and God said to them, "Be fertile and increase, fill the earth *and master it*, and rule the fish of the sea, the birds of the sky, and all living things that creep on the earth."' The Hebrew for 'master it' is vocalized as though it is in the plural (both of you master...) with a suffix indicating the object (the earth). Clearly the process is meant to come about by way of procreation. However, if we ignore the masoretic vocalization, the word would read as a command in the masculine singular, and thus we would understand that the command to be fertile and fill the world is directed only at the male. R. Johanan b. Berokah, however, draws our attention to the beginning of the verse where we are told that 'God blessed *them*,' which would indicate that the following commandment applies to both men and women.

'וְכִבְשֻׁהָ' 'וְכִבְשָׁהּ' כְּתִיב הָאִישׁ כּוֹבֵשׁ אִשְׁתּוֹ שֶׁלֹּא תֵצֵא לַשּׁוּק שֶׁכָּל אִשָּׁה שֶׁיּוֹצְאָה
לַוּק סוֹפָהּ לְהִכָּשֵׁל מִנָּא לָן מִן דִּינָה שֶׁנֶּאֱמַר 'וַתֵּצֵא דִינָה' (בראשית לד, א) וּלְבַסּוֹף
נִכְשְׁלָה הֲדָא הוּא דִכְתִיב 'וַיַּרְא אֹתָהּ שְׁכֶם וְגוֹ'' (שם שם, ב)

**'And master it – *ve-khivshuhah.*' 'And master *her*' is written! A man
must master his wife that she should not go out into the market
place, for any woman who goes out into the market place will eventually come to grief. Whence do we know this? From Dinah, as it is
written, 'Now Dinah... went out...' (Genesis 34:1), and ultimately she
came to grief, as it is written 'And Shechem... saw her' (ibid. verse 2).**

This section of the *midrash* takes the key word out of its context and sees
the feminine suffix as referring not to the earth, but to Eve! Thus a man
must master his wife by not allowing her to put herself in a position of
danger, as did the biblical Dinah when she 'went out' to visit the daughters
of the land, with the result that she was forcibly taken by Shechem. Had
she stayed at home, it would not have happened. Thus, the commandment is that a wife must allow herself to be mastered by her husband and
obey him when he asks her not to flaunt herself in public. (*Tiferet Tzion*)
It would have been helpful if the *midrash* had quoted not only the verse
'and Dinah went out' but also the subsequent words, 'and Shechem took
her,' because that is the real point of the story. Everyone saw Dinah, not
only Shechem. But the point is that he saw her in the market place and
assumed that she had abandoned the ways of modesty and, in
consequence, he dared to take her. But if he had seen her in her father's
house, he would never have dared to approach her.

רַבִּי יִרְמְיָה וְרַ' אַבָּהוּ וְרַ' יִצְחָק בַּר מַרְיוֹן בְּשֵׁם רַבִּי חֲנִינָא הֲלָכָה כְּרַבִּי יוֹחָנָן

**R. Jeremiah and R. Abbahu and R. Isaac bar Marion said in R.
Ḥanina's name: The law is as stated by R. Joḥanan b. Berokah.**

The law referred to is that both man and woman are commanded to
procreate.

* * *

Seed Thoughts

Three times in these scriptural passages is the concept of power
mentioned – to have dominion, to subdue, or to master. The question I
would raise has been beautifully put by the *Tiferet Tzion* (See below,
Additional Commentary). Is it the purpose of the creation of man for him

to subdue the fish? Is it not rather for him to rise along the ladder of the spiritual life whose top reaches to heaven?

Of course man's purpose is spiritual. But spirituality does not mean ethereal. Power is not a bad word. Like every other concept it can be used morally or immorally. In fact, the spiritual life is best tested by its relationship to power, and to the handmaiden of power, which is possession.

There is no relationship in human society in which power is not a factor. We are accustomed to power in the political sphere or the military. Upon reflection, however, there is a relationship of power between husband and wife. The power can be shared or it can be unilateral, but it exists in the concept of authority between parents and children, teachers and pupils, employers and employees, and other relationships too numerous to mention. The question that always has to be asked, the criterion that must always be used, is this: Is the power tyrannical and ego-serving or has it been transformed into stewardship?

The *Ethics of the Fathers* says, 'Beauty, strength, wealth, honor, wisdom, sagacity, old age, and children are good for the righteous and good for the world.' These items imply qualities that are moral. If they are held by the wicked the world is damaged, if by good people the world benefits.

The world will not be helped if good people try to escape the responsibility of power and pretend that by doing so they are acting in a saintly manner. In reality, they are copping out and betraying the original mandate that God gave to Adam and Eve.

That mandate is the gift of power. But, as R. Jacob of Kefar Ḥanan insisted, it can only be properly employed by one who lives consciously aware that he or she is created in the image of God.

* * *

Additional Commentary

Contradictions

The expression 'If he merits' or 'if he does not merit' is a favorite interpretation of the Sages when two biblical verses seem to contradict each other. It was obviously the view of the Sages that here we have two contradictory verses. In the verse 'Let us make man,' we find the expression *ve-yirdu* – 'and they shall rule' and in the verse 'and God blessed them,' the verb used is *u-redu* – 'and rule!' *U-redu* can only be read as a positive verb, while *ve-yirdu* can be read as *ve-yeradu*, in the passive, meaning 'they will be ruled.' The *midrash*, therefore, interprets *u-redu* as applying 'if they have merit' and *ve-yeradu*, 'if they do not have merit.' The fact that *u-redu* is in a verse that contains a blessing seems to confirm that interpretation.

R. Jacob of Kefar Ḥanan takes an opposite position. The verse, 'Let us make man in our image after our likeness' is the one that contains *ve-yirdu*, meaning that if man acts in the spirit of God's likeness he will have dominion, and the context implies that this is a good thing. By the same token, if man does not act in the spirit of God's likeness he will not dominate. But this is not implied by the verse *u-redu*. Maybe it could be interpreted that since the verse does not say *yirshu*, they will conquer, the implication is that *u-redu* might imply either dominion or *yeridah*, meaning downfall. If they have merit they will conquer and, if not, they will fall. According to R. Jacob, living in God's image will bring dominion and not living in God's image will bring *yeridah*, downfall. The reader can choose whatever interpretation he prefers. (RZWE)

*

R. Jacob of Kefar Ḥanan

He intends to teach why it is that man is entitled to rule over the animal world. The reason is that man was created in the image and likeness of God. That entitles him to rule over those who are lower than him in the scale of creation. The three Sages quoted in this *midrash* all come to emphasize three special attributes by virtue of which the human being is preeminent over all other creatures. The first of these is that the human being has the ability to make choices, unlike other creatures who are the slaves of their natural instincts. That is what R. Ḥanina means when he says, 'If he will merit he will have dominion,' for all his actions are under his control for constructive or destructive purposes, depending upon the choices he makes. Man's second attribute is that his form and likeness is complete and more beautiful in appearance than any other creature. In this connection R. Jacob of Kefar Ḥanan says, 'Of him who is in Our likeness I say rule!' The meaning is that man is of a special and unique configuration as Rashi interprets it in the Torah. He is there described as more handsome than any other creature. The third attribute has to do with his possession of the faculty of intelligence. In this connection R. Jacob of Kefar Ḥanin says, 'Let the one in Our image and likeness come to rule over the one who is not in Our image and likeness,' for in this capacity he resembles the beings of the upper world. Maimonides says that this refers to the faculty of intelligence and this is the principle reason why man can rule over the animal kingdom, for they do not possess this intelligence. (*Yefei To'ar*)

*

R. Jacob said

The intent of this teaching is to strengthen the words of R. Ḥanina by reference to the preceding verse where it is written, 'Let us make man in our image' and then 'they shall rule.' Is the whole purpose of the creation of man to rule over the fish in the sea? Is not his purpose to climb the ladder of the spiritual life whose top reaches heaven?

Therefore, said R. Jacob, the meaning of the verse is whoever lives in the image of God, namely the righteous, will have dominion over the fish, and so on, and since within the context of 'Let us make man' are included the wicked, Scripture also uses the expression *ve-yirdu*, implying that whoever does not live in the image of God *ve-yeradu*, will be dominated, namely, the animals will have dominion over them. There is a real *ḥiddush* (*novella*) here. God only permitted those who live in His image to dominate over the animal world, namely, the pious. As for the *am ha-aretz*, the ignorant, where the only difference between them and the animals is that they walk on two legs, they are prohibited from dominating animals. That, by the way, is the reason that our Sages prohibited an ignoramus from eating meat. (*Tiferet Tzion*)

*

It is taught elsewhere

The creation of man took place in the daytime and at that time they were commanded to be fruitful. In fact, they immediately fulfilled that command, as stated in *The Fathers according to Rabbi Natan* (*Avot de-R. Natan*) Chapter One: 'On that very day they climbed into bed as two and came off the bed as four.' From this source it would be quite likely to err and assert that the commandment to be fruitful could be observed in the daytime. In actual fact, the Rabbis have said that Israel is meant to be holy and should not engage in marital relations in the daytime. Therefore, the *midrash* cited a *mishnah* from Tractate Ketubbot from which it is quite clear that the commandment of 'be fruitful' applies only at night, as it states, 'A virgin is married on the fourth day of the week in order that the intercourse in fulfillment of the *mitzvah* take place on the night of the fifth day.' We thus know from this that the main time for the fulfillment of this *mitzvah* is at night. It is said of one who engages in sexual relations in the daytime, that because of this sin, that other evil one (the snake) alighted upon them. He had seen them engaged in sexual relations and desired Eve. (*Tiferet Tzion*)

*

A man is commanded to be fruitful

From the fact that the verse is repetitive in the sense that it says 'and God blessed them' followed immediately by 'and God said to them,' one derives that two things are meant: 1. The blessing to them that they be fruitful and 2. the commandment to them that they be fruitful, which is the reason why it also says 'and God said to them.' Similarly, in connection with the command to have dominion over the fish of the sea, they were told that if they followed in the way of the spiritual life, all of the animal world would submit to them. Since the word, 'and master it,' is also included (but without the *vav* that would make it plural) it applies only to man, Adam and not to Eve. We interpret, therefore, that the commandment was intended for Adam alone and that the blessing also included Eve, for there is no way of excluding her from the blessing (see Babylonian Talmud, Bava Batra 110b). Therefore we separate the Divine word by saying that 'be fruitful' in the case of Adam, meant both blessing and commandment, but in the case of Eve it implied only blessing. (*Tiferet Tzion*)

Parashah Eight, Midrash Thirteen

אָמַר רַ׳ אַבָּהוּ נָטַל הַקָּדוֹשׁ בָּרוּךְ הוּא כּוֹס שֶׁל בְּרָכָה וּבֵרְכָן

R. Abbahu said: The Holy One, blessed be He, lifted a goblet of benediction and blessed them.

R. Abbahu derives his teaching from the fact that verse 28 repeats itself. First, 'and God blessed them,' immediately followed by, 'and God said to them.' He interpreted that 'and God blessed them' is a self-contained entity, and, since it is never the style of Scripture to curtail a verse but to elaborate upon it, we must say that the intention of Scripture is that God blessed them with the blessing most appropriate to the context, namely, wedding blessings. We would then have to say that He blessed them with a goblet of blessing as the law requires, for surely God followed the custom of weddings in terms of the cup. He also did the same in terms of the attendants for the groom at Adam's wedding. (*Tiferet Tzion*)

אָמַר רַ׳ יְהוּדָה בַּר סִימוֹן מִיכָאֵל וְגַבְרִיאֵל הֵם הָיוּ שׁוֹשְׁבִינִין שֶׁל אָדָם הָרִאשׁוֹן

R. Judah b. R. Simon said: [The angels] Michael and Gabriel were Adam's 'best men.'

The normal procedure at wedding ceremonies is for the groom to be accompanied on his way to the *huppah*. This is where the custom of the 'best man' who holds the ring originated. When a man and a woman behave in a good way, the Divine Presence is manifest in their lives, but if, heaven forfend, they do not act in such a manner, then it is as though they are fire as our Sages have said. For this reason the wedding attendants were the angels Michael and Gabriel. They symbolize justice and mercy, and their presence indicates to the bride and groom that their marriage will develop in accordance with their behavior. (*Tiferet Tzion*)

אָמַר רַבִּי שַׂמְלַאי מָצִינוּ שֶׁהַקָּדוֹשׁ בָּרוּךְ הוּא מְבָרֵךְ חֲתָנִים וּמְקַשֵּׁט כַּלּוֹת וּמְבַקֵּר חוֹלִים וְקוֹבֵר מֵתִים

R. Simla'i said: We find that the Holy One, blessed be He, recites the benedictions over bridegrooms, adorns brides, visits the sick, and buries the dead.

By virtue of the fact that the Torah told us that God recited the appropriate wedding benedictions at Adam's wedding, we must perforce conclude that this is His way with all human beings. The *midrash* continues to supply the sources for the other good deeds God performs.

מְבָרֵךְ חֲתָנִים מִנַּיִן 'וַיְבָרֶךְ אֹתָם אֱלֹהִים'

Whence do we know that He recites the benedictions over bridegrooms? – 'And God blessed them.'

What we find is that when a man is single he exhausts himself in acquiring a livelihood, but if God gives him a wife and children he is able to maintain them without too much additional effort on his part at the beginning. All this stems from the blessing with which God blesses the groom in return for his trust in God that He would provide for him and therefore he takes a wife. (*Tiferet Tzion*) 'And God blessed them' means that He blessed them with the subject matters that are part of our wedding benedictions, namely, that their creation and what they create, the perfection of their home and marriage will last permanently, that they rejoice and that they be blessed with the fruit of the womb, with nourishment and with all their needs.

וּמְקַשֵּׁט כַּלּוֹת מִנַּיִן 'וַיִּבֶן ה' אֱלֹהִים אֶת הַצֵּלָע וְגוֹ'' (בראשית ב, כב)

Whence do we know that He adorns brides – 'And the Lord God fashioned the rib [that He had taken from the man into a woman]' (Genesis 2:22).

The main idea here is how to translate the word יבן, *va-yiven*. Does it only mean 'to fashion' or 'to build'? In certain islands of the sea, say the Sages, the Aramaic translation for 'decorate' is *beniyata*, also derived from the same root as *va-yiven*. It should therefore be translated not as to build, but to decorate. Furthermore, when it says in Genesis 2:7 that God created man from earth, *va-yiven* was not used at all, but וייצר, *va-yitzer*. How much more so should one not ascribe the act of building in the literal sense to the creation of woman from flesh. It should therefore rightly be translated as 'adorn.' (Mirkin)

מְבַקֵּר חוֹלִים מִנַּיִן שֶׁנֶּאֱמַר 'וַיֵּרָא אֵלָיו ה' בְּאֵלֹנֵי מַמְרֵא' (שם יח, א)

Whence do we know that He visits the sick? As it is written, 'And the Lord appeared to him by the terebinths of Mamre' (Genesis 18:1).

The reference in the verse is to the third day of Abraham's circumcision when he was visited by three messengers, angelic figures, one of whom was assigned the task of healing his pain.

קוֹבֵר מֵתִים מִנַּיִן 'וַיִּקְבֹּר אֹתוֹ בַגַּיְא' (דברים לד, ו)

Whence do we know that He buries the dead? – 'And He buried him in the valley…' (Deuteronomy 34:6).

God Himself looked after the burial of Moses, whose place of burial remains unknown to this day.

אָמַר רַ' שְׁמוּאֵל בַּר נַחְמָן בְּשֵׁם רַבִּי יוֹנָתָן אַף מַרְאֶה פָנִים לָאָבֵל הָדָא הוּא דִכְתִיב 'וַיֵּרָא אֱלֹהִים אֶל יַעֲקֹב עוֹד וְגוֹ' (בראשית לה, ט) מַה בְּרָכָה בֵּרְכוֹ רַבִּי יוֹנָתָן אָמַר בִּרְכַּת אֲבֵלִים

R. Samuel b. Naḥman said in the name of R. Jonathan: He also visits mourners, as it is written, 'And God appeared again to Jacob [on his arrival from Paddan-Aram, and He blessed him]' (Genesis 35:9). **With which benediction did He bless him? R. Jonathan said: With the benediction of mourners.**

Although the text itself does not specify the blessing, one cannot say that it was the change of name from Jacob to Israel because there is an intervening clause, 'And God said.' This forces us to conclude that a different blessing is meant and the interpretation is directed to the previous verse, which says, 'And Deborah died.' A *midrash* will later inform us that in addition to Deborah, his childhood nurse, his mother Rebecca also died at that time, which is why it is said that Jacob was blessed with a mourner's blessing. In the case of a mourner it is not what is said to him that is important only that one make an appearance before him. So the *midrash* is able to say that the mere appearance of God to Jacob at this time was a mourner's blessing.

* * *

Seed Thoughts

A most important concept in religion is *imitatio dei*, the imitation of God. In the Jewish tradition it is expressed in the phrase, מה הוא רחום אף אתה רחום – 'As He is merciful so you too be merciful.' It is not only God that is the model of imitation, but also those personalities in and out of the Bible who were touched by God in some fashion and in the imitation of them there is reflected an imitation of God.

The concept of imitation is a springboard for the ethical life and, in particular, that aspect of the ethical life that is involved with person-to-person relationships where mercy, charity, and compassion are involved and required.

Is religion, therefore, social work? Of course it is and why should it not be? A true religious commitment must involve working with the poor, the infirm, the aged, the lonely, the deprived, in one form or another. Social work has its own professional criteria and standards and, to be sure, not all social work is religious nor are social workers. But there is a vast realm where religious values must express themselves in human terms and that which we call social work is certainly one of them.

One would have to say, however, that religion is also more than social work. Certainly Judaism is more. Indeed, the *midrash* before us emphasizes the more. There is brought to our attention for imitation of the Divine, a series of great pastoral moments in which God Himself is involved in the personal lives of great biblical personalities. We would call them today 'rites of passage' and they are fraught with ritual and symbolic significance.

God blessed Adam and Eve at their wedding and so should we bless all brides and grooms. But surely more is involved than reciting a benediction. If, indeed, marriage has a special relationship to God, it must be marriage in its entirety. Jewish marriage involves seeking Jewish partners, building a home on religious foundations, raising children to the Torah way, mutual respect of husband and wife as a religious duty, as well as the availability of parents to children and vice versa. Each of these areas covers a vast value system as well as an infrastructure of communal institutions that are needed in order to make this all possible.

God healed Abraham from his circumcision. So, of course, *bikkur ḥolim*, visiting the sick is a great *mitzvah*. But much more than visiting is demanded – helping, nursing, caring, and doing whatever is needed for the patient as a human being. But God healed Abraham from his circumcision! So the circumcision is also a factor. In order to become a Jew, one's sexuality has to be dedicated to its highest purpose. And, indeed, the rite of circumcision and whatever is related to it can and, indeed, should be used as a stepping-stone in our education to the world of sexuality and its sanctification.

God visited Jacob in mourning and so should we visit each other. Mutual care and concern and the giving of oneself are the key to our living in the image of God. The various dimensions of bereavement require sensitivity, mutual respect, and consideration.

The point that is being made in all of this is that the rites of passage are demeaned by calling them rites. They are great and momentous occasions. They can be used to humanize us and each other. They should be so used.

* * *

Additional Commentary

The Holy One, blessed be He, lifted a goblet of benediction
From this we derive that the wedding blessings have to be recited over a cup of wine. (*Hidushei ho-Rashash*)

*

We find that the Holy One, blessed be He
Since the Holy One, whose greatness is beyond compare, occupies Himself with such good deeds, how much more so is it appropriate for those of flesh and blood to cleave to His commandments, to humble their pride and dignity if necessary, to perform acts of loving-kindness even with those who are lower and less important in their eyes. (*Yefei To'ar*)

*

This proves that human beings must do acts of kindness. (Rashi)

Parashah Nine, Midrash One

וַיַּרְא אֱלֹהִים אֶת כָּל אֲשֶׁר עָשָׂה וְגוֹ' (א, לא) רַבִּי לֵוִי פָּתַח 'כְּבֹד אֱלֹהִים הַסְתֵּר דָּבָר
וּכְבֹד מְלָכִים חֲקֹר דָּבָר' (משלי כה, ב)

'And God saw all that He had made, [and, behold, it was very good]'
(Genesis 1:31). R. Levi began [his exposition], 'It is the glory of God to
conceal a matter, and the glory of a king to examine a matter'
(Proverbs 25:2).

Some of the verses describing the earlier days of creation have already
told us that 'God saw that it was good.' Why did it have to be repeated
with the added description that 'it was *very* good'? R. Levi begins his
exposition with a verse from Proverbs which, as we shall see, he interprets
as a stricture against speculation. Up to the creation of the world – no
speculation. After the world was created, investigation is not only
permitted, but even commanded. He now goes on to offer more detail.

רַבִּי לֵוִי בְּשֵׁם רַבִּי חָמָא בַּר חֲנִינָא אָמַר מִתְּחִלַּת הַסֵּפֶר וְעַד כָּאן כְּבֹד אֱלֹהִים הוּא
הַסְתֵּר דָּבָר מִכָּאן וְאֵילָךְ 'כְּבֹד מְלָכִים חֲקֹר דָּבָר' כְּבוֹד דִּבְרֵי תוֹרָה שֶׁנִּמְשְׁלוּ
בַּמְּלָכִים שֶׁנֶּאֱמַר 'בִּי מְלָכִים יִמְלֹכוּ' לַחְקֹר דָּבָר (שם ח, טו)

Said R. Levi in the name of R. Ḥama b. Ḥanina: From the beginning
of the book [of Genesis] up to this point, 'it is the glory of God to
conceal a matter'; but from this point onward, 'the glory of a king
[is] to examine a matter.' It is to the glory of the words of the Torah,
which are likened to kings, as it is said, 'Through me [i.e., the Torah]
kings reign' (Proverbs 8:15), to examine a matter.

From the beginning of creation until the end of creation where it says,
'And, behold, it was very good,' an overview of creation is possible only
for God. On the other hand, the honor due to kings, which is a reference
to Torah, demands constant searching and seeking for meaning. This
exposition is, in fact, interpreting the verse, 'And God saw all that He had
made, and, behold, it was very good.' We are being warned that man
should not make the mistake of thinking that he knows God's purpose in
the creation story. 'And *God* saw' – only God is capable of seeing all that

He had accomplished and then saying 'behold it was very good.' That is not in man's power, and he must glorify God by refraining from speculation about the act of creation. (*Tiferet Tzion*) However, this is not the case with regards to Torah, which man must glorify by constant and intense study in an attempt to understand it.

* * *

Seed Thoughts

The idea that man should not investigate God's motives, because man's intellectual capacity is limited, is true, significant, even very beautiful from a certain point of view, but completely wishful thinking.

Those human beings who have exceptional brain power are going to think and are going to think about everything, what is above, what is below, and what is anywhere and everywhere. Such investigation almost becomes an imperative, when one considers the evil in the world. Surely, evil cannot be accepted with an attitude of helplessness and throwing up one's hands! Who would disagree that this horrendous phenomenon should be studied and pursued relentlessly until ameliorated if not totally eliminated?

Would infant mortality at birth have been reduced so dramatically if physicians and researchers had piously said, 'It is the will of God'? How did we know it was the will of God? What right does anyone have to say such a thing?

How could God have created a human being in His image and after His likeness and not have expected him to imitate God in this attitude of relentless and utter curiosity, all in the pursuit of truth.

'He who sits in the heavens laughs.' I have the peculiar feeling that the Holy One, blessed be He, is watching this expenditure of energy by His pious followers and getting a big kick, so to speak, out of the fact that R. Levi's restriction on human curiosity is not being obeyed, even to the extent of saying, 'My children have vanquished Me.'

If, indeed, there are moral boundaries to be placed upon the human intellect, perhaps they can be found in another direction. Genetic research is beyond the radical concept of *in vitro* fertilization and is almost at the point where cloning is possible. Animal husbandry and research can give us a clue into the directions that such research into human genetics will be taking us. The real areas for our concerns and moral inhibitions should be in the development of moral norms not to put an end to the research, but to enable it to function along lines that will maintain the sanctity of life even in the most advanced stages of science and technology. If we can succeed in discovering such standards and maintaining them in cooperation with the scientific world, we will be fulfilling both the mandate and the warning of the Creator in a way that hopefully He will also approve.

* * *

Additional Commentary

R. Levi said

It is impossible to explain the verse from Proverbs literally. How can you equate the glory of kings who are flesh and blood to the glory of God? For this reason R. Levi explains by means of this verse that there are two levels of authority: the Divine and the human. The first is the honor of God, the fact that He conducts His world in line with His will and not by virtue of the will of those who receive his decisions and are often the cause of His exercising His will. In this connection Scripture writes, 'It is the glory of God to conceal a thing.' We have no business investigating what existed before man's emergence on this planet. It is not within our intellectual power to understand what we call 'God's acts of creation.' (*Tiferet Tzion*)

*

The honor of kings

The Torah, however, speaks of what happened after the creation of man, for then God began to conduct His world in relation to man's behavior. This is what is described as the 'honor of kings,' for kings have to conduct their affairs of state and judge the world in accordance with the demands of time and space. When Scripture says, 'Through me kings reign,' it means that kings are obliged to learn from the Torah how God ruled generation after generation in accordance with time and place. It is our obligation to study this Torah material and to learn how God judges with righteousness, out of His desire for the good of the world. (*Tiferet Tzion*)

Parashah Nine, Midrash Two

דָּבָר אַחֵר וַיַּרְא אֱלֹהִים אֶת כָּל אֲשֶׁר עָשָׂה וְהִנֵּה טוֹב מְאֹד רַבִּי תַּנְחוּמָא פָּתַח 'אֶת
הַכֹּל עָשָׂה יָפֶה בְעִתּוֹ' (קהלת ג, יא) אָמַר רַבִּי תַּנְחוּמָא בְּעוֹנָתוֹ נִבְרָא הָעוֹלָם לֹא
הָיָה הָעוֹלָם רָאוּי לִבָּרֵאת קֹדֶם לָכֵן

**Another interpretation: 'And God saw all that He had made, and,
behold, it was very good' (Genesis 1:31). R. Tanḥuma commenced [his
exposition]: 'He brings everything to pass precisely at its time'
(Ecclesiastes 3:11). Said R. Tanḥuma: The world was created when it
was due, and the world was not fit to be created earlier.**

R. Tanḥuma also addresses the question why it was necessary to say 'it
was very good' at the end of the creation story, when the same idea had
been expressed several times before. He bases his interpretation on the
verse from Ecclesiastes and thus says that our verse must mean that this
particular time was ideal for the creation of the world – and, therefore, it
was very good. The idea is elaborated upon, in a sensational fashion, in
the following sections.

אָמַר רַ' אַבָּהוּ מִכָּאן שֶׁהַקָּדוֹשׁ בָּרוּךְ הוּא הָיָה בוֹרֵא עוֹלָמוֹת וּמַחֲרִיבָן בּוֹרֵא
עוֹלָמוֹת וּמַחֲרִיבָן עַד שֶׁבָּרָא אֶת אֵלּוּ אָמַר דֵּין הֲנָיָין לִי יָתְהוֹן לָא הֲנָיָין לִי

**R. Abbahu said: Hence we learn that the Holy One, blessed be He,
went on creating worlds and destroying them until He created these
[heaven and earth] and then He said: 'These please Me; those did
not please Me.'**

R. Abbahu takes R. Tanḥuma's idea even further. The earlier worlds that
God created did not live up to His expectations, so he destroyed them.
This world, however, was very good.

אָמַר רַבִּי פִּינְחָס טַעֲמֵהּ דְּרַבִּי אַבָּהוּ 'וַיַּרְא אֱלֹהִים אֶת כָּל אֲשֶׁר עָשָׂה וְהִנֵּה טוֹב
מְאֹד' דֵּין הֲנָיָין לִי יָתְהוֹן לָא הֲנָיָין לִי

**R. Pinḥas said: The reason for R. Abbahu's statement is, 'And God
saw all that He had made, and, behold, it was very good,' [which
means] 'These please Me; those did not please Me.'**

340

R. Pinḥas is supplying the unstated source of R. Abbahu's idea. The statement, 'and, behold, *it* was very good,' implies that there was something else that was not very good. Another interpretation is that the exclamation, 'behold,' is to be understood as 'now' – God saw that the world He had created *now* was very good, implying that those that He had created earlier were not so. (Soncino)

* * *

Seed Thoughts

With this *midrash* a Jew who believes in the Torah can remove most of his fears of evolution. The principle of evolution is that the world experienced development. Even man had his evolutionary ancestors. Darwinian evolution is not the only kind. There are many other hypotheses. All of them share the same basic principles: The world as we know it has developed and evolved.

I am not saying that the believer in the Bible has no problems with the evolutionary theory. If one takes a fundamentalist position that every word in the Genesis story has to be taken literally, there is no escape from the problems. But then, even a cursory glance at our *midrash* would make it very clear that literalism is a dead-end, not to be sought.

If we approach evolution in a generalized way as a theory of development, we can confront it without blinking an eyelash, for this *midrash* says it all.

Before this world was created, other worlds were built and destroyed by God. What were those other worlds like? Did they have human precursors? Were those worlds populated by dinosaurs, mammoth reptiles, and all the other *dramatis personnae* of the Darwinian vision? We do not know. It does not say. But it is not precluded.

In the beautiful interpretation of the *Tiferet Tzion*, the building and destroying of worlds is not to be seen as an arbitrary divine whim, but rather as the process of growth in stages. Just as a seed is planted, takes root, blossoms, and bears fruit so, we are told, every stage was a preparation for what followed.

This is not scientific evolution, but it is far removed from a static conception of creationism. It is a handle with which to confront many challenges. With it, evolution need not even be confronted. It can be adapted into the *weltanschauung* of the Jew who obeys the commandments without loss of integrity.

* * *

Additional Commentary

Creating worlds and destroying them

There seems to be a difference of opinion as to the intention of this *midrash*. According to Rashi and the vast majority of commentators, the implication was that before the creation of this world, the other worlds that God created were not beautiful or not yet ripe or, whatever the reason, not suitable and had to be replaced. Not so, says the *Yefei To'ar*. He writes, 'All the worlds that He created before this one were also beautiful in their time. Later on, with the passage of time and, presumably, other purposes that God had in mind, He destroyed them and replaced them by this one.' The concern of the *Yefei To'ar* seems to be that he cannot, by definition, contemplate a situation whereby God would do something unsatisfactory.

R. Tanḥuma began

The difficulty that prompted R. Tanḥuma's remarks lies in the problem: How can Scripture say 'And God saw… and, behold, it was very good.' The implication is that something now happened that makes everything very good. But then, does not God know everything from beginning to end? Surely nothing new happened to His knowledge after the creation of the world than had obtained before!

Therefore, he has to interpret why God brought this world into being at that particular time and not before, and that there was no change in God's mind, heaven forbid. So the verse says, 'And God saw,' intransitive as above, and when did God see? All that He had created from a state of non-existence to a state of existence, at a time when it would be very good for those whom He had created. So the verse says 'and, behold, it was very good,' meaning that at this particular time it was very good and not before and not after in accordance with His divine understanding that the world could not have accepted a creation that was good except at this particular time. That is why R. Tanḥuma cites the verse, 'He bring everything to pass precisely at its time.' (*Tiferet Tzion*)

*

Said R. Abbahu

The word 'very' is not to be understood as always being comparative to something else, for then it should have said that it was very much better than something else. But then, how can R. Abbahu be so certain that this world is the main goal of all the other worlds? Maybe it, too, is a preparation for other worlds yet to come. Therefore, said R. Abbahu, from the use of 'very good,' we learn that God created other worlds and destroyed them. But this should be understood in the same sense as the process of planting. Each previous world was a preparation for the world that followed it. (*Tiferet Tzion*)

Parashah Nine, Midrash Three

דָּבָר אַחֵר וַיַּרְא אֱלֹהִים אֶת כָּל אֲשֶׁר עָשָׂה וְהִנֵּה טוֹב מְאֹד רַבִּי יוֹחָנָן אָמַר מֶלֶךְ
בָּשָׂר וָדָם בּוֹנֶה פָּלָטִין מַבִּיט בָּעֶלְיוֹנִים רְאִיָּה אַחַת וּבַתַּחְתּוֹנִים רְאִיָּה אַחַת אֲבָל
הַקָּדוֹשׁ בָּרוּךְ הוּא מַבִּיט בָּעֶלְיוֹנִים וּבַתַּחְתּוֹנִים רְאִיָּה אַחַת

**Another interpretation: 'And God saw all that He had made, and,
behold, it was very good.' R. Joḥanan said: When a mortal king
builds a palace, he looks at the upper stories with one look and at
the lower stories with another, but the Holy One, blessed be He,
casts but a single look at the upper and the lower portions
simultaneously.**

The problem here is that the verse says, 'And God saw all that He had
made,' even though it has already been stated several times, 'And God
saw that it was good.' R. Joḥanan therefore explains that the Holy One
personally supervised both the upper and lower worlds, and not as might
be erroneously believed that God is above it all and only the heavens are
the seat of His majesty and concern. In this respect the parable of the king
of flesh and blood is revealing. A king builds a palace in such a way that
the upper chambers are more important. They are designed to suit his
majestic taste. The lower level, however, is designed for use of the servants
and other staff. He has a special criterion for the upper level and a
different one for the lower level. But God has only one vision for both the
upper and lower levels, which to Him are equal. In this connection we
have the verse, 'And God saw *all* that He had made,' meaning that He
supervises them both at the same time. (*Tiferet Tzion*)

אָמַר רַבִּי שִׁמְעוֹן בֶּן לָקִישׁ 'הִנֵּה טוֹב מְאֹד' זֶה הָעוֹלָם הַזֶּה 'וְהִנֵּה טוֹב מְאֹד' זֶה
הָעוֹלָם הַבָּא הָעוֹלָם הַזֶּה וְהָעוֹלָם הַבָּא הִבִּיט בָּהֶן הַקָּדוֹשׁ בָּרוּךְ הוּא רְאִיָּה אַחַת

**R. Simon b. Lakish said: 'Behold, it was very good' refers to this
world; '*And*, behold, it was very good' refers the next world. The
Holy One, blessed be He, took them both in with one glance.**

This is what R. Simon means. If Scripture had only written הנה טוב מאד,
hineih tov me'od – behold it was very good, it would certainly have been a

344

reference to this world because the word *hineih* has an immediacy that relates to the subject matter at hand and in the creation story that is certainly the reality of this world. But the moment *ve-hineih* appears with a *vav*, which transforms the meaning of the phrase, one can only conclude that something else is also intended and that can only be the world-to-come. The verse is further meant to tell us that God sees both worlds together, that is, that when God created the world He already had a vision of the world-to-come. Indeed, He planned this world so that it might be a preparation for the world-to-come. The explanation of the verse would thus be as follows: God oversaw everything that He had made so that it would be a preparation for the world-to-come, a preparation for *ve-hineih tov me'od*, meaning that through this world man will be renewed so that He will experience the 'very good' of the world-to-come. (*Tiferet Tzion*)

רַבִּי שִׁמְעוֹן בֶּן לָקִישׁ בְּשֵׁם ר' אֶלְעָזָר בֶּן עֲזַרְיָה אָמַר 'אֲהָהּ ה' אֱלֹהִים הִנֵּה אַתָּה עָשִׂיתָ אֶת הַשָּׁמַיִם וְאֶת הָאָרֶץ בְּכֹחֲךָ הַגָּדוֹל וּבִזְרוֹעֲךָ הַנְּטוּיָה לֹא יִפָּלֵא מִמְּךָ כָּל דָּבָר' (ירמיה לב, יז) מֵאוֹתָהּ שָׁעָה 'לֹא יִפָּלֵא מִמְּךָ כָּל דָּבָר'

R. Simon b. Lakish said in R. Eleazar b. Azariah's name: 'Ah! Lord God! You made heaven and earth with Your great might and outstretched arm. Nothing is too wondrous for You!' (Jeremiah 32:17). From that moment on [when You created the world] nothing is too wondrous for You!

According to this interpretation the verse, 'And God saw,' means that God saw at the very beginning of the world that man would become worthy of the world-to-come by virtue of his good deeds in this world and this, despite the fact that man has free will. Since that moment, 'nothing is too wondrous for You,' that is, from the time He created the world He saw everything that would happen until the end of time. (*Tiferet Tzion*)

רַבִּי חַגַּי בְּשֵׁם רַבִּי יִצְחָק אָמַר 'וְאַתָּה שְׁלֹמֹה בְנִי דַע אֶת אֱלֹהֵי אָבִיךָ וְעָבְדֵהוּ בְּלֵב שָׁלֵם וּבְנֶפֶשׁ חֲפֵצָה כִּי כָל לְבָבוֹת דּוֹרֵשׁ ה' וְכָל יֵצֶר מַחֲשָׁבוֹת מֵבִין אִם תִּדְרְשֶׁנּוּ יִמָּצֵא לָךְ וְאִם תַּעַזְבֶנּוּ יַזְנִיחֲךָ לָעַד' (דה"א כח, ט) קֹדֶם עַד שֶׁלֹּא נוֹצְרָה מַחֲשָׁבָה בְּלִבּוֹ שֶׁל אָדָם כְּבָר הִיא גְלוּיָה לְפָנֶיךָ

R. Ḥaggai said in R. Isaac's name: 'And you, my son Solomon, know the God of your father, and serve Him with a whole heart and with a willing mind, for the Lord searches all hearts and discerns the design (*yetzer*) of every thought; if you seek Him He will be available to you, but if you forsake Him He will abandon you forever'

(I Chronicles 28:9). **Even before a thought is born (*notzrah*) in a man's heart, it is already revealed before You.**

From the verse 'nothing is too wondrous for You' cited by R. Simon in the previous section, we learn that actions that will in the future be executed were known to God from the beginning. R. Ḥaggai cites the verse from I Chronicles to show that God also knew at the time of creation all the thoughts that man would ever think. (*Tiferet Tzion*)

רַבִּי יוּדָן בְּשֵׁם רַבִּי יִצְחָק קֹדֶם עַד שֶׁלֹּא נוֹצַר יְצוּר כְּבָר מַחֲשַׁבְתּוֹ גְלוּיָה לְפָנֶיךָ

R. Judan said in R. Isaac's name: Even before a creature is created, his thought is already known to You.

Since the verse from I Chronicles reads 'for the Lord searches all hearts,' it means He knows all of man's thoughts. Why then does it continue 'and discerns the design of every thought'? The answer is now given in the rubric 'even before a thought is born....' The meaning is that the existence of thoughts and desires comes before the choices made by the heart. The soul brings many visions to the forefront of the imagination, some of them potentially evil such as visions of temptation, pride, anger, and so forth, and then the person has to fight his evil inclination. The heart is the controlling organ that decides which path to choose.

אָמַר רַ' יוּדָן לְגַרְמֵהּ 'כִּי אֵין מִלָּה בִּלְשׁוֹנִי הֵן ה' יָדַעְתָּ כֻלָּהּ' (תהלים קלט, ד) קֹדֶם עַד שֶׁלֹּא יֵאָרֵשׁ לְשׁוֹנוֹ דִּבּוּר כְּבָר 'הֵן ה' יָדַעְתָּ כֻלָּהּ'

R. Judan said on his own behalf: 'There is not a word on my tongue but that You, O Lord, know it well' (Psalms 139:4) – even before [a man's] tongue gives expression to speech, 'You, O Lord, know it well.'

From what we have learned above, we know only in a general way that God foresees man's thoughts whether they are for good or evil. R. Judan, therefore, brings a verse as a proof-text that even the details of man's thoughts are known. That is the force of the phrase, 'You know it well.' This, then, now becomes the interpretation of our original text: 'And God saw all that He had made and behold' – He beheld all that would ever be.

* * *

Seed Thoughts

There is a medical expression known as tunnel vision. That means that a person can see directly in front of him, but not the wider perspective that includes also some perception of the visual area to the right or to the left without turning his head.

Many people have mental tunnel vision. Their ideological commitments are so intense that they only see what they want to see and can only comprehend that which fits into their concept of things. If a point of view that is even slightly to the left or right is expressed, it is seen as an instant challenge.

Tunnel vision exists in religion, in politics, and wherever human beings compete with each other. We cannot see everything in one glance as does the Almighty. But we can make a major effort to deepen our perspective, widen our horizons, expand the threshold of our tolerance, and widen the tunnel that limits our vision of life.

* * *

Additional Commentary

R. Simon b. Lakish says

He is responding to the use of the *vav* in *ve-hineih.* The word *hineih* makes a statement and the letter *vav* changes the meaning and adds something new. So he interprets the phrase, 'behold it was very good,' to refer to this world. But as for '*and* behold…' he adds his interpretation. God created man to lead a life of difficulty by having to struggle for a livelihood, face the anxieties in raising children, experience illnesses that afflict him from time to time, and many other things. So Scripture comes to tell us that the main goal of man's life is the world-to-come, which is achievable only through suffering. These sufferings motivate a person to want to repent, to change his ways and perform as many acts of charity as he can, as it is written, 'The way to the moral life is through chastisement.' In this respect the verse says, 'and God saw all that He had made,' which refers to this world with its six days of labor, bringing in their train bothersome obligations, suffering, and aggravation. But the verse continues, 'and behold it was very good,' which means that all the aforementioned help transform the person so that he may be entitled to eternal life. (*Tiferet Tzion*)

Parashah Nine, Midrash Four

רַבִּי חָמָא בַּר חֲנִינָא וְרַבִּי יוֹנָתָן רַבִּי חָמָא בַּר חֲנִינָא אָמַר מָשָׁל לְמֶלֶךְ שֶׁבָּנָה פְּלָטִין
רָאָה אוֹתָהּ וְעָרְבָה לוֹ אָמַר פְּלָטִין פְּלָטִין הַלְוַאי תְּהֵא מַעֲלַת חֵן לְפָנַי בְּכָל עֵת
כְּשֵׁם שֶׁהֶעֱלֵית חֵן לְפָנַי בְּשָׁעָה זוֹ כַּךְ אָמַר הַקָּדוֹשׁ בָּרוּךְ הוּא לְעוֹלָמוֹ עוֹלָמִי
עוֹלָמִי הַלְוַאי תְּהִי מַעֲלֶה חֵן לְפָנַי בְּכָל עֵת כְּשֵׁם שֶׁהֶעֱלֵית חֵן לְפָנַי בְּשָׁעָה זוֹ

R. Ḥama b. R. Ḥanina and R. Jonathan [exposited on the verse 'And
God saw all that He had made, and, behold, it was very good']. R.
Ḥama b. R. Ḥanina said: It can be compared to a king who built a
palace. When he saw it, it pleased him. He then exclaimed, 'O
palace, O palace, may you find favor before me at all times, just as
you find favor before me at this moment.' So too, the Holy One,
blessed be He, said to His world: 'O My world, O My world, may
you find favor before Me at all times just as you have found favor
before Me at this moment.'

These two Rabbis are explaining why on the sixth day it says *very* good,'
whereas on other days of creation it only says 'good.' R. Ḥama explains
the matter with his parable about the king who builds a palace. The
project turns out well and the king likes it. However, he is apprehensive
lest it deteriorate with the passage of time, and therefore articulates his
ardent desire that it should always remain in its beautiful pristine state.
The moral of the parable is that the Almighty blessed the world so that it
should always remain as it was at creation and not be ruined by man's
behavior. The word מאד, *me'od* – very, has the sense of continuity into the
future and being always on the increase. R. Jonathan also explained the
verse by way of a parable, but with a different thrust, as we shall see in the
next section.

רַבִּי יוֹנָתָן אָמַר לְמֶלֶךְ שֶׁהָיָה מַשִּׂיא אֶת בִּתּוֹ וְעָשָׂה לָהּ חֻפָּה וּבַיִת וְסִידָה וְכִיְּרָהּ
וְצִיְּרָהּ וְרָאָה אוֹתָהּ וְעָרְבָה לוֹ אָמַר לָהּ בִּתִּי הַלְוַאי תְּהֵא הַחֻפָּה הַזֹּאת מַעֲלַת חֵן
לְפָנַי בְּכָל עֵת כְּשֵׁם שֶׁהֶעֱלֵית חֵן לְפָנַי בַּשָּׁעָה הַזוֹ כַּךְ אָמַר הַקָּדוֹשׁ בָּרוּךְ הוּא
לְעוֹלָמוֹ עוֹלָמִי עוֹלָמִי הַלְוַאי תְּהֵא מַעֲלַת חֵן לְפָנַי בְּכָל עֵת כְּשֵׁם שֶׁהֶעֱלֵיתָ חֵן
לְפָנַי בַּשָּׁעָה הַזוֹ

348

R. Jonathan said: [The matter can be compared] to a king who gave his daughter in marriage and arranged a bridal chamber and a home for her, which he plastered, paneled, and had murals painted. When he saw it, it pleased him and he said to the bride, 'O my daughter, O my daughter, may this bridal chamber find favor before me at all times just as it finds favor before me at this moment.' So too, the Holy One, blessed be He, said to His world: 'O My world, O My world, may you find favor before Me at all times just as you find favor before Me at this moment.'

R. Jonathan rejects the parable of the palace because a palace is an inanimate object that cannot be held responsible for anything that happens to it. He therefore offers a parable of a princess who is to be married. The princess and her husband can be held responsible for the upkeep and maintenance of the bridal canopy and their new home. Thus mankind is held responsible for the welfare of the world. That is the meaning of the verse, 'And God saw all that He had made and behold it was very good.' God hoped that the creation, which was now so good, would remain good forever. (*Ha-Midrash ha-Mevo'ar*)

* * *

Seed Thoughts

A parent can do the maximum possible for a child's growth, welfare, and education. At a certain point, however, it is no longer up to him. He can only hope and pray that the teachings, the values, and the personal examples shown will have the proper influence. In this respect God is like a parent. He created a good world but He also created man. He filled the world with breathtaking complexity and beauty, but He endowed man with free will. Having created a choosing human being, God Himself limited His own powers. He saw the world and, behold, it was very good. But would it stay good? After all, man was in it. Who could tell, in advance, what man would provoke?

'O My world, O My world, would that you will find favor in My sight at all times.' How poignant that God cannot act differently from any other father. 'O My world,' or, as in the second parable, 'O, my daughter,' would that you should be as pleasant in my eyes in the future as you are now.

There is, however, one respect where God should expect more from us than an ordinary father. We who study His writings know that God is dependent upon man for the Divine Presence in the world to be meaningful. The Dubnow Magid interpreted the text of the priestly benediction as follows: the text reads, 'May the Lord bless you...,' which the Magid said means, '*Let* the Lord bless you and keep you!' God loves you and wants you. Act in such a way that His blessing will reach you.

* * *

Additional Commentary

And God saw

He looked – with the hope that the world would remain in this good condition forever. (*Matnot Kehunah*)

*

The palace and the daughter

R. Ḥama follows the view of Hillel that earth was created first. It has priority as the palace of the king, as we read earlier in the Midrash. There we were told that at the creation of the world God desired to create a close partnership with the lower world and that His abode should be on the earth. Therefore, R. Ḥama compared the world to a palace built by a king. R. Jonathan, however, follows the opinion of the School of Shammai that heaven was created first and is the principle palace of the king. Therefore, he compares heaven to a throne and earth to an ordinary receptacle, and states that the main connection of God to the world is through the Torah, which is the daughter of God, that was given to us. He gives the parable of a king who created a canopy for his daughter. So did God do with the world for the sake of Torah so that in this world the Torah would be coupled with the holy nation. God then blessed the canopy that the coupling would work out so that through it God's abundance and grace would descend from above to the world. (*Tiferet Tzion*)

Parashah Nine, Midrash Five

בְּתוֹרָתוֹ שֶׁל רַבִּי מֵאִיר מָצְאוּ כָתוּב 'וְהִנֵּה טוֹב מְאֹד' וְהִנֵּה טוֹב מוֹת

In R. Meir's Torah they found written, '"And, behold, it was very good" – And, behold, death is good.'

Among the commentators there is a difference of opinion as to the meaning of 'In R. Meir's Torah.' Some believe that the words were written in the margin of his Torah scroll, while others are of the opinion that the reference is to a book of homilies that R. Meir wrote. The rather strange note they found written can be explained as follows: *hineih tov me'od* would mean that life was very good. However, when you add the prefix *vav* and make it *ve-hineih*, it suggests the opposite and it is as though you are saying not only that life is good but that death, too, is good.

אָמַר רַ' שְׁמוּאֵל בַּר נַחְמָן רָכוּב הָיִיתִי עַל כְּתֵפוֹ שֶׁל זְקֵנִי וְעוֹלֶה מֵעִירוֹ לִכְפַר חָנָן דֶּרֶךְ בֵּית שְׁאָן וְשָׁמַעְתִּי אֶת רַ' שִׁמְעוֹן בֶּן רַבִּי אֶלְעָזָר יוֹשֵׁב וְדוֹרֵשׁ בְּשֵׁם רַ' מֵאִיר 'הִנֵּה טוֹב מְאֹד' הִנֵּה טוֹב מוֹת

R. Samuel b. Naḥman said: I was riding on my grandfather's shoulder going up from his own town to Kefar Ḥanan via Bet She'an and I heard R. Simon b. R. Eleazar as he sat and exposited in R. Meir's name: '"Behold, it was very good" – behold, death is good.'

R. Samuel is giving evidence of something he experienced when he was very young – young enough to be carried on his grandfather's shoulders for not a short hike. This additional evidence strengthens the tradition that the aphorism, 'Death is good,' was indeed R. Meir's. Of interest is the fact that, according to R. Simon b. Eleazar, R. Meir's deduction was not based on the *vav* of *ve-hineih* and the question as to how R. Meir derived this idea arises. The RaSHaSH (Rabbi Samuel Sassoon) explains it by what is known as the *At-Bash* method of hermeneutics, by which the first letter of the alphabet is replaced by the last letter of the alphabet, the second letter by the next to last letter, and so on. By this method, the letter *alef* of מאד can replace the letter *taf,* and the letter *daled* can replace the letter *vav.* Thus אדם can become מות = death. There are other interpretations. For

351

example, the word 'very' implies that creation has reached its maximum and thereafter only a process of deterioration can begin ultimately resulting in death. How then do you interpret the extra *vav*, 'and'? Here the innovative idea is that death was decreed even for the righteous even though that appeared to be against the purposes of creation. That is why the text reads *ve-hineih* with a *vav* to indicate that the very opposite is intended from what we expect. The entrance of death as a theme now brings into play reflections on the meaning of death.

רַבִּי חָמָא בַּר חֲנִינָא וְרַבִּי יוֹנָתָן רַבִּי חָמָא בַּר חֲנִינָא אָמַר רָאוּי הָיָה אָדָם הָרִאשׁוֹן
שֶׁלֹּא לִטְעֹם טַעַם מִיתָה וְלָמָּה נִקְנְסָה בּוֹ מִיתָה אֶלָּא צָפָה הַקָּדוֹשׁ בָּרוּךְ הוּא
שֶׁנְּבוּכַדְנֶצַּר וְחִירָם מֶלֶךְ צוֹר עֲתִידִין לַעֲשׂוֹת עַצְמָן אֱלֹהוּת וּלְפִיכָךְ נִקְנְסָה בּוֹ
מִיתָה הֲדָא הוּא דִכְתִיב 'בְּעֵדֶן גַּן אֱלֹהִים הָיִיתָ' (יחזקאל כח, יג) וְכִי בְגַן עֵדֶן הָיָה
חִירָם אֶתְמָהָא אֶלָּא אָמַר לוֹ אַתָּה הוּא שֶׁגָּרַמְתָּ לְאוֹתוֹ שֶׁבְּעֵדֶן שֶׁיָּמוּת

R. Ḥama b. R. Ḥanina and R. Jonathan [offered explanations]. R. Ḥama b. R. Ḥanina said: Adam deserved to be spared the experience of death. Why then was the penalty of death decreed against him? Because the Holy One, blessed be He, foresaw that Nebuchadnezzar and Hiram, king of Tyre, would make gods of themselves. Therefore was death decreed against [Adam], as it is written, 'You were in Eden, the garden of God' (Ezekiel 28:13). Was then Hiram in Eden? Surely not! [God] said thus to him: 'It is you who caused him who was in Eden (i.e., Adam) to die.'

The proof-verse is from the dirge that the prophet Ezekiel recited over Hiram, king of Tyre. Since the verse, taken literally, is almost incomprehensible, R. Ḥama was able to interpret it with respect to the death of Adam. Adam did not deserve the punishment of death for what in reality was a relatively minor sin, and for which he repented. The punishment was not intended for Adam, but rather for future generations. Nebuchadnezzar and Hiram claimed to be gods, and the way to prove to humanity that they were not gods was to have them die. However, they as individuals could not be sentenced to death, so the whole of humanity, starting with Adam, had to have the experience of death. Mirkin points out that in the case of Hiram the texts quoted are much more appropriate for Adam. There is the reference to the Garden of Eden, which certainly could not apply to Hiram, as well as verses not quoted in the *midrash* but from the same context in Ezekiel, 'Every precious stone… and gold beautifully wrought for you, mined for you, prepared the day you were

created,' which certainly applies more to Adam and thus enabled the
midrash to make its connection. But, then, how could it be that because of
these two wicked men and other individuals like them that all mankind
should suffer the penalty of death? The answer is that the purpose of death
is not punishment, but to create the greatest of all motivations for
repentance – fear of death and the punishment of hell. (RZWE)

רַבִּי חִיָּא בַר בְּרַתֵּהּ דְּרַ' בֶּרֶכְיָה בְּרֶכְיָה מִשּׁוּם רַבִּי בֶּרֶכְיָה 'אַתְּ כְּרוּב מִמְשַׁח' (שם שם, יד)
אַתְּ הוּא שֶׁגְּרַמְתָּ לְאוֹתוֹ כְרוּב שֶׁיָּמוּת

**R. Ḥiyya, the son of R. Berekhiah's daughter, in the name of R.
Berekhiah: 'You were the far-covering cherub (*kheruv*)' (Ezekiel 28:14).**

Ezekiel 28:13 reads, 'You were in Eden, the garden of God' and verse 14
goes on to say 'you were the far-covering cherub.' The entire section refers
to Hiram, king of Tyre, and the *midrash* uses the words Eden and cherub
to make the connection to Adam. You, Hiram, made it inevitable that the
cherub, Adam, would die. The reference is to the time after Adam was
expelled from the Garden of Eden and the cherubs prevented him from
entering, even though he had repented for his sin. Apparently, even the
repentance did not influence the decree to be changed because God
foresaw that Hiram would be descended from him. (*Tiferet Tzion*)

אָמַר לוֹ רַבִּי יוֹנָתָן אִם כֵּן יִגְזֹר מִיתָה עַל הָרְשָׁעִים וְאַל יִגְזֹר מִיתָה עַל הַצַּדִּיקִים
אֶלָּא שֶׁלֹּא יְהוּ הָרְשָׁעִים עוֹשִׂים תְּשׁוּבָה שֶׁל רְמִיּוּת וְשֶׁלֹּא יְהוּ הָרְשָׁעִים אוֹמְרִים
כְּלוּם הַצַּדִּיקִים חַיִּים אֶלָּא שֶׁהֵן מְסַגְּלִין מִצְוֹת וּמַעֲשִׂים טוֹבִים אַף אָנוּ נְסַגֵּל
מִצְוֹת וּמַעֲשִׂים טוֹבִים נִמְצֵאת עֲשִׂיָּה שֶׁלֹּא לִשְׁמָהּ

**R. Jonathan said to [R. Ḥama b. R. Ḥanina]: If so, He should have
decreed death for the wicked and not decreed death for the
righteous! The reason is lest the wicked perform fraudulent repentance, and so that the wicked should not say, 'Surely the righteous
live only because they treasure up religious acts and good deeds; so
shall we too lay up a store of religious acts and good deeds,' and
their performance of such would not be with the correct motives.**

After the diversion by R. Ḥiyya, R. Jonathan responds to R. Ḥama. Death
was decreed for the righteous so that the wicked would not benefit from
fraudulent penitence. If righteous people did not die, the wicked would
realize that they were being rewarded for their good deeds and they, too,
would observe *mitzvot* even though they did not really believe in them. In
order to prevent this fraud the righteous also had to experience death.

רַבִּי יוֹחָנָן וְר' שִׁמְעוֹן בֶּן לָקִישׁ רַבִּי יוֹחָנָן אָמַר מִפְּנֵי מָה נִגְזְרָה מִיתָה עַל הָרְשָׁעִים
אֶלָּא כָּל זְמַן שֶׁהָרְשָׁעִים חַיִּים הֵם מַכְעִיסִים לְהַקָּדוֹשׁ בָּרוּךְ הוּא הָדָא הוּא דִּכְתִיב
'הוֹגַעְתֶּם ה' בְּדִבְרֵיכֶם' (מלאכי ב, יז) כֵּיוָן שֶׁהֵם מֵתִים הֵן פּוֹסְקִים מִלְהַכְעִיס
לְהַקָּדוֹשׁ בָּרוּךְ הוּא שֶׁנֶּאֱמַר 'שָׁם רְשָׁעִים חָדְלוּ רֹגֶז' (איוב ג, יז) שָׁם חָדְלוּ
מִלְהַכְעִיס לְהַקָּדוֹשׁ בָּרוּךְ הוּא מִפְּנֵי מָה נִגְזְרָה מִיתָה עַל הַצַּדִּיקִים אֶלָּא כָּל זְמַן
שֶׁהַצַּדִּיקִים חַיִּים הֵם נִלְחָמִים עִם יִצְרָן כֵּיוָן שֶׁהֵם מֵתִים הֵם נָחִין הָדָא הוּא
דִּכְתִיב 'וְשָׁם יָנוּחוּ יְגִיעֵי כֹחַ' (שם שם, שם) דַּיֵּנוּ מַה שֶּׁיָּגַעְנוּ

R. Joḥanan and R. Simon b. Lakish [discussed this matter]. R. Joḥanan said: Why was death decreed against the wicked? Because as long as the wicked live they anger the Holy One, blessed be He, as it is written, 'You have wearied the Lord with your talk' (Malachi 2:17), but when they die they cease to anger the Holy One, blessed be He, as it is said, 'There the wicked cease from troubling' (Job 3:17), which means, there the wicked cease from enraging the Holy One, blessed be He. Why was death decreed against the righteous? Because as long as the righteous live they must struggle against their evil inclinations, but when they die they enjoy rest, as it is written, 'There rest those whose strength is spent' (ibid.) — [they say,] 'We have labored enough!'

R. Joḥanan refused to accept the theory that the righteous have to die because of the wicked. Therefore he posits another theory, for which he finds support in the Bible. The wicked die because throughout their life they anger God. The righteous die because throughout their life they have fought the evil inclination and for them death brings relief, freedom, and peace.

וְר' שִׁמְעוֹן בֶּן לָקִישׁ אָמַר לִתֵּן שָׂכָר לְאֵלּוּ בְּכִפְלַיִם וּלְהִפָּרַע מֵאֵלּוּ בְּכִפְלַיִם לִתֵּן
שָׂכָר לַצַּדִּיקִים שֶׁלֹּא הָיוּ רְאוּיִים לִטְעֹם טַעַם מִיתָה וְקִבְּלוּ עֲלֵיהֶם טַעַם מִיתָה
לְפִיכָךְ 'לָכֵן בְּאַרְצָם מִשְׁנֶה יִירָשׁוּ' (ישעיה סא, ז) וּלְהִפָּרַע מִן הָרְשָׁעִים שֶׁלֹּא הָיוּ
צַדִּיקִים רְאוּיִים לִטְעֹם טַעַם מִיתָה וּבִשְׁבִילָן קִבְּלוּ עֲלֵיהֶן מִיתָה לְפִיכָךְ 'וּמִשְׁנֶה
שִׁבָּרוֹן שָׁבְרֵם' (ירמיהו יז, יח)

But R. Simon b. Lakish said: [Death was decreed] in order to reward [the righteous] in double measure and to punish [the wicked] in double measure. To reward the righteous, who do not deserve to experience death, but accepted on themselves the experience of death — 'therefore in their land [Gan Eden] they shall inherit double' (Isaiah 61:7); and to punish the wicked, since the righteous had not deserved death yet accepted it on their account; therefore 'they will be shattered with double destruction' (Jeremiah 17:18).

R. Simon b. Lakish disagreed with his mentor and colleague. He believed that death does comes to the righteous because of the wicked, but there is still some consolation. The righteous will receive a double reward in Paradise because they did not deserve death but accepted it so that the principle of free choice and true and sincere repentance should prevail in the world. The wicked will receive a double punishment – for the evil of their ways and because they forced death on the righteous as well.

* * *

Seed Thoughts

Sometimes you have to take exception even to what a *midrash* says. On the one hand, who can argue with someone of the stature of R. Jonathan? On the other hand, he states that the reason death was decreed for the righteous was so that the wicked should not be allowed a fraudulent repentance. That is to say, when they see the righteous flourishing with long life and ascribe it to their observance of the commandments they would do the same without believing in it and without meaning it but only to reap the reward.

The commentators fall over each other in condemning this kind of be-havior. To perform holy acts and not believe an iota in what they were doing! Can there be anything more spiritually fraudulent than that? Who can disagree with such pious sentiments?

And yet, let it be stated as forcefully as possible that this view flies in the face of one of the most beautiful of all Jewish teachings. מתוך שלא לשמה בא לשמה – 'Doing *mitzvot* for non-altruistic reasons leads to doing them for their own sake.' Or, to put it another way, very often a person will begin to do something for the wrong reasons, and will end up doing it for the right reasons.

How does this happen? The person gets to like what he is doing. He begins to realize that the experience can become meaningful for him. In the case of Judaism we have the confidence of what is called המאור שביהדות, 'the light of Judaism' – the belief that in every Jewish symbol there is contained something of the great message of Judaism. Sooner or later that message – that light – will reveal itself.

The Jewish teaching of 'what is not for its own sake may become for its own sake' has a deep foundation in the very psychology of the human being. In the early beginnings of psychology there was the James–Lange theory of the emotions that expressed itself in this way: You do not see the bear, are afraid, and run. You see the bear, run, and are afraid. It is the action that stokes the emotion and not the other way round. John Dewey in his classic book, *Human Nature and Conduct*, sees in the formation of good routine habits, the way – the only way – to influence moral conduct.

If someone were to tell me that a group of Jews decided to observe the commandments, but would not accept the theological foundations that are usually associated with them, I might not be overjoyed, but I would certainly look upon it as a great opportunity. I have great confidence in the light of Judaism that would ultimately reveal itself. They might be beginning for the wrong reasons, but they may very well end up for the right reasons. I would invite all the 'wicked' of our *midrash* to observe the commandments for all the 'fraudulent reasons.' For many of them it will turn out to be מתוך שלא לשמה בא לשמה.

* * *

Additional Commentary

In R. Meir's Torah

Maybe R. Meir saw some similarity in the pronunciation and meaning of *mavet* (death) and *me'od* (very). For example Jonah 4:9, 'I am greatly angry even unto death' where the meaning is I am very angry, or Song of Songs 8:6, 'For love is fierce as death,' meaning it is very strong, or Jeremiah as quoted in *Exodus Rabbah* 31:10, 'Beat us until we die, as it is written, "For You have despised us very much,"' or the commentary of RaSHaSH quoted in our commentary to the text. (Mirkin).

*

Lest the wicked perform fraudulent repentance

There are two categories of the wicked. The first try to hide their inner thoughts from God because of their belief that He does not know the thoughts of man. The second category try to hide their acts under the mistaken notion that God does not see their acts if they are hidden in the dark. Thus, in private they act like the wicked Zimri and in public like the pious Pinḥas. They assumed that a pretended public repentance would suffice. But this is fraudulent. The first group who think they can hide their thoughts figure that the righteous achieve eternal life because of the accumulation of good deeds. They assume, incorrectly, that the true worship of God is external. Therefore it is easy for them to do the same even though their heart is not in it. Such people do not deserve eternal life. (*Tiferet Tzion*)

*

You have wearied the Lord

How can the term weary be used in connection with God? The answer is that this remains the intention of the wicked, namely to weary God. The verse says 'with their talk' and not with their deeds. From this we learn that even when they do not have the power to do evil deeds they still anger God with their words. That is why he says, so long as the wicked live they anger God. (*Tiferet Tzion*)

*

We have labored enough

But surely a real *tzaddik* would want to live longer in order to do more good deeds? The response to this is that they have done enough. God does not remove a righteous one from the earth until he has accomplished all that he is meant to accomplish, at which point he no longer has to be in the world and his reward is as though he had lived forever and conquered the evil inclination forever.

*

Is there hope for the wicked?

The righteous die because of the sins of their generation (*Shir ha-Shirim Rabbah*) and by their death they atone for the generation. They, therefore, are entitled to that portion of Paradise that would have belonged to the wicked in the world-to-come, had they not been wicked. After all, it was because of the wicked that they, the righteous, tasted death. This is what the verse means in saying, 'Therefore in their land will they inherit double.' It is also very good for the wicked that God gives their portion to the *tzaddik* because that enables them to start paying back the tremendous debt that they owe him. For, if the righteous would not receive this portion, nothing would then help the wicked; he would never be able to enter Paradise and use his portion because he doesn't have the record of doing commandments and good deeds. He would be like a debtor who possesses a large sum of money that is hidden in a place beyond the reach of man. He must then pay back his obligations through hard work and effort. Similarly, if the wicked were not allowed to pay back their debt to God by means of God taking their portion in Paradise and giving it to the *tzaddikim*, their only alternative would be to suffer the tortures of hell forever because of their terrible deeds. Now, however, that God accepts their share in Gan Eden as partial payment of their obligations, their burden of obligation is lightened. (*Tiferet Tzion*)

*

Special Note

Many Hebrew editions of our text quote the verse from Jeremiah 17:18 that concludes our *midrash* incorrectly. Instead of the word שָׁבְרֵם, *shovrem*, which means 'to shatter,' they have substituted the word יִירָשׁוּ, *yirashu*, meaning 'they will inherit.' Most commentators regard the last three words as a scribal or printer's error and assume it is a corruption of Jeremiah 17:18. The *Tiferet Tzion* does not appear to agree. As I understand his interpretation, he has taken two words from Jeremiah – *double* and *destruction* – and combined it with one word of the verse from Isaiah 61:7 meaning to inherit. That has resulted in his most unusual interpretation. I have left the translation of the verse as though it were entirely from Jeremiah, not being certain how else to treat it.

Parashah Nine, Midrash Six

אָמַר רַבִּי שִׁמְעוֹן בֶּן אֶלְעָזָר 'הִנֵּה טוֹב מְאֹד' וְהִנֵּה טוֹבָה שֵׁנָה וְכִי שֵׁנָה טוֹבָה מְאֹד
אַתְמְהָא לֹא כֵן תְּנֵינַן יַיִן וְשֵׁנָה לָרְשָׁעִים נָאֶה לָהֶם וְנָאֶה לָעוֹלָם אֶלָּא מִתּוֹךְ
שֶׁאָדָם יָשֵׁן קִמְעָא הוּא עוֹמֵד וְיָגֵעַ בַּתּוֹרָה הַרְבֵּה

R. Simon b. Eleazar said: 'Behold, it was very good' [is not written;
'*And*, behold it was very good'] means: and, behold, sleep was good.
Is sleep very good?! I am amazed! Were we not taught, 'Wine and
sleep are beneficial to the wicked and beneficial to the world'?! But
[R. Simon meant] that when a man sleeps a little, he can arise and
toil much in the study of the Torah.

This thought is also derived from the letter *vav* – '*and* behold,' which,
according to R. Simon, indicates that something else was also very good,
and he decides that the something else is sleep. It is possible that the
interpretation is influenced by the earlier interpretations that refer to
death as very good – sleep being a form of death, in that it is a condition
of inactivity. The objection of the *midrash* is based on a *mishnah* (Tractate
Avodah Zarah 71b) that states that sleep and wine are good for the wicked
and good for the world because while he is sleeping the wicked person is
not sinning, but it continues that sleep is bad for the righteous. The *midrash*
therefore re-interprets R. Simeon to mean that he meant a little sleep is
very good because it refreshes and enables the person to study more
Torah.

* * *

Seed Thoughts

It is no accident that immediately after the *midrash* that interprets 'very
good' as death, we have another exposition that defines 'very good' as
referring to sleep.

In the Jewish tradition sleep has always been used as a popular way of
speaking about death. This is not surprising when you consider that death
is the greatest of all mysteries. There is very little that a person who is alive
can say about death since no one has come back from the other side.
Even testimony from those who have reached the brink and returned is

not necessarily proof of anything. In the face of this lack of real knowledge, any analogy that will help is acceptable and the parable of sleep is one of them.

Sleep is defined in the tradition as representing one sixtieth of death. What it means is that the body functions but without consciousness. This is somewhat surprising since in death the body does not function either and there may be consciousness depending upon how you define the concept of soul. Perhaps the parable resides in the fact that the human being cannot function during sleep, which is a sort of paralysis, and this is its resemblance to death.

Sleep is also explained as one of life's greatest miracles. The fact that you go to sleep at night, lose consciousness, and then get up in the morning with the return of your strength is perceived as a great miracle. The parable here is not death *per se*, but the concept of resurrection. The last verse of the *piyyut* 'Adon Olam' might be perceived as applying in both dimensions: 'Into Your hand I commit my spirit when I sleep and when I awake, and, with my spirit my body also. The Lord is with me, I shall not fear.'

This, then, is the real comparison with sleep – not death but resurrection. Sleep prepares us with strength to study more Torah; resurrection prepares us to serve God fully and exclusively with our good inclination.

Since resurrection (*tehiat ha-meitim*) is a concept that is meant to take place on this earth and as a precursor to the Messiah, even the wicked can be included in it. In sleep they do not sin. At the resurrection sin would be meaningless. They, too, will then have an opportunity to repent and be included in the final redemption.

* * *

Additional Commentary

Behold sleep was good

The expression, 'very good,' does not necessarily have to be used as a means of comparison to something else or to some earlier time. R. Simon b. Eleazar interprets it as referring to sleep. Sleep transforms a person into a new and refreshed being, better than what he was before. The adjective 'very good' is thus most appropriate. Another fact to be taken into consideration is the fact that in the context of the creation story sleep was a new phenomenon never before experienced. This was alluded to in an earlier *midrash*, when at the creation story the angels mistakenly took Adam to be a divine being and wanted to adore him with the paean, 'Holy, holy, holy.' God prevented them by placing man in a deep sleep, at which the angels realized that he was not divine. It is thus appropriate that the text says 'very good' because the word *ve-hineih* begins with a *vav* whose purpose is to indicate an opposite meaning from what is stated or something innovative. So, He showed the heavenly angels something different, namely, that by means of sleep man becomes 'very good' in the sense that he can no longer be mistaken for someone else. It is also the purpose of the text to issue a warning to the righteous (who might be tempted to divert their sleeping time to the study of Torah) not to curtail their sleeping time because if they have enough sleep, in the long run they will be able to study much more Torah. (*Tiferet Tzion*)

Parashah Nine, Midrash Seven

רַבִּי נַחְמָן בַּר שְׁמוּאֵל בַּר נַחְמָן בְּשֵׁם רַב שְׁמוּאֵל בַּר נַחְמָן אָמַר 'הִנֵּה טוֹב מְאֹד'
זֶה יֵצֶר טוֹב 'וְהִנֵּה טוֹב מְאֹד' זֶה יֵצֶר רָע

R. Naḥman b. R. Samuel b. R. Naḥman said in R. Samuel b. R. Naḥman's name: 'Behold it was very good' is the good inclination; 'And behold it was very good' is the evil inclination.

The style of this *midrash* is the same as in the previous one. I would have thought that only the good inclination was meant by the word *good*. Now that the *vav* has been added to *ve-hineih*, which usually alludes to something that is opposite, it must also refer to the evil inclination.

וְכִי יֵצֶר הָרַע טוֹב מְאֹד אַתְמָהָא אֶלָּא שֶׁאִלּוּלֵי יֵצֶר הָרַע לֹא בָּנָה אָדָם בַּיִת וְלֹא
נָשָׂא אִשָּׁה וְלֹא הוֹלִיד וְלֹא נָשָׂא וְנָתָן

Can then the evil inclination be [described as] very good?! That would be extraordinary! But, were it not for the evil inclination, no man would build a house, marry a woman, or beget children, or engage in commerce.

The usual meaning of 'evil inclination' is sexual desire and, indeed, sexual desire is an important motivation in building a home and family. This *midrash*, however, adds an extra dimension and interprets 'evil inclination' as referring also to jealousy, which leads to competitiveness and is a driving force in domestic as well as economic activity.

וְכֵן שְׁלֹמֹה אוֹמֵר 'כִּי הִיא קִנְאַת אִישׁ מֵרֵעֵהוּ' (קהלת ד, ד)

And thus said Solomon: 'I have also noted that all labor and skillful enterprise come from men's envy of each other' (Ecclesiastes 4:4).

The verse from Ecclesiastes says it all. Only competition, which Solomon described as jealousy, motivates society. This is the significance of the addition of the *vav*. The fact that a person wishes to emulate the good things possessed by his neighbor and even add to it is very good for the progress and development of the world. The word *me'od*, very, also has a special accentuation. The fact that people make an effort to acquire

362

possessions is good. It is *me'od*, which means *midah merubah* – a greater effort or extra effort in strength as well as in property. The *me'od* is good. (*Ha-Midrash ha-Mevo'ar*)

* * *

Seed Thoughts

The conflict between spirituality and materialism has no basis in reality. The same can be said of spirituality and secularism, if by that is meant a concern with worldly needs.

Our *midrash* identifies the good inclination with spirituality and the evil inclination with materialism. Of course, it is well aware that there is evil in the world and that human beings make wicked choices. It is the choices that are wrong, however, and not the substance.

Sex is not evil because it is sex. It can be used for building a marriage, a home, and a family. Used in that manner it fulfills the purpose of creation and civilization. Used to exploit women or children, or men for that matter, or to cater to lasciviousness for fun and games, it is guilty of besmirching and belittling one of the greatest of all human attributes. The same could be said of and applied to money, power, honor, and the various other goals of human ambition.

The true saint is not the one who wallows in spirituality. The true saint in Judaism is the one who has found the right balance between spirituality and materialism that will elevate man to his highest.

* * *

Additional Commentary

If not for the evil inclination
For the purpose of the higher life and true fear of the Lord, unquestionably the good inclination is superior because it educates and brings one to the good life. The evil inclination is not good in itself, but when a moral vacuum is created it can be controlled and re-directed and one can receive a reward for this. When it comes to material matters, the evil inclination is very effective. It arouses envy in the heart of a person to try to imitate his neighbor ('keep up with the Cohens') and through this kind of competition the world is built. (*Yefei To'ar*)

*

And behold it was very good is the evil inclination
The expression, 'very good,' should not be seen merely as a point of comparison to something else or to an earlier time. Through the good inclination man elevates himself from day to day. The *vav* in *ve-hineih* has the

effect of changing the meaning around and being innovative. It makes the point about the evil inclination that although it starts out with bad potential, it can have the effect of making man 'very good.' What happens is that the good inclination makes him 'very good' spiritually, while the evil inclination makes him 'very good' materially, and these material things are also very important as underpinnings to spirituality.

Parashah Nine, Midrash Eight

אָמַר רַב הוּנָא 'הִנֵּה טוֹב מְאֹד' זוֹ מִדַּת הַטּוֹב 'וְהִנֵּה טוֹב מְאֹד' זוֹ מִדַּת יִסּוּרִין

R. Huna said: 'Behold, it was very good' is happiness; 'And behold it was very good' is suffering.

If it had only said, 'Behold it was very good,' I would have said it refers to the life of happiness, for that is God's purpose in providing the environment of the world for man. The addition of the *vav* which, as explained in earlier *midrashim*, directs our attention to the opposite quality, in this case suffering, that can sometimes motivate a person to surrender himself to God.

וְכִי מִדַּת יִסּוּרִין טוֹבָה מְאֹד אַתְמָהָא אֶלָּא שֶׁעַל יָדֶיהָ הַבְּרִיּוֹת בָּאִים לְחַיֵּי הָעוֹלָם הַבָּא

But can suffering [be described as] very good?! That is amazing! It is in fact so, because through it men attain life of the future world.

But can suffering really be considered good? It can for some persons who can only be awakened to life's purposes through suffering.

וְכֵן שְׁלֹמֹה אוֹמֵר 'וְדֶרֶךְ חַיִּים תּוֹכְחוֹת מוּסָר' (משלי ו, כג) אֲמַרְתְּ צֵא וּרְאֵה אֵיזֶהוּ דֶרֶךְ מְבִיאָה אֶת הָאָדָם לְחַיֵּי הָעוֹלָם הַבָּא הֱוֵי אוֹמֵר זוֹ מִדַּת יִסּוּרִין

And so said Solomon: 'And the way to life is the rebuke that disciplines' (Proverbs 6:23). Now, go forth and see which path leads man to the life of the future world? Surely it is [the path of] suffering.

The text in Proverbs designates chastisement as the way to life. But the term מוסר, *musar*, which is rendered as chastisement or instruction, is from the same root as יסורין, *yissurin*, meaning suffering. From this the conclusion is derived that suffering can be a source of meaning and a way to the future world. Thus the term *ve-hineih* would indicate that even the opposite of the good, that is, suffering, can be a vehicle that leads to the good.

* * *

Seed Thoughts

The classic literature of Judaism uses the concept of suffering as being good rather freely. Our *midrash* is a good example. In the Book of Job (6:2 and 3 et al) the argument is summarily and decisively rejected by Job himself, yet it continues to appear.

First of all, says Job, you cannot prove that the purpose of suffering is moral and ethical. Secondly, who is to judge what is light suffering and what is major. All I can tell you, says Job, is that my suffering made life so unbearable that I know that it is not possible to suffer as I did and so many others do and still serve God. Even after it is all over, its meaning paralyzes you and makes it very difficult to come to moral decisions.

Why, then, does the ploy with suffering persist? Because it is always with us. Because we cannot suffer without meaning. Sometimes even an unconvincing meaning is better than no meaning at all.

* * *

Additional Commentary

And the way to life is the rebuke that disciplines

The first part of the verse quoted from Proverbs reads, 'For the command-ment is a lamp and the Torah is a light,' and it may be said that even though a person studied Torah and fulfilled commandments he will not inherit eternal life unless he experiences suffering. By means of suffering the heart surrenders and becomes humble. At that moment the Torah enters the heart, whereas for the wicked their Torah knowledge is only skin deep. Note the connection between *musar* and *yissurin.* (RZWE)

*

The dispensation of happiness

There is a type of person who is inner directed and can motivate himself to follow the good way, the good inclination that God has implanted in his heart. It was with such a person in mind that R. Samuel b. Naḥman interpreted the expression 'very good' as referring to the good inclination as stated in the preceding *midrash.* But there is another type of person who is not inner directed and does not motivate himself so that God must arouse him in some external manner. Some people can be aroused intel-lectually by examining logically all the good things that God has provided for them from their birth to the present moment. There are also those who seem to be in a deep sleep, unaware of what is going on in their lives. They have to be aroused through suffering, which forces a person to confront himself and awaken to life's purposes and demands. (*Tiferet Tzion*)

Parashah Nine, Midrash Nine

אָמַר רַ' זְעֵירָא 'הִנֵּה טוֹב מְאֹד' זוֹ גַּן עֵדֶן 'וְהִנֵּה טוֹב מְאֹד' זוֹ גֵּיהִנָּם

R. Ze'ira said: 'Behold it was very good' is the Garden of Eden; 'And behold, it was very good' is Gehenna.

Once again the *midrash* is expositing the additional *vav*. The Garden of Eden, Paradise, was created to reward the righteous; Gehenna was created to punish the wicked.

וְכִי גֵּיהִנָּם טוֹב מְאֹד אֶתְמְהָא מָשָׁל לְמֶלֶךְ שֶׁהָיָה לוֹ פַּרְדֵּס וְהִכְנִיס לְתוֹכוֹ פּוֹעֲלִים וּבָנָה אוֹצָר עַל פִּתְחוֹ אָמַר כָּל מִי שֶׁהוּא מִתְכַּשֵּׁר בִּמְלֶאכֶת הַפַּרְדֵּס יִכָּנֵס לְאוֹצְרוֹ וְכָל מִי שֶׁאֵינוֹ מִתְכַּשֵּׁר בִּמְלֶאכֶת הַפַּרְדֵּס אַל יִכָּנֵס לְאוֹצְרוֹ כָּךְ כָּל מִי שֶׁהוּא מְסַגֵּל בְּמִצְוֹת וּמַעֲשִׂים טוֹבִים הֲרֵי גַּן עֵדֶן וְכָל מִי שֶׁאֵינוֹ מְסַגֵּל בְּמִצְוֹת וּמַעֲשִׂים טוֹבִים הֲרֵי גֵּיהִנָּם

But can Gehenna [be described as] very good?! How remarkable! This, however, can be compared to a king who had an orchard into which he brought workers. He built a treasure house by its entrance and said: 'Whoever proves himself in the work of the orchard may enter the treasure house, but he who does not prove himself in the work of the orchard may not enter the treasure house.' Thus for him who accumulates religious acts and good deeds, behold there is Paradise; while for him who does not lay up religious acts and good deeds, behold there is Gehenna.

But how could Gehenna ever be considered good? The answer is as a motivation for good behavior which is the point of the parable of the orchard. Or, as the *midrash* says elsewhere, only when God created Gehenna could He say, 'And the Lord saw all that He had made and behold it was very good,' meaning that the existence of hell where the wicked will be punished spurs on humans to do good.

* * *

Seed Thoughts

The *Tiferet Tzion* is one of the most traditional commentators. He uses concepts which, at first glance, may appear to be quite unsophisticated.

367

Thus, it took me quite a while to understand what he was saying about this particular *midrash*. But, if I am correct, what he says is quite sensational.

Heaven and hell are concepts of the mind. They are not to be conceived as having a territorial location. The Garden of Eden in the past may have been associated with space and time. The Garden of Eden of the future is neither space nor time but a state of mind.

If a person does the right thing and feels that it is the right thing, and accumulates *mitzvot*, he then feels an inner glow that is happiness of the highest sort. Paradise cannot be greater than that right here in this world. Of course the same concept is applicable to the world-to-come.

By the same token, if one does the wrong thing, nobody has to speak to him of punishment. He feels it intrinsically. For him, this is Gehenna.

Now, although these concepts on an individual human level are in this world, they are not man made. God has implanted these concepts into the universe together with many other influences as a way of helping man to make the most of his possibilities.

Of course the human being is free – 'Everything is in the hand of heaven except fear of Heaven.' But God did create enabling influences to help us and we should use them to our advantage.

* * *

Additional Commentary

Very good is the Garden of Eden

There are some people who are only aroused or motivated by material things either in the dispensation of happiness or in the dispensation of suffering about which the previous *midrash* spoke. There are others who are motivated by spirituality. The very pious, for example, are excited by the joy that comes to them from doing a commandment or in contemplating the reward that will come to them from it in the world-to-come. Even though they never experienced it, they nonetheless believe they know what their reward in this connection will be.

Those who are not rooted in sin are aroused by remorse when they stumble into sin. They are despondent when they contemplate the degree of their punishment in the world-to-come. This anguish leads them to penitence.

Now it so happens that all creatures that God created in this material world have their counterparts in great abundance in the upper worlds. We know from the stories of Elijah and Elisha that some of these influences are positive. But some can also be negative as the Psalmist says, 'Save my life... from the clutches of a dog' (Psalms 22:21). Through these influences, God is able to offer a good reward to the righteous in Paradise and to the wicked, punishment in Gehenna. That is why the text is able to say about Gehenna and about Gan Eden, 'And God saw all that He had made (i.e., all the influences that He created by which to reward man for his behavior whether in this world or the next) and behold it was very good,' because through them man was able to be elevated to the point where he could be described as 'very good.' (*Tiferet Tzion*)

*

Is Gehenna very good?

The questioner was convinced that R. Ze'ira in his interpretation meant that the time spent in Gehenna is very good, which is absurd, since in Gehenna man cannot repair his behavior. The answer is that the point of reference is this world and that is why the parable of the king and the orchard is introduced. Those who do their work properly will perceive with their own eyes the magnitude of their reward, and those who do not do their work properly also perceive their punishment with their own eyes. Similarly, whoever gathers up good deeds sees Paradise before his eyes literally, meaning he experiences great inner rapture. He who has neglected his work and has not built up a store of good deeds experiences a Gehenna in this world by virtue of the despondency that then comes over him. This prompts him to begin his way back to God and merits the designation 'very good.'

Parashah Nine, Midrash Ten

אָמַר רַבִּי שְׁמוּאֵל בַּר יִצְחָק 'הִנֵּה טוֹב מְאֹד' זֶה מַלְאַךְ חַיִּים 'וְהִנֵּה טוֹב מְאֹד' זֶה
מַלְאַךְ הַמָּוֶת וְכִי מַלְאַךְ הַמָּוֶת טוֹב מְאֹד אַתְמָהָא אֶלָּא לְמֶלֶךְ שֶׁעָשָׂה סְעוּדָה וְזִמֵּן
אֶת הָאוֹרְחִים וְהִכְנִיס לִפְנֵיהֶם תַּמְחוּי מָלֵא כָּל טוֹב אָמַר כָּל מִי שֶׁהוּא אוֹכֵל
וּמְבָרֵךְ אֶת הַמֶּלֶךְ יֹאכַל וְיֶעֱרַב לוֹ וְכָל מִי שֶׁהוּא אוֹכֵל וְאֵינוּ מְבָרֵךְ אֶת הַמֶּלֶךְ יֻתַּז
רֹאשׁוֹ בְּסָיִף

R. Samuel b. R. Isaac said: 'Behold it was very good' is the angel of
life; 'And behold it was very good' is the angel of death. But can the
angel of death [be described as] very good? How remarkable! [It can
be compared] to a king who made a feast, invited the guests, and set
a dish filled with all good things before them. He said, 'Whoever will
eat and bless the king, let him eat and enjoy it; but he who would
eat and not bless the king, let him be decapitated with a sword.'

R. Samuel b. R. Isaac is following the same tack as the other Rabbis in
this *Parashah*, albeit with a different message, as follows in the moral of
the parable.

כָּךְ כָּל מִי שֶׁהוּא מְסַגֵּל בְּמִצְווֹת וּמַעֲשִׂים טוֹבִים הֲרֵי מַלְאַךְ חַיִּים וְכָל מִי שֶׁאֵינוּ
מְסַגֵּל בְּמִצְווֹת וּמַעֲשִׂים טוֹבִים הֲרֵי מַלְאַךְ הַמָּוֶת.

Similarly, for him who lays up precepts and good deeds, lo! there is
the angel of life; while for him who does not lay up precepts and
good deeds, lo! there is the angel of death.

The meaning of the parable is that God invites man to benefit from this
world and says, whoever gathers good deeds will be guarded in life, and
those who do not will merit death. The implication of the additional *vav*
is that this threat motivates people to choose the good way and to reach
that which produces life and the good. (*Ha-Midrash ha-Mevo'ar*)

* * *

Seed Thoughts

The *Tiferet Tzion* once again seems to have gotten the drift of this *midrash*
better than the other commentators. We are not dealing here with a real

entity in using terms like 'the angel of death.' We are dealing with and using a concept to help us understand man. Man can become an angel of death in the sense of ruining his life. Or, he can become an angel of life by affirming his potentialities and making the right moral decisions.

Furthermore, the food that is mentioned in the parable is more than the food we eat. It symbolizes all the good things of this world. The king in the parable is not a worldly king; he is the King of the universe. If, therefore, you handle the affairs of this world in the spirit of the King and His will in creating the universe, you will find great satisfaction. Otherwise, your life will be meaningless.

However, even if the wrong choices are made, all is not lost. Man has that most precious of all possessions – the power to change. Once he realizes that he has chosen the way that leads to death, he can change and often will. It is this quality that makes even the 'angel of death' in him 'very good.'

* * *

Additional Commentary

This is the angel of life
'The angel of life' is a literary way of referring to life eternal. (RZWE)

*

Is the angel of death really 'very good'?
The questioner was quite certain in posing his question that 'angel of death' was to be taken literally and referred to the being who has this tremendous power to create and impose death. So his question is in order: What good comes to man from such an entity that it should be described as 'very good'? The answer is that nothing literal is implied here, but rather the power of good and the power of evil that resides in good itself. That is why we have the parable of the king who made a feast and said whoever eats and blesses the king will find satisfaction. Similarly, whoever eats for the sake of heaven will also find the food tasty and it will become for him the food of life. Whoever eats, however, merely to satisfy his bodily hungers will thereby become an angel of death, that is to say, he will become a victim of severe illnesses through which he will be aroused to repentance and will then also become 'very good.' (*Tiferet Tzion*)

Parashah Nine, Midrash Eleven

אָמַר רַ' שִׁמְעוֹן בַּר אַבָּא 'הִנֵּה טוֹב מְאֹד' זוֹ מִדַּת הַטּוֹב 'וְהִנֵּה טוֹב מְאֹד' זוֹ מִדַּת
הַפֻּרְעָנוּת וְכִי מִדַּת הַפֻּרְעָנוּת טוֹבָה הִיא מְאֹד אֶלָּא שׁוֹקֵד עַל הַפֻּרְעָנוּת הֵיאַךְ
לַהֲבִיאָהּ

**R. Simon b. Abba said: 'Behold, it was very good' is the dispensation
of the good; 'And behold, it was very good' is the dispensation of
punishment. But is the dispensation of punishment very good? It
means that He considers well how to bring it.**

This *midrash* follows the same rubric as the previous *midrashim* in this
parashah and is indeed very similar to *Midrash Eight*. The good is that the
Almighty is very meticulous to see that the punishment fits the sin exactly.
Never does He punish more than necessary in order always to leave an
opening for repentance. (*Ha-Midrash ha-Mevo'ar*)

אָמַר רַבִּי סִימוֹן בְּשֵׁם רַבִּי שִׁמְעוֹן בַּר אַבָּא כָּל הַמִּדּוֹת בָּטְלוּ מִדָּה כְּנֶגֶד מִדָּה לֹא
בָּטְלָה

**R. Simon said in R. Simon bar Abba's name: All measures have
ceased, yet the rule of measure for measure has not ceased.**

Even though all the principles by which the Sanhedrin judged were
suspended after the destruction of the Temple and the end of Jewish
sovereignty, one principle still remains in operation, that of measure for
measure. This refers to matters that will be judged by the heavenly, not
earthly, courts. This is an elaboration of the thought R. Simon bar Abba
expressed in the previous section.

רַבִּי הוּנָא בְּשֵׁם רַ' יוֹסֵי מִתְּחִלַּת בְּרִיָּתוֹ שֶׁל עוֹלָם צָפָה הַקָּדוֹשׁ בָּרוּךְ הוּא שֶׁבַּמִּדָּה
שֶׁאָדָם מוֹדֵד בָּהּ מוֹדְדִין לוֹ לְפִיכָךְ אָמְרוּ חֲכָמִים 'וְהִנֵּה טוֹב מְאֹד' הִנֵּה טוֹב מִדָּה

**R. Huna said in R. Jose's name: From the very beginning of the
world's creation the Holy One, blessed be He, foresaw that it will be
measured to man in the same measure that he measures [for
himself], therefore the Sages said that 'And, behold, it was very
good' means that there is a 'good' measure.**

All of this started at the creation of the world when these principles were also created. This is deduced from וירא, *va-yar* – [God] saw, and מאד, *me'od,* which resembles the word מדה, *middah* – a measure. God favored the principle of measure for measure. (Our text follows the version of Mirkin based on the Theodor-Albeck text, which reads הנה טוב מדה, to be translated as 'There is a fitting dispensation.' Most traditional editions [including *Ha-Midrash ha-Mevo'ar*] end with the phrase זו מדה טובה, translated as 'This is a good measure.' However, as can be seen from the sentence above, the meaning does not change.) This is similar to the interpretation of בכל מאדך, *bekhol me'odekha* – 'with all your might,' in the first paragraph of the *Shema.* There the Sages interpreted the phrase to mean 'You shall love the Lord, your God, wth every measure that He metes out to you.' (*Matnot Kehunah*) Thus, there is a precedent for interpreting the word *me'od* as meaning *middah.*

* * *

Seed Thoughts

Measure for measure is a great principle because it is just. What can be more just than that evil should be punished and good rewarded and all in equal measure? What a unique argument, that by this principle man could engage in self-judgment. There is only one trouble with it. It does not work. This may be too extreme a judgment. It sometimes works in simplistic terms and in areas that are not too serious.

But it did not work in the case of Job, who kept asking God, 'If I am a sinner let me know my sin. I am not aware of having sinned.' We know from the Book of Job that measure for measure was not the principle by which he was being judged. He was being tested by God and Satan. So that measure for measure is only one of the principles by which God rules the world. Putting human beings through a test is another way – witness Job and Abraham.

This, however, does not deny the fact that measure for measure is the principle by which God governs the world. The only problem is that we cannot always see it. Only God can.

Whereas it is true that there is great merit and comfort in the knowledge that God knows what He is doing, the idea of self-reflection in terms of discovering our own inadequacies is only a partial truth and partial answer. In so many areas that have to do with the moral life, we are dealing with faith. Measure for measure works. We may not always understand it but God does. And we'd better believe it, is what the *midrash* is saying.

* * *

Additional Commentary

Therefore Scripture said

Punishment that comes measure for measure is a great blessing for man. It enables him to reflect upon his deeds in order to recognize what aspect of his behavior could have merited punishment and that would open the door to repentance. (RDL; RZWE)

*

He considers well how to bring it

God took good care that the Temple should be destroyed and the Jews be deported to Babylon in summer and not in winter, for they would never have survived the rigors and hardships of that long journey in winter. He was anxious how to make the punishment fit the wrongs committed so that the victims, recognizing this, would be led to repentance. Others say: He caused the Temple to be destroyed two years before its time for had He waited longer, Israel's sins would have condemned them to complete destruction. (Soncino)

*

'Very good' is the dispensation of good

Some people can only be aroused to change their ways by facts that they see with their own eyes. For them God created both the measure of good and the measure of punishment in a relationship of measure for measure. Such a person would be motivated to do good when he is able to perceive why he was punished. He will then see that he was punished in exact accord to what he perpetrated. Therefore, the verse says, 'And God saw all that He had made,' that by means of all of them man could be motivated to be 'very good.'

Parashah Nine, Midrash Twelve

רַבָּנָן אָמְרִי לַהּ בְּשֵׁם רַבִּי חֲנִינָא בַּר אִידִי וְרַבִּי פִּינְחָס וְרַ' חִלְקִיָּה הוּא 'מְאֹד' הוּא
אָדָם הִנּוּן אוֹתִיּוֹת דְּדֵין הִנּוּן אוֹתִיּוֹת דְּדֵין הָדָא הוּ דִכְתִיב 'וַיַּרְא אֱלֹהִים אֶת כָּל
אֲשֶׁר עָשָׂה וְהִנֵּה טוֹב מְאֹד' זֶה אָדָם

Some Rabbis said in the name of R. Ḥanina b. R. Idi, R. Pinḥas, and
R. Ḥilkiah: *Me'od* is identical with *adam* [man], for the letters of one
word are [the same] as the letters of the other. Thus it is written,
'And God saw all that He had made, and, behold, *me'od* was good,'
that is, Adam was good.

This interpretation breaks the continuity of the *vav* rubric and is based on
a straightforward interpretation that does not see *me'od* as meaning 'very'
and describing 'good,' but rather as a noun, meaning man. The logic
seems to be that since man is the pinnacle of the creation story, what the
Almighty saw and described as good must be him.

* * *

Seed Thoughts

Of all the various interpretations that have been presented in the *midrash*
thus far in the interpretation of the word *me'od,* this is the most appealing.
'Very good' now means 'man is good,' for he was the goal of creation. In
the case of all the possibilities that have heretofore been offered, there is
a feeling that the interpretations have been forced. This one is a natural.

Why was the creation of man 'very good'? Because God was satisfied
with His handiwork. He was happy, if such a term can be used about God.
It is, therefore, our job to keep Him happy, so to speak, or, to express it
better, to keep Him satisfied.

Rabbi Ashlag in the preface to his commentary on the Zohar expresses
the purpose of man in this very way – לתת נחת רוח ליוצרו, to give *nachas* to
his creator. I have used the Yiddish word in the translation, rather than
the English 'satisfaction,' because it more aptly describes what man's duty
is – to offer the Almighty on a continual basis proof that He can be satisfied with the fact of man's creation.

The second interpretation continues the development of this theme.

The unique characteristic of man is that in his old age he can and usually does try to rectify the errors of his youth. That is to say, even though we may not always have brought *nachas* to our Maker, we can make it our goal now and in the future.

It is in our hands to make the world stay 'very good.'

* * *

Additional Commentary

Me'od – Adam

In rendering the expression *tov me'od*, the Holy One, blessed be He, was using the name of man (with inverted letters) to hint at the fact that He was very satisfied with the creation of man. This was not said specifically but only by allusion in the same way that one should not state all of a person's good attributes in his presence. (Mirkin)

*

Because most men become repentant and, in their old age, try to make amends for having gone astray in their youth (Tractate Sukkah 53a), therefore, God advanced the letter *mem*, the last letter of *adam*, and placed it at the beginning of the word *me'od* to teach that at the end of his days he corrects and perfects his youth. (*Tiferet Tzion*)

Parashah Nine, Midrash Thirteen

אָמַר רַבִּי שִׁמְעוֹן בֶּן לָקִישׁ 'הִנֵּה טוֹב מְאֹד' זוֹ מַלְכוּת שָׁמָיִם 'וְהִנֵּה טוֹב מְאֹד' זוֹ
מַלְכוּת הָרוֹמִיִּים וְכִי מַלְכוּת הָרוֹמִיִּים טוֹב מְאֹד אֶתְמְהָא אֶלָּא שֶׁהִיא תּוֹבַעַת
דִּיקָיוֹן שֶׁל בְּרִיּוֹת שֶׁנֶּאֱמַר 'אָנֹכִי עָשִׂיתִי אֶרֶץ וְאָדָם עָלֶיהָ בָרָאתִי' (ישעיה מה, יב)

R. Simon b. Lakish said: 'Behold, it was very good' is the kingdom
of heaven; 'And, behold, it was very good' is the Roman Empire. But
can the Roman Empire [be described as] very good?! How strange!
[It can be so described] because it exacts justice for men, as it is
written, 'It was I who made the earth, and created man (*adam*) upon
it' (Isaiah 45:12).

How can the Roman Empire be good, that power that destroyed our
Temple? Indeed, it is often referred to as the evil kingdom. Yet, even the
worst government has this in its favor, that it provides law and order and
gives a citizen an opportunity, through its laws, to seek redress if his rights
are violated. Indeed, the Sages advised, 'Pray for the welfare of the state,
for if it were not for fear of it, a man would swallow his neighbor alive'
(*Ethics of the Fathers* 3:2), and the reference is also to a non-Jewish state.
Isaiah 35:13, which is the continuation of the verse quoted, begins 'I
spurred him on for justice,' implying that God gives man rulership only
so that he could enforce justice. Furthermore, the appearance of the word
adam in the verse from Isaiah, which has the same letters as *me'od*, seems
to be an allusion to our source verse. Thus, R. Simon b. Lakish made the
connection and interpreted 'very good' as referring even to a wicked
government, if it follows the rule of law. The verse in Isaiah refers to
Cyrus; God through the prophet is saying that He brought Cyrus to the
forefront so that justice should be safeguarded. In the case of Cyrus it was
justice for Israel, who had suffered so much under Nebuchadnezzar. But,
in general justice protects human beings from oppression. (Mirkin)

* * *

Seed Thoughts

One version of our *midrash* uses the term 'earthly kingdom,' as opposed to
the 'Kingdom of Heaven,' to imply government. Another text, preferred

in the Theodor-Albeck edition, uses the term 'Roman Empire.' When the latter is used the true intent of the *midrash* becomes clear in a very dramatic fashion.

Rome was the largest empire and greatest government of its day. It brought with it many important contributions to civilization, such as Roman law, which remains the basis for many legal systems to the present day. But Rome was also the most hated of all governments, particularly by the nations and countries that it conquered.

This enables R. Simon b. Lakish to make an extreme point, which I would render to the effect that bad government is better than no government. Even bad government by its very nature has to do something worthwhile even in its own interest. So Mussolini, the fascist dictator, used to boast that in his Italy the trains always ran on time; even bad government has rules. A person can learn to live with it and even protect himself against it.

But 'no government' is anarchy. It is everyone doing 'that which is right in his own eyes.' There is no basis in such a set-up for social living, commerce, or security. Man is a social animal and therefore requires government.

The *midrash* also makes a further point. Granted that we are spiritual beings and as spiritual beings our minds and hearts should be directed to higher things. Certainly, by any standard the rule of God is better then that of man. Unfortunately, we do not have a choice. We have only the earth to contend with and man's rule upon it. We have no right to spend our time in contemplating 'pie in the sky when we die.' The Kingdom of Heaven is not in our hands, only the kingdom of earth. That means government of man by man. God has removed Himself directly from the earth through the process of placing Himself behind the scenes. But He placed man on earth to govern it.

So what are our choices? It could be dog eat dog and every man devouring his neighbor. Or it could be government of the people, by the people, and for the people. The choice is ours.

* * *

Additional Commentary

The kingdom of earth

Some texts read the Roman Empire, possibly because of the close proximity in sound between *adam, me'od,* and *Edom,* which is the term by which Rome is designated in Rabbinic literature. They all have the same letters.

Parashah Nine, Midrash Fourteen

וַיְהִי עֶרֶב וַיְהִי בֹקֶר יוֹם הַשִּׁשִּׁי (בראשית א, לא)

**'And there was evening and there was morning, the sixth day'
(Genesis 1:31).**

The problem is that the word *ha-shishi*, the sixth day, has the prefix of the
letter *heh*, the definite article, which does not occur with any other of the
days of creation.

אָמַר רַבִּי יוּדָן זוֹ שָׁעָה יְתֵרָה שֶׁמּוֹסִיפִין מֵחֹל עַל קֹדֶשׁ וּבָהּ נִגְמְרָה מְלֶאכֶת הָעוֹלָם
עַל כֵּן כְּתִיב 'הַשִּׁשִּׁי'

**R. Judan said: This intimates the extra hour that we add from the
profane to the sacred, and in it the work of creating the world was
finished, therefore it is written '*the* sixth.'**

The letter *heh* is an allusion to the extra hour of the sixth day that is usually
observed as the Sabbath. God, of course, does not need this extra hour
as a precaution because He knows exactly when the Sabbath begins and,
for Him, that last hour of the sixth day is truly the sixth day. But we
humans need that extra protection in order not to transgress the Sabbath.
It may be Sabbath for us, but it is the sixth day for God.

אָמַר רַבִּי סִימוֹן בַּר מָרְתָא עַד כָּאן מוֹנִין לְמִנְיָנוֹ שֶׁל עוֹלָם מִיכָּן וְאֵילַךְ מוֹנִין
לְמִנְיָן אַחֵר

**R. Simon bar Marta said: Hitherto world time was counted, but
henceforth we count by a different reckoning.**

The special lesson has to do with counting time. From the first day of
creation to the sixth day is a time pattern of its own. From the sixth day,
which is the creation of man and onwards, we count from a different point
of departure – the anniversary of man's creation and the completion of
creation. That is the meaning of the emphasis placed on the sixth day,
ha-shishi, *the* sixth day, the last day according to the old counting, the first
day according to the new counting.

* * *

Seed Thoughts

With man a new system of counting began. We are told that the world existed for billions of years. If so, it was the kind of time that does not matter.

Without man, time is meaningless. What is time to God, who is infinite? 'For a thousand years in Your sight are but as yesterday when it is past.' Only with the creation of man does time begin to have meaning. For time is consciousness. People who have lost consciousness say, 'Where am I? What happened?' 'What day is it?' They have no conception of time from the moment they lost consciousness.

The important question for all of us is: What can we do with our time to use it most constructively?

It is of interest to note that the biblical structures for time always seemed to be related to some kind of purpose. The Sabbath is a form of time. It is also related to a purpose, which, though it may not be fulfilled during that time period is meant to be emphasized and repeated. The purpose of Sabbath is to re-create the world as God intended it to be. And if not the entire world, at least the little world of our own creation. That is the meaning of the term זכר למעשה בראשית, *zekher le-ma'aseh breishit* – a remembrance of the work of creation. The Sabbatical year and the Jubilee also had purposes, notably in the areas of social justice, the elimination of debts, and the release from slavery.

All of these structures of time were seen as opportunities to fulfill in greater or lesser form some of the objectives of creation. Even the months of the year were not merely ways of counting. Rosh Ḥodesh, the beginning of the month, with its symbol of the moon became a form of human renewal.

Time is made for man. We cannot extend it. It is not given to us as an open-ended gift. But we can deepen it by adding to it meaning and significance.

* * *

Additional Commentary

The sixth day
The question being raised is not only that of the extra letter *heh*. It is also the fact that 'the sixth day' is followed by *va-yekhulu* – heaven and earth were completed, which applies to the end of the sixth day and not the beginning of it. (RZWE)

*

R. Simon bar Marta

Nowhere is such an Amora mentioned. Theodor explains that the proper reading is *ba meitash ma'aseh*, meaning 'on it creation was weakened.' R. Simon was treating the word *ha-shishi* not as a numeral, but as a verb derived from the root 'to weaken' and was saying that in some fashion creation was weakened on the sixth day just as humans slacken their efforts when they know things are coming to an end. R. Simon seems to be drawing two conclusions from his remarks. The first, that the work slackened toward the end, the second that the *heh* seems to indicate the end of the work and the beginning of something quite new and different on the seventh day. (Mirkin)

*

Hitherto

Up to the sixth day one counted in terms of creation. After the sixth day one counts in other dimensions, weeks, months, Sabbatical year, Jubilee, and so forth. Or, perhaps, he is indicating that after the six thousandth year, a new form of counting will be instituted. (*Matnot Kehunah*)

*

Before the sixth day there was no complete week, so one counted in terms of creation. After the sixth day there took place the first week and the system of counting changed. (Rashi)

*

Up to the sixth day we count from creation: first day, second day, and so forth. But from the creation of man on the sixth day we count the years. Rosh ha-Shanah dates from the creation of man. (*Ha-Midrash ha-Mevo'ar*)

Parashah Ten, Midrash One

וַיְכֻלוּ הַשָּׁמַיִם וְהָאָרֶץ וְכָל צְבָאָם (בראשית ב, א)

'And the heaven and the earth were finished (*va-yekhulu*)' (2:1).

The intention of this *midrash* is to explain the use of the term *va-yekhulu*. The assumption is that it derives from the root כלה, which means 'to cease.' After all, did the heavens cease to exist? It would have been enough for the text to have said 'were completed.' It is in response to this question that a proof-text is brought from Psalms.

כְּתִיב 'לְכָל תִּכְלָה רָאִיתִי קֵץ רְחָבָה מִצְוָתְךָ מְאֹד' (תהלים קיט, צו) לַכֹּל יֵשׁ סִיקוֹסִים שָׁמַיִם וָאָרֶץ יֵשׁ לָהֶן סִיקוֹסִים חוּץ מִדָּבָר אֶחָד שֶׁאֵין לוֹ סִיקוֹסִים וְאֵי זוֹ זוֹ הַתּוֹרָה שֶׁנֶּאֱמַר 'אֲרֻכָּה מֵאֶרֶץ מִדָּהּ וּרְחָבָה מִנִּי יָם' (איוב יא, ט)

It is written, 'I have seen that all things have their limit (*tikhlah*), but Your commandment is broad beyond measure' (Psalms 119:96) — everything has a measure, heaven and earth have a measure. Except one thing which has no measure. What is that? That is the Torah, as it says, 'Its measure is longer than the earth and broader than the sea' (Job 11:9).

The word *tikhlah* derives from the same root as *va-yekhulu* and so the interpretation is as follows: Everything has limitations and boundaries, even heaven and earth, which appear so strong and enduring. Indeed, the Psalmist specifies, 'They shall perish, but You shall endure' (102:27). One thing, however, has no limit — besides, of course, God and Israel — and that is the Torah. Its endurance is limitless, because it represents God's will and wisdom and He is eternal. By contrast, heaven and earth are finite with a beginning and an end.

דָּבָר אַחֵר 'לְכָל תִּכְלָה רָאִיתִי קֵץ' זוֹ מְלֶאכֶת שָׁמַיִם וָאָרֶץ שֶׁנֶּאֱמַר 'וַיְכֻלוּ הַשָּׁמַיִם וְהָאָרֶץ'

Another interpretation: 'I have seen that all things have their limit' refers to the work of the heaven and earth, as it is said, 'And the heaven and the earth were finished.'

The 'other' interpretation now clarifies the literal meaning of the *midrash.* It is not that heaven and earth will cease. God wants them to continue and every day He renews their mandate. It is the work of the creation of heaven and earth that will cease, whereas the work of Torah will never cease.

* * *

Seed Thoughts

What remains so permanently fascinating about Midrash is its ability to yield so much to so many different eyes. In studying the material I discover that I am just as interested in what the commentators have to say as I am about what the Midrash itself says. Midrash is like poetry. It yields multiple meanings. Just as beauty is in the eyes of the beholder, Midrash depends upon the beholder and such insights that his experience and background will help him discern.

Certainly our *midrash* is as clear and simple a document as one would expect to find. After it is handled by the *Tiferet Tzion,* however, it turns out to be complicated and full of allusions and secondary meanings.

The *Tiferet Tzion* brings forward a concept that is quite new to me. The soul is not a static concept; it has reference to many layers of meaning. That which the world regards as the highest form of earthly wisdom, the *Tiferet Tzion* describes as *nefesh.* There is, however, a higher form of wisdom than that which is found on earth. That wisdom has its source in the higher life. It is revealed wisdom and the *Tiferet Tzion* calls it *neshamah,* meaning a higher aspect of the soul.

I find a startling similarity between the *Tiferet Tzion* and his concept of *neshamah* and that of the term *hokhmah,* wisdom, as defined by the *Malbim.* According to the *Malbim* (in his commentary to Proverbs, Chapter 1) *hokhmah* differs from *da'at,* knowledge, and *binah,* understanding, which are the other very high expressions of wisdom, in the sense that the values and assumptions of *hokhmah* go beyond logic and are based upon divine revelation.

Hokhmah is to the *Malbim* what *neshamah* is to the *Tiferet Tzion.* Both agree that Torah is the source of this unique kind of knowledge, whether it is expressed as *neshamah* or as *hokhmah.*

There is one aspect of the *Tiferet Tzion*'s presentation that I still find hard to grasp. If, indeed, *neshamah* has Torah as its source and main nourishment, why should there be such an abyss between the great Torah authorities and lesser scholars. Surely even the disciples of the learned would have some glimmer of the greater truth. How could it be otherwise? But, according to the *Tiferet Tzion* and the many sources that he quotes, that is, indeed, the reality.

Perhaps someone with greater insight will be able to help us understand what is here being claimed.

And again, there is no such thing as a simple *midrash*. It all depends upon who looks at it.

* * *

Additional Commentary

Except one thing

In the case of finite objects, whenever their purpose is accomplished they deteriorate. This holds true for all living things. It applies also to all materialistic forms of knowledge that earthly people possess. This knowledge has its source in *nefesh*, not in *neshamah*, which comes from on high. This requires an explanation.

When heaven and earth come to an end so will these types of knowledge, for they are only needed for this world. So, they, too, will deteriorate. Their great men are not really different in kind from those on a more mediocre level because all the assumptions that they share they know equally well. But in the case of Torah knowledge, you cannot compare the great scholars with those on a secondary level, even when it comes to fundamental assumptions. Thus, R. Eliezer in *Shir Hashirim Rabbah* says, 'If all the seas were ink and all the lakes quills and the heavens and earth parchment and all human beings scribes, they would not be able to write down all the Torah that I learned. But, for all that, I did not diminish them [my masters, i.e., their knowledge] even by as much as a dog is able to lap up from the sea. Nor did my pupils, who learned much from me, take as much as a brush would take that is dipped in pigment.' The reason is that the greater a person is in Torah, the more he is able to broaden and deepen its foundation in both revealed and mystical knowledge. Those on a higher level in learning cannot even be compared to them. This indicates that there are no limits or end to Torah. It is forever growing *ad infinitum*.

Since the verse does not specify that Torah has no end, the *midrash* brings the verse that says, 'Your commandment is broad beyond measure,' that is, Torah knowledge does not come to a person via the *nefesh*, whose foundation is in the earth, for how could the offspring be larger than the earth from which it was taken? We can only say, therefore, that it comes from the *neshamah* on high, which is limitless. The point here is that the text attests to the fact that the wisdom of the Torah is greater than the wisdom with which God established the earth (see Tractate Bava Batra 12a where the *ḥakham*, the one who has *ḥokhmah*, is considered to be greater than a prophet). It will be as the verse says, 'God established the earth with wisdom.' On earth the wisdom is that of nature, which has a limitation but the Torah is higher wisdom, which is infinite.

*

Another explanation

The 'other explanation' relates the verse to living beings whose power is limited. That is why the noun *tikhlah* is used. It means that their strength ebbs. The Psalmist testifies that he actually saw their end (in a vision). The second explanation adds something to the first. In the first, David did not actually visualize their demise, but expected it by definition. The second explanation is that David reflected on the nature of living beings and surmised that the weaker the species the sooner it deteriorated. The real innovation here is that he so reflected on heaven and earth. Even though they are so strong and established in the universe, nevertheless he concludes that they too will come to an end. So, the *midrash* interprets the use of *va-yekhulu* as being an expression of limitation, that the powers of heaven to stretch will someday disappear. (*Tiferet Tzion*)

Parashah Ten, Midrash Two

רַבִּי חָמָא פָּתַח 'הָגוֹ סִיגִים מִכָּסֶף וְגוֹ''' (משלי כה, ד)

R. Ḥama b. R. Ḥanina commenced [his exposition]: 'The dross having been separated from the silver [a vessel emerged for the smith]' (Proverbs 25:4).

This *midrash*, too, is addressing the term *va-yekhulu*. Why did the verse not use a word like *va-yishlemu*, which means 'they were completed,' and thus its meaning would have been clearer? R. Ḥama quoted the verse from Proverbs in response to this problem. The refiner has to remove the dross from the silver and only then so can he produce a beautiful product. This is what happened at the end of creation, and *va-yekhulu* means the dross was removed. The *midrash* goes on to clarify this concept.

אָמַר רַבִּי אֱלִיעֶזֶר בְּשֵׁם רַבִּי יַעֲקֹב מָשָׁל לְאַמְבָּטִי שֶׁהָיְתָה מְלֵאָה מַיִם וְהָיוּ בָהּ
שְׁנֵי דְיוֹסְקוֹסִים נָאִים כָּל זְמַן שֶׁהָיְתָה מְלֵאָה מַיִם לֹא הָיְתָה מְלֶאכֶת דְּיוֹסְקוֹסִים
נִרְאֵית כֵּיוָן שֶׁפְּתָקָהּ וְנֵעֵר הַמַּיִם שֶׁבְּתוֹכָהּ נִרְאֵית מְלֶאכֶת דְּיוֹסְקוֹסִים כָּךְ כָּל זְמַן
שֶׁהָיָה הָעוֹלָם תֹּהוּ וָבֹהוּ לֹא נִרְאֵית מְלֶאכֶת שָׁמַיִם וָאָרֶץ כֵּיוָן שֶׁנֶּעֱקַר תֹּהוּ וָבֹהוּ
מִן הָעוֹלָם נִרְאֵית מְלֶאכֶת שָׁמַיִם וָאָרֶץ 'וַיֵּצֵא לַצֹּרֵף כֶּלִי'' (שם שם, שם) נַעֲשׂוּ כֵלִים
הֲדָא הוּא דִכְתִיב 'וַיְכֻלּוּ הַשָּׁמַיִם וְהָאָרֶץ וְכָל צְבָאָם'

R. Eliezer said in the name of R. Jacob: This may be compared to a bath full of water, in which were two beautiful bas-reliefs; as long as it was full of water the work of the bas-reliefs could not be seen, but when the plug was removed and the water emptied, the bas-reliefs could be seen. So too, as long as formlessness and void were in the world, the work of heaven and earth could not be seen, but as soon as formlessness and void were eradicated from the world, the work of heaven could be seen – 'a vessel (*keli*) emerged for the smith,' that is, [heaven and earth] became finished articles (*kelim*); that is what is written, 'And the heaven and the earth became completed utensils.'

R. Eliezer explains R. Ḥama's opening verse. Formlessness and void (*tohu va-vohu*), which had been created on the first day, had to be removed before heaven and earth could be revealed in all their glory. This was done by means of the various acts of creation during the six days. Removal of the formlessness was like removing the dross from the metal so that a properly refined article could be produced. Heaven and earth were the beautiful instruments that emerged. Thus the phrase *va-yekhulu* should be perceived as coming from the same root as *keli*, vessel. When heaven and earth were created their beauty could not be seen because of the *tohu va-vohu* that were still in existence. By the end of the creation, which is where our verse appears, the *tohu va-vohu* – the dross in the silver – had been removed and heaven and earth emerged as beautiful vessels.

* * *

Seed Thoughts

A beautiful note is added in the interpretation we have just read and studied. The creation of the world was done backstage, so to speak. While the various acts of creation were taking place, the *tohu va-vohu*, which is here personified as a specific entity, a sort of veil over the universe, was still in place. Everything that was created did, indeed, take place, but they could be discerned only fleetingly as openings appeared in the veil, however that veil is interpreted.

But, on the sixth day, when all the other acts of creation were completed, the veil was removed.

Why then? Because man and woman had been created. After all, God did not need the world as a stage. But man did. Would there be any point in raising the curtain for a play if the actors were not ready and only the scenery was in place? How, then, could the curtain of the world be raised unless and until the actors, man and woman, had taken their position and were ready to perform?

The world is an empty vessel without man. He gives it its libretto and cast of characters. *Va-yekhulu* – Heaven and earth were now fully completed. The producer, God, could now raise the curtain.

On with the show!

* * *

Additional Commentary

Became finished articles

In the previous *midrash* Psalm 119:96 was quoted, 'I have seen that all things have their limit (*tikhlah*),' as an allusion to *va-yekhulu*, and we can now apply the message of this *midrash* to the verse, since *tikhlah* also derives from the same root as *keli*. The verse can now be interpreted as 'I have seen that all things became vessels, but Your commandment is broad beyond measure.' (*Matnot Kehunah*)

*

Removing the dross from the silver

R. Ḥama's opening verse is a continuation of verses we have already seen in the discussion about the final stages of creation: 'It is the glory of God to conceal a matter, and the glory of a king to examine a matter. Like the heavens in their height, like the earth in its depths, is the mind of kings – unfathomable' (Proverbs 24:1-2). The verse then goes on to say that when the dross was taken away from the silver, that is to say, when God removed the formlessness and void, there then came forth a vessel for the refiner, meaning that heaven and earth were revealed. However, it is not possible to interpret the event in this way. For, in creating heaven and earth God did not merely remove the formlessness and void that had covered the universe up to that time, for to say that is to deny creation *ex nihilo*. The explanation here seems to be as quoted in Tractate Ḥagigah, Chapter 2, that *tohu*, formlessness, refers to a green band that circled the universe and *va-vohu*, void, refers to the great boulders imbedded into the structure of the universe. In the beginning, the earth was covered and hidden by them. God then removed the *tohu*, meaning the green band, which encircled the world externally and the *bohu*, meaning the rocks in the deep. This is what is meant by 'The dross having been separated from the silver, a vessel emerged for the smith.' *Va-yekhulu* should now be understood as coming from the word *keli*, for then heaven and earth were complete just as a finished vessel. (*Yefei To'ar*)

*

The verses in Proverbs (as indicated by *Yefei To'ar*) can all be related to the creation. It can then be understood in the following manner:

'In the beginning God created heaven and earth,' but 'the earth was formless and void' and not visible because of this *tohu va-vohu*. During the six days of creation God removed the *tohu va-vohu* and then '*va-yekhulu* – the earth became revealed as a complete vessel.' This also resolves the verse in Proverbs, 'The dross having been separated from the silver, a vessel emerged for the smith.' The problem with this verse is that the end does not flow from the beginning. Taking away the dross from the silver does not produce a vessel and conversely, one can produce a vessel without taking the dross away from the silver. But this reference is to creation and there the vessel was already created, but not visible because of the dross, the *tohu va-vohu*. The plain meaning is that if the refiner wants to produce a perfect vessel he should first remove the dross from the silver or, as the section in Proverbs continues, 'Remove the wicked from the king's presence; and his throne will be established in justice' (verse 5). Even without this the king's throne can be established, but not in justice. (Mirkin)

*

As soon as formlessness and void were eradicated
In the beginning the world was *tohu va-vohu* – formless and void. The reason is that God created the world and all within it so that they could be strong 'as a mirror of cast metal' (Job 37:18) and remain strong. It was necessary, therefore, to create it from the sources of *tohu va-vohu* so that it would have the quality of being finite like that from which it was created. Throughout the six days of creation, during which time heaven and earth were outstretched and through whom God created all of creation, it was necessary that the *tohu va-vohu* serve them so that they could become the foundation for all creation. At the end of the sixth day, however, when all creatures had been created, God removed the *tohu va-vohu* from the world because they were no longer needed. This is what the verse means in saying *va-yekhulu*, which means that the conclusion of creation came about by itself, by the very fact that God removed the *tohu va-vohu*. Then the beauty and glory of this world were exposed. Scripture thus also informs us that good waits forever and only evil behavior, which is referred to by the term *tohu va-vohu*, covers up the good and keeps it away from man. When we return to God in truth, and the veil of *tohu va-vohu* will be removed by the power of His love, then the true good will be revealed to us by the power of His love, speedily and in our days, Amen! (*Tiferet Tzion*)

Parashah Ten, Midrash Three

כֵּיצַד בָּרָא הַקָּדוֹשׁ בָּרוּךְ הוּא אֶת עוֹלָמוֹ אָמַר רַבִּי יוֹחָנָן נָטַל הַקָּדוֹשׁ בָּרוּךְ הוּא
שְׁתֵּי פַקְעִיוֹת אַחַת שֶׁל אֵשׁ וְאַחַת שֶׁל שֶׁלֶג וּפְתָכָן זֶה בָּזֶה וּמֵהֶן נִבְרָא הָעוֹלָם

**How did the Holy One, blessed be He, create His world? R. Johanan
said: The Holy One, blessed be He, took two coils, one of fire and
the other of snow, and worked them into each other, and from these
the world was created.**

This is another explanation as to why Scripture uses the verb *va-yekhulu*
in preference to a verb like *va-yishlemu,* which also means completed. God
produced the world from the four basic elements He had originally
created. The coil of fire included the elements of fire and air; the coil of
snow included the basic elements of water and earth. These were worked
together into one ball and the world emerged. This follows the view that
the world was created from the center and then expanded outward until
stopped by God's command. (*Ha-Midrash ha-Mev'oar*)

רַבִּי חֲנִינָא אָמַר אַרְבַּע לְאַרְבַּע רוּחוֹת הַשָּׁמָיִם

**R. Hanina said: [He took] four [balls] for the four directions of
heaven.**

R. Hanina follows the view that the creation of the world began from the
perimeter and that the four balls, representing the basic elements, then
converged at the center.

רַבִּי חָמָא בַּר חֲנִינָא אָמַר שֵׁשׁ אַרְבַּע לְאַרְבַּע רוּחוֹת וְאַחַת מִלְמַעְלָן וְאַחַת
מִלְמַטָּן

**R. Hama b. R. Hanina said: Six – four for the four directions and one
for above them and one for below them.**

This interpretation adds two other dimensions, those of above and below,
but the theory is the same. The world was created first from its outer parts
and then converged at the middle. All the various views agree that the
world started as balls of energy that converged or expanded by God's
command. This, then, is what *va-yekhulu* means. The world only reached

completion when its expansion had reached the boundaries that God wanted. The word ויכלו would then be seen as deriving from כלל, meaning, inclusive (*kollel*) of many elements.

אַדְרִיָנוֹס שְׁחִיק עֲצָמוֹת שָׁאֲלָה לְרַ' יְהוֹשֻׁעַ בַּר חֲנַנְיָא אָמַר לֵהּ כֵּיצַד בָּרָא הַקָּדוֹשׁ
בָּרוּךְ הוּא אֶת עוֹלָמוֹ אָמַר לֵהּ כְּהַהוּא דַאֲמַר רַבִּי חָמָא בַּר חֲנִינָא אָמַר לֵהּ אֶפְשָׁר
כֵּן אַתְמָהָא הִכְנִיסוֹ לְבֵית קָטָן אָמַר לֵהּ פְּשׁוֹט יָדְךָ לַמִּזְרָח וְלַמַּעֲרָב לַצָּפוֹן וְלַדָּרוֹם
אָמַר לֵהּ כָּךְ הָיָה מַעֲשֵׂה לִפְנֵי הַקָדוֹשׁ בָּרוּךְ הוּא

[The Emperor] Hadrian – may his bones rot! – asked R. Joshua b. R. Hananiah: How did the Holy One, blessed be He, create the world? He answered him in accordance with what R. Hama had said. 'Is that actually possible?' exclaimed he, 'It is very strange!' Thereupon [R. Joshua] led [Hadrian] into a small chamber and said to him: 'Stretch out your hand to east, west, north, and south. Even so was the work [of creation] before the Holy One, blessed be He.'

Hadrian is 'honored' with a special curse because of the great persecutions he instigated against the Jews in the Holy Land. The point of the story is that it was as simple for God to create the world as described above as it would be for an adult to touch all dimensions of a very small room. All this is merely in a manner of speaking. In essence everything happened at God's command. (*Ha-Midrash ha-Mevo'ar*)

* * *

Seed Thoughts

Does it really matter how and with what God created the world? Not if the answer is restricted to chemical and physical substances and processes. But suppose the act of creation of the world in some way determined its moral and physical character?

The *Tiferet Tzion* tries to move us in this direction. For one thing, fire and water symbolize justice and mercy. We know this from other sources. Justice and mercy are sometimes incompatible qualities as are fire and water. But the first quality is as indispensable to the moral life as the second is to the physical world.

The second question, which is a follow-up from this discussion, is: Can man influence the world or is he subject to the influence of the unchanging rules of the universe?

That is why the concepts of upper and lower worlds are introduced into the discussion. Man has to have the power to influence earth and heaven.

There must also be some way in which he can respond to that influence. The whole question of whether or not the stars have control is part of this discussion.

But there is more that can be said. Justice and mercy are the great principles of the world. But what about beyond this world? What hope is there beyond this world? Is it worth struggling to make justice and mercy compatible with each other?

It is in this respect that the upper and lower worlds should be perceived, as ways of adding depth to this discussion. There is no ceiling on the universe. Man's hope lies in the upper world where in some fashion he will ascend to complete his spiritual mission. The lower world represents the failure to achieve this mission.

Whether the movement of the world in the act of creation was outwards as R. Johanan says or inwards as R. Hanina implies does not seem to be decisive. But the movement upwards and downwards – that represents the moral challenge of the human being.

* * *

Additional Commentary

The Holy One, blessed be He, took two coils, one of fire and the other of snow
The interpretation of *va-yekhulu* is that they were finished by themselves. God simply took two coils that He held by cords and intertwined them. When He let the cords go heaven and earth came into being. Maybe the terms fire and snow are a reference to the fact that *shamayim*, as we have seen in earlier *midrashim*, consists of fire and water. (Mirkin)

*

One of fire and and the other of snow
God conducts His world by means of justice and mercy, which is why His glorious presence is sometimes described as *Ha-Shem Elokim*, Lord God, as is well known. We must then conclude that He created the world with fire, which symbolizes justice, and snow, which symbolizes mercy. He then mixed them together since justice has to be blended with mercy (see above *Parashah Four, Midrash Nine*). (*Tiferet Tzion*)

*

He worked them into each other
The difference of opinion among R. Johanan, R. Hanina, and R. Hama can be explained as follows: R. Johanan follows the view that whatever is found in heaven and earth has its source in earth. This is consistent with his view that the stars do not affect Israel, because the conduct of the

world reflects the behavior of man. He therefore affirms that the main part of creation took place on earth and from earth heaven was created. In this connection the *midrash* says, 'He worked them into each other,' meaning that from the two balls that became one were created all the worlds.

R. Ḥanina follows the view of R. Joshua that whatever is in heaven and earth was created in heaven, that the stars do affect Israel, that the main source of creation was in heaven and that earth issues from heaven. That means that the behavior on earth is influenced by heaven. It was in this connection that he said four balls (not two like R. Joḥanan), referring to the four directions of heaven. From the heavens earth was also created, for every wind has a special talent to influence the world.

R. Ḥama b. R. Ḥanina follows the view of R. Eliezer that whatever is in heaven is a product of heaven and whatever is on earth is the product of earth. He also follows the view that the nature of the winds is fixed and unchanging, but that the constellations are sometimes influenced by man and sometimes they are not. He therefore said four, referring to the four directions and also one ball that was needed above to create the constellations and one that was needed below to create earth. (*Tiferet Tzion*)

*

Is such a thing possible?

Hadrian, may his name rot, follows the view that the existence of heaven and earth is through the power of attraction (gravity) – each one attracts the other and thus they are sustained. When, therefore, he was answered that God created the world by six coils, one for each wind and two for the dimensions of top and bottom, all of which could not be done at one time due to the vast distances between east and west and from heaven to earth, he therefore wondered whether such a thing could be possible. How could each one remain extant after they no longer had the power to attract each other. In response R. Joshua took him to a small room and spread his hands to east and west. He thus proved that just as it is possible to spread your hands to east and west at one time because of the small size of the room, so is the size of the world in relationship to God. (*Tiferet Tzion*)

Parashah Ten, Midrash Four

אָמַר ר' הוֹשַׁעְיָא דָּרַשׁ רַבִּי אֶפֶס בְּאַנְטוֹכְיָא אֵין לְשׁוֹן 'וַיְכֻלּוּ' אֶלָּא לְשׁוֹן מַכָּה
וּלְשׁוֹן כְּלָיָה

R. Hoshaya said: R. Efes preached in Antioch, 'The word *va-yekhulu* connotes nought but blows and destruction (*kelayah*).'

R. Efes offered another interpretation as to why *va-yekhulu* is used and not *va-yishlemu*, which means completed without other ambiguous possibilities. The word *va-yekhulu*, says R. Hoshaya, does not at all have the meaning of completion, but rather the meaning of destruction. It is to be associated with the word כליה, *kelayah*, which means destruction, and it implies that all the former good and blessing that was bestowed on the world was removed.

מָשָׁל לְמֶלֶךְ שֶׁנִּכְנַס בִּמְדִינָה וְקִלְּסוּ אוֹתוֹ בְּנֵי הַמְּדִינָה וְעָרֵב לוֹ קִלּוּסָן הִרְבָּה לָהֶן
בְּדִיצָה הִרְבָּה לָהֶן בְּהַדְיוֹכִין לְאַחַר זְמַן הִכְעִיסוּ אוֹתוֹ וּמִעֵט לָהֶן בְּדִיצָה וּמִעֵט
לָהֶן בְּהַדְיוֹכִין

This may be compared to a king who entered a province, and its inhabitants praised him, which pleased him. Thereupon he became very fond of them and entertained them with many races and charioteers. Later they angered him and he liked them less and diminished the number of races.

In response to the praise the king encouraged them with many activities that would please them. But when they angered him, he deprived them of these entertainments as a result of which they were not able to perform their work with the same zeal.

כָּךְ עַד שֶׁלֹּא חָטָא אָדָם הָרִאשׁוֹן הָיוּ הַמַּזָּלוֹת מְהַלְּכִין דֶּרֶךְ קְצָרָה וּבִמְהִירוּת
מִשֶּׁחָטָא סִבְּבָן דֶּרֶךְ אֲרֻכָּה וּבִמְתִינוּת

Similarly, until Adam sinned the constellations followed a course that was short and swift. After he sinned, they followed a course that was long and deliberate.

The creation of man was the goal and purpose of the world. Therefore the constellations that influenced the seasons of the year moved faster so that man would not have to wait long for his harvests. But when Adam sinned creation was cursed and the constellations then followed a slower course and covered a much larger circumference. This is an explanation of R. Efes' opinion that *va-yekhulu* means that the heavens and earth were smitten.

יֵשׁ מַזָּל שֶׁגּוֹמֵר הִלּוּכוֹ לִשְׁנֵים עָשָׂר חֹדֶשׁ כְּגוֹן כּוֹכַב חַמָּה

There is a planet that completes its circuit in twelve months, e.g., the sun;

וְיֵשׁ מַזָּל שֶׁהוּא גוֹמֵר הִלּוּכוֹ לִשְׁלֹשִׁים יוֹם וְהִיא לְבָנָה

And there is planet that completes its circuit in thirty days, viz. the moon;

וְיֵשׁ מַזָּל שֶׁהוּא גוֹמֵר הִלּוּכוֹ לִשְׁתֵּים עֶשְׂרֵה שָׁנָה וְהוּא צֶדֶק

And there is planet that completes its circuit in twelve years, viz. Jupiter;

וְיֵשׁ מַזָּל שֶׁגּוֹמֵר הִלּוּכוֹ לִשְׁלֹשִׁים שָׁנָה וְהוּא שַׁבְּתַי

And there is planet that completes its circuit in thirty years, viz. Saturn;

חוּץ מִן כּוֹכַב נֹגַהּ וּמַאְדִּים שֶׁאֵין גּוֹמְרִין הִלּוּכָן אֶלָּא לְאַרְבַּע מֵאוֹת וּשְׁמֹנִים שָׁנָה

Besides Mercury, Venus, and Mars, which complete their circuits in 480 years.

It can be seen that the various constellations travel at different speeds and cover different distances. The following table will be helpful in understanding what the text is saying.

Ḥama	חמה	Sun	365 days
Levanah	לבנה	Moon	29 days, 12 hours
Tzedek	צדק	Jupiter	11 years, 316 days
Shabbetai	שבתי	Saturn	29 years, 167days
Nogah	נגה	Venus	225 days, 584 days around the sun
Ma'adim (Mirkin)	מאדים	Mars	687 days around the sun

(וּבְעֵי שְׁאֵלָה שֶׁנֹּגַהּ מְהַלֶּכֶת שְׁנֵים עָשָׂר מַזָּלוֹת לַעֲשָׂרָה חֳדָשִׁים כָּל מַזָּל עֶשְׂרִים
וַחֲמִשָּׁה יוֹם וּמַאְדִּים חֹדֶשׁ וָחֵצִי כָּל מַזָּל מַהֲלַךְ שְׁנֵים עָשָׂר שָׁנָה וָמֶחֱצָה וְהֵיאַךְ
אוֹמֵר כֵּן נֹגַהּ וּמַאְדִּים אֵין גּוֹמְרִין הִלּוּכָן אֶלָּא לְאַרְבַּע מֵאוֹת וּשְׁמֹנִים שָׁנָה חֲזֵינָא
תְּמִיהָא לְפִיכָךְ בָּעֵי שְׁאֵלָה)

(A question can be asked: Venus is able to overtake the twelve
constellations of the zodiac which ordinarily complete their circuit
in one year, in just ten days. A constellation that ordinarily takes
thirty days is overtaken by Venus on the twenty-fifth day. Mars, on
the other hand, takes one-and-a-half months to complete what the
ordinary constellations are able to do in one month. How then can
[the *midrash*] say that Venus and Mars complete their circuit in 480
years! I found this problem and therefore I am posing the question.)

The above section is not part of the original *midrash*. It is probably the
work of a later Sage who found a difficulty in the text. Theodor responds
to this problem by reading 480 days instead of 480 years.

רַ' פִּינְחָס בְּשֵׁם רַ' חָנָן דְּצִפּוֹרִין תַּנֵּי בְּנוֹת שׁוּחַ בְּשָׁנָה שְׁנִיָּה שֶׁל שְׁמִטָּה נוֹהֵג
קְדֻשַּׁת שְׁבִיעִית שֶׁלָּהֶן לְפִי שֶׁעוֹשׂוֹת פֵּרוֹת לְשָׁלֹשׁ שָׁנִים וְאוֹתוֹ הַיּוֹם עָשׂוּ פֵרוֹת
בֶּן יוֹמָן

**R. Pinḥas said in the name of R. Ḥama of Sepphoris: It has been
taught that for white figs the sabbatical year is in the second year [of
the second cycle and only then the] sanctity of the sabbatical year
[applies to them], because they produce fruit [once] in three years,
but on that day the fruits were produced in one day.**

We learn in the Mishnah (Shevi'it 5:1) that white figs have their sabbatical
restrictions in the second year of the sabbatical cycle. That is because they
take three years to ripen. Thus, counting the seventh year as one, two
more years would have to transpire before the figs would ripen, at which
time the sanctity of sabbatical fruits would apply to them. But on the third
day of the creation of the world the white figs and all the other fruits were
produced in one day. This proves that the passage of the constellations
must have been very swift to make this possible. This, then, is what
va-yekhulu means – the fruits were 'smitten' for the future to require such
a long time to ripen.

אֲבָל לֶעָתִיד לָבוֹא הַקָּדוֹשׁ בָּרוּךְ הוּא מְרַפֵּא אוֹתָהּ מַכָּה שֶׁנֶּאֱמַר 'וּמַחַץ מַכָּתוֹ
יִרְפָּא' (ישעיה ל, כו)מַחַץ מַכָּתוֹ שֶׁל עוֹלָם יִרְפָּא

But in the time to come the Holy One, blessed be He, will heal that injury, for it is said, 'And He will heal the force of its injury' (Isaiah 30:26), **that is, He will heal the injury which the world suffered.**

In the Messianic future when the sin of Adam will be forgiven and atoned for, God will heal the wound that He inflicted on the constellations and, consequently, on the seasons of the year and on the ripening processes of the fruits and all growing things, and will restore the world to the original system set up at creation.

* * *

Seed Thoughts

The process of film-making has perfected the technique of slow motion and fast-forward film. Slow motion is very important in investigative material where you look for every imaginative detail, and I am sure that we can all remember how humorous fast-forward film can be especially when it is unexpected and deals with people whose appearances are familiar. Some understanding of that kind of technique is necessary to come to grips with the extraordinary statements we find in the midrashic text now under study.

The whole notion that the pace of the constellations used to be faster as well as their effects upon the natural world, particularly on the harvest, comes to a climax in the interpretation of the day of man's creation. On that famous sixth day of creation man was created, endowed with the divine image, was supported by the creation of woman, and then sinned by disobeying God.

No wonder that *va-yekhulu* is rendered as meaning tainted or destroyed. That wonderful world that God had made would now be forfeited. Not the forces of nature; they would remain intact. But the collapse of man destroys the purpose of the world and renders creation irrelevant.

In that wonderful paragraph of *va-yekhulu* God celebrates the creation of the world as symbolized by the Sabbath, but man is not even mentioned. No wonder chapter two of Genesis has to start from scratch and tell the story of man's creation all over again.

The lesson is obvious, but it needs stating again and again. Man can be angel or devil. As devil he jeopardizes the world; as angel he sanctifies it. But nobody wants man to be an angel; only that he try to be a human being.

It is the goal of Judaism to make him try.

* * *

Additional Commentary

The way that is short and swift

The growth of fruit is dependent upon the constellations that govern the seasons. Each fruit has its own star or angel that helps it grow. By growing quickly fruit can ripen even every day. It is the view of the Sages that Adam's sin took place on the sixth day, the very same day he was created. *Va-yekhulu* here becomes interpreted as a combination of *va-yakh*, 'and He struck,' and *va-yikhleh*, 'He ended or destroyed,' the meaning being towards evening at the close of that day. (RZWE)

*

He entertained them with races

Antioch was famous in its day for its speedy chariots and its races and competitors. הַדְיוֹכִין, *hadyuchin*, refers to the charioteers. The paths of the stars in the heavens resembles a race of chariot drivers. A short course refers to a brief season and the ripening of food right away. (Mirkin)

*

The intent of the parable is to indicate that the constellations were then very large and therefore the light they cast upon the earth very strong. That is the meaning of the term דִּיצָה *ditzah*. It refers to the light that makes all life rejoice and even influenced the fruit to ripen each day. This latter is the meaning of *dyuchin*, which in the *Arukh* (a Talmudic dictionary) is translated as the language of success and good will. (*Tiferet Tzion*)

*

The word *va-yekhulu* connotes

When man was being created, vegetation had not yet started as it is written, 'No shrub of the earth was yet in the field,' and only because of the rain necessary for the creation of man did the shrubbery begin to grow (as is explained in *Parashah* 13, *Midrash* 1). On that very day Adam ate from the tree of knowledge, which was a fig tree and which today requires three years to produce fruit. One can only conclude, therefore, that the constellations changed their course and speed. This is the force of the curse, 'By the sweat of your brow shall you eat bread': because the constellations changed their course and became slower, the earth was no longer able to produce except by the sweat of the farmer's brow, with great effort. (*Tiferet Tzion*)

A question is raised

This question is not part of the original *midrash*. It is probably the gloss of a scholar. It may be that the comment of the *midrash* about the circuits of the constellations does not include times of their complete circuit, but only that aspect of their journey that affects the earth, which is the meaning of the phrase, גּוֹמֵר הִלּוּכוֹ, *gomer hilukho* – concludes its circuit. As for Mars, its cycle is not over until the passage of 480 years, which is why Pharaoh said to Moses, 'Behold, evil lies ahead of them'; and the Sages said, 'He saw in his crystal ball that Mars, which stands for blood and killing, was approaching them, but the Almighty changed the blood Pharaoh saw to the blood of circumcision.' Despite that, Israel was not able to approach its objective until after 480 years after they left Egypt when the Temple was established, which was the goal of the Exodus. It appears that their goal was not achieved until after 480 years.(*Tiferet Tzion*)

As it is said

At first Scripture says, 'When the Lord binds up His people's wounds' (Isaiah 30:26) and then continues 'And He will heal the force of its injury.' The second sentence cannot, therefore, be referring to Israel, which has already been mentioned. It must refer to the light of the sun, which was mentioned earlier in the verse, 'And the light of the moon shall be as the light of the sun and the light of the sun shall become sevenfold.' (*Tiferet Tzion*)

Parashah Ten, Midrash Five

אָמַר רַ' יְהוֹשֻׁעַ בֶּן לֵוִי נִשְׁתַּכְלְלוּ שָׁמַיִם בַּחַמָּה וּלְבָנָה וּבַמַּזָּלוֹת וְנִשְׁתַּכְלְלָה הָאָרֶץ בָּאִילָנוֹת וּבַדְּשָׁאִין וְגַן עֵדֶן

R. Joshua b. Levi said: The heaven was adorned with the sun, moon, and planets; the earth was adorned with trees, herbs, and the Garden of Eden.

Another interpretation as to why *va-yekhulu* was used and not the more direct *va-yishlemu*. The word *va-yekhulu* is translated by Onkelos into Aramaic as *va-eshtakhlelu*, meaning 'they were adorned,' or 'they became beautiful,' and therefore R. Joshua b. Levi interpreted *va-yekhulu* as meaning that on the sixth day, heaven and earth reached their completion in the sense that they were adorned and perfected with the sun, the moon, and the planets in the heavens and with trees, herbs, and the Garden of Eden on earth.

רַבִּי סִימוֹן בְּשֵׁם רַבִּי יְהוֹשֻׁעַ בֶּן לֵוִי מְכוֹלָלִים הָיוּ הַמַּעֲשִׂים וְהָיוּ מוֹתְחִין וְהוֹלְכִין

R. Simon said in the name of R. Joshua b. Levi: The works [of creation] were included [in the creation of heaven and earth] and went on emerging [during the six days of creation].

R. Simon is offering another of R. Joshua b. Levi's interpretations of *va-yekhulu*, according to which it derives from the root כלל, meaning 'to include.' The meaning of our verse will now be that all the details of creation were included in the creation of heaven and earth and were actualized during the six days. The process was completed when *va-yekhulu* was said.

וְכָל צְבָאָם אָמַר רַ' אֶלְעָזָר ג' צְבָאִים הֵן צָבָא לַשָּׁמַיִם וְלָאָרֶץ וְצָבָא לַתַּלְמִידִים וְצָבָא לַיִּסּוּרִין

'And all their period (*tzeva'am*)' – R. Eleazar said: There are three periods: a period for heaven and earth, a period for disciples, and a period for suffering.

The word צָבָא, *tzava*, is usually translated as 'army,' 'host,' or, as in the JPA

400

Bible, 'array.' If the intention of this verse was to refer to those hosts associated with heaven and earth, the term should have been *ve-tziv'otam*, 'their hosts.' Why then *tzeva'am*, meaning 'their host' in the singular? In this connection R. Eleazar translated the term 'fixed periods,' which are a fixed period for heaven and earth, for God has established a fixed time for the duration of heaven and earth; a fixed period for disciples who, when their time comes, take the place of their teachers; and a fixed period for suffering, very well thought out and fixed timewise, depending upon the decree established in advance.

צָבָא לַשָּׁמַיִם וָאָרֶץ שֶׁנֶּאֱמַר 'וַיְכֻלּוּ הַשָּׁמַיִם וְהָאָרֶץ וְכָל צְבָאָם' צָבָא לַתַּלְמִידִים מִנַּיִן שֶׁנֶּאֱמַר 'כָּל יְמֵי צְבָאִי אֲיַחֵל עַד בֹּא חֲלִיפָתִי' (איוב יד, יד) עַד יָקוּם חֲלוּפִי וְצָבָא לַיִּסּוּרִים מִנַּיִן שֶׁנֶּאֱמַר 'הֲלֹא צָבָא לֶאֱנוֹשׁ עֲלֵי אָרֶץ' (שם ז, א)

A fixed period for heaven and earth, as it is written, 'And the heavens and earth were finished and all their fixed periods.' Where [do we learn that there is] a fixed period for disciples? As it is written, 'All the time of my service I wait until my replacement comes' (Job 14:14). Where [do we learn that there is] a fixed period for suffering? As it is written, 'Truly man has a term of service on earth' (ibid. 7:1).

The *midrash* continues with the proof-verses for R. Eleazar's statement regarding the three fixed periods. The first is our verse itself. In both of the verses quoted from Job the word *tzava* appears and in the context it must mean a period of time. Rashi writes that the first verse from Job is in a discussion about sages and their disciples. The other verse from Job is in his complaint about his suffering.

וְכָל צְבִיוֹנוֹ שֶׁל אָדָם אֵינוֹ אֶלָּא עַל הָאָרֶץ וּמַה הֲנָיָה לוֹ 'וְכִימֵי שָׂכִיר יָמָיו' (שם שם,

שם)

Yet the whole desire of man is [to remain upon the] earth. What pleasure can he have from that, seeing that 'his days are like those of a hireling' (ibid.).

This is another interpretation of the verse in Job based on a different understanding of the word צבא, which can also mean 'desire.' Man's whole desire is to stay alive, although his days are fixed, like a hireling. When his time comes he will depart and whatever he has will go with him. Therefore, let him take all these things to heart and work not only for the goals of this world but also of the world-to-come.

נַחְמָן בְּרֵהּ דְּרַ' שְׁמוּאֵל בַּר נַחְמָן אָמַר אִם זָכָה צָבָא לוֹ וְאִם לָאו צָבָא עָלָיו בָּנָה
בִּנְיָן עָלָה בְּיָדוֹ צָבָא לוֹ נָפַל מִמֶּנּוּ וָמֵת צָבָא עָלָיו אָכַל פִּתּוֹ וַהֲנָיָתוּ צָבָא לוֹ עָמְדָה
בְּתוֹךְ גְּרוֹנוֹ וַחֲנָקַתּוּ צָבָא עָלָיו

Naḥman, the son of R. Samuel b. Naḥman, said: If a man merits it,
the host [of divine powers] are his; if not, the host is against him. If
he erects a building and his work is successful, the host is for him; if
he falls from it and dies, there is a host against him. If he eats his
bread and it benefits him, there is a host for him; if it lodges in his
throat and chokes him, there is a host against him.

Still dealing with the verse 'Truly man has a term of service on earth' (Job
7:1), R. Naḥman posed the question, when it says *tzeva le-enosh*, a fixed
time for man, is it a good thing for him or is it bad? His answer is that it
depends on the person's behavior. Of interest is the fact that R. Naḥman
is interpreting the word as 'a host,' thus taking the meaning in our verse
in Genesis and applying it to the verse in Job. He is also stressing that
anything good or bad that happens to a person is the result of that person's
piety or lack of it, the implication being that so was ordained from the
very creation of the world. He continues in the next passage to elaborate
his point.

הַרְבֵּה צְבָאִים מִנָּה הַקָּדוֹשׁ בָּרוּךְ הוּא לְאָדָם הַזֶּה לִתְבֹּעַ דִּיקְיוֹן שֶׁלּוֹ הַרְבֵּה דֻּבִּים
הַרְבֵּה אֲרָיוֹת הַרְבֵּה נְחָשִׁים הַרְבֵּה שְׂרָפִים הַרְבֵּה עַקְרַבִּים וְלֹא עוֹד אֶלָּא 'כִּימֵי
שָׂכִיר יָמָיו'

Many hosts has the Holy One, blessed be He, appointed against man
to exact his penalties – many bears, many lions, many snakes, many
fiery serpents, many scorpions. And furthermore, 'his days are like
those of a hireling.'

All the natural elements are seen as agents of the Holy One, blessed be
He, the function of which is to punish man for his transgressions. For the
dangerous animals listed there is evidence in the Bible: bears, as in the
story of Elisha (II Kings 2:24); lions, as was the case with the nations
re-settled by the king of Assyria (II Kings 17:25); snakes and fiery
serpents, as was the case with the Children of Israel in the wilderness
(Numbers 21:6). Moreover, not only will all the efforts to accumulate
possessions in this world be to no avail, man's days are as the days of a
hireling, that is, his life span is limited.

* * *

Seed Thoughts

In this *midrash*, for the first time in the creation story, beauty makes its appearance and with it art, design, space, color and all those variations that sight and sound and creativity make possible.

What did the aesthetic dimension that we are now describing bring into the creation picture that had not been there before? What was lacking hitherto?

For one thing, enjoyment. In the beginning everything was assembled in potpourri fashion until heaven and earth were properly extended. Then the various creations had a perspective through which they could be perceived. This beauty, this fantastic achievement, this attention to detail, this miracle of growth, contributed an enjoyment that had hitherto not obtained. First and foremost, this enjoyment belonged to God even though sensual things cannot be applied to Him. But this enjoyment is surely what is meant by the Sabbath, which gave God the opportunity to contemplate His creation. The enjoyment was also that of man who not only learned to appreciate his habitat but to imitate it in creativity and reproduce it in art.

Was there also enjoyment by all other living things not excluding the inanimate? One can only resort to poetry and parable. The Psalmist said it for us, 'Day speaks to day and night utters words of wonder to night.'

The second category that the dimension of the aesthetic brings with it is the sense of individuality. Nothing is the same as anything else. Everything is unique – plants and animals. Even members of the same species have something about them that is singularly their own. The aesthetic dimension helps us understand, appreciate, and advocate the sense of uniqueness.

The third element that the aesthetic life brings to bear is that the whole is greater than its parts. The magic of the whole universe helps us understand the miracle of every specific created thing. It also sets forth as a good dramatic vehicle would, the necessity of having the world as a proper stage and scenic background for the drama of man.

No attempt is being made in this *midrash* to make comparisons between the ethical and the aesthetic. Obviously, without ethics and man's moral behavior, the aesthetic dimension would be of no value. On the other hand, as the *Ethics of the Fathers* points out, the skill of the aesthetic achievement adds to the value of the world and makes us more responsible for preserving and sustaining it.

* * *

Additional Commentary

Was completed

Va-yekhulu is here rendered as *nishtakhlelu* meaning 'was perfected, improved and became more beautiful.' (RZWE)

*

The creation started out poorly on the first day, but began improving over the six days until God said, '*va-yekhulu*' – 'Enough!' The world was already sufficiently perfected and developed, *meshukhlal.* (*Matnot Kehunah*)

*

Va-yekhulu is here understood as to be crowned or adorned. The *midrash* can also be understood as interpreting וכל צבאם, *ve-khol tzeva'am* – '*and* all their host,' as בכל צבאם, *be-khol tziv'am* – *in* all their beautiful colors or variations. (Mirkin)

*

Fixed time

The word צבא, *tzava,* always refers to muliplicity or a multitude. Here are listed three hosts upon whom the world depends:
1. The host of heaven and earth by which are meant the multitude of galaxies and constellations that are in the heavens and the multitude of species that are on the earth. If even one of them were to be removed, the world would be destroyed, as is well known.
2. The host of pupils that cause the Torah to multiply as they study it; the existence of the world depends upon the Torah.
3. The host of sufferings and afflictions that motivate a person to repentance, and this repentance is for the benefit of the world.

Some interpreters maintain that the word *tzava* refers to a fixed time and lists three that are constrained by time. The hosts of heaven are limited by the fact that there is a time for every species in the universe. In the case of pupils there is a time span within which they must learn before going out into the world. There is even a set time for afflictions that leave a person after they have fulfilled their purpose of spurring him on to penitence. The *midrash* uses both interpretations. (*Yefei To'ar*)

*

Perfected

The word *va-yekhulu* is here seen as an allusion to *kelilat yofi,* 'the epitome of beauty.' The meaning is that before heaven and earth reached their proper dimensions, the beauty of the sun, moon, and constellations were not discernible and the same holds for the vegetation, because they were not properly organized. After the sixth day, however, when the dimensions of heaven and earth were revealed, then was the beauty of all the other acts of creation revealed. (*Tiferet Tzion*)

*

A fixed period for man on earth

The term אנוש, *enosh*, applies to man as sufferer. For example, a fatal wound is described in Hebrew as *enooshah*. When, therefore, Scripture uses *tzava* in connection with *enosh* it can only mean that it is referring to the host of afflictions which are the emissaries of God sent to motivate man.

*

The whole desire of man is to be upon the earth

This interpretation is based on the fact that the expression *alei eretz* – 'on earth,' is unnecessary. *Tzava* is therefore given two interpretations: 1. As meaning the host of afflictions, as above. 2. As being a derivative of *zivyon* (Tractate Rosh ha-Shanah 11a), which means 'desire.' The interpretation would then be: Although the purpose of the host of afflictions is to motivate a person to penitence so that his chief desire should be the world-to-come, nevertheless, his desires remain on the earth, that is, his desires are directed to material things.

Parashah Ten, Midrash Six

בַּר סִירָא אָמַר אֵלֶּה הֶעֱלָה סַמִּים מִן הָאָרֶץ בָּהֶם הָרוֹפֵא מְרַפֵּא אֶת הַמַּכָּה וּבָהֶם הָרוֹקֵחַ מְרַקֵּחַ אֶת הַמִּרְקַחַת

Ben Sira said: God caused medicaments to spring forth from the earth; with them the physician heals the wound and the apothecary compounds his preparations.

This *midrash* is also proposing an interpretation of צבאם, *tzeva'am*, 'hosts.' It approaches the translation in its simplest form as meaning a gathering of soldiers. They are commanded to institute law and order. The word *tzava* seems appropriate even when referring to the hosts of heaven – sun, moon, stars, and constellations – since they are charged with the direction of nature. Who, however, are the hosts of earth? It cannot refer to those who were created, since they are consumers of the earth's goods and not supervisors of it. The answer is that anyone can become part of God's hosts if God commands him to do something. Thus, Ben Sira teaches that God commanded the plants to produce medicaments and they did so. What is done with medicaments is the responsibility of man. Both the physician and the apothecary use these drugs to good purpose. But they can be used for evil purposes as well.

אָמַר רַ' סִימוֹן אֵין לְךָ כָּל עֵשֶׂב וְעֵשֶׂב שֶׁאֵין לוֹ מַזָּל בָּרָקִיעַ שֶׁמַּכֶּה אוֹתוֹ וְאוֹמֵר לוֹ גְּדַל הֲדָא הוּא דִכְתִיב 'הֲיָדַעְתָּ חֻקּוֹת שָׁמָיִם אִם תָּשִׂים מִשְׁטָרוֹ בָאָרֶץ וְגוֹ'' (איוב לח, לג) לְשׁוֹן שׁוֹטֵר 'הַתְקַשֵּׁר מַעֲדַנּוֹת כִּימָה אוֹ מוֹשְׁכוֹת כְּסִיל תְּפַתֵּחַ' (שם שם, לא)

R. Simon said: There is not a single herb which does not have a constellation in heaven which strikes it and says, 'Grow!,' as it is written, 'Do you know the laws of the heaven or impose its authority (*mishtaro*) on earth?' (Job 38:33) The language used is of a policeman (*shoter*): 'Can you tie cords to Pleiades, or undo the reins of Orion?' (ibid. verse 31).

The use of the term שוטר, meaning one who enforces order, from the verse in Job, is the proof-text that the constellations act as policemen, law enforcers, imposing their authority on the plant world and ordering them to grow. Pleiades and Orion are the constellations that are responsible for cold and heat. As the Talmud puts it, were it not for the heat of Orion, the world could not sustain the cold of Pleiades. (Tractate Berakhot 58:2)

רַבִּי חֲנִינָא בַּר פָּפָּא וְרַ' סִימוֹן אָמַר כִּימָה מְעַדֶּנֶת אֶת הַפֵּרוֹת וּכְסִיל מוֹשֵׁךְ בֵּין
קֶשֶׁר לְקֶשֶׁר הֲדָא הוּא דִכְתִיב 'הֲתֹצִיא מַזָּרוֹת בְּעִתּוֹ וְעַיִשׁ עַל בָּנֶיהָ תַנְחֵם' (שם
שם, לב) רַבִּי תַּנְחוּם בַּר חִיָּא וְרַ' סִימוֹן אָמְרוּ מַזָּל הוּא שֶׁהוּא מְמַזֵּר אֶת הַפֵּרוֹת.

R. Ḥanina b. Papa and R. Simon said: Pleiades enhances the fruit and Orion draws out [the stalk] between knot and knot, as it is written, 'Can you lead out the constellations (*mazarot*) in their season, conduct the Bear with her sons?' (ibid. verse 32). **R. Tanḥum b. R. Ḥiyya and R. Simon said: [*Mazarot* connotes] the constellation which ripens (*memazer*) the fruits.**

These two constellations are also responsible for the growth of plants. Pleiades helps keep the plants moist (מעדנת, *me'adenet*) from the dryness of the atmosphere and thus ripens them satisfactorily. Orion, through its heat, makes the branches extend. This is derived from the verb *moshekh*, draw out. The use of the term *mazarot* when, probably, *mazalot*, constellations, was intended, is used to show that this constellation, כימה, *kimah*, spreads out the plantings so that the chaff is separated from the kernel or fruit as the case may be. We now have an explanation of צבאות, 'the hosts.' They refer to those influences that affect and sustain agricultural growth.

* * *

Seed Thoughts

When I first saw this *midrash* I was overpowered by what seemed to me a most romantic process. A force above us was encouraging every plant, twig, and natural being to grow, grow, grow.

Isn't that force meant to parallel what should happen spiritually? That a force, external or internal, should be beating down upon us and saying grow, discover yourself, develop your talents, improve them, sensitize them; grow, grow, grow!

Along comes the *Tiferet Tzion* and other commentators to dash all of these thoughts into irrelevance. That is not what the *midrash* means at all! The plants have a mind of their own. They do not want to grow. They know that if they do grow, human beings will exploit them for unproductive, maybe even immoral, purposes. Therefore a special angel had to be appointed over each plant to beat them, if necessary, and, at all costs, to get them to grow even against their better judgment. Don't allow man to prevail and destroy the world. The minority of good people deserve the opportunity to try their best and do their best.

I read these commentaries and am duly impressed by their insights, but unsatisfied. The original interpretation seems to be so much better.

If we are created, then let us grow. If we are here, let us do something about our own reality.

The School of Hillel and the School of Shammai debated for years whether man should or should not have been created. Finally they concluded that, while theoretically it might have been better for man had he not been created, nevertheless, since creation is now a fact, let man do the best he can.

Similarly, the world is here. It is a fact. Therefore, grow. Maybe our *midrash* is casting new light on the meaning of *tzeva'am*, 'their hosts.' Maybe as noted by RZWE the term is closely related to the word *retzonam*, meaning 'their desire.' Maybe the purpose of the angels was to help human beings cultivate their desire to live and to create. Therefore they say to all of us, 'Grow, grow, grow!'

* * *

Additional Commentary

What is the meaning of *tzeva'am*?
One view interprets *tzeva'am* as deriving from the word *ratzon*, meaning will or desire. Everything in creation has a desire that becomes its purpose, though the purpose takes different forms such as drugs. (RZWE)

*

Another interpretation is that God through intermediaries forces a particular purpose on various types of creation. (Mirkin)

*

Ben Sira says
Ben Sira's point is that the goal of all the hosts is the betterment of man. Even those that appear hostile are also for his benefit, for they can heal him from illness. In this connection he says that God causes medicaments to come from the earth. Just as in the case of drugs, if he doesn't have merit he will require them for medicine and if he does have merit he will use them for enjoyment, similarly all things in the world will be used for medicine or for enjoyment. But everything is for the good of man because the Holy One, blessed be He, only does good things for both the wicked and the good. (*Tiferet Tzion*)

*

There is no blade of grass

All creatures have only one desire – to do the will of their Maker so that through them His name will be sanctified. However, in view of the deterioration of the world to the point where only one person in a thousand eats so that the body will be strengthened in order to serve God, and the majority eat only in order to fulfill their own hedonistic desires, the plants do not want to grow. The plants see that they are used by humans to increase their desires and be diverted from the service of God. The Holy One, blessed be He, wants the world to be preserved and relies upon the righteous to preserve it for Him. But the righteous can only function in a settled and inhabited world. For this reason God created the hosts in the heavens so that they would force all elements in the world to function as required by the laws of nature. That is their whole purpose, but, as shown above, sometimes the laws of nature are used by people to desecrate God's name. That is why they cannot be referred to as the hosts of God, but only as the hosts of heaven and the hosts of earth since their function, after all, is to enforce the natural laws of heaven and earth. (*Tiferet Tzion*)

Parashah Ten, Midrash Seven

רַבָּנָן אָמְרִי אֲפִלּוּ דְּבָרִים שֶׁאַתָּה רוֹאֶה אוֹתָן שֶׁהֵן יְתֵירָה בָּעוֹלָם כְּגוֹן זְבוּבִין
וּפַרְעוֹשִׁין וִיתוּשִׁין אַף הֵן בִּכְלָל בְּרִיָּתוֹ שֶׁל עוֹלָם הֵן וּבַכֹּל הַקָּדוֹשׁ בָּרוּךְ הוּא
עוֹשֶׂה שְׁלִיחוּתוֹ אֲפִלּוּ עַל יְדֵי נָחָשׁ אֲפִלּוּ עַל יְדֵי יְתוּשׁ אֲפִלּוּ עַל יְדֵי צְפַרְדֵּעַ

The Rabbis said: Even those things which you may regard as
superfluous in the world, such as flies, fleas, and gnats, are also
included in the creation of the world, and the Holy One, blessed be
He, carries out His purpose even through snakes, scorpions, gnats,
and frogs.

The intention of this *midrash* is to explain the presence of the word כל, *kol*,
'*all* their hosts,' in the biblical text, which seems to be unnecessary. The
word *kol* thus refers to all those many creatures whose presence seems to
be superfluous in the world on the ground that they merely harass human
beings. Nevertheless, they were included in creation and are part of the
'hosts' of the earth. God uses them for His purpose as with other creatures.

רַבִּי תַּנְחוּמָא אָמַר לַהּ בְּשֵׁם רַבִּי מְנַחֲמָה רַבִּי בְּרֶכְיָה בְּשֵׁם רַבִּי חֶלְבּוֹ רַבִּי אַחָא
הֲוָה מִשְׁתָּעֵי הָדֵין עוֹבָדָא חַד בַּר נָשׁ הֲוָה קָאֵם עַל כֵּיף נַהֲרָא חֲמָא חַד עוּרְדְּעָן
טָעֲנָא חֲדָא עַקְרָב וּמִגִּיזָה יָתֵהּ נַהֲרָא וְכֵיוָן דַּעֲבַדַת שְׁלִיחוּתֵהּ אַחֲזַרְתֵּא לְאַתְרֵהּ

R. Tanḥuma said in the name of R. Menaḥamah and R. Berakhiah
in the name of R. Ḥelbo: R. Aḥa told the [following] story. A man
was standing by the bank of a river when he saw a frog bearing a
scorpion and carrying it across the river; as soon as [the scorpion]
had carried out its commission, [the frog] carried it back to its place.

Three kinds of creations are found on land: cattle, creeping things and
wild beasts. Cattle were created to serve man, but wild beasts and
creeping things were created to serve the purposes of God. This is what
the *midrash* means: God accomplishes His purpose by means of wild
beasts even by means of snakes, which do not even have feet. In
connection with creeping things, it is written, 'even by means of an insect,'
which is the smallest of all creeping things. The waters contain most of the
creatures found on earth and in connection with them the *midrash* says,

'even by means of a frog,' which is the smallest of all the water creatures and does not attack others. Even so, God performs His will by means of a frog as well. Since God arranges all punishments to fit the crime, He needs many types of messengers for His purpose. The point of the story about the frog is that God's purpose is not fulfilled accidentally, but deliberately and with great sophistication. The idea of a frog ferrying a scorpion back and forth is surely not a usual occurrence.

רַבִּי פִּינְחָס בְּשֵׁם רַבִּי חָנָן דְּצִפּוֹרִין אֲמַר עוֹבָדָא הֲוָה בְּחַד גְּבַר דַּהֲוָה קָאֵם לְמֶחֱצַד בְּהָדָא בִּקְעַת בֵּי טַרְפָּא חֲמָא חַד עֵשֶׂב וְלִקֵט יָתֵהּ וְעֲבָדֵהּ כְּלִילָא לְרָאשֵׁהּ אֲזַלָא חַד חִוְיָא וּמְחָא יָתֵהּ וּקְטִיל יָתֵהּ אֲתָא חַד גְּבַר וְקָם לְמִסְקַר בְּהַהוּא חִוְיָא אֲמַר תָּמַהּ אֲנִי עַל מַן דְּקְטַל הָדֵין חִוְיָא אֲמַר הַהוּא גַּבְרָא אֲנָא קְטָלִית יָתֵהּ תְּלָה תְּלָה אַפוֹי וַחֲמָא לְהַהוּא עֵשְׂבָּא עֲבִידָא כְּלִילָא לְרָאשֵׁהּ אֲמַר מִן קוּשְׁטָא אַתְּ קְטָלִית יָתֵהּ אֲמַר לֵהּ אִין אֲמַר לֵהּ יָכֵל אַתְּ מָרִים הָדֵין עִשְׂבָּא מִן רֵאשָׁךְ אֲמַר לֵהּ אִין אִין כֵּיָן דַּאֲרִים יָתֵהּ אֲמַר לֵהּ אַתְּ יָכוֹל קָרִיב הָכָא וּמָרִים הָדֵין חִוְיָא בְּהָדֵין חוּטְרָא אֲמַר לֵהּ אִין כֵּיָן דִּקְרַב לְהַהוּא חִוְיָא מִיָּד נָשְׁרוּ אֲבָרְיו

R. Pinḥas related in the name of R. Ḥanan of Sepphoris: It once happened that a man was about to reap [produce] in the Bei Tarpa valley when he saw some grass which he plucked and plaited into a covering for his head. A snake came, but he struck and killed it. Another man then came along, examined the snake and said, 'I wonder who could have killed this snake!' 'I killed it,' said the first man. [The second man] then noticed the grass wreath on his head and said, 'Did you in truth kill it?' 'Yes,' he answered. 'Can you remove that herb from your head?' he continued. 'Yes,' replied [the first man]. When he had removed it, he said to him, 'Can you come here and lift up the snake with your staff?' 'Yes,' replied he, but as soon as he approached the snake, his limbs fell off.

This is an intriguing story that requires a great deal of examination. When the farmer came to reap produce, it was very hot weather and he plucked the grass in order to make a covering to protect his head. It is possible that when he did so he disturbed the snake's lair and when it emerged he killed it. The second man, who was probably a snake charmer, wondered who was so powerful as to be able to kill the snake and surmised that there was something about the grass from which the hat had been made that had some powerful protection against the poison of snakes. When the first man took off the hat and approached the snake, he died. There are several possible explanations for his death. It could be that he had been bitten when he had killed the snake and that the grass really did protect him. Another possibility is that he had not really killed the snake and when he approached it, it sprang up and bit him. Yet another possibility is that he inadvertently touched the snakes fangs and thus the poison entered his body. Our *midrash* pays no attention to this aspect of the story. Its main point is that the Almighty's messengers fulfill their missions even after their deaths.

רַבִּי יַנַּאי הָיָה יוֹשֵׁב וְדוֹרֵשׁ בְּפֶתַח עִירוֹ רָאָה נָחָשׁ מַרְתִּיעַ וּבָא וַהֲוָה מְרַדֵּף לֵהּ מִן הָדֵין סִטְרָא וַהֲוָה חָזַר מִן דֵּין סִטְרָא וְעוֹד הֲוָה רָדֵף לֵהּ מִן הָדֵין סִטְרָא וַהֲוָה חָזַר מִן דֵּין סִטְרָא אֲמַר זֶה הוֹלֵךְ לַעֲשׂוֹת שְׁלִיחוּתוֹ מִיָּד נָפְלָה הֲבָרָה בָּעִיר פְּלוֹנִי בֶּן פְּלוֹנִי נְשָׁכוֹ נָחָשׁ וָמֵת

R. Jannai was sitting and lecturing at the entrance to his town, when he saw an angry snake coming. He chased after it [to kill it] from this side, but it returned from the other side. He chased after it from the other side, but it returned from this side. [Seeing its determination to enter the town, R. Jannai] said, 'It is going to carry out a mission.' Immediately a report spread in the town, 'So-and-so has been bitten by a snake and died.'

When R. Jannai saw that all of his efforts to catch the snake and kill it failed, he realized that the snake was on a mission that man could not stop. Sure enough, shortly thereafter they heard that someone had been killed by a snake.

רַבִּי אֶלְעָזָר הֲוָה יָתֵב מְטַיֵּל בְּבֵית הַכִּסֵּא אֲתָא חַד רוֹמָאי וְתִרְכֵהּ וּקְדִים יָתֵהּ וִיתֵב לֵהּ אֲמַר לֵית דֵּין עַל מַגָּן מִיָּד נְפַק חַד חִוְיָא וּמְחָא יָתֵהּ וּקְטַל יָתֵהּ וְקָרָא עָלָיו 'וְאֶתֵּן אָדָם תַּחְתֶּיךָ' וְאֶתֵּן אֱדוֹם תַּחְתֶּיךָ (ישעיה מג, ד)

R. Eleazar was sitting to ease himself in a privy, when a Roman came and drove him away and sat down [where R. Eleazar had been sitting]. 'This is not for nothing,' [R. Eleazar] remarked. Immediately a snake emerged and struck and killed [the Roman]. [R. Eleazar] applied to [the Roman] the verse, 'Therefore will I give a man (*adam*) in your place' (Isaiah 43:4) – I give *edom* (a Roman) in your place.

When R. Eleazar was rudely pushed away from a privy that was then taken over by a Roman, he couldn't understand why he had been singled out and not another of the many who were present. But he understood

when a snake killed the Roman in the privy. The verse quoted includes
the term *adam*, man, which the *midrash* reads as *edom*, often applied as an
epithet for Rome or Romans, since both words are spelled the same.

רַבִּי יִצְחָק בַּר אֶלְעָזָר הֲוָה קָאֵם וּמְטַיֵּל עַל מְשׁוּנִיתָא דְּיַמָּא דְּקֵיסָרִין רָאָה שָׁם
קוּלִית אַחַת וַהֲוָה מַצְנַע לַהּ וַהֲוַת מִתְגַּלְגְּלָא מַצְנַע לַהּ וַהֲוַת מִתְגַּלְגְּלָא אֲמַר זֹאת
מוּכֶנֶת לַעֲשׂוֹת שְׁלִיחוּתָהּ עֲבַר חַד בַּלְדָּר וְנִכְשַׁל בָּהּ וְנָפַל וָמֵת אֲזַל פַּשְׁפְּשׁוּנֵהּ
וְאַשְׁכְּחוּנֵהּ טָעֵן כְּתָבִין בִּישִׁין עַל יְהוּדָאֵי דְּקֵיסָרִין

**R. Isaac b. R. Eleazar was strolling on the cliffs of the sea at
Caesarea, when he saw a thigh bone. He buried it, but it rolled out;
he buried it again, and again it rolled out. 'This is intended to
perform its mission,' he remarked. Then a messenger passed by,
stumbled over [the bone], fell and died. They went and searched
him and found that he was bearing evil decrees against the Jews of
Caesarea.**

The point of this story is God's will can be achieved even through
inanimate objects.

טִיטוּס הָרָשָׁע נִכְנַס לְבֵית קָדְשֵׁי הַקֳּדָשִׁים וְחַרְבּוֹ שְׁלוּפָה בְיָדוֹ וְגִדֵּר אֶת שְׁתֵּי
הַפָּרוֹכוֹת וְנָטַל שְׁתֵּי זוֹנוֹת וּבְעָלָן עַל גַּבֵּי הַמִּזְבֵּחַ וְיָצָא חַרְבּוֹ מְלֵאָה דָם אִית
דְּאָמְרִי מִדַּם הַקֳּדָשִׁים וְאִית דְּאָמְרִי מִדַּם שָׂעִיר שֶׁל יוֹם הַכִּפּוּרִים וְחֵרֵף וְגִדֵּף
וְנָטַל כָּל כְּלֵי בֵית הַמִּקְדָּשׁ וַעֲשָׂאָן כְּמִין גּוּרְגּוּתְנִי אַחַת וְהִתְחִיל מְחָרֵף וּמְגַדֵּף
כְּלַפֵּי מַעְלָה וְאָמַר לָא דָמֵי הַהוּא דְּעָבֵד קְרָבָא עִם מַלְכָּא בְּמַדְבְּרָא וּנְצַח לֵהּ
לְהַהוּא דְּעָבֵד קְרָבָא עִם מַלְכָּא בְּגוֹ פָּלָטִין דִּידֵהּ וּנְצַח לֵהּ

**The wicked Titus entered the Holy of Holies with a drawn sword in
his hand and pierced the two veils. He then took two prostitutes and
had sexual intercourse with them on the surface of the altar. When
he went out, his sword was drenched in blood, some say from the
blood of the holy offerings, some say it was the goat of the Day of
Atonement. And he blasphemed and reviled God, and took all the
vessels of the Temple and bundled them. He then began to
blaspheme and revile God saying, 'You cannot compare a hero who
battles a king in a wilderness and defeats him to one who defeats a
king in his own palace.'**

Titus was the Roman general who destroyed the Temple in Jerusalem.
This *midrash* describes his blasphemous attitude. He was not content to
defeat the Jews and conquer their country; he had to exhibit his disdain

for everything the Jews held holy. The two veils were the two curtains that separated the Holy of Holies from the main hall of the Temple, which hung about a handbreadth from each other. His behavior on the altar speaks for itself. The blood of the sacrificial goat of the Day of Atonement was usually sprinkled on the veil, which is how it reached his sword. He bundled the sacred vessels into the veil itself, which he then tied in a four-cornered way for ease in carrying, and then he boasted of his own prowess in that he had defeated his enemy, the God of Israel, in His own palace, the Temple.

The *midrash* continues:

יָרַד לַסְּפִינָה כֵּיוָן שֶׁיָּרַד מְחָאַה נַחְשָׁלָא בְּיַמָּא אָמַר דּוֹמֶה זֶה שֶׁאֵין כֹּחוֹ שֶׁל אֱלֹהַּ שֶׁל אֻמָּה זוֹ אֶלָּא בַּמַּיִם דּוֹר אֱנוֹשׁ לֹא פָרַע מֵהֶן אֶלָּא בַּמַּיִם דּוֹר הַמַּבּוּל לֹא פָרַע מֵהֶן אֶלָּא בַּמַּיִם פַּרְעֹה וְכָל חֵילוֹ לֹא פָרַע מֵהֶן אֶלָּא בַּמַּיִם אַף אֲנִי כְּשֶׁהָיִיתִי בְּתוֹךְ בֵּיתוֹ וּבִרְשׁוּתוֹ לֹא הָיָה יָכוֹל לַעֲמֹד בִּי וְעַכְשָׁו לְכָאן קְדָמַנִי סָבוּר הוּא שֶׁיַּהַרְגֵנִי בַּמַּיִם אָמַר לוֹ הַקָּדוֹשׁ בָּרוּךְ הוּא רָשָׁע חַיֶּךָ מִבְּרִיָּה שֶׁהִיא פְּחוּתָה מִכָּל הַבְּרִיּוֹת שֶׁבָּרָאתִי מִשֵּׁשֶׁת יְמֵי בְרֵאשִׁית בָּהּ אֲנִי נִפְרָע מֵאוֹתוֹ רָשָׁע מִיָּד רָמַז הַקָּדוֹשׁ בָּרוּךְ הוּא לַשַּׂר שֶׁל יָם וְעָמַד מִזַּעְפּוֹ

He then embarked on a ship [for Rome] and the ship was hit by a great wave. He said, 'It appears to me that the strength of this nation's God is [only] in water. He punished the generation of Enosh with water; He punished the generation of the Flood with water; He could only punish Pharaoh and his armies with water. When I was in His house and in His power he could not withstand me, but now he is confronting me, expecting to defeat me by means of water.' God said to him, 'Evil man! By your life, I will punish you by the very lowest of creatures of all that I created in the six days of creation!' The Holy One, blessed be He, signaled the angel in charge of the sea and the storm subsided.

The *midrash* goes on to describe Titus' blasphemous attitude even further. It was as though the Roman general considered himself God's equal and as though he was saying, 'I am an army general who fights on land. You could not defeat me on land because all Your power is in water.' He was mocking God.

כֵּיוָן שֶׁהִגִּיעַ לְרוֹמִי יָצְאוּ כָּל גְּדוֹלֵי רוֹמִי לִקְרָאתוֹ וְקִלְּסוּ אוֹתוֹ כֵּיוָן שֶׁעָלָה לְרוֹמִי נִכְנַס לַמֶּרְחָץ כֵּיוָן שֶׁיָּצָא הֵבִיאוּ פְּיָלֵי פּוֹטִירִין שֶׁל יַיִן לִשְׁתּוֹתוֹ וְנִכְנַס יִתּוּשׁ בְּתוֹךְ חוֹטְמוֹ וְהָיָה נוֹקֵר אֶת מֹחוֹ וְהוֹלֵךְ עַד שֶׁנַּעֲשָׂה גָדוֹל כְּמוֹ גוֹזָל שֶׁל שְׁתֵּי לִיטְרָאוֹת

וְהָיָה מְצֻוֶּה וְאוֹמֵר פִּצְעוּ מֹחוֹ שֶׁל אוֹתוֹ הָאִישׁ וְדְעוּ בַּמֶּה אֱלֹהֵיהֶם שֶׁל יְהוּדִים
נִפְרַע מֵאוֹתוֹ הָאִישׁ

When Titus reached Rome, all the great men of Rome came out to meet him. In Rome he entered a bathhouse and when he came out they brought him a goblet of wine to drink. A gnat entered his nostril and burrowed into his brain until it grew as large as a dove weighing two liters. [Titus] then ordered, 'Open the head of "this man" so that we might know by what means the God of the Jews is punishing "this man".'

On his arrival in Rome, Titus prepared himself for the great banquet to celebrate his victory. The motif of the bathhouse and the wine are revealing. Flies and gnats are common in the hot, damp atmosphere of a bathhouse and wine attracts insects. The arrival of a gnat on the scene therefore appeared to be perfectly natural. The insect in Titus' head reached the size of a dove weighing two liters and, apparently looked like a dove, which is most appropriate because Israel, whom he had conquered, is compared to a dove. Furthermore, Israel's distinguishing marks are the positive and negative commandments symbolized by the size of two liters. (*Tiferet Tzion*) Titus realized that this was his punishment and referred to himself as 'this man,' in the furtive mode, in order not to associate the catastrophe with himself.

מִיָּד קָרְאוּ לָרוֹפְאִים וּפָצְעוּ מֹחוֹ וְהוֹצִיאוּ כְּגוֹזָל שֶׁל שְׁתֵּי לִיטְרָאוֹת אָמַר רַ'
אֶלְעָזָר בַּר רַבִּי יוֹסֵי אֲנָא חֲמֵיתֵהּ בְּרוֹמִי תַּרְתֵּין לִיטְרִין מֵהָכָא וְגוֹזָלָא מֵהָכָא
וּתְקַל חַד לָקֳבֵל חַד וְנָטְלוּ אוֹתוֹ וְנָתְנוּ אוֹתוֹ בְּתוֹךְ קְעָרָה אַחַת כָּל מַה דַּהֲוָה הָדֵין
שַׁנִּי הֲוָה הָדֵין שַׁנִּי פְּרַח יְתוּשָׁה פְּרַחָה נַפְשֵׁהּ דְּטִיטוּס הָרָשָׁע

They immediately called the physicians who opened his head and removed a dove-like creature weighing two liters. R. Eleazar b. R. Jose said: I saw [this insect] in Rome; when it was weighed [on a scale] against a weight of two liters. They took it and put it on a plate. The more [its health] improved, the more the condition of Titus deteriorated until the insect flew away and the soul of the wicked Titus flew away.

The moral of this story about Titus is that the Almighty can perform His will and His mission even with the very smallest of creatures. This is the meaning of 'all their hosts' – 'All' can become the army of God.

* * *

Seed Thoughts

The idea of purpose is central to the religious conception of the world. The world must have been created for a purpose, and the purpose had to be disseminated and shared among all the various aspects of creation and be evident in them.

The idea of purpose does not have any significance in the secular world, because purpose is connected with the idea of a Creator. Therefore, secularists who deny a creator are implicitly denying the idea of purpose. The closest one comes to the concept of purpose in the secular world is Darwin's theory of natural selection; but even this lacks the theoretical basis that we ascribe to purpose. Recent scientific discoveries do give us some insight into a more theologically friendly conception of purpose. I have in mind some of the most recent theories in modern physics; but these theories are still speculative and not universally accepted in the scientific world.

The *midrash* before us ascribes this sense of purpose in a very special way to the animal world. The least of God's creatures fulfills His will. Even in death, as the *midrash* startlingly explains, a snake can fulfill its mission. The animal world does all of this by instinct or by some intuition we can only marvel at but not understand. But what about the human being? Was not the world created with man in mind? In the final analysis, the overall purpose of the world must be fully dependent upon him.

That is our real problem. Man is free to accept or reject a purpose or anything else for that matter. Unlike the animals, which live and react by instinct, man can only accept a purpose consciously and with a sense of awareness.

That is the real educational challenge. First to acknowledge and accept that man has been given a purpose. Second, to define that purpose as succinctly as possible. Third, to make every effort in preparation and in action to fulfill that purpose.

As to what this purpose might be in specific terms, I am reminded of the *mishnah* in the *Ethics of the Fathers* (3:5): 'Beloved is man for he was created in the divine image. An extra special act of love was bestowed upon him in being told and becoming aware that he was created in God's image.' In other words, the purpose of man is to fulfill the divine image in which we are created. This is an objective fact, but it must become subjective. We must become aware of this purpose and internalize it. That is the purpose of the Torah and the Jewish religion.

* * *

Additional Commentary

They opened his head

Titus warned the physicians on two points: 1. to open his head in order to relieve his pain; and 2. not to harm the insect so that all may see how God is paying him back. The implication is that as a result of his pain he wanted to repent. (*Tiferet Tzion*)

*

The more the insect improved, the more Titus deteriorated

When they removed the insect, it was like a dove; it then gradually diminished until it became an ordinary insect. It then flew away as insects do and, at that point, Titus died. So long as the insect remained different from others, God kept Titus alive so that everyone should see his humiliation and his punishment for having oppressed Israel. But when it became an insect there was no longer any reason to keep Titus alive. (*Tiferet Tzion*)

*

A goblet of wine

After a period of time in a steam bath a person becomes very thirsty and therefore is given to drink from a large vessel. Because of the intensity of his thirst Titus didn't realize that an insect had entered his nostril. It was an appropriate punishment. He had entered the Holy of Holies, a place where ordinary mortals were forbidden to enter, and similarly the insect had entered his nostril where ordinarily this does not happen. The fact that the insect began boring into his brain is a measure-for-measure punishment for his own blasphemy. (*Tiferet Tzion*)

Parashah Ten, Midrash Eight

וַיְכַל אֱלֹהִים בַּיוֹם הַשְּׁבִיעִי וְגוֹ' (בראשית ב, ב)

'And God finished on the seventh day' (Genesis 2:2).

But we know that the work ended on the sixth day. It means that creation ended in the last hour of the sixth day as above (*Parashah Nine Midrash Thirteen*). It is called the seventh day because we add from the secular to the sacred, thus sanctifying the last hour of the sixth day.

אָמַר רַ' חֲנִינָא מְשָׁכַנִי רַבִּי יִשְׁמָעֵאל בְּ"רַ יוֹסֵי אֵצֶל פֻּנְדָּק אֶחָד וְאָמַר לִי כָּאן הִתְפַּלֵּל אַבָּא שֶׁל שַׁבָּת בְּעֶרֶב שַׁבָּת

R. Ḥanina said: R. Ishmael b. R. Jose once persuaded me to come to a certain inn and said to me, 'Here my father once recited the Sabbath prayer [evening service] on the eve of the Sabbath.'

This anecdote illustrates the point made above. Although it was still day on Friday, R. Jose recited the Sabbath liturgy, on the principle of adding from the secular to the sacred and the Sabbath is sanctified in prayer even though, strictly speaking, it is not yet Sabbath.

רַ' יִרְמְיָה וְרַ' אַחָא אָמְרִי רַ' יוֹחָנָן מַקְשֵׁי כָּאן הִתְפַּלֵּל אַבָּא שֶׁל שַׁבָּת בְּעֶרֶב שַׁבָּת אַתְמָהָא וְלָא צְרִיךְ מַקְשֵׁי דְּהָא חַמָּרַיָּא הֲווֹ סָלְקִין מִן עֲרָב לְצִפּוֹרִין וַהֲווֹ אָמְרִין כְּבָר שָׁבַת רַבִּי חֲנִינָא בֶּן דּוֹסָא בְּעִירוֹ

R. Jeremiah and R. Aḥa said: R. Joḥanan objected [to the report]. [How can it be] that 'Here my father recited the Sabbath prayer on the eve of the Sabbath? I am amazed!' But R. Joḥanan should not have objected, because donkey drivers used to travel from [the town of] Arav to Sepphoris [on Friday] and [when they arrived] they said, 'R. Ḥanina b. Dosa had [already] commenced the Sabbath in his town [Arav].'

R. Joḥanan's objection to R. Ḥanina's anecdote was that it was inconceivable that R. Jose would recite the Sabbath evening prayers on Friday. The reason is that R. Joḥanan disagreed with the law stated above and held that the Sabbath prayers should be recited only after nightfall.

He could not accept the fact that R. Jose, a great authority, acted in such a manner. However, the *midrash* continues, there is other evidence of such behavior. The town of Arav is situated approximately fifteen kilometers from Sepphoris and the donkey drivers, who arrived there before the onset of Shabbat, used to say that in Arav R. Ḥanina b. Dosa, who was famous for his piety, had already begun the Sabbath before they left!

וְאִי בָּעֵית מַקְשָׁיָא עַל הָדָא קַשְׁיָא דַּאֲמַר רַבִּי חֲנִינָא מְשָׁכַנִי רַבִּי יִשְׁמָעֵאל בְּרַבִּי יוֹסֵי אֵצֶל פֻּנְדָּק אֶחָד וְאָמַר לִי כָּאן הִתְפַּלֵל אַבָּא שֶׁל אַחַר שַׁבָּת בַּשַּׁבָּת

But if you wish to object, it is to the following [anecdote that you should object]: R. Ḥanina said, 'R. Ishmael b. R. Jose once persuaded me to enter a certain inn and said, "Here my father recited the post-Sabbath prayer on the Sabbath".'

Clearly this second anecdote – or perhaps this version of the anecdote – does raise a difficulty. Whereas we add to the sacred, that is, add time from Friday to the Sabbath, we certainly cannot take time from the Sabbath and add it to Sunday. How could R. Jose recite the evening prayers for the close of Shabbat while it was still Shabbat? The *amidah* for the close of Shabbat contains the special *havdalah* prayer, *ata ḥonantanu*, distinguishing between the sacred and the secular.

אָמַר רַבִּי אַבָּא אַף עַל דָּא לָא הֲוֵי צְרִיךְ לְמַקְשֵׁי דְּהָא רַבִּי הֲוָה יָתֵב וְדָרֵשׁ וַהֲוָה אָמַר לְאַבָּא יוּדָן אָמוֹרֵהּ אַכְרוֹז קוֹמֵי דְצִבּוּרָא יְצַלּוֹן דְּחוֹלָא עַד יוֹמָא קָאֵם

Said R. Abba: To this [anecdote too] he need not have objected. Rabbi [Judah the Patriarch] was once sitting and lecturing when he said to Abba Yudan, his spokesman, 'Announce to the congregation that they should recite the weekday prayer while it is still day.'

This report constitutes a very weighty precedent. R. Judah ha-Nasi, the compiler of the Mishnah, was the undisputed halakhic authority of his time and if he allowed the post-Sabbath prayers to be recited while it was still daylight on the Sabbath, it must be permitted to do so. What probably happened was that the lecture ended early and it was doubtful whether the assembled congregation would remain for *ma'ariv* or, even if he felt that there would be *minyan*, the required quorum, he may have been reluctant to place an unnecessary burden on the community. Nor can this be considered adding from the secular to the sacred for everyone knows that weekday does not come until the appearance of three stars. (Mirkin) At any rate, we see from all this that such procedures were practiced.

* * *

Seed Thoughts

There is a concept in Jewish traditional law and custom known as *Tirchah de-tzibburah*, which, roughly translated, could be rendered, 'placing unnecessary burdens on the community.' Preachers are advised against overly long sermons and cantors are admonished not to prolong the liturgy – all because of this principle.

In modern times this practice can be discerned in the custom of many synagogues in Israel, but more especially in the Diaspora, to advance the time of prayer of the Friday evening service. This is particularly stressed in northern climates where the sun might set as late as ten o'clock P.M. or even later as one goes farther north. To pray at this hour and expect a family to dine together at a Sabbath meal is to impose a requirement that only few could tolerate.

One would have thought that this kind of pragmatism was a modernism that true pietists would never contemplate. But behold! A *midrash* where we have not one, but two illustrations of this practice dating back to the second century and condoned by the greatest halakhic authorities.

Donkey drivers would go from the town of Arav to Sepphoris on the eve of the Sabbath. They would arrive before the onset of Sabbath, but would inform the community that even before they left Arav, a distance of fifteen kilometers, R. Ḥanina ben Dosa had already ushered in the Sabbath, his purpose being to add hours of holiness to the Sabbath. Even so, it also had some pragmatic benefits for certain households. Did it create confusion, because different people followed a different time schedule? Possibly. But one can live with that kind of pluralism.

The second illustration is even more illuminating. It was recalled by R. Abba that no less an authority than R. Judah the Patriarch, the head of the Sanhedrin, instructed the congregation to recite the evening service on Saturday night before it became dark. His concern was that the *derashah*, the lesson, would finish at an early hour after which, if there were a long time interval, people would leave for home before *ma'ariv*. They would not be praying with a *minyan* and, very possibly, a *minyan* might not even remain. R. Judah made the judgment that it was better to advance the service before the 'emergence of three stars.' Might that not affect the observance of the Sabbath? That could be rectified educationally by teaching that the ending of the Sabbath is not determined by prayer but by the objective standards of time.

I remember such a service in London, England, in 1973 where the evening service on Saturday night was recited while it was yet daylight. The Rabbi of the congregation explained to me that this was the only way they could have a *minyan* and mourners could recite *kaddish*. The practice astonished me. We can see, however, that there is ample precedence from our *midrash*.

If we were to render this material into an ideological framework, it could be explained as the difference between time and timeliness. The Sabbath is limited by strictures of time; but other matters such as prayers, Sabbath meals, reciting *kiddush*, have to be seen within the more flexible structure of timeliness.

This same principle operated for the Almighty. Did God create the world in six or seven days? On which day was it concluded? Obviously on the seventh. But why does it sometimes say the sixth and sometimes the seventh? Because creation went on until the very last moment. Certain things required an accentuation in importance so they were rushed in at the last moment to show how much they were needed by the world. But nothing was created during the last hour of the sixth day to make room for the Sabbath and to symbolize that time would always be modified by timeliness.

* * *

Additional Commentary

Here my father recited the Sabbath prayer

This story is brought in order to explain the verse, 'And on the seventh day God finished the work.' The interpretation is, 'before the seventh day.' (*Yefei To'ar*)

*

'And on the seventh day the Lord finished…' But did God really finish on the seventh day? Here the most important part is missing and the *midrash* should have stated, 'From this we learn that one can add from the secular to the sacred.' And it will thus appear that the creation did end on the seventh day (as it encroached upon the hours of the sixth day). God, however, doesn't require this additional time. It is only because of this whole question of adding from the secular to the sacred that these stories are brought forward. (RZWE)

*

They prayed in a place that was lowland whereas on the plateau it was still light. Thus in some places it appeared as though it were the seventh day. That is what often happens during the last hour of the sixth day. (Mirkin)

*

R. Ishmael persuaded me

Where the righteous pray becomes a holy site where everyone's prayer has a better chance of being heard, especially the son of a righteous man where the merit of the father is retained in the very place. This why Jacob said, 'Could this be a place where my forefathers prayed and I would not know about it, and prayed there?' So when R. Ishmael passed this inn where his father had prayed, he, too, wanted to enter and pray there. He explained why, and, *en passant*, told R. Hanina that his father recited the Sabbath evening prayers while it was yet day. (*Tiferet Tzion*)

*

The prayers at the termination of the Sabbath

He had a very important mitzvah to perform at the conclusion of the Sabbath, so he followed the view of the Tractate Berakhot that the prayers of post-Sabbath may be recited on Sabbath. (*Tiferet Tzion*)

*

Announce that the congregation should pray

Many people had gathered there to hear the lecture of Rabbi Judah and after the lecture everyone would go home. He, therefore, requested that they recite tomorrow's prayer while it was still day so that they might all pray together on the principle that 'the king is honored by a multitude of people.' (*Tiferet Tzion*)

Parashah Ten, Midrash Nine

רַבִּי שָׁאֲלֵהּ לְרַבִּי יִשְׁמָעֵאל בְּ"רַ יוֹסֵי אָמַר לוֹ שָׁמַעְתָּ מֵאָבִיךָ מַהוּ 'וַיְכַל אֱלֹהִים בַּיּוֹם הַשְּׁבִיעִי' אַתְמְהָא

Rabbi [Judah ha-Nasi] asked R. Ishmael b. R. Jose: Have you heard from your father what 'And God finished on the seventh day' (Genesis 2:2) means? [The matter is] perplexing!

The reason for R. Judah's difficulty with the verse is the same question raised in the previous *midrash*. Was not the world completed on the sixth day?

אֶלָּא כָּזֶה שֶׁהוּא מַכֶּה בְּקָרְנוֹס עַל גַּבֵּי הַסַּדָּן הִגְבִּיהָהּ מִבְּעוֹד יוֹם וְהוֹרִידָהּ מִשֶּׁתֶּחְשַׁךְ

[He answered]: It is like a man striking the hammer on the anvil, raising it while it is still day but bringing it down after nightfall.

Like a workman using a hammer, God lifted up the hammer on the sixth day and lowered it at nightfall just at the beginning of the seventh day. The end point of bringing down the hammer was close to the first minute of the Sabbath so that the conclusion of the work was on the Sabbath. That is why the verse can say *va-yekhal*, meaning that God finished on the seventh day. Why did the Creator not add from the secular to the holy?

אָמַר רַ' שִׁמְעוֹן בֶּן יוֹחַאי בָּשָׂר וָדָם שֶׁאֵינוֹ יוֹדֵעַ לֹא עִתָּיו וְלֹא רְגָעָיו וְלֹא שְׁעוֹתָיו הוּא מוֹסִיף מֵחֹל עַל הַקֹּדֶשׁ אֲבָל הַקָּדוֹשׁ בָּרוּךְ הוּא שֶׁהוּא יוֹדֵעַ רְגָעָיו וְעִתָּיו וּשְׁעוֹתָיו נִכְנַס בּוֹ כְּחוּט הַשַּׂעֲרָה

R. Simon b. Yoḥai said: Mortal man, who does not know his (exact) times, his minutes, or his hours, must add from the profane to the sacred; but the Holy One, blessed be He, who knows his minutes, his times, and his hours, can enter it by a hair's breadth.

A human being can never be absolutely sure when it comes to time and is liable to desecrate the Sabbath if he works too close to its advent, but God knows time absolutely so that on the very last hour of the sixth day, which we use as an addition from the profane to the sacred, God was able to finish His work. The verse is thus able to say 'the seventh day' because the conclusion of the work approached the seventh day, but did not enter into it.

גְּנִיבָא וְרַבָּנָן גְּנִיבָא אָמַר מָשָׁל לְמֶלֶךְ שֶׁעָשָׂה לוֹ חֻפָּה וְצִיְּרָהּ וְכִיְּרָהּ וּמֶה הָיְתָה חֲסֵרָה כַּלָּה שֶׁתִּכָּנֵס לְתוֹכָהּ כָּךְ מֶה הָיָה הָעוֹלָם חָסֵר שַׁבָּת רַבָּנָן אָמְרִי מָשָׁל לְמֶלֶךְ שֶׁעָשׂוּ לוֹ טַבַּעַת מֶה הָיְתָה חֲסֵרָה חוֹתָם כָּךְ מֶה הָיָה הָעוֹלָם חָסֵר שַׁבָּת

Genivah and the Rabbis discussed this [matter]. Genivah said: This may be compared to a king who made a bridal chamber, which he plastered, painted, and adorned; now what did the bridal chamber lack? A bride to enter it. Similarly, what did the world still lack? The Sabbath. The Rabbis said: Imagine a king who made a ring; what did it lack? A signet. Similarly, what did the world lack? The Sabbath.

In the word ויכל, *va-yekhal*, one can discern the root of the word *kallah*, meaning 'bride.' This is the textual source that prompted Genivah to describe the Sabbath as a bride. Just as the presence of a bride completes the arrangements for a wedding, so did the oncoming of the Sabbath on the seventh day complete the world. Furthermore, just as the signet is the purpose for which a king wears a ring, so is the Sabbath the purpose for which God created the world. Both Genivah and the Rabbis agree that the use of the wording 'seventh day' is appropriate. The Sabbath is described as 'a sign between Me and the Children of Israel' and with the creation of the Sabbath, this sign, this signet, marked the formal completion of the creation of the world.

וְזֶה אֶחָד מִן הַדְּבָרִים שֶׁשִּׁנּוּ לְתַלְמַי הַמֶּלֶךְ וַיְכַל אֱלֹהִים בַּיּוֹם הַשִּׁשִּׁי וַיִּשְׁבֹּת בַּיּוֹם הַשְּׁבִיעִי

And this is one of the texts they changed for King Ptolemy, [making it read], 'And God finished on the sixth day and rested on the seventh.'

With regard to the translation of the Bible commissioned by King Ptolemy of Egypt, see *Parashah Eight Midrash Eleven*. This verse was one of those that were deliberately 'mistranslated' by the Rabbinic translators in creating the *Septuagint* in order to avoid passages that would raise questions, the answers to which the Greek-speaking readers would have difficulty in understanding.

תַּלְמַי הַמֶּלֶךְ שָׁאַל אֶת הַזְּקֵנִים בְּרוֹמִי בְּכַמָּה יָמִים בָּרָא הַקָּדוֹשׁ בָּרוּךְ הוּא עוֹלְמוֹ
אָמְרוּ לוֹ לְשִׁשָּׁה יָמִים אָמַר לָהֶם וּמֵאוֹתָהּ שָׁעָה גֵּיהִנָּם נִסֶּקֶת לִרְשָׁעִים אוֹי
לָעוֹלָם מִדִּינָיו

**King Ptolemy asked the elders in Rome, 'In how many days did the
Holy One, blessed be He, create His world?' 'In six days,' they
replied. He said to them, 'And since then Gehenna has been stoked
up for the wicked?! Woe to the world because of His laws!'**

Most of the manuscripts of *Bereishit Rabbah* have a different reading. They
infer that instead of King Ptolemy asking the elders in Rome, the correct
reading should be, 'A philosopher asked...' (cf. the 'philosopher' mentioned above, *Parashah One Midrash Nine, Parashah Eight Midrash Nine*).
The reference would then be to one of the sectarians who was
theologically close to the Christians. He realized that according to Jewish
theology Gehenna has been in existence since that time and those who
do not observe the Sabbath are doomed to be sent to it – thus 'Woe to the
world because of these laws.' Presumably he meant that his religion would
be more compassionate. (Mirkin) Many emendations have been suggested
for this difficult passage but none have achieved a consensus.

'מְלַאכְתּוֹ' לֹא כֵן אָמַר ר' בֶּרֶכְיָה בְּשֵׁם רַבִּי סִימוֹן לֹא בְעָמָל וְלֹא בִיגִיעָה בָּרָא
הַקָּדוֹשׁ בָּרוּךְ הוּא אֶת עוֹלְמוֹ וְאַתְּ אוֹמֵר 'מִכָּל מְלַאכְתּוֹ' אַתְמָהָא אֶלָּא לְהִפָּרַע
מִן הָרְשָׁעִים שֶׁהֵן מְאַבְּדִין אֶת הָעוֹלָם שֶׁנִּבְרָא כֻלּוֹ בְּעָמָל וּבִיגִיעָה וְלִתֵּן שָׂכָר טוֹב
לַצַּדִּיקִים שֶׁהֵן מְקַיְּמִין אֶת הָעוֹלָם שֶׁנִּבְרָא כֻלּוֹ בְּעָמָל וּבִיגִיעָה

**['And God finished on the seventh day] His work.' Did not R.
Berekhiah in the name of R. Simon say, 'Neither with labor nor with
toil did the Holy One, blessed be He, create His world,' yet it says,
'[And He rested] from all his *work*! This is amazing! [It is so written]
only in order to punish the wicked who destroy the world, which
was as though created entirely with labor and toil, and to give a
goodly reward to the righteous who uphold the world which was as
though created entirely with labor and toil.**

It is not to be understood from this that God worked in any physical way.
It is simply the use of the language of work as in the passage of the *Ethics
of the Fathers* (5:1) that God created the world with ten sayings. Why then
use the term 'work' at all? It is a way of putting an evaluation on the world
and making both the good and the wicked cognizant of how great the
stakes are in the preservation of the world.

וּמַה נִּבְרָא בּוֹ לְאַחַר שֶׁשָּׁבַת שַׁאֲנָן נַחַת וְשַׁלְוָה וְהַשֶּׁקֶט

And what was created on [the seventh day] after He rested? Tranquility, ease, peace, and quiet.

Actual work was really done on the seventh day. The creation of the Sabbath is a new phenomenon and is considered work. (*Yefei To'ar*) The four qualities listed are actual creations since they liberate the person from fear, worry, and anxiety about the very problems that come from trying to observe the Sabbath. This corresponds beautifully with the four occasions that work is used in the Sabbath paragraph: 'And God finished on the seventh day the *work* which He had done... and He rested on the seventh day from all the *work*...because thereon He rested from all His *work*...which God in *creating* had made.' (*Ha-Midrash ha-Mevo'ar*)

רַבִּי לֵוִי בְּשֵׁם רַ' יוֹסֵי בְּ"רַ נְהוֹרַאי כָּל זְמַן שֶׁהָיוּ יְדֵי קוֹנֵיהֶם מְמַשְׁמְשִׁין בָּהֶם הָיוּ מוֹתְחִים וְהוֹלְכִין כֵּיָן שֶׁנָּחוּ יְדֵי קוֹנֵיהֶם מֵהֶן נִתַּן לָהֶם נִיחָה 'וַיָּנַח' (שמות כ, יא) לְעוֹלָמוֹ 'בַּיּוֹם הַשְּׁבִיעִי'

R. Levi said in the name of R. Jose b. R. Nehorai: As long as the hands of their master were working on them they went on expanding; but when the hands of their master rested, rest was afforded to them, and thus 'He gave rest' to his world 'on the seventh day' (Exodus 20:11).

This interpretation is given in response to the question asked above. What was created on the Sabbath that was actually new? The answer is that God moved from the act of expansion to the experience of fulfillment. While God was actively creating, every element of the cosmos was expanding. At a certain stage God said, 'Enough!' At that point what was given to all creatures was rest. This was the new creation. The verse does not say 'He rested,' for which the correct term would be נח, *naḥ*, but rather וינח, *va-yonaḥ*, which means He gave the concept of rest to the world. Therefore it says that on the seventh day He rested from all the work He had done during the previous six days.

אָמַר רַ' אַבָּא בָּשָׂר וָדָם בְּשָׁעָה שֶׁהוּא עוֹשֶׂה אַסְטְרַטְיָא אֵינוֹ נוֹתֵן דּוֹנָטִיבָה וּבְשָׁעָה שֶׁהוּא נוֹתֵן דּוֹנָטִיבָה אֵינוֹ עוֹשֶׂה אַסְטְרַטְיָא אֲבָל הַקָּדוֹשׁ בָּרוּךְ הוּא עָשָׂה אַסְטְרַטְיָא וְנָתַן דּוֹנָטִיבָה 'וַיִּשְׁבֹּת' 'וַיְבָרֶךְ.'

R. Abba said: When a mortal [king] takes his army into quarters, he does not distribute largesse, whereas when he distributes largesse,

he does not order a halt. But the Holy One, blessed be He, ordered a halt and distributed largesse, [as it is written,] 'And He rested... and He blessed.'

When an army prepares for battle they are not only provided with equipment and provisions but also given many inducements to serve well beyond the call of duty. However, when they are demobilized, the equipment is withdrawn and the provisions cease. But when God gave His creatures 'rest,' which corresponds to demobilization in the parable, He gave them gifts as well, in the form of a blessing. That is why it says *va-yishbot*, and He gave them rest, followed by *va-yevorekh*, and He blessed. A person of flesh and blood gives a gift in exchange for effort and work, but God gives a gift even at a time of cessation from work. (*Yefei To'ar*)

* * *

Seed Thoughts

The Sabbath is here compared to a bride and to a signet ring. Can you imagine a wedding ceremony without a bride? By the same token a world without the Sabbath would be an empty shell. Insofar as the signet ring is concerned, there is no point in a king having such a ring unless it bore his seal to be used for official documents. That is its purpose. By the same token, the Sabbath is the purpose for which the world was created.

These views were expressed by Genivah and the Sages, respectively. The more one reflects upon them, however, the more one realizes that we are not dealing with a controversy, but with views that complement each other. Granted that a canopy without a bride is an empty vessel; on the other hand, a bride without a ring is not sanctified. The ring is the promise of both commitment and a sanctified purpose. In the same vein, the world requires not merely a theoretical purpose but a framework of commitment so that its purpose be embedded in the life of every human being. How can this be done? Who will do it?

Set me as a seal upon thy heart,
As a seal upon thine arm;
For love is strong as death. (Song of Songs 8:6)

In the metaphorical language of the Song of Songs, it is Israel that calls upon God and beseeches, 'Set me as a seal upon thy heart as a seal upon thine arm.' In its highest reaches, the Jewish people wants to be used not only to fulfill the purpose of the world, but also as a vehicle of commitment. Israel will adopt the Sabbath and make it part of its way of life and through it rehearse weekly in its form and content the purpose for which the world was created.

But in the Song of Songs Israel also calls out, 'Set me as a seal upon thine arm.' Emotion of the heart is not enough. Ideals and even commitment require power. They require muscle!

In the first place, that which we are calling muscle depends upon numbers. With all due respect to the individual and his integrity, one person cannot be compared to a community. A community does more than multiply numbers; it provides a continuity that goes beyond the individual.

'Muscle' also requires a political structure dedicated to a spiritual purpose. That is why the Jewish religion was mandated to a particular land and a particular holy site. It is difficult for Jews in the lands in which they live to function in any capacity other than that of individuals and citizens. In a state of Israel, however, the power structure itself could be dedicated to the goals of creation, assuming a peaceful world.

It does not take too vivid an imagination to see in the symbolism of the mind, the heart, and the arm, an oblique reference to the equally dramatic symbol of the *tefillin* as well. This is another of the signs of commitment. This and the Sabbath and the festivals and all the other emotional and intellectual commandments are the vehicles through which Israel in the past and Jews at their highest levels are called upon for their involvement and their identification. The world needs both a bride and a signet ring; it needs purpose and commitment.

* * *

Additional Commentary

And God finished on the seventh day

This should be understood as though it read, *'im yom ha-shevi'i*, meaning that, together with the seventh day, God finished His work. (*Matnot Kehunah*)

*

The use of the term 'seventh day' in this context simply means that the seventh day met the sixth day precisely at the moment of its completion. From our point of perception it seemed to be the seventh day because we are not able to shrink the day or observe minutiae, and our only recourse is to add from the secular to the sacred. (RZWE)

*

When it says *va-yekhulu ha-shomayim* it means *kolu ha-shomayim*, the heavens completed themselves. That is the explanation of raising up the hammer, after which it will come down by itself. (Mirkin)

*

In how many days did God create the world?

There is no contradiction between what R. Berakhiah is saying and what follows. R. Berakhiah is talking about the beginning of creation which was by God's word, and our text, *melakhto*, is talking about the conclusion of creation. In the beginning God created the world in small dimensions as was mentioned in connection with the creation of heaven and earth, that the cedars of Lebanon were the size of grasshoppers at their beginnings. The same holds for all creation. Only afterwards did God extend them to their proper dimensions as mentioned by R. Levi later on. 'As long as the hands of their master were working they went on expanding.' So, the beginning of creation required no physical effort, but the end of creation where God had to expand them to their proper size did require some effort on the part of all the creatures themselves in accordance with the powers that God had assigned to them.

The question of the *midrash* really has to do with why effort was required because this does not seem to be in His Honor. That is the explanation of the answer: all this was required in order to motivate the wicked to mend their ways in the world where even God had to struggle in order to create it.

The purpose of creation is to improve things for man's ultimate end. That is why the world at the beginning was created in miniature form without effort, but concluded in expanded form with effort. The ground was then prepared to punish those who destroy the world and reward those who build it up. (*Tiferet Tzion*)

*

Tranquility, ease, peace, and quiet

The *midrash* uses the above four terms to describe the spiritual condition and opportunity of the Sabbath. The person who has experienced the rush of life such as urbanization and competition achieves rest from this external pressure, but his heart does not yet achieve inner peace, which is called *naches*. So far all that has been achieved is the absence of evil. Now he is ready to receive the good that is that peace and unity with man and his fellow and that tranquility that is inner and that happens whenever the human will is not in conflict with the human intellect. When this happens there occurs the true tranquility of soul. (*Tiferet Tzion*)

Parashah Eleven, Midrash One

'וַיְבָרֶךְ אֱלֹהִים אֶת יוֹם הַשְּׁבִיעִי וַיְקַדֵּשׁ אֹתוֹ' (בראשית ב, ג) כְּתִיב 'בִּרְכַּת ה' הִיא תַעֲשִׁיר וְלֹא יוֹסִף עֶצֶב עִמָּהּ' (משלי י, כב)

**'And God blessed the seventh day and declared it holy' (Genesis 2:3).
It is written, 'It is the blessing of the Lord that enriches' (Proverbs
10:22).**

The 'blessing' mentioned in Proverbs is taken as an allusion to 'And God
blessed the seventh day.' What was the blessing given to the Sabbath? It
was that man would not have to exhaust himself and work himself to the
bone in order to make a living. God's blessing by itself will suffice. This
is the literal meaning, but there is a homiletical one as well.

'בִּרְכַּת ה' הִיא תַעֲשִׁיר' זוֹ הַשַּׁבָּת שֶׁנֶּאֱמַר 'וַיְבָרֶךְ אֱלֹהִים אֶת יוֹם הַשְּׁבִיעִי' 'וְלֹא יוֹסִף עֶצֶב עִמָּהּ' (משלי שם, שם) זֶה הָאֵבֶל הֵיךְ מַה דְּאַתְּ אָמַר 'נֶעֱצַב הַמֶּלֶךְ עַל בְּנוֹ' (ש"ב יט, ג)

**'It is the blessing of the Lord that enriches' (ibid.); this refers to the
Sabbath, as it is written, 'And God blessed the seventh day' and
'grief adds nothing to it' (ibid.) refers to mourning, as it says, 'The
king was grieving for his son' (II Samuel 19:3).**

The principle of the blessing is that the Sabbath will guard those who
observe it. This is perceived more effectively from the second half of the
verse from Proverbs. We know that when a person is sitting *shiv'ah*, in the
first seven days of mourning for a close relative, Shabbat interrupts the
mourning. The word עצב, *'etzev*, in many places is interpreted as
mourning. It is as though the Sabbath helps those in grief transcend the
heavy burden of bereavement. Thus the Sabbath helps those that help it.
Thus, when the verse says that God blessed the Sabbath day it means that
He invited the Sabbath to bless those who observe it and guard it. The
verse from Samuel is quoted merely to show that in the case of David *'etzev*
means mourning.

* * *

Seed Thoughts

The Jewish tradition says that all the blessings that exist can be subsumed under three categories – children, livelihood and life.

When we pray for our children it is because we want them to be blessed with the very same things that we want for ourselves, namely, life, livelihood, and children of their own. What about those who have no children, has this blessing passed them by? Not at all, says the prophet Isaiah in a beautiful section that we read on fast days: 'For thus says the Lord, to those without children who keep my Sabbaths, who choose the things that please Me and hold fast to My covenant. I will give in My house and within My walls a monument and a memorial better than sons and daughters. I will give them an everlasting memorial which shall not be cut off.'

The blessing of a livelihood means first and foremost the ability of people to sustain themselves financially as independent human beings. But it also means more. There are many people with adequate funds who idle away their time in life. The goal is to do something useful at every stage of existence. It means also to work for a society that will help individuals in their effort to lead useful lives.

The blessing of life itself is, first and foremost, quantitative. Who is there that would not want to live for many years? Long life is the most popular of all the blessings. That part, however, is not in our hands and one can only hope that our will conforms to God's will. There is an aspect of life, however, that is qualitative and that is largely in human hands. That means making life worth living, making it meaningful by devoting it to good deeds.

The fifth commandment says, 'Honor your father and your mother that your days may be prolonged.' Not 'your years,' but 'your days.' A good life is not one of many years, but one of many days of achievement, of giving, and of worth.

* * *

Additional Commentary

And God blessed the seventh day

Since it says, 'And God blessed,' but does not specify what the blessing is, one must conclude that it includes all the blessings that exist. In actual fact, all the possible blessings can be reduced to three categories: children, life and livelihood. It is in this connection that the verse in Proverbs is quoted, 'It is the blessing of the Lord that enriches.' This implies that in this verse there will be found all three categories of blessing. In connection with livelihood, the verse is crystal clear, and in connection with children and life there is the second part of the verse, 'grief adds nothing to it.' The explanation is that even if David's sins contributed to the death, heaven forfend, of one of his children, nevertheless by means of Sabbath observance, he will merit that there will be no further grief and he and his remaining children will be blessed with long life, riches, and honour. (*Tiferet Tzion*)

Parashah Eleven, Midrash Two

וַיְבָרֶךְ אֱלֹהִים אֶת יוֹם הַשְּׁבִיעִי וְגוֹ' רַבִּי יִשְׁעָאֵל אוֹמֵר בֵּרְכוֹ בַּמָּן וְקִדְּשׁוֹ בַּמָּן בֵּרְכוֹ
בַּמָּן שֶׁכָּל יְמוֹת הַשַּׁבָּת הָיָה יוֹרֵד עֹמֶר בְּעֶרֶב שַׁבָּת שְׁנֵי עוֹמָרִים וְקִדְּשׁוֹ בַּמָּן שֶׁלֹּא
יָרַד בּוֹ כָּל עִקָּר

'And God blessed the seventh day and declared it holy' – He blessed
it with the manna and declared it holy with the manna. He blessed
it with the manna, for every day of the week there descended one
omer [of manna], but on the eve of the Sabbath, two *omers*. And He
declared it holy with manna, which did not descend on the Sabbath
at all.

One has to understand how the Sabbath was blessed and how it was
sanctified. It was blessed by virtue of the fact that every day for the forty
years in the wilderness an *omer* (a measure of approximately 2.5 liters) per
person of manna fell. It was sanctified by the fact that this manna did not
fall on the Sabbath, but on the eve of the Sabbath for the Sabbath. There
is a view that in anticipation of the Sabbath on Friday, two *omers* of manna
appeared in addition to the portion for Friday. That means three *omers*
were gathered Friday. From the fact that God blessed the seventh day at
the time of creation we can conclude that the blessing was intended for
the future. (*Yefei To'ar*)

רַבִּי נָתָן אוֹמֵר בֵּרְכוֹ בַּמָּן וְקִדְּשׁוֹ בַּמָּן וְקִדְּשׁוֹ בִּבְרָכָה רַבִּי יִצְחָק אָמַר בֵּרְכוֹ בַּמָּן וְקִדְּשׁוֹ
בַּמְקוֹשֵׁשׁ

R. Nathan said: He blessed it with the manna and declared it holy
with a blessing. R. Isaac said: He blessed it with the manna and
declared it holy through the man who gathered [sticks on the
Sabbath].

The idea of hallowing the Sabbath with a blessing is based on the idea that
those who observe it are obligated to recite blessings over it. From this is
derived the law that the Sabbath is hallowed by the blessing of *kiddush* as
it begins and ends with the phrase *mekadesh ha-shabbat*, 'who sanctifies the
Sabbath.' The reference to the man who gathered sticks (Numbers
16:32-36) implies that the strict punishment recorded in the Bible

whereby Sabbath desecration became a capital offence was a way in which it was sanctified in the legal system.

וּבֵרְכוֹ בַּעֲטִיפָה רַב הוּנָא אָמַר צָרִיךְ לְהַחֲלִיף רַ' חִיָּא בְּשֵׁם רַ' יוֹחָנָן אָמַר צָרִיךְ לְעָרֵב אָבִין בַּר חַסְדַּאי אָמַר צָרִיךְ לְשַׁלְשֵׁל רַבִּי יִרְמְיָה וְרַ' זְעֵירָא הֲווֹן מְהַלְּכִין כַּחֲדָא וְאִסְתַּלַּקַת גְּלִתֵּהּ דְּרַ' יִרְמְיָה וְשִׁלְשְׁלָהּ רַבִּי זְעֵירָא הָדָא אָמְרָה צָרִיךְ לְשַׁלְשֵׁל

He blessed it with [the distinction of] robing. R. Huna said: A man must change [his garments] for the Sabbath. R. Ḥiyya said in R. Joḥanan's name: A man must mingle [his garments]. Avin b. Ḥasdai said: He must let [his cloak] hang down. R. Jeremiah and R. Ze'ira were walking together and R. Jeremiah's cloak being tucked up [when the Sabbath commenced], R. Ze'ira pulled it down. This was [in accordance with] what [Avin b. Ḥasdai] had said, 'One must let one's cloak hang down.'

We have to try to resemble God as much as possible. He adorns Himself with garments on the Sabbath, symbolically speaking, and so should we. One who cannot afford to have a separate wardrobe for the Sabbath should at least have one garment set aside for Sabbath. If even this is beyond his capacity let him wrap his garments in such a way as to make a difference on the Sabbath. (*Tiferet Tzion*) R. Jeremiah had his cloak tucked up to facilitate easier walking and when Shabbat began, his companion, R. Ze'ira, pulled it down. Having the garment hang down was the manner in which the rich dressed to indicate that they did not have to work. Wearing the garments hanging down on the Sabbath was therefore considered a form of Sabbath honor and also an indication that on that day no work is to be done.

רַ' אֶלְעָזָר אוֹמֵר בֵּרְכוֹ בְּנֵר וּבִי הָיָה הַמַּעֲשֶׂה פַּעַם אַחַת הִדְלַקְתִּי אֶת הַנֵּר בְּלֵילֵי שַׁבָּת וּבָאתִי וּמְצָאתִי אוֹתוֹ בְּמוֹצָאֵי שַׁבָּת דָּלוּק וְלֹא חָסֵר כְּלוּם

R. Eleazar said: [God] blessed [the seventh day] in the matter of a lamp, and this happened in my case. I once kindled a lamp for the Sabbath night and when I came at the termination of the Sabbath I found it still burning and [the oil] not at all diminished

The blessing of light is a symbol of the plenitude of blessings. Since the fire that burns is a spiritual symbol it indicates that whatever a person sacrifices for the Sabbath will not be felt as a lack. The abundance of blessings will more than make up for the expense incurred.

בֵּרְכוּ בְּאוֹר פָּנָיו שֶׁל אָדָם קִדְּשׁוֹ בְּאוֹר פָּנָיו שֶׁל אָדָם לֹא דוֹמֶה אוֹר פָּנָיו שֶׁל אָדָם
כָּל יְמוֹת הַשַּׁבָּת כְּמוֹ שֶׁהוּא דוֹמֶה בַּשַּׁבָּת

[God] blessed [the seventh day] with the light of a man's face and
declared it holy through the light of a man's face. The light of a
man's face all the days of the week is not the same as it is on the
Sabbath.

God bestowed on the Sabbath both material and spiritual blessings. This
is implied in the text *va-yevorekh* and *va-yekadesh.* The face of a person is
the image of God and therefore these blessings are visible on his face.
(*Tiferet Tzion*)

בֵּרְכוּ בַּמְּאוֹרוֹת רַ' שִׁמְעוֹן בַּר יְהוּדָה אִישׁ כְּפַר עַכּוֹ אוֹמֵר מִשּׁוּם רַ' שִׁמְעוֹן אַף
עַל פִּי שֶׁנִּתְקַלְלוּ הַמְּאוֹרוֹת מֵעֶרֶב שַׁבָּת אֲבָל לֹא לָקוּ עַד מוֹצָאֵי שַׁבָּת

[God] blessed [the seventh day] in respect of the luminaries. R.
Simon b. R. Judah, a man of Acre, said in the name of R. Simon:
Although the luminaries were cursed on the eve of the Sabbath, yet
they were not [actually] smitten until the termination of the
Sabbath.

We learned in an earlier *midrash* (*Parashah Ten, Midrash Four*) that as part
of the punishment of Adam, the luminaries were also punished in the
sense that the pace of their traversing the heavens was altered. This
affected the seasons of the year and the pace of productivity of the
vegetation. However, although the sin of Adam was on a Friday, the
punishment of the luminaries was delayed until after the Sabbath.

אַתְיָא כְּרַבָּנָן וְלֹא אָתְיָא כִּדְרַבִּי אַמִּי דַּאֲמַר רַ' אַמִּי אָדָם הָרִאשׁוֹן לֹא לָן כְּבוֹדוֹ
עִמּוֹ מַה טַעַם 'וְאָדָם בִּיקָר בַּל יָלִין נִמְשַׁל כַּבְּהֵמוֹת נִדְמוּ' (תהלים מט, יג) וְרַבָּנָן
אָמְרִי לָן כְּבוֹדוֹ עִמּוֹ וּמוֹצָאֵי שַׁבָּת נִטַּל מִמֶּנּוּ זִיווֹ וּטְרָדוֹ מִגַּן עֵדֶן הֲדָא הוּא דִכְתִיב
'מְשַׁנֶּה פָנָיו וַתְּשַׁלְּחֵהוּ' (איוב יד, כ)

This [opinion] is in accordance with the Rabbis' [opinion], but not
with that of R. Ammi, since R. Ammi said: Adam's glory did not
abide the night with him. What is the proof? 'Man (*adam*) does not
abide in glory, he is like the beasts that perish' (Psalms 49:13). The
Rabbis said: His glory did abide with him, but at the termination of
the Sabbath his splendor was taken from him and [the Almighty]
expelled him from the Garden of Eden, as it is written, 'You alter
his visage and dispatch him' (Job 14:20).

According to R. Ammi the special dignity that Adam acquired at his creation disappeared when he sinned and he did not have it even for the first Friday night. In the proof-text the word *adam* is personified as referring to Adam the first man and not, as is the obvious intention of the text, to mankind as a whole. The verse from Job cited by the Rabbis has also been applied to Adam in the Garden of Eden (see *Bereishit Rabbah* 16:1).

כֵּיוָן שֶׁשָּׁקְעָה חַמָּה בְּלֵילֵי שַׁבָּת בִּקֵּשׁ הַקָּדוֹשׁ בָּרוּךְ הוּא לִגְנֹז אֶת הָאוֹרָה וְחָלַק
כָּבוֹד לַשַּׁבָּת הָדָא הוּא דִכְתִיב 'וַיְבָרֶךְ אֱלֹהִים אֶת יוֹם הַשְּׁבִיעִי וַיְקַדֵּשׁ אֹתוֹ' בֵּרְכוֹ
בְּאוֹרָה כֵּיוָן שֶׁשָּׁקְעָה הַחַמָּה בְּלֵילֵי הַשַּׁבָּת הִתְחִילָה הָאוֹרָה וְהָיְתָה מְשַׁמֶּשֶׁת
הִתְחִילוּ הַכֹּל מְקַלְּסִין הָדָא הוּא דִכְתִיב 'תַּחַת כָּל הַשָּׁמַיִם יִשְׁרֵהוּ וְאוֹרוֹ עַל
כַּנְפוֹת הָאָרֶץ' מִפְּנֵי מָה 'וְאוֹרוֹ עַל כַּנְפוֹת הָאָרֶץ' (שם לז, ג)

As soon as the sun set on the night of the Sabbath, the Holy One, blessed be He, wished to hide the light, but he showed honor to the Sabbath, as it is written, 'And God blessed the seventh day and declared it holy' – with what did He bless it? With light. When the sun set on the Sabbath eve, the light continued to function, whereupon all began praising, as it is written, 'Under the whole heaven they sing praises to Him' (Job. 37:3). Why? Because 'His light [reaches] unto the ends of the earth' (ibid.).

The original light at the beginning of the world shone until the fourth day when the luminaries were created, and then it was hidden by God. At the creation of man this light was returned in his honor and it would have remained had not Adam sinned. However, God, out of respect for the Sabbath, allowed the original light to remain over the Sabbath.

אָמַר ר' יְהוּדָה בַּר רַבִּי סִימוֹן אוֹר שֶׁבָּרָא הַקָּדוֹשׁ בָּרוּךְ הוּא בַּיּוֹם רִאשׁוֹן אָדָם
צוֹפֶה וּמַבִּיט בּוֹ מִסּוֹף הָעוֹלָם וְעַד סוֹפוֹ כֵּיוָן שֶׁהִסְתַּכֵּל הַקָּדוֹשׁ בָּרוּךְ הוּא בְּאַנְשֵׁי
דוֹר הַמַּבּוּל וּבְאַנְשֵׁי דוֹר הַפְּלָגָה שֶׁמַּעֲשֵׂיהֶן מְקֻלְקָלִין עָמַד וּגְנָזָה וְהִתְקִינָה
לַצַּדִּיקִים לֶעָתִיד לָבוֹא וּמִנַּיִן שֶׁגְּנָזָה שֶׁנֶּאֱמַר 'וַיִּמְנַע מֵרְשָׁעִים אוֹרָם וּזְרוֹעַ רָמָה
תִּשָּׁבֵר' (שם לח, טו) וּמִנַּיִן שֶׁהִתְקִינָה לַצַּדִּיקִים לֶעָתִיד לָבוֹא שֶׁנֶּאֱמַר 'וְאֹרַח
צַדִּיקִים כְּאוֹר נֹגַהּ הוֹלֵךְ וָאוֹר עַד נְכוֹן הַיּוֹם' (משלי ד, יח)

R. Judah b. Simon said: Adam could see from one end of the world to the other by the light which the Holy One, blessed be He, created on the first day. When God looked at the men of the generation of the Flood and at the men of the generation of the Tower of Babel, whose actions were corrupt, He hid the light and installed it for the

righteous in the world to come. Whence do we know it was hidden? As it says, 'Their light is withheld from the wicked, and the upraised arm is broken' (Job 38:15). And whence do we know that He installed it for the righteous in the world to come? As it says, 'The path of the righteous is like radiant sunlight, ever brightening until noon' (Proverbs 4:18).

The light that God created on the first day illuminated the Garden of Eden for Adam, as well as providing light in the other constellations. It enabled Adam to foresee all the generations yet to come. It was more than seeing. He was given an insight into all the secrets of the universe, which is why it was later hidden. When God saw the corrupt behavior of the generation of the Flood, and the generation of the Tower of Babel who would rebel against Him, He realized they might do even worse with the powerful help of this extraordinary light. So He hid the light away and prepared it for the righteous in the world-to-come.

רַ' לֵוִי בְּשֵׁם רַבִּי זְעִירָא אָמַר ל"ו שָׁעוֹת שִׁמְּשָׁה אוֹתָהּ הָאוֹרָה שְׁנֵים עָשָׂר שֶׁל עֶרֶב שַׁבָּת וְי"ב שֶׁל לֵילֵי שַׁבָּת וְי"ב שֶׁל שַׁבָּת כֵּיוָן שֶׁשָּׁקְעָה הַחַמָּה בְּמוֹצָאֵי שַׁבָּת הִתְחִיל הַחֹשֶׁךְ מְמַשְׁמֵשׁ וּבָא וְנִתְיָרֵא אָדָם הָרִאשׁוֹן שֶׁנֶּאֱמַר 'וָאֹמַר אַךְ חֹשֶׁךְ יְשׁוּפֵנִי וְלַיְלָה אוֹר בַּעֲדֵנִי' (תהלים קלט, יא) אוֹתוֹ שֶׁכָּתוּב בּוֹ 'הוּא יְשׁוּפְךָ רֹאשׁ וְאַתָּה תְּשׁוּפֶנּוּ עָקֵב' (בראשית ג, טו) בָּא לְהִזְדַּוֵּג לִי

R. Levi said in the name of R. Ze'ira: That light functioned thirty-six hours, twelve on the eve of the Sabbath [i.e., Friday], twelve during the night of the Sabbath, and twelve on the Sabbath [day]. When the sun sank at the termination of the Sabbath, darkness began to set in. Adam was terrified, as its says, 'And I said, "Surely darkness will cover me [*yeshufeini*, also 'bruise me'] and [from now on] night will be the light for me" (Psalms 139:11); shall he of whom it was written, 'It shall strike at your head and you shall strike at its heel' (Genesis 3:15), now come to attack me!'

How do we know that Adam became fearful? It is derived from the use of the verb in the quoted Psalm, the authorship of which is traditionally attributed to Adam (*Eitz Yosef*), יְשׁוּפֵנִי, *yeshufeini*, meaning 'will envelop me' or, in this case, 'will bruise me,' which also occurs in the verse regarding the punishment given to the serpent for enticing Eve to eat of the Tree of Knowledge. Adam knew that the darkness was a punishment for the sin and feared that it was a sign that he would be attacked by the serpent.

מֶה עָשָׂה הַקָּדוֹשׁ בָּרוּךְ הוּא זִמֵּן לוֹ שְׁנֵי רְעָפִים וְהִקִּישָׁן זֶה לָזֶה וְיָצָא מֵהֶן אוֹר
וּבֵרַךְ עָלֶיהָ הָדָא הוּא דִכְתִיב 'וְלַיְלָה אוֹר בַּעֲדֵנִי' (תהלים שם, שם) מַה בֵּרַךְ עָלֶיהָ
'בּוֹרֵא מְאוֹרֵי הָאֵשׁ' אָתְיָא כִּשְׁמוּאֵל דַּאֲמַר שְׁמוּאֵל מָה מְבָרְכִין עַל הָאוֹר
בְּמוֹצָאֵי שַׁבָּת מִפְּנֵי שֶׁהִיא תְּחִלַּת בְּרִיָּתָה

What did the Holy One, blessed be He, do? He prepared for him two flints, which he struck against each other; light came forth from them and he recited a blessing over it; hence it is written, 'night will be the light for me (ba'adeini).' What blessing did he recite? 'Who creates the light of the fire.' This agrees with Samuel, for Samuel said: Why do we recite a blessing over light at the termination of the Sabbath? Because it was then created for the first time.

The word בַּעֲדֵנִי, *ba'adeini*, which appears in the verse from Psalms is a difficult word. However, according to this *midrash* it becomes significant in that it is interpreted as meaning 'in my Eden.' The whole verse will now mean: 'I was terrified of the darkness because I feared that the serpent would attack me, but I was given a way to make light in the night.' The fact that two flints are mentioned does not mean that Adam invented fire. It merely means that he used what had already been created. Creation *ex nihilo* only took place during the six days of creation. (*Tiferet Tzion*) Since all of this took place on Saturday night, which is when the original light was hidden, it is offered as a source for the benediction of light at the *Havdalah* ceremony.

רַב הוּנָא בְשֵׁם רַב וְרַבִּי אַבָּהוּ בְּשֵׁם רַבִּי יוֹחָנָן אָמַר אַף מוֹצָאֵי יוֹם הַכִּפּוּרִים
מְבָרְכִין עָלָיו מִפְּנֵי שֶׁשָּׁבַת הָאוֹר כָּל אוֹתוֹ הַיּוֹם

R. Huna in Rav's name and R. Abbahu in R. Joḥanan's name said: At the termination of the Day of Atonement, too, we recite a blessing over it, because the fire rested the whole day.

The interpretation given in the previous paragraph can only apply to *Havdalah* after the Sabbath that commemorates creation. On the Day of Atonement there is another reason that also applies to the Sabbath – it was forbidden to use light during the holy day. At the termination of the Sabbath we acknowledge the renewal of the use of fire, and at the termination of the Day of Atonement we acknowledge the light kindled on the eve of the Day of Atonement that subsided because of the prohibition. The blessing is to express a feeling of renewal because he did not benefit from the light of that day. (Rashi) It is possible that the Rabbis of this *midrash* are, in fact, disagreeing with Samuel's statement, recorded in the previous *midrash*, and are saying that the fact that we also recite the benediction at the close of the Day of Atonement proves that Samuel's explanation is not correct.

* * *

Seed Thoughts

'And God blessed the seventh day and declared it holy.' The plain meaning of the Hebrew verse is that God blessed the Sabbath day by declaring it holy. There is a similar construct in the blessing that is recited when called to the Torah, 'Who has chosen us from among all the peoples and given us His Torah,' which should be understood as meaning, 'He has chosen us from among the peoples by giving us the Torah.'

So God blessed the Sabbath day by hallowing it. But how does one hallow it? At this point the *midrash* suggests the principle of change or difference. In ancient times God Himself established the principle of difference when the manna did not fall on the Sabbath. We are also called upon to make those changes, or to emphasize those differences that would help emphasize the importance of Sabbath: changing clothes, putting on our best garments and adornments, making the Sabbath meal different and festive, doing whatever we can to make the day special. The result of this special effort is that even a person's countenance takes on a more radiant look on the Sabbath.

This brings us to a most interesting Rabbinic saying: 'It is incumbent upon a person to make his face lighten up on the Sabbath.' What does this mean?

William James, many years ago, originated the concept of 'The Will to Believe.' Belief is more than ideological and intellectual. It has to do with the entire temperament of the person. It is an emotive commitment – one wills to believe.

By the same token one wills to love. If one is prepared for marriage, the decision will not be made by chemistry alone, but by an act of will and a determination to find the right person.

Herman Wouk in his volume, *This is My God*, uses the expression 'The Leap of Observance' to apply this concept to the world of the commandments. One has to make the decision to observe even before one knows all the religious answers.

This is probably what the Rabbis had in mind in saying that it is incumbent upon us to make our face lighten up on the Sabbath. We cannot wait for the Sabbath to do things to us. We ourselves must create the Shabbat atmosphere, do what has to be done, motivate others, if necessary, put on an appearance of joy, and the result, believe it or not, will be well-being and light and radiance.

This applies not only to the Sabbath, but to all challenges of the moral and spiritual life. They do not happen by themselves! Of course the Sabbath occurs once a week. But one has to 'make Shabbos.' It does not make itself. We have to make the Sabbath and then the Sabbath will make us.

* * *

Additional Commentary

Sanctified by manna

The concept of holiness means to sanctify oneself through that which is permitted. This means to add prohibitions where it is otherwise permitted. (Ramban on the *sidrah Kedoshim*) The intention of the text in saying 'and He declared it holy' was that He ceased work even from those activities that were permitted on the Sabbath. Since they merely resembled work done in the weekday, the Sages decreed that they should be included as part of the cessation from work. The best proof of this is the manna, which did not fall on Sabbath even though the reason for it not to fall was only Rabbinical prohibition regarding boundaries.

R. Ishmael said that God sanctified the Sabbath with the manna, because by not falling on the Sabbath at all, it indicated that God sanctified the Sabbath also by means of things that were otherwise permitted. R. Nathan, on the other hand, operates on the principle that boundaries do not exist beyond the height of ten handbreadths, and the fact that the manna did not fall on the Sabbath was for the benefit of Israel to prevent them from the temptation of Sabbath desecration by gathering objects in the public domain. Therefore he maintains that He sanctified it with a blessing. This blessing was to be the revelation of God's presence in public, His seal of approval of the Sabbath as the conclusion of creation. That is what is meant in the statement of the *Pesikta* in the name of R. Ammi. He sanctified it by a blessing, and from this we learn that the Sabbath has to be blessed over a goblet of wine when it is ushered in. Just as God sanctified the original Sabbath by celebrating the abundance of this world, so must we. (*Tiferet Tzion*)

*

And God blessed

Based on the juxtaposition of the two verbs, *va-yevorekh* and *va-yekadesh*, we have the source for the Sabbath blessing – *mekadesh ha-shabbat.* (Mirkin)

*

When God saw the actions of the generation of the Flood

Even though God knew from the outset that there would be evil doers in the world, particularly after the sin of the first man, he nevertheless issued the Supreme Light, even if only temporarily, so that He could then hide it and keep it in store for those righteous who would earn its privilege.

*

R. Isaac said

R. Isaac accepts the principle that God wants us to sanctify ourselves in those matters that are permitted, but he refrains from using the example of the manna because he also accepts the limitation that boundaries do not exist beyond ten handbreadths. He uses the example of the gatherer of wood. Although the gatherer only desecrated a Rabbinical precept, the punishment was not related to the essence of the type of work, but rather in order to dramatize that desecration of the Sabbath merits punishment by death. This was *hora'at sha'ah*, a decision rendered only for that particular moment in time. God revealed through this extraordinary decision that He observes the concept of *shevut*, that is, Rabbinical ordinances, in relationship to the Sabbath. (*Tiferet Tzion*)

*

It is part of the mystery and sanctity of the Sabbath that those who are guilty of its desecration are subject to the death penalty. (*Ha-Midrash ha-Mevo'ar*)

Parashah Eleven, Midrash Three

בֵּרְכוֹ בִּיצִיאָה

He blessed it by providing for additional expenditures.

This is an alternative interpretation of the text, 'And God blessed the seventh day and declared it holy.' How did He bless it? By encouraging man to spend money in order to honor the Sabbath with the assurance that God will pay him back so that he will not suffer any loss. This assurance was needed because of the saying in Tractate Betzah (15b) that a person's income during the year is part of the decrees of judgment between Rosh Hashana and Yom Kippur with the exception of expenditures made for the Sabbath. (*Ha-Midrash ha-Mevo'ar*)

רַבִּי לֵוִי בְּשֵׁם רַ' יוֹסֵי בַּרַ' חֲנִינָא אָמַר כָּל יוֹם שֶׁיֵּשׁ בּוֹ חֶסְרוֹן כָּתִיב בּוֹ בְּרָכָה וְאֵינוֹ חָסֵר כְּלוּם

R. Levi said in the name of R. Jose b. R. Ḥanina: A blessing is written in connection with every day in which there is a decrease, and so it suffers no loss at all.

Everything that was created during the six days of creation has a built-in liability that is permanent and yet, every such creation has a blessing written on its day that makes up the loss, as illustrated in the next section.

בַּחֲמִישִׁי נִבְרְאוּ עוֹפוֹת וְדָגִים וּבְנֵי אָדָם שׁוֹחֲטִין עוֹפוֹת וְאוֹכְלִים וְצָדִים דָּגִים וְאוֹכְלִין וּכְתִיב בּוֹ בְּרָכָה וְאֵינוֹ חָסֵר כְּלוּם בַּשִּׁשִּׁי נִבְרָא אָדָם וּבְהֵמָה וּבְנֵי אָדָם שׁוֹחֲטִין בְּהֵמָה וְאוֹכְלִין וּבְנֵי אָדָם מֵתִים וּכְתִיב בּוֹ בְּרָכָה וְאֵינוֹ חָסֵר כְּלוּם

On the fifth day birds and fish were created; now people kill birds and eat them, and catch fish and eat them, yet since a blessing is written [for that day], the [numbers] never decline at all. On the sixth day human beings and animals were created; human beings slaughter animals and consume them as food, and human beings themselves die, but a blessing for that [day] and [their numbers] do not decline at all.

442

On the fifth day of creation the blessing was "Be fertile and increase, fill the waters in the seas, and let the birds increase on the earth' (Genesis 1:22). On the sixth day, the blessing was 'Be fertile and increase, fill the earth and master it' (ibid., verse 28). Therefore, although fish, fowl, and animals are slaughtered for food, their numbers do not decrease, and although human beings die, the population of the world never decreases. That means that the blessing makes up for any loss that is suffered.

בַּשְּׁבִיעִי מַאי אִית לָךְ לְמֵימַר ר' לֵוִי בְּשֵׁם ר' חָמָא בַּר' חֲנִינָא אָמַר מִפְּנֵי הַיְצִיאָה ר' אֶלְעָזָר בְּשֵׁם ר' יוֹסֵי אָמַר מִפְּנֵי אִיסְטְנִיסִים

But what can you say about the seventh day? R. Levi said in the name of R. Ḥama b. R. Ḥanina: the [additional] expenditure. R. Eleazar said in R. Jose's name: [The blessing helps] people with delicate digestions.

The seventh day also has a blessing written in it, but what loss can that blessing make up for seeing that nothing was created on seventh day? It can only refer therefore to the expenditures for the Sabbath day that a person must undertake in order for the Sabbath to be truly honored. This occasions a financial loss and therefore a special blessing is needed for the seventh day. In the edition of *Ha-Midrash ha-Mevo'ar*, R. Eleazar in R. Jose's name is given as the first section in the next *midrash*, although it clearly belongs here in that it is an alternative answer to R. Ḥama b. R. Ḥanina's. The thrust of the answer seems to be that people ate more on Shabbat than they did on other days – a fact which is certainly true nowadays – and that may very well upset their stomachs.

* * *

Seed Thoughts

The message of this *midrash* is the message of courage. In the creation story we have evidence not only of plenitude but of decimation. Animals kill other animals. Humans slaughter animals and even each other in wars. How will creation maintain itself? That is the meaning of the blessing. Don't worry! 'Be fertile and increase' will prevail over the behavior of 'dog eat dog.'

This is the message of courage. There are always signs and portents of despair. Do not worry that the clouds will bring a storm. Maybe they will; maybe they will not. Go ahead with your life courageously.

I am reminded of another text, also in the Book of Genesis. There it says that Abraham gave everything he had to Isaac. But the very next verse says that he gave presents to his other children, so that he could not have given all to Isaac. One Sage says that he gave to Isaac the blessing he had received from God. Another says that he gave him the gift of courage. But both are one. The greatest gift of all is courage.

We need courage in facing any number of challenges. Even getting up in the morning to face a new day requires courage. There are problems between parents and children, between spouses, between co-workers, between rival political ideologies and parties. Any one of these problems can be overwhelming. We must have courage. We must have the faith that produces courage. We must have God who makes faith possible and has given us courage as His blessing.

* * *

Additional Commentary

Additional expenditures
The expenditures that are involved in preparing for the Sabbath can be very difficult for a person. Therefore man was blessed in the spirit of the Sages who have God say, 'Borrow from Me and I will pay back as well.' (*Matnot Kehunah*)

Parashah Eleven, Midrash Four

רַבֵּינוּ עָשָׂה סְעוּדָה לְאַנְטוֹנִינוֹס בַּשַּׁבָּת הֵבִיא לְפָנָיו תַּבְשִׁילִין שֶׁל צוֹנֵן אָכַל מֵהֶם
וְעָרֵב לוֹ עָשָׂה לוֹ סְעוּדָה בַּחֹל הֵבִיא לְפָנָיו תַּבְשִׁילִין רוֹתְחִין אָמַר לוֹ אוֹתָן עָרְבוּ
לִי יוֹתֵר מֵאֵלּוּ אָמַר לוֹ תָּבֵל אֶחָד הֵן חֲסֵרִין אָמַר לוֹ וְכִי יֵשׁ קֵילָרִין שֶׁל מֶלֶךְ חָסֵר
כְּלוּם אָמַר לוֹ שַׁבָּת הֵן חֲסֵרִין אִית לָךְ שַׁבָּת

Our teacher [R. Judah the Prince] made a meal for Antoninus on the
Sabbath. He served him with cold dishes; he ate them and found
them delicious. [On another occasion] he made a meal for him
during the week and served him with hot dishes. Said [Antoninus]
to [R. Judah], 'Those others I enjoyed more than these.' 'These lack
a certain condiment' he replied. 'Does the royal pantry lack
anything?' [Antoninus] exclaimed. 'They lack the Sabbath,' he
retorted, 'do you indeed possess the Sabbath?'

R. Judah the Prince was the official representative of the Jewish
population of Eretz Israel to the Roman rulers, and he therefore had close
contacts with the Roman imperial house. The *midrash* describes two
occasions when Rabbi, as he is called, invited the Emperor Antoninus for
dinner. The first was on a Sabbath when the food had to be served cold
due to the Sabbath restrictions. The second was served hot during a
weekday and should have tasted better. At the beginning he thought that
the superior taste of Rabbi's food was due to the superiority of his chefs;
however, when the Emperor realized that the same menu served hot did
not taste better, he realized that another factor was involved. It was this
that prompted his question, 'Does the royal pantry lack anything?' He was
told that it did – the Sabbath. (*Tiferet Tzion*) The emperor meant that if an
ingredient was missing he would immediately send for it, so Rabbi asked,
'Does your pantry possess the Sabbath?'

רַבִּי יִשְׁמָעֵאל בַּר' יוֹסֵי שִׁיְלֵהּ לְרַבִּי אָמַר לוֹ בְּנֵי בָבֶל בִּזְכוּת מָה הֵן חַיִּים אָמַר לוֹ
בִּזְכוּת הַתּוֹרָה וּבְנֵי אֶרֶץ יִשְׂרָאֵל בִּזְכוּת מָה אָמַר לוֹ בִּזְכוּת מַעַשְׂרוֹת וְאַנְשֵׁי חוּצָה
לָאָרֶץ בִּזְכוּת מָה אָמַר לוֹ בִּזְכוּת שֶׁהֵן מְכַבְּדִין אֶת הַשַּׁבָּתוֹת וְיָמִים טוֹבִים

R. Ishmael b. R. Jose asked Rabbi [a question]; he said to him, 'On
account of what virtue do the Babylonian [Jews] live [a life of wealth

445

and honor]?' He answered, 'By virtue of the Torah [which they study].' 'And by what virtue do those in Eretz Israel?' He answered, 'By virtue of the tithes [they separate].' 'And those in the Diaspora?' 'By virtue of the fact that they honor the Sabbaths and festivals.

The verb 'live' in our context should not be taken literally. We have followed the interpretation of *Ha-Midrash ha-Mevo'ar*, the Soncino translation suggests that it means a life of prosperity; and the *Tiferet Tzion* maintains that it means long life. At any rate what is involved is a life of well-being. It is this that prompts the questions put to Rabbi. That the Jews of Babylonia prospered because of the Torah can be seen from the fact that tremendous institutions of Torah were created there and great scholars were sustained and honored there. The same could not be said for the Jews in the land of Israel at this point in time because many great Torah scholars had emigrated to Babylonia. That is why in the case of the Jews in the Land of Israel their special merit is in giving tithes, which is a unique commandment applying only in Eretz Israel. And the Jews of the Diaspora? By virtue of the Sabbath. Babylonia had its own special status, because of its stature as a Torah center, and it was not considered part of the Diaspora. The rest of the Jews in the world were not known for their Torah learning, which only developed a long time after Rabbi's day, and they did not separate tithes. As we learned in the first *midrash* of this *Parashah*, the verse, 'It is the blessing of God that enriches' refers to the Sabbath, and those who observe it in the proper way are blessed with rich life in all senses of the term.

אָמַר רַ' חִיָּא בַּר אַבָּא פַּעַם אַחַת זִמְּנַנִי אָדָם אֶחָד בְּלוּדְקִיָּא וְהֵבִיא לְפָנֵינוּ דְיוּסְקוֹס אֶחָד טָעוּן בִּי"ו מוֹטוֹת וּבוֹ מִכָּל מַה שֶּׁנִּבְרָא בְּשֵׁשֶׁת יְמֵי בְרֵאשִׁית

R. Ḥiyya b. Abba said: A man in Laodicea once invited me [to his home] and served us from a platter borne on sixteen staves, and on it was [an assortment] of everything created in the first six days of creation.

This story is brought to illustrate that the reward of Sabbath observance according to the law is prosperity. Laodicea is a town in Northern Syria, and the 'sixteen staves' imply that thirty-two persons were carrying it. This corresponds to the thirty-two miraculous ways of wisdom with which the Almighty created the world. (*Tiferet Tzion*) Since the Sabbath testifies to the renewal of the world, therefore thirty-two men were carrying the table to symbolize the manner in which the world was created. The fact that the table contained a sample of all that was created, meaning every manner of food and spice as well as their containers (the goblets and every manner of serving utensil) is meant to testify that by means of the Sabbath God created all of them.

וְתִינוֹק אֶחָד הָיָה יוֹשֵׁב בְּאֶמְצָעִיתוֹ וְהָיָה מַכְרִיז וְאוֹמֵר 'לַה' הָאָרֶץ וּמְלוֹאָהּ תֵּבֵל וְיֹשְׁבֵי בָהּ' (תהלים כד, א)

And a child sat in the middle and recited, 'The earth is the Lord's and all that it holds' (Psalms 24:1).

The presence of a small child is also significant. The breath of children is holy to God and the use of a child in this story is to indicate that we live by virtue of the children and our stewardship of them.

כָּל כָּךְ לָמָּה שֶׁלֹּא תָזוּחַ דַּעְתּוֹ שֶׁל בַּעַל הַבַּיִת עָלָיו אָמַרְתִּי לוֹ בְּנִי מֵהֵיכָן זָכִיתָ לְכָל הַכָּבוֹד הַזֶּה אָמַר לִי טַבָּח הָיִיתִי וְכָל בְּהֵמָה יָפָה שֶׁהָיִיתִי רוֹאֶה כָּל יְמוֹת הַשַּׁבָּת הָיִיתִי מַפְרִישָׁהּ לַשַּׁבָּת וְאָמַרְתִּי לוֹ לֹא עַל מַגָּן זָכִיתָ

Why so much? So that the owner should not become conceited. I said to him, 'My son, whence did you merit all this glory?' 'I was a butcher,' replied he, 'and whenever during all the days of week I saw a beautiful animal I set it aside for the Sabbath.' I said to him, 'Not for nothing did [you deserve this] merit.'

Generally speaking, wealth that comes upon a person as a result of good luck usually has the effect of distancing him from God. When, however, R. Ḥiyya saw that this man's wealth had drawn him closer to God, he realized that the man must have possessed special merit on the principle that one commandment leads to another, leading one ultimately all the way to the world-to-come. (*Tiferet Tzion*)

אָמַר רַ' תַּנְחוּמָא עוֹבָדָא הֲוָה בְּרוֹמִי בְּעַרוֹבַת צוֹמָא רַבָּה וַהֲוָה תַּמָּן חַד חַיָּט וַאֲזַל דְּיִזְדְּבַן לֵהּ חַד נוּן אַשְׁתְּכַח הוּא וְטַלְיָא דְּאִיפַּרְכוֹס קָיְמִין עֲלֵוֵהּ

R. Tanḥuma said: It once happened in Rome on the eve of the great fast that a tailor went to buy a fish, and it fell out that he and the governor's servant had to bid for it.

The great fast is the Day of Atonement and the fish was the only good one left in the market. The Jewish tailor, a simple man, was presumably buying the fish for the festive meal before the fast.

הֲוָה הָדֵין מַסִּיק לֵהּ בְּטִימֵי וְהָדֵין מַסִּיק לֵהּ בְּטִימֵי עַד דִּמְטָא לְי"ב דֵּינָרִין וּנְסָבָא הַהוּא חַיָּטָא

This one made a bid and then the other one made a bid until it reached twelve dinars, at which price the tailor bought it.

Twelve dinars was an enormous price to pay for a fish; it was the equivalent of sixty grams of silver!

בְּעַנְתָּא דַאֲרִיסְטוֹן אָמַר אִיפַּרְכוֹס לְטַלְיָא לְמָה לָא אַיְתֵית לִי נוּן אֲמַר לֵהּ מָרִי מָה לִכְפּוּר מִנָּךְ אֲזַלִּית וְלָא הֲוָה תַמָּן אֶלָּא חַד נוּן וְאִשְׁתְּכַחִית אֲנָא וְחַד יְהוּדָאי קָיְמִין עִלָוֵהּ וַהֲוָה הוּא מַסִּיק לֵהּ בְּטִימֵי וַאֲנָא מַסִּיק לֵהּ בְּטִימֵי עַד דִּמְטָא לִשְׁנֵים עֲשַׂר דֵּינָרִין מָה הֲוַת בָּעֵי דְּנַיְיתָא לָךְ בִּתְרֵי עֲשַׂר דֵּינָרִין אַתְמָהָא

At dinner the governor demanded of his servant, 'Why have you not served me fish?' 'Master, should I lie to you?' he replied. 'I went [to the market to buy a fish] and there was only one [good] fish [left]. A a certain Jew bid for it against me. He and I raised our bids until the price reached twelve dinars. Would you really want me to bring you a single fish for twelve dinars? I would be amazed!'

It seems that the governor recognized the truth of the story the servant told, but his curiosity was aroused.

אֲמַר לֵהּ מַאן הוּא אֲמַר לֵהּ בַּר נָשׁ פְּלָן שָׁלַח בָּתְרֵהּ וַאֲתָא לְגַבֵּיהּ אֲמַר לֵהּ מַה חֲמֵית חַיָּט יְהוּדָאי דַּאֲכַלְתְּ נוּן בִּתְרֵי עֲשַׂר דֵּינָרִין אֲמַר לֵהּ מָרִי אִית לָן חַד יוֹם בְּכָל חוֹבִין דְּאֲנַן עָבְדִין כָּל יוֹמֵי שַׁתָּא הוּא מְכַפֵּר עֲלֵינָן וְכַד הוּא אָתָא לֵית אֲנַן צְרִיכִין לְיַקּוּרֵי יָתֵהּ אָמַר כֵּיוָן שֶׁהֵבֵאתָ רְאָיָה לִדְבָרֶיךָ הֲרֵי אַתָּה פָּטוּר

[The governor then] said to [the servant], 'Who was it?' 'So-and-so, the Jew,' he answered. He had him summoned and [the Jew] came. [The governor] said to him, 'What did you see, Jewish tailor, that you can eat a fish at twelve dinars!' 'Sir,' he replied, 'we have one day when all our sins we do all the days of the year are forgiven us, and when it comes around should we not honor it greatly?' [The governor] replied, 'Since you have explained yourself, you are free to go!'

Why did the governor want to interview the tailor who had outbid his servant in buying the fish? He thought that the tailor had found a secret treasure. Such things either belong completely to the government or they are highly taxed. Another possibility is that he suspected that the Jew had

had an ulterior motive in bidding up the price of the fish, and thus his question, 'What did you see...?' Was there something about this fish that was special? There was, but the tailor did not know it yet.

מַה פָּרַע לוֹ הַקָּדוֹשׁ בָּרוּךְ הוּא הָלַךְ וְקָרַע אוֹתָהּ וְזִמֵּן לוֹ בְּתוֹכָהּ מַרְגָּלִיּוֹת טוֹבָה
וְהָיָה מִתְפַּרְנֵס הֵימֶנָּה כָּל יָמָיו

How did the Holy One, blessed be He, repay [the tailor]? He returned home, opened the fish [to prepare it for the meal] and found within it a precious pearl from which he was able to earn a livelihood for the rest of his life.

According to the Rabbis, eating on the eve of Yom Kippur is as important as fasting, which probably accounts for the extreme behavior of the tailor. The tailor was rewarded by finding a precious pearl in the fish. This brings the story in line with the *midrash* that the Jews of the Diaspora merit a great reward because of their observance of the Sabbath and the festivals.

* * *

Seed Thoughts

To what do the people of Babylonia owe their prosperity? To the fact that they study the Torah intensively. To what do the inhabitants of the Land of Israel owe their material success? To the fact that they give tithes from their agricultural harvest with great scrupulousness. To what do the communities in the Diaspora owe their wealth? To the fact that they celebrate the Sabbath and the festivals with great honor.

The *midrash* here lists three fundamental pillars of the Jewish religious experience. The most important of them all is Torah, since, when learning is combined with commitment and practice, it automatically brings with it tithing and observance of the festivals. The inhabitants of the Land of Israel are mentioned second because at that particular time, Torah institutions were weak in the Land of Israel; but they did observe their unique opportunity in Israel of giving tithes. The community of the Diaspora had neither Torah nor the commandment of tithing, but they did do with great sincerity that which was available to them – honoring the Sabbath and festivals.

But we have learned in so many Rabbinic writings that reward and punishment are not necessarily visible in this world. More often than not, the righteous suffer and the wicked prosper. Material success is a matter of *mazal*, luck. How can the *midrash* be so emphatic in accounting for the prosperity of the various communities as a reward for their good religious behavior?

Maybe we have to approach this material from a different perspective. Maybe the true meaning of this passage should be perceived inversely. The community of Babylonia was prosperous. It is not a question of what caused it. We do not know what causes these things. But what should they have done with their prosperity? How should they express their gratitude? How can they render their privilege – and the consequent social inequity – into a source of social redemption? The way to do so is through Torah, through the act of giving, and through the life of celebration.

The life of Torah involves learning in its primary formulation. But it also involves much more. It involves the art of honoring scholars and scholarship, the obligation of maintaining *yeshivot* and institutions of Jewish learning. It means making the very experience of learning itself associated with a lifestyle of status and emulation. The Jews of Babylonia were famous for the wonderful structure of their society and the many important institutions of learning they supported.

Tithing is giving. But it implies more than the giving of money. It postulates the giving of oneself to causes of worth and altruism. It involves sacrifice, if necessary, and the giving of oneself without thought of reward or recognition.

A life of celebration is relatively easier. But more than celebration is involved. The towering commitment of the Sabbath and festivals is to refrain from work on them. Outside of Israel, that becomes the greatest of all challenges. It may sometimes demand changing one's professional occupation. It may involve restrictions of many kinds. It subsumes as well commitments such as *kashrut,* prayer, and ritual behavior. All of these have to be equally celebrated.

The question is not to what do we owe our prosperity. The question – nay, the proposition – is that if we have been granted a livelihood and, in some cases much more than a livelihood, let us express our gratitude by becoming worthy of it.

* * *

Additional Commentary

You are lacking the Sabbath
This was not mentioned at the outset because the taste of food depends upon two factors, cooking and ingredients. If the cause of the tastiness of the menu in question was the cooking, that could certainly have been improved during the weekday; but because the problem resided in the in-

gredients, one of which was the Sabbath, there was no way to rectify this on a weekday. That is why Rabbi first mentioned that an ingredient was missing and then he explained about the Sabbath. (*Tiferet Tzion*)

*

By what virtue do the Babylonians live?

The point here is to understand not why they live, but rather why they are privileged to live lives of prosperity and material success. (Mirkin)

*

How did God reward him?

Whatever a man does over and beyond the call of duty he is repaid by God even in this world. This was the answer given by God to the angels, 'How can I not favor Israel since they have scrupulously taken upon themselves the obligation to recite a benediction over a morsel of food the size of an olive that they were not required to do from the written Torah.' (*Tiferet Tzion*)

Parashah Eleven, Midrash Five

טוּרְנוֹסְרוּפוּס הָרָשָׁע שָׁאַל אֶת רַבִּי עֲקִיבָא אָמַר מַה יוֹם מִיוֹמַיִם אָמַר לֵהּ וּמַה
גְּבַר מִן גְּבְרִין

The wicked Tinneus Rufus asked R. Akiva [a question]. He said:
'How is this day [the Sabbath] different from other days?' 'How does
one man differ from other men?' he retorted.

The conversations recorded in this *midrash* should be understood as
offering a variant interpretation of the text, 'And God blessed the seventh
day and declared it holy.' The question revolves around the meaning of
holy, which here will be defined as worthy of honor. Tinneus Rufus was
one of the Roman governors of Jerusalem, which explains his desire to
want to know about Judaism. R. Akiva's response to Rufus may not have
been understood by him at first, but it was most appropriate. He had
asked, 'How is the Sabbath day different from other days?' R. Akiva
answered with a question that meant, why are you, Rufus, different from
other men in the sense that you have been appointed a high officer of
Rome.

אָמַר מָה אֲמַרִית לָךְ וּמָה אֲמַרְתְּ לִי אָמַר לֵהּ אֲמַרְתְּ לִי מַה יוֹם מִיוֹמַיִם מַאי שְׁנָא
יוֹמָא דְשַׁבַּתָא מִכָּל יוֹמָא וַאֲמַרִית לָךְ וּמַן גְּבַר מִגּוּבְרִין מַאי שְׁנָא טוּרְנוֹסְרוּפוּס
מִכָּל גְּבְרִין אָמַר לוֹ שֶׁרָצָה הַמֶּלֶךְ לְכַבְּדֵנִי אָמַר לוֹ אַף זוֹ שֶׁרָצָה הַקָּדוֹשׁ בָּרוּךְ הוּא
לְכַבְּדָהּ

'What did I ask you and what did you answer me?' inquired he. 'You
asked me,' he replied, 'why does the Sabbath differ from all other
days,' and I answered you, 'Why is Rufus different from other men.'
[Rufus] said, 'Because the Emperor desired to honor him.' 'Then this
day, too, the Holy One, blessed be He, wished to honor,' [R. Akiva]
retorted.

Rufus also meant by his question, why do you need the Sabbath at all? So
R. Akiva responded, why is it necessary for you to be an officer? That, he
answered, was because the king wanted to honor me. So, implied R.
Akiva, God wanted to honor the Sabbath.

אָמַר לֵהּ מִנָּאן אַתְּ מוֹדַע לִי אָמַר לוֹ הֲרֵי נָהָר סַמְבַּטְיוֹן יוֹכִיחַ שֶׁמּוֹשֵׁךְ אֲבָנִים כָּל
יְמוֹת הַשַּׁבָּת וּבַשַּׁבָּת הוּא נָח אָמַר לֵהּ לְנַגְדָּא אַתְּ נָגֵד לִי אַתְמְהָא

[Rufus] said to [R. Akiva], 'How can you prove it to me?' [To which
R. Akiva] answered, 'The River Sambatyon proves it, which carries
stones all the days of the week but rests on the Sabbath.' 'You are
pulling me along [to a far-off place]. I am amazed [at that answer!],'
exclaimed Rufus.

The first proof offered to prove the uniqueness of the Sabbath was the
river Sambatyon, which rested on the Sabbath. (The name Sambatyon is
probably a corruption of Shabbatyon, which would mean to observe the
Sabbath. Naḥmanides identifies this river as bearing the name of 'Gozen.'
[*Ha-Midrash ha-Mevo'ar*]) Rufus dismissed this answer, because it was
based on a fact about which he knew nothing. Rufus had most probably
never heard of the Sambatyon. The word נגדא, *nagda*, which the *midrash*
puts in Rufus' mouth, could mean either a river or a map or a guide, but
the lesson would be the same. (Mirkin)

אָמַר לֵהּ וַהֲרֵי הַמַּעֲלֶה אֶת הַמֵּת בִּזְכוּרוֹ יוֹכִיחַ שֶׁהוּא עוֹלֶה כָּל יְמוֹת הַשַּׁבָּת
וּבַשַּׁבָּת אֵינוֹ עוֹלֶה וְהַהוּא גַבְרָא לִיהֱוֵי בָּדֵק בַּאֲבוּהוֹ חַד זְמַן צְרִיךְ וּבָדֵק בַּאֲבוּהוֹ
וּסְלֵק כָּל יוֹמָא דְשַׁבְּתָא וּבְשַׁבְּתָא לָא סְלֵק

[R. Akiva then] said to him, 'Then let him who brings up the dead
by his male genital prove it, for every day [the dead] will come up,
but not on the Sabbath. Go and try it with your father!' [Rufus] went
and made a test with his own father: Every day of the week he came
up, but on the Sabbath he did not come up.

The second proof offered by R. Akiva is more difficult since it deals with
necromancy. However, Rufus almost certainly believed in magic, so the
proof would be acceptable if it worked. The word זכורו, *zekhuro*, is
translated literally as 'the male organ,' and its meaning here is difficult. It
probably indicates that the voice of the necromancer seemed to come
from the lower part of the body. (Mirkin)

בְּחַד שַׁבְּתָא אַסְקֵהּ אָמַר לֵהּ אַבָּא מִן דְּמִיתְתְּ אִיתְעַבְדִית יְהוּדִי אַתְמְהָא מִפְּנֵי
מָה עָלִיתָ כָּל יְמוֹת הַשַּׁבָּת וְשַׁבָּת לֹא עָלִיתָ אָמַר לוֹ כָּל מִי שֶׁאֵינוֹ מְשַׁמֵּר אֶת
הַשַּׁבָּת אֶצְלְכֶם בִּרְצוֹנוֹ כָּאן הוּא מְשַׁמֵּר אוֹתוֹ בְּעַל כָּרְחוֹ אָמַר לוֹ וְכִי עָמָל יֵשׁ
לָכֶם שֶׁאַתֶּם עֲמֵלִים כָּל יְמוֹת הַשַּׁבָּת וּבַשַּׁבָּת אַתֶּם נוֹחִין אָמַר לוֹ כָּל יְמוֹת הַשַּׁבָּת
אָנוּ נִדּוֹנִין וּבַשַּׁבָּת אָנוּ נוֹחִין

On Sunday he brought him up (again). 'Father,' he said to him, 'have you become a Jew after death?! I am amazed! Why did you come up on all the days of the week but not on the Sabbath?' [His father] answered him, 'He among you [the living] who does not observe the Sabbath of his own free will, here is forced to observe it.' [Rufus] said to him, 'But what work have you there, that the whole week you work and must rest on the Sabbath?' [His father] said to him, 'On all the days of the week we are judged, but on the Sabbath we rest.'

The seance with his father apparently worked and the story indicates that the Sabbath has spiritual power even in the case of non-Jews who are not commanded to observe it in this world and even after death.

חָזַר אֵצֶל רַ' עֲקִיבָא אָמַר לוֹ אִם כִּדְבָרֶיךָ שֶׁהַקָּדוֹשׁ בָּרוּךְ הוּא מְכַבֵּד אֶת הַשַּׁבָּת אַל יַשֵּׁב בָּהּ רוּחוֹת אַל יוֹרִיד אַל גְּשָׁמִים אַל יַצְמִיחַ בָּהּ עֵשֶׂב אָמַר לוֹ תִּפַּח רוּחֵהּ דְּהַהוּא גַּבְרָא

[Rufus] went back to R. Akiva and said to him: 'If it is as you say that the Holy One, blessed be He, honors the Sabbath, then he should not stir up winds on it, or cause the rain to fall on it, or let grass grow on it!' 'May the spirit of that man [Rufus] fly away!' he exclaimed.

Rufus must have had some knowledge of Jewish law (*Ha-Midrash ha-Mevo'ar*), otherwise in response to the question why God works on the Sabbath day by having nature continue in its activities, he would never have understood R. Akiva's response, which follows. By his exclamation, which, out of politeness, refers to Rufus in the third person, R. Akiva was accusing him of blasphemy.

אֶמְשֹׁל לְךָ מָשָׁל לִשְׁנַיִם שֶׁהָיוּ דָרִין בְּחָצֵר אַחַת אִם אֵין זֶה נוֹתֵן עֵרוּב וְזֶה נוֹתֵן עֵרוּב שֶׁמָּא מֻתָּרִין לְטַלְטֵל בֶּחָצֵר אֲבָל אִם הָיָה דָר אֶחָד בֶּחָצֵר הֲרֵי הוּא מֻתָּר בְּכָל הֶחָצֵר כֻּלָּהּ אַף כָּאן הַקָּדוֹשׁ בָּרוּךְ הוּא לְפִי שֶׁאֵין רְשׁוּת אַחֶרֶת עִמּוֹ וְכָל הָעוֹלָם כֻּלּוֹ שֶׁלּוֹ מֻתָּר בְּכָל עוֹלָם כֻּלּוֹ וְלֹא עוֹד אֶלָּא שֶׁהֲרֵי אוֹכְלֵי הַמָּן מְעִידִין עָלָיו שֶׁכָּל יְמוֹת הַשַּׁבָּת הָיָה יוֹרֵד וּבַשַּׁבָּת לֹא הָיָה יוֹרֵד

I will give you an illustration. [Suppose] two were dwelling in the same courtyard; if both do not put down an *eruv*, would they be permitted to carry in the courtyard [on the Sabbath]? But if only one person dwells in an enclosed courtyard, he is permitted [to carry on the Sabbath] in the whole courtyard. Similarly here, since the Holy One, blessed be He, does not share authority with anyone and the entire world is His, He is certainly permitted [to move things] throughout the whole universe. And furthermore, those who ate the manna give testimony on the matter, since [the manna] fell every day of the week, but it did not fall on the Sabbath.

R. Akiva's final and conclusive explanation is based on the laws of *eruv ḥatzerot*. The law is that if two persons share the same courtyard they must each put down in the courtyard an *eruv*, that is, the makings of a meal, before the onset of the Sabbath, as a symbol that the courtyard belongs to each one of them; otherwise they are not permitted to carry things in it on the Sabbath, because each is then carrying in a domain that belongs to the other. R. Akiva's point was that the Almighty does not share His domain, that is, as far as He is concerned the entire universe is His private domain. Apparently, this rather complicated halakhic answer was acceptable to the Roman.

* * *

Seed Thoughts

The main lesson of this *midrash* is that to sanctify means to honor. God honored the Sabbath and therefore so should we.

This beautiful teaching, however, is encrusted by a series of stories and observations that are strictly within the parameters of magic and superstition. The story of the River Sambatyon that rests on the Sabbath can be seen as an interesting legend with a Sabbath teaching. But what are we to make of necromancy and calling up the dead and the assertion that the dead cannot be recalled on Sabbath? Does not the Torah warn us against necromancy? Is it not a specific prohibition?

One can only add that every generation is influenced by its environment and reflects it. Who is there in the Talmudic tradition greater than R. Akiva? Yet he had no compunctions about bringing necromancy into the conversation. It was something accepted by the Romans and the Jews had to live with it.

It is the same in our generation. Sometimes we do not even realize how much we have been influenced by our environment. It takes someone from the outside to notice this lack of authenticity.

Does this lessen R. Akiva's status and that of others like him? It merely makes him more human. It also makes us appreciate all the more the efforts he and others had to make to keep Judaism authentic even while they were compromising, unwittingly to be sure, in other unimportant areas.

* * *

Additional Commentary

God wanted to honor it

Basically, the Sabbath is a rule without a reason. However, there is a reason given in the Torah, 'On the seventh day He ceased from work and rested.' Thus, the Sabbath is a sign that the world was created *ex nihilo*. This is what R. Akiva could have replied to Tinneus Rufus. But then, the Roman probably thought that the idea of creation could have been expressed in many ways that did not require rest on the seventh day. Why not the sixth day or the first day Why the seventh day when creation ended? Why not while it was happening? It was for this reason that R. Akiva answered the way he did. We honor you because the emperor chose you. We honor the Sabbath because God chose it. (*Yefei To'ar*)

Parashah Eleven, Midrash Six

פִּילוֹסוֹפוֹס אֶחָד שָׁאַל אֶת רַבִּי הוֹשַׁעְיָה אָמַר לוֹ אִם חֲבִיבָה הִיא הַמִּילָה מִפְּנֵי
מָה לֹא נִתְּנָה לְאָדָם הָרִאשׁוֹן

A philosopher asked R. Hoshaya a question. He said: 'If circumcision is so precious, why was it not given to Adam?'

The verse, 'God ceased from all the work of creation which He had done' (Genesis 2:3), has to be understood as the text on the basis of which this *midrash* emerges. The Hebrew for 'which He had done,' לעשות, *la'asot*, is literally translated as 'in order to do' and seems to be superfluous. It would have been enough to say 'God ceased from all the work of creation.' The question of the philosopher must be understood as, 'Why was Adam not born circumcised?' He probably did not know or did not believe in the Rabbinic statement that Adam *was* born circumcised. (*Ha-Midrash ha-Mevo'ar*) There is also implied in his remarks the question, 'why is not every male child born circumcised?'

אָמַר לוֹ מִפְּנֵי מָה אוֹתוֹ הָאִישׁ מְגַלֵּחַ פְּאַת רֹאשׁ וּמַנִּיחַ אֶת פְּאַת זְקָנוֹ אָמַר לוֹ
מִפְּנֵי שֶׁגָּדַל עִמּוֹ בְּשְׁטוּת אָמַר לוֹ אִם כֵּן יְסַמֵּא אֶת עֵינוֹ וִיקַטֵּעַ אֶת יָדָיו וִישַׁבֵּר
אֶת רַגְלָיו עַל יְדֵי שֶׁגָּדְלוּ עִמּוֹ בְּשְׁטוּת

He answered him, 'Why did you shave the corners of your head and leave your beard?' [The philosopher] said: 'Because it grew with me in folly.' 'If so, you should blind your eye, cut off your hands, and break your legs, because they grew with you in folly!'

The hair of the head exists when a person is born, whereas the beard only grows after puberty. 'Folly' should be understood as 'when I had no sense.' R. Hoshaya's question was based on the assumption that it is more logical for a man to shave his beard and not his head, since the hair of the head is there before the hair of the beard. The implication is one shaves the hair of the head because it must be important for the body or for one's appearance to act this way. The philosopher's answer was not that at all. He claimed that the hair of his head came in infancy, but the hair of his beard came at an age of maturity and, therefore, has to be cherished more.

457

But for the same reason should you not blind your eye, cut off your hands, and break your legs since they, too, came in infancy?

אָמַר לֵהּ וּלְאִלֵּין מִלַּיָּא אֲתֵינַן אִתְמָהָא

[The philosopher] retorted, 'To such an argument have we come! I am amazed!'

'Look here,' said the philosopher, 'I asked you a logical question and you turned the conversation in a trivial direction. Everyone knows that the limbs of the human body are indispensable, whereas the hair of one's head, or of one's beard for that matter, are not vital and are even replaceable. When I ask about circumcision I am talking about an organ of the human body that is indispensable.'

אָמַר לוֹ לְהוֹצִיאֲךָ חָלָק אִי אֶפְשָׁר אֶלָּא כָּל מַה שֶּׁנִּבְרָא בְּשֵׁשֶׁת יְמֵי בְרֵאשִׁית צְרִיכִין עֲשִׂיָּה כְּגוֹן הַחַרְדָּל צָרִיךְ לְמִתּוֹק הַתּוּרְמוֹסִים צָרִיךְ לְמִתּוֹק הַחִטִּין צְרִיכִין לְהִטָּחֵן אֲפִלּוּ אָדָם צָרִיךְ תִּקּוּן

'I cannot send you away empty-handed,' said [R. Hoshaya], 'whatever was created in the first six days requires further preparation, mustard needs sweetening, vetches need sweetening, wheat needs grinding, and even man needs completing.'

I cannot reveal to you the reasons God may have had for circumcision, but this much I can tell you so that you should not go away empty-handed. Many things in our world have to be worked over from their natural state. Mustard seed cannot be used in its original state and has to be processed with a sweetener for human consumption; the wide beans used for animal feed also have to undergo a sweetening process. Wheat has to be ground into flour and then kneaded into dough before bread can be produced. By the same token, man also has to be completed. This is what circumcision does. It purifies his character. (*Ha-Midrash ha-Mevo'ar*) This is the meaning of the text, 'God ceased from all the work of creation *but left something still to be done [la'asot].*' We have to be prepared to do the perfecting and completion of creation.

* * *

Seed Thoughts

Let us begin with the comment of the *Yefei To'ar*. He offers three reasons to justify circumcision, bearing in mind that no commandment depends upon rational justification. It is enough that it is a divine decree. On the other hand, good arguments help in the never-ending process of explaining ancient practices to a skeptical generation.

The three reasons for circumcision are its effect upon character, its hygienic advantages, and its role in the act of creation itself. I can only handle two of these arguments, for it seems to me that the first and third arguments overlap.

Let us begin with the hygienic aspects of circumcision. This has varied with the passing fashions of medicine. There was a time when the health profession advocated the circumcision of all boys without regard to religion. The pendulum has now moved in the other direction and modern medicine seems to be reluctant to 'mutilate' the body when you do not have to. All of this is beginning to change again with the dreadful epidemic of AIDS. A recent study has indicated that circumcised males are far less prone to contract AIDS than those who are not circumcised. Of late, a special committee of the medical profession has been given the task of examining and researching this study and asked to come up with a definite recommendation.

What is meant by the claim that circumcision affects one's character? I believe we are dealing here with only one aspect of moral behavior as it relates to character and that is sexuality. Sexuality has always been central to civilization and has become even more important since the teachings of Freud. Circumcision involves the sexual genitals of the male. It proclaims a sexual message. It says that sex was given to us for procreation and sanctification. That is to say, out of the sexual act we produce not only a fetus, but a human being in the image of God. The sexual act should be seen as a holy experience, not only because of the end product, but because the man and woman who are partners in the act should see themselves as partners in spiritual creation as well.

The *Tiferet Tzion* makes the point that circumcision helps diminish lust. I do not know whether this is meant to refer to the inner experience of sexual urges. If so, the same point has been made in medical literature, albeit critically. The criticism is that circumcision makes it more difficult for the sexual urge to be aroused. But is that a criticism? Is that not precisely the kind of social discipline that our society requires? On the other hand, we can never be sure that this is what the *Tiferet Tzion* has in mind. Maybe what he means is that the emphasis on sexuality as being the vehicle through which God and man and, in particular, God and the Jew, express their covenant, will have the effect of transmuting lust into love and affection.

* * *

Additional Commentary

Circumcision

Why not give the commandment of circumcision to Adam at a later stage? Because he did not obey the easy commandment (not eating from the Tree of Knowledge). How then can he be expected to obey a more difficult commandment like circumcision? (Rashi)

*

Adam was one of thirteen (in the Bible) who were born circumcised. (RZWE)

*

Mustard needs sweetening

There are three reasons for circumcision. The first is to perfect one's ethical qualities. This point is made by Maimonides in his *Guide for the Perplexed* (Book 3, Chapter 49). This is the point of the illustration of the mustard seed, which by beating and pressing is relieved of its bitterness. Similarly, disciplining the material or animal in man removes many of his bad qualities. The second reason is the perfection of the body. What is involved here is the protection of the body from afflictions that have to do with sexuality. The author of *The Akeidah* states that circumcision is most important because it prevents many afflictions. In this respect we have the illustration of the peas whose bitterness is removed when the pod or shell is removed by means of cooking. The third reason is the perfection of the very act of creation itself. This is the meaning of the illustration of the wheat, which has to be ground in order to remove the chaff. (*Yefei To'ar*)

*

Man needs completing

You might think that the verse 'And God saw everything that He had made and behold it was very good' includes man, who therefore needs no further improvement. Not so. He still needs perfection and that is the meaning of the last phrase of the creation story as interpreted by the *midrash*: God ceased from all the work of creation *la'asot* in order to be perfected or which God created so that man should complete it. (Rashi)

*

If circumcision is so precious

The philosopher did not ask about all the other commandments given to Israel after the Exodus from Egypt, since they may have all been connected in some way with the Exodus. Circumcision, however, was commanded to Abraham in order to produce a holy progeny – 'And I will set

My covenant between you and Me and I will multiply you very much.' His question was why was not this given to Adam so that he could produce a holy progeny for the whole world. This is the same question that Abraham posed and God answered that it was enough that He and Abraham were in the same world. The explanation is that Abraham's great virtue was that he fought against the evil inclination even before he was circumcised, and the power of evil was therefore very great within him and yet he was victorious; therefore, he grew greatly in stature to the point that the whole world existed because of his merit.

But God foresaw that coming generations would not be able to withstand this powerful temptation and therefore He commanded circumcision. This was the answer that R. Hoshaya gave to the philosopher. In asking why does a person shave his head and retain his beard, he had in mind to show that man's great virtue was that he can overcome evil things by means of acquired wisdom much better than by purely natural means. The hair on the head signifies natural wisdom and that of the beard testifies to the efforts one made in trying to acquire wisdom. All this was to show that a person is not nearly as proud of his natural wisdom as of that which he acquired with effort. But since he could not tell this to the gentile directly because that would mean teaching him Torah, he told it to him as a hint as to why the commandment of circumcision could not be given to Adam.

However, the philosopher did not take the hint. He uttered one foolish thought and he was answered with another. Finally the philosopher said, 'You have answered me very cutely about the hair of my head and beard, but that was not my real question. My real question is about circumcision.' To this R. Hoshaya answered, 'I cannot answer you directly (*halak*) and you did not understand the hint. Apparently you are making the argument that circumcision was not necessary and that man can improve himself without it. Here I must point out that most of what has been created can only improve themselves through the process of changing themselves. This should teach man that he, too, requires a change and that perfection will only come if he changes the body with which he was created by means of circumcision.' Circumcision has the quality of removing lust or at least diminishing it and thus enabling man to climb the ladder that leads heavenward. (*Tiferet Tzion*)

* * *

Concluding Seed Thought

The story of creation should not end with a period but with an exclamation point.

That is actually what has happened. The final words of the creation story are 'which God has created (for man) to do.' It need not have ended that way. It could have ended 'which God has created.' But by adding the phrase *la'asot*, '[in order] to do,' the entire emphasis has now changed. We are now told that God created an incomplete world.

The key word here is *la'asot*. It does not say that man should complete the work, for who are we to claim that we are able to complete God's work. Nor does it say that man should perfect God's work. It says only that God created this world for man 'to do.' But what does that mean?

In the first place, 'to do' means to do exactly what God has been doing, namely, to create. But God is able to create *ex nihilo*, from nothing, while we can only create from something. It so happens that modern man has exceled in this kind of creating. The breakthroughs in science, the information revolution, the Internet, the medical breakthroughs: This kind of creativity is only possible by gifted individuals, but all of us benefit and have a great opportunity to do many things that otherwise would have been impossible for us to had these developments not taken place.

But 'to do' means much more than that. It means to make the most of our lives. God created this world so that man should make the most of his life.

The story is told of a ḥasid (member of an ultra-orthodox group) who paid a visit to his Rebbe (spiritual leader). The Rebbe asked him in Yiddish, 'Vos tust du?' (What do you do?). He answered that he had a warehouse and that he imported clothing that he sold to the retail trade. But the Rebbe persisted. What do you do? He answered in the same vein, but when the Rebbe persisted with his question, he threw up his hands and asked the Rebbe what he meant. 'I mean what do you do for the *mitzvot* (commandments)? What do you do for good deeds, charity, and so forth?' That is what a man is supposed to do with his life.

Someone once said that a human being needs three things: something to do, someone to love, and something to hope for. All of these elements are referred to in the last line of the creation story.

La'asot, 'to do,' is the challenge to make the most of our lives. The seventh day, Sabbath, is the festival of love. It is the day in which husband and wife are expected to share their love with each other, when children and parents celebrate their affection, when all members of the family circle celebrate their kinship, when love of Torah is also mandated. And as for something to hope for, the verse says 'and God rested from His work.' What is His work? It is to create hope for the world, to give it purpose and significance.

The prayerbook says about God that in His goodness He 'reviews every day the work of creation.' The creation story never ends. It is ongoing, continuous for man 'to do' until the end of time.

Bibliographical Abbreviations

Ha-Midrash ha-Mevo'ar – Under the general editorship of Rabbi Abraham Steinberger presiding over a faculty of scholars, the first four volumes, *Bereishit Rabbah*, were published in 1984 in Jerusalem. The final volume of the *Midrash Rabbah* was completed fifteen years later. This commentary leaves nothing undone or unexplained. Every new interpretation is traced to its source. The use of different type styles (bold, italics, etc.) helps the reader follow the various levels of interpretation. Every volume ends with additional commentary from a plethora of sources.

Ḥidushei ho-Rashash – The work of Rabbi Samuel Strashun (acronym *Rashash*). This commentary first appeared as annotations to the first Vilna edition of the *Midrash Rabbah* in 1851.

Matnot Kehunah – This commentary is the work of Rabbi Issachar Ber ben Naftali of the town of Mishbershin in Poland. The work first appeared in the Cracow edition (1587) of the *Midrash Rabbah* and has appeared in every compilation ever since. This commentary sparkles with brevity and has been used by all who study Midrash.

Mirkin – This commentary by Moshe Aryeh Mirkin was the first of the modern Hebrew commentaries. Published in Tel Aviv in 1968, the author emphasizes the plain meaning of the text. He leans heavily on the edition of Theodore and Albeck, the great textual scholars, and bases many of his interpretations on manuscript emendations and corrections that they suggested. He has a great talent for brevity without compromising the meaning, and this is a most valuable contribution to understanding Midrash.

RDL – This is the acronym of Rabbi David Luria. His work first appeared in the Vilna edition (5647/1887, second edition) from which work our quotations have been taken.

RZWE – These are the initials of Rabbi Zev Wolf Einhorn. His Hebrew commentary is entitled מהרז"ו, which are his Hebrew initials. His commentary is a very large work and appears also in abridged form; both forms are presented side by side in the Vilna edition. His interpretation tries to apply the thirty-two hermeneutical principals of Rabbi Elazar ben Azariah. Our quotations are from the Vilna edition.

Rashi – Rabbi Solomon Yitzḥaki (1040–1105) is the great interpreter of the Bible and Talmud. According to the Vilna edition, Rashi also wrote a commentary to *Bereishit Rabbah*, but authorities disagree and feel that the commentary is culled from his views as written in his other commentaries. There are even some scholars who argue that the commentary to *Bereishit Rabbah* was written by someone else. However, Rashi's name is associated with these ideas and probably always will be.

Soncino – The Soncino Press, from its headquarters for many years in London, England, pioneered the translation of the great classics of Judaism into English, including the Bible, the Talmud, the *Zohar*, and the *Midrash Rabbah*. The *Midrash Rabbah* was translated in 1939, and in the 1980s the rights to Soncino Press were acquired by Judaica Press in New York, through whose permission their translation has been used. In addition to the translation, the Soncino editions include explanatory notes.

Tiferet Tzion – The author of *Tiferet Tzion*, Rabbi Yitzḥak Zev Yadler, passed away in 1917 and his great work, *Tiferet Tzion*, was not published until 1958. It is a tremendous work by one person, who, according to his own testimony, spent fourteen years of unremitting work, night and day, to produce this monumental commentary on the *Midrash Rabbah*. A *ḥasid* and mystic by belief, upbringing, and conviction, he was able to relate to many of the difficult mystical passages of the *Midrash Rabbah* as no one else has been able to do. The present work relies heavily on his insights.

Yedei Moshe – This commentary was first published in 1691. It was included in the second edition of the Vilna Midrash in 1887, from which the present quotations were taken.

Yefei To'ar – This work, by Rabbi Samuel Yaffe Ashkenazi, is the most important of the early commentaries on the *Midrash Rabbah*. It appeared in 1607, more or less around the same time as the Venice edition of the *Midrash Rabbah*. Unfortunately the author passed away ten years before its publication. Already in his day he was interested in comparing the different texts of Midrash to be found in many manuscripts. The *Yefei To'ar* has since been included in every anthology of the *Midrash Rabbah*. Our quotations are from the Vilna edition.